HERMAN MELVILLE:

A REFERENCE BIBLIOGRAPHY

1900-1972

With Selected Nineteenth Century Materials

Compiled by

Beatrice Ricks

Joseph D. Adams

G. K. HALL & CO., 70 LINCOLN STREET, BOSTON, MASS.

1973

Library of Congress Cataloging in Publication Data

Ricks, Beatrice.
    Herman Melville: a reference bibliography, 1900-1972.

    1.   Melville, Herman, 1819-1891--Bibliography.
I.   Adams, Joseph D., joint author.   II.   Title.
Z8562.58.R53   016.813'3   72-14197
ISBN 0-8161-1036-0

This publication is printed on permanent/durable acid-free paper.

ISBN 0-8161-1036-0

To the gracious and competent staff
of The Ward Edwards Library of
Central Missouri State University

PREFACE

The bibliography is comprised mainly of two parts: a masterlist of bibliographic items, alphabetically arranged, the items consecutively numbered; and an index where references are numerically listed under works and various topics. Since computerization has already appeared in much bibliographical work, the numerical index, it is hoped, will be readily adaptable to computerized production.

This bibliography provides information as to individual books and articles by and about Herman Melville, and reflects the history and revivals of interest in Melville and his work.

No attempt has been made to evaluate the critic's thought; the aim has been to bring together the bulk of scholarship directed toward Melville study. Brief annotations have been inserted to indicate the principal areas of study, or pertinent issues raised.

The bibliography centers mainly upon the twentieth century. Since Melville is such a focus of scholarly interest, it has been necessary to limit the coverage to approximately 3500 items in order to involve as many topics of study as possible. Notable nineteenth-century items have been included to indicate Melville's place in his contemporary cultural and literary milieu.

Melville's own writings, chronologically arranged, are divided into representative *Complete Collections;* representative *Partial Collections; Journals; Letters; Poetry; Reviews by Melville and Miscellaneous Pieces;* and *Melville's Prose Writings.* A representative listing of editions of the various works of Melville has been included for the reason that the first nineteenth-century editions have particular interest to historians, while those of the twentieth century, particularly those having introductions of critical significance, indicate revival of interest in Melville. Since the 1920's, however, the production of Melville texts has gained such momentum that only representative listing can be provided.

This arrangement of bibliographical references and textual material has been designed to serve students and scholars in their research on the cultural, historical, literary, and social aspects of Melville study.

BEATRICE RICKS
JOSEPH D. ADAMS

TABLE of CONTENTS

vii

TABLE OF ABBREVIATIONS
AND PUBLICATIONS

A&A	Art and Action: Twice a Year
Academy	London Academy
Accent	
Adelphi	
AHRF	Annales Historiques de la Révolution Francaise
AI	American Imago
AION-SG	Annali Instituto Universitario Orientale, Napoli, Sezione Germanica
AJGE	Aoyama Journal of General Education (Tokyo)
AL	American Literature
Albion	New York Albion
AlWk	Princeton Alumni Weekly
Am	American
AmArt	American Artist
AmBC	American Book Collector
America	America: A Journal of To-Day
AmLAB	American Library Association Bulletin
AmLR	American Literary Review (Tokyo)
AmM	American Mercury
AmMag	American Magazine
AmNor	Americana Norvegica
AmR	American Review
AmSch	American Scholar
Andvari	
Anglica	Anglica (Kansai U., Osaka)
AN&Q	American Notes & Queries (New Haven, Conn.)
AntigR	Antigonish Review
Approdo	L'Approdo Letterario (Roma)
AQ	American Quarterly
Arbor	
ArlQ	Arlington Quarterly
ArQ	Arizona Quarterly
ArtN	Art News
AS	American Speech

Asia	
Athenea	
Athenaeum	Athenaeum (London)
Atl	Atlantic Monthly
Atlántico	
ATQ	American Transcendental Quarterly
BAS	Bulletin of the Atomic Scientists
BB	Bulletin of Bibliography
BBMB	Bernice P. Bishop Museum Bulletin
BBPL	Bulletin of Boston Public Library
BBr	Books at Brown
BC	Book Collector
BCA	Buffalo Commercial Advertiser
BentMis	Bentley's Miscellany
BLM	Bonniers Litterära Magasin (Stockholm)
BNYPL	Bulletin New York Public Library
Bookman	
BostonP	Boston Post
BPLQ	Boston Public Library Quarterly
BSAA	Bulletin of the Society of American Authors
BSAP	Bulletin de la Society d'Anthrolologie de Paris
BSL	Bay State Librarian
BSUF	Ball State University Forum
BuR	Bucknell Review
BUSE	Boston University Studies in English
BwM	Blackwoods Magazine
BzJA	Beihefte zum JA
CamJ	Cambridge Journal
CamR	Cambridge Review
CanL	Canadian Literature
Carrell	The Carrell: Journal of the Friends of the University of Miami (Fla.) Library
CathW	Catholic World
CE	College English
CEA	CEA Critic
CEAAN	Center for Editions of American Authors Newsletter (MLA)
CEMW	Columbia Essays on Modern Writers
CentM	Century Magazine

Table of Abbreviations and Publications

CentR	The Centennial Review (Michigan State)
Century	
ChicagoR	Chicago Review
ChrE	Christian Examiner
ChrObs	Christian Observatory
ChrP	Christian Parlor Magazine
ChS	Christian Scholar
ChT	Christianity Today
Cithara	
CJ	Classical Journal
CL	Comparative Literature
CLAJ	College Language Association Journal (Morgan State College, Baltimore)
ClearH	Clearing House
CLS	Comparative Literature Studies (University of Illinois)
Colliers	
Colophon	
ColQ	Colorado Quarterly
ColS	The Columbian Sentinel
Comm	Commentary
CommAd	New York Commercial Advertiser
CompD	Comparative Drama
Complex	
ConnR	Connecticut Review
Conrad	Conradiana
ContempR	Contemporary Review
Conv	Convivium
CP	Concerning Poetry
CR	The Critical Review (Melbourne; Sydney)
CraneR	The Crane Review (Tufts University)
Crit	Critique: Studies in Modern Fiction
Criterion	
Critic	
Critica	
Criticism	(Wayne State)
Critique	Critique (Paris)
CritQ	Critical Quarterly
Crit&R	Criticism and Research (Banaras Hindu University)
CS	Cahiers du Sud
CuaAm	Cuadernos Americanos (Mexico)
Cuadenos	Cuadenos (Paris)
CurOp	Current Opinion

Cw	Commonweal
DA	Dissertation Abstracts
DAI	Dissertation Abstracts International (Supersedes DA)
DD	Double Dealer
Delineator	
Delta	
DenverQ	Denver Quarterly
Descant	
Dickensian	
DilR	Diliman Review
Discourse	(Concordia College)
DosL	Doshisha Literature
DR	Dalhousie Review
DRund	Deutsche Rundschau
DubR	Dublin Review
DubUM	Dublin University Magazine
DVLG	Deutsche Vierteljahrsschrift für Literaturwissenschaft und Geistesgeschichte
EA	Études Anglaises
E&AL	English and American Literature
Eagle	Pittsfield, Mass.
EclR	Eclectic Review
EcrC	Les Ecrivains Célèbres
EdinR	Edinburgh Review
EIC	Essays in Criticism (Oxford)
EigoS	Eigo Seinen (The Rising Generation) (Tokyo)
EiT	Eibungaku Tenbo (Meiji Gakuin University)
EJ	English Journal
ELH	Journal of English Literary History
ELN	English Language Notes (University of Colorado)
EngRec	English Record
EngRev	English Review
ES	English Studies
ESQ	Emerson Society Quarterly
ESQ:JAR	Emerson Society Quarterly: Journal of the American Renaissance
ESRS	Emporia State Research Studies
Etc	Etc. A Review of General Semantics

Table of Abbreviations and Publications

ETJ	Educational Theatre Journal
Etudes	
E-WR	East-West Review
ExExc	Exercise Exchange
Expl	Explicator
FCHQ	Filson Club Historical Quarterly
FI	Friends' Intelligencer
FilmQ	Film Quarterly
FL	Figaro Littéraire
Fle	La Fiera Letteraria (Italy)
Forum	The Forum
ForumH	Forum (Houston)
FR	French Review
Freeman	
Furioso	
FurmS	Furman Studies (Furman University, Greenville, South Carolina)
GaR	Georgia Review
Geibun	Geibun (Kinki University)
GentM	Gentlemen's Magazine
The Griffin	
HAB	Humanities Association Bulletin (Canada)
Harb	Harbinger
HarpMM	Harper's Monthly Magazine
HB	Horn Book
HeM	Hommes et Mondes
Herald	New York Herald
HGM	Harvard Graduates' Magazine
H&H	Hound and Horn
HistM	Historical Messenger
HistN	Historic Nantucket
HLB	Harvard Library Bulletin
HLQ	Huntington Library Quarterly
H&M	Hommes et Monde
HM	Hunt's Merchant's Magazine
HNMM	Harper's New Monthly Magazine
Holiday	
HopR	Hopkins Review
HSELL	Hiroshima Studies in English Language and Literature (Hiroshima, Japan)
HudR	Hudson Review

Humanist	
HumR	Humane Review
IJPsy	International Journal of Psychiatry
ILondN	Illustrated London News
Independent	
IndRes	Indian Response
Insula	Insula (Madrid)
IntlBR	International Book Review
Inventario	
InvitL	Invitation to Learning
IowaR	Iowa Review
Ipna	(Lima)
IrishD	Irish Digest
Italia	Italia che scrive
JA	Jahrbuch für Amerikastudien
JAAC	Journal of Aesthetics and Art Criticism
JAE	Journal of Aesthetic Education
JAF	Journal of American Folklore
JAmS	Journal of American Studies.
JAP	Journal of Analytical Psychology (London)
JdD	Journal des Debats
JdJ	Journal des Journaux
JEGP	The Journal of English and Germanic Philology
JewN	The Jewish News (Newark, New Jersey)
JGE	Journal of General Education
JH	Journal of Humanities (Hosei University, Japan)
JHI	Journal of the History of Ideas
JHR	Journal of Human Relations
JISHS	Journal of Illinois State Historical Society
JJQ	James Joyce Quarterly (University of Tulsa, Oklahoma)
JNH	Journal of Negro History
JO'L	John O'London's
JO'LW	John O'London's Weekly
JosB	Joshidai Bungaku
JR	Journal of Religion
JRUL	Journal of Rutgers University Library
Judaism	
KAL	Kyushu American Literature (Fukuoka, Japan)

Table of Abbreviations and Publications

KB	Kleine Beitrage
KbM	Knickerbocker Magazine
KFR	Kentucky Folklore Record
KM	Kansas Magazine
KR	Kenyon Review
LaCul	La Cultura
L'Arche	
LC	Literary Criterion (University of Mysore, India)
LCUT	Library Chronicle of the University of Texas
LesEC	Les Ecrivains Célèbres
Let	Letteratura
LetN	Lettres Nouvelles
LH	Lincoln Herald
LHB	Lock Haven Bulletin
LHR	Lock Haven Review (Lock Haven State College, Pa.)
Life	
Line	
List	Listener
LitD	Literary Digest
LitDIBR	Literary Digest International Book Review
LitG&JBL	Literary Gazette, and Journal of the Belles Lettres, London
LitGuide	The Literary Guide
LitHY	Literary Half-Yearly
LitR	Literature Review (Fairleigh Dickinson University, Teaneck, New Jersey)
LitRNYEP	Literary Review, New York Evening Post
LitW	Literary World
LivA	Living Age
LLA	Littell's Living Age
LonMer	London Mercury
L&P	Literature and Psychology (University of Hartford)
LSUSHS	Louisiana State University Studies, Humanities Series
LugR	Lugano Review
LV	Lenguas Vivas

Table of Abbreviations and Publications

Mainstream	
MASJ	Midcontinent American Studies Journal (University of Kansas, Lawrence, Kansas)
MB	More Books
MD	Modern Drama
MdS	Mar del Sur (Lima)
M&E	The Mail and Express
Measure	
MelbCR	Melbourne Critical Review
MFS	Modern Fiction Studies
MHM	Maryland Historical Magazine
MHSB	Missouri Historical Society Bulletin
MichA	Michigan Academician
MinnR	Minnesota Review
MissQ	Mississippi Quarterly
MLN	Modern Language Notes
MLQ	Modern Language Quarterly
MLR	Modern Language Review
ModA	Modern Age (Chicago)
ModSpr	Moderna Språk
Month	
MP	Modern Philology
MQ	Midwest Quarterly (Pittsburg, Kansas)
MQR	Michigan Quarterly Review
MR	Massachusetts Review (University of Massachusetts)
MSE	Massachusetts Studies in English
MSN	Melville Society Newsletter
MSS	Manuscripts
MTJ	Mark Twain Journal
Musicology	
NA	Nuova Antologia (Roma)
N&A	Nation and Athenaeum
NAdV	Nouvelles Annales des Voyages (Paris)
Nation	London Nation
NAR	North American Review
NatlGeo	National Geographic
NatlMis	National Miscellany
NBMM	New Bedford Morning Mercury
NC&A	Nineteenth Century and After
NCF	Nineteenth Century Fiction
N&Q	Notes and Queries

NEQ	New England Quarterly
NewCol	New Colophon
NewEng	New Englander
NewL	New Leader
NewRep	New Republic
NL	Nouvelles Littéraires
NLeftR	New Left Review
NLH	New Literary History
NMM	New Monthly Magazine
NMQ	New Mexico Quarterly
NoSav	The Noble Savage
Novel	Novel: A Forum on Fiction (Brown University)
NQR	New Quarterly Review
NR	New Republic
NRF	Nouvelle Revue Francaise
NS	Die Neueren Sprachen
NS&N	New Statesman and Nation
NStm	New Statesman
NVT	Nieuw Vlaams Tijdschrift
NY	New Yorker
NYCrit	New York Critic
NYDT	New York Daily Tribune
NYEP	New York Evening Post
NYES	New York Evening Sun
NYFQ	New York Folklore Quarterly
NYG&BR	New York Genealogical and Biographical Record
NYH	New York History
NYHSQ	New York Historical Society Quarterly
NYHTBR	New York Herald Tribune Book Review
NYM&E	New York Mail and Express
NYT	New York Times
NYTBR	New York Times Book Review
NYTrib	New York Tribune
NYW	New York World
ODHS&WMB	Old Dartmouth Historical Society and Whaling Museum Bulletin
Open Court	
Orient/West	
OSA&HQ	Ohio State Archaeological and Historical Quarterly
Outlook	
OutlookInd	Outlook and Independent

Overland	
PacS	Pacific Spectator
PADS	Publications of the American Dialect Society
PaMak	Paper Maker
Panorama	
PAPS	Proceedings of the American Philosophical Society
Par	Paragone
Paunch	(Buffalo, New York)
PBSA	Papers of the Bibliographical Society of America
PEB	Providence Evening Bulletin
PELL	Papers on English Language and Literature
Person	Personalist
Perspective	Washington University
PhilF	Philadelphia Forum
Phylon	
PLL	Papers on Language and Literature (Southern Illinois University)
PMASAL	Papers of the Michigan Academy of Science, Arts, and Letters
PMLA	Publications of the Modern Language Association of America
PN	Poe Newsletter (Washington State University)
Poetry	
PopSM	Popular Science Monthly
PQ	Philological Quarterly
PR	Partisan Review
PragSE	Prague Studies in English
PrAPS	Proceedings of the American Philosophical Society
Preuves	
PrS	Prairie Schooner
PS	Pacific Spectator
PSA	Papeles de Son Armadans (Mallorca)
PsyR	Psychoanalytic Review
PubW	Publisher's Weekly
PULC	Princeton University Library Chronicle
Pursuit	
PutM	Putnam's Monthly
QH	Quaker History

Table of Abbreviations and Publications

QQ	Queen's Quarterly
RAA	Revue Anglo-Américaine
Ramparts	
RDM	Revue des deux mondes
RdP	Revue de Paris
RdPac	Revista del Pacífico
ReadD	Reader's Digest
Realidad	
RelLif	Religion in Life
Ren	Renascence
Rendezvous	Journal of Arts and Letters (Idaho State University)
Reporter	
RES	Review of English Studies
RevCam	Revista Camoniana
Review	
RevR	Review of Reviews
RiceIP	Rice Institute Pamphlet
RikR	Rikkyo Review (Tokyo)
RinL	Religion in Life
RLC	Revue de Littérature Comparée
RLM	Revue des Lettres Modernes
RLMC	Revista di Letterature Moderne e Comparate (Firenze)
RLV	Revue des Langues Vivantes (Brussels)
RLz	Radjans'ke Literaturoznavstvo (Kiev)
RO	Revista de Occidente
RS	Research Studies (Washington State University)
RSSCW	Research Studies of the State College of Washington
SA	Studi Americani (Roma)
SAB	South Atlantic Bulletin
Sage	(University of Wyoming)
SailM	The Sailor's Magazine
Salmagundi	
SAQ	South Atlantic Quarterly
SatR	Saturday Review
SatRL	Saturday Review of Literature
SB	Studies in Bibliography: Papers of the Bibliographical Society of the University of Virginia
ScAR	Scottish Art Review

SCE	Study of Current English (Tokyo)
SchM	Schweizer Monatshefte
SDR	South Dakota Review
SEL	Studies in English Literature, 1500-1900
SELit	Studies in English Literature (English Literary Society of Japan, University of Tokyo)
Serif	The Serif (Kent, Ohio)
SFQ	Southern Folklore Quarterly
ShAB	Shakespeare Association Bulletin
ShakR	Shakespeare Survey
Show	
SHR	Southern Humanities Review
SIR	Studies in Romanticism
SLett	Studi Letterari
SLitI	Studies in the Literary Imagination (Georgia State College)
SNNTS	Studies in the Novel (North Texas State University)
SoL	Soviet Literature
SoLM	Southern Literary Messenger
SoQ	Southern Quarterly (Hattiesburg, Miss.)
SoR	Southern Review (Louisiana State University)
SoRA	Southern Review: An Australian Journal of Literary Studies (University of Adelaide)
Southerly	(Sydney)
SovL	Soviet Literature
SP	Studies in Philology
Spec	Spectator (99 Gower Street, London)
Sp-ital	Lo Spettatore italiano
Spectator	
SpT	Spirit of the Times
SQ	Shakespeare Quarterly
SR	Sewanee Review
SRo	Studi Romani
SRom	Studies in Romanticism
SSF	Studies in Short Fiction
StLU	Studia de Literatura Universala (Bucharest)
SuL	Sprache und Literatur Englands und Amerikas, Lehrgangsvorträge der Akademie Comburg

SUS	Susquehanna University Studies (Selingsgrove, Pa.)
SWR	Southwest Review
Sym	Symposium
TA	Table Ronde (France)
T&C	Town and Country
TCEL	Thought Currents in English Literature (Tokyo)
TCL	Twentieth Century Literature
TFSB	Tennessee Folklore Society Bulletin
ThA	Theatre Arts
Thought	
Thoth	Department of English, Syracuse University
TigE	Tiger's Eye
TimeM	Time Magazine
TLS	(London) Times Literary Supplement
TM	Temps Modernes
ToJ	Today's Japan
Tomorrow	
Tribune	New York Tribune
TriQ	TriQuarterly
TSB	Thoreau Society Bulletin
TSE	Tulane Studies in English
TSL	Tennessee Studies in Literature
TSLL	Texas Studies in Literature and Language
TWA	Transactions of the Wisconsin Academy of Sciences, Arts, and Letters
TwYr	Twice a Year
UCB	Union College Bulletin
UCM	University of Chicago Magazine
UCQ	University College Quarterly
UFMH	University of Florida Monographs, Humanities Series
UKCR	University of Kansas City Review
UMPAW	University of Minnesota Pamphlets on American Writers
Universitas	
UnR	Universal Review
UR	University Review (Kansas City)
USDemR	United States Democratic Review
UTLC	University of Texas Library Chronicle

UTQ	University of Toronto Quarterly
UTSE	University of Texas Studies in English
UWR	University of Windsor Review
VBQ	Visva-Bharati Quarterly (Santiniketan, India)
Verri	
Views	
VP	Vita e Pensiero
VQR	Virginia Quarterly Review
VS	Victorian Studies (Indiana University)
WAL	Western American Literature
WBEP	Wiener Beiträge zur Englischen Philologie
WestmR	Westminster Review
WF	Western Folklore
WHR	Western Humanities Review
WisSL	Wisconsin Studies in Literature
Word	
WordS	Word Study
WorldR	World Review (London)
WR	Western Review
WyR	Weekly Review (New York)
Yankee	
YR	Yale Review
Y/T	Yale/Theatre
YULG	Yale University Library Gazette
ZAA	Zeitschrift für Anglistik und Amerikanistik

Masterlist of Bibliographic Entries

1   A., S. P. "Toward the Whole Evidence on Melville as a
         Lecturer," AN&Q, 2 (October, 1942), 111-112.

         Did Melville withdraw his lecture in New Haven,
     scheduled for December 30, 1857, because of local opinion
     as evidenced in an editorial in the Journal and Courier?

2   Aaron, Daniel. "An English Enemy of Melville," NEQ, 8
         (1935), 561-567.

         Edward Lucett's ROVINGS IN THE PACIFIC FROM 1837
     TO 1849 WITH A GLANCE AT CALIFORNIA (London: 1851),
     adds to the history of Melville in the South Seas.

3   Aaron, Daniel. "Melville and the Missionaries," NEQ, 8
         (1935), 404-408.

         Reviews in the Honolulu Polynesian and the Friend
     between 1846 and 1850 show the antagonism which Melville's
     writing provoked in the South Seas.

4   Abbot, Rev. John, S. C. "The Missionary--A Sailor Story,"
         SailM, 17 (1845), 361-63.

5   Abcarian, Richard. "The World of Love and the Spheres of
         Fright: Melville's 'Bartleby the Scrivener,'"
         SSF, 1 (1964), 207-215.

         The theme is reflected in the changes undergone
     by the narrator who finally realizes that "Bartleby's
     condition represents the human condition."

6   Abel, Darrel. AMERICAN LITERATURE. Great Neck: Barron's
         Educational Series, 1963. Vol. 2, pp. 449-51.

7   Abel, Darrel. "The American Renaissance and the Civil War:
         Concentric Circles," ESQ, 44 (3rd Qt., 1966), 86-91.

         Although Melville and Hawthorne did not enter into
     anti-slavery activities, they viewed slavery as an evil.

8   Abel, Darrel. "'Laurel Twined with Thorn': The Theme of
         Melville's TIMOLEON," Person, 41 (July, 1960), 330-340.

         One theme, reiterated throughout the poems in
     TIMOLEON (1891), unifies them into a work of art--the
     idea that intellectuals and artists are alienated from
     their fellowmen by their innovative, nonconformist
     thinking.

9   Abel, Darrel. SIMPLIFIED APPROACH TO MOBY DICK.
           Woodbury, New York: Barron's Educational Series, Inc.,
           1971.

           Biographical sketch, the rhetoric and symbolism of
       the novels, chapter-by-chapter summaries and commentary.

10   Abernethy, Julian W. "Present Schools and Tendencies,"
           AMERICAN LITERATURE. New York: Maynard Merrill & Co.,
           1902, pp. 456-457.

           Herman Melville, a "forgotten New York novelist,"
       whose TYPEE and OMOO were "once the sensation of two
       continents."

11   Adamic, Louis. A NATION OF NATIONS. New York and London:
           Harper & Bros., Publishers, 1944, p. 100.

           It was not well known that Herman Melville's
       mother was of "Early Dutch stock."

12   Adams, Frederick B., Jr. "The Crow's Nest," Colophon, n. s.,
           2 (1936), 148-154.

           Satire of Scoresby's AN ACCOUNT OF THE ARTIC REGIONS
       in "The Mast-head" Chapter 35 of MOBY DICK.

13   Adams, James Truslow. THE EPIC OF AMERICA. Illus. by
           M. J. Gallagher. Boston: Little, Brown, and Company,
           1932, pp. 234, 272.

           Melville had written an American classic, but
       America, so preoccupied with the impending Civil War,
       neither knew nor cared "what the 'White Whale' signified
       or whether there was evil in the universe."

14   Adams, James Truslow. THE MARCH OF DEMOCRACY: THE RISE
           OF THE UNION. New York; London: Charles Scribner's
           Sons, 1932, passim.

           Melville, possessing "a profound sense of evil,"
       reacted most deeply against the conditions of American
       life, as well as against the terms imposed on man by the
       cosmos itself. In MOBY DICK, he cloaked his thoughts in
       a romanticism to which "most of his contemporaries found
       no key."

15   Adams, Richard P. "American Renaissance: An Epistemological
         Problem," ESQ, 35 (2nd Qt., 1964), 2-7.

         The "epistemological effort" of Hawthorne and
      Melville was to find "the right relation between the
      subjective and objective aspects of experience," and
      to know "who they were, in relation to what was, both
      within them and outside of them."

16   Adams, Richard P. "The Apprenticeship of William
         Faulkner," TSE, 12 (1962), 113-156.

         Faulkner's work deeply influenced by his early
      reading in Melville.

17   Adams, Richard P. "Permutations of American Romanticism,"
         SIR, 9, iv (Fall, 1970), 249-268.

         Romantic writers concentrate on dynamism--energy--
      as opposed to classical staticism--control. Organicism
      is merely one type of control and is actually static.
      The "American renaissance" writers (Melville for one)
      try to reconcile the contradiction between organicism
      and dynamism.

18   Adams, Richard P. "Romanticism and the American
         Renaissance," AL, 23 (1952), 419-432.

      MOBY DICK as "negative Romanticism."

19   Adams, Robert Martin. "Masks, Screens, Guises: Melville
         and Others," in NIL: EPISODES IN THE LITERARY
         CONQUEST OF VOID DURING THE NINETEENTH CENTURY.
         New York: Oxford University Press, 1966, pp. 131-148.

         Chapter 6 in MOBY DICK deals with nothingness.

20   Aderman, Ralph M. "When Melville Lectured Here,"
         HistM, 9 (June, 1953), 3-5.

21   Adkins, Nelson F. "A Note on Herman Melville's TYPEE,"
         NEQ, 5 (1932), 348-351.

         An account of Dr. Thomas L. Nichols, probably the
      first outside the Melville family to read TYPEE and
      advise its publication. This contemporary reference to
      Melville in Nichols' FORTY YEARS OF AMERICAN LIFE,
      published in London, 1864, reprinted in above "Note."

22   Aguirre, José L. "MOBY DICK of Herman Melville,"
         Atlántico, No. 5 (1957), 33-48.

23   Aigner, Helmut. DIE ENTWICKLUNG DES PESSIMISMUS IN
        PROSAWERK HERMAN MELVILLES. Vienna, 1953.

24   Aiken, Conrad. /"MOBY DICK and the Puritan Dream"7, THE
        COLLECTED CRITICISM OF CONRAD AIKEN FROM 1916 TO THE
        PRESENT: A REVIEWER'S ABC. New York: Meridian Books,
        Inc., 1958, pp. 91-92.

25   Aiken, Conrad. "MOBY-DICK and the Puritan Dream," in
        STUDIES IN MOBY-DICK. Howard P. Vincent, comp.
        Columbus, Ohio: Charles E. Merrill Publishing
        Company, 1969, pp. 160-161.

26   Alcott, Bronson. THE JOURNALS OF BRONSON ALCOTT. Selected
        and edited by Odell Shepard. Boston: Little, Brown,
        and Company, 1938, p.185.

        December 9, 1846. "Read TYPEE, by Melville--a
        charming volume,...I almost found myself embarked to
        spend the rest of my days with those simple islanders
        of the South Seas."

27   Alden, John R. PIONEER AMERICA. New York: Alfred A.
        Knopf, 1966, pp. 253-255, passim.

        The appearance of MOBY DICK marked the end of
        Melville's popularity. Contemporary Americans did not
        read books offering a tragic view of existence. "Melville
        was much closer to Marcus Aurelius than he was to John
        Calvin or John Wesley...."

28   Allen, Don Dameron. "Symbolic Color in the Literature of
        the English Renaissance," PQ, 15 (1936), 81-92.

29   Allen, Gay Wilson. "The Influence of Space on the American
        Imagination," in ESSAYS ON AMERICAN LITERATURE IN HONOR
        OF JAY B. HUBBELL. Clarence Gohdes, ed. Durham,
        North Carolina: Duke University Press, 1967, pp.
        329-342.

        America's space consciousness and her writers and
        adventurers. "...MOBY DICK is no less space-conscious
        than LEAVES OF GRASS...."

30   Allen, Gay Wilson. MELVILLE AND HIS WORLD. London:
        Thames & Hudson, 1971; New York: Viking Press,
        1971.

31   Allen, Jerry. Introduction, GREAT SHORT WORKS OF HERMAN
        MELVILLE. New York: Harper & Row, Publishers, 1966.
        A Perennial Classic.

31.1 Allen, Jerry. Afterword. MOBY DICK; OR, THE WHALE.
New York: Harper & Row, 1966.

32 Allen, Walter. THE MODERN NOVEL IN BRITAIN AND THE UNITED
STATES. New York: E. P. Dutton & Co., Inc., 1964,
pp. 50, 319.

Comparison of J. C. Powys's novels with Melville's
work.

Melville's THE CONFIDENCE-MAN as one of the possible
sources for Ralph Ellison's THE INVISIBLE MAN.

33 Allen, Walter. THE URGENT WEST: THE AMERICAN DREAM AND
MODERN MAN. New York: E. P. Dutton & Co., Inc.,
1969, pp. 130ff, 205-206, passim.

Rev. by Richard Lehan, NCF, 24 (1969), 123-126.

34 Almy, R. R. "J. N. Reynolds: A Brief Biography with
Particular Reference to Poe and Symmes," Colophon,
n. s., 2 (1937), 224-245.

Melville students know J. N. Reynolds as the author
of MOCHA DICK; others remember Poe's admiration of him;
still others note his connection with the hollow earth
theory of Captain Symmes.

35 Alter, Robert. "The Apocalyptic Temper," Comm, 41
(June, 1966), 61-66.

35.1 Altick, Richard D. THE ART OF LITERARY RESEARCH.
New York: W. W. Norton & Company, Inc., 1963,
pp. 50, 120-121, passim.

F. O. Matthiessen might not have so greatly
admired the discordia concors of the "soiled fish"
image in WHITE JACKET (Chapter XCII) had he known
that "soiled" was a printer's error for "coiled"
which Melville had written.

36 Altick, Richard D. THE SCHOLAR ADVENTURERS. New York:
The Free Press; London: Collier-Macmillan Limited,
1950, passim.

Use of infrared light have enabled technicians at
the Pierpont Morgan Library to read the passage inked out
by Mrs. Hawthorne in the account given by Hawthorne of his
long evening chat with Melville: "...and if truth must
be told, we smoked cigars even within the sacred precincts
of the sitting room."

37   Ament, William S. "Bowdler and the Whale: Some Notes
          on the First English and American Editions of
          MOBY DICK," AL, 4 (1932), 39-46.

          At least thirty-five passages were expurgated in
      the English edition.

38   Ament, William S. "Introduction," MOBY DICK. New York:
          1928, pp. xxxvii.

39   Ament, William S. "Some Americanisms in MOBY DICK,"
          AS, 7 (1932), 365-67.

40   AMERICAN ACADEMY OF ARTS AND LETTERS: THE GREAT DECADE
          IN AMERICAN WRITING, 1850-1860. New York: American
          Academy of Arts and Letters, 1954, pp. 12-15.

41   "American Books Published in Great Britain Before 1848,"
          ESQ, 51 (2nd Qt., 1968), 129-136.

          Melville's TYPEE and OMOO are listed, but name(s)
      of publisher(s) not given.

41.1 THE AMERICAN HERITAGE BOOK OF GREAT HISTORIC PLACES.
          By the Editors of American Heritage, THE MAGAZINE
          OF HISTORY. Narrative by Richard M. Ketchum.
          Introduction by Bruce Catton. New York: American
          Heritage Publishing Co., Inc., in cooperation with
          Simon and Schuster, Inc., 1957, pp. 23, 26, 56.

          Illustrations and account of places memorable to
      Melville and his tales of whaling.

42   THE AMERICAN WRITER IN ENGLAND: AN EXHIBITION ARRANGED
          IN HONOR OF THE SESQUICENTENNIAL OF THE UNIVERSITY
          OF VIRGINIA. Charlottesville: University Press of
          Virginia, 1969, pp. 50-54.

          Among Melville items is a signed presentation copy
      of the first American edition of MOBY DICK from Melville
      to Dr. Robert Tomes, and prints of two of his letters:
      the first written (1852) to introduce Lemuel Shaw to
      John Murray, published here for the first time. The
      second to Havelock Ellis (1890), "presumably unpublished"
      but in fact printed before. (See LETTERS, Davis and
      Gilman, eds., 1960, #258).

43   Ames, Nathaniel. A MARINER'S SKETCHES. Providence: 1830.

44   Amoruso, Vito. "Alla ricerca d'Ismaele: Melville
         e l'arte," SA, 13 (1967), 169-233.

         Melville's development through MOBY DICK.

45   Anderson, Betty C. "The Melville-Kierkegaard Syndrome,"
         Rendezvous, 3, ii (1968), 41-53.

46   Anderson, Charles R. "Contemporary American Opinions of
         TYPEE and OMOO," AL, 9 (1937), 1-25.

         A survey of reviews of the two novels, favorable
and unfavorable.

47   Anderson, Charles R. "The Genesis of BILLY BUDD,"
         AL, 12 (1940), 329-346.

         "The Mutiny on the Somers" in The American Magazine,
June 1888, "may very well have been what stimulated
Melville to give his interpretation of the same theme."

48   Anderson, Charles R., ed. JOURNAL OF A CRUISE IN THE
         PACIFIC OCEAN, 1842-1844, IN THE FRIGATE UNITED
         STATES. With Introduction and Notes on Herman
         Melville. Durham, North Carolina: Duke University
         Press, 1937; New York: AMS Press, 1966.

         First hand evidence of Melville's fourteen months
on a United States naval vessel. Reveals what is literal
and what is fictitious in WHITE-JACKET.

         Rev. by Charles J. Olson, Jr., NEQ, 12 (1939), 148-149.

49   Anderson, Charles R. MELVILLE IN THE SOUTH SEAS. Diss.
         Columbia: 1936.

50   Anderson, Charles R. MELVILLE IN THE SOUTH SEAS. New York:
         Columbia University Press, 1939, 1940, 1949, 1951;
         repr., New York: Dover, 1966; London: Constable,
         1966.

         A record of Melville's journeyings, 1841-1844: the
autobiographical elements; the extent to which Melville
drew upon his reading; and the reception of the South Sea
novels.

         Rev. by Robert S. Forsythe, AL, 11 (1939), 85-92.

51   Anderson, Charles R. "Melville's English Debut,"
         AL, 11 (1939), 23-38.

         Examination of fifteen major British periodicals
shows the proportion of favorable and unfavorable reviews
similar in the United States and England.

52 Anderson, Charles R. "Melville's South Sea Romance,"
EigoS, 115 (1969), 478-482.

The single English-language contribution to the
Melville issue of THE RISING GENERATION (EigoS).

53 Anderson, Charles R. "A Reply to Herman Melville's
WHITE-JACKET by Rear-Admiral Thomas O. Selfridge, Sr.,"
AL, 7 (1935), 123-144.

Rear-Admiral Selfridge states his objections to
Melville's pictures of life on a man-of-war.

54 Anderson, Charles R. "The Romance of Scholarship:
Tracking Melville in the South Seas," Colophon, n. s.,
3 (1938), 259-279.

Sources of the author's two works: THE JOURNAL
OF A CRUISE OF THE FRIGATE UNITED STATES and MELVILLE
IN THE SOUTH SEAS.

55 Anderson, David D. "Melville Criticism: Past and
Present," MQ, 2 (1961), 169-184.

WHITE-JACKET (1850), interesting to its contemporary
critics because of its reform aspects, now attracts interest
as a work with philosophical content.

56 Anderson, David D. "Melville and Mark Twain in
Rebellion," MTJ, 11, iii (Fall, 1961), 8-9.

57 Anderson, Marilyn. "Melville's Jackets: REDBURN and
WHITE-JACKET," ArQ, 26 (1970), 173-181.

A study of the jacket motif in the two novels
reveals significant sophistication in Melville's early
experiments with literary symbolism.

58 Anderson, Quentin. "Introduction," MOBY-DICK, OR THE
WHITE WHALE. New York: Collier Books, 1962.

59 Anderson, Quentin. "Sailing to Byzantium," KR, 11
(Summer, 1949), 519-20.

Melville "approached his own nature in BILLY BUDD."
Christian doctrines are but the "tropes" to Melville's
"total feeling."

59.1 Anderson, Quentin. "Sailing to Byzantium," in TWENTIETH
CENTURY INTERPRETATIONS OF BILLY BUDD. Howard P.
Vincent, ed. Englewood Cliffs, New Jersey: Prentice-
Hall, Inc., 1971, pp. 97-98.

60   Anderson, Quentin. "Second Trip to Byzantium," KR, 11
          (1949), 516-520.

      An essay-review of the Freeman text of BILLY BUDD.

61   Anderson, Quentin, and Joseph Anthony Mazzeo, eds.
          THE PROPER STUDY: ESSAYS ON WESTERN CLASSICS.
          New York: St. Martin's Press, Inc., 1962.

62   André, Robert. "L'expérience d'autrui chez Melville,"
          CS, 54 (1962), 270-79.

      Melville's latent homosexuality, veiled and
      repressed by his Puritan education, exercised a
      profound influence on the evolution of his work.

63   André, Robert. "Melville et Shakespeare," Critique,
          20 (August-September, 1964), 705-715.

      Many aspects of Lear's sensibility seem to have
      affected Melville, but paternity, the major theme of
      the novel, not explained by the Shakespearean influence.

64   Andreev, K. Raziashchaia stal'Germana Melvilla--"Mobi
          Dik ili Belyi Kit" /The Cutting Edge of Herman
          Melville--"Moby-Dick, or, The White Whale"/.
          Literaturnaia gazeta, December 9, 1961.

65   Andrews, Deborah C. "Note on Melville's CONFIDENCE MAN,"
          ESQ, 63 (Spring, 1971), 27-28.

      "Moredock Hall" may be a reference to Judge James
      Hall, or to "Moore of Moore Hall," Thoreau's allusion in
      WALDEN. Further, the exchange between Goodman and Noble
      may also have been a private joke involving Melville
      and his neighbors, John and Sarah Morewood.

66   Angoff, Allan. ed. AMERICAN WRITING TODAY: ITS
          INDEPENDENCE AND VIGOR. Washington Square: New York
          University Press, 1957, pp. 94-95, 205-206, passim.

      Comparison of Herman Melville and Robert Penn
      Warren in their creation of "visions of horror that...
      seem true." Also, similarities between Melville's
      PIERRE and Warren's WORLD ENOUGH AND TIME are a matter
      of "common view of the human condition...."

67   Anon. ("Sir Nathaniel") "American Authorship," - No. IV.
          Herman Melville. NMM, 98 (1853), 300-308.

68   Anon. "Another Significant American Centenary,"
          CurOp, 67 (September, 1919), 184-185.

69   Anon.   "Catholic and Protestant Missions,"   ChrE, 44
       (May, 1848), 416, 441.

70   Anon.   Review of Frank T. Bullen's THE CRUISE OF THE
       "CACHALOT" ROUND THE WORLD AFTER SPERM WHALES.
       London Athenaeum, 3718 (January 28, 1899), 107.

       The author claimed his the first attempt to
       describe the cruise of a South Sea whaler from the
       seaman's viewpoint, but reviewer noted that nearly a
       half century before, Herman Melville had produced a
       work unrivalled for accuracy and of enthralling
       interest.

71   Anon.   "The Classic Story of Whaling Adventure," a review
       of C. M. Newell's THE VOYAGE OF THE FLEETWING.
       New York Nation, 46 (April 19, 1888), 330.

       Comparison with Melville's MOBY DICK, "the classic
       story of whaling adventure."

72   Anon.   /The Dramatic Force of Melville/. London Academy,
       57 (December 9, 1899), 691. Repr., MOBY-DICK AS
       DOUBLOON. Hershel Parker and Harrison Hayford, eds.
       New York: W. W. Norton, 1970, pp. 118-119.

73   Anon.   "Eutretiens de Polyèdre: Herman Melville,"
       Etudes, 331 (1969), 49-65.

74   Anon.   "Here in Boston," Boston Post (October 2, 1891).

       A reader, noting Melville's death, wonders if
       his books are still read by boys, but reports finding
       a copy of MOBY.DICK in the Public Library, "thumbed
       beyond repair."

74.1   Anon.   "Herman Melville," NYT, July 27, 1919, III, 1.

75   Anon.   "Herman Melville," TLS, July 26, 1923, pp. 493-94.

76   Anon.   "Herman Melville," TLS, March 9, 1922, p. 151.

77   Anon.   "Herman Melville--Mariner and Mystic," CathW,
       114 (1922), 686-687.

       One of the few hostile reviews of Weaver's book.

78   Anon. "Herman Melville's PIERRE," TLS, 1500 (1930), 884.

79   Anon. Herman Melville's Silence," TLS, 1173 (July 10, 1924), 433.

80   Anon. "Herman Melville's Whale," Spectator, 24 (1851), 1026-27.

81   Anon. "Journal of Melville's Voyage in a Clipper Ship," NEQ, 2 (1929), 120-139.

      An excerpt from the fragment of a journal Melville kept in 1860 when he sailed to San Francisco on the Meteor, commanded by his brother, Thomas. Apparently Raymond Weaver was mistaken when he wrote that Melville returned to New York on the Meteor in 1861; the ship sailed from San Francisco to England in 1861.

82   Anon. "Manuscript Division Accessions during 1942," BNYPL, 47 (February, 1943), 91-98.

      Includes letters of Washington and Herman Melville.

83   Anon. "Melville and His Public," AN&Q, 2 (August, 1942), 67-71.

      Newspaper accounts of Melville's lectures, January 9-February 20, 1858.

84   Anon. "Melville Issue," PULC, 13 (Winter, 1952).

85   Anon. "Melville's Journey: The Conflict of Heart and Mind," TLS, No. 45 (January 12, 1946), 18.

      Melville held fast to "doubts of all things earthly" with intuitions of "some things heavenly."

86   Anon. "Melville and Our Sea Literature," NYEP, August 2, 1919.

87   Anon. A Mention of Melville. Bookman, 1 (1891), 50.

88   Anon. "The Merchant Service," HM, 1 (December, 1839), 468-492.

89   Anon. "The Misanthrope," TimeM, 65 (1955), 114, 116, 118.

      A review of the Hendricks House edition.

90   Anon. "MOBY DICK; OR, THE WHITE WHALE," <u>Critic</u>, 22
       (1893), 232.

       In MOBY DICK, the author's "extraordinary vocabulary,
its wonderful coinages and vivid turnings and twistings
of worn-out words, are comparable only to Chapman's
translation of Homer...."

91   Anon. "Moby Dick and the Years to Come," NYTrib,
       August 4, 1919.

91.1   Anon. "The Mystery of Herman Melville," CurOp, 71
       (1921), 502-503.

92   Anon. "A Neglected American Classic," LitD, 70 (1921), 26.
       Neglect of Melville's greatest achievement, MOBY DICK.

93   Anon. "An Opera Text," TLS, No. 2601 (December 7, 1951),
       p. 785.
       Discussion of the libretto written by E. M. Forster
and Eric Crozier for the Benjamin Britten BILLY BUDD.

94   Anon. "The Parlor Table," ChrP, 3 (September, 1846).

95   Anon. "Retrospective Survey of American Literature,"
       WestmR, 57 (January and April, 1852), 304.

96   Anon. Review of the Stedman Edition of MOBY DICK.
       NYCrit, 22 (April 15, 1893), 232.
       Melville's vocabulary comparable only to Chapman's
translation of Homer. The "only wonder is that Melville
is so little known and so poorly appreciated."

97   Anon. "Sailor Melville Still Read," NYES, August 1,
       1919, p. 16

98   Anon. "Some Melville Letters," Nation&Ath, 29 (August 13,
       1921), 712-713.

99   Anon. "A Testimonial for MOBY DICK," <u>Nation</u>, 28 (January,
       1921), 572.

100   Anon. "Toward the Whole Evidence on Melville as a
       Lecturer," AN&Q, 2 (1942), 111-112.

101   Anon. "A Trio of American Sailor-Authors," DubUM, 47
         (January, 1856), 47-54. Repr. in LLA, 48 (March,
         1856), 560-566.

         The trio: Melville, Dana, and Cooper.

102   Anon. "TYPEE: A Peep at Polynesian Life," ChrObs, 1
         (May, 1847), 230-234.

103   Anon. "TYPEE: The Traducer of Missions," ChPM, 3
         (July 1846), 75.

         Assertion that Melville's books gained
"respectability and influence" because they were
published in Wiley and Putnam's LIBRARY OF AMERICAN
BOOKS.

104   Anon. "Unknown Writings of Moby Dick's Biographer,"
         NYTBR, January 21, 1923, p. 3.

105   Anon. "The Vogue of Herman Melville," N&A (London), 31
         (September 30, 1922), 857-58.

         A review of TYPEE and OMOO, the first volumes of
the Constable edition of Melville.

         So enthusiastic the admiration of English critics
for MOBY DICK that "the more intellectual of the American
critics have...retorted that the White Whale is not such
a fine whale after all. It might have been bigger, or
different...."

106   Archer, Lewis F. "Coleridge's Definition of the Poet and
         the Works of Herman Melville and William Faulkner,"
         DA, 28 (Drew: 1967), 1810A-11A.

         Coleridge's theory of the imagination is the method
for examination of Melville's symbolic art and prophetic
vision.

107   Arendt, Hannah. ON REVOLUTION. New York: The Viking
         Press, 1963, pp. 77-83.

         Compassion plays a role in BILLY BUDD, but its
topic is "goodness beyond virtue and evil beyond vice,"
and the plot of the story consists "in confronting these
two."

108   Armour, Richard. "Herman Melville," and "MOBY DICK -
         Strong Men Cry and Whales Blubber," in THE CLASSICS
         RECLASSIFIED. Illustrated by Campbell Grant. New
         York: Bantam Books. Pathfinder Editions. 1960,
         pp. 82-93.

         An "irreverent retelling" of Melville's classic.

109   Arms, George. "MOBY DICK and 'The Village Blacksmith,'"
        N&Q, 192 (1947), 187-188.

        Old Perth (Chapter 92) possibly a satire of
Longfellow's blacksmith.

110   Arnavon, Cyrille. HISTOIRE LITTÉRAIRE DES ETATS-UNIS.
        Lyons: 1953.

111   Arvin, Newton. HAWTHORNE. Boston: Little Brown & Co.,
        1929; New York: Russell & Russell, 1961, passim.

112   Arvin, Newton, ed. THE HEART OF HAWTHORNE'S JOURNALS.
        Boston: Houghton Mifflin, 1929; New York: Barnes
        & Noble, 1967, pp. 229-232, passim.

        Relationship of Melville and Hawthorne.

113 Arvin, Newton. HERMAN MELVILLE. New York: Sloane, 1950;
        Toronto: Macmillan, 1957; New York: Viking Compass
        Books, 1957.

        Rev. by Harrison Hayford, NCF, 5 (1950), 163-167;
        Sherman Paul, NEQ, 23 (1950), 405-407.

114   Arvin, Newton. "Introduction," MOBY DICK. New York
        Rinehart, Holt & Winston, 1948, 1957, 1966.

115   Arvin, Newton. "MARDI, REDBURN, WHITE-JACKET," in
        MELVILLE: A COLLECTION OF CRITICAL ESSAYS.
        Richard Chase, ed. Englewood Cliffs, New Jersey:
        Prentice Hall, 1962, pp. 21-38.

116   Arvin, Newton. "Melville and the Gothic Novel," NEQ,
        22 (March, 1949), 33-48.

        The Gothic or Radcliffean element was a "minor
ingredient" in the totality of Melville's imagination,
but the Gothic tradition lingered long enough to impart
"a delicate tincture."

117   Arvin, Newton. "Melville and the Gothic Novel," in
        AMERICAN PANTHEON. Daniel Aaron and Sylvan
        Schendler, eds. New York: Delacorte Press, 1966,
        pp. 106-122.

118   Arvin, Newton. "Melville's CLAREL," HudR, 14 (1961),
        298-300.

119   Arvin, Newton. "Melville's MARDI," AQ, 2 (1950), 71-81.

In MARDI Melville experimented unsuccessfully with different modes of writing: the type popularized by Cooper and Marryat, romantic allegory, sentimental symbolism, satire in the manner of Lucian, Rabelais, and Swift, as well as the legends and myths of Polynesia.

120   Arvin, Newton. "Melville's Shorter Poems," PR, 16 (October, 1949), 1034-1046.

Melville, following the direction of poetry which was "colloquial, prosaic, anti-poetic, and ironic," was, in a sense, a "precursor of a whole line of twentieth-century American poets."

121   Arvin, Newton. "A Note on the Background of BILLY BUDD," AL, 20 (1948), 51-55.

Additional evidence on the <u>Somers</u> affair.

122   Arvin, Newton. "The Whale," in LITERATURE IN AMERICA: AN ANTHOLOGY OF LITERARY CRITICISM SELECTED AND INTRODUCED BY PHILIP RAHV. Cleveland and New York: Meridian Books. The World Publishing Company, 1957, pp. 168-88.

123   Aschaffenburg, Walter. "Bartleby: Genesis of an Opera, 1," in MELVILLE ANNUAL 1965, A SYMPOSIUM: BARTLEBY THE SCRIVENER. Howard P. Vincent, ed. (Kent. Stud. in Eng., III). Kent, Ohio: Kent State University Press, 1966, pp. 25-41.

The "shaping" of a "fine work of literature" into an opera is justified if the result is more vivid, "more immediate" so as to move "the heart and mind of the beholder and listener."

124   Ashley, Clifford W. "A Possible Verse Parody of MOBY-DICK," AN&Q, 2 (July, 1942), 62-63.

125   Ashley, Clifford W. THE YANKEE WHALER. Boston: Houghton Mifflin, 1926, passim.

An account of whaling with illustrations and references to MOBY DICK.

126   Aspiz, Harold. "Phrenologizing the Whale," NCF, 23
        (1968), 18-27.

        Chapters 79 and 80 of MOBY DICK, in which Ishmael
        applies Lavater's physiognomy and Gall's "spinal"
        phrenology to the whale, mock "the uselessness of both
        'semi-sciences' to disclose the whale's real meaning."

126.1   Atkinson, Brooks. Foreword, BILLY BUDD, FORETOPMAN.
        The novel, edited by Frederic Barron Freeman,
        corrected by Elizabeth Freeman; the dramatic
        version, adapted by Louis O. Coxe and Robert
        Chapman. New York: Popular Living Classics
        Library, 1962.

127   Auden, W. H. "The Christian Tragic Hero," NYTBR, 50
        (December 16, 1945), 1, 21.

        Ahab contrasted with the Greek tragic hero.

128   Auden, W. H. "The Christian Tragic Hero," in TRAGEDY:
        MODERN ESSAYS IN CRITICISM. Englewood Cliffs:
        Prentice-Hall, 1963, pp. 234-38.

129   Auden, W. H. THE ENCHAFED FLOOD OR THE ROMANTIC
        ICONOGRAPHY OF THE SEA. London: Faber and Faber,
        Ltd., 1949 (?); New York: Random House, 1950, pp.
        93-149.

        Auden centers on the longing for the sea from
        Wordsworth to Mellarmé, with emphasis on MOBY DICK.

130   Auden, W. H. "Herman Melville," COLLECTED POEMS OF
        W. H. AUDEN. New York: Random House, 1945,
        pp. 146-147.

131   Auden, W. H. "The Passion of Billy Budd," in TWENTIETH
        CENTURY INTERPRETATIONS OF BILLY BUDD. Howard P.
        Vincent, ed. Englewood Cliffs, New Jersey: 1971,
        pp. 85-88.

        Claggart must corrupt innocence, and if he cannot,
        he must annihilate it, "which he does."

132   Augustin, Hermann. "Johann Jakob Bachofen und Herman
        Melville: Ein Hinweis," SchM, 46 (1967), 1124-46.

133   Ault, Nelson A. "The Sea Imagery in Herman Melville's
        CLAREL," RSSCW, 27 (June, 1959), 72-84.

134   Austin, Allen. "The Three-Stranded Allegory of MOBY DICK,"
       CE, 26 (February, 1965), 344-349.

       The three strands are pessimistic naturalism, satire
       of transcendentalism, and satire of Christianity.

135   Ayo, Nicholas. "Bartleby's Lawyer on Trial," ArQ, 28
       (1972), 27-38.

136   Bab, Julius. AMERIKAS DICHTER. Berlin: Christian-Verlag,
       1949, p. 49.

       MOBY DICK is permeated with fanatic pessimism,
       which accounts for its vogue among the younger generation
       after World War II.

137   Babcock, C. Merton. "Explication: 'Zadockprattsville,'"
       MSN, 14 (1958).

       Zadockprattsville, the headquarters for Braggadocio
       Incorporated in Melville's PIERRE, is derived from
       Zadock Pratt, a "familiar folk character" of the Catskill
       Mountain region, noted, among other things, for "his
       willingness to appreciate his own superior talents."

138   Babcock, C. Merton. GLOSSARY OF THE LANGUAGE. Michigan
       State College, 1954.

139   Babcock, C. Merton. "Herman Melville's Whaling
       Vocabulary," AS, 29 (October, 1954), 161-174.

140   Babcock, C. Merton. "Introduction," TYPEE: A REAL
       ROMANCE OF THE SOUTH SEAS. New York: Harper and
       Brothers. (Harper's Modern Classics). 1959.

141   Babcock, C. Merton. "The Language of Melville's
       'Isolatoes,'" WF, 10 (October, 1951), 285-289.

142   Babcock, C. Merton. "Melville's Backwoods Seamen,"
       WF, 10 (April, 1951), 126-133.

       Melville's use of folklore.

143   Babcock, C. Merton. "Melville's 'Moby Dictionary,'"
       WordS, 29 (December, 1953), 7-8.

       Melville's interest in etymology and his originality
       as a coiner of words.

144   Babcock, C. Merton. "Melville's Proverbs of the Sea,"
       WF, 11 (October, 1952), 254-265.

145   Babcock, C. Merton. "Melville's World's Language,"
            SFQ, 16 (September, 1952), 177-182.

            Melville in his sea tales employed folk language
        (folk idiom, proverbs, tall talk, and supernaturalism)
        to dramatize his "democratic theme."

146   Babcock, C. Merton, ed. "Of the Monstrous Pictures of
            Whales," - "Herman Melville," IDEAS IN PROCESS:
            AN ANTHOLOGY OF READINGS IN COMMUNICATION. New York:
            Harper and Brothers, 1958, pp. 291-296, 296-298.

            Excerpt from MOBY DICK with questions and exercises
        for teaching.

147   Babcock, C. Merton. "Some Expressions from Herman
            Melville," PADS, 31 (April, 1959), 3-13.

148   Babcock, C. Merton. "The Vocabulary of MOBY-DICK,"
            AS, 27 (May, 1952), 91-101.

            Melville's contribution to the English and American
        languages was more through the coining of new words than
        through adaptation of language to his own special purposes.

149   Babin, James L. "Melville and the Reformation of Being
            from TYPEE to Leviathan," SoR, 7, 1 (January, 1971),
            89-114.

150   Bach, Bert C. "Melville's Confidence-Man: Allegory,
            Satire, and the Irony of Intent," Cithara, 8, ii
            (1969), 28-36.

151   Bach, Bert C. "Melville's ISRAEL POTTER: A Revelation
            of Its Reputation and Meaning," Cithara, 7, 1
            (November, 1967), 39-50.

            The sustained irony and implicit social criticism
        make this "little esteemed" historical novel more than
        a mere adventure story, although it is weakened by
        "faulty handling of point of view."

152   Bach, Bert C. "Melville's Theatrical Mask: The Role of
            Narrative Perspective in His Short Fiction,"
            SLitI, 2, i (1969), 43-55.

            Each of the fifteen narrators of the tales is a
        bachelor or bachelor-like, fearful of change and defini-
        tions of moral or ethical concepts. However, by volition
        or circumstance, each is led to confront reality different
        from his earlier beliefs.

153   Bach, Bert C. "Narrative Point of View in the Fiction of Herman Melville After MOBY-DICK," DA, 27 (New York University: 1967), 2494A.

The first four chapters provide analysis of the later novels and fifteen tales and sketches. A fifth chapter is devoted to narrative function.

154   Bach, Bert C. "Narrative Technique and Structure in PIERRE," ATQ, 7 (1970), 5-8.

The shift from first-person to third-person narrator (after MOBY DICK) is the basis for study of PIERRE.

154.1   Bacon, Francis. "Memnon, or a Youth Too Forward," ESSAYS AND THE WISDOM OF THE ANCIENTS. London: 1696.

A possible source of Melville's story of Memnon.

155   Bader, A. L. "Marryat's 'THE OCEAN WOLF,'" PQ, 16 (1937), 80-82.

156   Bagley, Carol. "Melville's Trilogy: Symbolic Precursor of Freudian Personality Structure in the History of Ideas," DA, 27 (Washington State: 1966), 1778A.

Melville considered as a "symbolic and artistic" precursor of Freud's "scientifically articulated structure and development of human personality."

157   Baim, Joseph. "The Confidence-Man as 'Trickster,'" ATQ, 1 (1st Qt., 1969), 81-83.

The Confidence Man is an archetypal figure "in whom all opposition is resolved."

158   Baird, James R. HERMAN MELVILLE AND PRIMITIVISM. Diss. Yale: 1947.

159   Baird, James R. ISHMAEL: THE ART OF MELVILLE IN THE CONTEXTS OF INTERNATIONAL PRIMITIVISM. Baltimore, Md.: Johns Hopkins Press, 1956. Repr. New York: Harper Torchbook, 1960.

Historical and symbolic analysis of the disillusionment which Melville and other nineteenth-century travelers experienced in visiting Jerusalem.

160   Baird, James R. "Noble Polynesian," PacS, 4 (Autumn, 1950), 452-465.

161   Baker, Carlos. "Of Arts and Artifacts," NYTBR, 52 (1947), 2.

      MOBY DICK vitalizes the facts and artifacts of whaling.

161.1   Baker, Dr. Louis A. HARRY MARTINGALE: OR, ADVENTURES OF A WHALEMAN IN THE PACIFIC. Boston: 1848.

162   Bakhta, V. Posleslovie. Afterword, MELVILLE. OMU. Moscow, 1960, pp. 271-276.

163   Baldini, Gabriele. MELVILLE O LE AMBIGUITÀ. Milan: 1952.

      See review-article of Agostino Lombardo, "A Review of Gabriele Baldini's MELVILLE O LE AMBIGUITÀ," Sp-ital, 6 (1953), 275-278.

164   Balfour, Marie Clothilde. "Tahiti in 1842: As Melville Saw It," Appendix, OMOO. London: John Lane, 1904, pp. 447-462.

165   Ball, Roland C. "American Reinterpretations of European Romantic Themes: The Rebel-Hero in Cooper and Melville," in PROCEEDINGS OF THE IVth CONGRESS OF THE INTERNATIONAL COMPARATIVE LITERATURE ASSOCIATION. Francois Jost, ed. Fribourg, 1964, 2 vols. The Hague: Mouton, 1966, II, 1113-21.

166   Barbarrow, George. "Leyda's Melville--A Reconsideration," HudR, 7 (Winter, 1955), 585-593.

167   Barber, Edwin and Virginia Price Barber. BB, 25 (1967), 30.

      References to Melville.

168   Baritz, Loren. "The Demonic, Herman Melville," CITY ON A HILL: A HISTORY OF IDEAS AND MYTHS IN AMERICA. New York: John Wiley and Sons, 1964, pp. 271-331.

      Melville's intellectual journey began "in the buoyant temper of Young America" and ended in a private world of "unmitigated and unmediated torment." The climax of his disillusionment may be seen in CLAREL.

169   Barnet, Sylvan. "The Execution in BILLY BUDD," AL, 33 (January, 1962), 517-519.

      A survey of critical opinions and an analysis of the execution and hanging-scene ending.

170   Barnouw, Adriaan J. THE PAGEANT OF NETHERLANDS HISTORY.
       New York: Longmans, 1952.

       Melville's misspelling of "The Specksynder"
(MOBY DICK, Chapter 33) which should be spelled
"Specksnyder."

171   Barrett, Laurence N. "The Differences in Melville's
       Poetry," PMLA, 70 (September, 1955), 606-623.

       The "violence" of syntax and form in Melville's
poetry is purposeful. The differences arise from the
"history of his symbols."

172   Barrett, Laurence N. FIERY HUNT: A STUDY OF MELVILLE'S
       THEORY OF THE ARTIST. Diss. Princeton: 1949.

173   Barry, Sister Marie of the Trinity. THE PROBLEM OF
       SHIFTING VOICE AND POINT OF VIEW IN MELVILLE'S EARLY
       NOVELS AND MOBY-DICK. Diss. Catholic University:
       1952.

174   Barth, J. Robert. "Faulkner and the Calvinist Tradition,"
       Thought, 39 (Spring, 1964), 100-120.

       William Faulkner's protestantism descends from
Melville and others.

175   Bartlett, I. H. "The Democratic Imagination," in THE
       AMERICAN MIND IN THE MID-NINETEENTH CENTURY. New
       York: Crowell, 1967, pp. 94-113.

176   Barzun, Jacques. "Each Age Picks Its Literary Greats,"
       OPINIONS AND PERSPECTIVES FROM THE NEW YORK TIMES
       BOOK REVIEW. Introduction by Francis Brown, ed.
       Boston: Houghton Mifflin Company. The Riverside Press,
       Cambridge: 1955, 1964, pp. 18-23.

       Public response to Melville "then and now."

177   Basson, Maurice. HAWTHORNE'S SON: THE LIFE AND LITERARY
       CAREER OF JULIAN HAWTHORNE. Columbus, Ohio: Ohio
       State University Press, 1970.

       References to Melville.

178   Bates, Ernest Sutherland. AMERICAN FAITH: ITS RELIGIOUS,
       POLITICAL, AND ECONOMIC FOUNDATIONS. New York:
       W. W. Norton & Company, 1940, pp. 202, 417.

       Melville's satiric portrait in MOBY DICK of Captain
Bildad actually expressed the "driving force of all the
Protestant sects"--to unite "worldly and spiritual
advantage," to insure both the "good life on earth and a
better one in heaven."

179   Battenfeld, David H.   "I Seek for Truth: A Comparative
         Study of Melville's MOBY-DICK and PIERRE," DA, 18
         (Stanford: 1958), 1426-27.

180   Battenfeld, David H.   "The Source for the Hymn in
         MOBY DICK," AL, 27 (November, 1955), 393-396.

         The source is the rhymed version of the first
         part of Psalm 18, as found in the psalms and hymns of
         the Reformed Protestant Dutch Church.

181   Beach, Joseph Warren.   "Hart Crane and MOBY DICK,"
         WR, 20 (Spring, 1956), 183-196.

         Influence of MOBY DICK on Crane's "Voyages,"

181.1   Beale, Thomas. THE NATURAL HISTORY OF THE SPERM WHALE.
         London: 1839.

         A source for Melville.

182   Beatty, Lillian. "Typee and Blithedale: Rejected Ideal
         Communities," Person, 37 (Autumn, 1956), 367-378.

         Melville and Hawthorne both thought man must not
         isolate himself; "it is folly to reform an evil world";
         and intellect does not "take the place of heart."

183   Beaver, Harold Lawther, ed. AMERICAN CRITICAL ESSAYS:
         TWENTIETH CENTURY: SELECTED WITH INTRODUCTION.
         New York: Oxford University Press, 1959.

184   Beck, George Louis.   Introduction, MOBY DICK. London:
         Putnam, 1901.

185   Beebe, Maurice. IVORY TOWERS AND SACRED FOUNTS: THE
         ARTIST AS HERO IN FICTION FROM GOETHE TO JOYCE.
         New York: New York University Press, 1964, passim.

186   Beebe, Maurice, Harrison Hayford, and Gordon Roper.
         "Criticism of Herman Melville: A Selected Checklist,"
         Melville Special Number, MFS, 8 (1962), 312-346.

187   Beharriell, Stanley R. THE HEAD AND THE HEART IN THE
         MIND AND ART OF HERMAN MELVILLE. Diss. Wisconsin:
         1954.

188   Belgion, Montgomery. "Heterodoxy on MOBY DICK?"
       SR, 55 (1947), 108-125.

189   Belgion, Montgomery, ed. Introduction. MOBY-DICK.
       London: Cresset, 1946.

190   Bell, Millicent. "Hawthorne's 'Fire-Worship': Interpreta-
       tion and Source," AL, 24 (1952), 31-39.

       Comparison of views of Melville and Hawthorne.

191   Bell, Millicent. "The Irreducible MOBY DICK,"
       Melville Supplement, ESQ, 28 (1962), 4-6.

192   Bell, Millicent. "Melville and Hawthorne at the Grave of
       St. John (A Debt to Pierre Bayle)," MLN, 67
       (February, 1952), 116-118.

       The English translation of Pierre Bayle's
       DICTIONNAIRE HISTORIQUE ET CRITIQUE (London, 1734-1738),
       III, 576, the source of the story, alluded to by Melville
       and Hawthorne, that the earth over the grave of St. John
       heaves as if from the breathing of the saint.

193   Bell, Millicent. "Pierre Bayle and MOBY DICK," PMLA,
       66 (September, 1951), 626-648.

       Bayle's DICTIONARY a major source for MOBY DICK.

       See Arthur Sherbo, "Melville's Portuguese Catholic
       Priest," AL, 26 (1955), 563-564. Sherbo discusses a
       point about Chapter 83 puzzling to Bell.

193.1 Bellman, Samuel I. "American Literature Symmetrics (3)
       Melville," /poem/. CEA Critic, 34 (May, 1972),
       19.

194   Bellow, Saul. "Deep Readers of the World, Beware,"
       OPINIONS AND PERSPECTIVES FROM THE NEW YORK TIMES
       BOOK REVIEW. Introduction by Francis Brown, ed.
       Boston: Houghton Mifflin Company. The Riverside
       Press, Cambridge: 1955, 1964, pp. 24-28.

       Symbolism in MOBY DICK.

195   Benét, William R. "Poet in Prose," SatRL, 30 (1947), 17.

196   Bennett, Arnold. "PIERRE," THE SAVOUR OF LIFE: ESSAYS
       IN GUSTO. Garden City: Doubleday, Doran & Co., Inc.,
       1928, pp. 305-307.

       A defense of PIERRE.

197   Bennett, John. "Melville and Humanitarianism," DA, 16
       (Wis.: 1956), 961.

198   Bennett, John. THE STRUCK LEVIATHAN: POEMS ON MOBY DICK.
       Columbia, Mo.: Missouri University Press, 1970.

199   Benson, E. M. "Pierre or the Ambiguities," OutlookInd,
       152 (1929), 311.

       PIERRE is autobiographical.

200   Bentley, Richard. BentMis, 31 (January, 1852), 104-105.

       Early reaction to Herman Melville.

201   Benton, Richard P. "The Problem of Literary Gothicism,"
       ESQ: A JOURNAL OF THE AMERICAN RENAISSANCE, 18
       (1st Qt., 1972), 5-9.

       Survey of studies of the Gothic, listing those on
       Melville.

202   Berchan, M. "Le tatouage aux Iles Marquises," BSAP, 1
       (1860), 99-117.

203   Bercovitch, Sacvan. "Melville's Search for National
       Identity: Son and Father in REDBURN, PIERRE, and
       BILLY BUDD," CLAJ, 10 (March, 1967), 217-218.

204   Bergler, Edmund. "A Note on Herman Melville," AI, 2
       (Winter, 1954), 385-397.

       The white whale is the bad pre-Oedipal mother.

205   Bergmann, Johannes D. "The Original Confidence-Man,"
       AQ, 21 (1969), 560-577.

       The original Confidence Man was a "real life"
       criminal well known in the 1850's.

206   Bergmann, Johannes D. "The Original Confidence Man: The
       Development of the American Confidence Man in the
       Sources and Backgrounds of Herman Melville's THE
       CONFIDENCE-MAN: HIS MASQUERADE," DA, 30 (Conn.:
       1969), 678A-79A.

       William Thompson, prototype for THE CONFIDENCE-MAN.

207   Bergstrom, Robert F. "The Impulsive Counterchange: The
Development and Artistic Expression of Melville's
Religious Thought, 1846-1857," DA, 30 (Duke: 1969),
272A-73A.

208   Beringause, A. F. "Melville and Chrétien de Troyes,"
AN&Q, 2 (October, 1963), 20-21.

       Parallels between "Tartarus of Maids" and Chrétien
de Troyes's YVAIN.

209   Berkelman, Robert G. "MOBY DICK: Curiosity or Classic?"
EJ, 27 (1938), 742-755.

210   Berlind, Bruce. "Notes on Melville's Shorter Poems,"
HopR, 3 (1950), 24-35.

211   Bernard, Kenneth. "Lowell's 'Agassiz' and Mrs. Alexander,"
YULG, 45 (1971), 118-122.

212   Bernard, Kenneth. "Melville's MARDI and the Second Loss
of Paradise," LHR, 7 (1965), 23-30.

       MARDI is the story of paradise regained and then
lost again. It is also an allegory of the America that
was once a "Garden."

213   Bernstein, John. "BENITO CERENO and the Spanish
Inquisition," NCF, 16 (March, 1962), 345-350.

214   Bernstein, John. PACIFISM AND REBELLION IN THE WRITINGS
OF HERMAN MELVILLE. Diss. Pennsylvania, 1961.

215   Bernstein, John. PACIFISM AND REBELLION IN THE WRITINGS
OF HERMAN MELVILLE. The Hague: Mouton & Co., 1964.

       Pacificism and rebellion appear as themes in
virtually all of Melville's work, and an understanding
of the conflict of these two themes is essential.

216   Berthoff, Warner. "'Certain Phenomenal Men': The Example
of BILLY BUDD," ELH, 27 (December, 1960), 334-351.

       Billy and Vere represent complementary "motions of
magnanimity under the most agonizing worldly duress...."

217   Berthoff, Warner. THE EXAMPLE OF MELVILLE. Princeton:
Princeton University Press, 1962. New York: W. W.
Norton & Co., 1972.

       The four worlds of MOBY DICK: The first, that of
dry land; the second, the world of men; third, the men
of the Pequod and their exploits; fourth, non-human
elements, etc.

218   Berthoff, Werner. "The Example of BILLY BUDD," TWENTIETH
        CENTURY INTERPRETATIONS: A COLLECTION OF CRITICAL
        ESSAYS. Howard P. Vincent, ed. Englewood Cliffs,
        N. J.: Prentice-Hall, Inc., 1971, pp. 67-81.

        In the telling of BILLY BUDD there is no quarrel
with God or society or law or nature or any agency of
human suffering.

219   Berthoff, Warner. "Herman Melville: THE CONFIDENCE-MAN,"
        LANDMARKS OF AMERICAN WRITING. Hennig Cohen, ed.
        New York: Basic Books, 1969, pp. 121-133.

        The confidence man is not a deity or devil or
trickster, but a kind of teacher in an obscure moral
world "from which the blessings of grace and of moral
certitude appear to have been withdrawn." However,
the conclusion is that there is "a hopeful, benignant ending after all." It, too, is a "masquerade," but "there
may be more comfort and cheer in it, or at least less
terror, than we quite dare to think."

220   Berthoff, Warner, ed. Introduction, GREAT SHORT WORKS
        OF HERMAN MELVILLE. New York: Harper & Row,
        rev. ed., 1970.

221   Berthoff, Warner. "Melville's Lager Fiction: The Rites
        of Story Telling," FICTIONS AND EVENTS: ESSAYS IN
        CRITICISM AND LITERARY HISTORY. New York: E. P.
        Dutton & Co., Inc., 1971, pp. 219-229.

        Themes of Melville's shorter tales and "the truths
they predicate" are very likely as profound as interpretive
criticism has assumed them to be.

222   Berthoff, Warner. "Ponderous Stuttering in Chapter 5,"
        THE CONFIDENCE MAN: HIS MASQUERADE. Hershel Parker,
        ed. New York: W. W. Norton & Company, Inc., 1971,
        pp. 319-320.   o

        The excellent use of language in THE CONFIDENCE-MAN.

223   Berthoff, Warner. "Words, Sentences, Paragraphs, Chapters,"
        in THE RECOGNITION OF HERMAN MELVILLE: SELECTED
        CRITICISM SINCE 1846. Hershel Parker, ed. Ann Arbor,
        Mich.: Michigan University Press, 1967, pp. 313-332.

        Melville's use of language.

224   Berti, Luigi. "Fra Melville e Poe una affascinante
        parentela," FLe, 43 (October 26, 1952), 1.

        Similarities between Poe and Melville.

225   Berti, Luigi. "Melville viaggiatore o no," FLe, 26
        (June 29, 1952), 1.

226   Berti, Luigi. "Mr. Omoo," Inventario, 14 (January-December,
        1960), 335-37.

227   Berti, Luigi, ed. POESIE. 2nd ed. Firenze: Fussi,
        1957.

        Text of Melville's poems in English and Italian.

228   Betts, William W., Jr. "MOBY DICK: Melville's Faust,"
        LHB, 1, i (1959), 31-44.

        Goethe's FAUST influenced character of Ahab; the
Parsee is Ahab's Mephistopheles.

229   Beum, Robert. "Melville's Course," DR, 45 (Spring, 1965),
        17-33.

        Examination of Melville's failure in MARDI and
success in MOBY DICK.

230   Beverley, Gordon. "Herman Melville's Confidence,"
        TLS, 2493 (November 11, 1949), 733.

        THE CONFIDENCE-MAN shows true confidence in the
universe and in man.

231   Bewley, Marius. THE COMPLEX FATE: HAWTHORNE, HENRY
        JAMES AND SOME OTHER AMERICAN WRITERS. Introduction
        and Two Interpolations by F. R. Leavis. New York:
        Gordian Press, Inc., 1967, pp. 1-3.

        Melville, Hawthorne, Cooper, and James "form a line
in American writing based on a finely critical consciousness of the national society." Their resemblance lies in
their sense of the dangers and deficiencies which they
saw "encircling the possibilities they believed the
country possessed...."

232   Bewley, Marius. "Melville," THE ECCENTRIC DESIGN.
        New York: Columbia University Press, 1959, pp.
        187-219.

233   Bewley, Marius. "Melville and the Democratic Experience,"
       MELVILLE: A COLLECTION OF CRITICAL ESSAYS. Richard
       Chase, ed. Englewood Cliffs, N. J.: Prentice-Hall,
       1962, pp. 91-115.

       Captain Ahab is symbolic of the "representative
nineteenth-century American," and the fate that overtakes
him is "an indication of Melville's own reaction to the
American world of his day."

234   Bewley, Marius. MASKS AND MIRRORS: ESSAYS IN CRITICISM.
       New York: Atheneum, 1970, pp. 230-231, passim.

       No other writer of the American nineteenth-century
speaks as "profoundly and intimately to us as Melville."

235   Bewley, Marius. "Solitude and Society: Nathaniel
       Hawthorne," INTELLECTUAL HISTORY IN AMERICA:
       CONTEMPORARY ESSAYS ON PURITANISM, THE ENLIGHTENMENT
       AND ROMANTICISM. Cushing Strout, ed. New York:
       Harper & Row, 1968, pp. 179-191, passim.

       MOBY DICK is the story of a "theological quest,"
which issues, after years, in the tired disillusionment
of CLAREL.

236   Bewley, Marius. "A Truce of God for Melville," SR, 61
       (Autumn, 1953), 682-700.

       Objections to Lawrance Thompson's interpretations
of Melville.

237   Bezanson, Walter E. CLAREL. An Annotated Edition.
       Rutgers, 1954.

238   Bezanson, Walter E. "The Context of Melville's Fiction,"
       Melville Supplement, ESQ, 28 (1962), 9-12.

       MOBY DICK in relation to Melville's life, work,
and cultural milieu.

239   Bezanson, Walter E. "The Critical Furies of Edward
       Dahlberg," Criticism, 8 (Winter, 1966), 97-101.

       A review-article of Edward Dahlberg's ALMS FOR
OBLIVION. Minneapolis: Minneapolis U. P., 1964.

       "It makes one sad that the longest and most
ambitious essay among these bitter alms should be a
virulent attack on Melville...."

240   Bezanson, Walter E. "Herman Melville's CLAREL,"
       DAI, 30 (Yale: 1969), 2520A.

241   Bezanson, Walter E., ed. Introduction, CLAREL: A POEM
        AND PILGRIMAGE IN THE HOLY LAND. New York:
        Hendricks House, Inc., 1954, 1960.

        Luther Mansfield called it the best text to date.

        Rev. Stanley Brodwin, PMLA, 86 (1971, 375;
        Joseph G. Knapp, S. J., NEQ, 34 (1961), 539-541;
        Luther S. Mansfield, AL, 33 (1962), 537-538.

242   Bezanson, Walter E. "Melville's CLAREL: The Complex
        Passion," ELH, 21 (June, 1954), 146-159.

        Analysis of historical, theological, and psychological
        dilemma in the poem.

243   Bezanson, Walter E. "Melville's Reading of Arnold's
        Poetry," PMLA, 69 (June, 1954), 365-391.

244   Bezanson, Walter E. "MOBY DICK: Work of Art,"
        MOBY DICK CENTENNIAL ESSAYS. Tyrus Hillway and
        Luther S. Mansfield, eds. Dallas: Southern
        Methodist University Press, 1953, pp. 30-59.

245   Bezanson, Walter. "MOBY DICK: Work of Art,"
        CRITICISM: SOME MAJOR AMERICAN WRITERS. Selected
        by Lewis Leary. New York: Holt, Rinehart and
        Winston, Inc., 1971, pp. 95-114.

246   Bickley, Robert B., Jr. "Literary Influences and
        Technique in Melville's Short Fiction, 1853-1856,"
        DAI, 30 (Duke: 1970), 4935A.

247   Bier, Jesse. "Lapsarians on THE PRAIRIE: Cooper's
        Novel," TSLL, 4 (1962), 49-57.

        In THE PRAIRIE Cooper comes closest to the
        artistry of Melville and Hawthorne.

248   Bier, Jesse. THE RISE AND FALL OF AMERICAN HUMOR.
        New York: Holt, Rinehart and Winston, 1968,
        pp. 375-385, passim.

249   Bier, Jesse. "The Romantic Coordinates of American
        Literature," BuR, 18, ii (Fall, 1970), 16-33.

250   Bigelow, Gordon E. "The Problem of Symbolist Form in
        Melville's 'Bartleby the Scrivener,'" MLQ, 31
        (September, 1970), 345-358.

251   Bigsby, C. W. E. "Hemingway en de Amerikaanse Traditie
        van de Mens als Christus," NVT, 22, 8 (October,
        1969), 826-840.

            The central myth of American literature is the
        "ultimate incident in a society's revenge against non-
        conformity, the Crucifixion." The first Christ-figure
        in American literature was Melville's Billy Budd.

252   Billson, James. "Letter to the Editor," Nation&Ath, 29
        (1921), 396-397.

253   Billson, James. "Some Melville Letters," Nation&Ath,
        (1921).

254   Birdsall, Richard D. "Berkshire's Golden Age," AQ, 8
        (Winter, 1956), 328-355.

255   Birdsall, Richard D. THE FIRST CENTURY OF BERKSHIRE
        CULTURAL HISTORY. Diss. Columbia: 1954.

256   Birrell, Augustine. "The Great White Whale: A Rhapsody,"
        Athenaeum, 4735 (January 28, 1921), 99-100; repr. in
        LivA, 308 (1921), 659-661.

            Two striking features of this book are "its most
        amazing eloquence, and its mingling of an ever-present
        romanticism of style with an almost savage reality of
        narrative...."

256.1   Birss, John Howard. "An Obscure Melville Letter," N&Q,
        163 (1932), 275.

257   Birss, John Howard. "Another, but Later, REDBURN,"
        AN&Q, 6 (1947), 150.

            Another novel--not by Melville--dated 1896,
        bearing the title REDBURN has been found in the
        Harvard College Library.

257.1   Birss, John Howard, comp. A BOOK OF REVIEWS BY HERMAN
        MELVILLE. [n. p.], 1932.

258   Birss, John Howard. "A Book Review by Herman Melville," NEQ, 5 (1932), 346-348.

     An article on THE RED ROVER, LitW, 6 (March 16, 1850), 276-277, has been attributed to Melville.

259   Birss, John Howard. "Herman Melville and the Atlantic Monthly," N&Q, 167 (1934), 223-224.

     A letter from Melville, August 19, 1857, agreeing to contribute to the Atlantic Monthly.

260   Birss, John Howard. "Herman Melville and Blake," N&Q, 166 (1934), 311.

261   Birss, John Howard. "Herman Melville Lectures in Yonkers," AmBC, 5 (1934), 50-52.

262   Birss, John Howard. "International Copyright: A New Letter of Herman Melville," N&Q, 173 (1937), 402.

     An article on subject of international copyright from HOME JOURNAL, January 12, 1850, which includes a passage from a letter by Melville.

263   Birss, John Howard. "A Letter of Herman Melville," N&Q, 162 (1932), 39.

     Melville's letter in praise of Cooper.

264   Birss, John Howard. "Melville and James Thompson ('B.V.')," N&Q, 174 (1938), 171-172.

     A brief description of a copy of Thompson's A VOICE FROM THE NILE in which Melville made some notes.

265   Birss, John Howard. "Melville's Marquesas," SatRL, 8 (1932), 429.

266   Birss, John Howard. "'A Mere Sale to Effect' with Letters of Herman Melville," NewCol, 1 (July, 1948), 239-255.

     Letters (1846-1852) concerned with Melville's negotiations about London publication of his works.

267   Birss, John Howard. "MOBY-DICK under Another Name,"
          N&Q, 164 (1933), 206.

          A. M. Newell made use of MOBY-DICK in writing
PEHE NU-E, THE TIGER WHALE OF THE PACIFIC, Boston, 1877.

268   Birss, John Howard. "A Note on Melville's MARDI,"
          N&Q, 162 (1932), 404.

          A possible source of Hautia's name.

269   Birss, John Howard. "An Obscure Melville Letter,"
          N&Q, 163 (1932), 275.

          A letter to George McLaughlin to be sold at a
Sanitary Fair in 1864.

270   Birss, John Howard. "A Satire on Melville in Verse,"
          N&Q, 165 (1933), 402.

271   Birss, John Howard. "The Story of Toby, A Sequel to
          TYPEE," HLB, 1 (Winter, 1947), 118-119.

272   Birss, John Howard. "Toward the Whole Evidence on
          Melville as a Lecturer," AN&Q, 3 (1943), 11-12.

273   Birss, John Howard. "'Travelling,' A New Lecture by
          Herman Melville," NEQ, 7 (1934), 725-728.

          Report from the CAMBRIDGE CHRONICLE, February 25,
1860, of a lecture given at Dowse Institute, Cambridge,
Mass., on February 21, 1860. (A file of the CAMBRIDGE
CHRONICLE is preserved in the Harvard College Library.)

274   Birss, John Howard. "Whitman and Herman Melville,"
          N&Q, 164 (April, 1933), 280.

275   Bixby, William. REBEL GENIUS: THE LIFE OF HERMAN
          MELVILLE. New York: David McKay Company, Inc., 1970.

276   Blackmur, R. P. "The Art of Herman Melville," VQR, 14
          (Spring, 1938), 266-282.

          The "tools of craft" with which Melville secured
his effects in PIERRE and MOBY DICK.

277   Blackmur, R. P. "The Craft of Herman Melville:
       A putative Statement," THE EXPENSE OF GREATNESS.
       New York: Arrow Editions, 1940; repr., Gloucester,
       Mass.: Peter Smith, 1958, pp. 139-166.

       An expanded version of "The Art of Herman Melville."

       Repr., ACHIEVEMENT OF AMERICAN CRITICISM. C. A.
Brown, comp. New York: 1954, pp. 638-653; AMERICAN
LITERARY ESSAYS. Lewis Leary, ed. New York: Crowell,
1960, pp. 102-115; THE LION AND THE HONEYCOMB: ESSAYS
IN SOLICITUDE AND CRITIQUE. New York: Harcourt, Brace &
Co., 1935, 1955, pp. 124-144; MELVILLE: A COLLECTION OF
CRITICAL ESSAYS. Richard Chase, ed. Englewood Cliffs,
N. J.: Prentice-Hall, 1962, pp. 75-90.

278   Blackmur, R. P., ed. Introduction, AMERICAN SHORT
       NOVELS. New York: Thomas Y. Crowell Co., 1960.

       BILLY BUDD Melville's "continuing allegory of
how it is that we seek what we must shun."

279   Blanch, Robert J. "Captain Ahab, the Outsider,"
       EngRec, 18, 1 (October, 1967), 10-14.

       Ahab is the "Romantic Outsider," who believes
he can search out truth. The whale masks black blood
under a white skin, and Ahab hopes to "destroy the
massive symbol of matter."

279.1 Blanchott, Maurice. LE LIVRE À VENIR. Paris: Gallimard,
       1959, p. 15.

       "Ulysses understood a small part of what Ahab saw"
and "held firm,..." while Ahab was "lost in the image."

280   Blanck, Jacob, comp. BIBLIOGRAPHY OF AMERICAN
       LITERATURE. Vols. 2 and 3. New Haven: Yale
       University Press, 1957.

       Rev. by James D. Hart, AL, 33 (1961), 229-232.

281   Blanck, Jacob. "News from the Rare Book Sellers,"
       PW, 152 (August, 23, 1947), B122.

       Bibliographical details on the three issues of
the first edition of MOBY DICK.

282   Blank, Gustav. "Das Verhältnis von Dichtung, Dichter und
       Gesellschaft in der amerikanischen Literatur des 20.
       Jahr-hunderts," JAS, 6 (1961), 32-74.

283   Blankenship, Russell. AMERICAN LITERATURE AS AN
            EXPRESSION OF NATIONAL MIND. New York: 1931.

            Rev. by Reed Smith, AL, 4 (1932), 78-82.

284   Blansett, Barbara Nieweg. "'From Dark to Dark': MARDI,
            A Foreshadowing of PIERRE," SoQ, 1 (April, 1963),
            213-227.

            Contemporary critics deplored Melville's turn to
        philosophical skepticism in the two novels. Similar
        in theme, the novels make symbolic use of the light and
        dark female characters.

285   Blansett, Barbara Nieweg. "Melville and Emersonian
            Transcendentalism," DA, 24 (Texas: 1964), 2904.

            Melville's early attraction to Transcendental ideals
        as they are seen in MARDI, and his transition to the anti-
        Transcendentalism of PIERRE. Pierre is "a doomed trans-
        cendental man, motivated by a desire to follow absolute
        truth."

286   Bloom, Edward A. "The Allegorical Principle," ELH, 18
            (September, 1951), 163-190.

            Any possible critical doubts of Melville's final
        allegorical intention in his creation of MOBY DICK are
        resolved in a letter from Melville to Mrs. Hawthorne (1852).

            The letter is quoted in part by Willard Thorp,
        HERMAN MELVILLE. New York: 1938, p. lxxii, n. 116.

287   Blotner, Joseph. THE MODERN AMERICAN POLITICAL NOVEL,
            1900-1960. Austin: Texas University Press, 1966,
            passim.

            A survey of political views expressed in BILLY BUDD.

288   Bluefarb, Sam. "The Sea-Mirror and Maker of Character in
            Fiction and Drama," EJ, 48 (December, 1959), 501-510.

289   Bluestone, George. "Bartleby: The Tale, The Film,"
            MELVILLE ANNUAL 1965, A SYMPOSIUM: BARTLEBY THE
            SCRIVENER. Howard P. Vincent, ed. (Kent Stud. in
            Eng., III). Kent, Ohio: Kent State University
            Press, 1966, pp. 45-54.

            Description of the cast and production of the
        movie based on the story.

289.1   Bluestone, George. "Notes on BARTLEBY," University of
        Washington. Mimeographed. n. d. (c. 1962).

        Criticism of story, discussion of movie "Bartleby"
        written and directed by Bluestone, first shown at University
        of Washington, January 10, 1962.

289.2   Bluestone, George. NOVELS INTO FILM. Baltimore: The
        Johns Hopkins Press, 1957, passim.

        John Huston's production of MOBY DICK.

290   Boas, George. ROMANTICISM IN AMERICA. Baltimore: 1940.

291   Boas, Ralph Philip. THE STUDY AND APPRECIATION OF
        LITERATURE. New York: Harcourt, Brace and Company,
        1931, pp. 133, 144.

        MOBY DICK is "tangy" with the details of whaling.
        Captain Ahab, Queequeg and the rest of the crew "may
        seem a little hysterical," but the sea is there as
        nowhere else except in that master of setting, Joseph
        Conrad.

292   Bode, Carl. THE ANATOMY OF AMERICAN POPULAR CULTURE:
        1840-1861. Berkeley and Los Angeles. University
        of California Press, 1959, pp. 225-227, 271.

        In TYPEE, "the arch example of the South Sea Island
        adventure," Fayaway became the "prototype of a school
        of friendly South Pacific charmers."

293   Bode, Carl. "Foreign Ports and Exotic Places, 1840-1860,"
        THE HALF-WORLD OF AMERICAN CULTURE. Carbondale:
        Southern Illinois University Press, 1965, pp. 33-53.

294   Boewe, Charles. "Romanticism Bracketed," ESQ, 35
        (1st Qt., 1964), 7-10.

        Melville and other writers developed in a society
        in which boundless opportunity was possible. The 1830's
        were the seedtime, the 1840's the period of germination,
        the 1850's produced the harvest.

295   Bohn, William E. "Melville's Neglected Masterpiece,"
        NewL, 39 (1956), 5.

296   Boies, Jack Jay. "Existential Nihilism and Herman
       Melville," TWA, 50 (1961), 307-320.

       Melville, the "disillusioned serious man" of the
       existentialists, rejected the rationalism of Kant and
       the empiricism of Locke. He shows a strong preoccupation
       with symbolic, vicarious suicide, and it is in this area
       that his metaphysical nihilism is most evident.

297   Boies, Jack Jay. THE GROWTH OF NIHILISM IN AMERICAN
       PROSE FICTION AS EXEMPLIFIED BY HERMAN MELVILLE,
       MARK TWAIN, JACK LONDON, AND ERNEST HEMINGWAY.
       Diss. Wis.: 1959.

298   Boies, Jack Jay. "Melville's Quarrel with Anglicanism,"
       ESQ, 33 (4th Qt., 1963), 75-79.

       Melville's portraits of the clergy and references
       to particular sects suggest his "quarrel" lies more with
       Anglicanism, than with Calvinism.

299   Boies, Jack Jay. "THE WHALE Without Epilogue," MLQ, 24
       (June, 1963), 172-176.

       MOBY DICK is nihilistic, beginning and ending with
       death. (Ishmael is saved only physically.) This idea
       more strongly presented through absence of the epilogue
       (from early English edition, THE WHALE). Melville let
       Ishmael live, not because he shared Ishmael's viewpoint,
       but because he had been criticized for abandoning his
       narrator.

300   Bond, William H. "Melville and TWO YEARS BEFORE THE MAST,"
       HLB, 7 (1953), 362-365.

301   Bone, Robert A. THE NEGRO NOVEL IN AMERICA. New Haven:
       Yale University Press, 1958, passim.

       Melville's influence on Ralph Ellison.

302   Bonheim, Helmut. "The Vocabulary of BILLY BUDD," ExExc,
       10 (March, 1963), 13-14.

303   Booth, Edward Townsend. GOD MADE THE COUNTRY. New York:
       Alfred A. Knopf, 1946, passim.

304   Booth, Thornton Y. "MOBY DICK: Standing Up to God,"
       NCF, 17 (June, 1962), 33-43.

       Relationship of the Book of Job.

305   Booth, Wayne C. THE RHETORIC OF FICTION. Chicago:
      Chicago University Press, 1961, pp. 203-205.

      "Benito Cereno."

306   Borges, Jorge Luis. OTHER INQUISITIONS, 1937-1952. Trans.
      Ruth L. C. Simms. Introduction by James E. Irby.
      Austin, Texas: Texas University Press, 1964, passim.

      Melville devoted many pages of MOBY DICK to "an
      elucidation of the insupportable whiteness of the whale."

307   Borton, John. HERMAN MELVILLE: THE PHILOSOPHICAL
      IMPLICATIONS OF LITERARY TECHNIQUE IN MOBY DICK.
      (Amherst College Honors Theses No. 6). Amherst,
      Mass.: Amherst College Press, 1961.

      Melville's philosophy as exemplified in MOBY DICK
      and BILLY BUDD. "The Whiteness of the Whale" chapter is
      crucial.

308   Botta, Guido. "L'ultimo romanzo di Melville," SA, 3
      (1957), 109-131.

      THE CONFIDENCE MAN.

309   Boudreau, Gordon V. "Herman Melville: Master Mason of
      the Gothic," DA, 28 (Ind.: 1968), 5007A-08A.

      The recurrent metaphor of the gothic cathedral and
      its constituent symbols, light and rock from MARDI through
      BILLY BUDD, with emphasis on Melville's "religious intent."

      Billy Budd, "a true Christ figure," is presented as
      "the copestone (rock) and rose-window (light) of that
      cathedral."

310   Boudreau, Gordon V. "Of Pale Ushers and Gothic Piles:
      Melville's Architectural Symbology," ESQ, 18
      (2nd Qt., 1972), 67-82.

      Melville's use of the Gothic.

311   Bourne, W. O. "Missionary Operations in Polynesia,"
      NewEng, 6 (1848), 41-58.

312   Bowden, Edwin T. THE DUNGEON OF THE HEART: HUMAN
      ISOLATION AND THE AMERICAN NOVEL. New York:
      Macmillan, 1961, pp. 156-172, passim.

      The theme of "The Monkey Rope" Chapter is "human
      isolation," or man's moral obligation to other men.
      Ahab's chief sin is social irresponsibility, and Ishmael
      is "a likable, recognizable fellow."

      Rev. by Alexander Cowie, AL, 34 (1962), 439-440;
      Robert H. Knox, NEQ, 34 (1961), 558-560.

313   Bowen, James K. "'Crazy Ahab' and Kierkegaard's
        'Melancholy Fantastic,'" RS, 37 (March, 1969),
        60-64.

        Comparison of what Kierkegaard does through
        philosophic precept with what Melville does through
        creative incident indicates that the intent of each
        writer complements the other, providing an understanding
        of both the "melancholy fantastic" and "crazy Ahab."

314   Bowen, James K., and Richard Vanderbeets. A CRITICAL
        GUIDE TO HERMAN MELVILLE. Abstracts of Forty Years
        of Criticism. Glenview, Ill.: Scott, Foresman,
        1971.

315   Bowen, Merlin. THE LONG ENCOUNTER: SELF AND EXPERIENCE
        IN THE WRITINGS OF HERMAN MELVILLE. Chicago: Chicago
        University Press, 1960.

        Melville's works are "so many dramatic representations
        of the encounter of the self and the not-self."

        See Edward H. Rosenberry. "Awash in Melvilliana,"
        NEQ, 33 (1960), 525-528.

316   Bowen, Merlin. "REDBURN and the Angle of Vision," MP,
        52 (November, 1954), 100-109.

317   Bowen, Merlin. SELF AND EXPERIENCE IN THE WRITINGS OF
        HERMAN MELVILLE. Diss. Chicago: 1957.

318   Bowen, Merlin. "Tactics of Indirection in Melville's
        THE CONFIDENCE-MAN," SNNTS, 1, iv (Winter, 1969),
        401-420.

        The story is not a sermon "but a gesture, a life-
        sustaining and life-enhancing act. And the man who could
        write it was a man for whom life was clearly something
        still worth living."

319   Bowers, David. "Democratic Vistas," LITERARY HISTORY OF
        THE UNITED STATES. Robert E. Spiller, et al, eds.
        New York: Macmillan, 1948, I, 345-357.

        Melville in relation to Transcendentalism.

320   Boyle, Thomas E. "The Tenor in the Organic Metaphor:
        A view of American Romanticism," *Discourse*, 11, ii
        (Spring, 1968), 240-251.

        Comparison of Whitman's SONG OF MYSELF and Melville's
        MOBY DICK. The differentiation in tenor shows Melville
        essentially anti-romantic.

321   Boynton, Percy H. "Harriet Beecher Stowe and Herman
         Melville," A HISTORY OF AMERICAN LITERATURE.
         New York: Ginn & Co., 1919, pp. 304-309.

         The Melville revival can be accounted for partly
         by the post-war skepticism, but more because in Melville
         has been rediscovered one of "the immensely energetic
         and original personalities of the last hundred years."

322   Boynton, Percy H. "Herman Melville," MORE CONTEMPORARY
         AMERICANS. Chicago: Chicago University Press, 1927,
         pp. 29-50.

         MOBY DICK is as much an allegory as THE DIVINE
COMEDY or PARADISE LOST.

323   Boynton, Percy H. LITERATURE AND AMERICAN LIFE. Boston:
         1936.

324   Brack, Vida K., and O. M. Brack, Jr. "Weathering Cape
         Horn: Survivors in Melville's Minor Short Fiction,"
         ArQ, 28 (1972), 61-73.

325   Bradley, G. P. "Burial Customs Formerly Observed in the
         Naval Service," JAF, 7 (1894), 67-69.

326   Bradley, Scully, Richmond Croom Beatty and E. Hudson Long,
              eds. THE AMERICAN TRADITION IN LITERATURE. New York:
         1956. Revised, New York: W. W. Norton, 1962, Vol. I.

327   Branch, E. D. THE SENTIMENTAL YEARS. New York: 1934.

328   Branch, Watson G. "An Annotated Bibliography," in
              THE CONFIDENCE MAN: HIS MASQUERADE. Hershel Parker,
              ed. New York: W. W. Norton & Co., 1971, pp. 363-376.

         An annotated bibliography for THE CONFIDENCE MAN
from 1919 to 1971.

329   Branch, Watson G. "The Mute as 'Metaphysical Scamp,'"
              THE CONFIDENCE-MAN: HIS MASQUERADE. Hershel Parker,
              ed. New York: W. W. Norton, 1971, pp. 316-319.

330   Brashers, H. C. "Ishmael's Tattoos," SR, 70, 1
              (Winter, 1962), 137-154.

         Ishmael assimilates the significance of Queequeg's
tattoos, the micro and macrocosmic elements that enable
Ishmael alone to survive his voyage. Ishmael achieves
the balance between his ego and his "kinship to the
universe." Thus, his soul "tattooed, he outlives the
ego-maniacal Ahab, the unrational Queequeg, and the
crew."

331   Braswell, William. "The Early Love Scenes of Melville's
        PIERRE," AL, 22 (1950), 283-289.

        Melville's style in the early love scenes is a mock
romantic satire of sentimental, erotic romances. He
ridicules Pierre's "precious posturing," and satirizes
idyllic Eden.

332   Braswell, William. HERMAN MELVILLE AND CHRISTIANITY.
        Diss. Chicago University: 1934.

333   Braswell, William. HERMAN MELVILLE AND CHRISTIANITY.
        Chicago: Chicago University Libraries, 1934.

334   Braswell, William. "The Main Theme of MOBY DICK,"
        Melville Supplement, ESQ, 28 (1962), 15-17.

        Ahab and the "wickedness" of MOBY DICK.

335   Braswell, William. "Melville as a Critic of Emerson,"
        AL, 9 (November, 1937), 317-34.

        Melville's letters to E. A. Duyckinck (March 3,
1849), and other letters (See Minnigerode's SOME
PERSONAL LETTERS OF HERMAN MELVILLE), also Melville's
journals, comments on Emerson's lectures, etc., give
more information than scholars have had heretofore.

336   Braswell, William. "Melville's BILLY BUDD, as 'An Inside
        Narrative,'" AL, 29 (May, 1957), 133-146.

        The story may be considered an "inside narrative"
about a tragic conflict in Melville's own spiritual life.

337   Braswell, William. "Melville's Opinion of PIERRE,"
        AL, 23 (May, 1951), 246-250.

338   Braswell, William. MELVILLE'S RELIGIOUS THOUGHT: AN
        ESSAY IN INTERPRETATION. Durham: Duke University
        Press, 1943; repr. New York: Pageant Book Co., 1959.

        Melville came to believe that one senses the
ultimate truth more through the heart than through the
head.

        Rev. by F. Barron Freeman, NEQ, 17 (1944), 125-127.

339   Braswell, William. "Melville's Use of Seneca," AL, 12
        (1940), 98-104.

340   Braswell, William. "A Note on 'The Anatomy of Melville's
        Fame,'" AL, 5 (1934), 360-364.

        Corrects and extends article by O. W. Riegel,
"The Anatomy of Melville's Fame," AL, 3 (1931),
195-203.

341   Braswell, William. "The Satirical Temper of Melville's
       PIERRE," AL, 7 (1936), 424-438.

       Melville gratified the "satirical element" in his
       nature by mocking his too "idealistic self" and by defying
       the literary conventions of a world that fêted its clever
       authors and starved its geniuses.

342   Bratcher, James T. "MOBY DICK: A Riddle Propounded,"
       Descant, 4 (1959), 34-39.

       MOBY DICK is a riddle in that it leaves unanswered the
       question it propounds of whether or not evil underlies all
       apparent good.

343   Braude, William G. "Melville's MOBY DICK," Expl, 21
       (1962), Item 23.

       The name Pequod may have reference to the punishing
       of Leviathan mentioned in the fifty quotations in The
       Extracts, for it is the root of the word "punish" in
       Hebrew.

       Cf., Kenneth Walter Cameron, ESQ, 29 (1962), 3-4.

344   Braun, Julie Ann. "Melville's Use of Carlyle's SARTOR
       RESARTUS: 1846-1857," DA, 28 (U. C. L. A.: 1968),
       4622A.

       Carlyle's influence strongest in MOBY DICK and
       PIERRE.

345   Braunsperger, Elfriede. MELVILLE ALS MYSTIKER. Diss.
       Vienna, 1953.

346   Bray, Richard T. "Melville's MARDI: An Approach
       Through Imagery," DAI, 30 (Wis.: 1970), 5401A.

347   Bredahl, Axel C., Jr. "Melville's Angles of Vision: The
       Function of Shifting Perspective in the Novels of
       Herman Melville," DAI, 31 (Pittsburgh: 1970),
       1263A.

347.1 Bredahl, Axel C., Jr. MELVILLE'S ANGLES OF VISION.
       Gainesville, Florida: Florida University Press,
       1972.

348   Breinig, Helmbrecht. "The Destruction of Fairyland:
       Melville's 'Piazza' in the Tradition of the
       American Imagination," ELH, 35 (1968), 254-283.

       Examination of "fairyland" as an ideal world of
       actuality, especially in 19th century America. Melville
       becomes "one of the first 'moderns'" through his demonstra-
       tion that "the destruction of fairyland is a base for the
       development of art."

349   Breit, Harvey, C. L. R. James, and Lyman Bryson.
         "MOBY-DICK," InvitL, 2 (Spring, 1952), 41-47.

350   Brewer, D. S. "'Wanderer,' Lines 50-57," MLN, 67 (1952),
         398-399.

         Compared to Melville's "John Marr."

351   Brickell, Herschel. "Herman Melville," NR, 58 (1929),
         205-206.

         Acceptance of Mumford's reading of "organic vision"
into Melville's life and works.

352   Bridgman, Richard. THE COLLOQUIAL STYLE IN AMERICA.
         New York: Oxford University Press, 1966, pp. 69-72.

         Colloquial style in Chapter 43 of MOBY DICK.

         Rev., Guy A. Cardwell, AL, 39 (1967), 124-125.

353   Bridgman, Richard. "Melville's Roses," TSLL, 8 (Summer,
         1966), 235-244.

         Melville made "fresh and varied uses" of the
traditional rose symbol, beginning with MOBY DICK,
on through "Jimmy Rose," "Naples in the Time of Bomba,"
and most impressively in the rose poems of "Weeds and
Wildings, with a Rose or Two."

354   Briggs, C. F. WORKING A PASSAGE. New York: 1844.

355   Britten, Benjamin. BILLY BUDD /an opera/. New York:
         1953.

         See E. M. Forster and Eric Crozier for libretto.

356   Brodtkorb, Paul, Jr. "THE CONFIDENCE-MAN: The Con Man
         as Hero," SNNTS, 1, iv (Winter, 1969), 421-435.

         THE CONFIDENCE-MAN, a nihilistic gloss on "All the
world's a stage," "assumes with Ahab in his worst moments
that beyond the mask lies the naught. Which is why the
playful con-man, diffracted into various masquerades, is
the hero of the book,...and in his very playfulness even
its potential saviour,...."

357   Brodtkorb, Paul, Jr. "The Definitive BILLY BUDD: 'But
         Aren't it all sham?'" PMLA, 82 (December, 1967),
         602-612.

         The unity of the story stems from its theme of
understanding. Every major character tries to understand
those about him; at the same time the narrator attempts
to understand the characters.

358   Brodtkorb, Paul, Jr. HERMAN MELVILLE'S SYMBOLOGY. Diss.
        Yale: 1963.

359   Brodtkorb, Paul, Jr. ISHMAEL'S WHITE WORLD: A
        PHENOMENOLOGICAL READING OF MOBY DICK. New Haven:
        Yale University Press, 1965.

        Rev. by Richard Harter Fogle, AL, 37 (1966), 485-486.

360   Brodtkorb, Paul, Jr. "The White Hue of Nothingness,"
        TWENTIETH CENTURY INTERPRETATIONS. Howard P. Vincent,
        ed. Englewood Cliffs, N. J.: Prentice-Hall, Inc.,
        1971, pp. 29-33.

361   Brodwin, Stanley. "Herman Melville's CLAREL: An
        Existential Gospel," PMLA, 86 (May, 1971), 375-387.

        "The real structured drama of CLAREL is to be
   discovered in the 'inner' but 'unconcealed' nature of
   man's existence as he discovers it in his freedom and
   in facing death."

        Cf., S. C. Chamberlain. "Reply," PMLA, 87
   (1971), 103-104.

362   Bronson, Walter C. A SHORT HISTORY OF AMERICAN LITERATURE.
        Boston: D. C. Heath & Co., 1910, pp. 148-149.

        An early survey of American literature, listing
   TYPEE, MOBY DICK, THE PIAZZA TALES, BATTLE PIECES,
   POEMS, "and other poems and prose works; all showing
   much strength and talent."

363   Brooks, Cleanth. "The Language of Poetry. Some Problem
        Cases," NS, 6 (April, 1967), 401-414.

        Poets often have to "dislocate" language in order
   to express themselves successfully. Different strategies
   of dislocation are apparent in Melville.

364   Brooks, Van Wyck. EMERSON AND OTHERS. New York:
        Dutton 1927, pp. 195-205.

        Influence of Rabelais, Thomas Moore, Butler,
   and Carlyle on Melville.

365   Brooks, Van Wyck. THE FLOWERING OF NEW ENGLAND.
        New York: E. P. Dutton and Company, Inc., London:
        J. M. Dent and Sons, 1952, passim.

366   Brooks, Van Wyck. FROM A WRITER'S NOTEBOOK. New York:
       E. P. Dutton & Company, 1958, p. 101.

       The seventeenth-century "flavour" of certain passages
       of MOBY DICK, the "fruit of taste" developed by certain
       American painters--the "amber patina of age," often called
       the "brown sauce" of the school of Munich.

367   Brooks, Van Wyck. "Herman Melville," DICTIONARY OF
       AMERICAN BIOGRAPHY. New York: D. C. Heath, 1933,
       pp. 522-526.

368   Brooks, Van Wyck. (New) Introduction. OMOO. Designed
       by John Dreyfus. Wood Engravings by Reynolds Stone.
       Oxford: Printed for the members of the Limited
       Editions Club, 1961.

369   Brooks, Van Wyck. Introduction, OMOO. New York: Heritage
       Press, 1967.

370   Brooks, Van Wyck. "The Literary Life in America,"
       AMERICAN LITERARY CRITICISM, 1900-1950. Introduction
       by Charles I. Glicksberg. New York: Hendricks House,
       Inc., 1952, pp. 146-160.

       Add to poverty, the "want of a society devoted to
       intellectual things," and the result is a fate such as
       Herman Melville's in New York.

371   Brooks, Van Wyck. "Melville in the Berkshires,"
       TigE, 1 (October, 1947), 47-52.

372   Brooks, Van Wyck. "Melville the Traveller," and "Melville
       in the Berkshires," in THE TIMES OF MELVILLE AND
       WHITMAN. New York: Dutton, 1947. Reissued, New
       York: Dutton, 1953, pp. 145-164; 165-179, passim.

       Lives of great writers of the period as they were
       related to the nation and its struggles.

       Rev. by Robert E. Spiller, AL, 20 (1949), 459-461.

373   Brooks, Van Wyck. "Notes on Herman Melville,"
       EMERSON AND OTHERS. New York: 1927, pp. 171-205.

374   /Brooks, Van Wyck./ "A Reviewer's Notebook," Freeman, 4
       (October 26, 1921), 166-167; (December 21, 1921),
       258-259; 6 (February, 14, 1923), 550-551; 7 (May 9,
       1923), 214-215; (May 16, 1923), 238-239; (May 23,
       1923), 262-263; (May 30, 1923), 286-287.

       The Melville revival. The prediction is that a
       "few hundred or a few dozen readers," discovering Melville
       for the first time, will "seize upon his gift as a
       permanent possession."

375   Brooks, Van Wyck. THE WORLD OF WASHINGTON IRVING.
New York: E. P. Dutton, 1945, passim.

Recreation of the literary milieu.

376   Brooks, Van Wyck. WRITER IN AMERICA. New York: E. P.
Dutton, 1953, p. 20.

Melville's work is "defective in structure."

377   Brophy, Brigid, Michael Levey, and Charles Osborne.
"Moby Dick or The White Whale," FIFTY WORKS OF
ENGLISH (AND AMERICAN) LITERATURE WE COULD DO
WITHOUT. New York: Stein and Day, Publishers,
1967, 73-75.

MOBY DICK, American literature's "pseudo-founding
father, its false prophet in fake biblical prose."
American literature is now "old enough and good enough
to sell off the great white elephant."

378   Brophy, Robert J. "Benito Cereno, Oakum, and Hatchets,"
ATQ, 1 (1969), 89-90.

The oakum-pickers and hatchet-scourers are allusions
to two of the "Parcae of classical lore."

379   Brouwer, Fred E. "Melville's THE CONFIDENCE-MAN as Ship
of Philosophers," SHR, 3 (1969), 158-165.

Melville had in mind "specific philosophers"--
eighteenth-century ethical thinkers who wrote in reaction
to Thomas Hobbes.

380   Brower, Kenneth. "Moby Dick, Man, and Environment,"
VOICES FOR THE WILDERNESS. W. Schwartz, ed.
New York: Ballantine, 1969, pp. 176-178.

381   Brown, Cecil M. "The White Whale," PR, 36 (1969),
453-459.

Ishmael, the forerunner of the "modern white
liberal-intellectual."

382   Brown, Clarence Arthur. "The Aesthetics of Romanticism,"
THE ACHIEVEMENT OF AMERICAN CRITICISM. New York:
Ronald Press, 1954, pp. 149-182.

Rev. by Howard Mumford Jones, AL, 26 (1955), 597-598.

383   Brown, E. K. "Hawthorne, Melville and 'Ethan Brand,'"
AL, 3 (1931), 72-75.

Refutation of views of Lewis Mumford (HERMAN
MELTILLE, 1929), and Newton Arvin (HAWTHORNE, 1961),
that in Ethan Brand, Hawthorne drew a portrait of
Melville.

384.   Brown, E. K. RHYTHM IN THE NOVEL. Toronto: Toronto
        University Press, 1950, pp. 56-57. Repr. U. S. A.,
        1957, 1963, p. 52.

        Definition of an "expanding symbol" and the purpose
        it serves in a novel, followed by analysis of Melville's
        use of the whale as an "expanding symbol."

385   Brown, John Mason. "Hanged from the Yardarm," AS THEY
        APPEAR. New York: McGraw Hill Book Co., Inc.,
        1952, pp. 186-192.

        Comparison of the tale BILLY BUDD with the play.

386   Brown, Ruth Elizabeth. "A French Interpreter of New
        England Literature, 1846-1865," NEQ, 13 (1940),
        305-321.

        Survey of criticism of two French critics, Emile
        Montégut and Philarète Chasles, who reviewed American
        writers, including Melville and Hawthorne.

387   Brown, Sterling. THE NEGRO IN AMERICAN FICTION.
        Washington: Associates in Negro Folk Education,
        1937, pp. 11-13.

        "Benito Cereno."

388   Browne, J. Ross. ETCHINGS OF A WHALING CRUISE. New
        York: 1846.

389   Browne, Ray B. "The Affirmation of 'Bartleby,'"
        FOLKLORE INTERNATIONAL: ESSAYS IN TRADITIONAL
        LITERATURE, BELIEF, AND CUSTOM IN HONOR OF
        WAYLAND DEBS HAND. D. K. Wilgus, ed., assisted
        by Carol Sommer. Hatboro, Pa.: Folklore
        Associates, Inc., 1967, pp. 11-21.

        Melville's continuing interest in "heroic
        endurance." A line of "savior-figures" run from
        Bartleby and Hunilla to their culmination in Billy
        Budd, who is a more successful embodiment than
        Bartleby of the "universal hero-savior."

390   Browne, Ray B. "BILLY BUDD: Gospel of Democracy,"
        NCF, 17 (March, 1963), 321-337.

        The novel's form and its relationship to the
        political philosophies of Edmund Burke and Thomas
        Paine: The roles of Vere and of "Billy as common
        sailor," Melville's use of songs to strengthen the
        common man theme, all indicate the "ultimate victory
        of a democratic political philosophy over a conserva-
        tive one."

        Cf., Bernard Suits. "BILLY BUDD and Historical
        Evidence: A Rejoinder," NCF, 18 (1963), 288-291.

391   Browne, Ray B. "ISRAEL POTTER: Metamorphosis of
       Superman," FRONTIERS OF AMERICAN CULTURE. Ray B.
       Browne, Richard H. Crowder, Virgil L. Lokke, and
       William T. Stafford, eds. Lafayette, Ind.:
       Purdue University Press, 1968, pp. 88-98.

       The title character is the "true mountaineer, the
backwoodsman," who symbolizes a "kind of superman," who
is at last replaced by the "common man."

       ISRAEL POTTER and THE CONFIDENCE-MAN share an
"over-riding theme": the necessity for humanism, of
"man's faith in the human race in this man-of-war and
godless world."

391.1   Browne, Ray B. MELVILLE'S DRIVE TO HUMANISM. Lafayette,
       Indiana: Purdue University Press, 1972.

       Melville's themes show Melville's "humanism,"
and his belief that the solution to man's problems
lies with man himself.

392   Browne, Ray B. "Popular Theater in MOBY DICK,"
       NEW VOICES IN AMERICAN STUDIES. Ray B. Browne,
       Donald M. Winkelman, and Allen Hayman, eds.
       Lafayette, Ind.: Purdue Studies, 1966, pp. 89-101.

       Much of the humorous dialogue in MOBY DICK derives
from contemporary "burlesques, extravaganzas, farces,
variety acts, curtain raisers,...melodramas--and, of
course, Negro minstrels."

393   Browne, Ray B. "Two Views of Commitment: 'The Paradise
       of Bachelors' and 'The Tartarus of Maids,'" ATQ, 7
       (Summer, 1970), 43-47.

394   Browne, Ray B., and Martin Light, eds. CRITICAL APPROACHES
       TO AMERICAN LITERATURE. I. New York: Crowell, 1965.

395   Browne, Ray B., and Donald Pizer, eds. THEMES AND
       DIRECTIONS IN AMERICAN LITERATURE: ESSAYS IN HONOR
       OF LEON HOWARD. Lafayette, Indiana: Purdue
       University Studies, 1969.

396   Bruffee, Kenneth A. "Elegiac Romance," CE, 32, iv
       (January, 1971), 465-476.

       The term "Elegiac Romance" applies to such novels
as Melville's MOBY DICK, Conrad's LORD JIM and HEART OF
DARKNESS, and novels by various other authors.

       They are "romances" because a heroic figure in each
is embarked on some kind of quest. They are "elegiac"
because the narrator in each tells the story after the
heroic figure is dead.

397   Brumm, Ursula. "The Figure of Christ in American
         Literature," PR, 24 (Summer, 1957), 403-412.

         BILLY BUDD.

398   Brumm, Ursula. "Herman Melville: 'The Lexicon of
         Holy Writ,'" AMERICAN THOUGHT AND RELIGIOUS
         TYPOLOGY. Rutgers University Press, 1970,
         pp. 162-187.

399   Brumm, Ursula. DIE RELIGIOSE TYPOLOGIE IM AMERIKANISCHEN
         DENKEN. IHRE BEDEUTUNG FUR DIE AMERIKANISCHE
         LITERATUR UND GEISTESGESCHICHTE. Leiden: E. J.
         Brill, 1963; New Brunswick, N. J.: Rutgers University
         Press, 1970.

         The influence of Typology on American writers,
         among them Melville, viewed not as a symbolist in the
         modern sense, but as "ein symbolischer Realist," whose
         heroes are the ideal American, the Christlike Adam.

         Rev. by Henry A. Pochmann, AL, 36 (1965), 543-544;
         Jesper Rosenmeier, NEQ, 38 (1965), 121-122.

400   Bryan, William Alfred. GEORGE WASHINGTON IN AMERICAN
         LITERATURE, 1775-1865. New York: Columbia
         University Press, 1952, p. 166.

         "Lee in the Capital" from BATTLE PIECES AND
         ASPECTS OF THE WAR (1866), written some time after the
         cessation of hostilities, compares Washington and Robert
         E. Lee,--"Who looks at Lee must think of Washington;...."

401   Buchanan, Robert. "Imperial Cockneydom," UnR, 4 (1889),
         71-91.

402   Buchanan, Robert. "'Melville' from 'Socrates in Camden,
         with a Look Round," London Academy, 28 (August 15,
         1885), 102-103.

         The author sought everywhere for "this Triton,"
         Herman Melville. "No one seemed to know anything of
         the one great imaginative writer fit to stand shoulder
         to shoulder with Whitman on that continent."

403   Buckley, A. R. CRITICAL AND INTERPRETIVE READING OF
         "PIAZZA TALES." Diss. Long Island University,
         1954.

404   Buckley, Vincent. "The White Whale as Hero," CR, 9
         (1966), 1-21.

         MOBY DICK dramatizes the white whale as protagonist
         and initiator, so that Ahab assaults metaphysical order
         in the relationships of God, man, and the natural world.

405   Bulgheroni, Marisa. IL DEMONE DEL LUOGO: LETTURE
          AMERICANE. Milan: Instituto Editoriale Cisalpino
          di Varese, 1968.

          Discussion of THE CONFIDENCE-MAN.

406   Burgert, Hans. "William Faulkner on MOBY DICK: An
          Early Letter," SA, 9 (1963), 371-375.

          William Faulkner was asked what book he would like
       most to have written: "...the book which I put down
       with the unqualified thought 'I wish I had written that'
       is MOBY DICK...."

407   Bunker, Robert M. WHITMAN, MELVILLE, TWAIN: MOCKERY
          OF THEIR OWN WORLD SCHEMES. Diss. New Mexico:
          1954.

408   Burke, Kenneth. "Ethan Brand: A Preparatory Investigation,"
          HopR, 5 (Winter, 1952), 45-65.

409   Burke, Kenneth. THE PHILOSOPHY OF LITERARY FORM.
          Baton Rouge: Louisiana State University Press,
          1941, 2nd ed., 1967, pp. 24, 83, 88.

          MOBY DICK is frequently cited for examples of
       various literary devices.

410   Burnam, Tom. "Tennyson's 'Ringing Grooves' and Captain
          Ahab's Grooved Soul," MLN, 68 (June, 1952), 423-424.

          Apparently both Tennyson and Melville thought
       railroads were "grooved."

411   Burns, Graham. "The Unshored World of MOBY DICK,"
          CR, 13 (1970), 68-83.

          Melville as stylist.

412   Burns, Landon C., Jr. "A Cross-Referenced Index of
          Short Fiction and Author-Title Listing," SSF, 7
          (1970), 1-218.

          An indispensable aid for finding the "right"
       anthology for certain stories, particularly those of
       Melville.

413   Burton, Dwight L. LITERATURE STUDY IN THE HIGH SCHOOLS.
          3rd ed. New York, Chicago: Holt, Rinehart and
          Winston, Inc., 1959, 1964, 1970, pp. 309, passim.

          Of the books with the sea as background, treating
       man's moral condition and his relationship to the
       universe, perhaps the "greatest" is MOBY DICK, which
       high school students may read with profit.

414　　Buschmann, Johann. APERÇU DE LA LANGUE DES ILES
　　　　　MARQUISES. Berlin: 1843.

415　　Bush, C. W. "This Stupendous Fabric: The Metaphysics
　　　　　of Order in Melville's PIERRE and Nathaniel West's
　　　　　MISS LONELYHEARTS," JAmS, 1, ii (October, 1967),
　　　　　269-274.

　　　　　Both Pierre and Miss Lonelyhearts attempt a
　　　　synthesis of "ideality and life." Both, aspiring to
　　　　some form of Christian order, are frustrated, and
　　　　achieve their dreams of order only in death.

416　　Butler, John F. EXERCISES IN LITERARY UNDERSTANDING.
　　　　　Chicago: Scott, Foresman, 1956, pp. 22-25.

　　　　　"Benito Cereno."

417　　Cabau, Jacques. "Melville: La chasse à Dieu," NL, 47
　　　　　(1969), I, 10.

418　　Cady, Edwin H. THE GENTLEMAN IN AMERICA: A LITERARY
　　　　　STUDY IN AMERICAN CULTURE. Syracuse University
　　　　　Press, 1949, passim.

　　　　　Melville made his Pierre a Christian gentleman
　　　　to show how terribly the "abysses of moral ambiguity
　　　　opened beneath even the man conventionally recognized
　　　　as humanly perfect."

419　　Cady, Edwin H. THE ROAD TO REALISM: THE EARLY YEARS
　　　　　(1837-1885) OF WILLIAM DEAN HOWELLS. Syracuse
　　　　　University Press, 1956, p. 104, passim.

　　　　　Incidental remarks which place Melville in his
　　　　literary milieu.

420　　Cady, Edwin H. "The Teacher and the American Novel:
　　　　　1964," THE TEACHER AND AMERICAN LITERATURE: PAPERS
　　　　　PRESENTED AT THE 1964 CONVENTION OF NATIONAL COUNCIL
　　　　　OF TEACHERS OF ENGLISH. Lewis Leary, ed. Champaign,
　　　　　Ill.: 1965, pp. 21-30.

　　　　　A survey of criticism of various American novels,
　　　　including BILLY BUDD and MOBY DICK.

421　　Cahoon, Herbert. "Herman Melville: A Checklist of
　　　　　Books and Manuscripts in the Collections of the
　　　　　New York Public Library," BNYPL, 55 (1951),
　　　　　263-75; 325-338.

　　　　　Contains bibliography of Melville's contribution
　　　　to periodicals.

422   Cahoon, Herbert. "Herman Melville and W. H. Hudson,"
        AN&Q, 8 (December, 1949), 131-132.

        Hudson in IDLE DAYS IN PATAGONIA discusses
Melville's chapter on "The Whiteness of the Whale"
in MOBY DICK.

423   Cairns, William B. AMERICAN LITERATURE FOR SECONDARY
        SCHOOLS. New York: Macmillan, 1914, p. 226.

        Melville's "novels of adventure" are recommended
as "full of excitement, wholesome and well told."

424   Calhoun, Dorothy C. "TYPEE: A Fifteen-Minute Radio Play,"
        ONE HUNDRED NON-ROYALTY ONE-ACT PLAYS. William
        Kozlendo, ed. New York: 1940.

425   Calinescu, Adriana. "Structura Simbolului in 'MOBY DICK,'"
        StLu, 8 (1966), 187-206.

426   Callan, Richard J. "The Burden of Innocence in Melville
        and Twain," Ren, 17 (Summer, 1965), 191-194.

        Parallel situations in BILLY BUDD and HUCKLEBERRY
FINN indicate that Twain the humorist may be more
pessimistic about society than Melville.

427   Calverton, V. F. THE LIBERATION OF AMERICAN LITERATURE.
        New York: Scribner's, 1932, pp. 271-273.

428   Cambon, Glauco. "La Caccia Ermeneutica a MOBY DICK,"
        SA, 8 (1962), 9-19.

428.1   Cambon, Glauco. DANTE'S CRAFT: STUDIES IN LANGUAGE AND
        STYLE. Minneapolis: Minnesota University Press,
        1969.

        The first essay, Part II, Dante's influence on
American writers from Melville to Eliot.

429   Cambon, Glauco. "Giacobbe e l'angelo in Melville e
        Conrad," Let, 4 (1956), 53-69.

430   Cambon, Glauco. "Ishmael and the Problem of Formal
        Discontinuities in MOBY DICK," MLN, 76 (June,
        1961), 516-523.

        Ishmael, the artist, is present through his narration
when he ceases to be directly present. He is the "self-
ironizing" writer seeking realization through "self-
effacement in the work of art."

431   Cambon, Glauco. "Ismaele e it problema dell'unita
        formale in MOBY-DICK," Verri, 2 (1962), 133-142.

432   Cambon, Glauco. LA LOTTA CON PROTEO. Milano: Bompiani,
        1963.

        On Melville and others.

433   Cambon, Glauco. "Una Pagina di Melville," SLett (1957),
        419-431.

434   Cambon, Glauco. "Una Pagina di Melville," STUDI
        LETTERARI PER IL 250 ANNIVERSARIO DELLA NASCITA DI
        C. GOLDONI (Stuidia Ghisleriana. Pubblicazioni del
        Collegio Ghislieri in Pavia e dell 'Associazione
        Alumni. Ser. II, Vol. II). Pavia: Gepografia del
        Libro, 1957, pp. 419-431.

435   Cambon, Glauco. "Space, Experiment, and Prophecy,"
        THE INCLUSIVE FLAME: STUDIES IN AMERICAN POETRY.
        Bloomington: Indiana University Press, 1963,
        pp. 3-52.

436   Cameron, Kenneth W. "'BILLY BUDD' and 'An Execution at
        Sea,'" ESQ, 2 (1st Qt., 1956), 13-15.

        An earlier treatment of the BILLY BUDD theme.

437   Cameron, Kenneth W. "Emerson and Melville Lecture in
        New Haven (1856-1857)," ESQ, 19 (2nd Qt., 1960),
        85-96.

438   Cameron, Kenneth W. "Etymological Significance of
        Melville's Pequod," ESQ, 29 (1962), 3-4.

        Usually associated with a Connecticut Indian
        tribe (the Pequots), the word has more pertinent
        meaning if derived from the Hebrew root PKD: "to
        strike against, to go in search of, to punish, to
        terrify."

        Cf., William G. Braude. "Melville's MOBY DICK,"
        Expl. 21 (1962), Item 23.

439   Cameron, Kenneth W. HAWTHORNE AMONG HIS CONTEMPORARIES.
        Hartford: Transcendental Books, 1968, pp. 512-513,
        passim.

440   Cameron, Kenneth W. "Melville, Cooper, Irving and
         Bryant on International Matters," ESQ, 51 (2nd Qt.,
         1968), 108-121.

         Reproduction of six documents signed by American
authors calling for establishment of an international
copyright law. The Melville petition is Document 3.

441   Cameron, Kenneth W. "Melville, Cooper, Irving, and
         John Esaias Warren: Travel Literature and
         Patronage," ESQ, 47 (2nd Qt., 1967), 114-125.

         The correspondence reveals the problems which
men of letters have always encountered in seeking
government patronage.

442   Cameron, Kenneth W. "A Melville Letter and Stray Books
         from His Library," ESQ, 63 (Spring, 1971), 47-49.

         Letter to Richard Tobias Greene of Sandusky is
accompanied by the auction dealer's description.

         Four books recently sold are listed because they
do not appear in MELVILLE'S READING by Merton M.
Sealts, Jr.

443   Cameron, Kenneth W. "More Grist for Melville's MOBY
         DICK," ESQ, 1 (4th Qt., 1955), 7-8.

444   Cameron, Kenneth W. "A Note on the Corpusants in
         MOBY DICK," ESQ, 19 (2nd Qt., 1960), 22-24.

445   Cameron, Kenneth W. "Samoan Laws for Melville's Ships
         in 1839," ESQ, 33 (1963), 47-48.

         Reprint of two broadsides: <u>Samoan Laws</u> (November 5,
1839) and <u>Commercial Regulations Made by the Principle</u> /sic7
<u>Chiefs of the Samoa Group of Islands</u> (1839). A copy of the
was given to the captain of every ship visiting the islands.

446   Cameron, Kenneth W. "Scattered Melville Manuscripts,"
         ATQ, 1 (1969), 63-64.

         Reproduction of two items from dealer's catalogues:
an undated letter from Melville to Evert Duyckinck and
a quoted proverb with his signature.

447   Camillucci, Marcello. "Un Centenario MOBY-DICK,"
         VP, 36 (April, 1953), 183-189.

448   Camillucci, Marcello. "Il Grande Dio Assoluto," FLe, 10
         (March 8, 1953), 5.

449   Camp, James Edwin. "An Unfulfilled Romance: Image,
        Symbol and Allegory in Herman Melville's CLAREL,"
        DA, 27 (Mich.: 1966), 472A.

        Key images in relation to the developing allegory,
romantic plot, and philosophic dialectic.

450   Campbell, Harlan S. "CLAREL." Diss. Stanford: 1954.

451   Campbell, Harry Modean. "The Hanging Scene in Melville's
        BILLY BUDD FORETOPMAN," MLN, 66 (1951), 378-81.

        Cf., G. Giovannini. "The Hanging Scene in
Melville's BILLY BUDD," MLN, 70 (1955), 491-497.

452   Campbell, Harry Modean. "The Hanging Scene in Melville's
        BILLY BUDD: A Reply to Mr. Giovannini," MLN, 70
        (November, 1955), 497-500.

        Evidence for pessimism lies in the final hanging
scene.

453   Campbell, Marie A. "A Quiet Crusade: Melville's Tales
        of the Fifties," ATQ, 7 (Summer, 1970), 8-12.

        The fall of innocence a recurrent theme in THE
PIAZZA TALES, the real tragedy of the characters being
"the failure to mature."

454   Camus, Albert. "Herman Melville," EcrC, 3 (1953),
        128-129.

455   Camus, Albert. "Herman Melville," LYRICAL AND CRITICAL
        ESSAYS. Edited with Notes by Philip Thody; tr. by
        Ellen Conroy Kennedy. New York: Knopf, 1968,
        pp. 288-294.

        Melville's lyricism, like Shakespeare's, makes
use of the four elements.

456   Canaday, Nicholas, Jr. "Harry Bolton and Redburn: The
        Old World and the New," ESSAYS IN HONOR OF ESMOND
        LINWORTH MARILLA. Thomas Austin Kirby and William
        John Olive, eds. Baton Rouge: Louisiana State
        University Press, 1970.

457   Canaday, Nicholas, Jr. "Melville and Authority: A Study
         of Thematic Unity," DA, 17 (Florida: 1957), 2007.

458   Canaday, Nicholas, Jr. MELVILLE AND AUTHORITY. (UFMH 28)
         Gainesville: Florida University Press, 1968.

         The extent to which the theme of authority appears
in Melville's writing.

459   Canaday, Nicholas, Jr. "Melville's Pierre: At War with
         Social Convention," PLL, 5 (1969), 51-62.

         Out of Pierre's obedience to a "moral imperative"
in defiance of society, come both "heroism and foolish-
ness, knowledge and grief, independence and death."
Melville's attitude toward Pierre's "war" is ambivalent.

460   Canaday, Nicholas, Jr. "A New Reading of Melville's
         'Benito Cereno,'" STUDIES IN AMERICAN LITERATURE.
         Waldo McNeir and Leo B. Levy, eds. (LSUSHS, 8).
         Baton Rouge: Louisiana State University Press,
         1960, pp. 49-57.

         Chaos and disorder are the inevitable results of
"authority functioning without power and of power
exercised without authority."

461   Canaday, Nicholas, Jr. "The Theme of Authority in
         Melville's TYPEE and OMOO," ForumH, 4 (1963),
         38-41.

         The sailor's rebellion against intolerable ship
captains, and the theme of authority and the ship
captain's role. Also, the evil effects of European
civilization upon the islands.

462   Canby, Henry Seidel. AMERICAN MEMOIR. Boston: Houghton
         Mifflin Company. The Riverside Press, Cambridge:
         1947, pp. 319, 415.

         Thomas Carlyle's influence on Melville.

463   Canby, Henry Seidel. "Conrad and Melville," LitR, 2
         (1922), 383-394.

464   Canby, Henry Seidel. "Conrad and Melville," DEFINITIONS:
         ESSAYS IN CONTEMPORARY CRITICISM. First Series.
         New York: Harcourt Brace, 1922, pp. 257-268.
         Reissued: Kennikat Press, by arrangement with
         Harcourt, Brace and World, 1967, pp. 257-268.

         Conrad's achievement more complete than Melville;
his scope less.

465   Canby, Henry Seidel. "Hawthorne and Melville," CLASSIC
        AMERICANS: A STUDY OF EMINENT AMERICAN WRITERS
        FROM IRVING TO WHITMAN WITH AN INTRODUCTORY SURVEY
        OF THE COLONIAL BACKGROUND OF OUR NATIONAL LITERATURE.
        New York: Harcourt, Brace, 1931, pp. 226-262;
        Russell & Russell, Inc., 1959, pp. 226-262.

466   Canfield, Francis X. "MOBY DICK and the Book of Job,"
        CathW, 174 (1952), 254-260.

        Melville's copy of the Bible indicates that the
        Book of Job was a prevailing influence in the creation
        of MOBY DICK. Both the Book of Job and MOBY DICK have
        the same lesson to teach: "God directs the events of
        day-to-day living and even draws good out of evil."

467   Cannon, Agnes D. "Melville's Concept of the Poet and
        Poetry," DA, 29 (Pa.: 1969), 2207A.

468   Cannon, Agnes D. "Melville's Use of Sea Ballads and
        Songs," WF, 23, 1 (January, 1964), 1-16.

        Melville loved ballads and used them in three
        ways: to heighten realism of sea descriptions, to
        indicate emotions, to supply the base for ballads of
        his own.

        "Billy in the Darbies," an account of "Christ in
        Chains."

468.1   Canoll, J. W. Henry. New York CommAd, January 18, 1886.

        Reference to Melville as a "buried" author.

469   Caraber, Andrew J., Jr. "Melville's THE CONFIDENCE-MAN,"
        Expl, 29 (October, 1970), Item 9.

        If "Noah" is taken to be Noah Webster (to whom °
        Melville refers in Chapter 53 of MOBY DICK), then the
        "press" must be regarded as a symbol of the free press
        of America.

470   Cardwell, Guy A. "Melville's Gray Story: Symbols and
        Meaning in 'Benito Cereno,'" LV, 1 (1957), 4-13.

        Repr., BuR, 8 (May, 1959), 154-167; MELVILLE'S
        "BENITO CERENO": A TEXT FOR GUIDED RESEARCH. John P.
        Runden, ed. Boston: Heath, 1965, pp. 133-142;
        A "BENITO CERENO HANDBOOK. Seymour L. Gross, ed.
        Belmont, Calif.: Wadsworth, 1965, pp. 99-104.

471   Cargill, Oscar. INTELLECTUAL AMERICA: IDEAS ON THE
          MARCH. New York: The Macmillan Company, 1941.

         Comparison of Hart Crane's "The Bridge" and "the
mad prose" of MARDI.

472   Carlisle, E. F. "Captain Amasa Delano: Melville's
          American Fool," <u>Criticism</u>, 7 (Fall, 1965), 349-362.

         "Benito Cereno" indicates the failure of optimism,
"the inadequacy of the Great American Boob."

473   Carothers, Robert L. "Herman Melville and the Search
          for the Father: An Interpretation of the Novels,"
          DAI, 30 (Kent State: 1970), 4445A.

474   Carothers, Robert L. "Melville's 'Cenci': A Portrait
          of PIERRE," BSUF, 10, 1 (Winter, 1969), 53-59.

         The "incestuous motive" is the heart of the conflict
that eventually destroys Pierre. Pierre's wish for a
sister and his "basically sexual" image of his father
prepares the way for his difficulties.

475   Carpenter, Frederic I. "'The American Myth': Paradise
          (To Be) Regained," PMLA, 74 (December, 1959),
          599-606.

         The "experimental idealism" of the new Adam found
expression in Emerson and Thoreau, but was criticized
by Hawthorne and Melville.

476   Carpenter, Frederic I. "The Genteel Tradition:
          A Re-Interpretation," NEQ, 15 (1942), 427-443.

         The moral philosophy of Melville and Hawthorne
remained traditional. They illustrate the genteel
tradition at its best, recognizing the "beauty and
the heroism" of the Transcendental ideal but denouncing
its "romantic extravagances."

477   Carpenter, Frederic I. "Melville: The World in a Man
          of War," UKCR, 19 (Summer, 1953), 257-264.

         In MOBY DICK, an allegory of democracy, the
captain is a democratic leader of a crew who have
voluntarily signed on and who give up their democratic
rights in pursuit of profit and the war against evil,
with resulting disaster. The novel thus allegorizes
"two inherent dangers" of democracy: the possibility
that men may voluntarily surrender their freedom, and
the threat that "they may mix their dream of democracy
with the romantic dream of world dominion." Thus, in
MOBY DICK, Melville prophesies "the doom of democracy."

478   Carpenter, Frederic I. "Melville and the Men-of-War,"
       AMERICAN LITERATURE AND THE DREAM. New York:
       Philosophical Library, Inc., 1955, pp. 73-82,
       passim.

       Submission to "traditional authority" and
       rejection of "individual responsibility," which
       Melville approved in BILLY BUDD, run counter both
       to American experience and to American idealism.

479   Carpenter, Frederic I. "Puritans Preferred Blondes:
       The Heroines of Melville and Hawthorne," NEQ, 9
       (1936), 253-272.

       In MARDI and PIERRE blondness is an "ideal virtue"
       and darkness a serious and sometimes "unforgivable sin."

       MOBY DICK is the search of Ahab, the monomaniac of
       an idea, for the white whale. And, Yillah, the "personi-
       fication of whiteness," is an albino. Also, Moby Dick
       is an albino whale.

480   Carrington, George C., Jr. THE IMMENSE COMPLEX DRAMA:
       THE WORLD AND ART OF THE HOWELLS NOVEL. Columbus,
       Ohio: Ohio State University Press, 1966, pp. 30-31,
       passim.

       Comparison of William Dean Howells and Melville.

481   Carter, Angela. "REDBURN: HIS FIRST VOYAGE by Herman
       Melville," AntigR, 1, i (1970), 103-105.

482   Carter, Everett. HOWELLS AND THE AGE OF REALISM.
       Philadelphia, New York: J. B. Lippincott Company,
       1954, pp. 21-22, 32-33, passim.

       Explanation for Howells' loss of popularity and
       Melville's revival.

483   Casper, Leonard. "The Case Against Captain Vere,"
       Perspective, 5 (Summer, 1952), 146-152.

484   Cawelti, John G. "Some Notes on the Structure of THE
       CONFIDENCE-MAN," AL, 29 (1957), 278-288.

       THE CONFIDENCE-MAN is not a "random collection"
       of episodes, but the "bitter polemic of a despairing
       man," a serious attempt to present one man's "vision
       of reality."

484.1   Cecchi, Emilio. "Diario degli stretti," (1940),
        SCRITTORI INGLESI E AMERICANI: SAGGI NOTE E
        VERSIONI. 4th ed. Rev. and Enlarged. Milano:
        Il Saggiatore, 1962, I, 121-127.

        JOURNAL UP THE STRAITS (Oct. 11, 1856-May 5, 1857).

484.2   Cecchi, Emilio. "Hawthorne e Melville a Roma," (1950),
        SCRITTORI INGLESI E AMERICANI: SAGGI NOTE E
        VERSIONI. 4th ed. Rev. and Enlarged. Milano:
        Il Saggiatore, 1962, I, 127-130.

484.3   Cecchi, Emilio. "Incontro con MOBY DICK," (1931),
        SCRITTORI INGLESI E AMERICANI: SAGGI NOTE E
        VERSIONI. 4th ed. Rev. and Enlarged. Milano:
        Il Saggiatore, 1962, I, 108-111.

484.4   Cecchi, Emilio. "Melville minore," (1945),
        SCRITTORI INGLESI E AMERICANI: SAGGI NOTE E
        VERSIONI. 4th ed. Rev. and Enlarged. Milano:
        Il Saggiatore, 1962, I, 116-121.

        ISRAEL POTTER
        MOBY DICK

485   Cecchi, Emilio. "MOBY DICK dopo un Secolo," Fle, 10
        (March 8, 1953), 3.

485.1   Cecchi, Emilio. "Nuove Interpretazioni di Melville,"
        (1952), SCRITTORI INGLESI E AMERICANI: SAGGI NOTE
        E VERSIONI. 4th ed. Rev. and Enlarged. Milano:
        Il Saggiatore, 1962, I, 112-116.

        MOBY DICK

485.2   Cecchi, Emilio. SCRITTORI INGLESI E AMERICANI: SAGGI
        NOTE E VERSIONI. 4th ed. Rev. and Enlarged. Milano:
        Il Saggiatore, 1962. 2 vols, passim.

486   Cecchi, Emilio. "Two Notes on Melville," SR, 68
        (July, 1960), 398-406.

        Melville in MOBY DICK is almost prehistoric in
        his presentation of man against nature.

487   Cecil, L. Moffitt. "Symbolic Pattern in THE YEMASSEE,"
          AL, 35 (January, 1964), 510-514.

          The central serpent image of Chapter 20 proves
          that William Gilmore Simms experimented with the
          symbolic methods which were to characterize the works
          of Melville and Hawthorne.

488   Cellini, Ilva, and Giorgio Melchiori, eds. ENGLISH
          STUDIES TODAY. Fourth Series. Roma: Edizioni di
          Storia e Letteratura, 1966.

489   Cestre, Charles. LA LITTÉRATURE AMÉRICAINE. Paris:
          Librairie Armand Colin, 1945.

          An introduction of American literature to French
          readers. The violence of Melville is deplored.

          Rev. by Robert E. Spiller, AL, 18 (1947), 335-337.

490   Chamberlain, S. C. "Reply," PMLA, 87 (January, 1972),
          103-104.

          A reply to Stanley Brodwin. "Herman Melville's
          CLAREL: An Existential Gospel," PMLA, 86 (1971),
          375-387.

491   Chandler, Alice. "Captain Vere and the 'Tragedies of
          the Palace,'" MFS, 13 (Summer, 1967), 259-261.

          BILLY BUDD, Melville's "bleakest statement" of the
          way in which he saw injustice, tyranny, and hate at "the
          heart of things."

492   Chandler, Alice. "The Name Symbolism of Captain Vere,"
          NCF, 22 (June, 1967), 86-89.

          The name "Vere" had widespread pejorative use in
          19th century literature, but if Melville chose the name
          to suggest "aristocratic associations" then the story
          is indeed a "Gospel of Democracy."

493   Chapin, Henry, ed. Introductory Note, THE APPLE-TREE
          TABLE AND OTHER SKETCHES. Princeton: Princeton
          University Press, 1922; New York: Greenwood Press,
          1969.

494   Chapin, Henry, ed. JOHN MARR AND OTHER POEMS. Princeton:
          1922.

495   Chapman, John, ed. "'BILLY BUDD': Play in Three Acts,"
          by Louis O. Coxe and Robert Chapman, based on the
          Short Novel by Herman Melville. THE BEST PLAYS OF
          1950-1951 AND THE YEAR BOOK OF THE DRAMA IN AMERICA.
          New York, Toronto: 1951, pp. 100-124, 349.

496   Chapman, John, ed. THEATRE '56, Including "The Theatre
          in the United States and Canada," by George Freedley
          and "The Theatre in London," by C. B. Mortlock.
          New York: Random House, 1956, p. 34.

          A melodramatic adaptation of Melville's BILLY BUDD
          by Louis O. Coxe and Robert Chapman under the title of
          THE GOOD SAILOR; produced by Frith Banbury at the Lyric,
          Hammersmith, 1956.

497   Charters, Ann. OLSON/MELVILLE: A STUDY IN AFFINITY.
          Berkeley: Oyez, 1968.

498   Charvat, William. "James T. Fields and the Beginnings
          of Book Promotion, 1840-1855," HLQ, 8 (1944), 75-94.

499   Charvat, William. "Literary Economics and Literary
          History," ENGLISH INSTITUTE ESSAYS: 1949.
          Alan S. Downer, ed. New York: AMS Press, Inc.,
          1965, pp. 73-91.

          The artist was at his best when the two pressures--
          "creative and social"--were in equilibrium. It was the
          artist "in balance with society" who produced such works
          as MOBY DICK.

500   Charvat, William. LITERARY PUBLISHING IN AMERICA,
          1790-1850. Philadelphia: Pennsylvania University
          Press, 1959, passim.

          Melville's books were acclaimed when they were
          "solidly based on his travels," and neglected and abused
          when he moved into "the world of possibility."

501   Charvat, William. "Melville and the Common Reader,"
          SB, 12 (1959), 41-57.

          Melville and the 19th century reading public.

502   Charvat, William. "Melville's Income," AL, 15 (1943),
          251-261.

          Melville made a good living from his writing
          during the first years of his literary life (1846-1851),
          but his income shrank from 1851 to 1866.

503   Charvat, William. "Melville's Income," (1943); "Melville
         and the Common Reader," (1958)/an earlier version of
         "Melville and the Common Reader"/; also previously
         unpublished: "Melville," THE PROFESSION OF AUTHOR-
         SHIP IN AMERICA, 1800-1870: THE PAPERS OF WILLIAM
         CHARVAT. Matthew J. Bruccoli, ed. Columbus: Ohio
         State University Press, 1968.

504   Charvat, William. THE ORIGINS OF AMERICAN CRITICAL
         THOUGHT: 1810-1835. New York: A. S. Barnes and
         Company, Inc., 1961, (A Perpetua Book), passim.

        Melville was not indebted either to the criticism
or the fiction of the preceding period.

505   Chase, F. H. LEMUEL SHAW. Boston: 1918.

506   Chase, Owen. NARRATIVE OF THE MOST EXTRAORDINARY AND
         DISTRESSING SHIPWRECK OF THE WHALESHIP ESSEX OF
         NANTUCKET. New York: 1821. 1963 edition with
         Introduction prepared by B. R. McElderry, Jr.
         New York: Corinth Books, 1963.

        The work is important as a possible source for
the climax of MOBY DICK.

507   Chase, Richard. "An Approach to Melville," PR, 14
         (May-June, 1947), 285-294.

        Melville's "Promethean Hero" is no vaporous or
"irresponsible extravagance" of the Romantic Age. He
is "elementary psychology" for American moralists.

508   Chase, Richard. "An Approach to Melville," LITERARY
         OPINION IN AMERICA. Morton D. Zabel, ed. 3rd ed.
         rev., New York: Harper & Row, 1962, pp. 588-596.
         Also in PSYCHOANALYSIS AND AMERICAN FICTION. Irving
         Malin, ed. New York: Dutton, 1965, pp. 111-120.

509   Chase, Richard. "The Classic Literature: Art and Idea,"
         PATHS OF AMERICAN THOUGHT. Arthur M. Schlesinger, Jr.,
         and Morton White, eds. London: Chatto & Windus,
         1964, pp. 52-70.

        A study of the works which indicate Melville's
attitude toward injustice and suffering, and, as well,
toward American problems.

510   Chase, Richard. "Dissent on BILLY BUDD," PR, 15 (1948), 1212-1218. Expanded in HERMAN MELVILLE: A CRITICAL STUDY. New York: 1949.

        Melville's "definitive moral statement" is not made in BILLY BUDD, but in MOBY DICK, THE CONFIDENCE-MAN, and CLAREL. Billy Budd is preeminently the "beatified boy of the liberal-progressive myth," the figure who gets "pushed around." His suffering and death are without "moral content."

511   Chase, Richard. "Herman Melville," MAJOR WRITERS OF AMERICA. I. Perry Miller, gen. ed. New York: Harcourt, Brace & World, 1962.

512   Chase, Richard. HERMAN MELVILLE: A CRITICAL STUDY. New York: Macmillan, 1949.

        Melville's models of style, other than the great English authors, came from the popular American rhetoric and oratory of his own day.

513   Chase, Richard. "Innocence and Infamy," LITERATURE IN CRITICAL PERSPECTIVES. Walter K. Gordon, ed. New York: Appleton, 1968, pp. 741-752.

514   Chase, Richard, ed. Introduction, MELVILLE: A COLLECTION OF CRITICAL ESSAYS. Englewood Cliffs, N. J.: Prentice-Hall, 1962, pp. 1-10.

515   Chase, Richard, ed. Introduction, SELECTED TALES AND POEMS BY HERMAN MELVILLE. New York: Holt, Rinehart and Winston, 1950, 1960, pp. v-xix.

516   Chase, Richard. "Melville and MOBY DICK," THE AMERICAN NOVEL AND ITS TRADITION. Garden City, New York: Doubleday & Company, Inc., 1957, pp. 89-115.

517   Chase, Richard. "Melville and MOBY DICK," THE PROPER STUDY: ESSAYS ON WESTERN CLASSICS. Quentin Anderson and Joseph A. Mazzeo, eds. New York: St. Martin's Press, 1962, pp. 528-544.

        MOBY DICK is at once the "most startling" and the "most characteristic product" of the American imagination.

518   Chase, Richard. "Melville's CONFIDENCE MAN," KR, 11
       (Winter, 1949), 122-140.

       This book of folklore, "an attack on liberalism
       by a liberal," is a carefully planned and subtle satire
       on the American spirit.

519   Chasles, Philarète. ANGLO-AMERICAN LITERATURE AND MANNERS.
       Trans. Donald MacLeon. New York: Charles Scribner,
       1852, pp. 118-146.

520   Chasles, Philarète. "Séjour des deux Américains chez les
       Taipies, dans l'Ile Noukahiva," JdJ (June 22, 25,
       1846).

521   Chasles, Philarète. "Voyages réels et fantastiques
       d'Hermann Melville," RDM, 2 (15 Mai, 1849), 542-570.

522   Chatfield, E. Hale. "Levels of Meaning in Melville's
       'I and My Chimney,'" AI, 19 (Summer, 1962), 163-169.

523   Chittick, V. L. O. "Haliburton Postscript I: Ringtailed
       Yankee," DR, 37 (Spring, 1957), 19-36.

524   Chittick, V. L. O. "The Way Back to Melville: Sea-Chart
       of a Literary Revival," SWR, 40 (Summer, 1955),
       238-248.

       Melville, a much-less-forgotten man during his
       later years than supposed; his cult in England, particular-
       ly, was continuous. Archibald MacMechan, who relished
       especially "a western quality displayed in MOBY-DICK,"
       deserves credit for nourishing Melville's Englisn fame.

525   Clarens, Carlos. AN ILLUSTRATED HISTORY OF THE HORROR
       FILMS. New York: G. P. Putnam's Sons, 1967, p. 40.

       John Barrymore "incarnated" such physically or
       spiritually "deformed" characters as Captain Ahab in
       two versions of MOBY DICK.

526   Clark, Harry Hayden. "American Literary History and
       American Literature," THE REINTERPRETATIONS OF
       AMERICAN LITERATURE. Norman Foerster, ed. New
       York: Harcourt, Brace, 1928; New York: Russell
       & Russell, 1959, pp. 181-213.

       MOBY DICK is a spiritual epic symbolizing the
       struggle between the eternal ruthlessness of nature and
       the enmity of man.

527   Clark, Harry Hayden, ed. "Changing Attitudes in Early
        American Literary Criticism, 1800-1840," THE
        DEVELOPMENT OF AMERICAN LITERARY CRITICISM.
        Chapel Hill: North Carolina University Press,
        1955, pp. 15-73.

528   Clark, Harry Hayden, comp. "Herman Melville (1819-1891),"
        AMERICAN LITERATURE: POE THROUGH GARLAND. New York:
        Appleton-Century-Crofts, 1971, pp. 65-71.

529   Clark, Harry Hayden. "Intellectual History and Its
        Relation to a Balanced Study of American Literature,"
        ENGLISH INSTITUTE ANNUAL - 1940. New York: AMS
        Press, Inc., 1965, pp. 115-129.

530   Clark, Harry Hayden, ed. Introduction, TRANSITIONS IN
        AMERICAN LITERARY HISTORY. Durham, North Carolina:
        Duke University Press, 1953.

        Melville remained, "half of New York and half of
        New England, divided in his origins as in his life and
        mind."

531   Clarke, Katherine Ann. "'POUR SALUER MELVILLE,' Jean
        Giono's Prison Book," FR, 35, 5 (April, 1962),
        478-483.

        Comparison of Jean Giono and Melville.

532   Clarks, Justin Wright. "Major Thomas Melville," ColS
        (October 30, 1832).

533   Clavering, Rose. "The Conflict Between the Individual
        and Social Forces in Herman Melville's Works: TYPEE
        to MOBY-DICK," DA, 18 ((New York: 1958), 2137-38.

534   Cleopatra, Sister. "MOBY DICK: An Interpretation,"
        LitHY, 6 (1965), 49-54.

        MOBY DICK symbolizes God in vanquishing Ahab,
        the "ungodly, godlike man." The white whale combines
        the powers of Brahma, Vishnu, and Siva, as well as
        being representative of the Christian God.

535   Clive, Geoffrey. THE ROMANTIC ENLIGHTENMENT. New York:
        Meridian Books, 1960, pp. 161-165, passim.

536   Clive, Geoffrey. "Teleological Suspension of the Ethical
            in Nineteenth-Century Literature," JR, 34 (1954),
            75-87.

            Article appears as "BILLY BUDD, Kierkegaard's
       FEAR AND TREMBLING, and CRIME AND PUNISHMENT," in
       Clive's THE ROMANTIC ENLIGHTENMENT. New York: 1960.

537   Clough, Wilson O. THE NECESSARY EARTH: NATURE AND
            SOLITUDE IN AMERICAN LITERATURE. Austin: Texas
            University Press, 1964, pp. 125-131.

            Ahab within "the American pattern of the student
       of nature and solitude."

538   Clubb, Merrel D. "The Second Personal Pronoun in
            MOBY-DICK," AS, 35 (December, 1960), 252-260.

539   Cluny, Claude Michel. "'Le Samouraï,' de Melville,"
            NRF, 16 (janv 1968), 110-114.

540   Coan, Otis W., and Richard G. Lillard. AMERICA IN FICTION:
            AN ANNOTATED LIST OF NOVELS THAT INTERPRET ASPECTS
            OF LIFE IN THE UNITED STATES. Stanford, Calif.:
            Stanford University Press, 1945, pp. 96, 115.

            MOBY DICK, a "chaotic masterpiece" which
       dramatizes the problem of evil in the conflict between
       Ahab and the white whale.

541   Coan, T. M. "Herman Melville," LitW, 22 (1891), 492-493.

542   Cobb, Robert P. SOCIETY VS. SOLITUDE IN THE AMERICAN
            RENAISSANCE: STUDIES IN EMERSON, THOREAU, HAWTHORNE,
            MELVILLE AND WHITMAN. Diss. Michigan: 1954.

543   Cockcroft, George P. THE TWO HERMAN MELVILLES. Diss.
            Columbia: 1964.

544   Coffin, Tristram P. "Harden E. Taliaferro and the Use
of Folklore by American Literary Figures," SAQ,
64 (Spring, 1965), 241-246.

Comparison of Taliaferro's use of folklore and
Melville's use in MOBY DICK.

545   Cohen, B. Bernard. "SEPTIMIUS FELTON" AND "MOBY-DICK."
Diss. Georgia Tech: 1954.

546   Cohen, Hennig, ed. "THE CONFIDENCE-MAN," LANDMARKS OF
AMERICAN WRITING. Basic Books, 1969.

Repr. FICTIONS AND EVENTS: ESSAYS IN CRITICISM
AND LITERARY HISTORY. New York: E. P. Dutton & Co., Inc.,
1971, pp. 229-242.

547   Cohen, Hennig, ed. Introduction and Notes, THE BATTLE-
PIECES OF HERMAN MELVILLE. New York: Thomas
Yoseloff, 1963.

Rev. by Luther S. Mansfield, AL, 36 (1964), 87-88.

548   Cohen, Hennig, ed. Introduction, THE CONFIDENCE-MAN.
New York: Holt, Rinehart, and Winston, 1964.

549   Cohen, Hennig, ed. Introduction. WHITE JACKET. New York:
Holt, Rinehart, and Winston, 1967.

550   Cohen, Hennig, ed. Introduction and Notes, SELECTED
POEMS. Carbondale: Southern Ill. University Press,
1964.

551   Cohen, Hennig. "Melville and Webster's THE WHITE DEVIL,"
ESQ, 33 (4th Qt., 1963), 33.

Melville exploited the "Dirge" from Webster's
play in his poem "The Admiral of the White."

552   Cohen, Hennig. "Melville's Copy of Broughton's 'POPULAR
POETRY OF THE HINDOOS,'" PBSA, 61 (3rd Qt., 1967),
266-267.

A copy of this 1814 book in the Columbia University
Library bears Melville's signature, and the title should
become item 87a in Sealts's MELVILLE'S READING.

553   Cohen, Hennig. "Melville's Tomahawk Pipe: Artifact
and Symbol," SNNTS, 1, iv (1969), 397-400.

Melville's frequent literary use of tobacco as
"something soothing or sacred" appears significantly
in his treatment of Queequeg's tomahawk pipe.

554   Cohen, Hennig. "New Melville Letters," AL, 38 (January,
       1967), 556-559.

       Four letters, two of 1853, two of 1861, to Julius
       Rockwell, show Melville's interest in an Independence
       Day celebration in Pittsfield in 1853, and (two letters
       of 1861) his interest in obtaining a consulship in 1861.
       The four letters are printed for the first time.

555   Cohen, Hennig. "Wordplay on Personal Names in the
       Writings of Herman Melville," TSL, 8 (1963), 85-97.

       Melville's wordplay in names of individuals
       developed from simple appropriateness to rank and
       occupation in the early tales to rich complexity of
       suggestion in BILLY BUDD.

556   Cohn, Ruby. DIALOGUE IN AMERICAN DRAMA. Bloomington and
       London: Indiana University Press, 1971, pp. 288-290.

       Treatment of Robert Lowell's play "Benito Cereno."

557   Colacurcio, Michael J. "A Better Mode of Evidence--The
       Transcendental Problem of Faith and Spirit," ESQ,
       54 (1st Qt., 1969), 12-22.

       Melville's PIERRE, Emerson's "Divinity School
       Address," and Hawthorne's "Rappaccini's Daughter
       clearly illustrate the two sides of the philosophic
       conflict in the American Renaissance between spiritual
       and pragmatic faith.

558   Colcord, Lincoln. "Notes on MOBY DICK," Freeman, 5
       (August 23, 1922), 559-562; (August 30, 1922),
       585-587.

       Melville's ineptitude in handling the storm scenes
       in MOBY DICK.

            Cf., Sumner W. D. Scott. "Some Implications of
       the Typhoon Scenes in MOBY DICK," AL, 12 (1940), 91-98.

559   Coles Publishing Company. MOBY DICK NOTES. Toronto:
       Coles Publishing Co., 1967.

560   Collins, Carvel. "Melville's MARDI," Expl, 12 (May, 1954),
       Item 42.

561   Collins, Carvel. "Melville's MOBY DICK," Expl, 4
       (February, 1946), Item 27.

       Freedom of will in Chapter 46, "The Mat-Maker."

       Cf., G. Giovanni, "Melville's MOBY DICK," Expl, 5
       (1946), Item 7.

562   Colombo, Dario. "MOBY DICK (Interpretazione)," Italia,
       42 (December, 1959), 267-269.

563   Colum, Padraic. "MOBY DICK as an Epic: A Note,"
       Measure, 13 (1922), 16-18.

       Repr., as "Epic of the Sea," in A HALF-DAY'S
       RIDE. New York: 1932, pp. 175-179.

       MOBY DICK an epic rather than a novel.

564   Colvin, Sir Sidney, ed. THE LETTERS OF ROBERT LOUIS
       STEVENSON. London: William Heinemann, Ltd.,
       in Association with Chatto & Windus: Cassell &
       Company, Ltd., and Longmans, Green & Company,
       1924, III, 202, 254.

565   Colwell, James L., and Gary Spitzer. "'Bartleby' and
       'The Raven': Parallels of the Irrational," GaR,
       23 (1969), 37-43.

566   Commager, Henry Steele, and Allan Nevins, eds. HERITAGE
       OF AMERICA. New York: Little, Brown & Co., 1949,
       1951, pp. 308, 313-317.

       Flogging and hardships of naval life, and Melville
       on the Acushnet in 1841.

567   Conarroe, Joel O. "Melville's Bartleby and Charles
       Lamb," SSF, 5 (Winter, 1968), 113-118.

       Bartleby's unwillingness to function as a clerk,
       or "even as a human being," possibly suggested by
       Lamb's "The Superannuated Man."

568   Condon, Richard A. "The Broken Conduit: A Study of
       Alienation in American Literature," PacS, 8
       (Autumn, 1954), 326-332.

569   "'The Confidence Man' on a Large Scale," New York <u>Herald</u>,
        (July 11, 1849), p. 2, cols. 1-2.

570   Connolly, Thomas E. "A Note on Name Symbolism in
        Melville," AL, 25 (January, 1954), 489-490.

        Note to Rosalie Feltenstein's "Melville's 'Benito
        Cereno,'" AL, 19 (1947), 245-255.

571   Connor, C. H. "MOBY-DICK," CEA, 10 (1948), 3.

572   Conrad, Joseph. Letter to Humphrey Milford, January 15,
        1907. (See MacShane, Frank. "Conrad on Melville,"
        AL, 29 (1958), 463-464.

        "...Lately I had in my hand MOBY DICK. It struck
        me as a rather strained rhapsody with whaling for a
        subject and not a single sincere line in the 3 vols
        of it...."

573   Cook, Albert. PRISMS: STUDIES IN MODERN LITERATURE.
        London and Bloomington, Ind.: Indiana University
        Press, 1967, pp. 111, 120.

        Comparison of Melville and Kafka.

574   Cook, Albert. "Romance as Allegory: Melville and
        Kafka," THE MEANING OF FICTION. Detroit: Wayne
        State University Press, 1960, pp. 242-259.

        MOBY-DICK.

575   Cook, Charles H., Jr. "Ahab's 'Intolerable Allegory,'"
        BUSE, 1 (Spring-Summer, 1955), 45-52.

        Ahab, a warning to twentieth-century man who,
        giddy with scientific success, presumes to untangle
        the intricate knot of good and evil.

576   Cook, Dorothy E., and Estelle A. Fidell, comps. "Herman
        Melville," SHORT STORY INDEX: SUPPLEMENT 1950-1954:
        AN INDEX TO 9,575 STORIES TO 549 COLLECTIONS. New
        York: H. W. Wilson Company, 1956.

577   Cook, Dorothy E., and Isabel S. Monro, comps. "Herman
        Melville," SHORT STORY INDEX: SUPPLEMENT: AN
        INDEX TO 60,000 STORIES IN 4,320 COLLECTIONS.
        New York: H. W. Wilson Company, 1953, p. 875.

578   Cook, Reginald L. "Big Medicine in MOBY-DICK," <u>Accent</u>, 8 (Winter, 1948), 102-109.

         Also in MYTH AND LITERATURE: CONTEMPORARY THEORY AND PRACTICE. John B. Vickery, ed. Lincoln, Nebr.: 1966, pp. 193-199.

         Ahab's defeat is the failure of magic as an effective force in the manipulation of natural forces. Melville uses this "big medicine" romantically to heighten drama and "to infuse the magnificent...poetry with strange overtones."

579   Corey, James R. "Herman Melville and the Theory of Evolution," DA, 29 (Wash. State: 1969), 3093A.

580   Costner, Martha Izora. GOLDSMITH'S <u>CITIZEN OF THE WORLD</u> AND MELVILLE'S <u>THE CONFIDENCE-MAN</u>. Comanche, Okla.: 1971.

581   Couch, H. N. "MOBY DICK and the Phaedo," CJ, 28 (February, 1933), 367-368.

         Last paragraph of Chapter 7 is from Plato.

582   Cournat, Michael. "Essai sur Melville," <u>L'Arche</u>, 3 (August-September, 1946), 42-52.

583   Cournos, John. "Herman Melville--the Seeker" and "The Comparison of Melville with Rimbaud and Doughty," A MODERN PLUTARCH. London: T. Butterworth, 1928, pp. 77-89, 113-118; Indianapolis: 1928, pp. 78-95, 127-134.

584   Cournos, John. "A Visit to John Masefield," New York <u>Independent</u>, 73 (September 5, 1912), 537-538.

         See John Masefield.

585   Coursen, Herbert R., Jr. "Nature's Center," CE, 24 (March, 1963), 467-469.

         The views of nature held by Melville and others.

586   Cowan, S. A. "In Praise of Self-Reliance: The Role of
        Bulkington in MOBY DICK," AL, 38 (January, 1967),
        547-556.

        It is questionable that Melville was satirizing
        transcendental self-reliance in MOBY DICK. Bulkington
        is the "self-reliant hero" who rejects the shore in
        order to pursue his private vision of truth.

587   Cowen, W. W. HERMAN MELVILLE'S MARGINALIA. Diss.
        Harvard: 1965.

588   Cowen, Walker. "Melville's 'Discoveries': A Dialogue
        of the Mind with Itself," THE RECOGNITION OF HERMAN
        MELVILLE: SELECTED CRITICISM SINCE 1846. Hershel
        Parker, ed. Ann Arbor: Michigan University Press,
        1967, pp. 333-346.

        "The marginalia are the private journal of his
        discoveries, the documented history of Melville's half-
        century struggle with himself and his art...."

589   Cowie, Alexander. "Emerson in an Existential Age,"
        OPINIONS AND PERSPECTIVES FROM THE NEW YORK TIMES
        BOOK REVIEW. Introduction by Francis Brown, ed.
        Boston: Houghton Mifflin Company, 1955, 1964, passim.

        Melville's contemporary reputation.

590   Cowie, Alexander. "Herman Melville," THE RISE OF THE
        AMERICAN NOVEL. New York: American Book Company,
        1948; 1951, pp. 362-411.

591   Cowie, Alexander. "Symbols Ahoy," CEA, 11 (1949), 7-8.

        On teaching MOBY DICK.

592   Cowley, Malcolm. "American Myths, Old and New," SatR,
        45 (September 1, 1962), 6-8, 47.

        An incidental reference but pertinent: Romantic
        love was not a major theme in serious American literature
        nor in familiar folklore. After the first few chapters,
        MOBY DICK has no female characters "except mother whales."

593   Cowley, Malcolm. THE LITERARY SITUATION. New York:
        Viking Press, 1958, passim.

        There are no "real" epics in our poetry and,
        except for MOBY DICK, we have produced very few
        "epics in prose."

594   Cowley, Malcolm. A MANY-WINDOWED HOUSE: COLLECTED
        ESSAYS ON AMERICAN WRITERS AND AMERICAN WRITING.
        Introduction by Henry Dan Piper, ed. Carbondale
        and Edwardsville: Southern Illinois University
        Press, 1970, passim.

        Rev. by John Lydenberg, AL, 43 (1972), 673-675.

594.1   Coxe, Louis O. BILLY BUDD. London: Heineman, 1966.

595   Coxe, Louis O., and Robert Chapman. BILLY BUDD: Play
        in Three Acts, Based on the Short Novel by Herman
        Melville. London: Geoffrey Cumberlege, Oxford
        University Press, 1950.

596   Coxe, Louis O., and Robert Chapman. BILLY BUDD: Based
        on a Novel by Herman Melville. Foreword by Brooks
        Atkinson. Princeton: Princeton University Press,
        1951; New York: Hill and Wang, 1951.

        The Foreword is Atkinson's review of the play,
        New York *Times*, February 11, 1951.

597   Coxe, Louis O., and Robert Chapman. "BILLY BUDD,"
        ThA, 37 (February, 1952), 50-69.

        Script publication of the three-act play based
        on Melville's BILLY BUDD.

598   Coxe, Louis O., and Robert Chapman. "BILLY BUDD,"
        BEST AMERICAN PLAYS. Third Series, 1945-1951.
        John Gassner, ed. New York: Crown Publishers,
        1952.

599   Coxe, Louis O., and Robert Chapman. "BILLY BUDD": Play
        in Three Acts Based on Novel by Herman Melville;
        produced by Chandler Cowles and Anthony B. Farrell
        at the Biltmore Theatre, New York: February 10,
        1951, closed May 12, 1951.

        Produced as THE GOOD SAILOR by Frith Banbury at
        the Lyric, Hammersmith; Philip Bond as Billy, 1956.

599.1　Coxe, Louis O., and Robert Chapman. BILLY BUDD, FORETOPMAN.
The novel, ed. by Frederic Barron Freeman, corrected
by Elizabeth Freeman; the dramatic version adapted by
Coxe and Chapman. Foreword by Brooks Atkinson.
New York: Popular Living Classics Library, 1962.

600　Coy, Juan José. "Complicidad e inocencia en la
literatura americana," RO, 7 (June, 1969), 352-366.

Melville reflects the sociological phenomena in
counterpointing good with evil.

601　Cramer, Maurice B. "BILLY BUDD and BILLY BUDD," JGE,
10 (April, 1957), 78-91.

Melville's novel and the play by Louis O. Coxe
and Robert Chapman.

602　Crane, Hart. "At Melville's Tomb," COMPLETE POEMS AND
SELECTED LETTERS AND PROSE OF HART CRANE. New York:
Liveright Publishing Corp., 1933, 1958, 1966, p. 104.

Cf., Harriet Monroe. "A Discussion with Hart Crane,"
Poetry, 29 (1926), 34-41.

603　Crane, Hart. THE LETTERS OF HART CRANE, 1916-1932.
Brom Weber, ed. New York: Hermitage House, 1952,
pp. 404-405.

Letter of Hart Crane to Solomon Grunberg,
March 20, 1932; "...In MOBY DICK the whale is a
metaphysical image of the Universe...."

604　Craven, H. T. "Tahiti from Melville to Maugham,"
Bookman, 50 (November-December, 1919), 262-267.

605　Creeger, George Raymond. "Color Symbolism in the Works
of Herman Melville: 1846-1852." DA, 25 (Yale:
1965), 6620.

606　Creeger, George Raymond. "The Symbolism of Whiteness
in Melville's Prose Fiction," JA, 5 (1960), 147-163.

607　Crise, Stelio. "Ahab, Pizdrool, Quark," JJQ, 7 (1969),
65-69.

608　Cromphout, Gustaaf Van. "Herman Melville's REDBURN
Considered in the Light of the Elder Henry James's
THE NATURE OF EVIL," RLV, 29 (1963), 117-126.

609   Cronkhite, George F. LITERATURE AS LIVELIHOOD: THE ATTITUDE OF CERTAIN AMERICAN WRITERS TOWARD LITERATURE AS A PROFESSION FROM 1820 TO THE CIVIL WAR. Diss. Harvard: 1948.

610   Cross, John J. "Melville's THE CONFIDENCE-MAN: The Problem of Source and Meaning," NM, 60 (1959), 299-310.

611   Crothers, George D., ed. "Herman Melville," INVITATION TO LEARNING: ENGLISH AND AMERICAN NOVELS. New York: Basic Books, Inc., 1966, pp. 223-231.

       See for MOBY DICK dialogue of Alfred Kazin, Lawrance Thompson, and Lyman Bryson.

612   Crowley, Paul. "Melville's New Halo," Cw, 9 (1929), 687-688.

613   Crowley, William G. "Melville's Chimney," ESQ, 14 (1st Qt., 1959), 2-6.

614   Culhane, Mary. THOREAU, MELVILLE, POE, AND THE ROMANTIC QUEST. Diss. Minnesota: 1945.

615   Cunliffe, Marcus. "Herman Melville," THE LITERARY HISTORY OF THE UNITED STATES. Baltimore: Penguin Books, 1954, pp. 105-119.

616   Curl, Vega. PASTEBOARD MASKS: FACT AS SPIRITUAL SYMBOL IN THE NOVELS OF HAWTHORNE AND MELVILLE. Radcliffe Honors Theses No. 2. Radcliffe: 1931.

617   Curl, Vega. PASTEBOARD MASKS. FACT AS SPIRITUAL SYMBOL IN THE NOVELS OF HAWTHORNE AND MELVILLE. Cambridge: Harvard University Press, 1931.

618   Curle, Richard. COLLECTING AMERICAN FIRST EDITIONS. Indianapolis: 1930.

619   Current-García, Eugene, and Walter R. Patrick, eds. AMERICAN SHORT STORIES: 1820 TO THE PRESENT. Chicago: Scott, Foresman, 1952.

620　Curti, Merle. THE GROWTH OF AMERICAN THOUGHT. 3rd ed.
　　　　New York, Evanston, and London: Harper & Row,
　　　　Publishers, 1943, 1951, 1964, passim.

　　　References show Melville's place in the social
and political milieu.

621　Curti, Merle, Richard H. Shryock, Thomas C. Cochran, and
　　　　Fred Harvey Harrington. A HISTORY OF AMERICAN
　　　　CIVILIZATION. New York: Harper & Brothers, 1953,
　　　　pp. 239-241.

　　　References place Melville in his cultural milieu.

622　Curtis, George William. See Milne, Gordon. GEORGE
　　　　WILLIAM CURTIS AND THE GENTEEL TRADITION.
　　　　Bloomington, Ind.: Indiana University Press,
　　　　1956.

623　Dahl, Curtis. "MOBY-DICK and the Reviews of THE CRUISE
　　　　OF THE CACHELOT," MLN, 67 (November, 1952), 471-472.

　　　Evidence indicates the critics' ignorance of
Melville's works as late as fifty years after the
publication of MOBY DICK.

624　Dahl, Curtis. "MOBY DICK'S Cousin BEHEMOTH," AL, 31
　　　　(March, 1959), 21-29.

　　　Melville knew Cornelius Mathews' popular BEHEMOTH:
A LEGEND OF THE MOUND-BUILDERS (1839), which strikingly
foreshadows MOBY DICK. However, in spite of parallels,
BEHEMOTH is "a bad and often absurd book" while MOBY DICK
is "a superlatively good one."

625　Dahlberg, Edward. ALMS FOR OBLIVION. Minneapolis:
　　　　Minneapolis University Press, 1964, pp. 115-142.

　　　Terms Melville a "misogynist" who "lusted after
men and beasts."

　　　See rev-article by Walter E. Bezanson. "The
Critical Furies of Edward Dahlberg," Criticism, 8
(1966), 97-101.

626　Dahlberg, Edward. "Can These Bones Live," SING O BARREN.
　　　　London: Routledge, 1947; New York: New Directions,
　　　　1960, pp. 27-67.

627 Dahlberg, Edward. "Laurels for Borrowers," *Freeman*, 2 (1951), 187-190.

628 Dahlberg, Edward. "MOBY-DICK: An Hamitic Dream," LitR, 4 (Autumn, 1960), 87-118.

629 Dahlberg, Edward. "MOBY DICK: An Hamitic Dream," VARIETIES OF LITERARY EXPERIENCE. Stanley Burnshaw, ed. New York: New York University Press, 1962, pp. 183-213.

630 Daiber, H. "Der Alte Mann und Kapitan Ahab," DRund, 79 (1953), 618-620.

631 Daiker, Donald A. "The Motif of the Quest in the Writings of Herman Melville," DAI, 30 (Ind.: 1970), 4979A.

632 Dale, T. R. "Melville and Aristotle: The Conclusion of MOBY-DICK as a Classical Tragedy," BUSE, 3 (Spring, 1957), 45-50.

633 Damon, S. Foster. "Pierre, the Ambiguous," H&H, 2 (January-March, 1929), 107-118.

   Melville's was one of the first attempts in literary history to analyze incest. His realization that "problems of the soul" are rooted in the "subconscious" put him ahead of his time.

634 Damon, S. Foster. "Why Ishmael Went to Sea," AL, 2 (1930), 281-283.

635 Dana, Richard Henry, Sr. Letter to Evert Duyckinck, January 25, 1854. (New York Public Library, Duyckinck Collection).

636 Dana, Richard Henry. TWO YEARS BEFORE THE MAST. New York: 1842.

637 Daniels, Marvin. "Pathological Vindictiveness and the Vindictive Character," PsyR, 56, ii (1969), 169-196.

   Analysis of the three literary characters pathologically governed by hatred, one of which is Ahab; the other two are Milton's Satan and Hawthorne's Roger Chillingworth.

638   Dauner, Louise. "The 'Case' of Tobias Pearson:
        Hawthorne and the Ambiguities," AL, 21 (1950),
        464-472.

        Parallels with PIERRE.

639   D'Avanzo, Mario L. "'The Cassock' and Carlyle's
        'Church-Clothes,'" ESQ, 50 (1st Qt., 1968),
        74-76.

        Chapter 95, "The Cassock," of MOBY DICK may be
        read as "a crafty comic-ironic commentary" on Book III,
        Chapter 2 of SARTOR RESARTUS.

640   D'Avanzo, Mario L. "Melville's 'Bartleby' and Carlyle,"
        MELVILLE ANNUAL 1965, A SYMPOSIUM: BARTLEBY THE
        SCRIVENER. Howard P. Vincent, ed. (Kent Studies
        in English III). Kent, Ohio: Kent State University
        Press, 1966, pp. 113-139.

        Parallels between "Bartleby" and SARTOR RESARTUS,
        and also HEROES AND HERO WORSHIP, are keys to an under-
        standing of Melville's short story.

641   D'Avanzo, Mario L. "Melville's 'Bartleby' and John Jacob
        Astor," NEQ, 41 (1968), 259-264.

        Melville may be suggesting that were it not for the
        Bartlebys, the Astors and lawyers might be "dictating
        to the world of letters in a most utilitarian, devastat-
        ing way."

642   Davidson, Edward H. "American Romanticism as Moral
        Style," ESQ, 35 (1964), 10-14.

643   Davidson, Frank. "'Bartleby': A Few Observations,"
        ESQ, 27 (2nd Qt., 1962), 25-32.

644   Davidson, Frank. "Melville, Thoreau, and 'The Apple-Tree
        Table,'" AL, 25 (January, 1954), 479-488.

        Melville's debt to Thoreau for the story, and
        the story as statement of Melville's religious
        difficulties at time of writing.

645   Davis, David Brion. HOMICIDE IN AMERICAN FICTION,
        1798-1860: A STUDY IN SOCIAL VALUES. Ithaca,
        New York: Cornell University Press, 1957, passim.

646   Davis, Frank M. "Herman Melville and the Nineteenth-
              Century Church Community," DA, 27 (Duke: 1967),
              3866A-67A.

        Melville's treatment of churchmen "became
increasingly hostile," with emphasis on their
indifference to the primitive and the poor.

647   Davis, Merrell R. "The Flower Symbolism in MARDI,"
              MLQ, 2 (December, 1941), 625-638.

        Frances S. Osgood's THE POETRY OF FLOWERS AND
FLOWERS OF POETRY (1841) offers a key to the meaning
of Melville's flower symbolism.

648   Davis, Merrell R. "Herman Melville's MARDI: The
              Biography of a Book," DA, 30 (Yale: 1969),
              1522A-23A.

649   Davis, Merrell R. MELVILLE'S MARDI: A CHARTLESS
              VOYAGE. New Haven, Conn.: Yale University Press,
              1952, 1967.
              Rev. by Leon Howard, AL, 24 (1953), 557-558.

650   Davis, Merrell R. "Melville's Midwestern Lecture Tour,
              1859," PQ, 20 (1941), 46-57.

        Melville's tour took him to Chicago, Milwaukee,
Rockford, Illinois, and Quincy, Illinois. Some news-
paper reviews were disapproving, but the Milwaukee
Daily Wisconsin for February 26, 1859, printed a two-
column favorable review.

651   Davis, Merrell R., and William H. Gilman, eds. THE
              LETTERS OF HERMAN MELVILLE. New Haven, Conn.:
              Yale University Press, 1960.

        Collection of 271 letters, 42 are new, and 55
published in full for the first time.

        See Edward H. Rosenberry. "Awash in Melvilliana,"
NEQ, 33 (1960), 525-528; and also: Granville Hicks.
"Correspondence of a Gentle Man," SatR, June 18,
1960, p. 15.

        Revs. by Leon Howard, NCF, 16 (1961), 91-92;
Merton M. Sealts, Jr., AL, 32 (1961), 473-475.

652   Davison, Richard A. "Melville's MARDI and John Skelton,"
           ESQ, 43 (2nd Qt., 1966), 86-87.

           Echoes of Skelton's "Philip Sparrow" in the
       account of Yillah's milk-white bird.

653   Davison, Richard A. "Redburn, Pierre and Robin:
           Melville's Debt to Hawthorne?" ESQ, 47 (2nd Qt.,
           1967), 32-34.

           Although there are similarities between the three
       characters, there are also dissimilarities. Melville
       had noted the innocence-experience theme in Shakespeare
       long before he knew Hawthorne.

654   Day, A. Grove. "Hawaiian Echoes in Melville's MARDI,"
           MLQ, 18 (March, 1957), 3-8.

654.1 Day, A. Grove, ed. Introduction and Notes. MELVILLE'S
           SOUTH SEAS. New York: Hawthorne Books, 1970.

655   Day, Frank L. "Herman Melville's Use of THE REBELLION
           RECORD in His Poetry. Tennessee University Thesis,
           1959.

656   Day, Frank L. "Melville and Sherman March to the Sea,"
           AN&Q, 2 (May, 1964), 134-136.

           Evidence indicates that Melville drew heavily
       upon THE STORY OF THE GREAT MARCH for his poem "The March
       to the Sea" (1866).

657   D'Azevedo, Warren. "Revolt on the San Dominick,"
           Phylon, 17 (1956), 129-140.

           The theme is the "psychological impact" of
       slavery and revolt upon Captain Delano and particularly
       on Don Benito.

658   Deane, Paul. "Herman Melville: Four Views of American
           Commercial Society," RLV, 34 (1968), 504-507.

           Social criticism in four tales: "The Paradise of
       Bachelors and the Tartarus of Maids," "Bartleby,"
       "Jimmy Rose," and "The Fiddler."

659   Deane, Paul. "Herman Melville: The Quality of Balance,"
           Serif, 7, ii (1970), 12-17.

660   DEISTVITEL'NYE I FANTASTICHESKIE PUTESHESTVIIA GERMANA
MEL'VILLA. "Taipi" - Omu" - "Vtornik," (S publikatsiei
otryvkov) /THE REAL AND THE FANTASTIC JOURNEYS OF
MELVILLE. "TYPEE" -"OMOO" - "MARDI" (With excerpts)/.
Biblioteka dlia chteniia, 1849, t. 96, otd. VII,
pp. 77-90.

661   Dekker, George. "Lilies that Fester," NLeftR, 28
(November-December, 1964), 75-84.

       Melville and others shared the concern for
national racial destiny in America.

661.1   Delhumeau, Jean Paul. ILES DE GLÉNAN. Paris: Blondel la
Rougery, 1963.

       French version of BENITO CERENO.

662   Denny, M., and W. Gilman, eds. THE AMERICAN WRITER AND
THE EUROPEAN TRADITION. Minneapolis: Minneapolis
University Press, 1950.

       Rev. by Richard Chase, AL, 25 (1953), 378-380.

663   Dent, A. "BILLY BUDD." /Motion Picture Version/
ILondN, 241 (October 13, 1962), 574.

664   de Onis, José. "Melville y el mundo hispánico,"
Cuadenos, 70 (March, 1963), 53-60.

       In MOBY DICK, subtle use made of the myth that
Americans were to dislodge Spain from its place in
history.

665   de Onis, José. "Messianic Nationalism in the Literature
of the Americas: Melville and the Hispanic World,"
PROCEEDINGS OF THE IVTH CONGRESS OF THE INTERNATIONAL
COMPARATIVE LITERATURE ASSOCIATION. Francois Jost, ed.
Fribourg, 1964: The Hague: Mouton, 1966.

666   Detweiler, Robert. "Christ and the Christ Figure in
American Fiction," ChS, 47, 2 (Summer, 1964),
111-124.

       The Christ figure in faith and fiction, particularly
in BILLY BUDD.

667   Devers, James. "Melancholy, Myth, and Symbol in
            Melville's 'Benito Cereno': An Interpretive Study,"
            DA, 29 (U. C. L. A.: 1969), 2671A.

668   De Voto, Bernard. "Editions of TYPEE," SatRL, 5
            (1928), 406.

            When TYPEE appeared in England (1846), there was
        a greater outcry about Melville's treatment of the
        missionaries than when the book appeared in America
        the same year.

            Cf., G. Thomas Tanselle. "TYPEE and De Voto:
        A Footnote," PBSA, 64 (1970), 207-209; and "TYPEE
        and De Voto Once More," PBSA, 62 (1968), 601-604.

669   De Voto, Bernard. MARK TWAIN'S AMERICA. Boston: Little
            Brown, 1932, pp. 312-313. Repr. in Norton Critical
            Edition of MOBY DICK, 1967.

670   Dew, Marjorie. "The Attorney and the Scrivener: Quoth
            the Raven, 'Nevermore,'" MELVILLE ANNUAL 1965, A
            SYMPOSIUM: BARTLEBY THE SCRIVENER. Howard P.
            Vincent, ed. (Kent Stud. in Eng., III). Kent,
            Ohio: Kent State University Press, 1966, pp. 94-103.

            The attorney's realization of responsibility for
        Bartleby is existential guilt which every man feels
        when he recognizes an unlimited responsibility for
        another person without the resources to handle it.

671   Dew, Marjorie. "'Benito Cereno': Melville's Vision and
            Revision of the Source," A BENITO CERENO HANDBOOK.
            Seymour L. Gross, ed. Belmont, Calif.: Wadsworth,
            1965, pp. 178-184.

672   Dew, Marjorie. "Herman Melville's Existential View of
            the Universe: Essays in Phenomenological Interpre-
            tation," DA, 28 (Kent State: 1967), 672A.

            Melville's "preoccupation with the existential
        theme" as the basis for his appeal to moderns.

673   Dew, Marjorie. "The Prudent Captain Vere," ATQ, 7
            (Summer, 1970), 81-85.

            Vere's existential acceptance of guilt for
        Billy's execution, not with satisfaction, but in
        responsibility for maintenance of order.

674   Dibden, A. J. AN INTERPRETATION OF TRAGEDY AND THE PROMETHEAN SPIRIT IN SANTAYANA, MOODY, ROBINSON, AND MELVILLE. Diss. Columbia: 1952.

675   Dichmann, Mary E. "Absolutism in Melville's PIERRE," PMLA, 67 (1952), 702-715.

676   Dickinson, Leon T. "The 'Speksnyder' in MOBY DICK," MSN, 12 (Spring, 1956).

677   Dillingham, William B. AN ARTIST IN THE RIGGING: THE EARLY WORK OF HERMAN MELVILLE. Athens, Georgia: Georgia University Press, 1972.

      The heroes in Melville's novels (preceding MOBY DICK) can be viewed as the same man in different stages of life.

      Rev. by Franklin Gaige, ArQ, 28 (1972), 95-96.

678   Dillingham, William B. "Melville's Long Ghost and Smollett's Count Fathom," AL, 42 (May, 1970), 232-235.

      Melville's characterization of Dr. Long Ghost in OMOO strongly influenced by Smollett's Count Fathom in THE ADVENTURES OF FERDINAND COUNT FATHOM.

679   Dillingham, William B. "The Narrator of MOBY DICK," ES, 49 (February, 1968), 20-29.

      Puzzling tone of the book and its shifts in point of view are attributable to the narrator's state of mind which results from the situations Ishmael recreates as he tells his story.

680   Dillingham, William B. "'Neither Believer Nor Infidel': Themes of Melville's Poetry," Person, 46 (Autumn, 1965), 501-516.

      The four predominant themes in the poetry deal with innate depravity, the endless human search, man's eternal loneliness, and the folly of dogma.

681   Dillistone, Frederick W. "The Angel Must Hang," THE
        NOVELIST AND THE PASSION STORY. London: Collins,
        1960; New York: Sheed & Ward, 1961, pp. 45-68.

        Melville is feeling "after a way of reconciliation
        which he can accept with his mind as well as with his
        heart."

682   Dix, William S. "Herman Melville and the Problem of
        Evil," RiceIP, 35 (July, 1948), 81-107.

683   Dobbyn, Dermot. "Birthplace of MOBY DICK," CathW, 185
        (Summer, 1957), 431-435.

        MOBY-DICK and the Bible.

684   Dodds, John W. THE AGE OF PARADOX: A BIOGRAPHY OF
        ENGLAND, 1841-1851. New York: Toronto: Rinehart
        & Company, Inc., 1952, pp. 249, passim.

        Most of Melville's books appeared in England in
        advance of publication in United States. Murray printed
        5,000 copies of TYPEE, sold, 4,104; OMOO, 4,000 copies,
        sold, 2,512. Reissued in a 2s,6d. series TYPEE sold
        4,000 copies in 1847, OMOO, 2,500 copies.

684.1   Dodson, Daniel B. "Malcolm Lowry," CEMW, 51 (1970),
        3-48.
        The quality of Lowry's marine imagery suggests
        Melville's influence.

685   Donahue, Jane. "Melville's Classicism: Law and Order
        in His Poetry," PLL, 5 (Winter, 1969), 63-72.

        A classical theme exists in Melville's poetry as
        early as "Dupont's Round Fight," BATTLE PIECES. Melville
        provides the clearest example in nineteenth-century
        American poetry of the "fruitful interaction of classical
        and romantic themes."

686   Donaldson, Scott. "The Dark Truth of THE PIAZZA TALES,"
        PMLA, 85 (1970), 1082-1086.

        Three concerns run through the tales: the
        difficulty of human perception, artistic and otherwise;
        the dangers of human isolation; and the catastrophic
        effects of human servitude.

687   Donoghue, Denis. "Herman Melville," CONNOISSEURS OF
CHAOS: IDEAS OF ORDER IN MODERN AMERICAN POETRY.
New York: Macmillan, 1965, pp. 76-99.

688   Donoghue, Denis. "Melville," LugR, 1, i (1965), 67-82.

       When Melville turned to poetry after 1857, he sought
relief from private visions by expressing more conventional
normalcy.

689   Donoghue, Denis. "In the Scene of Being," HudR, 14
(1961), 232-246.

       The "intransigence of Ahab" in MOBY DICK and "the
genial and dynamic relation to the actual" are related
to the experience of reading literature.

690   Donow, Herbert S. "Herman Melville and the Craft of
Fiction," MLQ, 25 (June, 1964), 181-186.

       Melville's knowledge of the craft of fiction "was
no match for his vision of metaphysical immensity." He
was a novelist "only in the vaguest sense of that word."

691   Dorson, Richard M. "Israel Potter," AMERICAN REBELS:
NARRATIVES OF THE PATRIOTS. Richard M. Dorson, ed.
An edited version of the 1824 Providence edition
of LIFE AND REMARKABLE ADVENTURES OF ISRAEL R.
POTTER. New York: Pantheon, 1953.

692   Doubleday, Neal F. "Jack Easy and Billy Budd," ELN, 2
(September, 1964), 39-42.

       Parallels between Jack Easy of Marryat's novel,
MR. MIDSHIPMAN EASY, and Melville's Billy Budd.

693   Dow, Janet. "Ahab: The Fisher King," ConnR, 2, ii
(1969), 42-49.

       Archetypal parallels between MOBY-DICK and the
Trail legend.

694   Dow, Ralph. Introduction, MOBY DICK. New York:
Macmillan, 1929.

695   Dowling, Joseph A. Introduction, THE DEMOCRATIC
         IMAGINATION: A GUIDE TO AN EXHIBITION OF RARE
         BOOKS BY RALPH WALDO EMERSON, HENRY DAVID THOREAU,
         NATHANIEL HAWTHORNE, WALT WHITMAN, HERMAN MELVILLE.
         Bethlehem, Pa.: Rare Book Room, Lehigh University
         Library, October 1, 1968.

696   Downs, Robert B. FAMOUS AMERICAN BOOKS. New York:
         McGraw Hill, 1971.

         Essays on fifty books (among them MOBY DICK),
chosen for their influence, with literary excellence
a secondary criterion.

697   Drew, Philip. "Appearance and Reality in Melville's
         THE CONFIDENCE-MAN," ELH, 31 (1964), 418-442.

         Disagreement with three points: the confidence-man
is a trickster; those who trust him are fools, those who
distrust him are wise; the novel's message is that
innocence, faith and trust are doomed. It is in ourselves that we must "locate the failure of confidence
which is the subject of the book."

698   Drew, Philip. "The Two-Headed Symbol," List, 74
         (August 26, 1965), 300-301.

         Melville locates his stories at a point where the
general morality is not simply "vague" but in fact
continues to support "simultaneously two incompatible
doctrines."

699   Drummond, C. Q. "Nature: Meek Ass or White Whale?"
         Sage, 1 (Spring, 1966), 71-84.

         An attack on inconsistencies in Emerson's NATURE.
MOBY DICK explores the "Emersonian proclivity: first,
by extreme application; second, by question of spiritual
meaning behind fact."

700   Dryden, Edgar A. "Herman Melville's Narrators and the
         Art of Fiction: A Study in Point of View," DA, 26
         (Johns Hopkins: 1965), 3298-3299.

         Melville's narrators are "portraits of the artist
at work." The narrators through their ability to be
at one and the same time "involved in and detached from
experience, are able to create a fiction which is also
the vehicle of truth."

701 Dryden, Edgar A. MELVILLE'S THEMATICS OF FORM: THE
GREAT ART OF TELLING THE TRUTH. Baltimore: Johns
Hopkins University Press, 1968.

A study of "the internal morphology of Melville's
fictional world." Melville saw life as "an empty
masquerade" and the human and natural worlds as "lies."

Cf., Walter E. Bezanson, "MOBY DICK: Work of Art,"
MOBY DICK CENTENNIAL ESSAYS. Tyrus Hillway and Luther S.
Mansfield, eds. Dallas, Tex.: 1953; and Paul Brodtkorb,
Jr. ISHMAEL'S WHITE WORLD: A PHENOMENOLOGICAL READING
OF MOBY DICK. New Haven: 1965.

Revs. by Paul Brodtkorb, Jr., AL, 41 (1969), 434-37;
Wendell Glick, Criticism, 12 (1970), 79-82; Edwin
Gittleman, NEQ, 42 (1969), 599-602.

701.1 Duberman, Martin. JAMES RUSSELL LOWELL. Boston:
Houghton Mifflin Company; Cambridge: The Riverside
Press, 1966, pp. 168-169, passim.

702 Dubler, Walter. "Theme and Structure in Melville's THE
CONFIDENCE MAN," AL, 33 (November, 1961), 307-319.

The major dramatic form is a dialectical pattern
of thesis-antithesis, without a stated synthesis (or
satiric norm). Though the pattern portrays extremism
in somber episodes, it is counterpointed by the unstated
implied norm—The Golden Mean. What could be virtues in
moderation become evils in excess.

703 Duerksen, Roland A. "CALEB WILLIAMS, POLITICAL JUSTICE,
and BILLY BUDD," AL, 38 (November, 1966), 372-376.

Parallels of Melville's BILLY BUDD with William
Godwin's CALEB WILLIAMS, particularly in the scene of
the young farmer arraigned for murder before Squire
Faulkland, and that of Billy before Vere. Godwin in
POLITICAL JUSTICE deals with the problems of duty and
justice, but Melville's novel indicates that he could
not accept Godwin's solution.

704 Duerksen, Roland A. "The Deep Quandary in BILLY BUDD,"
NEQ, 41 (1968), 51-66.

Melville questions the validity of an "unnatural
power system" in which not only Dansker and Vere but
all the major characters acquiesce; the story thus
analyzes the problem of human society which "seemingly
cannot put into practice those moral concepts which it
values most highly."

705   Duffey, Bernard. "Romantic Coherence and Incoherence in
           American Poetry," CentR, 8 (Fall, 1964), 453-464.

           The poetry of both Melville and Whitman indicates
       decline of romantic coherence. Neither poet uses the
       coheren: world-view of American Protestantism found in
       Emerson and Bryant. Melville's poetry illustrates the
       "collapse of the Protestant world into fragments."

706   Duffield, Brainerd. "MOBY DICK: A Modern Adaptation,"
           Line, 1 (1948), 32-40.

707   Duffy, Charles. "A Source for the Conclusion of Melville's
           MOBY DICK," N&Q, 181 (November 15, 1941), 278-279.

           Thomas Campbell's "Death Boat of Heligoland" (1828),
       a possible source.

           Cf., Thomas O. Mabbott. "A Source for the Conclusion
       of Melville's MOBY DICK," N&Q, 181 (July 26, 1941), 47-48.

708   Duffy, Charles. "Toward the Whole Evidence on Melville
           as a Lecturer," AN&Q, 2 (July, 1942), 58.

           Reprint of report from Ithaca Journal and Advertiser,
       January 13, 1858, of a lecture by Melville.

709   Duncan, Robert W. "The London Literary Gazette and
           American Writers," PELL, 1 (Spring, 1965), 153-166.

           William Jerdan in the review he edited (1817-1850)
       dealt fairly with Melville and other American writers.

710   Durham, Philip. "Prelude to the Constable Edition of
           Melville," HLQ, 21 (May, 1958), 285-289.

711   Duyckinck, Evert. "MARDI," LitW, 4 (April 7, 14, 1849),
           309-310; 333-336.

712   Duyckinck, Evert. "Melville's MOBY DICK; OR, THE WHALE,"
           LitW, 9 (November 15, 1851), 381-383; (November 22,
           1851), 403-404.

713   Duyckinck, Evert A., and George L. Duyckinck. "Herman
        Melville," CYCLOPAEDIA OF AMERICAN LITERATURE:
        EMBRACING PERSONAL AND CRITICAL NOTICES OF AUTHORS,
        AND SELECTIONS FROM THEIR WRITINGS. FROM THE EARLIEST
        PERIOD TO THE PRESENT DAY: WITH PORTRAITS, AUTOGRAPHS
        AND OTHER ILLUSTRATIONS. New York: Charles Scribner,
        1855, II, 672-676; Laird Simons, ed. Philadelphia:
        Wm. Rutter & Co., 1875, II, 636-639; Detroit: Gale
        Research Co., 1965, II, 636-639.

        Evert Duyckinck proclaimed Melville and Hawthorne
    the "literary titans" of his day.

713.1 Dwight, Timothy. TRAVELS IN NEW ENGLAND AND NEW YORK.
        New Haven: 1821, II, 398.

        Relates an incident which might have been the
    source of "The Apple-Tree Table."

714   Earnest, Ernest. EXPATRIATES AND PATRIOTS: AMERICAN
        ARTISTS, SCHOLARS, AND WRITERS IN EUROPE. Durham,
        N. C.: Duke University Press, 1968.

        Herman Melville in England.

715   Eastman, Richard M. A GUIDE TO THE NOVEL. San Francisco:
        Chandler Publishing Co., 1965, p. 142ff.

        The Americans, Melville and Hawthorne, offered the
    first "full-blown illustrations" of modern philosophical
    fiction.

716   Eby, Cecil D., Jr. "Another Breaching of 'MOCHA DICK,'"
        ELN, 4 (June, 1967), 277-279.

        An 1849 source for MOBY DICK is suggested by a
    reference to Reynolds' tale in the March 1849 issue of
    The Knickerbocker. The 1849 mention is significant for
    its suggestion of an indestructible whale.

717   Eby, Cecil D., Jr. "William Starbuck Mayo and Herman
        Melville," NEQ, 35 (December, 1962), 515-520.

        William Starbuck Mayo's novel, KALOOLAH, OR,
    JOURNEYINGS TO THE DJEBEL KUMRI: AN AUTOBIOGRAPHY OF
    JONATHAN ROMER, a possible influence on Melville's
    MOBY DICK.

718   Eby, E. H. "Herman Melville's 'Tartarus of Maids,'"
        MLQ, 1 (1940), 95-100.

        The biological burdens of women conveyed by
        consistent and detailed symbolism.

719   Eckardt, Sister Mary Ellen. "An Interpretive Analysis
        of the Patterns of Imagery in MOBY-DICK and BILLY
        BUDD." DA, 23 (Notre Dame: 1962), 2134.

720   Eddy, D. Mathis. "Melville's Response to Beaumont and
        Fletcher: A New Source for THE ENCANTADAS,"
        AL, 40 (1968), 374-380.

        Melville marked his copy of the 1679 Folio of
        Beaumont and Fletcher's play, WIT WITHOUT MONEY (I, i),
        and therefore, the play is a possible source of the
        third epigraph to Sketch Sixth.

721   Eddy, Fern M. "A Dark Similitude: Melville and the
        Elizabethan-Jacobean Perspective," DA, 28
        (Rutgers: 1967), 626A.

        Melville's reading in the English dramatists,
        and his familiarity with nineteenth-century dramatic
        criticism and the New York stage of the 1840's,
        are possible influences on MOBY DICK, PIERRE, and
        THE CONFIDENCE MAN.

722   Edelstein, Tilden G. STRANGE ENTHUSIASM: A LIFE OF
        THOMAS WENTWORTH HIGGINSON. New Haven and London:
        Yale University Press, 1968, passim.

        Higginson's transcendental outlook made him see
        Melville as too unsympathetic with reform-minded optimists
        and too insistent upon the "world's ambiguities."

723   Edgar, Pelham. "Herman Melville and MOBY DICK," THE ART
        OF THE NOVEL. New York: Macmillan, 1933, pp.
        130-135.

724   The Editors. "Melville and His Public: 1858," AN&Q, 2
        (August, 1942), 67-71.

725   Egbert, Samuel O. MELVILLE AND THE IDEA OF PROGRESS.
        Diss. Wash U.: 1939.

726   Ehrlich, Heyward. "'Diving and Ducking Moralities':
          A Rejoinder," BNYPL, 70 (November, 1966), 552-553.

          Melville was interested in the "meaning" and not
the sound of the Duyckinck name. His complimentary
allusion of 1849 ("dive") reflects partiality to "the
literary nationalism of 'Young America'" as represented
by Duyckinck and Cornelius Mathews.

727   Ehrlich, Heyward. "The 'Mysteries' of Philadelphia:
          Lippard's QUAKER CITY and 'Urban' Gothic," ESQ, 18
          (1st Qt., 1972), 50-65.

          Melville was influenced through Carlyle and
Coleridge by the German branch represented by E. T. A.
Hoffman and Jean Paul Richter, and, as well, by the
French. His conflict with the Gothic sub-genres can
never be completely resolved.

728   Ehrlich, Heyward. "A Note on Melville's 'Men Who Dive,'"
          BNYPL, 69 (1965), 661-664.

          Evert in a letter (March 4, 1839) to his brother
George explains that "duycking" in the family coat of
arms "means diving--that is to say seeking the hidden
pearls of truth." Melville, who must have known this bit
of lore, is punning on the family name. Duyckinck, not
Emerson, is the man who "dives."

          Cf., James H. Pickering. "Melville's 'Ducking'
Duyckinck," BNYPL, 70 (1966), 551-552; and Heyward
Ehrlich, "'Diving and Ducking Moralities': A Rejoinder,"
BNYPL, 70 (1966), 552-553.

729   Eigner, Edwin M. "Faulkner's Isaac and the American
          Ishmael," JA, 14 (1969), 107-115.

          The majority of American fictional heroes are
not biblical Ishmaels but Isaacs. Comparison of such
heroes in Faulkner and Melville.

730   Eigner, Edwin M. "The Romantic Unity of Melville's
          OMOO," PQ, 46 (January, 1967), 95-108.

          The psychological development of the narrator
is the key to OMOO'S unity, and the irrelevant digressions
are symbolically related to it.

731   Ekner, Reidar. "THE ENCANTADAS and BENITO CERENO--On
        Sources and Imagination in Melville," ModSpr, 60
        (1966), 258-273.

        Comparison of Melville's work with Captain David
        Porter's JOURNAL, James Colnett's A VOYAGE TO THE SOUTH
        ATLANTIC and William Ambrosia Cowley's VOYAGE AROUND THE
        GLOBE, among others, reveals Melville's skillful imagery
        in "weaving this wreath of fictitious prose and putting
        flesh on borrowed bones."

732   Ekstrom, William F. A FURTHER EXPLORATION OF THE
        THEMATIC AND ARTISTIC PROBLEMS PRESENTED BY "THE
        CONFIDENCE MAN." Diss. Louisville: 1954.

733   Elder, Marjorie J. TRANSCENDENTAL SYMBOLISTS: NATHANIEL
        HAWTHORNE AND MELVILLE. Diss. Chicago: 1964.

734   Eldridge, Herbert G. "'Careful Disorder': The Structure
        of MOBY DICK," AL, 39 (May, 1967), 145-162.

        The "organic disorder" of MOBY DICK was supported
        by the architecture necessary for orderly growth.

        Cf., Walter E. Bezanson. "MOBY DICK: Work of
        Art," MOBY DICK CENTENNIAL ESSAYS. Tyrus Hillway
        and Luther S. Mansfield, eds. Dallas: 1953; and
        Paul Brodtkorb, Jr. ISHMAEL'S WHITE WORLD. New
        Haven: 1965.

735   Eliot, Alexander. "Melville and Bartleby," *Furioso*, 3
        (Fall, 1947), 11-21.

736   Elliott, Harrison. "A Century Ago an Eminent Author
        Looked Upon Paper and Papermaking," PaMak, 21
        (1952), 55-58.

737   Elliott, Patrick F. HERMAN MELVILLE'S TRAGIC VISION:
        AN ESSAY IN THEOLOGICAL CRITICISM. Diss. Chicago:
        1965.

738   Ellis, A. B. "On Polyandry," PopSM, 39 (1891), 802.

739   Ellis, Theodore R., III. "Another Broadside into MARDI,"
        AL, 41 (1969), 419-422.

        Albert Smith probably the author of the brief
        burlesque of MARDI, "A Page by the Author of MARDI,"
        published in THE MAN IN THE MOON, May 1849, issue of
        the British humor magazine.

740   Ellison, Jerome. "How to Catch a Whale: Evil, Melville,
         and the Evolution of Consciousness," MQR, 6 (Spring,
         1967), 85-89.

         MOBY DICK criticism indicates that critics have
generally eschewed "questions of good and bad, and Good
and Evil." Criticism demands a stable intellectual
basis which can be found in C. G. Jung's theories of
archetypes and of evolutionary nature of the consciousness.

741   Ellison, Ralph. "Society, Morality, and the Novel,"
         THE LIVING NOVEL: A SYMPOSIUM. Granville Hicks, ed.
         New York: The Macmillan Company, 1957, passim.

         Incidental references which place Melville in his
literary, cultural and social milieu.

742   Ellsberg, Edward. Foreword. MELVILLE: THE BEST OF MOBY
         DICK AND TYPEE: ALSO BILLY BUDD. New York: Platt
         & Munk, 1964.

743   Elsbree, Langdon. "Huck Finn on the Nile," SAQ, 69
         (1970), 504-510.

         Twentieth-century Egyptians appear to grasp
sympathetically nineteenth-century American problems
and attitudes as expressed in the works of Melville
and other American writers.

744   THE ENCYCLOPAEDIA BRITANNICA: A DICTIONARY OF ARTS,
         SCIENCES, LITERATURE AND GENERAL INFORMATION. 11th
         edition. Cambridge, England; New York: 1911,
         XVIII, 102-103.

         Melville was "the product of a period in American
literature when the fiction written by writers below
Irving, Poe, and Hawthorne was measured by humble artistic
standards."

745   THE ENCYCLOPAEDIA BRITANNICA. Chicago, London, Toronto:
         William Benton, Publisher, 1971, XV, 135-137.

         In MOBY DICK and in BILLY BUDD, Melville reached
the "heights of which he was capable as a writer of
prose. Allusive, eloquent, highly figurative, subtly
symbolic, it was strong enough to carry the mighty theme
for which it was constructed."

746   Engstrom, Alfred G. "The Single Tear: A Stereotype of
         Literary Sensibility," PQ, 42 (1963), 106-109.

         Ahab's tear within a literary tradition.

747   Ensslen, Klaus. "Melville's 'Benito Cereno,'" KB, 21
           (1961), 27-33.

748   Ensslen, Klaus. MELVILLES ERZAHLUNGEN: STIL- UND
           STRUKTURANALYTISCHE UNTER-SUCHUNGEN. Heidelberg:
           Carl Winter, 1966.

           An examination of sixteen prose pieces, beginning
       with "Bartleby" and including BILLY BUDD.

749   Ensslen, Klaus. STIL- UND STRUKTURANALYTISCHE
           UNTERSUCHUNGEN VON HERMAN MELVILLES TALES. (einschl.
           BILLY BUDD). Diss. Munich.

750   "Enoch Mudge - Ship Salvation," The Bulletin. OLD
           DARTMOUTH HISTORICAL SOCIETY AND WHALING MUSEUM.
           New Bedford: 1955, pp. 1-3.

751   Erdman, David V., and Ephim G. Fogel, eds. EVIDENCE FOR
           AUTHORSHIP: ESSAYS ON PROBLEMS OF ATTRIBUTION WITH
           AN ANNOTATED BIBLIOGRAPHY OF SELECTED READINGS.
           Ithaca, New York: Cornell University Press, 1966,
           p. 516.

           Evidence of style "found highly negative" as to
       whether Melville reviewed THE SCARLET LETTER.

       Cf.,Willard Thorp. "Did Melville Review THE SCARLET
       LETTER?" AL, 14 (1942), 302-305; R. E. Watters.
       Melville's 'Isolat es,'" PMLA, 60 (1945), 1138n.

752   Erskine, John. "MOBY-DICK," Chapter X in THE DELIGHT
           OF GREAT BOOKS. Indianapolis: 1928, pp. 223-240.

753   Erskine, John. "A Whale of a Story," Delineator, 115
           (October, 1929), 15, 68, 71, 72.

           Taken from a chapter in Erskine's THE DELIGHT
       OF GREAT BOOKS (1928).

754   ESSAY AND GENERAL LITERATURE INDEX, 1900-1972. New York:
           The H. W. Wilson Company.

755   Estrin, Mark W. "Dramatizations of American Fiction:
           Hawthorne and Melville on Stage and Screen,"
           DAI, 30 (New York University: 1970), 3428A.

756   Evans, William A. "The Boy and the Shadow: The Role of Pip and Fedallah in MOBY DICK," SLitI, 2, 1 (1969), 77-81.

757   Exman, Eugene. "Herman Melville, Novelist," THE BROTHERS HARPER. New York: 1965, pp. 282-302.

758   Fadiman, Clifton. "Herman Melville," Atl, 172 (October, 1943), 88-91.

        Melville who does not possess the trait of humor compared with Shakespeare who is "balanced" by a sense of humor.

759   Fadiman, Clifton. "Herman Melville," JUBILEE: ONE HUNDRED YEARS OF THE ATLANTIC. Boston: Little, Brown and Company, 1957, pp. 309-314.

        This is the Introduction to the 1943 Heritage Press edition of MOBY DICK.

760   Fadiman, Clifton, ed. Introduction, MOBY DICK. New York: Heritage Press, 1943; Harper and Brothers, 1950; Bantam Books, 1964.

761   Fadiman, Clifton. MOBY DICK. Illustrated by Robert Shore. New York: Macmillan, 1962.

762   Fadiman, Clifton. "MOBY DICK," PARTY OF ONE. New York: World, 1955, pp. 136-144.

763   Fagin, N. Bryllion. "Herman Melville and the Interior Monologue," AL, 6 (January, 1935), 433-34.

        The "interior monologue" used in MOBY DICK.

764   Faigelman, Steven H. "The Development of Narrative Consciousness in MOBY DICK," DA, 28 (Cornell; 1967), 2243A-44A.

        The main story is that of Ishmael to which "The Try-Works" chapter is central. Melville condemns the "Romantic Imagination" of Ahab's idealism and affirms it through Ishmael's "final survival" as a story teller.

765   Falk, Robert. "Shakespeare in America: A Survey to
       1900," ShakR, 18 (1965), 102-118.

       Performances and criticism of Shakespeare became
       common in the United States in the 18th and 19th
       centuries. Noteworthy results include the influence
       of "Lear" on Melville's novels, especially MOBY DICK.

766   Falwiler, Toby. "The Death of the Handsome Sailor:
       A Study of BILLY BUDD and THE RED BADGE OF COURAGE,"
       ArQ, 26 (1970), 101-112.

767   Farnsworth, Robert M. "From Voyage to Quest in Melville,"
       Melville Supplement, ESQ, 28 (1962), 17-20.

       Ishmael as narrator, rather than Redburn.

768   Farnsworth, Robert M. "ISRAEL POTTER: Pathetic Comedy,"
       BNYPL, 65 (February, 1961), 125-132.

       ISRAEL POTTER is a serious projection of Melville's
       beliefs. Here, Melville controlled the ironical themes
       which had caused the failure of PIERRE, "by focusing
       them ironically in the soft light of pathetic comedy."
       Israel's is the struggle of man to control his fate, and
       it reflects "the problem of America to realize her
       destiny."

769   Farnsworth, Robert M. "Ishmael to the Royal Masthead,"
       UKCR, 28 (1962), 183-90.

       Ahab, not Ishmael, the real center of meaning.

770   Farnsworth, Robert M. "Melville's Use of Point of View
       in His First Seven Novels," DA, 19 (Tulane: 1959),
       3294-95.

771   Farnsworth, Robert M. "Slavery and Innocence in 'Benito
       Cereno,'" ESQ, 44 (3rd Qt., 1966), 94-96.

       The story indicates that Melville understood the
       implications of slavery and its racial biases. He
       knew that the innocence of Captain Delano helped
       constitute the crime.

772   Fast, Howard. "American Literature and the Democratic
       Tradition," CE, 8 (March, 1947), 279-284.

       Same article in EJ, 36 (1947), 55-60.

       Incidental references which place Melville in his
       literary and social milieu.

773   Faulkner, William. "MOBY DICK: 'Golgotha of the Heart,'"
       <u>Tribune</u> (Chicago), "Books," July 16, 1927, p. 12.

       "...I think that the book which I put down with the
       unqualified thought 'I wish I had written that' is MOBY
       DICK...."

774   Faulkner, William. "MOBY DICK: 'Golgotha of the Heart,'"
       STUDIES IN MOBY-DICK. Howard P. Vincent, comp.
       Columbus, Ohio: Charles E. Merrill Publishing
       Company, 1969, p. 162.

775   Feidelson, Charles, Jr. THE IDEA OF SYMBOLISM IN
       AMERICAN WRITING, WITH PARTICULAR REFERENCE TO
       EMERSON AND MELVILLE. Diss. Yale: 1948.

776   Feidelson, Charles, Jr., ed. Introduction, MOBY-DICK.
       Indianapolis: Bobbs-Merrill, 1964.

777   Feidelson, Charles, Jr. "Melville," "The Fool of Truth,"
       SYMBOLISM AND AMERICAN LITERATURE. Chicago:
       Chicago University Press, 1953, pp. 27-35; 162-212,
       passim. Repr., Chicago University Press, 1959 (A
       Phoenix Book).

       Rev. by Richard Chase, AL, 25 (1953), 378-80.

778   Feidelson, Charles, Jr. "The World of Melville," <u>Show</u>,
       3 (1963), 47-55, 96.

       General article with photographs.

779   Felheim, Marvin. "Meaning and Structure in 'Bartleby,'"
       CE, 23 (1962), 369-370; 375-376.

       Repr., in THE DIMENSIONS OF THE SHORT STORY: A
       CRITICAL ANTHOLOGY. James E. Miller, Jr., and Bernice
       Slote, eds. New York: Dodd, Mead, 1964, pp. 534-539.

780   Feltenstein, Rosalie. "Melville's 'Benito Cereno,'"
       AL, 19 (November, 1947), 245-255.

       Melville's use of sources, adaptation of fact to
       fiction and symbol.

       Cf., Thomas E. Connolly. "A Note on Name Symbolism
       in Melville," AL, 25 (1954), 489-490.

781   Fenton, Charles A. "'The Bell Tower': Melville and
           Technology," AL, 23 (May, 1951), 219-232.

           Melville condemns technology in "The Bell Tower."
           Nature destroys the tower with an earthquake, but
           Bannadonna destroys himself. Technology threatens that
           which sustains man--his responsibility to his fellowman
           and to God.

782   Ferguson, Alfred. Introduction, BILLY BUDD, AND OTHER
           STORIES. Suggestions for Reading and Discussion by
           Allen Kirschner. Houghton, 1970.

783   Ferguson, DeLancey. "The Legacy of Letters," AmSch,
           29 (1960), 406-418.

           Recent editions of Melville and others.

784   Ferris, M. L. D. "Herman Melville," BSAA, 6 (1901),
           289-293.

785   Fidell, Estelle A., and Esther V. Flory, comps. "Herman
           Melville," SHORT STORY INDEX. SUPPLEMENT, 1955-1958,
           AN INDEX TO 6,392 STORIES IN 376 COLLECTIONS. New
           York: H. W. Wilson Company, 1960, p. 186.

786   Fidell, Estelle A., comp. "Herman Melville," SHORT
           STORY INDEX. SUPPLEMENT 1959-1963: AN INDEX TO
           9,068 STORIES IN 582 COLLECTIONS. New York:
           H. W. Wilson, 1965, p. 271.

787   Fidell, Estelle A., comp. "Herman Melville," SHORT
           STORY INDEX: SUPPLEMENT 1964-1968: AN INDEX TO
           11,301 STORIES IN 793 COLLECTIONS. New York:
           H. W. Wilson Co., 1969, p. 330.

788   Fiedler, Leslie A. "American Literature," CONTEMPORARY
           LITERARY SCHOLARSHIP: A CRITICAL REVIEW. Lewis
           Leary, ed. New York: Appleton-Century-Crofts,
           1958, pp. 157-185.

789   Fiedler, Leslie A. "Blackness of Darkness: The Negro
and the Development of American Gothic," IMAGES
OF THE NEGRO IN AMERICAN LITERATURE. Seymour L.
Gross and John Edward Hardy, eds. Chicago and
London: Chicago University Press, 1966, pp. 84-105.

In "Benito Cereno," Melville treats the tragic
encounter between comic stereotypes and a historic
instance of a slave mutiny. Captain Delano fails to
recognize rebellion on a Spanish slave ship precisely
because he is a good American. He will not believe the
"imputation of evil in man," but he is also incapable
of believing a Negro, a "body servant," anything but
"a faithful fellow."

790   Fiedler, Leslie A. "Come Back to the Raft Ag'in, Huck
Honey!" PR, 15 (1948), 664-671.

Repr., as "The Archetypal Approach: Literature
in the Light of Myth," FIVE APPROACHES OF LITERARY
CRITICISM: AN ARRANGEMENT OF CONTEMPORARY CRITICAL
ESSAYS. Wilbur S. Scott, ed. New York: Macmillan,
1963, pp. 303-312. Also, repr., in AN END TO INNOCENCE.
Boston: Beacon, 1955, pp. 142-151.

791   Fiedler, Leslie A. "The Failure of Sentiment and the
Evasion of Love," LOVE AND DEATH IN THE AMERICAN
NOVEL. Rev. ed. New York: Stein & Day, 1966,
pp. 337-390, passim.

792   Fiedler, Leslie A., ed. Introduction, Notes and Exercise
Questions, ART OF THE ESSAY. New York: Crowell,
1958.

793   Fiedler, Leslie A. "Ishmael's Trip," List, 78 (1967),
134-136.

Melville's democratic, romantic, "secret epic,"
and pseudo-novel contains a pseudo-drama. Ahab and
Ishmael fly from reality and death, as Melville flies
from form.

794   Fiedler, Leslie. "MOBY DICK: The Baptism of Fire and
       the Baptism of Sperm," LOVE AND DEATH IN THE
       AMERICAN NOVEL. New York: Criterion Books, 1960,
       pp. 520-552. Repr., Cleveland: Meridian Books,
       1962.

       MOBY DICK must be read not only as an account of a
whale hunt, but as a love story. The absence of women
in MOBY DICK indicates not the absence of love, but its
presence in "the peculiar American form of innocent
homosexuality."

       Revs. by Allen Hayman, NEQ, 34 (1961), 261-263;
Willard Thorp, New York Herald Tribune, Book Review,
April 10, 1960, p. 5.

795   Fiedler, Leslie A. NO! IN THUNDER: ESSAYS ON MYTH AND
       LITERATURE. Boston: Beacon Press, 1960, passim.

796   Fiedler, Leslie A. "Out of the Whale," Nation, 169
       (November 19, 1949), 494-496.

797   Fiedler, Leslie A. "From Redemption to Initiation,"
       NewL, 41 (1958), 20-23.

       Theme of the innocent child encountering evil
recurs in fiction. Only Pip remains unseduced by
Captain Ahab's madness.

798   Fiedler, Leslie A. THE RETURN OF THE VANISHING AMERICAN.
       New York: Stein and Day, 1968, passim.

799   Fiedler, Leslie A. "The Shape of MOBY DICK," THE
       COLLECTED ESSAYS OF LESLIE FIEDLER. New York:
       Stein & Day, 1971, II, 312-318.

800   Fiedler, Leslie A. WAITING FOR THE END. New York:
       Stein and Day, 1964, passim.

       CLAREL: An adaptation for Americans of the
archetypal pattern which has "most appealed to the
American imagination when it has sought at all to
deal with things Jewish."

       However, there are no Jews in that otherwise
universally representative crew: the Manx, African,
Irish, Spanish, Italian, Polynesian, and Middle-Eastern
human flotsam who, under a mad Yankee skipper, sail a
ship called after a defunct Indian tribe.

800.1 Field, D. D., ed. A HISTORY OF BERKSHIRE COUNTY.
Pittsfield, Mass.: 1829.

Relation of an incident which might have been the
source of "The Apple-Tree Table."

801 Field, M. B. MEMORIES OF MANY MEN AND OF SOME WOMEN.
New York: 1874.

802 Fields, James T. YESTERDAYS WITH AUTHORS. Boston:
1872, pp. 52-53.

803 Fiene, Donald M. "Bartleby the Christ," ATQ, 7 (Summer,
(1970), 18-23.

Melville meant the title character to "an
incarnation of Christ" and the tale itself "an
allegory dramatizing the apocalypse."

804 Fiene, Donald M. "A Bibliography of Criticism of
'Bartleby the Scrivener,'" MELVILLE ANNUAL 1965,
A SYMPOSIUM: BARTLEBY THE SCRIVENER. Howard P.
Vincent, ed. (Kent Stud. in Eng., III). Kent, Ohio:
Kent State University Press, 1966, pp. 140-190.

805 Fiess, Edward. "Byron and Byronism in the Mind and Art
of Herman Melville," DA, 25 (Yale: 1965), 4145.

806 Fiess, Edward. "Byron's Dark Blue Ocean and Melville's
Rolling Sea," ELN, 3 (June, 1966), 274-278.

807 Fiess, Edward. "Melville as a Reader and Student of
Byron," AL, 24 (1952), 186-194.

808 Fine, Ronald E. "Melville and the Rhetoric of Psychological
Fiction," DA, 27 (Rochester: 1966), 1364A.

Melville saw rhetoric as "an amoral force which
the artist wields." Consequently, he distrusted art,
which perhaps derived from the Platonic and Calvinistic
distrust of "uncanonical writing."

809 Finkelstein, Dorothée Metlitsky. HERMAN MELVILLE AND THE
NEAR EAST. Diss. Yale: 1957.

810 Finkelstein, Dorothee Metlitsky. MELVILLE'S ORIENDA.
New Haven: Yale University Press, 1961. New
York: Octagon Books, 1971.

Melville's interest in and literary use of the
Near East.

Revs., by Howard C. Horsford, AL, 34 (1962), 422-
423; Robert McElderry, Jr., Person, 43 (1962), 419;
Nathalia Wright, NEQ, 35 (1962), 418-420.

811 Finkelstein, Sidney. EXISTENTIALISM AND ALIENATION IN
AMERICAN LITERATURE. New York: International
Publishers, 1965; 2nd printing, 1967, pp. 32, 33.

Melville's use of the sermon.

812 Finkelstein, Sidney. "Six Ways of Looking at Reality,"
Mainstream, 13 (1960), 31-42.

Contrast of passages from Melville and others.

813 Firchow, Peter E. "BARTLEBY: Man and Metaphor,"
SSF, 5 (Summer, 1968), 342-348.

Melville's story stresses the human condition:
the isolation of man and his inability to communicate.
Bartleby himself is a "dead letter," whose address and
message the narrator attempts to decipher.

814 Firebaugh, Joseph J. "Humorist as Rebel: The Melville
of TYPEE," NCF, 9 (September, 1954), 108-120.

Melville's "richly tolerant humor is the palliative
of his rebellion." Much of the humor in TYPEE relies
upon verbal maneuvering, incongruity, and an ironic
juxtaposition of civilized and primitive societies.

815 Firkins, Ina Ten Eyck, comp. "Melville," INDEX TO
SHORT STORIES. SUPPLEMENT. New York: H. W. Wilson
Company, 1929, p. 188.

816 Firkins, Ina Ten Eyck, comp. "Melville," INDEX TO
SHORT STORIES. SECOND SUPPLEMENT. New York:
H. W. Wilson Company, 1936, p. 166.

817   Fisher, Marvin. "Bug and Humbug in Melville's 'Apple-Tree
        Table,'" SSF, 8 (Summer, 1971), 459-466.

818   Fisher, Marvin. "Focus on Herman Melville's 'The Two
        Temples': The Denigration of the American Dream,"
        AMERICAN DREAMS, AMERICAN NIGHTMARES. David Madden,
        ed. Preface by Harry T. Moore. Carbondale and
        Edwardsville: Southern Illinois University Press,
        1970; London and Amsterdam: Feffer & Simons, Inc.,
        pp. 76-86.

        Melville questioned, not the "meaning of the dream"
        or its connection with "the promised Kingdom of Christian
        thought." In his own way, he "seems to have affirmed
        these." It was, rather, the self-styled role of America
        as a "redeemer nation," the idea of America as the necessary
        locus for "realization of the American Dream" that he
        challenged.

819   Fisher, Marvin. "The Iconology of Industrialism,
        1830-1860," AQ, 13 (1961), 347-364.

        The conflict in nineteenth-century attitudes
        (Nature vs. Progress) may be traced in history, aesthetics,
        and technology. In America, this conflict is apparent from
        Emerson and Melville to Henry Adams and even Faulkner.

820   Fisher, Marvin. "'The Lightning-Rod Man': Melville's
        Testament of Rejection," SSF, 7 (Summer, 1970),
        433-438.

        The narrator, having freed himself of the
        Lightning-Rod man, has not freed mankind, for the
        Lightning-Rod man still dwells in the land and still
        "drives a brave trade with the fears of man."

821   Fisher, Marvin. "Melville's 'Bell-Tower': A Double
        Thrust," AQ, 18 (1966), 200-207.

        The story allegorizes mid-nineteenth-century
        America in two particulars. It is not only a "rejection
        of technological progress" but a response to Negro
        slavery. With its secondary thrust against a society
        which "enslaves human beings," the story may be likened
        to "The Tartarus of Maids" and "Benito Cereno."

822   Fisher, Marvin. "Melville's 'Jimmy Rose': Truly Risen?"
        SSF, 4 (Fall, 1966), 1-11.

        The tale is Melville's appraisal of Christianity
        in the America of his time. He found it "too often
        servile, self-seeking, and backward-looking, barely
        tolerated by an increasingly materialistic and mechanistic
        society which begrudged even its feeble support."

823   Fisher, Marvin. "Melville's TARTARUS: The Deflowering
        of New England," AQ, 23 (Spring, 1971), 79-100.

        The second part of Melville's diptych is a
        critique of industrialism and an example of Melville's
        artistry of concealment. The mechanistic values implicit
        in industrialism has precipitated a crisis. As portrayed
        by Melville, the machine threatens every physical,
        psychological, organic, and spiritual attribute of
        humanity.

824   Fisher, Richard E. "The American Repudiation of Melville's
        PIERRE," ModSpr, 55 (1961), 233-240.

        Critical reception of PIERRE was consistently
        hostile, and affected critical appraisal of Melville's
        earlier works.

825   Fiske, John C. "Herman Melville in Soviet Criticism,"
        CL, 5 (Winter, 1953), 30-39.

826   Fite, Olive L. "Billy Budd, Claggart, and Schopenhauer,"
        NCF, 23 (1968), 336-343.

        Melville's two figures may have grown out of
        what he found in Schopenhauer's exposition of the
        will to live.

827   Fite, Olive L. "The Interpretation of Melville's
        BILLY BUDD," DA, 17 (Northwestern: 1957), 354.

828   Flanagan, John T. "THE SPIRIT OF THE TIMES Reviews
        Melville," JEGP, 64 (January, 1965), 57-64.

        William T. Porter's journal published an announcement
        of every major novel of Melville, enthusiastically reviewed
        MOBY DICK, and was almost alone in sympathetic response to
        PIERRE.

829   Fletcher, Angus. ALLEGORY: THE THEORY OF A SYMBOLIC
        MODE. Ithaca, New York: Cornell University Press,
        1964, pp. 352-354, passim.

        The encounter of Ahab with the White Whale is the
        "apocalyptic vision of the war" between two powers,
        and thus it links Melville's romance to the main tradition
        established by THE REVELATION OF ST. JOHN THE DIVINE.

830   Fletcher, Richard M. "Melville's Use of Marquesan,"
        AS, 39 (May, 1964), 135-138.

        Melville proved himself a manipulator of language.
        He made some use of Marquesan in TYPEE, more in OMOO.
        He reproduced the language with reasonable accuracy,
        but often playfully devised alternative meanings.

831   Floan, Howard R. "MOBY-DICK y la lucha esperitual de
        Herman Melville," Arbor, 43 (1959), 421-430.

831.1   Floan, Howard R. "Melville," THE SOUTH IN NORTHERN EYES:
        1831 to 1861. Austin: Texas University Press, 1958,
        pp. 131-147.

832   Foerster, Norman, ed. THE REINTERPRETATION OF AMERICAN
        LITERATURE: SOME CONTRIBUTIONS TOWARD THE UNDER-
        STANDING OF ITS HISTORICAL DEVELOPMENT. New York:
        Harcourt, Brace & Co., 1928, 1955; Russell & Russell,
        1959, pp. 114-138, passim.

833   Foerster, Norman, and Robert P. Falk, eds. "Herman
        Melville," EIGHT AMERICAN WRITERS. New York:
        W. W. Norton & Co., 1963, pp. 781-795.

834   Fogle, Richard Harter. "'BENITO CERENO,'" MELVILLE:
        A COLLECTION OF CRITICAL ESSAYS. Richard Chase, ed.
        Englewood Cliffs, New Jersey: Prentice-Hall, 1962,
        pp. 116-124.

        After MOBY DICK, the tale of BENITO CERENO is
        "Melville's most fully achieved piece of writing."

835   Fogle, Richard Harter. "BILLY BUDD--Acceptance or Irony,"
        TSE, 8 (1958), 107-113.

        Repr., in LITERATURE IN CRITICAL PERSPECTIVES.
        Walter K. Gordon, ed. New York: Appleton-Century-
        Crofts, 1968, pp. 758-761; in TWENTIETH CENTURY
        INTERPRETATIONS OF BILLY BUDD. Howard P. Vincent, ed.
        Englewood Cliffs, N. J.: 1971, pp. 41-47.

        A survey of the "three principal conceptions" of the
        meaning of BILLY BUDD, those of Newton Arvin, Lawrance
        Thompson and Stanley Edgar Hyman. Conclusion is that
        the irony in the story is "neither a scream nor a sneer."

836   Fogle, Richard Harter. "BILLY BUDD: The Order of the
        Fall," NCF, 15 (1960), 189-205.

        A defense of Vere.

837   Fogle, Richard Harter. "Melville and the Civil War,"
        TSE, 9 (1959), 61-89.

        Melville's poetry.

838   Fogle, Richard Harter. "Melville's 'Bartleby': Absolutism,
        Predestination, and Free Will," TSE, 4 (1954), 124-
        135.

        Repr., in Richard Harter Fogle. MELVILLE'S SHORTER
        TALES. Norman: Oklahoma University Press, 1960, pp. 14-27.

839   Fogle, Richard Harter. "Melville's CLAREL: Doubt and
        Belief," TSE, 10 (1960), 101-116.

        CLAREL is Melville's treatment of the late 19th
        century conflict between faith and reason. Despite its
        merits, the poem lacks unity and development.

840   Fogle, Richard Harter. "Melville's Poetry," TSE, 12
        (1961-1962), 81-86.

        Melville's poetry, though impressive, is experimental
        and uneven, rarely subjective and lyrical.

841   Fogle, Richard Harter. MELVILLE'S SHORTER TALES. Norman:
        Oklahoma University Press, 1960.

        Cf., Edward H. Rosenberry, "Awash in Melvilliana,"
        NEQ, 33 (1960), 525-528.

        Rev. by William H. Gilman, AL, 34 (1962), 294-296.

842   Fogle, Richard Harter. MELVILLE'S TALES. Diss. Tulane:
        1954.

843   Fogle, Richard Harter. "The Monk and the Bachelor:
        Melville's BENITO CERENO," TSE, 3 (1952), 155-178.

844   Fogle, Richard Harter. "Organic Form in American Criticism:
        1840-1870," THE DEVELOPMENT OF AMERICAN LITERARY
        CRITICISM. Floyd Stovall, ed. Chapel Hill: North
        Carolina University Press, 1955, pp. 75-111.

        Melville accepted the doctrine of organic form
        more easily than did Hawthorne.

845   Fogle, Richard Harter. "The Themes in Melville's Later
       Poetry," TSE, 11 (1961), 65-86.

       In his later poetry Melville often uses the sea
       for imagery and background for his characters who
       have been "tried and almost broken," only to come
       to terms with life.

846   Foley, Mary. "The Digressions in BILLY BUDD,"
       MELVILLE'S BILLY BUDD AND THE CRITICS. William T.
       Stafford, ed. 2nd ed. Belmont, Calif.: Wadsworth,
       1968, pp. 220-223.

847   Foley, P. K. AMERICAN AUTHORS: 1795-1895: A BIBLIOGRAPHY
       OF FIRST AND NOTABLE EDITIONS CHRONOLOGICALLY ARRANGED
       WITH NOTES. New York: Milford House, Inc., 1969,
       pp. 195-196.

848   Fone, Byrne R., with George Marcelle. MELVILLE'S MOBY
       DICK AND OTHER WORKS. New York: Barrister Publishing
       Company, 1966.

       With notes and examination guides.

849   Forgues, E. D. "Moby Dick, Là Chasse a la Baleine,"
       RDM, 1 (February 1, 1853), 491-514.

850   Forrey, Robert. "Herman Melville and the Negro Question,"
       Mainstream, 15 (February, 1962), 23-32.

       "Benito Cereno"

851   Forster, E. M. "Prophecy," ASPECTS OF THE NOVEL. New
       York: Harcourt, Brace, 1927; repr., 1950, pp.
       138-143, 181-212.

852   Forster, E. M. "Letter," The Griffin, 1 (1951), 4-6.

       Explanation of the treatment of Vere as villain
       in his libretto for the Benjamin Britten opera
       of BILLY BUDD.

853   Forster, E. M., and Eric Crozier. "Libretto," for
       Benjamin Britten's BILLY BUDD: OPERA IN FOUR ACTS.
       London: Boosey & Hawkes, Ltd., 1951.

853.1　Forster, Margaret E. (Attributed). HAND-BOOK OF AMERICAN
　　　　　LITERATURE, HISTORICAL, BIOGRAPHICAL AND CRITICAL.
　　　　　Philadelphia: 1855(?), p. 189.

　　　　　"The wildness of Melville's stories--TYPEE, OMOO,
MARDI, and others--seems to be infectious...."

854　　Forsythe, Robert S. "Emerson and 'MOBY-DICK,'" N&Q, 177
　　　　　(December 23, 1938), 457-458.

　　　　　In 1834 Emerson heard the story of a white whale,
Old Tom, which attacked boats, and was finally taken by
the Winslow or the Essex. Thus, the legend of a ferocious
white whale was known five years before J. N. Reynolds'
account of Mocha Dick.

855　　Forsythe, Robert S. "Herman Melville in Honolulu,"
　　　　　NEQ, 8 (March, 1935), 99-105.

　　　　　An article (reprinted in above reference) appearing
in the Friend (Honolulu), New Series, 71 (August 1, 1873),
probably by Samuel C. Damon, editor, reports that Melville
resided there for several months in 1843 and left on
board the frigate United States in August of that year.

856　　Forsythe, Robert S. "Herman Melville in the Marquesas,"
　　　　　PQ, 15 (1936), 1-15.

857　　Forsythe, Robert S. "Herman Melville in Tahiti,"
　　　　　PQ, 16 (1937), 344-357.

　　　　　Melville's voyage on the Julia.

　　　　　Cf., Robert S. Forsythe. "More upon Herman
Melville in Tahiti," PQ, 17 (1938), 1-17.

858　　Forsythe, Robert S. "Herman Melville's Father Murphy,"
　　　　　N&Q, 172 (1937), 254-258; 272-276.

　　　　　A biographical sketch of Father Columba Murphy,
whom Melville met during his imprisonment on Tahiti,
and whom he portrayed accurately and favorably in
OMOO.

859　　Forsythe, Robert S. "Herman Melville's 'The Town-Ho's
　　　　　Story,'" N&Q, 168 (1935), 314.

　　　　　Chapter 54 of MOBY DICK first appeared in
Harper's New Monthly Magazine, October 1851, from
which it was printed in the Baltimore Weekly Sun,
November 8, 1851.

860   Forsythe, Robert S., ed. Introduction, PIERRE.
           (Americana Deserta Series). New York: Alfred A.
           Knopf, 1930.

           Rev. by Henry A. Murray, Jr. NEQ, 4 (1931), 333-337.

861   Forsythe, Robert S. "Mr. Lewis Mumford and Melville's
           PIERRE," AL, 2 (1930), 286-289.

           The discrepancies between Mumford's synopsis of
Melville's PIERRE and the novel itself.

862   Forsythe, Robert S. "More upon Herman Melville in
           Tahiti," PQ, 17 (1938), 1-17.

           Melville stayed in Tahiti from September 26 to
November 9, 1842, and in OMOO Melville incorporated,
on the whole, "much less fiction with his facts than
in TYPEE."

           Cf., Robert S. Forsythe. "Herman Melville in Tahiti,"
PQ, 16 (1937), 344-357.

863   Forsythe, Robert S. "An Oversight by Herman Melville,"
           N&Q, 172 (1937), 296.

864   Foster, Charles H. "Something in Emblems: A
           Reinterpretation of MOBY-DICK," NEQ, 34 (March, 1961),
           3-35.

           MOBY DICK is not two books--a picaresque sea story
and a Shakespearean tragedy--but three, its "top story
a fable of democratic protest" against slavery. In 1851,
Melville was angered by the Sims case in which a fugitive
Negro was remanded to Georgia under the Fugitive Slave
Act of 1850 by Chief Justice Shaw, Melville's father-in-law.
Shaw installed a chain around the courthouse and had to
pass under it himself, his genuflexion metaphorically
something in emblems.

865   Foster, Charles H. "The 'Theonomous Analysis' of
           American Culture," STUDIES IN AMERICAN CULTURE:
           DOMINANT IDEAS AND IMAGES. Joseph J. Kwiat and
           Mary C. Turpie, eds. Minneapolis: Minnesota
           University Press, 1960, pp. 189-206.

           Incidental references which place Melville in
his social and cultural milieu.

866   Foster, Edward F. "A Study of Grim Humor in the Works
           of Poe, Melville, and Twain," DA, 17 (Vanderbilt:
           1957), 1761-62.

867   Foster, Elizabeth S. "Another Note on Melville and
       Geology," AL, 22 (January, 1951), 479-487.

       A reply to Tyrus Hillway. "Melville's Geological
       Knowledge," AL, 21 (1949), 232-237, which was written
       to make additions to and to suggest "possible sources
       not named" in Elizabeth Foster's "Melville and Geology,"
       AL, 17 (1945), 50-65.

868   Foster, Elizabeth S. "Emerson as the Confidence-Man,"
       THE CONFIDENCE MAN: HIS MASQUERADE. Hershel
       Parker, ed. New York: W. W. Norton & Co., 1971,
       pp. 333-339.

       Any opponent of optimistic philosophy would
       naturally attack Ralph Waldo Emerson. Hence, Melville
       brings Emerson aboard the Fidèle, perhaps in the herb-
       doctor, and "certainly in the mystic Mark Winsome and
       his practical disciple Egbert."

869   Foster, Elizabeth S. HERMAN MELVILLE'S THE CONFIDENCE MAN,
       ITS ORIGINS AND MEANINGS. Diss. Yale: 1941.

870   Foster, Elizabeth S., ed. Introduction, THE CONFIDENCE
       MAN. New York: Hendricks House, 1954.

       Melville's various dealers in "confidence" satirize
       different forms of philosophical optimism.

871   Foster, Elizabeth S. "Melville and Geology," AL, 17
       (March, 1945), 50-65.

       Melville's knowledge of geology provided opportunity
       for humor in MARDI and furnished imagery in MOBY DICK.

       Cf., Tyrus Hillway. "Melville's Geological
       Knowledge," AL, 21 (1949), 232-237, and Elizabeth
       Foster. "Another Note on Melville and Geology,"
       AL, 22 (1951), 479-487.

872   Foster, Elizabeth S. "Melville's Revisions of Chapter 14,"
       in THE CONFIDENCE MAN: HIS MASQUERADE. Hershel Parker,
       ed. New York: W. W. Norton & Co., 1971, pp. 321-323.

       Perhaps for "fear of wounding religious sensibilities"
       Melville revised to "soften" statements. The other object
       of Melville's syntactical revisions was to produce "tension,
       tautness, strength in sentence structure." He "increased
       parallelism regularly and periodic structure frequently...
       as he combined and reduced sentences...."

873   Foster, Richard, ed. Introduction, SIX AMERICAN NOVELISTS
        OF THE NINETEENTH CENTURY. Minneapolis, Minn.:
        Minnesota University Press, 1968.

        Melville and others.

873.1   Fournier, Eliezer, adaptor. VESTE BLANCHE. Paris:
        Delagrave, 1957.

874   Fowler, Roger, ed. "Linguistic Theory and the Study of
        Literature," ESSAYS ON STYLE AND LANGUAGE:
        LINGUISTIC AND CRITICAL APPROACHES TO LITERARY
        STYLE. New York: The Humanities Press, 1966,
        pp. 1-28.

        Application of "convergence of style" to literary
        expression, particularly in MOBY DICK.

875   Fraiberg, Louis. PSYCHOANALYSIS AND AMERICAN LITERARY
        CRITICISM. Detroit: Wayne State University Press,
        1960, p. 152.

        A survey of Ludwig Lewisohn's views of the
        "troubled romancers," Melville, Hawthorne, and Poe.

876   Franciosci, Massimo. "'Taipi' eden realista," FLe, 10
        (March 8, 1953), 4.

877   Frank, Max. DIE FARB- UND LICHTSYMBOLIK IM PROSAWERK
        HERMAN MELVILLES. (BzJA 19.) Heidelberg: Winter,
        1967.

        Examination of prose from early "Fragments" to
        BILLY BUDD, omitting ISRAEL POTTER, THE CONFIDENCE MAN,
        and most of the shorter fiction, as well as poetry and
        miscellaneous writing.

878   Frank, Max. "Melville und Poe: Eine Quellen-Studie zu
        'Fragments from a Writing Desk No. 2,' 'Redburn' und
        'The Assignation,'" KLEINE BEITRAGE ZUR AMERIKANISCHEN
        LITERATURGESCHICHTE: ARBEITSPROBLEN AUS DEUTSCHEN
        SEMINAREN UND INSTITUTEN. Hans Galinsky and
        Hans-Joachim Lang, eds. Heidelberg: Winter,
        pp. 19-23.

879   Franklin, H. Bruce. "'Apparent Symbol of Despotic
          Command': Melville's BENITO CERENO," NEQ, 34
          (December, 1961), 462-477.

       The change Melville made i. Amasa Delano's plot
(NARRATIVE OF VOYAGES AND TRAVELS) by sending Benito
Cereno into monastic retirement (like Charles V),
suggests as a possible source, William Stirling's
CLOISTER LIFE OF THE EMPEROR CHARLES THE FIFTH. The
latter was quoted in the Edinburgh Review, January,
1855, and in Fraser's Magazine, April and May, 1851.

880   Franklin, H. Bruce. "Herman Melville and Science Fiction,"
          FUTURE PERFECT: AMERICAN SCIENCE FICTION OF THE
          NINETEENTH CENTURY. New York: Oxford University
          Press, 1966, pp. 144-150.

       "The Bell-Tower," Melville's only "complete science
fiction story," an important event in the history of the
genre. Melville included all the elements which were to
become conventional.

       The story also illustrates how technological creation
involves the "total design" of all of man's relationships:
the political, social, cultural.

881   Franklin, H. Bruce, ed. Introduction and Annotations,
          THE CONFIDENCE-MAN: HIS MASQUERADE. Indianapolis:
          Bobbs-Merrill, 1967.

882   Franklin, H. Bruce. Introduction, MARDI AND A VOYAGE
          THITHER. New York: Capricorn Books, 1964.

883   Franklin, H. Bruce. "The Island Worlds of Darwin and
          Melville," CentR, 11 (Summer, 1967), 353-370.

       Melville challenged and parodied THE VOYAGE OF THE
BEAGLE, which he owned and used, rejecting Darwin's
"particular observations, his use of these observations,
and his metaphoric structure."

884   Franklin, H. Bruce. "Melville's Mythology," DA, 22
          (Stanford: 1962), 3644.

885   Franklin, H. Bruce. "MOBY DICK: An Egyptian Myth
          Incarnate," THE WAKE OF THE GODS: MELVILLE'S
          MYTHOLOGY. Stanford: Stanford University Press,
          1963, pp. 53-98.

       The central myth is that of the struggle between
Osiris (Ahab), and Typhon, the Egyptian Leviathan (Moby
Dick).

886   Franklin, H. Bruce. "Redburn's Wicked End," NCF, 20
         (September, 1965), 190-194.

         Redburn's complete loss of innocence and
  initiation into guilt results from his betrayal,
  indifference and abandonment, of Harry Bolton who
  is the double of himself.

887   Franklin, H. Bruce. THE WAKE OF THE GODS: MELVILLE'S
         MYTHOLOGY. Palo Alto, Calif.: Stanford University
         Press, 1963.

         An analysis of Melville's major works within the
  context of mythology.

888   Franks, Jesse G. "Air and Brass: Faith, Philosophy,
         and Events in the First Six Novels of Herman Melville,"
         DAI, 30 (Ball State: 1969), 2482A.

889   Fraser, John. "THE TEMPEST Revisited," CR, 11 (1968),
         60-78.

         Although references to Melville are incidental,
  they place him in his literary and philosophic milieu.

890   Frear, W. F. ANTI-MISSIONARY CRITICISM WITH REFERENCE TO
         HAWAII. Honolulu: 1935, pp. 25-28.

         Melville is considered, with particular reference
  to OMOO.

891   Frederick, John T. THE DARKENED SKY: NINETEENTH-CENTURY
         AMERICAN NOVELISTS AND RELIGION. Notre Dame, Ind.:
         Notre Dame University Press, 1969, passim.

         A survey of Melville's "lifetime preoccupation
  with religious problems." A significant change seen
  in the later Melville reflected in BILLY BUDD, over-
  looked by those who read it only ironically. Melville
  "found peace--neither through victorious resolution of
  his dilemma nor in mere resignation," but in the "clear-
  sighted recognition of gains as well as losses and the
  acceptance of the total given fact of life itself."

892   Frederick, John T. "Melville's Early Acquaintance with
         Bayle," AL, 39 (1968), 545-547.

         Lord Lyttleton's LOCKE AND BAYLE, a fictitious
  dialogue between faith and skepticism, may have been
  a strong influence on Melville's skepticism. It was
  the longest selection in Lindley Murray's ENGLISH
  READER, which Melville studied at the Albany Academy
  in 1830.

893   Frederick, John T. "Melville's Last Long Novel: CLAREL,"
      ArQ, 26 (1970), 151-157.

      In theme and meaning, CLAREL constitutes the most
inclusive and penetrating analysis of the religious
ordeal of the nineteenth century.

894   Frederick, John T. "Symbol and Theme in Melville's
      ISRAEL POTTER," MFS, 8 (1962), 265-275.

      Israel Potter possesses an essential trait in
common with such figures as Bartleby, Hunilla, Don
Benito, Jimmy Rose, Clarel, or Billy Budd, which is
"the heart of their meaning for Melville," that is,
"bare endurance."

895   Frédérix, Pierre. HERMAN MELVILLE. Paris: 1950.

896   Freedman, Ralph. THE LYRICAL NOVEL: STUDIES IN HERMAN
      HESSE, ANDRE GIDE, AND VIRGINIA WOOLF. Princeton,
      New Jersey: Princeton University Press, 1963,
      pp. 14, 197.

      Incidental references but pertinent: Adaptation
of "episodic structure" to poetry produced types of
lyrical novels such as MOBY DICK in which emotions of
hero and reader "are caught in an atmosphere of poetry."

897   Freeman, F. Barron, ed. BILLY BUDD. Cambridge, Mass.:
      Harvard University Press, 1948. With corrections
      by Elizabeth Freeman, 1953. Repr., 1956.

      Extensive analysis of the biographical background,
sources, composition, text, style, technique, and
significance of BILLY BUDD.

      Rev., by Stanley T. Williams, AL, 21 (1950), 367-68.

897.1   Freeman, F. Barron, ed. BILLY BUDD, FORETOPMAN. The
      novel with corrections by Elizabeth Freeman; the
      dramatic version adapted by Louis O. Coxe and
      Robert Chapman. Foreword by Brooks Atkinson.
      New York: Popular Living Classics Library, 1962.

898   Freeman, F. Barron. A CRITICAL AND VARIORUM EDITION OF
      MELVILLE'S BILLY BUDD FROM THE ORIGINAL MANUSCRIPTS.
      Diss. Harvard: 1942.

899   Freeman, E. Barron. "The Enigma of Melville's 'Daniel Orme,'" AL, 16 (1944), 208-211.

       The sketch's autobiographical significance in relation to BILLY BUDD and WHITE JACKET. However, since the "Orme" fragment was written forty years before WHITE JACKET it is unwise to consider "Orme" a symbolic self-portrait of Melville's final spiritual status.

900   Freeman, John. HERMAN MELVILLE. London: Macmillan and Company, English Men of Letters Series, 1926; New York: Macmillan, 1926.

       This is one of the important studies in the Melville Revival of the twenties.

901   Freiberg, Louis. "The Westminster Review and American Literature, 1824-1885," AL, 24 (1953), 310-329.

       A survey of British interest in American literature, including Melville's work, as illustrated by the Westminster Review.

902   Freimarck, Vincent. "Mainmast as Crucifix in BILLY BUDD," MLN, 72 (November, 1957), 496-497.

903   French, Warren. THE SOCIAL NOVEL AT THE END OF AN ERA. Preface by Harry T. Moore. Carbondale and Edwardsville: Southern Illinois University Press, 1966, pp. 175-177.

       A comparison between Bigger Thomas in HOW "BIGGER" WAS BORN by Richard Wright, and the type of frontiersman described in THE CONFIDENCE MAN.

904   Freund, Philip. "Sea and Sky: Herman Melville," HOW TO BECOME A LITERARY CRITIC. New York: Beechhurst Press, 1947, pp. 80-96.

905   Freund, Philip. "Sea and Sky: Herman Melville," THE ART OF READING THE NOVEL. Rev. ed. New York: Collier Books, 1965, pp. 71-78, passim.

       BILLY BUDD is "idealism's most complete document."

906   Friederich, Werner P. WERDEN UND WACHSEN DER USA IN 300 JAHREN. Bern: 1939.

907   Friedman, Alan. THE TURN OF THE NOVEL. New York:
        Oxford University Press, 1966, p. 23.

        A comparison of WUTHERING HEIGHTS and MOBY DICK.

908   Friedman, Maurice. "Bartleby and the Modern Exile,"
        MELVILLE ANNUAL 1965, A SYMPOSIUM: BARTLEBY THE
        SCRIVENER. Howard P. Vincent, ed. (Kent Stud. in
        Eng., III). Kent, Ohio: Kent State University
        Press, 1966, pp. 64-81.

        The thesis is that the story is "modern": the
        "rupture" of the social expectation "catapults the
        nineteenth-century Bartleby into the absurd world of
        Camus' THE STRANGER and Kafka's 'The Judgement.'"

909   Friedman, Maurice. "Ishmael, Bartleby, and the Confidence
        Man," PROBLEMATIC REBEL: AN IMAGE OF MODERN MAN.
        New York: Random House, 1963, passim.

910   Friedman, Maurice. PROBLEMATIC REBEL: MELVILLE,
        DOSTOIEVSKY, KAFKA, CAMUS. Revised edition.
        Chicago: Chicago University Press, 1970.

        First edition, Random House, under title:
        PROBLEMATIC REBEL: AN IMAGE OF MODERN MAN, 1963.
        Revised edition contains further material.

911   Friedman, Maurice. "The Modern Job: On Melville,
        Dostoievsky, and Kafka," Judaism, 12 (Fall, 1963),
        436-455.

912   Friedrich, Gerhard. "The Melville Equation: His Truths
        of Fact and Fiction," HAB, 18 (Spring, 1967), 87-95.

        Melville employed fiction to "body forth" the
        implications of the facts of life.

913   Friedrich, Gerhard. "A Note on Quakerism and MOBY DICK:
        Hawthorne's 'The Gentle Boy' as a Possible Source,"
        QH, 54 (August, 1965), 94-102.

914   Friedrich, Gerhard. IN PURSUIT OF MOBY DICK: MELVILLE'S
        IMAGE OF MAN. (Pendle Hill Pamphlet, No. 98).
        Wallingford, Pa.: 1958.

        The name "Ishmael" may have its source in
        Hawthorne's "The Gentle Boy."

915   Frohock, W. M. THE NOVEL OF VIOLENCE IN AMERICA,
       1920-1950. Dallas, Texas: Southern Methodist
       University, p. 120, passim.

       Our renewed interest in Melville and Hawthorne
can be explained in part by the fact that "in our
lifetime something very like personification of evil
has walked the earth...."

916   Frohock, W. M. STRANGERS TO THIS GROUND: CULTURAL
       DIVERSITY IN CONTEMPORARY AMERICAN WRITING. Dallas:
       Southern Methodist University Press, 1961, passim.

       Incidental references which indicate the scholars
of the New Criticism had an appreciation of Melville.

917   Frost, O. W. JOAQUIN MILLER. New York: Twayne Publishers,
       Inc., 1967, p. 72.

       A comparison of Miller's LIFE AMONGST THE MODOCS
with Melville's TYPEE.

918   Frost, Robert. SELECTED LETTERS OF ROBERT FROST.
       Lawrance Thompson, ed. New York, Chicago, San
       Francisco: Holt, Rinehart and Winston, 1964,
       pp. 552-554.

       Frost's letter to Lawrance Thompson, c.May 1,
1952, disapproving of BILLY BUDD, but lauding
Melville as "a great story teller, one of America's
splendors in art...."

919   Frye, Northrop. "The Four Forms of Prose Fiction,"
       HudR, 2 (Winter, 1950), 582-595.

       The four chief strands are novel, confession,
anatomy, and romance. MOBY DICK a "fine modern example"
of romance-anatomy.

920   Frye, Northrop. "The Four Forms of Prose Fiction,"
       ANATOMY OF CRITICISM. Princeton: Princeton
       University Press, 1957, pp. 303-314.

921   Fukuma, Kin-ichi. "'BILLY BUDD': The Testament of
       Acceptance," KAL, 3 (May, 1960), 9-14.

922   Fuller, Margaret. (Attributed) Review of TYPEE.
       Tribune, (April 4, 1846).

923   Fuller, Roy, ed. Introduction, THE CONFIDENCE MAN.
       London: John Lehmann, 1948.

923.1   Fullerton, Bradford M. "Melville," SELECTIVE BIBLIOGRAPHY
        OF AMERICAN LITERATURE, 1775-1900. New York: Payson,
        1932, pp. 192-194.

924   Fulwiler, Toby. "The Death of the Handsome Sailor:
        A Study of BILLY BUDD and THE RED BADGE OF COURAGE,"
        ArQ, 26 (Summer, 1970), 101-112.

925   Fussell, Edwin S. "Herman Melville," FRONTIER:
        AMERICAN LITERATURE AND THE AMERICAN WEST.
        Princeton, New Jersey: Princeton University
        Press, 1965, pp. 232-326, passim.

        Rev. by Richard S. Kennedy, NEQ, 38 (1965), 544-546.

926   Gabriel, Joseph F. THE PROBLEM OF "GOOD AND EVIL" IN
        HAWTHORNE, MELVILLE AND HENRY JAMES. Diss. Pa.

927   Gabriel, Ralph Henry. "Melville, Critic of Mid-
        Nineteenth Century Beliefs," THE COURSE OF AMERICAN
        DEMOCRATIC THOUGHT: AN INTELLECTUAL HISTORY SINCE
        1815. New York: The Ronald Press Company, 1940,
        pp. 67-77, passim; rev. 2nd ed., New York: Ronald,
        1956, pp. 70-79.

        Rev. by H. G. Townsend, NEQ, 13 (1940), 597-550.

928   Gabriel, Ralph Henry, ed. "Whalers 'Trying Out,'"
        TOILERS OF LAND AND SEA: THE PAGEANT OF AMERICA:
        A PICTORIAL HISTORY OF THE UNITED STATES. London:
        Humphrey Milford, Oxford University Press; Toronto:
        Glasgow, Brook & Co.; New Haven: Yale University
        Press, 1926, III, 321.

        Illustrations of whaling, and excerpt from
        MOBY DICK.

929   Gaillard, T. L., Jr. "Melville's Riddle for Our Time:
        'BENITO CERENO,'" EJ, 61 (April, 1972), 479-487.

930   Gale, Robert L. "Bartleby--Melville's Father-in-Law,"
        AION-SG, 5 (1962), 57-72.

        Melville wrote into the story his feelings about
        his father-in-law, with Judge Shaw in the role of the
        Wall Street lawyer.

931   Gale, Robert L. "Evil and the American Short Story,"
        AION-SG, 1 (1958), 183-202.

932   Gale, Robert L. "Melville's MOBY DICK: Chapters 91-93," Expl, 22 (January, 1964), Item 32.

The three chapters form a unit which through the juxtaposition of ambergris and Pip emphasize the "essential worth and possible symbolic import of the little Negro."

933   Gale, Robert L. PLOTS AND CHARACTERS IN THE FICTION AND NARRATIVE POETRY OF HERMAN MELVILLE. Foreword by Harrison Hayford. Hamden, Conn.: Archon Books, 1969.

Chronologies of Melville's life and works, summaries of plots, and lists of "named or namable characters."

934   Gale, Robert L. "Redburn and Holden--Half-Brothers One Century Removed," ForumH, 3 (Winter, 1963), 32-36.

Comparison between REDBURN and CATCHER IN THE RYE.

935   Galland, René. "Herman Melville et 'MOBY DICK,'" RAA, 5 (1927), 1-9.

The crew of the Pequod is mankind, and Ahab its conscience, haunted by the idea of evil, which he must destroy, and the mystery of life which he must penetrate.

936   Galloway, David D. "Herman Melville's BENITO CERENO: An Anatomy," TSLL, 9 (Summer, 1967), 239-252.

The story is "a chiaroscuro of insinuation and reflection on the persistent intermingling of good and evil and a paradigm of the dangers of warped consciousness."

937   Garcia Blanco, Manuel. "Unamuno y el novelista norteamericano Melville," Insula, 19 (1964), 5, 216-217.

938   Gardner, John. "BARTLEBY: Art and Social Commitment," PQ, 43 (January, 1964), 87-98.

Bartleby as Christ-like, the lawyer as Jehovah-like, Turkey as Michael, Nippers as Lucifer, and Ginger Nut as Raphael.

939   Gargano, James W. "Melville's 'Jimmy Rose,'" WHR, 16 (Summer, 1962), 276-280.

940   Garnett, R. S. "MOBY DICK and MOCHA DICK: A Literary
           Find," BwM, 226 (December, 1929), 841-858.

       Reprints a large part of J. N. Reynolds's
MOCHA DICK.

941   Garnett, R. S. "Mocha Dick, or the White Whale of the
           Pacific," TLS (July 30, 1926), 509.

942   Garrison, D. H. "Melville's Doubloon and the Shield of
           Achilles," NCF, 26 (Summer, 1971), 171-184.

943   Gary, L. M. "Rich Colors and Ominous Shadows," SAQ, 37
           (1938), 41-45.

       Imagery in MOBY DICK.

944   Gaskins, Avery F. "Symbolic Nature of Claggart's Name,"
           AN&Q, 6 (December, 1967), 56.

       Melville may have coined the name to indicate
the character's action in relation to Billy. The word
clag suggests "stick," and Claggart "sticks like glue"
to Billy. Clag also means a "flaw in character", and,
as a verb, "to bedaub"; and Claggart attempts to bedaub
the character of Billy with false accusations.

945   Gassner, John. "Ebb Tide: Allegory: Coxe and Chapman's
           BILLY BUDD," in THEATRE AT THE CROSSROADS: PLAYS AND
           PLAYWRIGHTS OF THE MID-CENTURY AMERICAN STAGE.
           New York: Holt, 1960, pp. 139-141.

946   Geiger, Don. "Demonism in MOBY-DICK," *Perspective*, 6
           (1953), 111-124.

947   Geiger, Don. "Demonism in MOBY-DICK," in THE AGE OF THE
           SPLENDID MACHINE. Tokyo: Hukuseido Press, 1961,
           pp. 75-102.

       The techniques by which the theme of savage
reality is developed in Chapters 55-66.

948   Geiger, Don. "Melville's Black God: Contrary Evidence
           in 'The Town-Ho's Story,'" AL, 25 (January, 1954),
           464-471.

       Melville's "ultimate image of the Calvinist God
of the Puritan," just He may be but without love.

949   Geismar, Maxwell. Introduction, BILLY BUDD. New York:
           1962.

950   Geismar, Maxwell, ed. Introduction, BILLY BUDD, BENITO
           CERENO. Printed for Members of the Limited Editions
           Club, 1965.   -

           Contains ten paintings by Robert Shore.

951   Geismar, Maxwell, ed. Introduction, MOBY DICK: OR,
           THE WHITE WHALE. Abridged ed. New York:
           Washington Square Press, 1949, 1961.

952   Geismar, Maxwell, ed. Introduction, MOBY-DICK: OR, THE
           WHITE WHALE. New York: Pocket Books, 1956.

953   Geismar, Maxwell. Introduction, TYPEE. New York:
           1962

954   Geismar, Maxwell. "Was 'Papa' Truly a Great Writer?"
           OPINIONS AND PERSPECTIVES FROM THE NEW YORK TIMES
           BOOK REVIEW. Introduction by Francis Brown, ed.
           Boston: Houghton Mifflin Company, The Riverside
           Press, Cambridge: 1955, 1964, pp. 162-163.

           Melville's description of life in BILLY BUDD.

955   Geist, Stanley. HERMAN MELVILLE: THE TRAGIC VISION AND
           THE HEROIC IDEAL. Honors thesis. Harvard: 1939.

956   Geist, Stanley. HERMAN MELVILLE: THE TRAGIC VISION
           AND THE HEROIC IDEAL. Cambridge, Mass.: Harvard
           University Press, 1939. Repr., New York: Octagon
           Books, Inc., 1966.

           The isolation of Melville was neither "the
           aristocrat's scorn of the mob, the snob's vanity,"
           nor the "rugged individualist's confident self-reliance."
           It derived from a "consciousness of tragedy so acute...
           that true kinship with any man but one who shared his
           tragic vision was a grotesque mockery...."

957   Gerlach, John. "Messianic Nationalism in the Early
           Works of Herman Melville: Against Perry Miller,"
           ArQ, 28 (1972), 5-26.

           Cf., Perry Miller. THE RAVEN AND THE WHALE.
       New York: 1956.

958   Gerould, Gordon Hall. "Interpreters: I. Hawthorne,
           Melville, and the Brontes," THE PATTERNS OF ENGLISH
           AND AMERICAN FICTION: A HISTORY. Boston: Little,
           Brown & Co., 1942, pp. 341-366; New York: Russell
           & Russell, 1966, pp. 341-366, passim.

959   Gerstenberger, Donna., and George Hendrick. THE AMERICAN
        NOVEL, 1789-1959: A CHECKLIST OF TWENTIETH-CENTURY
        CRITICISM. Denver: Alan Swallow, 1961.

        Volume II: Criticism Written, 1960-1968. Chicago:
        Swallow Press, 1970. Extends first volume (1960),
        which covered 1900 to 1959.

960   Gessner, Robert. THE MOVING IMAGE: A GUIDE TO CINEMATIC
        LITERACY. New York: E. P. Dutton & Co., Inc.,
        1968, pp. 200-203.

        The mysticism, the discourses and lore about the
        whale, are the elements ignored in the two motion
        picture versions: THE SEA BEAST (1925) with John
        Barrymore "grimacing over the gunwales," and MOBY
        DICK (1956) with the "jaw of Gregory Peck hardly a
        match for the grin of the White Whale...."

961   Gettmann, Royal A. A VICTORIAN PUBLISHER: A STUDY OF
        THE BENTLEY PAPERS. Cambridge: 1960, passim.

        The publication dates are also recorded in A LIST
        OF THE PRINCIPAL PUBLICATIONS ISSUED FROM NEW BURLINGTON
        STREET DURING THE YEAR 1949 (London: 1897), 1850 (1898),
        and 1851 (1902).

962   Gettmann, Royal A., and Bruce Harkness. "BILLY BUDD:
        FORETOPMAN," TEACHER'S MANUAL FOR A BOOK OF
        STORIES. New York: Rinehart & Co., Inc., 1955,
        pp. 71-74.

963   Gibbings, Robert. Introduction, TYPEE. London: 1951.

964   Gibbs, Robert J. "The Living Contour: The Whale Symbol
        in Melville and Pratt," CanL, 40 (1969), 17-25.

965   Gibson, William M. "Herman Melville's 'BARTLEBY THE
        SCRIVENER' and 'BENITO CERENO,'" NS, Beiheft 9
        (1961), 107-116.

965.1   Gibson, William M. "Herman Melville's 'BARTLEBY THE
        SCRIVENER' and 'BENITO CERENO,'" THE AMERICAN
        RENAISSANCE, THE HISTORY OF AN ERA: ESSAYS AND
        INTERPRETATIONS. George Hendrick, ed. Frankfurt:
        Diesterweg, 1961, pp. 107-116.

        Parallels between the "dead-wall" confronting
        Bartleby, the "dead, impregnable, uninjurable wall"
        of Moby Dick's immense head, and the "impenetrable"
        blackness at the center of "Benito Cereno."

966   Gibson, William M., ed. Introduction, MOBY DICK.
       New York: Dell Publishing Company, 1959.

967   Gibson, William M., and George Arms, eds. TWELVE
       AMERICAN WRITERS. New York: Macmillan, 1962,
       pp. 267-268.

968   Gifford, George E., Jr. "Melville in Baltimore,"
       MHM, 51 (September, 1956), 245-246.

969   Gilenson, Boris. "Melville in Russia: For the 150th
       Anniversary of His Birth," SoL (1969), 171-173.

970   Gilman, William H. "The Hero and the Heroic in
       American Literature: An Essay in Definition,"
       PATTERNS OF COMMITMENT IN AMERICAN LITERATURE.
       Marston LaFrance, ed. Toronto: Published in
       association with Carleton University of Toronto
       University Press, 1967, pp. 3-17.

971   Gilman, William H. MELVILLE'S EARLY LIFE AND REDBURN.
       Diss. Yale: 1947.

972   Gilman, William H. MELVILLE'S EARLY LIFE AND REDBURN.
       New York: New York University Press, 1951; New
       York: Russell & Russell, 1972.

973   Gilman, William H. "Melville's JOURNAL OF A VOYAGE TO
       EUROPE AND THE LEVANT. II. A Reply to a Rejoinder,"
       AL, 28 (January, 1957), 523-524.

            Cf., William H. Gilman, Review, "JOURNAL OF A VISIT...
       AL, 28 (March, 1956), 82-93; Howard C. Horsford, "Melville's
       JOURNAL OF A VOYAGE...A Rejoinder to a Review," AL, 28
       (1957), 520-523.

974   Gilman, William H. "Melville's Liverpool Trip,"
       MLN, 60 (December, 1946), 543-547.

            Doubtful that Redburn is Melville and that the
       novel is Melville's autobiography.

975   Gilman, William H. "A Note on Herman Melville in
       Honolulu," AL, 19 (1947), 169.

            A letter from H. R. Hawkins, December 10, 1849,
       indicates that Melville may have set up pins in a
       bowling alley in Honolulu.

976   Ginoux, Edmond de. "La Reine Pomaré: femmes de Taïti et
         des Marquises," NAdV, 3 (1844), 365.

977   Giono, Jean. "Pour Saluer Melville," NRF, 28 (1940),
         433-468.

978   Giono, Jean. POUR SALUER MELVILLE. Paris: 1943.

979   Giono, Jean, et Joan Smith. MOBY DICK: ROMAN.
         Traduit de l'anglais par Lucien Jacques. Paris:
         Gallimard, 1941, 1956.

980   Giorcelli, Cristina. "Le poesie 'italiane' di Herman
         Melville," SA, 14 (1968), 165-191.

         The article illustrates the continuing Italian
    interest in Melville.

981   Giovannini, G. "The Hanging Scene in Melville's BILLY
         BUDD," MLN, 70 (November, 1955), 491-497.

         Cf., H. M. Campbell. "The Hanging Scene in
    Melville's BILLY BUDD: A Reply to Mr. Giovannini,"
    MLN, 70 (1955), 497-500.

982   Giovannini, G. "Melville and Dante," PMLA, 65 (1950),
         329.

         Cf., J. Chesley Mathews, "Melville and Dante,"
    PMLA, 64 (1949), 1238; and G. Giovannini, "Melville
    and Dante," PMLA, 64 (1949), 70-78.

983   Giovannini, G. "Melville's MOBY DICK," Expl, 5 (1946),
         Item 7.

         Further explanation of "the ball of free will"
    in Chapter 47.

         A reply to Carvel Collins, Melville's MOBY DICK,"
    Expl, 4 (1946), Item 27.

984   Giovannini, G. "Melville's PIERRE and Dante's INFERNO,"
         PMLA, 64 (March, 1949), 70-78.

         Cf., J. Chesley Mathews. "Melville and Dante,"
    PMLA, 64 (1949), 1238; and G. Giovannini, "Melville
    and Dante," PMLA, 65 (1950), 329.

985   Glasser, William. "MOBY DICK," SR, 77 (July-September,
         1969), 463-486.

986   Gleason, Philip. "MOBY-DICK: Meditation for Democracy," *Person*, 44 (November, 1963), 499-517.

Analysis is possible from a political point of view.

987   Gleim, William S., ed. "Journal of Melville's Voyage in a Clipper Ship," NEQ, 2 (1929), 120-125.

988   Gleim, William S. THE MEANING OF MOBY DICK. New York: Brick Row Bookshop, 1938. Repr., New York: Russell & Russell, 1962.

An expansion of the author's "A Theory of MOBY DICK," NEQ, 2 (1929), 402-419.

The novel is "really two stories"--one treating material things and another treating abstract things.

Rev. by Robert S. Forsythe, AL, 11 (1939), 308-09; F. Barron Freeman, NEQ, 11 (1938), 850-53.

989   Gleim, William S. "A Theory of MOBY DICK," NEQ, 2 (1929), 402-419.

Cf., WILLIAM S. GLEIM. THE MEANING OF MOBY DICK. New York: 1962.

990   Glick, Wendell. "Expediency and Absolute Morality in BILLY BUDD," PMLA, 68 (March, 1953), 103-110.

In BILLY BUDD, Melville finally resolves the conflict between expediency and absolute morality in favor of the former.

991   Glicksberg, Charles I. "Melville and the Negro Problem," *Phylon*, 11 (3rd Qt., 1950), 207-215.

992   Godard, Alice L. A STUDY OF MELVILLE'S SOCIAL CRITICISM AS REFLECTED IN HIS PROSE WRITINGS. Diss. Illinoia: 1946.

993   Goforth, David S. "Melville's Shorter Poems: The Substance and the Significance," DA, 29 (Ind.: 1969), 3097A.

994   Gohdes, Clarence. AMERICAN LITERATURE IN NINETEENTH CENTURY ENGLAND. New York: Columbia University Press, 1944, passim.

995   Gohdes, Clarence. BIBLIOGRAPHICAL GUIDE TO THE STUDY OF
        THE LITERATURE OF THE U. S. A. Durham, North
        Carolina: Duke University Press, 1959, 1963;
        3rd. ed., revised and enlarged, 1970.

996   Gohdes, Clarence. "British Interest in American
        Literature During the Latter Part of the Nineteenth
        Century as Reflected by Mudie's SELECT LIBRARY,"
        AL, 13 (1941-1942), 356-362.

        In Mudie's offerings for 1896, Melville is
        represented by TYPEE, OMOO, WHITE-JACKET, and MOBY-
        DICK, the first two being classified as non-fiction.

997   Gohdes, Clarence, ed. ESSAYS ON AMERICAN LITERATURE IN
        HONOR OF JAY B. HUBBELL. Durham, North Carolina:
        Duke University Press, 1967, passim.

998   Gohdes, Clarence. "Gossip about Melville in the South
        Seas," NEQ, 10 (1937), 526-531.

        A letter of "R. S.," (Lt. Henry Wise), written in
        1868, provided gossip about Melville and a description
        of the Typee valley, twenty years after Melville's visit.

        Cf., James Baird. ISHMAEL. Baltimore: 1956, p. 111.

999   Gohdes, Clarence. "Melville's Friend 'Toby,'" MLN, 59
        (January, 1944), 52-55.

        Information about Richard T. Greene who while
        editing the Mirror (Sandusky, Ohio) from August, 1854,
        to January 31, 1855), occasionally wrote of his
        associations with Melville.

1000   Gohdes, Clarence. THE PERIODICALS OF AMERICAN
        TRANSCENDENTALISM. Durham, North Carolina: Duke
        University Press, 1931, passim.

        Notes the tendency to include such literary
        figures as Melville and Whitman, who "assuredly did
        not regard themselves as transcendentalists...."

1001   Gohdes, Clarence. "The Reception of Some Nineteenth-
        Century American Authors in Europe," THE AMERICAN
        WRITER AND THE EUROPEAN TRADITION. Margaret Denny
        and William H. Gilman, eds. Minneapolis: University
        of Minnesota Press, 1950, pp. 106-120.

1002   Gohdes, Clarence. RUSSIAN STUDIES OF AMERICAN LITERATURE.
        Valentina A. Libman, comp. Trans. by Robert V.
        Allen. Chapel Hill: North Carolina University
        Press, 1969, pp. 136-137.

        From 18th century to 1963: lists of articles,
reviews, dissertations, and monographs on 148 American
authors, including Herman Melville.

1003   GOLD STAR LIST OF AMERICAN FICTION. Fiftieth Anniversary
        Edition, 1966. Syracuse, New York: Syracuse Public
        Library, 1966, p. 27.

1004   Goldberg, Gerald Jay, and Nancy Marmer Goldberg, eds.
        THE MODERN CRITICAL SPECTRUM. Englewood Cliffs,
        New Jersey: Prentice-Hall, 1962 (Prentice-Hall
        English Literature Series).

1005   Goldfarb, Russell, and Clare Goldfarb. "The Doubloon
        in MOBY DICK," MQ, 2 (Spring, 1961), 251-258.

1006   Goldsmith, Arnold L. "The 'Discovery Scene' in BILLY
        BUDD," MD, 3 (February, 1961), 339-342.

        Comparison of the book with the dramatic version
by Coxe and Chapman.

1006.1 Gold Star List of American Fiction. Fiftieth Anniversary
        Edition. New York: Syracuse Public Library, 1966,
        p. 27.

1007   Gollin, Richard Andrita, and Rita Gollin. "Justice in
        an Earlier Treatment of the BILLY BUDD Theme,"
        AL, 28 (January, 1957), 513-515.

        Douglas Jerrold's BLACK-EY'D SUSAN (1829) as
a possible source for part of Melville's plot and
theme.

        Cf., B. R. McElderry, Jr., "Three Earlier
Treatments of the BILLY BUDD Theme," AL, 27 (1955),
251-257.

1008   Gollin, Rita. "PIERRE'S Metamorphosis of Dante's
        INFERNO," AL, 39 (January, 1968), 542-545.

        For Dante, knowledge of sin was the means of over-
coming it, but Melville uses scenes from Dante to bring
Pierre to the extremity of guilt and despair.

1009   Gordan, John D. "An Anniversary Exhibition: The Henry W., and Albert A. Berg Collection 1940-1965," BNYPL, 69 (December, 1965), 665-677.

Description of manuscripts of many authors, including Melville.

1010   Gordon, Walter K., ed. LITERATURE IN CRITICAL PERSPECTIVES. New York: Appleton-Century-Crofts, 1968.

1011   Gorlier, Claudio. "Due classici dissepolti: WIELAND e CLAREL," Approdo, 12 (January-March, 1966), 3-8.

1012   Gorman, Herbert. HAWTHORNE: A STUDY IN SOLITUDE. New York: George H. Doran Company on Murray Hill, 1927, p. 92.

Description of the friendship between Hawthorne and Melville.

1013   Gorman, Herbert. "That Strange Genius Melville," NYTBR, March 19, 1929, pp. 1, 14 (sec. IV).

1014   Gosse, Sir Edmund. "Herman Melville," SILHOUETTES. London: William Heinemann, Ltd., 1925, pp. 355-361.

1014.1 Gostwick, Joseph. HAND-BOOK OF AMERICAN LITERATURE. HISTORICAL, BIOGRAPHICAL AND CRITICAL. London: 1856. New York: Kennikat Press. Kennikat Press Scholarly Reprints, 1971, p. 189.

1015   Goto, Shoji. "Philosophy of the Fatalist: A Note on PIERRE, OR THE AMBIGUITIES," RikR, 24 (March, 1963), 53-65.

1016   Gould, Jean. YOUNG MARINER MELVILLE. New York: Dodd, 1956.

Juvenile literature.

1017   Gow, Gordon. SUSPENSE IN THE CINEMA. London: A Zwemmer Limited; New York: A. S. Barnes & Co., 1968, pp. 61-62.

Successful creation of suspense in John Huston's film of MOBY DICK (1955).

1018   Gozzi, Raymond. "Melville's REDBURN: CIVILIZATION AND
ITS DISCONTENTS," L&P, 13 (Fall, 1963), 104.

A sailor in REDBURN presents part of Freud's
argument in CIVILIZATION AND ITS DISCONTENTS: "the
overcritical superego plus psychological castration
contributes to making civilized life hard to bear."

1019   Graham, Philip. "The Riddle of Melville's MARDI: A
Reinterpretation," UTSE, 36 (1957), 93-99.

Time is the key to understanding MARDI. The
different sections symbolize certain phases of man's
development, past, present, and future--a pattern
which gives the book a unifying theme: man's development through the ages.

1020   Granger, Bruce Ingham. "The Gams in MOBY DICK," WHR, 8
(Winter, 1953-1954), 41-47.

1021   Grauman, Lawrence, Jr. "Suggestions on the Future of
THE CONFIDENCE-MAN," PELL, 1 (Summer, 1965),
241-249.

From the second chapter, the confidence man
appears in seven guises, each "an avatar of the Devil."
However, Melville has not despaired, for man is not a
villain, but a victim, and Melville's grief is that of
compassion.

1022   Graves, Robert D. "Polarity in the Shorter Fiction of
Herman Melville," DA, 27 (Duke: 1966), 1821A-22A.

1023   Grdseloff, Dorothee. "A Note on the Origin of Fedallah
in MOBY DICK," AL, 27 (November, 1955), 396-403.

Melville drew on the published accounts of the
Ismailiya movement for the character of Fedallah,
the Parsee harpooner with a Mohammedan name.

Cf., Dorothee Metlitsky Finkelstein. MELVILLE'S
ORIENDA. New Haven: Yale University Press, 1961.

1024   Greeger, George R. "The Symbolism of Whiteness in
Melville's Prose Fiction," JA, 5 (1960), 147-163.

1025   Greeley, Horace (Attributed). Review of MOBY-DICK.
NYDT, November 22, 1851.

1026   Green, Jesse D. "Diabolism, Pessimism, and Democracy:
         Notes on Melville and Conrad," MFS, 8 (Autumn,
         1962), 287-305.

         Comparison of Melville and Conrad on various
         levels.

1027   Green, Martin B. "Melville and the American Romance,"
         RE-APPRAISALS: SOME COMMONSENSE READINGS IN AMERICAN
         LITERATURE. New York: W. W. Morton, 1965, pp. 87-
         112.

1028   Green, R. T. /Toby corroborates TYPEE/, BCA (July 11,
         1846).

1029   Greene, Daniel W. "Melville's NEVERSINK," AN&Q, 5
         (1966), 56-58.

1030   Greene, Maxine. "Man Without God in American Fiction,"
         Humanist, 25 (May-June, 1965), 125-128.

         Melville and other American writers show America
         as a nation of "diverse men and women, cast out on their
         own to find themselves."

1031   Greene, Maxine. "The Whale's Whiteness: On Meaning
         and Meaninglessness," JAE, 2 (1968), 51-72.

         Focus is on Ahab and Moby Dick in tracing the
         genesis of "meaninglessness" or "absurdity."

         Cf., Robert S. Guttchen. "Meaning and Meaning-
         lessness: A Response to Professor Greene," JAE, 2
         (1968), 79-84.

         Also, Sheldon W. Liebman. "The 'Body and Soul'
         Metaphor in MOBY-DICK," ESQ Sup. 50 (1st Qt., 1968),
         29-34.

1032   Greet, T. Y., Charles E. Edge, and John M. Munro, eds.
         THE WORLDS OF FICTION: STORIES IN CONTEXT. Boston:
         Houghton Mifflin, 1964.

1033   Greiner, Jean. "L'Utopie du mal," NRF, 14 (October,
         1966), 678-688.

         A comparison of Melville and Sade.

1033.1   Grejda, Edward S. "The Common Continent of Men: The
         Non-White Characters in the Fiction of Herman
         Melville," DA, 30 (Pittsburgh: 1969), 1566A.

1034   Grenander, M. E.   "Sonnet V from Dylan Thomas'
       ALTARWISE BY OWL-LIGHT Sequence," NEQ, 5
       (June, 1958), 263.

       Allusions to MOBY DICK in the poem.

1035   Grenberg, Bruce Leonard.   "Thomas Carlyle and Herman
       Melville: Parallels, Obliques, and Perpendiculars,"
       DA, 24 (North Carolina: 1964), 3323.

       Carlyle's influence on Melville's work from TYPEE
       through PIERRE.

1036   Griffith, Clark.   "Caves and Cave Dwellers: The Study
       of a Romantic Image," JEGP, 62 (1963), 551-568.

       The use of cave-imagery by Emerson, Melville, Poe,
       and Hawthorne indicates "the four major view points of
       which the American Romantic movement as a whole appears
       to have been composed."

1036.1 Griffith, Clark.   "'Emersonianism' and 'Poeism': Some
       Versions of the Romantic Sensibility," MLQ, 22
       (June, 1961), 125-134.

       The Emersonian reverences language as magical in
       MOBY DICK and scorns it as inadequate in PIERRE.

1037   Griffith, Frank C.   MELVILLE AND THE QUEST FOR GOD.
       Diss. Iowa: 1953.

1038   Grimm, Dorothy F.   MELVILLE AS SOCIAL CRITIC.   Diss.
       Penn.: 1948.

1039   Grimwood, A. A.   A STUDY OF THE SOURCES AND ALLEGORY OF
       MELVILLE'S MARDI.   Diss. New York University: 1949.

1040   Gross, John J.   "The Face of Plinlimmon and the 'Failures'
       of the Fifties," ESQ, 28, Melville Supplement (1962),
       6-9.

       A knowledge of Plinlimmon in PIERRE important for
       understanding of the short stories of THE ENCANTADAS.

1041   Gross, John J.   "Forward from Tocqueville," ESQ, 35
       (1964), 14-19.

1042   Gross, John J.   "Herman Melville and the Search for
       Community," DA, 15 (Iowa: 1955), 1619.

1043   Gross, John J.   "Melville, Dostoevsky, and the People,"
       PS, 10 (Spring, 1956), 160-170.

       Parallel between the two writers in their search
       for "a resolution of the conflict between the individual
       and his community."

1044   Gross, John J. "Melville's THE CONFIDENCE-MAN: The
         Problem of Source and Meaning," NM, 60 (Summer,
         1959), 299-310.

1045   Gross, John J. "The Rehearsal of Ishmael: Melville's
         'REDBURN,'" VQR, 27 (Autumn, 1951), 581-600.

         Redburn prefigures an archetypal Ishmael who
         loses innocence and develops an awareness of sin.

1046   Gross, John J. "Religion and Community in the American
         Renaissance," ESQ, 44 (3rd Qt., 1966), 59-64.

         Incidental remarks which place Melville in his
         social milieu: Melville, Emerson, and others inherited
         only the individualism of the Puritan, and instead of
         the sense of community, shared a nascent nationalism,
         not sufficiently cohesive.

1047   Gross, Seymour L., ed. A BENITO CERENO HANDBOOK.
         Belmont, Calif.: Wadsworth, 1965.

1048   Gross, Seymour L. "Hawthorne Versus Melville," BuR,
         14 (December, 1966), 89-109.

         The "differences of 'blackness'" in Melville and
         Hawthorne are primarily in terms of comparative readings:
         "My Kinsman, Major Molineux" and REDBURN, "Young Goodman
         Brown" and BENITO CERENO.

1049   Gross, Seymour L. "Introduction: Stereotype to
         Archetype: The Negro in American Literary Criticism,"
         IMAGES OF THE NEGRO IN AMERICAN LITERATURE. Seymour
         L. Gross and John Edward Hardy, eds. Chicago and
         London: Chicago University Press, 1966, pp. 1-26.

         Critical debate has "literally raged" over whether
         Melville agreed with Delano's view of the Negro as
         "frolicsome primitive" or Cereno's "vision of the black
         man as Evil;...."

         Cf., Sidney Kaplan. "Herman Melville and the
         American National Sin: The Meaning of BENITO CERENO,"
         JNH, 41 (1956), 311-338; JNH, 42 (1957), 11-37.

1050   Gross, Seymour L. "Mungo Park and Ledyard in Melville's
         BENITO CERENO," ELN, 3 (December, 1965), 122-123.

         Substitution of Ledyard for Mungo Park in revision
         of BENITO CERENO possibly the result of an article in
         Putnam's Monthly Magazine.

1051 Gross, Theodore. "Herman Melville: The Nature of
Authority," ColQ, 16 (1968), 397-412.

Tension in Melville's work grows out of fear of
power, ranging from absolute authority of a captain
over the crew, to the "ultimate authority" of nature.
In earlier books, men challenge all authority; later
fiction presents "a series of victims" whose wills have
been broken by authority in "some adamant form." The
resolution would appear in terms of "the authority that
ought to be," rather than that authority which "actually
exists."

1052 Gross, Theodore L. "Herman Melville: The Nature of
Authority," THE HEROIC IDEAL IN AMERICAN LITERATURE.
London: Collier-Macmillan, Ltd., New York: The
Free Press, 1971, pp. 34-50, passim.

As we become more aware of "the dangers of...
ruthless power and authority, we find the image of
ourselves reflected in the mirror of Melville's
fiction and seek to escape that image."

Revs., Thomas F. Gossett, AL, 44 (1972), 339-340;
Richard Slotkins, CE, 33 (1972), 941-947.

1053 Gross, Theodore L., and Stanley Wertheim, comps.
HAWTHORNE, MELVILLE, STEPHEN CRANE: A CRITICAL
BIBLIOGRAPHY. New York: Free Press, 1971.

1054 Grube, John. Introduction, THE CONFIDENCE MAN. New
York: Airmont, 1966.

1055 Guerard, Albert J. "THE NIGGER OF THE 'NARCISSUS,'"
THE ART OF JOSEPH CONRAD: A CRITICAL SYMPOSIUM.
Edited with Introduction by R. W. Stallman.
Michigan State University Press, 1960, pp. 121-139.

Comparisons of the novel with BENITO CERENO.

1056 Guerin, Wilfred L., et al. MANDALA: LITERATURE FOR
CRITICAL ANALYSIS. New York: 1970.

1057 Guetti, James L. "The Failure of the Imagination:
A Study of Melville, Conrad, and Faulkner,"
DA, 25 (Cornell: 1965), 4145-56.

1058 Guetti, James L. "The Languages of MOBY-DICK," THE
LIMITS OF METAPHOR: A STUDY OF MELVILLE, CONRAD,
AND FAULKNER. Ithaca: Cornell University Press,
1967, pp. 12-45, passim.

A study of the various vocabularies and linguistic
devices employed in MOBY DICK.

1059   Guidi, Augusto. "Aspetti dell'uomo e del male," FLe, 10
         March 10, 1953), 3.

         Melville's conflict is between Rousseau-like
         optimism and Puritan pessimism.

1060   Guidi, Augusto. "Considerazioni su BARTLEBY," SA, 3
         (1957), 99-108.

1061   Guidi, Augusto. "Di alcuni racconti di Melville,"
         AION-SG, 9 (1966), 119-140.

1962   Guidi, Augusto. "Melville e la statuaria classica,"
         SRo, 15 (1967), 289-297.

1063   Guido, John F. "Melville's MARDI: Bentley's Blunder?"
         FB3A, 62 (3rd Qt., 1968), 361-371.

         Bentley's publication of MARDI (1849) as a
         "three-decker" (because such a form was economically
         advantageous) probably caused failure of the book in
         England.

1064   Gullace, Giovanni. "Melville: natura umana e civiltà
         in TYPEE e in WHITE-JACKET," RLMC, 14 (June, 1961),
         34-40.

1065   Gupta, R. K. "Form and Style in Herman Melville's
         PIERRE: OR THE AMBIGUITIES," DA, 26 (Pittsburgh:
         1965), 1631-32.

         A study of the epic and dramatic conventions,
         symbolism, and imagery of the novel with the conclusion
         that PIERRE is not a failure, but "a successful literary
         performance and one of Melville's greatest artistic
         achievements."

1066   Gupta, R. K. "Hautboy and Plinlimmon: A Reinterpretation
         of Melville's 'The Fiddler,'" AL, 43 (1971), 437-
         442.

1067   Gupta, R. K. "Imagery in Melville's PIERRE," KAL, 10
         (1967), 41-49.

         In PIERRE, Melville uses imagery to establish
         tonal and atmospheric effects congruent with the
         moods and emotions of the novel, and also to clarify
         and sharpen his characterizations." Recurrent imagery,
         however, does not constitute the "basic pattern" or
         define major themes.

1068   Gupta, R. K. "Melville's Use of Non-Novelistic
       Conventions in PIERRE," ESQ, 48 (3rd Qt., 1967),
       141-145.

       Although in PIERRE Melville perhaps came closest to
the traditional novel, yet he found the conventions inade-
quate and restrictive and, therefore, "pushed beyond the
apparent limits" of his form to make use of certain
specific devices from the epic and drama.

1069   Gupta, R. K. "Pasteboard Maska: A Study of Symbolism
       in PIERRE," INDIAN ESSAYS IN AMERICAN LITERATURE:
       PAPERS IN HONOUR OF ROBERT E. SPILLER. Mukherjee,
       Sujit, and D. V. K. Raghavacharyulu, eds. Bombay:
       Popular Prakashan, 1969, pp. 121-128.

       Discussion of the Memnon Stone and the vision of
Enceladus.

1070   Guttchen, Robert S. "Meaning and Meaninglessness:
       A Response to Professor Green," JAE, 2 (1968),
       79-84.

       To Ahab the whale is not a symbol; it is evil.

       Cf., Maxine Greene. "The Whale's Whiteness:
On Meaning and Meaninglessness," JAE, 2 (1968), 51-72.

1071   Guttmann, Allen. "The Enduring Innocence of Captain
       Amasa Delano," BUSE, 5 (Spring, 1961), 35-45.

1072   Guttmann, Allen. "From TYPEE to MOBY-DICK: Melville's
       Allusive Art," MLQ, 24 (September, 1963), 237-244.

       Unlike allusions of the earlier romances, those
of MOBY-DICK are "fully woven into the fabric...The
allusions expand into complex metaphors. Even casual
references are, for the most part, pertinent."

1073   Haag, John. "Bartleby-ing for the Camera," MELVILLE
       ANNUAL 1965, A SYMPOSIUM: BARTLEBY THE SCRIVENER.
       Howard P. Vincent, ed. (Kent Stud. in Eng., III).
       Kent, Ohio: Kent State University Press, 1966,
       pp. 55-63.

       The making of the film, as a consequence of
"assorted frustrations and fits of general despair,
turned out to be conducive to a mood suitable for
Bartleby...Actually it was an exhilarating experience,
though being Bartleby was not...."

1074   Haave, Ethel-Mae. "Herman Melville's PIERRE: A Critical
        Study," DA, 30 (Yale: 1969), 1527A-28A.

1075   Haber, Tom Burns. "A Note on Melville's BENITO CERENO,"
        NCF, 6 (September, 1951), 146-147.

        The razor-cut in the shaving episode.

        Cf., Ward Pafford and Floyd C. Watkins. "BENITO
        CERENO: A Note in Rebuttal," NCF, 7 (1952), 68-71.

1076   Hagopian, John V. "BARTLEBY THE SCRIVENER," in INSIGHT I:
        ANALYSES OF AMERICAN LITERATURE. John V. Hagopian
        and Martin Dolch, eds. Frankfurt: Hirschgraben
        Verlag, 1962, pp. 145-149.

1077   Hagopian, John V. "BENITO CERENO," INSIGHT I: ANALYSES
        OF AMERICAN LITERATURE. John V. Hagopian and Martin
        Dolch, eds. Frankfurt: Hirschgraben, 1962, pp. 150-
        154.

1078   Hagopian, John V. "Melville's 'l'homme révolté,'"
        ES, 46 (October, 1965), 390-402.

        In his three most important stories--BARTLEBY,
        BENITO CERENO, and BILLY BUDD--Melville uses the theme
        of "l'homme révolté," a revolt which is both "necessary
        and hopeless."

1079   Hagopian, John V. "Seeing Through 'The Pupil' Again,"
        MFS, 5 (1959), 169-171.

        Like Captain Vere in BILLY BUDD, Pemberton of
        James's "The Pupil" made a tragic decision out of
        "stern necessity."

        A reply to Terence Martin. "James's 'The Pupil':
        The Art of Seeing Through," MFS, 4 (1958-59), 335-45.

1080   Hagopian, John V., and Martin Dolch. With assistance of
        W. Gordon Cunliffe and Arvin R. Wells. "BILLY BUDD,"
        INSIGHT I: ANALYSES OF AMERICAN LITERATURE. John V.
        Hagopian and Martin Dolch, eds. Frankfurt:
        Hirschgraben Verlag, 1962, pp. 144-165.

1081   Hakutani, Yoshinobu. "Hawthorne and Melville's
        BENITO CERENO," HSELL, 10 (1963), 58-64.

1082   Hall, James B. "MOBY DICK: Parable of a Dying System," WR, 14 (Spring, 1950), 223-226.

       MOBY DICK is an exposure of the weaknesses of the capitalistic system: as such, it can be read as "an industrial saga."

       Cf., Eugene R. Spangler, "Harvest in a Barren Field: A Counter-comment," WR, 14 (Summer, 1950), 305-307.

1083   Hall, Joan Joffe. "The Historical Chapters in BILLY BUDD," UKCR, 30 (October, 1963), 35-40.

       Melville employs the context of the mutinies under Admiral Nelson at Trafalgar to account for Vere's execution of Billy Budd. Vere acts "in favor of appearances, but with no illusions that appearance is reality."

1084   Hall, Joan Joffe. "Melville's Use of Interpolations," UR, 33 (Autumn, 1966), 51-59.

       In his earlier work, Melville made use of material easily separable from plot. By the time he reached MOBY DICK, he had mastered his technique of "alternating facts with plot and of selecting those facts which made the action credible, coherent, and meaningful." He had also developed another kind of interpolation, the parable, which parallels the plot "by interpreting and proposing alternatives to the protagonist's behavior."

1085   Hall, Joan Joffe. "NICK OF THE WOODS: An Interpretation of the American Wilderness," AL, 35 (1963), 173-182.

       Robert Montgomery Bird's novel rejects Cooper's "noble savage," and presents Bird's concept of the moral battle for the wilderness. Slaughter's dual role as the pacifist Quaker and the vengeful Nick parallels Melville's paradox in THE CONFIDENCE MAN.

1086   Hall, Joan Joffe. "Some Problems of Structure in Melville's Novels," DA, 22 (Stanford: 1962), 3663-64.

1087   Hall, Susan Corwin, comp. "Herman Melville," HAWTHORNE TO HEMINGWAY: AN ANNOTATED BIBLIOGRAPHY OF BOOKS FROM 1945 TO 1963 ABOUT NINE AMERICAN WRITERS. Robert H. Woodward, ed. New York: Garrett Pub. Co., 1965, pp. 7-15, passim.

1088   Halliburton, David G. "The Grotesque in American Literature: Poe, Hawthorne and Melville," DA, 27 (Calif., Riverside: 1967), 3840A-41A.

       The grotesque is not a genre but "a way of creating and perceiving," particularly in Melville for whom "the grotesque is a spatial configuration which must be penetrated to its essence."

1089   Halverson, John. "The Shadow in MOBY DICK," AQ, 15 (Fall, 1963), 436-446.

        A Jungian interpretation. Ahab, Ishmael, Queequeg, and Pip are archetypal figures undergoing archetypal experiences, moving in or out of, accepting or rejecting, their "shadows."

1090   Hamada, Masajiro. "Two Utopian Types of American Literature: TYPEE and THE CRATER," SEL, 40 (March, 1964), 199-214.

1091   Hamalian, Leo. "Melville's Art," Expl, 8 (March, 1950), Item 40.

1092   Hamer, Philip M., ed. A GUIDE TO ARCHIVES AND MANUSCRIPTS IN THE UNITED STATES. Compiled for the National Historical Publications Commission. New Haven: Yale University Press, 1961, pp. 256, 274, 427.

        Harvard: Mass.: Harvard University Archives. Widener Library. Herman Melville, 545 pieces.

        Massachusetts, Pittsfield. Berkshire Athenaeum: more than 50 letters of Herman Melville and his family.

        New York Law Institute Library, 120 Broadway, New York. Herman Melville, 128 pieces.

1093   Hand, Harry E. "'And War Be Done': BATTLE-PIECES and Other Civil War Poetry of Herman Melville," JHR, 11 (1963), 326-340.

1094   Handy, E. S. C. "Native Culture in the Marquesas," BBMB, 9 (1923).

1095   Handy, E. S. C. "Polynesian Religion," BBMB, 34 (1927).

1096   Handy, W. C. TATTOOING IN THE MARQUESAS. Honolulu: 1922.

1097   Hanley, James. Introduction, MOBY DICK. London: 1952.

1098   Hanley, James. Introduction, MOBY-DICK: OR, THE WHALE. New York: Coward-McCann, 1953.

1099   Hansen, Martin A. "Herman Melville og MOBY-DICK," Andvari, 92 (1967), 65-75.

1100   Hansen, Martin A. VED KORSVEJEN. Litteraere essays i
         udvalg ved Thorkild Bjornvig og Ole Wivel.
         Copenhagen: Gyldendal, 1964.

         I. a., Blicher, Johs. V. Jensen, Herman Melville,
    Jorgen Niesen.

1101   Harada, Keiichi. "Melville and Puritanism," SELit, 32
         (1956), 1-20.

1102   Harada, Keiichi. "The Theme of Incest in THE SOUND AND
         THE FURY and in PIERRE," AmLR, 14 (May, 1956), 1-7.

1103   Haraszti, Zoltan. "Melville Defends TYPEE," BBPL, 20
         (June, 1947), 203-208.

         Letter of Melville, May 23, 1846, offering an
    article to substantiate truthfulness of TYPEE. Toby
    Greene's unexpected substantiation probably explains
    why Melville's article was never published.

1104   Harding, Walter. Introduction, BATTLE PIECES AND ASPECTS
         OF THE WAR. Facsimile Reproductions. Gainesville,
         Florida: Scholars' Facsimiles & Reprints, 1960.

1105   Harding, Walter. "A Note on the Title 'MOBY-DICK,'"
         AL, 22 (January, 1951), 500-501.

         Captain Austin Braise's yacht Moby Dick carried
    a slave from Albany to Boston in 1847: Perhaps Melville
    got his title from the name of that yacht.

         Cf., Sidney Kaplan. "The Moby Dick in the service
    of the Underground Railroad," Phylon, 12 (1951), 173-
    176.

1106   Harkness, Bruce. "Bibliography and the Novelistic
         Fallacy," SB, 12 (1958), 59-73.

         Errors in texts of novels, including works of
    Melville.

1107   Hart, James D. "Melville and Dana," AL, 9 (1937), 49-55.

         Questionable whether Dana's TWO YEARS BEFORE THE
    MAST gave Melville the incentive to go to sea in 1841.

1108   Hart, James D. "A Note on Sherman Kent's 'Russian
               Christmas before the Mast,'" AL, 14 (November,
               1942), 294-298.

               Dana was not "irresponsible" in his use of factual
          data: "Perhaps the Russians in the near-by brig were
          celebrating Saint Nicholas Day" (December 18) rather
          than Christmas.

1109   Hart, John S. "Melville," A MANUAL OF AMERICAN LITERATURE:
               A TEXT-BOOK FOR SCHOOLS AND COLLEGES. Philadelphia:
               Eldredge & Brother, 1872, p. 486.

1109.1   Hart, Joseph C. MIRIAM COFFIN: OR, THE WHALE FISHERMAN.
               London and New York: 1834.

               A possible source of MOBY DICK.

1110   Hartman, Jay H. "VOLPONE as a Possible Source for
               Melville's THE CONFIDENCE-MAN," SUS, 7, 1v (1965),
               247-260.

1111   Harvey, Evelyn. MOBY-DICK. Colliers, 135 (March 4,
               1955), 70-73.

1112   Harvey, W. J. CHARACTER AND THE NOVEL. Ithaca, New
               York: Cornell University Press, 1965.

1113   Hashiguchi, Minoru. "Melville no Shi," EigoS, 115
               (1969), 485-486.

               Melville's poetry.

1114   Hauck, Richard Boyd. "The Descent into Faith: Herman
           o   Melville," A CHEERFUL NIHILISM: CONFIDENCE AND
               "THE ABSURD" IN AMERICAN HUMOROUS FICTION.
               Bloomington: Indiana University Press, 1971,
               pp. 77-132.

1115   Haven, Gilbert, and Thomas Russell. FATHER TAYLOR, THE
               SAILOR PREACHER. Boston: 1872.

               Similarity of the painting at the back of Father
          Taylor's pulpit and that of Father Mapple.

1116   Haverstick, Iola S. "A Note on Poe and PYM in Melville's
               OMOO," PN, 2, 1-11 (1969), 37.

1117   Havlice, Patricia Pate. INDEX TO AMERICAN AUTHOR
BIBLIOGRAPHIES. Metuchen, New Jersey: The
Scarecrow Press, Inc., 1971, pp. 114-115.

1118   Hawley, Hattie L. Introduction, MOBY DICK. New York:
1924.

1119   Hawthorne, Hildegarde. "Hawthorne and Melville,"
LitRNYEP, 2 (1922), 406.

1120   Hawthorne, Julian. "Man-Books," *America*, 1 (September 27,
1888), 11-12.

Melville in TYPEE and OMOO, MOBY DICK and WHITE
JACKET, wrote books of adventure, not woman books, nor
exactly "man-books," but rather boys' books, admirable
and unequaled, but which "did not quite fill the bill."

1121   Hawthorne, Julian. NATHANIEL HAWTHORNE AND HIS WIFE: A
BIOGRAPHY. Boston and New York: Houghton Mifflin
Company, Riverside Cambridge Press, 1884, 2 vols,
passim.

Hawthorne and Melville as neighbors.

1122   Hawthorne, Julian. "When Herman Melville was 'Mr. Omoo,'"
LitDIBR, 4 (1926), 561-562, 564.

1123   Hawthorne, Julian, and Leonard Lemmon. "An Early
Sea-Novelist," AMERICAN LITERATURE: A TEXT-BOOK
FOR USE IN HIGH SCHOOLS AND ACADEMIES. Boston:
D. C. Heath & Co., 1891, pp. 210-211.

Melville's position in literature "secure and
solitary"; he surpasses Cooper, "when Cooper writes of
the sea." No subsequent writer has even challenged
"a comparison with him on that element."

1124   Hawthorne, Julian, and Leonard Lemmon. "Herman Melville
(1819-1891)," BOOK FOR THE USE OF SCHOOLS AND
COLLEGES. Boston: D. C. Heath & Co., 1901, pp.
208-209.

Melville's imagination has a "tendency to wildness
and metaphysical extravagance," and "when he trusted to
it alone, he becomes difficult and sometimes repulsive...."

1125   /Hawthorne, Nathaniel7. THE AMERICAN NOTEBOOKS BY
NATHANIEL HAWTHORNE. Randall Stewart, ed. New
Haven: 1932, passim.

1126   Hayashi, Nobuyuki. A STUDY OF HERMAN MELVILLE. Tokyo:
Nanundo, 1958.

1126.1 Hayford, Harrison. Afterword, TYPEE. New York: New
           American Library (Signet Classic), 1964.

1127   Hayford, Harrison. "Hawthorne, Melville, and the Sea,"
           NEQ, 19 (December, 1946), 435-452.

           Hawthorne may have been attracted to Melville
        partly because of his own interest in things of the
        sea, though "by no means did he have Melville's
        romantic, irresistible itch for things remote."

1128   Hayford, Harrison. HAWTHORNE AND MELVILLE: A BIOGRAPHICAL
           AND CRITICAL STUDY. Diss. Yale: 1945.

1129   Hayford, Harrison. MELVILLE HANDBOOK. New York:
           Hendricks House, 1954.

1130   Hayford, Harrison. "Melville's Freudian Slip," AL, 30
           (November, 1958), 366-368.

           Errors in the official birth record of Stanwix
        Melville.

1131   Hayford, Harrison. "Melville's Usable or Visible Truth,"
           MLN, 74 (December, 1959), 702-705.

1132   Hayford, Harrison. "Poe in THE CONFIDENCE-MAN," NCF,
           14 (December, 1959), 207-218.

           A possible portrait.

1132.1 Hayford, Harrison. "Poe in THE CONFIDENCE-MAN," in
           THE CONFIDENCE MAN: HIS MASQUERADE. Hershel
           Parker, ed. New York: W. W. Norton & Company,
           1971, pp. 344-353.

1133   Hayford, Harrison. "The Sailor-Poet of WHITE-JACKET,"
           BPLQ, 3 (July, 1951), 221-228.

           Ephraim Curtiss Hine, who was author of THE HAUNTED
        BARQUE (1848) and who served on the frigate United States
        with Melville, qualifies as the original of the sailor-poet,
        Lemsford.

1134   Hayford, Harrison. "The Significance of Melville's
       'Agatha' Letters," ELH, 13 (December, 1946),
       299-310.

       The "Agatha" letters throw light on the problem
    of Melville's intentions in writing PIERRE.

1135   Hayford, Harrison, ed. THE SOMERS MUTINY AFFAIR.
       Englewood Cliffs, New Jersey: Prentice-Hall, 1959.

       Background for BILLY BUDD.

1136   Hayford, Harrison. "Two New Letters of Herman Melville,"
       ELH, 11 (March, 1944), 76-83.

       Letters to R. H. Dana, Jr., October 6, 1849, and
    May 1, 1850, possible indication that TWO YEARS BEFORE
    THE MAST may have influenced Melville to embark on the
    Acushnet.

1137   Hayford, Harrison, and Walter Blair, eds. OMOO.
       New York: Hendricks House, 1957.

1138   Hayford, Harrison, and Merrill Davis. "Herman Melville
       as Office-Seeker," MLQ, 10 (1949), 168-183; 377-388.

1139   Hayford, Harrison, Hershel Parker, and G. Thomas Tanselle,
       eds. With Historical Note by Elizabeth S. Foster.
       MARDI: AND A VOYAGE THITHER. Evanston and Chicago:
       Northwestern University Press, and the Newberry
       Library, 1970.

       Rev., Lawrence Thompson, AL, 43 (1971), 450-451.

1140   Hayford, Harrison, and Hershel Parker. "The Text:
       History, Variants, and Emendations," "Glossary of
       Nautical Terms," MOBY-DICK. New York: W. W.
       Norton, The Norton Critical Edition, 1967,
       pp. 471-498, 499-507.

1141   Hayford, Harrison, Hershel Parker, and G. Thomas Tanselle,
       eds. OMOO: A NARRATIVE OF ADVENTURES IN THE SOUTH
       SEAS. Historical Note by Gordon Roper. Evanston
       and Chicago: Northwestern University Press and
       The Newberry Library, 1968.

1142   Hayford, Harrison, Hershel Parker, and G. Thomas Tanselle,
       eds. PIERRE. Evanston and Chicago: Northwestern
       University Press and The Newberry Library, 1971.

1143 Hayford, Harrison, Hershel Parker, and G. Thomas Tanselle, eds. REDBURN: HIS FIRST VOYAGE. Historical Note by Hershel Parker. Evanston, Illinois: Northwestern University Press, 1969.

1144 Hayford, Harrison, Hershel Parker, and G. Thomas Tanselle, eds. TYPEE: A PEEP AT POLYNESIAN LIFE. Historical Note by Leon Howard. Evanston and Chicago: Northwestern University Press and The Newberry Library, 1968.

1145 Hayford, Harrison, Hershel Parker, and G. Thomas Tanselle, eds. WHITE-JACKET: OR THE WORLD IN A MAN-OF-WAR. Historical Note by Willard Thorp. Evanston and Chicago: Northwestern University Press and The Newberry Library, 1970.

   Rev. by Howard P. Vincent, AL, 43 (1971), 292.

1146 Hayford, Harrison, and Merton M. Sealts, Jr., eds. Introduction and Notes. BILLY BUDD, SAILOR (AN INSIDE NARRATIVE): READING TEXT AND GENETIC TEXT. Chicago: Chicago University Press, 1962.

   Cf., William T. Stafford. "The New BILLY BUDD and the Novelistic Fallacy: An Essay-Review," MFS, 8 (1962), 306-311.

1147 Hayman, Allen. HERMAN MELVILLE'S THEORY OF PROSE FICTION: IN CONTRAST WITH CONTEMPORARY THEORIES. Diss. Illinois: 1961.

1148 Hayman, Allen. "The Real and the Original: Herman Melville's Theory of Prose Fiction," MFS, 8 (Autumn, 1962), 211-232.

   Melville's fiction, as stated in Chapter 33 of THE CONFIDENCE MAN, was primarily concerned not with "actuality," but with "reality," with, indeed, "more reality, than real life itself can show."

1149 Hays, Peter. "Slavery and BENITO CERENO: An Aristotelian View," EA, 23 (January-March, 1970), 38-46.

   An "Aristotelian reading" focuses attention on the title character as a tragic hero who finally achieves self-realization denied Captain Delano. The "transcribed depositions," however, detract from the "tone and mood" though they contribute to the unity of theme—the difficulty of true perception—by revealing the obtuseness of officialdom.

1150   Head, Brian F. "Camoes and Melville," RevCam, 1
        (1964), 36-77.

        A source study.

1151   Hefferman, William A. "Melville's Primitives: Queequeg
        and Fedallah," LHR, Ser. 1, No. 6 /Ser. 2, No. 1/
        (1964), 45-52.

        Conflict of values represented by Queequeg and
Fedallah, "the core of MOBY DICK."

1152   Heflin, Wilson L. HERMAN MELVILLE'S WHALING YEARS.
        Diss. Vanderbilt: 1952.

1153   Heflin, Wilson L. "A Man-of-War Button Divides Two
        Cousins," BPLQ, 3 (January, 1951), 51-60.

        Incident in Chapter 59, WHITE-JACKET, in which
Frank, a seaman, fears he may be recognized by his
brother, a commissioned officer, has an autobiographical
basis: Stanwix Gansevoort, Melville's cousin, was
granted a "reefer's warrant," and saw duty in the same
bay in which Melville was stationed on the United States.

1154   Heflin, Wilson L. "Melville and Nantucket," MOBY DICK
        CENTENNIAL ESSAYS. Tyrus Hillway and Luther S.
        Mansfield, eds. Dallas: Southern Methodist
        University Press, 1953, pp. 165-179.

1155   Heflin, Wilson L. "Melville and Nantucket," PROCEEDINGS
        OF THE NANTUCKET HISTORICAL ASSOCIATION. 1951.

1156   Heflin, Wilson L. "Melville's Third Whaler," MLN, 64
        (1949), 241-245.

1157   Heflin, Wilson L. "The Source of Ahab's Lordship over
        the Level Lodestone," AL, 20 (1948), 323-327.

        Melville probably indebted to William Scoresby, Jr.,
JOURNAL OF A VOYAGE TO THE NORTHERN WHALE-FISHERY (1823),
for idea of having lightning of the typhoon reverse
polarity of the Pequod's compasses and for the dramatic
solution of Ahab's navigational difficulties.

1158   Heilman, Robert. MAGIC IN THE WEB: ACTION AND LANGUAGE
        IN OTHELLO. Lexington: Kentucky University Press,
        1956, pp. 247-248, passim.

        Comparison of Iago and Claggart.

1159 Heimert, Alan. "MOBY DICK and American Political
Symbolism," AQ, 15 (Winter, 1963), 498-534.

In MOBY DICK, there are at least three reflections
of the controversy over the Compromise of 1850: dangers
encountered by the <u>Pequod</u> similar to the perils to the Ship
of State; American invasion of rights of other nations
(Mexico and Canada); and Ahab is made "to act and even
look like the demonic, yet admirable Senator /Calhoun/
who to many Americans seemed an incarnation of Ahab of
Old."

Cf., Charles H. Foster. "Something in Emblems:
A Reinterpretation of MOBY DICK," NEQ, 34 (1961), 3-35.

1160 Heinz, Heide. "Hermann Melvilles Erzählung 'Bartleby' im
Vergleich zu Franz Kafkas Roman DER PROZESS," in
SAARBRUCKER BEITRAGE ZUR ASTHETIK. Rudolf Malter
and Alois Brandstetter, eds. Saarbrucken: Verl.
der Saarbrücker Zeitung, 1966, pp. 59-66.

1161 Heiser, M. F. "The Decline of Neoclassicism, 1801-1848,"
TRANSITIONS IN AMERICAN LITERARY HISTORY. Harry
Hayden Clark, ed. Durham, North Carolina: Duke
University Press, 1953, pp. 93-159.

Incidental references to Melville, but important
for placing him in his literary and political milieu.

1162 Heitner, John A. "Melville's Tragic Triad: A Study of
His Tragic Visions," DA, 29 (Rochester: 1968),
229A-30A.

1163 Heller, Louis G. "Two Pequot Names in American Literature,"
AS, 36 (February, 1961), 54-57.

Name in MOBY DICK and THE LAST OF THE MOHICANS.

1164 Helmcke, Hans. DIE FUNKTION DES ICH-ERZAHLERS IN HERMAN
MELVILLES ROMAN "MOBY-DICK." Diss. Mainz: 1955.

1165 Helmcke, Hans. DIE FUNKTION DES ICH-ERZAHLERS IN HERMAN
MELVILLES ROMAN "MOBY-DICK" MIT EINEM VERGLEICHENDEN
BLICK AUF MELVILLES FRUHERE ROMANE. München: Max
Hueber, 1957.

The narrator is a participant in and observer of
events, but not the main protagonist.

Rev. by Horst Frenz, AL, 32 (January, 1961), 475-76.

1165.1 Hemingway, Ernest. THE GREEN HILLS OF AFRICA. New York: Charles Scribner's Sons, 1935, p. 20.

Laudatory of Melville's knowledge, "unwrapped in pudding."

1166 Henchey, Richard F. "Herman Melville's ISRAEL POTTER: A Study in Survival," DAI, 31 (Mass.: 1970), 1758A-59A.

1167 Hendrick, George. "Literary Comments in the Letters of Henry S. Salt to W. S. Kennedy," ESQ, 19 (1960), 25-29.

Salt's extant letters (1889-1929) to William Sloane Kennedy commenting on contemporary writers expecially Melville and Thoreau.

1168 Hendrickson, John. "BILLY BUDD: Affirmation of Absurdity," A&L, 2, 1 (Spring, 1969), 30-37.

Meaning of the work has been obscured by definitions in terms of Christian theology, Schopenhauerism, Freudianism, Lockean philosophy, and social expediency. Melville's point is that man is potential victim to self-definitions of others which are absurd and limit his own self-definitions.

1169 Henn, T. R. THE HARVEST OF TRAGEDY. New York: Barnes & Noble, Inc., n. d., passim.

Symbols in MOBY DICK.

1170 Herbert, T. Walter, Jr. "Calvinism and Cosmic Evil in MOBY-DICK," PMLA, 84 (1969), 1613-19.

Cosmic evil in the conflict of Ahab and the whale.

1171 Herbert, T. Walter, Jr. "Spiritual Exploration in MOBY-DICK: A Study of Theological Background," DAI, 31 (Princeton: 1970), 1278A.

1171.2 "Herman Melville's Silence," TLS, 1173 (1924), 433.

BILLY BUDD and PIERRE deal with central problem of Christianity.

1171.1 "Herman Melville's PIERRE," TLS, 1500 (1930), 884.

1172   Herring, Thelma. "THE ESCAPE OF SIR WILLIAM HEANS:
        Hay's Debt to Hawthorne and Melville," <u>Southerly</u>,
        26, 11 (1966), 75-92.

1173   Hetherington, Hugh W. "Early Reviews of MOBY DICK,"
        MOBY DICK CENTENNIAL ESSAYS. Tyrus Hillway and
        Luther S. Mansfield, eds. Dallas: Southern
        Methodist University Press, 1953, pp. 89-122.

1174   Hetherington, Hugh W. MELVILLE'S REVIEWERS, BRITISH AND
        AMERICAN, 1846-1891. Chapel Hill, North Carolina:
        North Carolina University Press, 1961.

        A detailed account of public response to Melville's
        work, book by book, explaining biases of reviewers.
        Conclusion to each section summarizes criticism, and
        places early criticism against present-day judgments.

        Cf., Hershel Parker. "A Reexamination of MELVILLE'S
        REVIEWERS," AL, 42 (1970), 226-32.

        Rev., by William Braswell, AL, 33 (1962), 538-39;
        Richard Harter Fogle, NEQ, 35 (1962), 264-266.

1175   Hetherington, Hugh W. THE REPUTATION OF HERMAN MELVILLE
        IN AMERICA. Diss. Michigan U.: 1933.

        First doctoral dissertation on Melville.

1176   Hetherington, Hugh W. "A Tribute to the Late Hiram
        Melville," MLQ, 16 (December, 1955), 325-331.

        "...whoever was responsible for the weird misnomer,
        it is highly symptomatic of the state of knowledge about
        Herman Melville at the time of his death."

1177   Hewett-Thayer, Harvey W. "The Voice of New England and
        Melville," AMERICAN LITERATURE AS VIEWED IN GERMANY,
        1818-1861. Chapel Hill: North Carolina University
        Press, 1958, pp. 38-56.

1178   Heyen, William. "Three Poems from MOBY DICK," MTJ,
        12 (Summer, 1965), 17.

        The poems in MOBY DICK confirm that Melville is
        one of the best nineteenth-century poets.

1179   Hibler, David J.   "DRUM-TAPS and BATTLE-PIECES: Melville
           and Whitman on the Civil War," Person, 50 (Winter,
           1969), 130-147.

           The poetry shows continuity with Melville's
           earlier writing; however, the war heightened his "sense
           of suffering and death."

1180   Hicks, Granville. "Correspondence of a Gentle Man,"
           SatR, June 18, 1960, p. 15.

           Rev.-art., of H. H. Davis and W. H. Gilman.
           THE LETTERS OF HERMAN MELVILLE. New Haven, Conn.:
           1960.

1181   Hicks, Granville. "Heritage," THE GREAT TRADITION: AN
           INTERPRETATION OF AMERICAN LITERATURE SINCE THE
           CIVIL WAR. New York: Macmillan, 1933, 1968, passim.

           Rev. by Robert E. Spiller, AL, 6 (1934), 358-61.

1182   Hicks, Granville. "A Re-Reading of MOBY DICK,"
           TWELVE ORIGINAL ESSAYS ON GREAT AMERICAN NOVELS.
           Charles Shapiro, ed. Detroit: Wayne State
           University Press, 1958, pp. 44-68.

1183   Higgins, Brian. "Mark Winsome and Egbert: 'In the
           Friendly Spirit,'" THE CONFIDENCE-MAN: HIS
           MASQUERADE. Hershel Parker, ed. New York:
           W. W. Norton & Company, 1971, pp. 339-343.

           "...Along with PIERRE, THE CONFIDENCE-MAN is a
           study of the practicability of biblical Christianity...."

1184   Hillway, Tyrus. "BILLY BUDD: Melville's Human
           Sacrifice," PacS, 6 (Summer, 1952), 342-347.

           Billy Budd's death as "heroic tragedy."

1184.1   Hillway, Tyrus. DOCTORAL DISSERTATIONS ON HERMAN MELVILLE:
           A CHRONOLOGICAL SUMMARY (1933-1952). Greeley, Col.:
           Melville Society, 1953; repr., Lansdowne Press, 1971.

1185   Hillway, Tyrus. HERMAN MELVILLE. New York: Twayne,
           1963. (United States Authors Series).

           Rev. by William Braswell, AL, 36 (1964), 88-89.

1186   Hillway, Tyrus. "Herman Melville's Major Themes,"
         AMERICANA-AUSTRIACA: FESTSCHRIFT DES AMERIKA-
         INSTITUTS DER UNIVERSITAT INNSBRUCK ANLASSLICH
         SEINES ZEHNJAHRIGEN BESTEHENS. Klaus Lanzinger, ed.
         (Beitrage zur Amerikakunde, Band 1.) Wien, Stuttgart:
         W. Braumüller Univ.-Verl., 1966, pp. 170-180.

         The themes are: 1. The shock of discovering reality
    to be vastly different from the "truth" propagated by
    organized institutions of society; 2. The disparity
    consciously or unconsciously existing between man's
    professions and his acts; 3. The relative helplessness
    of the individual to control his own destiny; and 4. The
    need for a moral ideal.

1187   Hillway, Tyrus. "Hollywood Hunts the White Whale,"
         ColQ, 5 (Winter, 1957), 298-305.

         Research for the film of MOBY-DICK.

1188   Hillway, Tyrus. "Melville and Nineteenth Century Science,"
         DA, 29 (1969), 3578A.

1189   Hillway, Tyrus. "Melville and the Spirit of Science,"
         SAQ, 48 (January, 1949), 77-88.

1190   Hillway, Tyrus. MELVILLE AND THE WHALE. Stonington,
         Connecticut: Stonington Publishing Co., 1950.

1191   Hillway, Tyrus. "Melville as Amateur Zoologist,"
         MLQ, 12 (June, 1951), 159-164.

         In MARDI, Melville seems unaware of the real
    nature of the nineteenth-century scientific movement.
    His reliance on semi-scientific works and his own
    uninformed observations lead to many ichthyological
    errors.

1192   Hillway, Tyrus. "Melville as Critic of Science,"
         MLN, 65 (June, 1950), 411-414.

1192.1   Hillway, Tyrus, ed. MELVILLE SOCIETY NEWSLETTER.

1193   Hillway, Tyrus. "Melville's Art: One Aspect," MLN, 62
         (November, 1947), 477-480.

         When Melville had finished MOBY DICK in 1851
    he had emptied his "reservoir of experience and
    reading"--the two elements which, with transcendental
    speculations, comprise his books.

1194   Hillway, Tyrus. "Melville's BILLY BUDD," Expl, 4 (1945),
         Item 12.

         It is the suffering of "Starry" Vere, far greater
         than that of Billy Budd, that makes this a "great work
         of art."

1195   Hillway, Tyrus. "Melville's Geological Knowledge,"
         AL, 21 (May, 1949), 232-237.

         Cf., Elizabeth S. Foster. "Melville and Geology,"
         AL, 17 (1945), 50-65, and "Another Note on Melville and
         Geology," AL, 22 (1951), 479-487.

1196   Hillway, Tyrus. "Melville's Use of Two Pseudo-Sciences,"
         MLN, 64 (March, 1950), 145-150.

         Phrenology and physiognomy.

1197   Hillway, Tyrus. "A Note on Melville's Lecture in
         New Haven," MLN, 60 (1945), 55-57.

         Melville's New Haven lecture, scheduled for
         December 30, 1857, was not the subject of an unfavor-
         able editorial but "merely received the normal
         journalistic treatment of the day."

1198   Hillway, Tyrus. "Pierre, the Fool of Virtue," AL, 21
         (May, 1949), 201-211.

         Melville did not propagate any philosophical
         system. In his novels, generally, "the search for
         truth proves futile, the defiance of destiny wholly
         foolhardy, and the apparent distinction between virtue
         and vice horrifyingly ambiguous."

1199   Hillway, Tyrus. "A Preface to MOBY DICK," in MOBY DICK
         CENTENNIAL ESSAYS. Tyrus Hillway and Luther S.
         Mansfield, eds. Dallas: Southern Methodist
         University Press, 1953, pp. 22-29.

1200   Hillway, Tyrus. "Some Recent Articles Relating to
         Melville (January 1947 to September 1948)," MSN, 4
         (November, 1948).

1201   Hillway, Tyrus. "Taji's Abdication in Herman Melville's
         MARDI," AL, 16 (1944), 204-207.

         The significance of Taji's suicide: A powerful
         effect is achieved by the extension of Taji's quest
         into eternity. To seek his lost happiness, he is
         willing to sever all ties with life.

1202   Hillway, Tyrus. "Taji's Quest for Certainty," AL, 18
        (March, 1946), 27-34.

        "A parallel of the main allegory in Herman
        Melville's MARDI is to be found...in the adventure
        of the fifth pilgrim on the island of Maramma."

1203   Hillway, Tyrus. "Two Books in Young Melville's Library,"
        BNYPL, 71 (Summer, 1967), 474-476.

        The books are Levi W. Leonard's THE LITERARY AND
        SCIENTIFIC CLASS BOOK (1826), a text assigned at the
        New York Male High School when Melville was in
        attendance, and THE YOUNG MAN'S OWN BOOK: A MANUAL
        OF POLITENESS, INTELLECTUAL IMPROVEMENT, AND MORAL
        DEPORTMENT (1832).

1204   Hillway, Tyrus. "The Unknowns in Whale-Lore," AN&Q, 8
        (August, 1948), 68-69.

        A Melville scholar on beached whales.

1205   Hillway, Tyrus, and Luther S. Mansfield, eds. MOBY DICK
        CENTENNIAL ESSAYS. Edited for the Melville Society.
        Dallas, Texas: Southern Methodist University Press,
        1953.

        Rev. by Howard P. Vincent, AL, 26 (1954), 444-45.

1205.1 Hillway, Tyrus, and Hershel Parker, comps. A DIRECTORY
        OF MELVILLE DISSERTATIONS. Compiled for the Melville
        Society. Evanston, Illinois: 1962.

        An expansion of Tyrus Hill's DOCTORAL DISSERTATIONS
        ON HERMAN MELVILLE (1953).

1206   Hinchcliffe, A. P. SYMBOLISM IN THE AMERICAN NOVEL:
        1850-1950: AN EXAMINATION OF THE FINDINGS OF RECENT
        LITERARY CRITICS IN RESPECT OF THE NOVELS OF HAWTHORNE,
        MELVILLE, JAMES, HEMINGWAY, AND FAULKNER. Diss.
        Manchester: 1962-1963.

1206.1 Hind, C. Lewis. MORE AUTHORS AND I. New York: Dodd,
        Mead and Co., 1922.

        Reminiscences about acquaintance with Herman
        Melville, among others.

1207   Hirsch, David H. "The Dilemma of the Liberal
        Intellectual: Melville's Ishmael," TSLL, 5
        (Summer, 1963), 169-188.

        Ishmael (and, by implication, Melville) found it
        possible to fuse a Biblical world-view with the liberalism
        of the Enlightenment through fraternal love.

1208   Hirsch, David H. "Melville's Ishmaelite," AN&Q, 5
             (April, 1967), 115-116.

1209   Hitt, Ralph E. "Melville's Poems of Civil War Controversy,"
             SLitI, 2, i (1969), 57-68.

             The war may have brought to Melville some release
        from the melancholy of his earlier years.

1210   Hoar, Victor M. "The Confidence Man in American
             Literature," DA, 27 (Ill.: 1965), 2753-2754.

             A survey of the subject, from the early Southern
        humorists through Faulkner.

1210.1 Hobbes, Thomas. LEVIATHAN: OR, THE MATTER, FORME, AND
             POWER OF A COMMONWEALTH ECCLESIASTICALL AND CIVILL.
             London: 1651

1211   Hobsbaum, Philip. "Eliot, Whitman and the American
             Tradition," JAmS, 3, 2 (December, 1969), 239-264.

             Eliot an expression of a distinctly American
        literary tradition of which Melville and others are
        the best manifestations.

1211.1 Hodgskin, Thomas. "Abolition of Impressment," EdinR, 41
             (1824), 154-181.

             A possible source for WHITE JACKET.

1212   Hoefer, Jacqueline J. "After MOBY DICK: A Study of
             Melville's Later Novels," DA, 28 (Wash.: 1968),
             2647A.

             PIERRE, ISRAEL POTTER, and THE CONFIDENCE MAN are
        stages in the examination of moral dilemma which Melville
        resolved in BILLY BUDD through creation of "a character
        who accepts his imperfect humanity and is not incapacitated
        by this knowledge." Captain Vere is Melville's interpre-
        tation of the "highest human potential."

1213   Hoeltje, Hubert H. "Hawthorne, Melville, and 'Blackness,'"
             AL, 37 (March, 1965), 41-51.

             Melville's analysis of Hawthorne's work presents
        a misreading of most of the stories and a complete
        distortion of Hawthorne's themes by stress upon
        melancholy and blackness.

1214   Hoeltje, Hubert H. INWARD SKY: THE MIND AND HEART OF
         NATHANIEL HAWTHORNE. Durham, North Carolina: Duke
         University Press, 1962, pp. 317-331, passim.

1215   Hoffman, Daniel G. "Melville," FORM AND FABLE IN
         AMERICAN FICTION. New York: Oxford University
         Press, 1961, pp. 221-313, passim.

         "...The great European satires are works of comic
         imagination based on the affirmation of man's ideals;
         Melville's, though their equal in indignation, attacks
         not only human institutions and human folly, but, as
         they never do, human nature itself."

1216   Hoffman, Daniel G. "Melville in the American Grain,"
         SFQ, 14 (September, 1950), 185-191.

1217   Hoffman, Daniel G. "Melville's 'Story of China Aster,'"
         AL, 22 (1950), 137-149.

         This chapter (in THE CONFIDENCE MAN) explicates
         the conflict between two dominating forces: "the
         Promethean-creative-civilizing impulse versus its
         opposite, the surrender of moral judgments and the
         perversion of the Promethean spirit to private ends
         at the expense of mankind."

1218   Hoffman, Daniel G. "MOBY DICK: Jonah's Whale or Job's?"
         SR, 69 (Spring, 1961), 205-224.

         Melville employs contrasting myths of many cultures
         which create unifying tensions, chiefly between Ahab and
         Ishmael, between narcissism and love for mankind. Ahab,
         anti-Christ and anti-Jonah, commands the Pequod in an
         assault on God and perishes without resurrection. Ishmael
         is a Jonah cast forth from the ship, but his God is
         Job's, the God of creation.

1219   Hoffman, Daniel G. "Myth, Magic, and Metaphor in
         MOBY-DICK," FORM AND FABLE IN AMERICAN FICTION.
         New York: Oxford University Press, 1961, pp. 233-278.

1220   Hoffman, Leonard R. "Problems in Melville: The Style
         from the Beginnings through MOBY DICK," DA, 14
         (Stanford: 1954), 2346-47.

1221   Hoffman, Michael J. "The Anti-Transcendentalism of
        MOBY-DICK," GaR, 23 (Spring, 1969), 3-16.

        MOBY-DICK mocks the Transcendental style; its
        major symbol "symbolizes absolutely nothing"; its central
        figure, a man "blinded by his own vision," "mouths the
        ideas of an author Melville thought a 'humbug,' and is
        ultimately a parody of the Transcendentalist 'great man.'"
        Ishmael is "the new post-transcendental man," whose
        "ironic detachment" will become a pose of the new hero
        of the "realist novel."

1222   Hoffmann, Charles G. THE DEVELOPMENT TOWARD THE SHORT
        NOVEL FORM IN AMERICAN LITERATURE WITH SPECIAL
        REFERENCE TO HAWTHORNE, MELVILLE, AND JAMES.
        Diss. Wis.: 1952.

1223   Hoffmann, Charles G. "The Shorter Fiction of Herman
        Melville," SAQ, 52 (July, 1953), 414-430.

        Melville's publications in 1855 indicate growing
        competence in shorter prose fiction. Despite his
        "exaggerated" style in MOBY DICK and PIERRE, in his
        subsequent short works he returns to the simple natural
        style characteristic of his early writing.

1224   Hogan, Robert. "The Amorous Whale: A Study in the
        Symbolism of D. H. Lawrence," MFS, 5 (Spring, 1959),
        39-46.

        The influence of Melville and Whitman on symbolism
        in AARON'S ROD and KANGAROO.

1225   Hohman, Elmo Paul. THE AMERICAN WHALEMAN. New York:
        Longmans, Green, 1928.

1226   Holder, Alan. "Style and Tone in Melville's PIERRE,"
        ESQ, 60 (1970), 76-86.

        A summary of the critical disagreements about the
        novel. Conclusion is that there are "major inconsistencies
        in Melville's handling of his material," particularly in
        the later chapters, which cause the book's ultimate
        "collapse into contradictions and fragments."

1227   Holland, Laurence Bedwell. THE EXPENSE OF VISION:
        ESSAYS ON THE CRAFT OF HENRY JAMES. Princeton,
        New Jersey: Princeton University Press, 1964,
        pp. 59, 73, passim.

1228   Hollis, Sophie. "MOBY-DICK: A Religious Interpretation,"
        CathW, 163 (May, 1946), 158-162.

        MOBY DICK is a religious allegory of fate and
        free will, revealing the "tragedy of the man who is
        neither believer nor infidel."

1229   Holman, C. Hugh. "The Defense of Art: Criticism Since
        1930," THE DEVELOPMENT OF AMERICAN LITERARY CRITICISM.
        Floyd Stovall, ed. Chapel Hill: North Carolina
        University Press, 1955, pp. 199-245.

        A survey of criticism.

1230   Holman, C. Hugh. "The Reconciliation of Ishmael: MOBY-
        DICK and the Book of Job," SAQ, 57 (Autumn, 1958),
        477-490.

        Thematically the story is that of passive Ishmael;
        in plot and action, Ahab is the center. An imperfect
        fusion of the two elements results from Melville's having
        written on two different levels at two different times.
        It results, too, from Melville's failure to define
        relationship of the narrator to his story.

1231   Holmes, Oliver Wendell, Jr. HOLMES-POLLOCK LETTERS:
        THE CORRESPONDENCE OF MR. JUSTICE HOLMES AND SIR
        FREDERICK POLLOCK, 1874-1932. Mark DeWolfe Howe,
        ed. Introductions by John Gorham Palfrey and
        Sir John Pollock, Bart. (2 vols. in one; second ed.)
        Cambridge, Mass.: The Belknap Press of Harvard
        University Press, 1961, II, 68, 227.

1232   Holt, Henry. GARRULITIES OF AN OCTOGENARIAN EDITOR:
        WITH OTHER ESSAYS SOMEWHAT BIOGRAPHICAL AND
        AUTOBIOGRAPHICAL. Boston and New York: Houghton
        Mifflin Company, 1923, p. 189.

        "...notwithstanding the hermit-like character
        I have known ascribed to Melville,...I often recall
        him as one of the very most agreeable men I have ever
        met...."

1233   Homans, George C. "The Dark Angel: The Tragedy of
        Herman Melville," NEQ, 5 (October, 1932), 699-730.

        In MARDI, MOBY DICK, and PIERRE, Melville dramatizes
        his search for the secret of the universe.

1234   Homberger, Eric. "I Am I," CamR, 90, #2187 (February 7, 1969), 251-253.

Comparison of Sylvia Plath's poetry with Melville's "The Whiteness of the Whale."

1235   Honig, Edwin. DARK CONCEIT: THE MAKING OF ALLEGORY. Evanston: Northwestern University Press, 1959, passim.

For Melville, the challenge was "to map out the relation of the unknown country of allegory to the known countries and conditions of contemporary actuality...."

1236   Honig, Edwin. "In Defense of Allegory," KR, 20 (Winter, 1958), 1-19.

1236.1   Hopkins, Vivian C. "Margaret Fuller: American Nationalist Critic," ESQ, 55 (2nd Qt., 1969), 24-41.

Margaret Fuller, as a reviewer for Horace Greeley's Tribune, criticized Melville and other American writers with "much vigor and enthusiasm."

1237   Horsford, Howard C. "The Design of the Argument in MOBY DICK," Herman Melville Special Number, MFS, 8 (1962), 233-251.

MOBY DICK, Melville's response to the disintegration of faith.

1238   Horsford, Howard C. "Evidence of Melville's Plans for a Sequel to THE CONFIDENCE-MAN," AL, 24 (March, 1952), 85-89.

During his European trip of 1856-1857, Melville apparently planned a sequel; perhaps the failure of his American publishers and the reception by the public of THE CONFIDENCE-MAN caused him to abandon the plan.

1239   Horsford Howard C. "Journal of a Visit to Europe and the Levant, October 11, 1856-May 6, 1857, by Herman Melville," DA, 15 (Princeton: 1955), 584-585.

1240   Horsford, Howard C., ed. MELVILLE'S JOURNAL OF A VISIT
          TO EUROPE AND THE LEVANT, OCTOBER 11, 1856-MAY 6,
          1857. Princeton: Princeton University Press, 1954;
          Oxford University Press, 1955.

          Rev. by William H. Gilman, AL, 28 (1956), 82-93.

          Cf., Howard C. Horsford. "Melville's JOURNAL...:
          A Rejoinder to a Review," AL, 28 (1957), 520-523;
          William H. Gilman. "Reply to a Rejoinder," AL, 28
          (1957), 520-524.

1241   Horsford, Howard C. "Melville's JOURNAL OF A VOYAGE TO
          EUROPE AND THE LEVANT: A Rejoinder to a Review,"
          AL, 28 (January, 1957), 520-523.

          Cf., William H. Gilman. "A Reply to a Rejoinder,"
          AL, 28 (1957), 523-524.

1242   Hoskins, Katherine. "Continuing Pursuit of Herman
          Melville," NewRep, 126 (1952), 18-19.

1243   Houghton, Donald E. "The Incredible Ending of Melville's
          TYPEE," ESQ, 22 (1st Qt., 1961), 28-31.

1244   Houston, Neal B. "Silent Apostles: Melville's Animus
          Against the Clergy," RS, 34 (December, 1966), 230-
          239.

          Portrayal of clergymen from TYPEE to BILLY BUDD
          shows Melville's three major criticism: They possess
          a "certain impracticability," they lack Father Mapple's
          "compulsion to preach the Truth in the face of Falsehood,"
          and they are silent "when face to face with the tragedy
          of life."

1245   Hovey, Richard B. JOHN JAY CHAPMAN: AN AMERICAN MIND.
          New York: Columbia University Press, 1959, p. 325.

          In a letter to Robert Nichols, June 24, 1923,
          Chapman mentioned that he had discovered Melville and
          was so fascinated by MOBY DICK "that he could hardly
          put it down."

1246   Howard, Frances K. "The Catalyst of Language: Melville's
          Symbol," EJ, 57 (September, 1968), 825-831.

          The lawyer's office is a kind of Plato's cave in
          which the lawyer personifies "the deceived rationalism,"
          called "common sense." The lawyer's final failure to
          understand his experience with Bartleby shows that
          "language becomes its own wall."

1247   Howard, Leon. "Americanization of the European Heritage,"
THE AMERICAN WRITER AND THE EUROPEAN TRADITION.
Margaret Denny and William H. Gilman, eds.
Minneapolis: Minnesota University Press, 1950,
pp. 78-89.

Melville's most powerful expression in prose the
result of the conflict between a heritage of European
philosophy and a characteristically American attitude
of mind, the "realistic demand to be shown."

1248   Howard, Leon. "The Case of the Missing Whaler," MSS, 12
(Fall, 1960), 3-9.

Leon Howard's research in Melville biography.

1249   Howard, Leon. "Die Entstehung von 'MOBY DICK,'" ZWEI
VÖLKER IM GESPRÄCH. Frankfurt am Main: Europäische
Verlagsanstalt, 1961, pp. 146-156.

1250   Howard, Leon. HERMAN MELVILLE. University of Minnesota
Pamphlets on American Writers, No. 13, Minneapolis,
Minn.: Minnesota University Press, 1961.

1251   Howard, Leon. "Herman Melville," TRES ESCRITORES
NORTEAMERICANOS: HERMAN MELVILLE, EDITH WHARTON,
GERTRUDE STEIN. Traducción Angela Figuera. Madrid:
Gredos, 1962, pp. 7-54.

1252   Howard, Leon. HERMAN MELVILLE (Arabic translation).
Beirut: Al Maktaba Al Ahliyya, 1963.

1253   Howard, Leon. HERMAN MELVILLE. (Korean translation of
II-3 with parallel English text). Seoul: English
Literary Society of Korea, 1964.

1254   Howard, Leon. HERMAN MELVILLE. (Portuguese translation
of II-3). Sao Paulo: Livraria Martins Editora,
1963.

1254.1 Howard, Leon. "Herman Melville," EIGHT AMERICAN WRITERS:
AN ANTHOLOGY OF AMERICAN LITERATURE. Norman Foerster
and Robert P. Falk, gen. eds. New York: W. W. Norton
& Co., 1963, pp. 781-970.

1255   Howard, Leon. "Herman Melville," SIX AMERICAN NOVELISTS
OF THE NINETEENTH CENTURY: AN INTRODUCTION.
Richard Foster, ed. Minneapolis: Minnesota
University Press, 1968, pp. 82-117.

1256   Howard, Leon. "Herman Melville," SERIES OF AMERICAN
         AUTHORS. (Japanese translation of II-3). Tokyo:
         Hokuseido, 1964, III, 139-193.

1257   Howard, Leon. HERMAN MELVILLE: A BIOGRAPHY. Berkeley,
         Calif.: California University Press, 1951; repr.
         1958. Toronto: Cambridge and Oxford, 1952; London:
         Cambridge University Press, 1958; Berkeley and
         Los Angeles: California University Press, 1967.

         Rev. William Braswell, AL, 24 (1952), 245-247;
         Harrison Hayford, NCF, 7 (1952), 61-67.

1258   Howard, Leon. "Herman Melville, MOBY DICK," THE AMERICAN
         NOVEL FROM COOPER TO FAULKNER. Wallace Stegner, ed.
         New York: Basic Books, 1965, pp. 25-34.

1259   Howard, Leon. "Herman Melville's MOBY DICK," The Voice
         of America Forum Lectures, The American Novel Series,
         No. 3. Washington: The Voice of America, 1965,
         pp. 1-7.

1260   Howard, Leon. Introduction, MOBY DICK; OR, THE WHALE.
         New York: Random House. Modern Library, 1950.

1261   Howard, Leon. Introduction, MOBY-DICK. (Yugoslav
         translation of III-2), Zagreb: Kultura, 1954.

1262   Howard, Leon. LITERATURE AND THE AMERICAN TRADITION.
         New York: Doubleday, 1960, pp. 181-182.

         Rev. by Floyd Stovall, AL, 32 (1960), 328-330.

1263   Howard, Leon. "Melville and Spenser--A Note on Criticism,"
         MLN, 46 (1931), 291-292.

         Epigraphs for the sketches of "The Encantadas"
         are mostly from Spenser.

1264   Howard, Leon. "Melville's Struggle with the Angel,"
         MLQ, 1 (June, 1940), 195-206.

         Advanced the theory that there were two
         MOBY DICKS.

1265   Howard, Leon. "The Mystery of Melville's Short Stories,"
         AMERICANA-AUSTRIACA: FESTSCHRIFT DES AMERIKA-
         INSTITUTS DER UNIVERSITÄT INNSBRUCK ANLÄSSLICH SEINES
         ZEHNJAHRIGEN BESTEHENS. (Beiträge zur Amerikakunde,
         Band 1.) Wien, Stuttgart: W. Braumüller, Univ.-Verl.
         1966, pp. 204-16.

         The stories suggest a pattern which controlled
     Melville's art of literary creation. Few of the tales,
     however, "gave expression to what he was deeply moved to
     write" (except perhaps "Bartleby" and "The Bell Tower"),
     but none was entirely free from "an internal emotional
     quality closely related to its author's known or probably
     serious personal concerns."

1266   Howard, Leon. "A Predecessor of MOBY DICK," MLN, 49
         (1934), 310-311.

         Hart's MIRIAM COFFIN, a whaling novel, a possible
     source.

1267   Howard, Leon. "The Quest for Confidence," HERMAN MELVILLE:
         THE CONFIDENCE-MAN: HIS MASQUERADE. Hershel Parker, ed.
         New York: W. W. Norton, 1971, pp. 286-298.

1268   Howe, Irving. "Anarchy and Authority in American
         Literature," DenverQ, 2 (Autumn, 1967), 5-30.

         Description of the conflict between American
     anarchism and the American notion of authority depicted
     by Melville and other American writers.

1269   Howe, Irving. "THE CONFIDENCE MAN, Tomorrow, 8 (1949),
         55-57.

1270   Howe, M. A. D. "Tale of Tanglewood," YR, n. s. 32
         (1942), 323-336.

1271   Howes, Jeanne C. "Melville's Sensitive Years,"
         MELVILLE AND HAWTHORNE IN THE BERKSHIRES: A
         SYMPOSIUM. Howard P. Vincent, ed. Kent, Ohio:
         Kent State University Press, 1968, pp. 22-41.

         A survey of the Pittsfield newspapers, particularly
     the Sun of 1833-1838, when young Melville visited his
     uncle's farm and became a Berkshire schoolmaster during
     a period of controversy over the district's schools.

1272   Howington, Don S. "Melville's 'The Encantadas': Imagery
         and Meaning," SLitI, 2, i (1969), 69-75.

1273   Howorth, R. G. "Melville and Australia," N&Q, 193
         (1948), 188.

1274   Howson, Alice Guest. MELVILLE AS LYRIC POET. Diss.
              Columbia: 1952.

1275   Hoyle, Norman Eugene. MELVILLE AS A MAGAZINIST. Diss.
              Duke: 1960.

1276   Hubbell, Jay B. THE SOUTH IN AMERICAN LITERATURE,
              1607-1900. Durham: Duke University Press, 1954,
              3rd printing, 1964, pp. 421-22, passim.

              William Gilmore Simms reviewed Melville's MARDI
         in the Southern Quarterly Review, October, 1849, praising
         it briefly, then adding: "...he spoils everything to
         the Southern reader when he paints a loathsome picture
         of Mr. Calhoun, in the character of a slave-driver,
         drawing mixed blood and tears from the victim at every
         stroke of the whip...."

1277   Hubbell, Jay B. WHO ARE THE MAJOR AMERICAN WRITERS?
              A STUDY OF THE CHANGING LITERARY CANON. Durham,
              North Carolina: Duke University Press, 1972.

              Melville's literary reputation.

1278   Hubben, William. "Ahab, the Whaling Quaker," RelLif,
              18 (Summer, 1949), 363-373.

              MOBY DICK in light of the 1940's confrontation
         of evil.

1279   Hudson, H. E., IV. "'Billy Budd': Adam or Christ?"
              CraneR, 7 (Winter, 1965), 62-67.

1280   Hudson, Hoyt H. "God's Plenty About Melville," Nation,
              114 (1922), 20.

1281   Hudson, Hoyt H. "The Mystery of Herman Melville,"
              Freeman, 3 (1921), 156-157.

1282   Hudson, William Henry. "Fear of Whiteness," excerpt from
              IDLE DAYS IN PATAGONIA in THE BEST OF WILLIAM HENRY
              HUDSON. Odell Shepard, ed. New York: Dutton,
              1949, pp. 35-42.

1282.1   Hudson, William Henry. "Snow, and the Quality of
              Whiteness," IDLE DAYS IN PATAGONIA. New York:
              E. P. Dutton & Co., 1917, pp. 108-120.

              Reference to Melville's description in MOBY DICK
         of whiteness in nature.

1283   Hughes, Raymond G. "Melville and Shakespeare," ShAB, 7
              (1932), 103-112.

1284   Hull, Raymona E. "London and Melville's ISRAEL POTTER," ESQ, 47 (2nd Qt., 1967), 78-81.

Melville's use of impressions recorded in his journal during his visit to London in 1849.

1285   Hull, Raymona E., ed. STUDIES IN THE MINOR AND LATER WORKS OF MELVILLE. Hartford: 1970.

1286   Hull, William. "MOBY DICK: An Interpretation," Etc, 5 (Autumn, 1947), 8-21.

1287   Hultin, Neil C. "Melville's Search for Meaning," Discourse, 7 (Autumn, 1964), 454-461.

The search for Moby Dick "is a search for possible answers to the riddle of the universe." The failure of the search is foreshadowed in the Etymology and Extracts opening the book.

1288   Humbach, Anne. ASPEKTE DER WORTBILDUNG BEI HERMAN MELVILLE. Diss. Freiburg, 1959.

1289   Hume, Robert D. "Gothic versus Romantic: A Revaluation of the Gothic Novel," PMLA, 84 (1969), 282-290.

The Gothic novel should be defined by its use of "a particular atmosphere for essentially psychological purposes." MOBY DICK is an "almost perfect example" of the form.

1290   Humphreys, A. R. "Herman Melville," JO'L, 4 (July 6, 1961), 18-19.

On MOBY DICK and BILLY BUDD.

1291   Humphreys, A. R. HERMAN MELVILLE. London: Oliver and Boyd, Ltd., 1962; New York: Barnes & Noble, Inc., 1966.

1292   Humphreys, A. R., ed. Introduction, Notes, Variant Readings, WHITE-JACKET, OR THE WORLD IN A MAN-OF-WAR. London: Oxford University Press, 1966.

1292.1 Hun, Henry. A SURVEY OF THE ACTIVITY OF THE ALBANY ACADEMY. Albany: 1934.

1293   Hunt, Livingston. "Herman Melville as a Naval Historian," HGM, 39 (1930), 22-30.

The satire in WHITE-JACKET.

1294   Huntress, Keith. "'Guinea' of WHITE-JACKET and Chief
            Justice Shaw," AL, 43 (1972), 639-641.

1295   Huntress, Keith. "Melville, Henry Cheever, and 'The
            Lee Shore,'" NEQ, 44 (Summer, 1971), 468-475.

            Henry Cheever as a reviewer of several of Melville's
    novels, and as a possible source for Chapter XXIII of
    MOBY DICK.

1296   Huntress, Keith. "Melville's Use of a Source for
            WHITE-JACKET," AL, 17 (1945), 66-74.

            Many of the incidents and even chapters in
    WHITE-JACKET were borrowed from LIFE IN A MAN-OF-WAR,
    OR SCENES IN OLD IRONSIDES (Philadelphia, 1841).
    However, Melville's superiority to his source provides
    an illustration of his technical ability.

1297   Huntress, Keith. "A Note on Melville's REDBURN,"
            NEQ, 18 (1945), 259-260.

            No discoveries have been made by which Melville's
    story of his first voyage as given in REDBURN can be
    checked. However, he may have read R. Thomas's
    INTERESTING AND AUTHENTIC NARRATIVES OF THE MOST
    REMARKABLE SHIPWRECKS...and this may have led him
    to read Owen Chase's NARRATIVE OF THE SHIPWRECK OF
    THE WHALE SHIP ESSEX OF NANTUCKET. Both stories
    contain the account of the wreck of the Essex, on
    which the tragic climax of MOBY DICK is based.

1298   Hurley, Leonard Burwell. THE AMERICAN NOVEL, 1830-1850.
            Diss. North Carolina: 1932.

1299   Hurt, James R. "SUDDENLY LAST SUMMER: Williams and
            Melville," MD, 3 (February, 1961), 396-400.

1300   Hutchens, John K. "Field Report on Mr. Melville's New
            One," NYHTBR (July 22, 1956).

1300.1 Hutchins, Robert Maynard, ed. MOBY-DICK: OR, THE WHALE
            by Herman Melville, in GREAT BOOKS OF THE WESTERN
            WORLD. Chicago, London, Toronto: Encyclopaedia
            Britannica, Inc., 1952.

1301   Hutchinson, William H. "A Definitive Edition of MOBY
            DICK," AL, 25 (January, 1954), 472-478.

            The Vincent-Mansfield edition.

1302   Hutchinson, William H. "Demonology in Melville's
            Vocabulary of Evil," DA, 27 (Northwestern: 1967),
            2132A-33A.

1303   Hyman, Stanley Edgar. THE ARMED VISION: A STUDY IN THE
       METHODS OF MODERN LITERARY CRITICISM. New York:
       Alfred A. Knopf, 1948, passim.

       A critical analysis of the work of various critics
       of Melville and others.

1304   Hyman, Stanley Edgar. "Melville the Scrivener," NMQ,
       23 (Winter, 1953), 381-415.

       BARTLEBY, BENITO CERENO, and BILLY BUDD each
       develops a single aspect of MOBY DICK'S totality.

1305   Hyman, Stanley Edgar. THE PROMISED END: ESSAYS AND
       REVIEWS, 1942-1962. New York: World, 1963.

1306   Ilson, Robert. "Benito Cereno from Melville to Lowell,"
       Salmagundi, 1, iv (Winter, 1966-67), 78-86.

       Differences between Melville's story and Robert
       Lowell's recent play; the latter as a tract for the
       times requiring certain changes in characterization
       and perspective.

1307   "Information into Wisdom," TLS, 3146 (June 15, 1962), 444.

1308   Ingalls, Jeremy. "The Epic Tradition: A Commentary,"
       E-WR, 1 (Spring, 1964), 42-69.

       The classic tragedy of Ahab within the epic of
       Ishmael.

1309   Irvine, Peter L. "The 'Witness' Point of View in Fiction,"
       SAQ, 69 (1970), 217-225.

       The indirect method of the "witness" in fiction
       provides the author greater freedom than other first-
       person methods. Among the significant examples of
       the method are novels by Melville.

1310   Isaacs, Neil D., and Louis H. Leiter, eds. APPROACHES
       TO THE SHORT STORY. San Francisco: Chandler, 1963.

1311   Isani, Mukhtar Ali. "Melville and the 'Bloody Battle in
       Afghanistan,'" AQ, 20 (Fall, 1968), 645-649.

       Possible sources for Melville's knowledge of the
       Khoord Kabul battle of 1842 mentioned in Chapter 1,
       where Ishmael is "spoofing the contemporary taste for
       the unusual, the spectacular, and the exotic."

1312　　Isani, Mukhtar Ali. "The Naming of Fedallah in MOBY DICK," AL, 40 (1968), 380-385.

　　　　The Spectator, Moore's LALLAH ROOKH, and Goodrich's revision of Webster's AMERICAN DICTIONARY, all contributed to Melville's creation of the Parsee and the selection of his name.

1313　　Ishag, Saada. "Herman Melville as an Existentialist: An Analysis of TYPEE, MARDI, MOBY DICK, and THE CONFIDENCE MAN," ESRS, 14 (December, 1965), 5-41, 60-62.

　　　　Structural and thematic affinities between Melville's works and the "Theater of the Absurd" school.

1314　　Itofuji, Hiromi. "Another Aspect of BILLY BUDD," KAL, 10 (1967), 29-40.

　　　　The Dansker and Vere are both servants of an unjust social system against which they should take action. One of the implicit "messages" of BILLY BUDD is "a political protest."

1315　　Ives, C. B. "BILLY BUDD and the Articles of War," AL, 34 (March, 1962), 31-39.

　　　　The Articles of War were Captain Vere's excuse for hanging Billy. He invoked the Mutiny Act, not applicable to sailors, and the Articles of War, which for persons convicted of striking officers required the death sentence by a general court-martial. His options were: pardon, light punishment, hanging, or general court-martial.

1316　　Ives, Sidney. "A Melville Ghost," PBSA, 59 (July, 1965), 318.

　　　　One of the Harvard copies of TYPEE, described by Bernard De Voto in 1928 as a "variant of the first edition," consisted in actuality of Part I of the first edition bound with Part II of the revised edition.

　　　　Cf., G. T. Tanselle, "Replies," PBSA, 62 (1968), 601-604; and Vol. 64 (October, 1968, April, 1970), 207-209.

1317　　Izzo, Carlo. "Vita silenziosa di Bartleby," FLe, 10 (March 8, 1953), 4.

1318　　Jackson, Holbrook. "Southward Ho!" ROMANCE AND REALITY: ESSAYS AND STUDIES. New York: Kennerly, 1912.

　　　　TYPEE.

1319   Jackson, Kenny. "ISRAEL POTTER: Melville's 'Fourth of July' Story," CLAJ, 6 (March, 1963), 194-204.

Melville had a purpose for his subtitle: "It presents a more mature writer and thinker who sums up his tirades of earlier works and introduces the subtleties...more explicitly expressed in THE CONFIDENCE MAN." Less vitriolic, ISRAEL POTTER is a serious commentary on the American scene.

1320   Jackson, Margaret. "Melville's Use of a Real Slave Mutiny in 'BENITO CERENO,'" CLAJ, 4 (December, 1960), 79-93.

1321   Jacobs, Jay. "Sails Ho!" Reporter, 27 (December 6, 1962), 42-43.

Robert Chapman and Louis O. Coxe's play, BILLY BUDD, is a "decided improvement on the master's novella," in its divesting of the novella's irrelevances. Peter Ustinov's film version, while "much better than most" films, is less than superb because it has added irrelevances in a mistaken effort to achieve verisimilitude.

1322   Jacoby, J. E. "Herman Melville, Gentleman and Scholar," LE MYSTICISME DANS LA PENSÉE AMÉRICAINE. Paris: 1931, pp. 206-240.

1323   Jacque, Valentina. "MOBY DICK in Russian," SovL, 6 (1962), 185-187.

The 1961 Russian translation.

1323.1   Jaffe, Adrian H., and Virgil Scott. Instructor's Manual, STUDIES IN THE SHORT STORY. New York: Holt, Rinehart and Winston, 1968, pp. 65-69.

BARTLEBY THE SCRIVENER.

1324   Jaffé, David. "The Captain Who Sat for the Portrait of Ahab," BUSE, 4 (Spring, 1960), 1-22.

Captain Charles Wilkes as model for Ahab.

1325   Jaffé, David. "Some Origins of MOBY-DICK: New Finds in an Old Source," AL, 29 (November, 1957), 263-277.

The "old source" is Wilkes's NARRATIVE OF THE U. S. EXPLORING EXPEDITION (1845).

1326   Jaffé, David. "Some Sources of Melville's MARDI,"
        AL, 9 (1937), 56-69.

        Possible sources: William Ellis, POLYNESIAN
        RESEARCHES (New York, 1833); Daniel Tyerman and
        George Bennet, JOURNAL OF VOYAGES AND TRAVELS (Boston,
        1832); Charles Wilkes, NARRATIVE OF THE UNITED STATES
        EXPLORING EXPEDITION (Philadelphia, 1845); and Frank
        DeBell Bennett, NARRATIVE OF A WHALING VOYAGE ROUND
        THE GLOBE (London, 1840).

1327   James, Cyril Lionel Robert. MARINERS, RENEGADES, AND
        CASTAWAYS: THE STORY OF HERMAN MELVILLE AND THE
        WORLD WE LIVE IN. New York: C. L. R. James, 1953.

        Ahab as a capitalist.

1328   Jarrard, Norman E. MELVILLE STUDIES: A TENTATIVE
        BIBLIOGRAPHY. Melville Society Special Publication,
        1 (December, 1958). Second impression with addenda
        (December, 1959).

        Mimeographed 49-page bibliography arranged
        chronologically.

1329   Jarrard, Norman E., ed. POEMS BY HERMAN MELVILLE: A
        CRITICAL EDITION OF THE PUBLISHED VERSE. Diss.
        Texas Univ.: 1960.

1329.1 Jarrard, Norman E., ed. POEMS BY HERMAN MELVILLE: A
        CRITICAL EDITION OF THE PUBLISHED VERSE. Ann Arbor:
        and Austin: Texas University Press, 1960 (University
        Microfilms).

1330   Jarrell, Randall. POETRY AND THE AGE. New York: Knopf,
        1953.

1331   Jaster, Frank. "Melville's Cosmopolitan: The Experience
        of Life in THE CONFIDENCE-MAN: HIS MASQUERADE,"
        SoQ, 8 (January, 1970), 201-210.

        Melville's cosmopolitan is a synthesis of life's
        experiences, neither wholly good nor wholly bad; in
        him man sees his own reflection. Since the mirror of
        man's intentions is neutral, man reveals himself as
        either good or bad. The novel's ambiguity is symbolic
        of Nature's indifference; man determines his own fate.

1332   Jeffrey, Lloyd N. "A Concordance to the Biblical
        Allusions in MOBY DICK," BB, 21 (May-August, 1956),
        223-229.

1333   Jerman, Bernard R. "With Real Admiration: More
        Correspondence between Melville and Bentley,"
        AL, 25 (November, 1953), 307-313.

        Six new letters, one from Melville, five from
        Bentley, dealing with the English reception of
        Melville's works.

1334   Jewell, Ross M. RECURRENT THEMES IN MELVILLE'S WORK.
        Diss. Indiana: 1954.

1335   Johnson, Arthur. "A Comparison of Manners," NewRep,
        20 (August 27, 1919), 113-115.

        Comparison with Henry James.

1336   Johnson, Jeanne. "The White Jacket," Thoth, 1 (1960),
        15-19.

1337   Johnson, Merle. "Herman Melville," MERLE JOHNSON'S
        AMERICAN FIRST EDITIONS. Bibliographic Check Lists
        of the Works of 199 American Authors. Revised by
        Jacob Blanck. 3rd ed. New York: R. R. Bowker Co.,
        1936, pp. 328-329.

1338   Johnson, Richard Colles. "An Attempt at a Union List
        of Editions of Melville, 1846-1891," BC, 19
        (Autumn, 1970), 333-347.

        Locations in American and English libraries of
        editions of Melville published during his lifetime,
        compiled in conjunction with the preparation of the
        Northwestern University-Newberry Library Edition
        begun in 1965.

1339   Jones, Bartlett C. "American Frontier Humor in
        Melville's TYPEE," NYFQ, 15 (Winter, 1959), 283-
        288.

        Understatement, hyperbole, braggadocio, rustic
        speech, the tall tale, and other devices employed in
        frontier humor, probably why nineteenth-century readers
        could not accept TYPEE as an accurate portrayal of
        South Sea life.

1340   Jones, Buford. "Melville's Buccaneers and Crébillon's
        Sofa," ELN, 2 (December, 1964), 122-126.

        References to James Colnet (A VOYAGE TO THE
        SOUTH ATLANTIC AND ROUND CAPE HORN INTO THE PACIFIC
        OCEAN. London, 1798), the poet Thomas Gray, and
        Claude-Prosper-Jolyot de Crébillon as aids in
        explication of the stone-sofa passage in "Barrington
        Isle and the Buccaneers."
            Cf., Russell Thomas. "Melville's Use of Some
        Sources in THE ENCANTADAS," AL, 3 (1932), 432-456.

1341   Jones, Buford. "Spenser and Shakespeare in THE
          ENCANTADAS, Sketch VI," ESQ, 35 (2nd Qt., 1964),
          68-73.

1342   Jones, Howard Mumford. "American Studies in Higher
          Education," ESSAYS ON AMERICAN LITERATURE IN
          HONOR OF JAY B. HUBBELL. Clarence Gohdes, ed.
          Durham, North Carolina: Duke University Press,
          1967, pp. 3-20.

          The question of nationalism in American letters.

1343   Jones, Howard Mumford. BELIEF AND DISBELIEF IN AMERICAN
          LITERATURE. Chicago: Chicago University Press,
          1967, passim.

          Incidental references which place Melville in
        his milieu.

1343.1 Jones, Howard Mumford. IDEAS IN AMERICA. Cambridge,
          Mass.: Harvard University Press, 1944, p. 219.

          "I hear much talk of MOBY DICK, which...is
        supposed to prove that the universe is evil. I had
        thought it had something to do with the dauntless
        spirit of man."

1344   Jones, Howard Mumford. HISTORY AND THE CONTEMPORARY:
          ESSAYS IN NINETEENTH-CENTURY LITERATURE. Madison:
          Wisconsin University Press, 1964, passim.

          A survey of criticism.

1345   Jones, Howard Mumford. JEFFERSONIANISM AND THE AMERICAN
          NOVEL. New York: Teachers College Press, Columbia
          University, 1966, pp. 36-38, passim.

          A survey of criticism: "...which Melville is one
        talking about--the nineteenth-century Melville, or the
        Melville who is the construction of twentieth-century
        criticism?...."

1345.1 Jones, Howard Mumford. O STRANGE NEW WORLD: AMERICAN
          CULTURE: THE FORMATIVE YEARS. New York: The
          Viking Press, 1964, p. 349.

          References help to place Melville in his literary
        milieu.

1346   Jones, Howard Mumford. THE THEORY OF AMERICAN LITERATURE.
         Ithaca, New York: Cornell University Press, 1948.
         Reissued with new Concluding Chapter and Revised
         Bibliography, 1965.

         Survey of the taste and views of American critics.
"Modern criticism wonders at the omission of Melville"
from W. C. Brownell's AMERICAN PROSE MASTERS (1901).

1347   Jones, Joseph. "Ahab's 'Blood-Quench': Theatre or
         Metallurgy?" AL, 18 (1946), 35-37.

         The spectacular episode of the "blood-quench"
at the forge, "unplausible as it sounds, has a long
tradition of practice behind it."

1348   Jones, Joseph. "Humor in MOBY-DICK," UTSE, 25 (1945-
         1946), 51-71.

         The philosophical meaning in MOBY DICK should
not obscure "the distinction that the book is
fundamentally a realistic story which has overtones..."
rather than a "full-feathered allegory which comes to
roost on a yard-arm of the Pequod."

1349   Jones, Joseph. "Melville: A 'Humorist' in 1890,"
         AN&Q, 8 (1948), 68.

         Melville is listed among humorists of minor
rank in an article by Henry Clay Lukens, "American
Literary Comedians," Harper's, April, 1890.

1350   Jones, Walter Dickinson. "A Critical Study of Herman
         Melville's ISRAEL POTTER," DA, 23 (Ala.: 1963),
         4357-58.

1351   Josephs, Lois. "Teaching MOBY DICK: A Method and an
         Approach," EJ, 56 (November, 1967), 1115-1119.

         The English major might approach MOBY DICK with
a thematic emphasis in high school, a chronological
emphasis in an undergraduate class in American
literature, a critical emphasis in an undergraduate
Seminar in the American Renaissance, and an even
more critical emphasis in a graduate Seminar on
Melville.

1352   Josephson, Matthew. "Libertarians and Others," PORTRAIT
         OF THE ARTIST AS AMERICAN. New York: 1930, repr.,
         Octagon Books, 1964, pp. 26-36.

1353   Josephson, Matthew. "The Transfiguration of Herman
              Melville," Outlook, 150 (September 19, 1928),
              809-811, 832, 836.

1354   Jung, Carl G. THE SPIRIT IN MAN, ART, AND LITERATURE.
              Trans. by R. F. C. Hull. London: Routledge & Kegan
              Paul, 1966, p. 88.

         MOBY DICK, "the greatest American novel."

1355   Jünger, Ernest. GÄRTEN UND STRASSEN: AUS DEN
              TAGEBÜCHERN VON 1939 UND 1940. Berlin: E. S.
              Mittler & Sohn, 1942.

1355.1   Justus, James. "Arthur Mervyn, American," AL, 42 (1970),
              304-324.

         Charles Brockden Brown's work portrays the
         American prototype, anticipating the American of
         Hawthorne, Melville, and later writers.

1356   Justus, James. "Beyond Gothicism: WUTHERING HEIGHTS
              and an American Tradition," TSL, 5 (1960), 25-33.

             The tradition includes Hawthorne, Melville, and
         Faulkner.

1357   Kael, Pauline. "BILLY BUDD," FilmQ, 16 (Spring, 1963),
              53-56.

             Rev.-art., of the film produced and directed by
         Peter Ustinov; screenplay by Ustinov from the novel
         of Herman Melville and the play by Robert Chapman
         and Louis O. Coxe. Photography: Robert Krasker;
         music: Anthony Hopkins.

1358   Kahn, Sholom J. "Herman Melville in Jerusalem: Excerpts
              from a Journal," Comm, 23 (February, 1957), 167-172.

1358.1   Kalem, T. E. "Harpooning Fate," Time, 97, (April 26, 1971),
              74.

             Appreciative review of Jack Aranson's ninety-minute
         one-man theatre piece, MOBY DICK. "Melville was a born
         monologuist, which helps Aranson mightily."

1359   Kaplan, Charles. "Jack Burden: Modern Ishmael," CE,
              22 (1960), 19-24.

             Ishmael and Warren's character in ALL THE KING'S
         MEN move from isolation to identity with humanity.

1360 Kaplan, Harold. THE PASSIVE VOICE: AN APPROACH TO
      MODERN FICTION. Athens, Ohio: Ohio University
      Press, 1966, passim.

1361 Kaplan, Sidney, ed. BATTLE-PIECES AND ASPECTS OF WAR.
      A facsimile Reproduction with Introduction.
      Gainesville, Fla.: Scholars' Facsimiles and
      Reprints, 1960.

1362 Kaplan, Sidney. "Can a Whale Sink a Ship? THE UTICA
      DAILY GAZETTE vs. THE NEW BEDFORD WHALEMAN'S
      SHIPPING LIST," NYH, 33 (April, 1952), 159-163.

      An argument in 1851 between the Utica DAILY
      GAZETTE and the NEW BEDFORD WHALEMAN'S SHIPPING LIST.

1362.1 Kaplan, Sidney. HERMAN MELVILLE AND THE AMERICAN NATIONAL
      SIN. Diss. Harvard.

1363 Kaplan, Sidney. "Herman Melville and the American
      National Sin: The Meaning of BENITO CERENO,"
      JNH, 41 (October, 1956), 311-338.

      First of two articles on Melville's treatment
      of the Negro and slavery.

      Cf., Sidney Kaplan. "Herman Melville and the
      American National Sin: The Meaning of BENITO CERENO,"
      JNH, 42 (1957), 11-37.

1364 Kaplan, Sidney. "Herman Melville and the American
      National Sin: The Meaning of BENITO CERENO,"
      JNH, 42 (January, 1957), 11-37.

      Melville does not take the humanitarian view of
      the Negro in BENITO CERENO.

      Cf., first article: Sidney Kaplan. "Herman
      Melville and the American National Sin: The Meaning
      of BENITO CERENO," JNH, 41 (1956), 311-338.

1365 Kaplan, Sidney. "Herman Melville and the American
      National Sin," IMAGES OF THE NEGRO IN AMERICAN
      LITERATURE. Seymour L. Gross and James E. Hardy,
      eds. Chicago: Chicago University Press, 1966,
      pp. 135-162.

1366 Kaplan, Sidney. "Herman Melville and the Whaling
      Enderbys," AL, 24 (May, 1952), 224-230.

      MOBY-DICK.

1367   Kaplan, Sidney. "The Moby Dick in the Service of the
        Underground Railroad," Phylon, 12 (2nd Qt., 1951),
        173-176.

        Correction of the statement by Walter Harding in
        "A Note on the Title of 'MOBY-DICK,'" AL, 22 (1951),
        500-501, that a vessel by the name of Moby Dick existed
        in the year 1847.

1368   Kaplan, Sidney. "'OMOO,' Melville's and Boucicault's,"
        AN&Q, 8 (January, 1950), 150-151.

1369   Kaplan, Sidney. "Towards Pip and Daggoo: Footnote on
        Melville's Youth," Phylon, 29 (Fall, 1968), 291-
        302.

1370   Karcher, Carolyn L. "The 'Spiritual Lesson' of
        Melville's 'The Apple-Tree Table,'" AQ, 23
        (Spring, 1971), 101-109.

        Melville's story clearly a topical satire on the
        Spiritualist cult of the 1850's.

1371   Karcher, Carolyn L. "The Story of Charlemont:
        A Dramatization of Melville's Concepts of Fiction
        in THE CONFIDENCE MAN: HIS MASQUERADE," NCF, 21
        (June, 1966), 73-84.

        The three chapters about fiction-writing embody
        Melville's techniques. "They identify the fictional
        representation of human reality with the mythical
        representation of divine reality; they ultimately
        redefine every detail in the book."

1372   Kasegawa, Koh. "Emerson, Thoreau, Melville," AJGE
        (Tokyo), 5 (November, 1964), 15-24.

1373   Kasegawa, Koh. "MOBY DICK as a Symbolic Myth," SEL, 36
        (1960), 251-272.

1374   Kasegawa, Koh. "MOBY DICK: A Tragedy of Madness,"
        TCEL, 30 (Autumn, 1957), 63-88.

1375   Kauffer, E. McKnight, illustrator. BENITO CERENO.
        New York: Random House, 1927.

        Called "a collector's item."

1376   Kauffmann, Stanley. "BILLY BUDD," A WORLD ON FILM:
        CRITICISM AND COMMENT. New York: Harper & Row,
        Publishers, 1958, 1966, passim.

1377   Kaufman, Paul. "Defining Romanticism," MLN, 40 (1925), 193-204.

1378   Kaufman, Paul. "The Romartic Movement," THE REINTERPRE-
        TATION OF AMERICAN LITERATURE: SOME CONTRIBUTIONS
        TOWARD THE UNDERSTANDING OF ITS HISTORICAL DEVELOP-
        MENT. Norman Foerster, ed. Preface by Robert P.
        Falk. New York: Russell & Russell, 1959, pp.
        114-138.

        The milieu of Hawthorne and Melville.

1379   Kaul, A. N. "Herman Melville: The New-World Voyageur,"
        THE AMERICAN VISION: ACTUAL AND IDEAL SOCIETY IN
        NINETEENTH-CENTURY FICTION. New Haven: Yale
        University Press, 1963, pp. 214-279.

1380   Kauvar, Gerald B. "Chapter 54 of MOBY DICK," ArlQ, 2
        (Winter, 1969-1970), 133-141.

        The story narrated in Chapter 54 is important
        for its themes, characters, and unusual structure
        (that of a tall tale). It is organically related
        to the entire novel.

1381   Kazin, Alfred, ed. Introduction, MOBY DICK. Boston:
        Houghton Mifflin Co. Riverside Editions, 1950,
        1956.

        Introduction repr., under various titles: Atl, 198
        (1956), 81-85; DISCUSSIONS OF MOBY DICK. Milton R. Stern,
        ed. Boston: Heath, 1960; CONTEMPORARIES. Boston: Little,
        Brown, 1962, pp. 29-46; MELVILLE: A COLLECTION OF
        CRITICAL ESSAYS. Richard Chase, ed. Englewood Cliffs:
        Prentice-Hall, 1962, pp. 39-48.

1382   Kazin, Alfred. "The Inmost Leaf," NR, 111 (1944), 840-841.

1383   Kazin, Alfred. "Ishmael and Ahab," Atl, 198 (November,
        1956), 81-85.

        The "poetic power" of MOBY DICK.

1383.1 Kazin, Alfred. "Ishmael and Ahab," AMERICAN CRITICAL
        ESSAYS: TWENTIETH CENTURY. H. L. Beaver, ed.
        London: Oxford University Press, 1959, pp. 332-47.

1383.2 Kazin, Alfred. "Ishmael and Ahab," CONTEMPORARIES.
        Boston: Little, Brown, 1962, pp. 29-40.

1384   Kazin, Alfred. "Ishmael in His Academic Heaven,"
        NY, 24 (February 12, 1949), 77, 84, 87-89.

1385   Kazin, Alfred. "On Melville as Scripture," PR, 17
        (1950), 67-75.

1385.1 Kazin, Alfred. "On Melville as Scripture," THE INMOST
        LEAF: A SELECTION OF ESSAYS. New York: Harcourt,
        Brace and Company, 1941, 1955, pp. 197-207.

1386   Kazin, Alfred. "MOBY-DICK," THE OPEN FORM. New York:
        Harcourt, Brace & World, 1961, pp. 112-123.

1387   Kazin, Alfred. ON NATIVE GROUNDS: AN INTERPRETATION OF
        AMERICAN PROSE LITERATURE. New York: Reynal &
        Hitchcock, 1942, passim.

        A survey of past attitudes and interpretations
        of various American writers, including Melville.

1388   Kazin, Alfred, Lawrance Thompson, and Lyman Bryson.
        "MOBY DICK," in INVITATION TO LEARNING: ENGLISH
        AND AMERICAN NOVELS. George D. Crothers, ed.
        London, New York: Basic Books, Inc., Publishers,
        1966, 224-231.

        Dialogue between the above critics as to MOBY DICK.

1389   Kazin, Alfred, Lawrance Thompson, and Lyman Bryson.
        "MOBY-DICK," InvitL, 11 (1953), 205-211.

1390   Kearns, Edward A. "Omniscient Ambiguity: The Narrators
        of MOBY-DICK and BILLY BUDD," ESQ, 58 (1st Qt.,
        1970), 117-120.

        Ambiguities of the two works are "necessary
        complements" to the omniscient narrative form and
        to Melville's investigation of "human perception
        and conception, Being and Identity."

1391   Keeler, Clinton. "Melville's Delano: Our Cheerful
        Axiologist," CLAJ, 10 (September, 1966), 49-55.

        Captain Delano's views aligned with Emersonian
        optimism.

1392   Kellogg, Remington. "Whales, Giants of the Sea,"
        NatlGeo, 67 (1940), 35-90.

1393   Kemp, Robert. "Les secrets de Melville," NL, 30
        (August 23, 1951), 3.

1394   Kendall, Lyle H., Jr. "On 'The Whiteness of the Whale,'"
        N&Q, 200 (1955), 266.

1395   Kennedy, Richard S. "The Theme of the Quest," EngRec,
        8 (Winter, 1957), 2-17.

        Ahab's quest for and conflict with the powers of
        the universe, and Ishmael's quest for self-knowledge.

1396   Kenney, Alice P. THE GANSEVOORTS OF ALBANY: DUTCH
        PATRICIANS IN THE UPPER HUDSON VALLEY. Syracuse,
        New York: Syracuse University Press, 1969.

1397   Kenny, Vincent S. "Clarel's Rejection of the Titans,"
        ATQ, 7 (1970), 76-81.

1398   Kenny, Vincent S. "Herman Melville's CLAREL," DA, 27
        (N. Y. U.: 1966), 458A-459A.

1399   Kent, Rockwell, illustrator. MOBY DICK. New York:
        Random House, 1930.

1400   Kern, Alexander. "The Rise of Transcendentalism, 1815-
        1860," TRANSITIONS IN AMERICAN LITERARY CRITICISM.
        Harry Hayden Clark, ed. Durham, North Carolina:
        Duke University Press, 1953, pp. 245-314.

        Hawthorne and Melville were affected by
        Transcendentalism, "if negatively."

1401   Kerr, Howard. MEDIUMS AND SPIRIT-RAPPERS AND ROARING
        RADICALS: SPIRITUALISM IN AMERICAN LITERATURE,
        1850-1900. Urbana: Illinois University Press, 1972.

        The personal and literary responses of American
        writers to spiritualism--from Lowell, Hawthorne and
        Melville to Howells and others.

1401.1 Kesey, Ken. ONE FLEW OVER THE CUCKOO'S NEST. New York:
        The Viking Press; London: Methuen & Co., Ltd.,
        1962, p. 81.

1402   Ketterer, David. "Some Co-ordinates in BILLY BUDD,"
        JAmS, 3 (December, 1969), 221-237.

1403   Key, Howard C. THE INFLUENCE OF TRAVEL LITERATURE UPON
        MELVILLE'S FICTIONAL TECHNIQUE. Diss. Stanford:
        1953.

1404   Key, James A. "An Introduction to Melville's Bird
        Imagery," DA, 27 (Tulane: 1966), 1369A.

        Melville uses birds to "symbolize predatory
        instincts, the conscious and unconscious mind, the
        ruling class, and the general nature of art and man."
        MARDI has the most birds.

1405   Keyes, Charlotte E. HIGH ON THE MAINMAST. A BIOGRAPHY
        OF HERMAN MELVILLE. New Haven: College and
        University Press, 1966. (Masterworks of Literature
        Series).

        Juvenile literature.

1406   Keyssar, Alexander. MELVILLE'S ISRAEL POTTER:
        REFLECTIONS ON THE AMERICAN DREAM. (LeBaron
        Briggs Prize Honors Essays in English) Cambridge:
        Harvard University Press, 1969.

        Melville's reappraisal of "the value of
        civilization," particularly in America.

1407   Kieft, Ruth M. Vande. "'When Big Hearts Strike Together':
        The Concussion of Melville and Sir Thomas Browne,"
        PLL, 5 (1969), 39-50.

        Melville's reading: A study of a major influence
        on the early Melville.

1408   Kieran, John, ed. "Concerning Whales," TREASURY OF
        GREAT NATURE WRITING. With Comments and Biographical
        Notes. New York: Hanover House, 1957, pp. 161-173.

1409   Kilbourne, W. G., Jr. "Montaigne and Captain Vere,"
        AL, 33 (January, 1962), 514-517.

        Similarity between Vere and Montaigne.

1410   Killinger, John. "The Death of God in American
        Literature," 3HR, 2 (Spring, 1968), 149-172.

        American roots include the 17th century quarrel
        between Calvinistic theocrats and atheists, 18th century
        Deism, 19th century Unitarianism, and the vision of evil
        associated with Puritan godliness in Hawthorne and
        Melville.

1411   Kimball, William J. "Charles Sumner's Contribution to
           Chapter XVIII of BILLY BUDD," SAB, 32 (November,
           1967), 13-14.

           Sumner's article, "The Mutiny of Somers"
           (North American Review, LVII, July 1843), stresses
           that Commodore Mackenzie, acting under martial law,
           did his duty in executing the mutinous members of
           his crew. The distinctions Captain Vere makes
           between natural and martial law may have been suggested
           to Melville by Sumner's arguments.

1412   Kimball, William J. "The Melville of BATTLE-PIECES:
           A Kindred Spirit," MQ, 10 (1969), 307-16.

           Melville's themes of nationalism and reconciliation
           are worked out in the direction of universality.

1413   Kimmey, John L. "Pierre and Robin: Melville's Debt to
           Hawthorne," ESQ, 38 (1st Qt., 1965), 90-92.

           Importance of "My Kinsman, Major Molineux" to
           Melville for its theme and technique.

1414   Kimpel, Ben Drew. HERMAN MELVILLE'S THOUGHT AFTER 1851.
           Diss. North Carolina: 1942.

1415   Kimpel, Ben Drew. "Melville's 'The Lightning-Rod Man,'"
           AL, 16 (1944), 30-32.

1416   Kimpel, Ben Drew. "Two Notes by Herman Melville: A
           Possible New Article by Melville?" AL, 16 (1944),
           29-32.

           1. An anonymous article on Lucian in the Cornhill
           Review (September, 1877) may be "connected" with Melville.

           2. "The Lightning-Rod Man" (1856), unless written
           several years before publication, shows Melville still
           had moments of "uncertain and unorthodox" but firm faith
           in a beneficent God.

1417   Kimura, Harumi. "Tensai yue no Shippai," EigoS, 115
           (1969), 483-484.

           Failure because of genius: Melville's PIERRE.

1417.1 Kinglake, Alexander William. EOTHEN; OR TRACES OF
           TRAVEL BROUGHT HOME FROM THE EAST.

           The first book to appear in Wiley Putnam's
           LIBRARY OF CHOICE READING, 1845.

1418　　Kinnamon, Jon M.　"BILLY BUDD:　Political Philosophies
　　　　　　in a Sea of Thought,"　ArQ, 26 (1970), 164-172.

　　　　　　　　Political confrontations in the story:　(1) The
　　　　conflict between the societies of two ships; (2) The
　　　　conflict between man's duty to his own society or to
　　　　his private moral sense; (3) The conflict in human
　　　　relations, Claggart and Billy being prototypes of
　　　　different political ideals.

1419　　Kirby, Thomas Austin, and William John Olive, eds.
　　　　　　ESSAYS IN HONOR OF ESMOND LINWORTH MARILLA.
　　　　　　Baton Rouge:　Louisiana State University Press,
　　　　　　1970.

1420　　Kirchner, Gustav.　"Amerikanisches in Wortschatz,
　　　　　　Wortbildung und Syntax von Herman Melvilles MOBY-
　　　　　　DICK," in MÉLANGES DE LINGUISTIQUE ET DE PHILOLOGIE:
　　　　　　FERNAND MOSSÉ IN MEMORIAM.　Ouvrage publie avec le
　　　　　　concours du Centre National de la Recherche
　　　　　　Scientifique.　Paris:　Didier, 1959, pp. 208-217.

1421　　Kirkham, E. Bruce.　"The Iron Crown of Lombardy in
　　　　　　MOBY DICK," ESQ, 58 (1970), 127-129.

1422　　Kirkland, James W.　"Animal Imagery in the Fiction of
　　　　　　Herman Melville,"　DAI, 31 (Tenn.:　1970), 1803A-04A.

1423　　Kirsch, James.　"The Enigma of MOBY DICK," JAP (London),
　　　　　　3 (1958), 131-148.

1424　　Kissane, James.　"Imagery, Myth, and Melville's PIERRE,"
　　　　　　AL, 26 (January, 1955), 564-572.

　　　　　　　　Cf., Charles Moorman.　"Melville's PIERRE and the
　　　　Fortunate Fall," AL, 25 (1953), 13-30.

1425　　Kissane, Leedice.　"Dangling Constructions in Herman
　　　　　　Melville's 'Bartleby,'"　AS, 36 (October, 1961),
　　　　　　195-200.

1426　　Klingerman, Charles.　"The Psychology of Herman Melville,"
　　　　　　PsyR, 40 (April, 1953), 125-143.

1427　　Knapp, Joseph G.　"Melville's CLAREL:　Dynamic Synthesis,"
　　　　　　ATQ, 7 (1970), 67-76.

　　　　　　　　Interpretation of the poem as "a continued
　　　　dissonance struggling toward a harmony" ultimately
　　　　achieved only in the imagery.　The imagery reveals
　　　　"a certitude that is learned only through suffering--
　　　　which is real even though infra-conceptual."

1428   Knapp, Joseph G. TORTURED SYNTHESIS: THE MEANING OF
        MELVILLE'S CLAREL. New York: Philosophical
        Library, 1971.

        Emphasis on "the negative pole of Melville's
        bipolar thought (though with hardly any reference
        to his other writing)," but suggests that Melville
        "finally accepted the orthodox Christian (Roman)
        position."

1429   Knapp, Joseph G. "Tortured Torturer of Reluctant Rhymes:
        Melville's CLAREL, an Interpretation of Post-Civil
        War America," DA, 24 (Minn.: 1963), 2035.

1430   Knapp, L. M. "The Naval Scenes in RODERICK RANDOM"
        PMLA, 49 (1934), 593-598.

1431   Knight, George Wilson. THE CHRISTIAN RENAISSANCE: WITH
        INTERPRETATIONS OF DANTE, SHAKESPEARE AND GOETHE
        AND NEW DISCUSSIONS OF OSCAR WILDE AND THE GOSPEL
        OF THOMAS. Toronto: Macmillan Company, 1933;
        London: Methuen & Co., Ltd., 1962, passim.

1432   Knight, Grant C. "Herman Melville," AMERICAN LITERATURE
        AND CULTURE. New York: Ray Long and Richard R.
        Smith, 1932, pp. 214-221.

1433   Knight, Grant C. THE STRENUOUS AGE IN AMERICAN LITERATURE.
        Chapel Hill: North Carolina University Press, 1954,
        passim.

1434   Knight, Karl F. "Melville's Variations of the Theme of
        Failure in BARTLEBY and BILLY BUDD," ArlQ, 2
        (Fall, 1969), 44-58.

        Parallels in Melville's writing of the 1850's.
        The two works appear "so remarkably similar that it is
        as if Melville had determined...to go back over the
        previous ground and make his point more tellingly."

1435   Knox, G. A. "Communication and Communion in Melville,"
        Ren, 9 (Autumn, 1956), 26-31.

1435.1 Knox, George. "Lost Command: BENITO CERENO Reconsidered,"
        Person, 40 (Summer, 1959), 280-291.

1436   Koerner, James D. "The Wake of the White Whale,"
        KM, 4 (1954), 42-50.

        Survey of scholarship and interpretation of
        MOBY DICK.

1437   Kohn, Hans. AMERICAN NATIONALISM: AN INTERPRETATIVE
        ESSAY. New York: The Macmillan Company, 1957,
        passim.

1438   Kolb, Harold H., Jr. THE ILLUSION OF LIFE: AMERICAN
        REALISM AS A LITERARY FORM. Charlottesville:
        Virginia University Press, 1969, passim.

1439   Kosok, Heinz. DIE BEDEUTUNG DER GOTHIC NOVEL FÜR DAS
        ERZÄHLWERK HERMAN MELVILLES. Diss. Marburg, 1962.

1440   Kosok, Heinz. DIE BEDEUTUNG DER GOTHIC NOVEL FÜR DAS
        ERZÄHLWERK HERMAN MELVILLES. Hamburg: Cram, de
        Gruyter & Co., 1963.

1441   Kosok, Heinz. "Ishmael's Audience in 'The Town Ho's
        Story,'" N&Q, 14 (1967), 54-56.

        Ishmael's narrative at Lima is "an abbreviated
        and simplified version" of the entire book; his
        listeners constitute "an image of Melville's reading
        public...."

1442   Kosok, Heinz. "Redburn's Image of Childhood," ESQ, 39
        (2nd Qt., 1965), 40-42.

        Melville's artistry seen in his reminiscences
        of the New York harbor, which helped his hero through
        a stage of inner development to acceptance of the
        world of adulthood.

1443   Kosok, Heinz. "'A sadder and a wiser boy': Herman
        Melville's REDBURN as Novel of Initiation," JA, 10
        (1965), 126-152.

1444   Kouwenhoven, John A. MADE IN AMERICA: THE ARTS IN
        MODERN CIVILIZATION. Introduction by Carl Van Doren,
        Garden City, New York: Doubleday & Company, Inc.,
        1948, pp. 131-132, 164-165.

        Rev., Richard E. Amacher, AL, 21 (1979), 131-132.

1445   Kramer, Aaron. MELVILLE'S POETRY: TOWARD THE ENLARGED
        HEART. Teaneck, New Jersey: Fairleigh-Dickinson
        University Press, 1972.

        A thematic study of three "ignored" poems:
        "Bridegroom Dick," "The Scout Toward Aldie," and
        "Marquis de Grandvin."

1446   Kramer, Aaron. THE PROPHETIC TRADITION IN AMERICAN
        POETRY, 1835-1900. Rutherford, Madison, Teaneck:
        Fairleigh Dickinson University Press, 1968, passim.

1446.1 Krause, Sydney J., ed. ESSAYS ON DETERMINISM IN AMERICAN
        LITERATURE. Kent, Ohio: Kent State University
        Press, 1964.

        Rev., by Harry Hayden Clark, *Criticism*, 8 (1966),
        300-302.

1447   Kreuter, Kent Kirby. "The Literary Response to Science,
        Technology and Industrialism: Studies in the Thought
        of Hawthorne, Melville, Whitman and Twain," DA, 24
        (Wis.: 1963), 2446.

1447.1 Kreymborg, Alfred, ed. LYRIC AMERICA: AN ANTHOLOGY OF
        AMERICAN POETRY (1630-1930). New York: Coward-
        McCann, Inc., 1930.

        Rev. by Robert Spiller, AL, 4 (1932), 220-222.

1448   Kriegel, Leonard. Introduction, LIFE AND REMARKABLE
        ADVENTURES OF ISRAEL POTTER. New York: Corinth
        Books, 1962.

        Source of Melville's work on ISRAEL POTTER.

1449   Krieger, Murray. "Melville's 'Enthusiast': The
        Perversion of Innocence," THE TRAGIC VISION:
        VARIATIONS ON A THEME IN LITERARY INTERPRETATION.
        New York: Holt, Rinehart & Winston, Inc., 1960;
        Chicago: Chicago University Press, 1960, pp. 257-
        260.

        Thematic significance of Ishmael's survival
        in context of the New Criticism.

1450   Krieger, Murray. THE PLAY AND PLACE OF CRITICISM.
        Baltimore: The Johns Hopkins Press, 1967, passim.

1451   Krim, Seymour. "What's *This* Cat's Story?" NoSav, 3
        (1961), 201-222.

        BARTLEBY

1451.1 Kronenberger, Louis, ed. NOVELISTS ON NOVELISTS: AN
        ANTHOLOGY. New York: Doubleday and Company,
        1962 (Anchor Books).

1452   Krutch, Joseph Wood. MORE LIVES THAN ONE. New York:
        William Sloane Associates, 1962.

1453   Krutch, Joseph Wood. "Taming Leviathan," <u>Nation</u>, 127
        (May 8, 1929), 561.

1454   Kühnelt, Harro H. "The Bell-Tower: Herman Melvilles
        Beitrag zur Roboterliteratur," WBEP, 66 (1958),
        139-157.

1455   Kühnelt, Harro H. "Der Humor in Melvilles MOBY DICK,"
        WBEP, 62 (1955), 111-121.

1456   Kühnelt, Harro H. "The Reception of Herman Melville's
        Works in Germany and Austria," INNSBRUCKER BEITRÄGE
        ZUR KULTURWISSENSCHAFT, 4 (1956), 111-121.

1457   Kulkarni, H.B. "Significance of Sacrifice in MOBY DICK,"
        IndRes (1969), 29-37.

1458   Kummer, George. "Herman Melville and the Ohio Press,"
        OSA&HQ, 45 (1936), 34-36.

        Newspaper notices of lectures.

1459   Kwiat, Joseph J., and Mary C. Turpie, eds. STUDIES IN
        AMERICAN CULTURE: DOMINANT IDEAS AND IMAGES.
        Minneapolis: Minnesota University Press, 1960,
        passim.

1460   Kyria, Pierre. "Begards sur la Littérature Américaine,"
        RdP, (March, 1968), 117-122.

        Survey of works of Melville and others as
        examples of the "Bible of Great Individualism" and
        of dissent.   o

1461   Lacy, Patricia. "The Agatha Theme in Melville's Stories,"
        UTSE, 35 (1956), 96-105.

1462   LaFrance, Marston, ed. PATTERNS OF COMMITMENT IN
        AMERICAN LITERATURE. Toronto: Published in
        Association with Carleton University of Toronto
        Press, 1967.

        Rev. by C. Carroll Hollis, AL, 40 (1969), 580-81.

1463   Lamont, E. H. <u>Athenaeum</u>, 2061 (April 27, 1867), 542.

1464　Lang, Hans-Joachim. "Ein Ärgerteufel bei Hawthorne und
　　　　Melville: Quellenuntersuchung zu THE CONFIDENCE-MAN,"
　　　　JA, 12 (1967), 246-251.

　　　　Hawthorne's "Seven Vagabonds" as source for
　　Melville's THE CONFIDENCE-MAN.

1465　Lang, Hans-Joachim. "Melville und Shakespeare,"
　　　　SHAKESPEARE: SEINE WELT--UNSERE WELT: RINGVORLESUNG
　　　　DER PHILOSOPHISCHEN FAKULTÄT DER UNIVERSITÄT
　　　　TÜBINGEN ZUM 400. GEBURTSTAG WILLIAM SHAKESPEARES.
　　　　Gerhard Müller-Schwefe, ed. Tübingen: Max Niemeyer,
　　　　1964, pp. 134-161.

1466　Lang, Hans-Joachim. "Melville's BILLY BUDD und seine
　　　　Quellen: Eine Nachlese," FESTSCHRIFT FÜR WALTHER
　　　　FISCHER. Heidelberg: Carl Winter, 1959, pp.
　　　　225-249.

1467　Lang, Hans-Joachim. "Melvilles Dialog mit Captain
　　　　Ringbolt," JA, 14 (1969), 124-139.

　　　　Melville's first book review dealt with J. Ross
　　Browne's ETCHINGS OF A WHALING CRUISE and Captain
　　Ringbolt's LIFE AND SAILOR YARNS. The former has been
　　examined as a source for Melville, the latter has not.
　　Ringbolt's book contains thirteen stories which may
　　have served as a source for Chapters 19 and 22 of
　　REDBURN.

1468　Langford, Richard E., Guy Owen, and William E. Taylor, eds.
　　　　ESSAYS IN MODERN AMERICAN LITERATURE. DeLand:
　　　　Stetson University Press, 1963, pp. 22-25.

　　　　BILLY BUDD.

1469　Lannon, Diedre. "A Note on Melville's BENITO CERENO,"
　　　　MSE, 2 (Spring, 1970), 68-70.

1470　Lanzinger, Klaus. DIE EPIK IM AMERIKANISCHEN ROMAN:
　　　　EINE STUDIE ZU JAMES F. COOPER, HERMAN MELVILLE,
　　　　FRANK NORRIS UND THOMAS WOLFE. (Studien zur
　　　　Sprache und Literatur Amerikas, 1). Frankfurt am
　　　　Main: Moritz Diesterweg, 1965.

　　　　MOBY DICK.

　　　　Rev. by George Hendrick, AL, 38 (1967), 561-562.

1471　Lanzinger, Klaus. "Melvilles Beschreibung des Meeres
　　　　in MARDI im Hinblick auf MOBY-DICK," NS, 9 (Jan.,
　　　　1960), 1-15.

1472   Lanzinger, Klaus, ed. "The Mystery of Melville's Short
         Stories," AMERICANA-AUSTRIACA. (Festschrift des
         Amerika-Instituts der Universität Innsbruck).
         Wien-Stuttgart: Wilhelm Braumüller, 1966, pp.
         204-216.

1473   Lanzinger, Klaus. PRIMITIVISMUS UND NATURALISMUS IM
         PROSASCHAFFEN HERMAN MELVILLES. Innsbruck:
         Universitatsuerlag Wagner, 1959.

         A biographical and critical study of Melville
         with some reference to naturalism and primitivism.

         Rev. by Henry A. Pochmann, AL, 32 (1960), 333-334.

1474   Larrabee, H. A. "Herman Melville's Early Years in Albany,"
         NYH, 15 (1934), 144-159.

1475   Larrabee, H. A. "Melville Against the World," SAQ, 34
         (1935), 410-418.

         The "aspirations, vanities, injustices, and
         failings" of the mid-nineteenth century are analyzed
         in MARDI.

1475.1   Larsen, Charles R. "MOBY-DICK, Circa 1972," CEA Critic,
         34 (May, 1972), 17-19.

         An irreverent commentary on the 20th century
         "relevance" of Melville's classic.

1476   Lash, Kenneth. "Captain Ahab and King Lear," NMQ, 19
         (Winter, 1949), 438-445.

1477   Laski, Harold J. THE AMERICAN DEMOCRACY: A COMMENTARY
         AND AN INTERPRETATION. New York: The Viking Press,
         1948, passim.

         References place Melville in his cultural and
         political milieu.

1477.1   Lasky, Melvin J. "America and Europe: Transatlantic
         Images," PATHS OF AMERICAN THOUGHT. Arthur M.
         Schlesinger, Jr., and Morton White, eds. London:
         Chatto & Windus, 1964, p. 475.

1478   Las Vergnas, Raymond. "Lettres Anglo-Américaines--Melville,"
         H&M, 6 (1951), 461-463.

1478.1   Lathers, Richard. THE REMINISCENCES OF RICHARD LATHERS.
         New York: The Grafton Press, 1907.

1479   Lathrop, George Parsons. A STUDY OF HAWTHORNE. Boston:
       James R. Osgood and Company, 1876. Repub.,
       Scholarly Press, Michigan, 1970, pp. 226, 230-231.

1480   Lathrop, Rose Hawthorne. MEMORIES OF HAWTHORNE. Boston:
       1897, passim.

1481   Lawall, Sarah N. CRITICS OF CONSCIOUSNESS: THE
       EXISTENTIAL STRUCTURES OF LITERATURE. Cambridge,
       Mass.: Harvard University Press, 1968, passim.

1482   Lawrence, D. H. "Herman Melville's MOBY-DICK," THE
       SYMBOLIC MEANING: THE UNCOLLECTED VERSIONS OF
       STUDIES IN CLASSIC AMERICAN LITERATURE. Armin
       Arnold, ed. Preface by Harry T. Moore. New York:
       Viking Press, 1961; With Introduction, Notes and
       Other Material, 1962, pp. 211-228.

1483   Lawrence, D. H. "Herman Melville's MOBY-DICK," STUDIES
       IN CLASSIC AMERICAN LITERATURE. New York: Seltzer,
       1923. Repr., Garden City, New York: Doubleday & Co.,
       1951, pp. 156-174.

1484   Lawrence, D. H. "Herman Melville's TYPEE and OMOO,"
       STUDIES IN CLASSIC AMERICAN LITERATURE. New York:
       Seltzer, 1923. Repr., Garden City, New York:
       Doubleday & Co., 1951, pp. 142-156.

1485   Lawrence, D. H. "Herman Melville's TYPEE and OMOO,"
       THE SYMBOLIC MEANING: THE UNCOLLECTED VERSIONS
       OF STUDIES IN CLASSIC AMERICAN LITERATURE. Armin
       Arnold, ed. New York: Viking Press, 1962, pp. 197-
       209.

1486   Lawrence, D. H. THE LETTERS OF D. H. LAWRENCE.
       Aldous Huxley, ed. New York: The Viking Press,
       1936, p. 322.

1487   Lawrence, Thomas Edward. THE LETTERS OF THOMAS EDWARD
       LAWRENCE. David Garnett, ed. London: Jonathan
       Cape, Ltd., 1938; New York: Doubleday & Company,
       Inc., 1938.

1488   Lawson, John Howard. THE HIDDEN HERITAGE. New York:
       Citadel Press, 1950, pp. 427-432.

       BENITO CERENO.

1489   Leaf, M. "MOBY-DICK by Herman Melville," Am, 131 (1941),
       58.

1490   Leary, Lewis. "Doctoral Dissertations in American
          Literature, 1933-1948," AL, 20 (1948-1949), 182-183.

1490.1   Leary, Lewis, ed. "Hawthorne and His Mosses," AMERICAN
          LITERARY ESSAYS. Reader's Bookshelf of American
          Literature. New York: Crowell, 1960, pp. 90-92.

1491   Leary, Lewis, comp. "Herman Melville," ARTICLES ON
          AMERICAN LITERATURE, 1900-1950. Durham, North
          Carolina: Duke University Press, 1954.

          Rev. by Nelson F. Adkins, AL, 27 (1955), 449-450.

1492   Leary, Lewis, comp., with assistance of Carolyn Bartholet
          and Catharine Roth. "Herman Melville," ARTICLES ON
          AMERICAN LITERATURE, 1950-1967. Durham, North
          Carolina: Duke University Press, 1970, pp. 367-390.

1493   Leary, Lewis. Introduction, HIS FIFTY YEARS OF EXILE.
          (ISRAEL POTTER). New York: Sagamore Press, 1957.

1494   Leary, Lewis. "An Introduction: Somewhat Personal,"
          CRITICISM: SOME MAJOR AMERICAN WRITERS. Selected
          by Lewis Leary. New York: Holt, Rinehart and Winston,
          Inc., 1971.

1494.1   Leary, Lewis, ed. Introduction, THE TEACHER AND AMERICAN
          LITERATURE: PAPERS PRESENTED AT THE 1964 CONVENTION
          OF THE NATIONAL COUNCIL OF TEACHERS OF ENGLISH.
          Champaign, Illinois: National Council of Teachers
          of English, 1965.

1495   Lease, Benjamin. "The Chemistry of Genius: Herman
          Melville and Anton Bruckner," Person, 48 (Spring,
          1967), 224-241.

1496   Lease, Benjamin. "Melville and the Booksellers,"
          MSN, 7 (June, 1951), 2.

1497   Lease, Benjamin. "Melville's Gally, Gallow," AS, 25
          (October, 1950), 186.

          A lexical Melvillean note in the British edition
          of THE WHALE, (London, 1851), III, 9-10.

1498   Lease, Benjamin. "Two Sides to a Tortoise: Darwin and
          Melville in the Pacific," Person, 49 (1968), 531-539.

1499   Leavitt, Hart D., ed. BILLY BUDD, FORETOPMAN. New York:
          Bantam, 1965.

1500   Lebowitz, Alan. HERMAN MELVILLE'S AHAB: THE EVOLUTION
        AND EXTINCTION OF THE HERO. Diss. Harvard: 1964.

1501   Lebowitz, Alan. PROGRESS INTO SILENCE: A STUDY OF
        MELVILLE'S HEROES. Bloomington: Indiana University
        Press, 1970.

        Rev. by Hennig Cohen, AL, 43 (1971), 453-454;
        Robert C. Ryan, Sym, 10 (1971), 230-240.

1502   Ledbetter, Kenneth. "The Ambiguity of BILLY BUDD,"
        TSLL, 4 (Spring, 1962), 130-134.

1503   Leeson, Ida. "Mutiny on the LUCY ANN," PQ, 19 (1940),
        370-379.

        OMOO.

1504   Lefcowitz, Allan, and Barbara Lefcowitz. "Ahab's
        Other Leg: Notes on Melville's Symbolic Method,"
        ESQ, 47 (2nd Qt., 1967), 23-28.

        The leg's symbolic pattern suggests that Melville's
        methodology encompasses various phases. From a mere
        token, the leg is enriched until it becomes a symbol
        of "limitation, dependence, death, and the material-
        idealist paradox...."

1505   Leisy, Ernest E. "Fatalism in MOBY DICK," MOBY DICK
        CENTENNIAL ESSAYS. Tyrus Hillway and Luther S.
        Mansfield, eds. Dallas: Southern Methodist
        University Press, 1953, pp. 76-88.

1506   Leisy, Ernest E. "Herman Melville," AMERICAN LITERATURE:
        AN INTERPRETATIVE SURVEY. New York: Thomas Y. Crowell
        Company, 1929, pp. 102-105, passim.

1507   Leisy, Ernest E. THE AMERICAN HISTORICAL NOVEL. Norman,
        Oklahoma: Oklahoma University Press, 1950, p. 96.

        Rev. by Kenneth B. Murdock, AL, 22 (1950), 527-528.

1508   Leiter, Louis. "Queequeg's Coffin," NCF, 13 (December,
        1958), 249-254.

1509   Lemon, Lee T. "BILLY BUDD: The Plot Against the Story,"
        SSF, 2 (Fall, 1964), 32-43.

        Repr., in LITERATURE IN CRITICAL PERSPECTIVES.
        Walter K. Gordon, ed. New York: Appleton-Century-
        Crofts, 1968, pp. 723-731.

        Thematic implications of the plot often oppose
        those of the story. Sympathy is clearly with Billy
        and against society, but Billy is truly culpable in not
        effectively protecting society. Billy is "irresponsible,
        and also not responsible--in the sense in which children
        and feeble-minded persons are not responsible."

1510   Leonard, Sterling Andrus. Introduction, TYPEE. New York:
        1920.

1511   Lerner, Max. AMERICA AS A CIVILIZATION: LIFE AND
        THOUGHT IN THE UNITED STATES TODAY. New York:
        Simon and Schuster, 1957, passim.

1512   Lesser, Simon O. FICTION AND THE UNCONSCIOUS. Boston:
        Beacon Press, 1957, pp. 92-93.

        A psychological reading of BILLY BUDD.

1513   Levereng, David. "MOBY DICK," PSYCHOANALYSIS AND
        LITERARY PROCESS. Frederick C. Crews, ed. Cambridge,
        Mass.: Winthrop Pubs., Inc., 1970, pp. 66-117.

1514   Levin, Gerald. "BARTLEBY THE SCRIVENER," THE SHORT
        STORY: AN INDUCTIVE APPROACH. New York:
        Harcourt, Brace, and World, 1967, pp. 229-230.

1515   Levin, Harry. CONTEXTS OF CRITICISM. Cambridge: Harvard
        University Press, 1957, pp. 97-109, 203-206.

        MOBY DICK.

1516   Levin, Harry. "DON QUIXOTE and MOBY DICK," CERVANTES
        ACROSS THE CENTURIES. Angel Flores and M. J.
        Bernardete, eds. New York: Dryden Press, 1947,
        pp. 217-226.

        DON QUIXOTE a complementary and not a major
        influence.

1517   Levin, Harry. "Don Quijote y Moby-Dick," Realidad, 2
        (1947), 254-267.

1518   Levin, Harry. LEARNERS AND DISCERNERS. Robert Scholes,
        ed. Charlottesville: Virginia University Press,
        1964, passim.

        The four-fold scheme of interpretation, suggested
        by Dante: the literal, the allegorical, the moral, and
        the anagogical, applied to MOBY DICK.

1519   Levin, Harry. THE MYTH OF THE GOLDEN AGE IN THE
        RENAISSANCE. Bloomington: Indiana University
        Press, 1969, passim.

        Early Christian theologians dated the loss of
        paradise from the "creation of woman." This would
        perhaps accord with Melville's "Paradise of Bachelors"
        which he situated, not on Tahiti or in the Marquesas,
        but in the masculine society of the Temple at London.

1520   Levin, Harry. THE POWER OF BLACKNESS: HAWTHORNE, POE,
        AND MELVILLE. New York: Alfred A. Knopf, 1958.

        Hawthorne's "power of blackness" which fascinated
        Melville was a power which "derives its force from its
        appeals to that Calvinistic sense of Innate Depravity
        and Original Sin...."

        Rev. by Newton Arvin, AL, 30 (1958), 380-381;
        Richard H. Fogle, NCF, 13 (1958), 167-170.

1521   Levin, Harry. REFRACTIONS: ESSAYS IN COMPARATIVE
        LITERATURE. New York: Oxford University Press,
        1966, p. 202, passim.

        The Cenci portrait was a "crucial link in the
        tenuous chain" that bound Hawthorne and Melville
        together, "an emblem of that sense of guilt for the
        world's corruption which they seem to have momentarily
        shared...."

1522   Levin, Harry. "Some European Views of Contemporary
        American Literature," THE AMERICAN WRITER AND
        THE EUROPEAN TRADITION. Margaret Denny and
        William H. Gilman, eds. Minneapolis: Minnesota
        University Press, 1950, pp. 168-183, passim.

        "...What is commonly regarded as peculiarly
        American is blatant and standardized...What is most
        original is most traditional: Melville."

1523   Levin, Harry. SYMBOLISM AND FICTION. Charlottesville:
         Virginia University Press, 1956, passim.

         Relationship between literal and symbolic
         meanings with examples from MOBY DICK.

1524   Levine, Stuart. "Melville's 'Voyage Thither,'" MQ, 3
         (Summer, 1962), 341-353.

1525   Le Vot, André. "Shakespeare et Melville: Le thème
         impérial dans MOBY DICK," EA, 17 (1964), 549-563.

1526   Levy, Leo. B. "Criticism Chronicle: Hawthorne, Melville,
         and James," SoR, 2 (1966), 427-442.

1527   Levy, Leo B. "Hawthorne and the Idea of 'Bartleby,'"
         ESQ, 47 (2nd Qt., 1967), 66-69.

         Melville's interest in the theme of "patient
         submission" shown in his "Agatha" correspondence with
         Hawthorne and in his characterizations of Bartleby and
         Hunilla. Also, common elements between Melville's
         story and Hawthorne's "The Old Apple Dealer."

1528   Levy, Leo B. "Hawthorne, Melville, and the Monitor,"
         AL, 37 (March, 1965), 33-40.

         Parallels between Melville's poems about the
         warship and Hawthorne's 1862 Atlantic essay, "Chiefly
         About War Matters," indicate the two men were thinking
         about the increasing mechanization of American life and
         the implications of the kind of warfare which the
         Monitor's engagement introduced.

1529   Lewes, George Henry. "Herman Melville--THE WHALE: OR
         MOBY DICK," LITERARY CRITICISM OF GEORGE HENRY
         LEWES. Alice R. Kaminsky, ed. Lincoln: Nebraska
         University Press, 1964, pp. 106-107.

1530   Lewin, Bruno. "Literarische Begegnungen Zwischen
         Amerika und Japan," JA, 14 (1969), 25-39.

         The first reference to Japan in American
         literature is made in Melville's MOBY DICK.

1531   Lewis, R. W. B. Afterword, THE CONFIDENCE MAN. New York:
        Signet, 1964, pp. 261-276.

1531.1 Lewis, R. W. B. "Baffling, Perverse, Demonic, Original,"
        NYHTBR, October 11, 1959, p. 5.

        Comparison of Malcolm of James Purdy's MALCOLM
        with Melville's Billy Budd.

1532   Lewis, R. W. B. "Crane's Visionary Lyric: The Way to
        the Bridge," MR, 7 (Spring, 1966), 227-253.

        Comparison of Hart Crane with Melville.

1532.1 Lewis, R. W. B. "Goneril and the Man with Gold Sleeve-
        Buttons: The Prose in Chapters 12 and 7," THE
        CONFIDENCE MAN: HIS MASQUERADE. Hershel Parker, ed.
        New York: W. W. Norton & Co., 1971, pp. 320-321.

1533   Lewis, R. W. B., ed. Introduction, HERMAN MELVILLE:
        STORIES, POEMS, AND LETTERS BY THE AUTHOR OF
        MOBY DICK. New York: Dell, 1962 (A Laurel Reader).

1534   Lewis, R. W. B. "Melville: The Apotheosis of Adam,"
        THE AMERICAN ADAM: INNOCENCE, TRAGEDY, AND TRADITION
        IN THE NINETEENTH CENTURY. Chicago: Chicago
        University Press, 1955, pp. 127-155.

        Rev. by Henry Nash Smith, AL, 28 (1956-57), 390-92.

1534.1 Lewis, R. W. B. "Melville: The Apotheosis of Adam,"
        THE MODERN CRITICAL SPECTRUM. G. J. Goldberg and
        N. M. Goldberg, eds. Englewood Cliffs, New Jersey:
        Prentice-Hall, 1962, pp. 321-341.

1535   Lewis, R. W. B. "Melville After MOBY-DICK," TRIALS OF
        THE WORD: ESSAYS IN AMERICAN LITERATURE AND THE
        HUMANISTIC TRADITION. New Haven: Yale University
        Press, 1965, pp. 36-76, passim.

1536   Lewis, R. W. B. "Melville on Homer," AL, 22 (1950),
        166-176.

        Melville as a reader of Homer.

1536.1 Lewis, Sinclair. "The American Fear of Literature,"
NOBEL LECTURES, INCLUDING PRESENTATION SPEECHES
AND LAUREATES' BIOGRAPHIES - LITERATURE - 1901-
1967. Horst Frenz, ed. Amsterdam, London, New
York: Published for the Novel Foundation by
Elsevier Publishing Company, 1969, pp. 278-289.

There were "surly and authentic fellows,"
Whitman and Melville, as well as others, who insisted
that our land had something more than "tea-table
gentility."

1537 Lewisohn, Ludwig. EXPRESSION IN AMERICA. New York:
Harper, 1932, pp. 186-193. Repr. as THE STORY OF
AMERICAN LITERATURE. New York: Modern Library,
1939, pp. 153-193.

Cf., Louis Fraiberg. PSYCHOANALYSIS AND AMERICAN
LITERARY CRITICISM. Detroit: Wayne State University
Press, 1960, p. 152ff.

1538 Leyda, Jay. "An Albany Journal by Gansevoort Melville,"
BPLQ, 2 (October, 1950), 328-329.

The manuscript journal kept by Gansevoort Melville
was inherited by the Misses Agnes, Helen, and Margaret
Morewood, grandnieces of Gansevoort and Herman Melville.

1539 Leyda, Jay. "Another Friendly Critic for Melville,"
NEQ, 27 (June, 1954), 243-249.

The Springfield Republican provided "fuller and
more careful" notices of Melville's works.

1540 Leyda, Jay. "The Army of the Potomac Entertains a Poet,"
A&A, 16 (1948), 259-272.

1541 Leyda, Jay. "Bartleby: Genesis of an Opera 2,"
MELVILLE ANNUAL 1965, A SYMPOSIUM: BARTLEBY THE
SCRIVENER. Kent Stud. in Eng., III. Kent, Ohio:
Kent State University Press, 1966, pp. 42-44.

1542 Leyda, Jay, ed. Introduction, THE COMPLETE STORIES OF
HERMAN MELVILLE. Now York: Random House, 1949.

A brief critical introduction and notes provide
data as to dates and circumstances of publication of
fifteen "short" stories.

Rev. by Perry Miller, NEQ, 22 (1949), 558.

1543   Leyda, Jay, ed. Introduction, THE PORTABLE MELVILLE.
New York: The Viking Press, 1952; Macmillan, 1969.

1544   Leyda, Jay. "Ishmael Melville: Remarks on Board Ship
Amazon," BPLQ, 1 (1949), 119-134.

Melville's cousin Thomas as model for Ishmael.

1545   Leyda, Jay. THE MELVILLE LOG: A DOCUMENTARY LIFE OF
HERMAN MELVILLE, 1819-1891. 2 vols. New York:
Harcourt, Brace, and Company, 1951. Repr. with
new supplement, New York: Gordian Press, 1969.

Rev. by William Braswell, AL, 24 (1952), 245-247.

1546   Leyda, Jay. "White Elephant vs. White Whale," T&C,
101 (August, 1947), 68ff.

1547   Leyris, Pierre, trans. COCORICOL ET AUTRES CONTES.
Paris: Gallimard, 1954.

1548   Libman, Valentina A., comp. "Melville," RUSSIAN STUDIES
OF AMERICAN LITERATURE: A BIBLIOGRAPHY. Robert
V. Allen, trans. Clarence Gohdes, ed. Chapel Hill:
North Carolina University Press, 1969, pp. 136-137.

Contains eight studies of Melville.

1549   Lid, R. W., ed. Instructor's Manual for THE SHORT STORY:
CLASSIC AND CONTEMPORARY. New York: J. B. Lippincott,
1967, pp. 32-35.

"Norfolk Isle and the Chola Widow."

1549.1 Lieber, Todd M. ENDLESS EXPERIMENTS. ESSAYS ON THE
HEROIC EXPERIENCE IN AMERICAN ROMANTICISM.
Columbus: Ohio State University Press, 1972,
passim.

The "ideal" tendencies for study of philosophical
and religious tensions of Romanticism found in the
writings of Melville and others, which link them to
modernists such as Williams and Stevens.

1550   Liebman, Sheldon W. "The 'Body and Soul' Metaphor in
MOBY-DICK," ESQ, Sup. 50 (1st Qt., 1968), 29-34.

The antagonism between body and soul, and the
paradoxes involved in the extension of these metaphors,
are reconciled in the sexual metaphor.

1551   Lindeman, Jack. "Herman Melville's Civil War," ModA,
         9 (Fall, 1965), 387-398.

           Melville's BATTLE-PIECES, mostly written after the
war, and the most vividly pictorial poems of the Civil
War, are the first poems in English to make "conscious
use of military technology."

1552   Lineman, Jack. "Herman Melville's Reconstruction,"
         ModA, 10 (Spring, 1966), 168-172.

           A number of Melville's BATTLE-PIECES (1866),
though primarily war poetry, are a plea for a justly
sane and charitable "reconstruction."

1553   Lish, Terrence G. "Melville's REDBURN: A Study in
         Dualism," ELN, 5 (December, 1967), 113-120.

           Redburn and Bolton are opposites--Redburn aloof,
inexperienced, innocent, never baptized into humanity,
Bolton outcast, yet generous and friendly. Redburn,
through Melville's heavy stress of dualism, defeats
himself and deserves the reader's contempt.

1554   Litman, Vicki H. "The Cottage and the Temple: Melville's
         Symbolic Use of Architecture," AQ, 21 (1969), 630-
         638.

           A survey, particularly of short stories, in light
of contemporary architectural theories such as those of
Andrew Jackson Downing, which established the farmhouse
and the temple as architectural ideals. Melville's own
"dystopian view of earthly possibilities," meant that
few, if any, perfect structures would appear in his
writing.

1555   Little, Thomas A. THE USE OF ALLUSION IN THE WRITINGS OF
         HERMAN MELVILLE. Diss. Nebraska: 1950.

1556   Lloyd Francis V., Jr. "A Further Note on Herman Melville,
         Lecturer," MHSB, 20 (July, 1964), 310-312.

           An invitation to lecture was extended by the
Mercantile Library Association of St. Louis. It is
not known whether Melville sent a reply.

1557   Lloyd, Francis V., Jr. "Melville's First Lectures,"
         AL, 13 (January, 1942), 391-395.

           Lectures in Lawrence, Mass., November 23, and
in Concord, New Hampshire, November 24, 1857, were
not successful.

1558   Lloyd, Francis V., Jr. "Melville's MOBY DICK," <u>Expl</u>, 29 (May, 1971), Item 72.

Argument as to whether it was the right or left leg of Ahab which was made of ivory. The Rockwell Kent illustrated edition shows three pictures of the left leg as ivory, but evidence in the story indicates it was the <u>right</u>.

1559   Lockerbie, D. Bruce. "The Greatest Sermon in Fiction," ChT, 8 (November 8, 1963), 9-12.

Father Mapple's sermon.

1560   Lodge, David. LANGUAGE OF FICTION: ESSAYS IN CRITICISM AND VERBAL ANALYSIS OF THE ENGLISH NOVEL. London: Routledge and Kegan Paul; New York: Columbia University Press, 1966, pp. 59-60.

Cf., Michael Riffaterre, "Criteria for Style Analysis," <u>Word</u>, 15 (1959), 172.

1561   Logan, John. "Psychological Motifs in Melville's PIERRE," MinnR, 7 (1967), 325-330.

The story is more melodramatic than tragic because Pierre "undergoes no <u>anagnorisis</u>, no self-understanding."

1561.1 Logasa, Hannah, comp. HISTORICAL FICTION: GUIDE FOR JUNIOR AND SENIOR HIGH SCHOOLS AND COLLEGES: ALSO FOR GENERAL READER. 9th rev. and enlarged edition. Brooklawn, New Jersey: McKinley Publishing Co., 1968, p. 319.

1561.2 Logasa, Hannah, comp. "Herman Melville," HISTORICAL FICTION AND OTHER READING REFERENCES FOR CLASSES IN JUNIOR AND SENIOR HIGH SCHOOLS AND COLLEGES. 6th rev. and enlarged edition. Philadelphia: McKinley Publishing Co., 1958, p. 214.

1562   Lombard, C. M. "The First American Salon," EA, 19 (January-March, 1966), 26-36.

Anne Charlotte Lynch Botta, known to many American writers, including Melville, frequently held literary soirees in her home in New York.

1563   Lombardi, Olga. "Il Mito Dell'America," NA, 508, 2030
        (February, 1970), 274-280.

        Rev-article of Dominique Fernandez, IL MITO
        DELL'AMERICA NEGLI INTELLETTUALI ITALIANI, A. Bocelli, ed.

1564   Lombardo, Agostino. "Introduzione a Melville," SA, 3
        (1957), 29-61.

1565   Lombardo, Agostino, ed. "Italian Criticism of American
        Literature: An Anthology," SR, 68 (July, 1960),
        353-515.

        Critical essays outlining Italian views of
        American writers including Melville.

1566   Lombardo, Agostino. "A Review of Gabriele Baldini's
        MELVILLE O LE AMBIGUITÀ," Sp-ital, 6 (June, 1953),
        275-278.

1567   Lombardo, Agostino. LA RICERCA DEL VERO: SAGGI SULLA
        TRADIZIONE LETTERARIA AMERICANA. Roma: Ed. di
        storia e letteratura, 1961.

1568   London Athenaeum, October 25, 1851.

        "...his interchapter on 'The Whiteness of the
        Whale' is full of ghostly suggestions for which a
        Maturin or a Monk Lewis would have been thankful.
        Mr. Melville has to thank himself only if his
        horrors and his heroics are flung aside by the
        general reader, as so much trash belonging to the
        worst school of Bedlam literature,...."

1569   London Atlas, November 1, 1851.

        "...the book before us /MOBY DICK/ offers no
        exception to the general rule which more or less applies
        to all Mr. Melville's fictions....Extravagance is the
        bane of the book, and the stumbling block of the author.
        He allows his fancy not only to run riot, but absolutely
        to run amuck, in which poor defenceless Common Sense is
        hustled and belaboured in a manner melancholy to
        contemplate...."

1570   London <u>Britannia</u>, November 8, 1851.

"THE WHALE is a most extraordinary work. There
is so much eccentricity in its style and in its con-
struction, in the original conception and in the
gradual development of its strange and improbable
story, that we are at a loss to determine in what
category of works of amusement to place it. It is
certainly neither a novel nor a romance, although it
is made to drag its weary length through three closely
printed volumes...."

1571   London <u>Leader</u>, November 8, 1851.

"...THE WHALE—Melville's last book—is a strange,
wild, weird book, full of poetry and full of interest.
To use a hackneyed phrase, it is indeed 'refreshing' to
quit the old wornout pathways of romance, and feel the
sea breezes playing through our hair, the salt spray
dashing on our brows, as we do here...."

1572   London <u>Morning Post</u>, November 14, 1851.

"There is much that is incredible...in this
latest effort /MOBY DICK/ of Mr. Melville's wayward
and romantic pen; but despite its occasional extrava-
gancies, it is a book of extraordinary merit....So
surprising are many of the adventures recorded...that
there are occasions when the reader is disposed to
believe that the whole book is one vast practical
joke. We are half inclined to believe that the author
is humbugging us,...but the spell of genius is upon
us, and we are powerless to resist...."

1573   London, Jack. CRUISE OF THE <u>SNARK</u>. New York: Harper
        & Bros., 1908; New York: The Regent Press, 1911,
        pp. 137-138.

Jack London told of reading TYPEE about 1886
which stirred in him a desire to go to Typee Valley,
as indeed he did, only to find the Marquesans sadly
degenerated.

1574   London, Jack. LETTERS FROM JACK LONDON. CONTAINING
        UNPUBLISHED CORRESPONDENCE BETWEEN LONDON AND
        SINCLAIR LEWIS. King Hendricks and Irving
        Shepard, eds. New York: The Odyssey Press,
        1965, pp. 255-256.

Letter to George P. Brett, January 16, 1908,
in which Jack London described the "historic valley"
of Typee—Melville's Typee—which he had visited.

1575 London, Jack. "Typee," <u>Pacific Monthly Magazine</u>,
    March, 1910.

    "'Taipi,' the chart spelled it, and spelled it
   correctly, but I prefer 'Typee,'....When I was a little
   boy I read a book spelled in that manner--Herman
   Melville's TYPEE; and many long hours I dreamed over
   its pages. Nor was it all dreaming. I resolved there
   and then, mightily come what would, that when I had
   gained strength and years I, too, would voyage to
   Typee....The years passed, but Typee was not forgotten."

1576 London, Philip W. "The Military Necessity: 'BILLY
    BUDD' and Vigny," CL, 14 (Spring, 1962), 174-186.

    Alfred de Vigny's SERVITUDE ET GRANDEUR
  MILITAIRES (1835) and BILLY BUDD compared.

1577 Long, Raymond. "The Hidden Sun: A Study of the
    Influence of Shakespeare on the Creative Imagination
    of Herman Melville," DA, 26 (U. C. L. A.: 1966),
    4634.

1578 Long, Raymond. THE HIDDEN SUN: A STUDY OF THE INFLUENCE
    OF SHAKESPEARE ON THE WRITINGS OF HERMAN MELVILLE.
    Los Angeles, Calif.: 1963.

1578.1 Long, William J. AMERICAN LITERATURE: A STUDY OF THE MEN
    AND THE BOOKS THAT IN THE EARLIER AND LATER TIMES
    REFLECT THE AMERICAN SPIRIT. Waltham, Mass.:
    Blaisdell Publishing Company, 1913, p. 247.

1578.2 Long, William J. OUTLINES OF ENGLISH AND AMERICAN
    LITERATURE. New York: Ginn & Co., 1917, pp. 399,
    500.

    In Melville, "we have an echo of Carlyle,...who
  affected Melville so strongly that the latter soon lost
  his bluff, hearty, sailor fashion of writing, which
  everybody liked, and assumed a crotchety style that
  nobody cared to read.

1579 Love, Gladys E., and Lillian C. West. "Melville and
    His Public," AN&Q, 2 (1942), 67-71.

1580 Lovette, Leland P., Lt. Commander, U. S. Navy. NAVAL
    CUSTOMS: TRADITION AND USAGE. United States Naval
    Institute, Annapolis, Maryland, 1939, passim.

    References to Melville's descriptions of life on
  naval vessels.

1581   Lowance, Mason I., Jr. "Veils and Illusions in BENITO
      CERENO," ArQ, 26 (Summer, 1970), 113-126.

1582   Lowell, James Russell. Letter to Charles F. Briggs.
      Putnam's Monthly Magazine (May 12, 1854).

      Lowell commented in his letter to Charles F.
Briggs that "the figure of the cross in the ass' neck
brought tears into his eyes, and he thought it the
finest touch of genius he had seen in prose." (THE
ENCANTADAS).

1583   Lowell, Robert. THE OLD GLORY. New York: Farrar, Straus
      & Giroux, 1965, 1968; London: Faber, 1966.

      Rev. ed., theater trilogy based on two stories
by Hawthorne and Melville's BENITO CERENO.

1584   Lowry, Malcolm. SELECTED LETTERS OF MALCOLM LOWRY.
      Harvey Breit and Margerie Bonner Lowry, eds.
      Philadelphia: J. B. Lippincott Company, 1965,
      pp. 197-199.

      Malcolm Lowry to Derek Pethick, March 6, 1950,
comparing Lowry's UNDER THE VOLCANO with MOBY DICK.

1585   Lowry, Thomas C. F. "Melville's MOBY DICK, XXXI,"
      Expl. 16 (January, 1958), Item 22.

1586   Lucas, F. L. "Herman Melville," NStm, 18 (April 1,
      1922), 730-731.

1587   Lucas, F. L. "Herman Melville," AUTHORS DEAD AND
      LIVING. London: Chatto and Windus, 1926, pp.
      105-114; New York: 1935, pp. 105-114.

1588   Lucas, Thomas Edward. "Herman Melville as Literary
      Theorist," DA, 24 (Denver: 1963), 2015.

1589   Luccock, Halford E. AMERICAN MIRROR: SOCIAL, ETHICAL
      AND RELIGIOUS ASPECTS OF AMERICAN LITERATURE, 1930-
      1940. New York: The Macmillan Company, 1940,
      passim.

1589.1   Lucett, Edward. ROVINGS IN THE PACIFIC FROM 1837 to
      1849 WITH A GLANCE AT CALIFORNIA. London: 1851.

1590   Lucid, R. F. "The Influence of TWO YEARS BEFORE THE MAST on Herman Melville," AL, 31 (November, 1959), 243-256.

1591   Lüdeke, Henry. GESCHICHTE DER AMERIKANISCHEN LITERATUR. Bern: A Francke Verlag, 1952.

Rev. by Ernest E. Leisy, AL, 25 (1953-54), 124.

1591.1 Ludwig, Jack Barry, and W. Richard Poirier. INSTRUCTOR'S MANUAL TO ACCOMPANY "STORIES: BRITISH AND AMERICAN." Boston: Houghton Mifflin, 1953, pp. 6-8.

BARTLEBY.

1592   Lueders, Edward G. "The Melville-Hawthorne Relationship in PIERRE and THE BLITHEDALE ROMANCE," WHR, 4 (Autumn, 1950), 323-334.

1592.1 Lukens, Henry Clay. "American Literary Comedians," Harpers (April, 1890).

Melville listed among the humorists of minor rank.

1593   Lundkvist, Artur. "Herman Melville," BLM, 11 (December, 1942), 773-786.

1594   Lunt, Dudley C. THE ROAD TO THE LAW. New York: Norton, 1965, pp. 14-15.

Melville's use of law in Chapter 89, "Fast-Fish and Loose-Fish."

1595   Lutwack, Leonard. "Herman Melville and ATLANTIC MONTHLY Critics," HLQ, 13 (August, 1950), 414-416.

1596   Lutwack, Leonard. HEROIC FICTION: THE EPIC TRADITION AND AMERICAN NOVELS OF THE TWENTIETH CENTURY. Southern Illinois University Press, 1971.

Early attempts at the American epic by American writers including Melville.

1597   Lutwack, Leonard. "Melville's Struggle with Style: The Plain, the Ornate, the Reflective," ForumH, 3 (Spring-Summer, 1962), 11-17.

1597.1   Lydenberg, John. "Emerson and the Dark Tradition,"
         CritQ, 4 (Winter, 1962), 352-358.

1598   Lynd, Richard. "Melville's Success in 'The Happy
         Failure': A Story of the River Hudson," CLAJ, 13
         (December, 1969), 119-130.

1599   Lynd, Robert. "Learned Sailorman," BOOKS AND WRITERS.
         Foreword by Richard Church. New York: Dent, 1952,
         pp. 142-146.

1600   Lynn, Kenneth S., ed. "Herman Melville," THE COMIC
         TRADITION IN AMERICA. New York: Doubleday, 1958,
         pp. 258-261.

1601   Lynn, Kenneth S., ed. "Herman Melville - 'Nantucket' -
         'Ethan Allen,'" THE AMERICAN SOCIETY. New York:
         George Braziller, 1963, pp. 83-87.

1602   Mabbott, Thomas O. "Herman Melville," N&Q, 162 (1932),
         151-152.

         A letter from Melville to Dr. William Sprague.

1603   Mabbott, Thomas O. "A Letter of Herman Melville,"
         N&Q, 176 (January, 1939), 60.

         Reprint of a letter of Melville, November 27,
   1857.

1604   Mabbott, Thomas O. "Melville's MOBY-DICK," Expl, 8
         (November, 1949), Item 15.

1605   Mabbott, Thomas O. "Melville's 'A Railroad Cutting Near
         Alexandria in 1855,'" Expl, 9 (June, 1951), Item 55.

         Poetry.

1606   Mabbott, Thomas O. "Poem by Herman Melville," N&Q, 149
         (July 18, 1925), 42-43.

1607   Mabbott, Thomas O. "A Source for the Conclusion of
         Melville's MOBY DICK," N&Q, 181 (July 26, 1941),
         47-48.

         A possible source, Robert Southey's COMMONPLACE
   BOOK, First Series, or direct from Southey's source,
   the Eastern Voyages of Johann Albrecht Mandelslo in
   1638-1640.

         Cf., Charles Duffy, "A Source for the Conclusion
   of Melville's MOBY DICK," N&Q, 181 (November 15, 1941),
   278-279.

1608   MacDonald, Allan. "A Sailor among the Transcendentalists,"
        NEQ, 8 (1935), 307-319.

        The original of Father Mapple.

1609   Macgowan, Kenneth. BEHIND THE SCREEN: THE HISTORY AND
        TECHNIQUES OF THE MOTION PICTURE. New York:
        A Delacorte Press Book, 1965, pp. 326, 342.

        The single year of 1956 saw the movie industry
        reach what then looked like the "peak of extravagance."
        Among the expensive films was MOBY DICK costing more
        than $5,000,000.

        After the war there were some eight or ten films
        without women or love stories, among them MOBY DICK
        (1956).

1610   MacIver, R. M., ed. GREAT MORAL DILEMMAS IN LITERATURE:
        PAST AND PRESENT. New York: Harper, 1956.

1611   MacLeish, Archibald. "A New Life of Melville," Bookman,
        69 (1929), 183-185.

        A review-article of Lewis Mumford's HERMAN MELVILLE.

1612   MacMechan, Archibald. "The Best Sea-Story Ever Written,"
        QQ, 7 (1899), 120-130.

        Article also in HumR, 7 (1901), 242-252.

            "One striking peculiarity of the book /MOBY DICK/
        is its Americanism....The theme and style are peculiar
        to this country. Nowhere but in America could such a
        theme have been treated in such a style...."

1613   MacMechan, Archibald. "The Best Sea Story Ever Written,"
        THE LIFE OF A LITTLE COLLEGE. Boston: Houghton
        Mifflin, 1914, pp. 179-198.

            Cf., Michael Zimmerman, "Herman Melville in the
        1920's," Part II, BB, 24 (January-April, 1965), 141.
        "...The fourth revival occurred in 1914 with Archibald
        MacMechan's 'Herman Melville.'"

1613.1 MacMechan, Archibald. Letter from Archibald MacMechan
        to Melville, from Halifax, Nova Scotia, December 23,
        1889.

            "...It is too much to ask you to correspond but
        I hope to do myself the pleasure of calling on you in
        New York in the spring months,.... I have enjoyed your
        books so much and, having had at least one adventure
        like 'Redburn,' I feel certain we should be at once
        on common ground." (Eleanor Melville Metcalf, HERMAN
        MELVILLE: CYCLE AND EPICYCLE. Cambridge: Harvard
        University Press, 1953, p. 277.)

1614 MacPhee, Laurence. REVIEW NOTES AND STUDY GUIDE TO
MELVILLE'S MOBY DICK. New York: Distributed by
Monarch Press, 1964.

1615 MacShane, Frank. "Conrad on Melville," AL, 29 (January,
1958), 463-464.

1616 Macy, John. "Leviathan," NewRep, 29 (1922), 185.

1617 Macy, John. THE SPIRIT OF AMERICAN LITERATURE. (First
copyright, Atlantic Monthly (c1908). New York:
Boni and Liveright, Inc., (n. d.), p. 16.

Criticism typical of the early twentieth-century.

1617.1 Macy, Obed. THE HISTORY OF NANTUCKET. Boston: 1835.

1618 Madden, David, ed. AMERICAN DREAMS, AMERICAN NIGHTMARES.
Preface by Harry T. Moore. London and Amsterdam:
Feffer & Simons, Inc.; Carbondale and Edwardsville:
Southern Illinois University Press, 1970, passim.

1619 Madson, Arthur L. "Melville's Comic Progression,"
WisSL, 1 (1964), 69-76.

TYPEE, OMOO, MARDI, REDBURN, MOBY DICK, and THE
CONFIDENCE-MAN are all comedies and each illustrates
one of Frye's phases of comedy. (Cf., Northup Frye.
ANATOMY OF CRITICISM. Princeton: 1957).

1620 Magaw, Malcolm O. "Apocalyptic Imagery in Melville's
'The Apple-Tree Table,'" MQ, 8 (Summer, 1967),
357-369.

Melville's allusions to John's vision on Patmos
in a story concerned with contrasting views of possibility
of after-life that "ends without a formulation of
conclusive judgment." The ambiguities are "deliberate
and meaningful; they reinforce the relativism of Melville's
metaphysics."

1621 Magaw, Malcolm O. "THE CONFIDENCE-MAN and Christian
Deity: Melville's Imagery of Ambiguity," EXPLORATIONS
OF LITERATURE. Rima D. Reck, ed. (LSUSHS 18) Baton
Rouge: Louisiana State University Press, 1966, pp.
81-88.

Both the confidence-man and the White Whale are
"masked images" of an unknowable God, and the qualities
man imputes to them are "merely projections of man's
own love or hate, faith or fear."

1622   Magaw, Malcolm O. "Herman Melville and the Christian
            Myth: The Imagery of Ambiguity." DA, 25 (Tulane:
            1965), 4126.

            Melville explores, not the Christian myth, but
            the "enigmas that have preoccupied human beings since
            the beginning of history." The ambiguity of his
            allusive Christian imagery "underscores the dualism
            and relativism of his metaphysics."

1623   Magowan, Robin. "Masque and Symbol in Melville's
            'BENITO CERENO,'" CE, 23 (February, 1962), 346-351.

            Melville incorporates ritual and symbol in his
            condemnation of the evils of slavery. Captain Delano,
            a "kind of Spenserian fairy hero, a temporarily be-
            charmed Knight of Civilization," survives evil because
            of his persistent faith.

1624   Mahoney, Mother M. Denis. CLAREL: AN INVESTIGATION OF
            SPIRITUAL CRISIS. Diss. Catholic University, 1957.

1625   Malbone, Raymond G. "How Shall We Teach the New BILLY
            BUDD, SAILOR?" CE, 27 (March, 1966), 499-500.

1626   Male, Roy R. HAWTHORNE'S TRAGIC VISION. Austin: Texas
            University Press, 1957, passim.

1627   Male, Roy R. TYPES OF SHORT FICTION. Belmont, California:
            Wadsworth, 1962.

1628   Male, Roy R. "The Story of the Mysterious Stranger in
            American Fiction," Criticism, 3 (Summer, 1961),
            281-294.

            The "mysterious stranger" in the works of Melville
            and others.

1629   Male, Roy R. "Sympathy--A Key Word in American
            Romanticism." ESQ, 35 (1964), 19-23.

1630   Malin, Irving. "The Compulsive Design," AMERICAN DREAMS,
            AMERICAN NIGHTMARES. David Madden, ed. Preface by
            Harry T. Moore. Carbondale and Edwardsville:
            Southern Illinois University Press, 1970, pp. 58-75.

            "The Bell Tower," an ironic "inversion" of "The
            Artist of the Beautiful." Both stories concern the
            "Faustian drive in art," but Owen Warland is a genuine
            artist and Bannadonna is a mechanician--like Ahab.

1631   Malin, Irving. NEW AMERICAN GOTHIC. Preface by Harry T.
        Moore. Carbondale, Illinois: Southern Illinois
        University Press, 1962.

        Ahab does not see Moby Dick as a living creature,
        good and bad, only as an "instrument" to be manipulated.

1632   Mandel, Ruth B. "Herman Melville and the Gothic Outlook,"
        DAI, 30 (Conn.: 1970), 3015A-16A.

1633   Mangold, Charlotte Weiss. "Herman Melville in German
        Criticism from 1900 to 1955," DA, 20 (Md.: 1959),
        4114.

1634   Mansfield, Luther S. "The Emersonian Idiom and the
        Romantic Period in American Literature," ESQ, 35
        (1964), 23-28.

1635   Mansfield, Luther S. "Glimpses of Herman Melville's Life
        in Pittsfield, 1850-1851: Some Unpublished Letters
        of Evert A. Duyckinck," AL, 9 (1937), 26-48.

        Information about Melville's life in Pittsfield
        an aid to understanding Melville as man and author.

1636   Mansfield, Luther S. HERMAN MELVILLE: AUTHOR AND NEW
        YORKER: 1844-1851. Diss. Chicago U.: 1935.

1637   Mansfield, Luther S. HERMAN MELVILLE: AUTHOR AND NEW
        YORKER, 1844-1851. Chicago: 1938.

1638   Mansfield, Luther S. "Melville and Hawthorne in the
        Berkshires," MELVILLE AND HAWTHORNE IN THE BERKSHIRES:
        A SYMPOSIUM. Howard P. Vincent, ed. Kent, Ohio:
        Kent State University Press, 1968, pp. 4-21.

1639   Mansfield, Luther S. "Melville's Comic Articles on
        Zachary Taylor," AL, 9 (1938), 411-418.

        Melville's seven articles to the Yankee Doodle
        in 1847 show his interests, his awareness of the life
        of his time, and his knowledge of current literary
        conventions.

1640   Mansfield, Luther S. "Some Patterns from Melville's
        'Loom of Time,'" ESSAYS ON DETERMINISM IN AMERICAN
        LITERATURE. Sydney J. Krause, ed. Kent, Ohio:
        Kent State University Press, 1964, pp. 19-35.

1641   Mansfield, Luther S.   "Symbolism and Biblical Allusion
         in MOBY DICK," ESQ, 28, Melville Supplement (1962),
         20-23.

1642   Mansfield, Luther S., and Howard P. Vincent, eds.
         MOBY-DICK; OR, THE WHALE. By Herman Melville.
         New York: Hendricks House, 1952, 1962.

         Revs. William H. Gilman, MLN, 69 (1954), 63-65;
         Leon Howard, NCF, 7 (1953), 303-304;
         William H. Hutchinson, "A Definitive Edition of
             MOBY DICK," AL, 25 (1954), 472-478;
         Sherman Paul, NEQ, 25 (1952), 423-424.

1643   Maquet, Jean. "Sur Melville," Critique, 1 (1946), 229-230.

         Rev.-art., W. E. Sedgwick's HERMAN MELVILLE:
         THE TRAGEDY OF MIND.

1644   Marcus, Mordecai. "Melville's Bartleby as a Psychological
         Double," CE, 23 (1962), 365-368.

         Repr., in THE DIMENSIONS OF THE SHORT STORY,
         James E. Miller and Bernice Slote, eds. New York:
         Dodd, Mead, 1964, pp. 539-545.

1644.1   Margoliouth, H. M., ed. "Upon Appleton House," THE
         POEMS AND LETTERS OF ANDREW MARVEL. Oxford: 1927,
         I, 81, 231.

         Sir William George Fairfax, from Marvel's poem,
         original of the character in BILLY BUDD, Captain Edward
         Fairfax Vere.

1645   Markels, Julian. "KING LEAR and MOBY-DICK: The Cultural
         Connection," MR, 9 (1968), 169-176.

         Ahab both Edmund and Lear; but Ishmael both Kent
         and Cordelia in recognizing the necessary "mutual
         responsibility of men in society."

1646   Marks, Barry A. "Retrospective Narrative in Nineteenth
         Century American Literature, CE, 31 (January, 1970),
         366-375.

         Ishmael, the narrator.

1647   Marsden, Walter. "Stories from the Deeps," JO'LW, 60
         (March 30, 1951), 181.

         Melville's short stories the "best" in the
         language.

1648   Marshall, H. P. "Herman Melville," LonMer, 11 (November,
         1924), 56-70.

         Symbolism in PIERRE and MOBY DICK.

1649   Marshall, Thomas F. THREE VOICES OF THE AMERICAN
TRADITION: EDGAR ALLAN POE, HERMAN MELVILLE,
ERNEST HEMINGWAY. Athens, Greece: 1955.

1650   Martin, Jay. HARVESTS OF CHANGE: AMERICAN LITERATURE,
1865-1914. Englewood Cliffs, New Jersey: Prentice-
Hall, Inc., 1967, passim.

1651   Martin, Lawrence H., Jr. "Melville and Christianity:
The Late Poems," MSE, 2 (1969), 11-18.

        "The Haglets," "The Maldive Shark," "The Berg"
from JOHN MARR; "Timoleon," "The Margrave's Birthnight,"
and "Herba Santa" from TIMOLEON.

1652   Martin, Sister M., O. P. BILLY BUDD and BENITO CERENO.
New York: Barnes & Noble, 1968.

1653   Martin, Terence. THE INSTRUCTED VISION: SCOTTISH COMMON
SENSE PHILOSOPHY AND THE ORIGINS OF AMERICAN FICTION.
Bloomington: Indiana University Press, 1961, p. 140.

1654   Martin, Terence. TEACHING A NOVEL: MOBY DICK IN THE
CLASSROOM. New York: College Entrance Examination
Board, 1965, pp. 3-14.

1655   Martineau, Stephen F. "Opposition and Balance: A
Characteristic of Structure in Hawthorne, Melville,
and James," DA, 28 (Columbia: 1967), 1441A.

1655.1 Martini, Carlo. Rev.-art., James Fenimore Cooper's
THE PILOT, NA, #1964 (August, 1964), 552-553.

        Cooper a precursor of Melville and others.

1655.2 Marx, Leo. "American Studies--A Defense of an Unscientific
Method," NLH, 1 (October, 1969), 75-90.

        Pre-Civil War attitudes toward industrialization
indicated in the works of Melville and others.

1656   Marx, Leo. "The Machine in the Garden," NEQ, 29 (1956),
27-42.

1657   Marx, Leo. THE MACHINE IN THE GARDEN: TECHNOLOGY AND
THE PASTORAL IDEAL IN AMERICA. New York: Oxford
University Press, 1964, pp. 277-319.

        Comparison of "Ethan Brand" and "The Try-Works,"
Chapter 96.

1658   Marx, Leo. "Melville's Parable of the Walls," SR, 61
        (Autumn, 1953), 602-627.

        Repr., AMERICAN LITERATURE: READINGS AND CRITIQUES.
        Robert W. Stallman and Arthur Waldhorn, eds. New York:
        Putnam, 1961, pp. 359-362; CRITICAL APPROACHES TO
        AMERICAN LITERATURE, I. Ray B. Browne and Martin
        Light, eds. New York: Crowell, 1965, pp. 290-309.

        "Bartleby," a parable of Melville as a writer in 1852,
        one who forsakes conventional modes because of irresistible
        preoccupation with "baffling philosophical questions."

1659   Mary Ellen, Sister, I. H. M. "Duplicate Imagery in
        MOBY DICK," Melville Special Number, MFS, 8
        (1962), 252-264.

        Similar imagery of Ahab and Moby Dick in the
        "wrinkled brow," the forehead, and the hump, which
        have Biblical connotations; images of God and King;
        the archeological imagery of pyramid, sphinx, and
        hieroglyphics. These are "projected images" in the
        sense of C. G. Jung, but the projection theory applies
        to Ahab, not Melville, who has complete artistic control.

1660   Mary Ellen, Sister, I. H. M. "Parallels in Contrast:
        A Study of Melville's Imagery in MOBY DICK and
        BILLY BUDD," SSF, 2 (Spring, 1965), 284-290.

        Images characterizing Ahab divided among three
        main characters of BILLY BUDD: hyperbolic heroic
        images to Billy, foreboding images to Claggart,
        images of authority to Captain Vere.

1660.1 Masefield, John. See John Cournos. "A Visit to John
        Masefield," New York Independent, 73 (September 5,
        1912), 537-538.

        Masefield's appreciative comment on Melville.

1661   Mason, Ronald. "BILLY BUDD and the Victory of Innocence,"
        THE SPIRIT ABOVE THE DUST: A STUDY OF HERMAN
        MELVILLE. London: John Lehmann, Ltd., 1951, pp.
        245-260.

        BILLY BUDD and THE TEMPEST.

1662   Mason, Ronald. "REDBURN: the assault upon Innocence,"
        THE SPIRIT ABOVE THE DUST: A STUDY OF HERMAN
        MELVILLE. London: John Lehmann, Ltd., 1951, pp.
        67-79.

1662.1 Mason, Ronald. THE SPIRIT ABOVE THE DUST: A STUDY OF
        HERMAN MELVILLE. London: John Lehmann, 1951, passim.

1662.2 Mason, Ronald. A STUDY OF MELVILLE'S POETRY. Diss.
        England: 1953.

1663   Mather, Edward. NATHANIEL HAWTHORNE: A MODEST MAN.
        New York: Thomas Y. Crowell Co., 1940, pp. 199-201,
        passim.

1664   Mather, Frank Jewett, Jr. "Herman Melville," WyR, 1
        (August 9, 1919), 276-278; (August 16, 1919), 298-
        301.

1665   Mather, Frank Jewett, Jr. "Herman Melville," SatRL, 5
        (April 27, 1929), 945-946.

           Rev.-art., Lewis Mumford. HERMAN MELVILLE.
    New York: 1929.

1666   Mather, Frank Jewett, Jr. "Reminiscences of a Melvillean,"
        Princeton AlWk, 38 (March 25, 1938), 555-556.

1666.1 Mathews, J. Chesley. "Lombardo on Emerson and American
        Art," ESQ, 38 (2nd Qt., 1965), 28-34.

1667   Mathews, J. Chesley. "Melville," Bibliographical
        Supplement: A Selective Checklist, 1955-1962,
        EIGHT AMERICAN AUTHORS: A REVIEW OF RESEARCH
        AND CRITICISM. Jay B. Hubbell, et al., eds.
        New York: W. W. Norton & Company, 1956, 1963,
        pp. 438-445.

1668   Mathews, J. Chesley. "Melville and Dante," PMLA, 64
        (1949), 1238.

           Cf., G. Giovannini. "Melville and Dante," PMLA,
    65 (1950), 329; and G. Giovannini, "Melville's PIERRE
    and Dante's INFERNO," PMLA, 64 (1949), 70-78.

1669   Mathews, J. Chesley. "Melville's Reading of Dante,"
        FurmS, 6 (Fall, 1958), 1-8.

1670   Matsumoto, M. "The Style of MOBY-DICK," Anglica, 4
        (1961), 33-58.

1671   Matteucci, G. "Herman Melville o delle ambiguità,"
        VP, 25 (February, 1952), 401-408.

        In Melville's novels ambiguity and predestination
    the dominant factors in shaping destiny of various
    characters.

1671.1   Matthews, Brander. AN INTRODUCTION TO THE STUDY OF
AMERICAN LITERATURE. New York: American Book
Company, 1896, pp. 15-16.

     Melville, a "writer of sea tales," shares only a
short paragraph with Richard H. Dana.

1672   Matthews, Brander. "Tellers of Sea Tales," NYTBR, 3
(1921), 5.

1673   Matthews, Cornelius. "Several Days in Berkshire,"
LitW, 7 (August 24, 1850), 145; (August 31, 1850),
166; (September 7, 1850), 185-186.

1674   Matthews, Herbert L. "Another Melville Take Is Rescued
from Oblivion," NYTBR, 3 (May 15, 1927), 9.

     BENITO CERENO, a "straight, unadorned yarn of the
sea...unadulterated by the introspection and mysticism
...of MARDI and PIERRE."

1675   Matthiessen, Francis O. "BILLY BUDD, FORETOPMAN,"
AMERICAN RENAISSANCE: ART AND EXPERIENCE IN THE
AGE OF EMERSON AND WHITMAN. New York: Oxford
University Press, 1941.

     Repr., MELVILLE: A COLLECTION OF CRITICAL ESSAYS.
Richard Chase, ed. Englewood Cliffs, New Jersey:
Prentice-Hall, 1962, pp. 156-168.

     In BILLY BUDD, Melville reaffirmed the democratic
state and "the universality of passion in common men
as well as in kings...."

1675.1   Matthiessen, Francis O. "A Bold and Nervous Lofty
Language," THE RECOGNITION OF HERMAN MELVILLE.
Hershel Parker, ed. Ann Arbor: Michigan University
Press, 1967, pp. 252-263.

1676   Matthiessen, Francis O., ed. Introduction, SELECTED
POEMS OF HERMAN MELVILLE. Norfolk, Conn.: 1944.

1677   Matthiessen, Francis O. "Melville," AMERICAN RENAISSANCE:
ART AND EXPRESSION IN THE AGE OF EMERSON AND WHITMAN.
New York: Oxford University Press, 1941, pp. 396-466,
passim; repr., New York: Oxford University Press,
1968, pp. 371-514, passim.

1678   Matthiessen, Francis O. "Melville: l'urto delle forze,"
Delta, n. s., 2 (August, 1952), 1-9.

1679   Matthiessen, Francis O. "Melville as Poet," THE
        RESPONSIBILITIES OF THE CRITIC. New York: Oxford
        University Press, 1952, pp. 77-80.

1680   Matthiessen, Francis O. "'Out of Unhandselled Savage
        Nature,'" THE MODERN CRITICAL SPECTRUM. G. J.
        Goldberg and N. M. Goldberg, eds. Englewood
        Cliffs, New Jersey: Prentice-Hall, 1962, pp.
        215-219.

1681   Maugham, W. Somerset. "Herman Melville and MOBY DICK,"
        THE ART OF FICTION: AN INTRODUCTION TO TEN NOVELS
        AND THEIR AUTHORS. Garden City, New York: Doubleday
        & Company, Inc., 1954, pp. 188-213.

1682   Maugham, W. Somerset, ed. Introduction, MOBY DICK.
        Philadelphia: 1949.

1683   Maugham, W. Somerset. "MOBY DICK," Atl, 181 (June,
        1948), 98-104.

1684   Maxwell, D. E. S. HERMAN MELVILLE. London: Routledge
        and K. Paul, 1968; New York: Humanities Press, 1968.

1685   Maxwell, D. E. S. "The Tragic Phase: Melville and
        Hawthorne," AMERICAN FICTION: THE INTELLECTUAL
        BACKGROUND. New York: Columbia University Press,
        1963, pp. 141-191, passim.

        WHITE-JACKET, MOBY-DICK, THE CONFIDENCE-MAN,
        BILLY BUDD.

1686   Maxwell, J. C. "Melville and Milton," N&Q, 12 (February,
        (1965), 60.

        The "barbarous hordes" nourished by Truth "in the
        loins of her frozen...North," (Book IX, PIERRE), echoes
        Milton, PARADISE LOST, I, 351-354.

1687   Maxwell, J. C. "Melville's Allusion to Pope," AN&Q, 3
        (September, 1964), 7.

        One of Melville's "neatest veiled allusions,"
        in Chapter XXX, REDBURN.

1688   Maxwell, J. C. "Three Notes on MOBY DICK," N&Q, 14
        (1967), 53.

        Allusions to Addison's "Cato" in Chapter 2 and
        Chapter 78; and adaptation of Coleridge's "Ancient
        Mariner" in Chapter 87.

1689   Mayoux, Jean-Jacques. "Le Douanier Melville," LetN, 2
        (June, 1954), 875-885.

1690   Mayoux, Jean-Jacques. "La Langue et le Style de Melville,"
        EA, 13 (July-September, 1960), 337-345.

1691   Mayoux, Jean-Jacques. MELVILLE PAR LUI MÊME. Paris:
        1958. Trans. by John Ashbery. New York: Grove
        Press, 1960; London: Evergreen Books, 1960.

1692   Mayoux, Jean-Jacques. "Myth et symbole chez Herman
        Melville," Inventario, 15 (1960), 43-54.

1693   Mayoux, Jean-Jacques. "PIERRE ou 'La saison en enfer'
        de Melville," LetN, 63 (September, 1958), 172-185.

1694   McAleer, John J. "Biblical Symbols in American
        Literature: A Utilitarian Design," ES, 46
        (August, 1965), 310-322.

        Influence of the "Mosaic Myth" of the New England
        Puritans in Melville and others.

1695   McAleer, John J. "Poe and Gothic Elements in MOBY DICK,"
        ESQ, 27 (2nd Qt., 1962), 34.

1696   McCarthy, Harold T. "ISRAEL R. POTTER as a Source for
        REDBURN," ESQ, 59 (1970), 8-9.

1697   McCarthy, Harold T. "Melville's REDBURN and the City,"
        MQ, 12 (July, 1971), 395-410.

1698   McCarthy, Paul. "Affirmative Elements in THE CONFIDENCE
        MAN," ATQ, 7 (1970), 56-61.

        Through Pitch, "the most important moral character,"
        the country may regain a sense of direction, at least
        "a greater awareness of both its potentialities and
        responsibilities."

1699   McCarthy, Paul. "Character and Structure in BILLY BUDD,"
        Discourse, 9 (Spring, 1966), 201-217.

1700   McCarthy, Paul. "The Extraordinary Man as Idealist in
        Novels by Hawthorne and Melville," ESQ, 54 (1st Qt.,
        1969), 43-51.

1701   McCarthy, Paul. "Melville's Use of Painting in PIERRE,"
        Discourse, 11 (Autumn, 1968), 490-505.

1702   McCarthy, Paul. "A Note on Teaching MOBY DICK,"
        ESQ, 35 (2nd Qt., 1964), 73-79.

1703   McCarthy, Paul. "The 'Soldier of Fortune' in Melville's
        THE CONFIDENCE MAN," ESQ, 33 (4th Qt., 1963), 21-24.

        The soldier, a minor figure, is a disciple of the
        devil and under the devil's tutelage, learning from him
        in order eventually to qualify "as a knowledgeable con
        man with skills and devices" that his master will approve.

1704   McCarthy, Paul. "Symbolic Elements in WHITE JACKET,"
        MQ, 7 (July, 1966), 309-325.

        The symbolic elements, the ship Neversink, the
        sailor, and the narrator, dominate the novel, and
        provide unity.

1705   McCarthy, Paul. "Theme and Structure in the Novels of
        Herman Melville," DA, 23 (Texas: 1962), 237.

1706   McCarthy, Paul. "The Use of Tom Brown in Melville's
        WHITE JACKET," ESQ, 47 (2nd Qt., 1967), 14-15.

        Tom Brown and men like him are not individualized
        because inhumanity of naval life reduce all but a few
        to anonymity and oblivion.

1707   McClary, Ben Harris. "Melville, Twain, and the Legendary
        'Tennessee Poet,'" TFSB, 29 (1963), 63-64.

        Melville in MOBY DICK and Twain in "Captain
        Stormfield's Visit to Heaven" referred to a notable
        Tennessee poet of whom no trace survives. Melville
        did not call him by name; Twain calls him Edward V.
        Billings.

1708   McClary, Ben Harris. "Melville's MOBY DICK," Expl, 21
        (1962), Item 9.

        Melville's use of prophecy, symbolic names, and
        play on words.

1709   McCloskey, John C. "MOBY-DICK and the Reviewers," PQ,
        25 (October, 1946), 20-31.

1710   McCorquodale, Marjorie Kimball. "Melville's Pierre as
        Hawthorne," UTSE, 33 (1954), 97-102.

1711   McCutcheon, R. P. "The Technique of Melville's ISRAEL
        POTTER," SAQ, 27 (1928), 161-174.

        Comparison of the novel with its source, THE LIFE
        AND REMARKABLE ADVENTURES OF ISRAEL POTTER (1824).

1712   McDermott, John F. "THE SPIRIT OF THE TIMES Reviews
        MOBY-DICK," NEQ, 30 (September, 1957), 392-395.

1713   McElderry, B. R., ed. Introduction, NARRATIVE OF THE
        MOST EXTRAORDINARY AND DISTRESSING SHIPWRECK OF
        THE WHALESHIP ESSEX. By Owen Chase. (Supplementary
        Accounts of Survivors and Herman Melville's Notes).
        New York: Corinth Books, 1963 (The American
        Experience Series).

        In 1851, Melville acquired the Harvard copy while
        writing MOBY DICK. The copy contains his notes, here
        reproduced in facsimile and transcription. McElderry
        adds two supplementary narratives: Thomas Chappel's
        AN ACCOUNT OF THE LOSS OF THE ESSEX, and Captain
        Pollard's "Narrative," contained in Tyerman and
        Bennet's JOURNAL OF VOYAGES AND TRAVELS (1832).

1714   McElderry, B. R. "THE NATIONAL ERA Review of WHITE-JACKET,"
        MSN, 15 (Winter, 1960), n. p.

1715   McElderry, B. R. "Three Earlier Treatments of the
        BILLY BUDD Theme," AL, 27 (May, 1955), 251-257.

        Parallels of BILLY BUDD with Douglas William
        Jerrold's BLACK-EYED SUSAN and THE MUTINY AT THE NORE,
        and Marryat's THE KING'S OWN.

        Cf., Richard Gollin, et al. "Justice in an
        Earlier Treatment of the BILLY BUDD Theme," AL, 28
        (1957), 513-515.

1716   McEniry, W. Hugh. "Some Contrapuntal Themes in Herman
        Melville," ESSAYS IN MODERN AMERICAN LITERATURE.
        Richard E. Langford, ed. DeLand, Florida: Stetson
        University Press, 1963, pp. 14-25.

        Melville's contrapuntal themes are "two conflicting
        understandings" of man's universe and his place in it.
        The first theme affirms that man can discover the
        ultimate truth about himself and his world; the second
        is that man's best chances in this life lie in daily
        adjustment to necessities and a rejection of the "lure
        of absolutes."

1717 McEniry, W. Hugh. THE YOUNG MELVILLE, 1819-1852. Diss. Vanderbilt: 1942.

1717.1 McEniry, W. Hugh. THE YOUNG MELVILLE. Nashville: 1942.

1718 McFee, William. "Blubber and Mysticism," Bookman, 55 (1922), 69-79.

1719 McFee, William. Introduction, MOBY DICK. Philadelphia: 1931, 1934.

1720 McGraves, Donald E. "The Steering Gear of the Pequod," AN&Q, 6 (May, 1946), 25.

1721 McHaney, Thomas L. "The Textual Editions of Hawthorne and Melville," SLitI, 2, 1 (1969), 27-41.

1722 McLean, Albert. "Spouter Inn and Whaleman's Chapel: The Cultural Matrices of MOBY DICK," MELVILLE AND HAWTHORNE IN THE BERKSHIRES: A SYMPOSIUM. Howard P. Vincent, ed. Kent, Ohio: Kent State University Press, 1968, pp. 98-108.

   The book's first twenty-three land-based chapters: Inn and chapel epitomize "the partial and conflicting values of the land," man's animal and spiritual needs. An individual will find "his freedom and seek his truth" by "heroic detachment" of "landlessness."

1723 McNally, William. EVILS AND ABUSES IN THE NAVAL AND MERCHANT SERVICE, EXPOSED; WITH PROPOSALS FOR THEIR REMEDY AND REDRESS. Boston: Cassady and March, 1839.

   A possible source for WHITE JACKET.

1724 McNamara, Anne. "Melville's BILLY BUDD," Expl, 21 (October, 1962), Item 11.

   The many classical allusions in BILLY BUDD are functional. They represent Billy as having qualities of hero, god, and bard; they underline his Vestal innocence; they emphasize his tragic flaw and his relation to the Fates.

1725 McNamara, Leo F. "Subject, Style, and Narrative Technique in BARTLEBY and 'Wakefield,'" MichA, 3 (1971), 41-46.

1725.1 McNeir, Waldo, and Leo B. Levy, eds. STUDIES IN AMERICAN
            LITERATURE. (LSUSHS, No. 8). Baton Rouge: Louisiana
            State University Press, 1960.

            Rev., James Baird, NEQ, 34 (1961), 284-286.

1725.2 McPherson, Hugo. HAWTHORNE AS MYTH-MAKER: A STUDY IN
            IMAGINATION. Toronto: Toronto University Press,
            1969, passim.

1726   McQuitty, Robert A. "A Rhetorical Approach to Melville's
            BARTLEBY, BENITO CERENO, and BILLY BUDD," DA, 29
            (Syracuse: 1969), 4010A-11A.

1727   McWilliams, J. P., Jr. "Drum Taps and BATTLE-PIECES:
            The Blossom of War," AQ, 23 (May, 1971), 181-201.

1728   Meldrum, Barbara. "The Artist in Melville's MARDI,"
            SNNTS, 1 (Winter, 1969), 459-467.

            In treatment of the theme of the artist, MARDI
        anticipates PIERRE and MOBY DICK. The quest of Taji,
        the protagonist, is not only for truth, but a movement
        away from the everyday world into that of the artist.

1729   Meldrum, Barbara. "Melville on War," RS, 37 (1969),
            130-138.

            Melville used the subject of war in WHITE JACKET
        and later to portray the theory and practice of both
        democracy and Christianity in a man-of-war world. His
        ideals did not change radically, though his hopes for
        realization of such ideals dimmed, possibly even flickered
        out by the time of BILLY BUDD.

1730   Meldrum, Barbara. Melville's MARDI, MOBY-DICK, and
            PIERRE: Tragedy in Recoil," DA, 28 (Claremont:
            1967), 686A.

            The hero as artist is one of the common elements
        uniting the three works. In the first and third, the
        "impersonality of the artist recoils and he destroys
        himself." Melville's own achievement as impersonal
        artist is "implicit in Ishmael's achievement" in
        MOBY DICK.

COMPLETE EDITIONS OF MELVILLE'S WORKS

1731   Melville, Herman. THE WORKS OF HERMAN MELVILLE. London:
        Constable and Company, 1922-1924, 16 vols. (Limited
        to 750 sets). Repr., New York: Russell & Russell,
        1963.

        Vols:
        1   TYPEE
        2   OMOO
        3-4   MARDI
        5   REDBURN, HIS FIRST VOYAGE
        6   WHITE JACKET; OR, THE WORLD IN A MAN-OF-WAR
        7-8   MOBY-DICK; OR, THE WHALE
        9   PIERRE; OR, THE AMBIGUITIES
        10   THE PIAZZA TALES
        11   ISRAEL POTTER, HIS FIFTY YEARS OF EXILE
        12   THE CONFIDENCE-MAN, HIS MASQUERADE
        13   BILLY BUDD, AND OTHER PROSE PIECES. Raymond Weaver, ed.
        14-15 CLAREL; A POEM AND PILGRIMAGE IN THE HOLY LAND
        16   POEMS, containing "BATTLE-PIECES," "JOHN MARR AND
              OTHER SAILORS," "TIMOLEON," and MISCELLANEOUS
              POEMS

1732   Melville, Herman. THE WORKS OF HERMAN MELVILLE. London:
        Jonathan Cape, pub., 1925.

1733   Melville, Herman. COMPLETE WORKS OF HERMAN MELVILLE.
        Howard P. Vincent, gen. ed. Chicago and New York:
        Hendricks House, 1947-

        The following have been published:

            COLLECTED POEMS (1947), Howard P. Vincent, ed.
            THE CONFIDENCE MAN (1954), Elizabeth Foster, ed.
            MOBY DICK (1952), Luther S. Mansfield and
                Howard Vincent, eds.
            THE PIAZZA TALES (1948), E. L. Oliver, ed.
            PIERRE; OR, THE AMBIGUITIES (1949),
                Henry A. Murray, ed.
            CLAREL: A POEM AND PILGRIMAGE IN THE HOLY LAND (1961),
                Walter E. Bezanson, ed.

1734   Melville, Herman. THE WRITINGS OF HERMAN MELVILLE.
       Harrison Hayford, Hershel Parker, and G. Thomas
       Tanselle, eds. Evanston and Chicago: Northwestern
       University Press and The Newberry Library, 1969.
       (In progress).

       Vols:
       1   TYPEE: A PEEP AT POLYNESIAN LIFE. Historical
            Note by Leon Howard; Textual Record by the
            editors.
       2   OMOO: A NARRATIVE OF ADVENTURES IN THE SOUTH SEAS.
            Historical Note by Gordon Roper.
       3   MARDI: AND A VOYAGE THITHER. Historical Note
            by Elizabeth S. Foster.
       4   REDBURN: HIS FIRST VOYAGE. Historical Note
            by Hershel Parker.
       5   WHITE-JACKET: OR, THE WORLD IN A MAN-OF-WAR.
            Historical Note by Willard Thorp.
       6   PIERRE.

                  PARTIAL COLLECTIONS OF MELVILLE'S WORKS

1735   Melville, Herman. THE APPLE TREE TABLE AND OTHER SKETCHES.
       Henry Chapin, ed. Princeton: Princeton University
       Press, 1922. New York: Greenwood Press, 1969.

       Apple-Tree Table
       Hawthorne and His Mosses
       Jimmy Rose
       I and My Chimney
       Paradise of Bachelors and Tartarus of Maids
       Cock-a-doodle Do!
       The Fiddler
       Poor Man's Pudding and Rich Man's Crumbs
       The Happy Failure
       The 'Gees

1736   Melville, Herman. BILLY BUDD AND OTHER PROSE PIECES.
       Raymond M. Weaver, ed. London: Constable and
       Company, 1924. New York: Russell & Russell, 1963.

       This is Volume 13 of the Constable edition and the
       Russell and Russell.

       BILLY BUDD, FORETOPMAN (first printing)
       Daniel Orme
       Hawthorne and His Mosses
       Cock-a-doodle-doo!
       The Two Temples
       Poor Man's Pudding and Rich Man's Crumbs
       The Happy Failure
       The Fiddler
       The Paradise of Bachelors and the Tartarus of Maids
       Jimmy Rose
       The Gees
       I and My Chimney
       The Apple-Tree Table
       Under the Rose
       The Marquis de Grandvin

1736   Melville, Herman. BILLY BUDD AND OTHER PROSE PIECES. Cont.

> Portrait of a Gentleman
> To Major John Gentian, Dean of the Burgundy Club
> Jack Gentian
> Major Gentian and Colonel J. Bunkum
> The Cincinnati Fragments from a Writing Desk

1736.1   Melville, Herman. ROMANCES OF HERMAN MELVILLE: TYPEE, OMOO, MARDI, MOBY DICK, WHITE JACKET, ISRAEL POTTER, REDBURN. New York: The Pickwick Publishers, 1928.

1737   Melville, Herman. SHORTER NOVELS OF HERMAN MELVILLE. Introduction by Raymond M. Weaver. New York: Horace Liveright, 1928, 1956, 1957. New York: Grosset and Dunlap. Grosset's Universal Library, 1957. Greenwich, Conn.: Fawcett Publications, 1960.

> Includes first American printing of BILLY BUDD in slightly different version from that of 1924 English edition. Also includes BENITO CERENO, BARTLEBY, and ENCANTADAS.

1738   Melville, Herman. ROMANCES OF HERMAN MELVILLE. New York: Tudor Publishing Company, 1931.

> One-volume collection containing seven of Melville's novels.

1739   Melville, Herman. HERMAN MELVILLE: REPRESENTATIVE SELECTIONS. Introduction, Bibliography, and Notes by Willard Thorp. New York: American Book Company (American Writer Series), 1938.

> TYPEE, eight chapters
> OMOO, seventeen chapters
> MARDI, seven chapters
> WHITE JACKET, nine chapters
> MOBY DICK, sixteen chapters and Epilogue
> POEMS, seventeen poems
> Selected Letters

1740   Melville, Herman. BILLY BUDD, BENITO CERENO AND THE ENCHANTED ISLES. Carl Van Doren, ed. New York: The Readers Club, Inc., 1942.

1741   Melville, Herman. COMPLETE STORIES OF HERMAN MELVILLE. Jay Leyda, ed. New York: Random House, 1949.

1742   Melville, Herman. SELECTED TALES AND POEMS BY HERMAN
        MELVILLE. Introduction by Richard Chase, ed.
        New York: Holt, Rinehart & Winston, 1950, 1960.

        Poems
        BENITO CERENO
        Jimmy Rose
        The Fiddler
        I and My Chimney
        The Bell Tower
        Paradise of Bachelors and Tartarus of Maids
        THE ENCANTADAS
        BILLY BUDD

1743   Melville, Herman. BILLY BUDD AND OTHER STORIES.
        Introduction by Rex Warner. London: John Lehmann,
        Ltd., 1951.

1744   Melville, Herman. BILLY BUDD, BENITO CERENO. London:
        Barmerlea Book Sales, Ltd., 1952.

1745   Melville, Herman. THE PORTABLE MELVILLE. Jay Leyda, ed.
        Toronto: Macmillan, 1952; New York: The Viking
        Press, 1952, Macmillan, 1969.

1746   Melville, Herman. SELECTED WRITINGS OF HERMAN MELVILLE.
        New York: Random House, 1952. Modern Library
        edition.

        Includes TYPEE, BILLY BUDD, and shorter pieces.

1747   Melville, Herman. COCORICO! ET AUTRES CONTES.
        Translated from English by Pierre Leyris. Paris:
        Gallimard, 1954.

1748   Melville, Herman. LE ENCANTADAS E ALTRI RACCONTI.
        Milano: Arnoldo Mondadori Editore, 1957.

1749   Melville, Herman. TYPEE AND BILLY BUDD. Introduction by
        Milton R. Stern. New York: Dutton Everyman
        Paperbacks, 1958.

1750   Melville, Herman. HERMAN MELVILLE: FOUR SHORT NOVELS.
        New York: Bantam Books, 1959. Bantam Classics.

1751   Melville, Herman. MELVILLE'S SHORTER TALES. Richard
        Harter Fogle, ed. Norman: Oklahoma University
        Press, 1960.

1752   Melville, Herman. BILLY BUDD AND OTHER TALES. Afterword
       by Willard Thorp. New York: New American Library,
       1961. Signet Classics.

1753   Melville, Herman. BILLY BUDD AND TYPEE. Introduction
       by Maxwell Geisman. New York: Washington Square
       Press, 1962.

1754   Melville, Herman. STORIES, POEMS, AND LETTERS BY THE
       AUTHOR OF MOBY DICK. Introduction by R. W. B. Lewis,
       ed. New York: Dell Publishing Co., 1962. A Laurel
       Reader.

1755   Melville, Herman. THREE SHORTER NOVELS OF HERMAN MELVILLE.
       Critical and biographical material by Joseph
       Schiffman. New York: Harper and Brothers, 1962.

       BENITO CERENO
       BARTLEBY THE SCRIVENER
       THE ENCANTADAS, OR THE ENCHANTED ISLES

1756   Melville, Herman. THE BEST OF MOBY DICK AND TYPEE: ALSO
       BILLY BUDD. Foreword by Edward Ellsberg. New York:
       Platt & Munk, 1964.

1757   Melville, Herman. BILLY BUDD, BENITO CERENO.
       Introduction by Maxwell Geisman, and ten paintings
       by Robert Shore. New York: Printed for members of
       the Limited Editions Club, 1965.

1758   Melville, Herman. GREAT SHORT WORKS OF HERMAN MELVILLE.
       Introduction and Selected Bibliography by Jerry
       Allen. New York: Harper & Row, 1966. A Perennial
       Classic.

       The Apple-Tree Table or Original Spiritual
          Manifestations.
       BARTLEBY THE SCRIVENER
       The Bell Tower
       BENITO CERENO
       BILLY BUDD
       Cock-a-doodle-doo!
       THE ENCANTADAS
       The Fiddler
       The Happy Failure
       I and My Chimney
       Jimmy Rose
       The Lightning Rod Man
       The Paradise of Bachelors and Tartarus of Maids
       The Piazza
       Poor Man's Pudding and Rich Man's Crumbs
       The Two Temples

1759   Melville, Herman. MOBY DICK AND OTHER WORKS. Byrne R.
         Fone and George Marcelle. New York: Barrister
         Publishing Company, 1966.

1760   Melville, Herman. FIVE TALES. With Illustrations of
         the Author and His Environment, and Introduction
         by James H. Pickering. New York: Dodd, Mead,
         1967.

         BARTLEBY
         BENITO CERENO
         I and My Chimney
         The Lightning Rod Man
         BILLY BUDD, FORETOPMAN

1761   Melville, Herman. THREE STORIES. With Wood Engravings
         by Garrick Palmer. London: Folio Society, 1967.

         BARTLEBY
         BENITO CERENO
         BILLY BUDD

1762   Melville, Herman. BILLY BUDD AND BENITO CERENO.
         Prepared for Barnes & Noble by Sister M. Martin,
         O. P., New York: Barnes & Noble, 1968.

1763   Melville, Herman. GREAT SHORT WORKS OF HERMAN MELVILLE.
         Introduction by Warner Berthoff, ed. New York:
         Revised edition, Harper & Row, Publishers, 1970.
         A Perennial Classic.

         The Town-Ho's Story
         BARTLEBY THE SCRIVENER
         Cock-a-doodle-doo!
         THE ENCANTADAS
         The Two Temples
         Poor Man's Pudding and Rich Man's Crumbs
         The Happy Failure: A Story of the River Hudson
         The Lightning Rod Man
         The Fiddler
         The Paradise of Bachelors and The Tartarus of Maids
         The Bell Tower
         BENITO CERENO
         Jimmy Rose
         I and My Chimney
         The 'Gees
         The Apple-Tree Table, or Original Spiritual
             Manifestations

         The Piazza
         The Marquis de Grandvin
         Three "Jack Gentian Sketches"
         John Marr
         Daniel Orme
         BILLY BUDD, SAILOR

         A Selected Bibliography
         Chronology

JOURNALS

1764 Melville, Herman. JOURNAL OF A CRUISE IN THE PACIFIC
      OCEAN, 1842-1844, IN THE FRIGATE UNITED STATES.
      With Introduction and Notes on Herman Melville by
      Charles Roberts Anderson, ed. Durham, North
      Carolina: Duke University Press, 1937.

1765 Melville, Herman. "Journal of Melville's Voyage in a
      Clipper Ship," /1860/. S. E. Morison, ed. NEQ, 2
      (1929), 120-125.

      An account of Melville's Cape Horn voyage in 1860
      on the Meteor, commanded by his brother, Thomas Melville.
      Fragment of journal preserved by his granddaughter,
      Mrs. Henry K. Metcalf.

1766 Melville, Herman. JOURNAL OF A VISIT TO LONDON AND THE
      CONTINENT BY HERMAN MELVILLE, 1849-1850. Eleanor
      Melville Metcalf, ed. Cambridge: Harvard University
      Press, 1948; London: Cohen & West, Ltd., 1949.

1767 Melville, Herman. JOURNAL UP THE STRAITS, October 11,
      1856-May 5, 1857. Raymond M. Weaver, ed. New York:
      The Colophon, 1935.

1768 Melville, Herman. JOURNAL OF A VISIT TO EUROPE AND THE
      LEVANT, OCTOBER 11, 1856-MAY 6, 1857. Howard C.
      Horsford, ed. Princeton, New Jersey: Princeton
      University Press, 1955.

1769 Melville, Herman. JOURNAUX DE VOYAGE: JOURNAL OF A
      VISIT TO LONDON AND THE CONTINENT. JOURNAL OF THE
      CLIPPER SHIP METEOR. JOURNAL OF A VISIT TO EUROPE AND
      THE LEVANT. Traduits de l'anglais par Francis Ledoux.
      Paris: Gillimard, 1956.

1769.1 Melville, Herman. DIARIO ITALIANO. Traduzione,
      Introduzione é note di Guido Botta. Roma:
      Opere Nuove, 1964.

LETTERS

1770   Melville, Herman. "Family Correspondence of Herman
        Melville, 1830-1904. In the Gansevoort-Lansing
        Collection," BNYPL, 33 (July, 1929), 507-525;
        (August, 1929), 575-625. V. H. Paltsits, ed.
        Repr., New York: New York Public Library, 1929.

        Copies or extracts of over one hundred letters.

1770.1 Melville, Herman. Family Correspondence of Herman Melville,
        1830-1904, in the Gansevoort-Lansing Collection.
        Victor Hugo Paltsits, ed. New York: New York
        Public Library, 1929. Folcroft, Pa.: Folcroft
        Press, 1969.

1771   Melville, Herman. THE LETTERS OF HERMAN MELVILLE.
        Merrell R. Davis and William H. Gilman, eds.
        New Haven: Yale University Press, 1960.

1772   Anon. "Manuscript Division Accessions During 1942,"
        BNYPL, 47 (1943), 91-98.

        Includes letters of Herman Melville.

1773   Melville, Herman. "Melville's 'Agatha' Letter to
        Hawthorne," S. E. Morison, ed. NEQ, 2 (1929),
        296-307.

1774   Melville, Herman. "Some Melville Letters," Nation&Ath,
        29 (1921), 712-713.

        Correspondence between Billson and Melville from
        1884 to 1888 dealing with the books Billson needed to
        collect a complete Melville.

1775   Melville, Herman. SOME PERSONAL LETTERS OF HERMAN
        MELVILLE. Meade Minnigerode, ed. New York:
        The Brick Row Book Shop, 1922; repr., Freeport,
        New York: Books for Libraries Press, 1969.

1776   Melville, Herman. STORIES, POEMS, AND LETTERS BY THE
        AUTHOR OF MOBY DICK. Introduction by R. W. B.
        Lewis, ed. New York: Dell Publishing Company,
        1962. A Laurel Reader.

1777   Melville, Herman. "An Unpublished Letter from Herman
        Melville to Mrs. Hawthorne in Explanation of 'MOBY
        DICK,'" American Art Association: Anderson
        Galleries Catalogue of Sale, No. 3911. New York:
        1931, p. 9.

POETRY

1777.1 Melville, Herman. POEMS, CONTAINING BATTLE-PIECES, JOHN
        MARR AND OTHER SAILORS, TIMOLEON AND MISCELLANEOUS
        POEMS, by Herman Melville. London, Bombay:
        Constable and Company, 1924.

1778   Melville, Herman. COLLECTED POEMS OF HERMAN MELVILLE.
        Howard P. Vincent, ed. Chicago: Packard & Co.,
        1947.

        Rev., by William Braswell, AL, 19 (1948), 366-368.

1779   Melville, Herman. POEMS BY HERMAN MELVILLE: A CRITICAL
        EDITION OF THE PUBLISHED VERSE. Norman Eugene
        Jarrard, ed. /Diss./ Texas University Press, and
        Ann Arbor: University Microfilms, 1960.

1780   Melville, Herman. POESIE. Luigi Berti, ed. 2nd ed.
        Firenze: Fussi, 1957.

        Text of Melville's poems in English and Italian.

1781   Melville, Herman. SELECTED POEMS OF HERMAN MELVILLE.
        William Plomer, ed. London: The Hogarth Press,
        1943.

1782   Melville, Herman. SELECTED POEMS OF HERMAN MELVILLE.
        Francis O. Matthiessen, ed. Norfolk, Conn.: New
        Directions, 1944.

1783   Melville, Herman. SELECTED TALES AND POEMS BY HERMAN
        MELVILLE. Richard Chase, ed. New York: Holt,
        Rinehart and Winston, 1950.

1784   Melville, Herman. MELVILLE'S SHORTER PUBLISHED POETRY:
        A CRITICAL STUDY OF THE LYRICS IN MARDI, OF BATTLE-
        PIECES, JOHN MARR, AND TIMOLEON. Diss. Dan Vogel,
        New York University: 1956.

1785   Melville, Herman. STORIES, POEMS, AND LETTERS BY THE
        AUTHOR OF MOBY DICK. Introduction by R. W. B.
        Lewis, ed. New York: Dell Publishing Co., Inc.,
        1962.

1786   Melville, Herman. SELECTED POEMS. Introduction and
        Notes by Hennig Cohen, ed. Carbondale: Southern
        Illinois University Press, 1964.

1787   Melville, Herman. SELECTED POEMS OF HERMAN MELVILLE:
        A READER'S EDITION. Introduction by Robert Penn
        Warren, ed. New York: Random House, 1970.

1788   Melville, Herman. BATTLE-PIECES AND ASPECTS OF THE WAR.
        New York: Harper and Brothers, 1866.

1788.1 Melville, Herman. POEMS, CONTAINING BATTLE-PIECES,
        JOHN MARR AND OTHER SAILORS, TIMOLEON AND MISCELLANEOUS
        POEMS, by Herman Melville. London, Bombay: Constable
        and Company, Ltd., 1924.

        BATTLE-PIECES

1789   Melville, Herman. BATTLE-PIECES AND ASPECTS OF THE WAR.
        Facsimile Reproductions. Introduction by Walter
        Harding. Gainesville, Florida: Scholars'
        Facsimiles & Reprints, 1960.

1789.1 Melville, Herman. BATTLE-PIECES AND ASPECTS OF THE WAR.
        Facsimile Reproductions. Introduction by Sidney
        Kaplan, ed. Gainesville, Florida: Scholars'
        Facsimiles & Reprints, 1960.

1790   Melville, Herman. THE BATTLE-PIECES OF HERMAN MELVILLE.
        Introduction and Notes by Hennig Cohen, ed. New
        York: T. Yoseloff, 1963.

1791   Melville, Herman. CLAREL: A POEM AND A PILGRIMAGE IN
THE HOLY LAND. By Herman Melville. In four Parts.
I. Jerusalem. II. The Wilderness. III. Mar Saba.
IV. Bethlehem. New York: G. P. Putnam's Sons,
1876. 2 vols.

This book was published in July, 1876. There was
no English edition.

1792   Melville, Herman. CLAREL. An Annotated Edition.
Walter E. Bezanson. Rutgers, 1954.

1793   Melville, Herman. CLAREL: A POEM AND PILGRIMAGE IN
THE HOLY LAND. Introduction by Walter E. Bezanson,
ed. New York: Hendricks House, Inc., 1960.

1794   Melville, Herman. CLAREL: A POEM AND PILGRIMAGE IN
THE HOLY LAND. New York: Russell, 1963.

1795   Melville, Herman. JOHN MARR AND OTHER SAILORS, WITH
SOME SEA PIECES. New York: De Vinne Press, 1888.

Privately printed in an edition of 25 copies
only. Reissued with other stories, Princeton: 1922,
of which there were also 175 copies on French handmade
paper.

1796   Melville, Herman. JOHN MARR AND OTHER POEMS. Henry
Chapin, ed. Princeton: 1922.

1796.1 Melville, Herman. POEMS, CONTAINING BATTLE-PIECES, JOHN
MARR AND OTHER SAILORS, TIMOLEON AND MISCELLANEOUS
POEMS, by Herman Melville. London, Bombay: Constable
and Company, Ltd., 1924.

JOHN MARR AND OTHER SAILORS

1797   Melville, Herman. "RAMMON": Text and Commentary by
Eleanor M. Tilton. "Off-print from Harvard
Library Bulletin,"Vol. 13, No. 1 (winter, 1959).

1798   Melville, Herman. TIMOLEON. New York: Canton Press, 1891.

Only twenty-five copies of this edition were printed.

1798.1 Melville, Herman. POEMS, CONTAINING BATTLE-PIECES, JOHN
MARR AND OTHER SAILORS, TIMOLEON AND MISCELLANEOUS
POEMS, by Herman Melville. London, Bombay: Constable
and Company, Ltd., 1924.

TIMOLEON

1799   ⎡Melville, Herman⎤. An Account of Major Thomas Melville
        in THE HISTORY OF PITTSFIELD, MASSACHUSETTS, FROM
        THE YEAR 1800 TO THE YEAR 1876. By J. E. A. Smith.
        Springfield, Mass.: C. W. Bryan and Co., 1876.

        Melville's name not given as author.

1800   Melville, Herman. A BOOK OF REVIEWS BY HERMAN MELVILLE.
        By John Howard Birss. ⎡n. p.⎤ 1932.

1801   Melville, Herman. "Hawthorne and His Mosses," LitW,
        7 (August 17, 1850; August 24, 1850), 125-127,
        145-147.

1802   Melville, Herman. "Hawthorne and His Mosses," LitW,
        1850. THE PORTABLE MELVILLE. Jay Leyda, ed.
        New York: Viking Press, 1952, 1967.

1803   Melville, Herman. "Hawthorne and His Mosses," in
        SHOCK OF RECOGNITION. Edmund Wilson, ed. New York:
        Farrar, Straus, 1955, pp. 187-204.

1804   Melville, Herman. "Hawthorne and His Mosses," in
        ART OF THE ESSAY. Leslie A. Fiedler, ed. With
        Introduction, Notes and Exercise Questions. New
        York: Crowell, 1958, pp. 571-584.

1805   Melville, Herman. "Hawthorne and His Mosses," in
        GOLDEN AGE OF AMERICAN LITERATURE. Perry Miller, ed.
        Braziller, 1959, pp. 407-419.

1806   Melville, Herman. A MEMORIAL OF JAMES FENIMORE COOPER.
        New York: Putnam, 1852, p. 30.

        A letter from Melville in praise of Cooper
        addressed to the committee organizing the Cooper
        Memorial.

1807   Melville, Herman. "Mr. Parkman's Tour," LitW, 4
        (March 31, 1849), 291-293.

1808   Melville, Herman. "Nathaniel Hawthorne," LitW, 6
        (March 30, 1850), 323-325.

REVIEWS BY MELVILLE AND

MISCELLANEOUS PIECES

1809   Melville, Herman. Review of THE CALIFORNIA AND OREGON
        TRAIL by Francis Parkman (1849) in LitW, 4 (March 31,
        1849), 291-293.

        Melville later regretted having attacked Parkman.
        Cf., THE LETTERS OF HERMAN MELVILLE. Merrell R. Davis
        and William H. Gilman, eds. New Haven: 1960, p. 96.

1810   Melville, Herman. Review of ETCHINGS OF A WHALING
        CRUISE and SAILORS' LIFE AND SAILORS' YARNS,
        by J. Ross Browne, (London: 1846), in LitW, 1
        (March 6, 1847), 105-106.

1811   Melville, Herman. Review of MOSSES FROM AN OLD MANSE,
        by Nathaniel Hawthorne. LitW (August 17, 24, 1850),
        125-127, 145-147.

1812   Melville, Herman. Review of THE SEA LIONS and THE RED
        ROVER by James Fenimore Cooper in LitW, 4 (April 28,
        1849), 370, and 6 (March 16, 1850), 277.

MELVILLE'S PROSE WRITINGS

1813   Melville, Herman. "A Thought on Book-Binding," LitW, 6
        (March 16, 1850), 276-277.

1814   Melville, Herman. THE APPLE-TREE TABLE AND OTHER SKETCHES.
        Henry Chapin, ed. Princeton, New Jersey: Princeton
        University Press, 1922. New York: Greenwood Press,
        1969.

1815   Melville, Herman. BARTLEBY THE SCRIVENER. First
        published anonymously in two issues of *Putnam's
        Monthly Magazine*, 1853.

1815.1 Melville, Herman. THE PIAZZA TALES. By Herman Melville.
        New York: Dix & Edwards, 1856; London: Sampson Low,
        Son and Co., 1856.

        BARTLEBY

1815.2 Melville, Herman. THREE SHORTER NOVELS. Quentin Anderson,
        ed. Afterword by Joseph Schiffman. New York: Harper,
        1962.

1816   Melville, Herman. GREAT SHORT WORKS OF HERMAN MELVILLE.
        Introduction by Jerry Allen. New York: Harper,
        1966.

        BARTLEBY THE SCRIVENER

1816.1 Melville, Herman. BARTLEBY. Traducción y prólogo de
        Jorge Luis Borges. Buenos Aires: EDICOM, 1969.

1816.2 Melville, Herman. THE PIAZZA TALES. By Herman Melville.
        New York: Dix & Edwards, 1856; London: Sampson
        Low, Son and Co., 1856.

        The Bell Tower.

1817   Melville, Herman. SELECTED TALES AND POEMS. Richard
        Chase, ed. New York: Holt, 1950.

        The Bell Tower

1818   Melville, Herman. GREAT SHORT WORKS OF HERMAN MELVILLE.
        Introduction by Jerry Allen. New York: Harper,
        1966.

        The Bell Tower

1818.1 Melville, Herman. THE PIAZZA TALES. By Herman Melville.
New York: Dix & Edwards; London: Sampson Low, Son
and Co., 1856.

BENITO CERENO.

1819 Melville, Herman. BENITO CERENO. London: 1926.

1,650 numbered copies only. First separate
edition. Reprinted from PIAZZA TALES, 1856.

1820 Melville, Herman. BENITO CERENO. Illustrations by E.
McKnight Kauffer. New York: Random House, Nonesuch
Ltd., edition, 1927.

A collector's item.

1821 Melville, Herman. BILLY BUDD, BENITO CERENO, AND THE
ENCHANTED ISLES. Carl Van Doren, ed. New York:
The Readers' Club, Inc., 1942.

1822 Melville, Herman. SELECTED TALES AND POEMS. Richard
Chase, ed. New York: Holt, 1950.

BENITO CERENO.

1822.1 Melville, Herman. THREE SHORTER TALES. Quentin
Anderson, ed. Afterword by Joseph Schiffman.
New York: Harper, 1962.

BENITO CERENO.

1823 Melville, Herman. BENITO CERENO in ILES DE GLÉNAN
by Jean Paul Delhumeau. Paris: Blondel la
Rongery, 1963.

1824 Melville, Herman. BENITO CERENO in BILLY BUDD, BENITO
CERENO. With Introduction by Maxwell Geismar and
ten paintings by Robert Shore. New York: Printed
for members of the Limited Editions Club, 1965.

1825 Melville, Herman. BENITO CERENO in A BENITO CERENO
HANDBOOK, Seymour Gross, ed. Belmont, Calif.:
Wadsworth Publishing Co., 1965.

1826 Melville, Herman. BENITO CERENO in THE OLD GLORY. Robert
Lowell. New York: Farrar, Straus & Giroux, 1965.
London: Faber, 1966.

1827   Melville, Herman. MELVILLE'S BENITO CERENO: A TEXT FOR
        GUIDED RESEARCH. John Paul Runden, ed. Boston:
        Heath, 1965.

1828   Melville, Herman. GREAT SHORT WORKS OF HERMAN MELVILLE.
        Introduction by Jerry Allen. New York: Harper,
        1966.

        BENITO CERENO.

1829   Melville, Herman. ARTHUR GORDON PYM, BENITO CERENO, AND
        RELATED WRITINGS. John Seelye, comp. Philadelphia:
        Lippincott, 1967.

1830   Melville, Herman. BILLY BUDD and BENITO CERENO. Prepared
        for Barnes & Noble by Sister M. Martin, O. P. New
        York: Barnes & Noble, 1968.

1831   Melville, Herman. BILLY BUDD, FORETOPMAN in BILLY BUDD
        AND OTHER PROSE PIECES. Raymond Weaver, ed. London:
        Constable and Company, 1924. New York: Russell &
        Russell, 1963.

1832   Melville, Herman. BILLY BUDD, BENITO CERENO AND THE
        ENCHANTED ISLES. Carl Van Doren, ed. New York:
        The Readers Club, Inc., 1942.

1832.1 Melville, Herman. BILLY BUDD, GABBIERE DI PARROCCHETTO.
        Eugenio Montale, ed. Milano: Bompiani, 1942.
        5th ed., 1965.

        First edition in Italian.

1832.2 Melville, Herman. FOUR GREAT AMERICAN NOVELS. Introduction
        by Raymond W. Short. New York: Henry Holt and Co.,
        1946.

        BILLY BUDD.

1833   Melville, Herman. BILLY BUDD, FORETOPMAN. Introduction
        by William Plomer. London: John Lehmann, Ltd.,
        1947.

1834   Melville, Herman. BILLY BUDD. F. Barron Freeman, ed.
        Cambridge, Mass.: Harvard University Press, 1948.
        With corrections by Elizabeth Freeman, 1953.
        Repr., 1956.

1835	Melville, Herman. SELECTED TALES AND POEMS. Richard Chase, ed. New York: Holt, 1950.
	BILLY BUDD.
1836	Melville, Herman. BILLY BUDD AND OTHER STORIES. Rex Warner, Introduction. London: John Lehmann, Ltd., 1951.
1837	Melville, Herman. BILLY BUDD AND THE PIAZZA TALES. Garden City, New York: Dolphin Books, 1956, 1961. A Dolphin Book.
1838	Melville, Herman. TYPEE AND BILLY BUDD. Introduction by Milton R. Stern, ed. New York: Dutton, 1958.
1839	Melville, Herman. BILLY BUDD in BILLY BUDD AND THE CRITICS. William T. Stafford, ed. San Francisco, Calif.: Wadsworth Publishing Co., 1961, 1968.
1840	Melville, Herman. BILLY BUDD AND OTHER TALES. Afterword by Willard Thorp, ed. New York: New American Library. Signet Classics, 1961.
	Based on the text edited by Frederic Barron Freeman and corrected by Elizabeth Freeman.
1841	Melville, Herman. BILLY BUDD, FORETOPMAN. Introduction by Alfred Weber. Karlsruhe: G. Braun, 1961.
1842	Melville, Herman. BILLY BUDD, FORETOPMAN. The novel edited by F. Barron Freeman, corrected by Elizabeth Freeman; the dramatic version, adapted by Louis O. Coxe and Robert Chapman. Foreword by Brooks Atkinson. New York: Popular Living Classics Library, 1962.
1843	Melville, Herman. BILLY BUDD AND TYPEE. Introduction by Maxwell Geismar. New York: Washington Square Press, 1962.
1844	Melville, Herman. BILLY BUDD, SAILOR (AN INSIDE NARRATIVE): READING TEXT AND GENETIC TEXT. Edited from the Manuscript with Introduction and Notes by Harrison Hayford and Merton M. Sealts, Jr., eds. Chicago: Chicago University Press, 1962, 1963.
1845	Melville, Herman. THE BEST OF MOBY DICK, TYPEE, AND BILLY BUDD. Foreword by Edward Ellsberg. New York: Platt and Munk, 1964.

1846　Melville, Herman. BILLY BUDD in BILLY BUDD, BENITO
CERENO. Introduction by Maxwell Geisman and ten
paintings by Robert Shore. New York: Printed for
members of the Limited Editions Club, 1965.

1847　Melville, Herman. BILLY BUDD, FORETOPMAN. With Special
Aids prepared by Hart Day Leavitt. New York:
Bantam, 1965.

1848　Melville, Herman. BILLY BUDD, GABBIERE DI PARROCCHETTO.
Traduzione dall'americano di Eugenio Montale. 5th
ed. Milano: Bompiano, 1965.

1848.1　Melville, Herman. BILLY BUDD. Przełożył Bronislaw
Zieliński. Illustrowala Ewa Frysztak. Wyd. 1.
Warszawa: Państwowy Instytut Wydawniczy, 1966.

1849　Melville, Herman. GREAT SHORT WORKS OF HERMAN MELVILLE.
Introduction by Jerry Allen. New York: Harper,
1966.

BILLY BUDD.

1849.1　Melville, Herman. BILLY BUDD. See Coxe, Louis O.
BILLY BUDD. London: Heineman, 1966.

1850　Melville, Herman. BILLY BUDD AND BENITO CERENO. Prepared
for Barnes and Noble by Sister M. Martin, O. P.,
New York: Barnes & Noble, 1968.

1851　Melville, Herman. BILLY BUDD AND OTHER STORIES.
Introduction by Alfred Ferguson. Suggestions
for Reading and Discussion by Allen Kirschner.
Boston: Houghton Mifflin, 1970.

1852　Melville, Herman. BILLY BUDD in TWENTIETH CENTURY
INTERPRETATIONS. Howard P. Vincent, ed. Englewood
Cliffs, New Jersey: Prentice-Hall, 1971.

1852.1　Melville, Herman. COCORICO! ET AUTRES CONTES. Traduit
de l'anglais par Pierre Leyris. Paris: Gallimard,
1954.

1852.2　Melville, Herman. KIKERIKI. Holzstiche von Otto Rohse.
Hamburg, Maxmillian--Gesellschaft, 1959.

1853　Melville, Herman. GREAT SHORT WORKS OF HERMAN MELVILLE.
Introduction by Jerry Allen. New York: Harper,
1966.

Cock-a-doodle-doo!

1854   Melville, Herman. THE CONFIDENCE MAN: HIS MASQUERADE.
By Herman Melville, author of THE PIAZZA TALES,
OMOO, TYPEE, etc. London: Longman, Brown, Green,
Longmans and Roberts, 1857.

1854.1 Melville, Herman. THE CONFIDENCE MAN: HIS MASQUERADE.
By Herman Melville, author of THE PIAZZA TALES,
OMOO, etc. New York: Dix Edwards and Co., 1857.

1855   Melville, Herman. THE CONFIDENCE MAN. Roy Fuller, ed.
London: John Lehmann, 1948.

1856   Melville, Herman. THE CONFIDENCE MAN: HIS MASQUERADE.
New York: Grove Press, 1949, 1953, 1955.

1857   Melville, Herman. THE CONFIDENCE-MAN. Elizabeth Foster,
ed. New York: Hendricks House, 1954.

1858   Melville, Herman. L'UOMO DI FIDUCIA. Introduzione,
si Sergio Perosa. Venezia, Neri Pozza, 1961.

1859   Melville, Herman. THE CONFIDENCE MAN: HIS MASQUERADE.
New York: Russell, 1963.

1860   Melville, Herman. THE CONFIDENCE MAN. Introduction by
Hennig Cohen, ed. New York: Holt, Rinehart, and
Winston, 1964.

1861   Melville, Herman. THE CONFIDENCE MAN. Afterword by
R. W. B. Lewis. New York: Signet, 1964.

1862   Melville, Herman. THE CONFIDENCE MAN. Introduction by
John Grube, New York: Airmont, 1966.

1863   Melville, Herman. THE CONFIDENCE MAN: HIS MASQUERADE.
Introduction and Annotations by Bruce Franklin, ed.
Indianapolis: Bobbs-Merrill, 1967.

Contains complete transcription of author's
manuscript fragment, "The River," pp. 354-355.

1864   Melville, Herman. THE CONFIDENCE MAN: HIS MASQUERADE.
Facsimile of first edition. Introduction and
Bibliography by John Seelye. San Francisco:
Chandler, 1968.

1865   Melville, Herman. THE CONFIDENCE MAN: HIS MASQUERADE.
            Hershel Parker, ed. New York: W. W. Norton &
            Company, 1971.

1865.1 Melville, Herman. THE PIAZZA TALES. By Herman Melville.
            New York: Dix & Edwards; London: Sampson Low, Son
            and Co., 1856.

            THE ENCANTADAS.

1866   Melville, Herman. THE ENCANTADAS: OR, ENCHANTED ISLES.
            Introduction, Critical Epilogue and Biographical
            Notes by Victor Wolfgang Von Hagen. Burlingame,
            Calif.: W. P. Wreden, 1940.

1867   Melville, Herman. BILLY BUDD, BENITO CERENO, AND THE
            ENCHANTED ISLES. Carl Van Doren, ed. New York:
            The Readers Club, Inc., 1942.

1868   Melville, Herman. SELECTED TALES AND POEMS. Richard
            Chase, ed. New York: Holt, 1950.

            THE ENCANTADAS.

1868.1 Melville, Herman. THREE SHORTER NOVELS. Quentin
            Anderson, ed. Afterword by Joseph Schiffman.
            New York: Harper, 1962.

1869   Melville, Herman. ENCANTADAS: Two sketches from
            ENCHANTED ISLES. With woodcuts by Rico Lebrun;
            cut by Leonard Baskin. Northhampton, Mass.:
            Printed at the Gehenna Press, 1963.

1870   Melville, Herman. GREAT SHORT WORKS BY HERMAN MELVILLE.
            Introduction by Jerry Allen. New York: Harper,
            1966.

            THE ENCANTADAS.

1871   Melville, Herman. SELECTED TALES AND POEMS. Richard
            Chase, ed. New York: Holt, 1950.

            The Fiddler.

1872   Melville, Herman. GREAT SHORT WORKS OF HERMAN MELVILLE.
            Introduction by Jerry Allen. New York: Harper,
            1966.

            The Fiddler.

1873 Melville, Herman. GREAT SHORT WORKS OF HERMAN MELVILLE.
      Introduction by Jerry Allen. New York: Harper,
      1966.

      The Happy Failure.

1874 Melville, Herman. SELECTED TALES AND POEMS. Richard
      Chase, ed. New York: Holt, 1950.

      I and My Chimney.

1874.1 Melville, Herman. ICH UND MEIN KAMIN; EINE ERZÄHLUNG.
      Übersetzt von Alfred Kuoni. Zürich: Verlag der
      Arche, 1965.

1875 Melville, Herman. GREAT SHORT WORKS OF HERMAN MELVILLE.
      Introduction by Jerry Allen. New York: Harper,
      1966.

      I and My Chimney.

1876 Melville, Herman. ISRAEL POTTER: HIS FIFTY YEARS OF
      EXILE. By Herman Melville, author of TYPEE, OMOO,
      etc. London: G. Routledge and Co., 1855.

1876.1 Melville, Herman. ISRAEL POTTER: HIS FIFTY YEARS OF
      EXILE. By Herman Melville. Author of TYPEE, OMOO,
      etc. New York: G. P. Putnam and Co., 1855.

1876.2 Melville, Herman. THE REFUGEE. /ISRAEL POTTER: HIS
      FIFTY YEARS OF EXILE/. Philadelphia: T. B.
      Peterson & Brothers, 1865.

      Pirated from the New York edition.

1877 Melville, Herman. ISRAEL POTTER. Introduction by
      Raymond M. Weaver. New York: 1924.

1878 Melville, Herman. ISRAEL POTTER. Introduction by C. A.
      Page. New York: L. C. Page, 1925.

1878.1 Melville, Herman. ISRAEL POTTER. Giuseppe Antonelli, ed.
      Roma: Belardetti, n. d.

      First edition of ISRAEL POTTER in Italian.

1878.2 Melville, Herman. ROMANCES OF HERMAN MELVILLE: TYPEE,
      OMOO, MARDI, MOBY DICK, WHITE JACKET, ISRAEL POTTER,
      REDBURN. New York: The Pickwick Publishers, Inc.,
      1928.

1879   Melville, Herman. ISRAEL POTTER. Translated from
          English by C. Cestre. Paris: Editions Corréa,
          1951.

1880   Melville, Herman. HIS FIFTY YEARS OF EXILE (ISRAEL POTTER).
          Introduction by Lewis Leary. New York: Sagamore
          Press, 1957. American Century Series.

1881   Melville, Herman. LIFE AND REMARKABLE ADVENTURES OF
          ISRAEL POTTER. Introduction by Leonard Kriegel.
          New York: Corinth Books, 1962.

1882   Melville, Herman. ISRAEL POTTER: HIS FIFTY YEARS OF
          EXILE. New York: Russell, 1963.

1883   Melville, Herman. ISRAËL POTTER; LES ADVENTURES D'UN
          PATRIOTE A L'ÉPOQUE DE LA RÉVOLUTION D'AMÉRIQUE.
          PRÉSENTATION PAR MICHEL HÉRUBEL. Paris: Union
          générale d'éditions, 1963.

1884   Melville, Herman. ISRAEL POTTER: HIS FIFTY YEARS OF
          EXILE. Garden City, New York: Doubleday, 1965.

1884.1   Melville, Herman. IZRAIL' POTTER; PIAT'DESIAT LET, EGO
          IZGNANIIA; ROMAN Perevod s angliiskogo I. Gurovoi.
          Moskva, Izd-vo, Khudozh. Lit-ra, 1966.

1885   Melville, Herman. SELECTED TALES AND POEMS. Richard
          Chase, ed. New York: Holt, 1950.

          Jimmy Rose.

1886   Melville, Herman. GREAT SHORT WORKS OF HERMAN MELVILLE.
          Introduction by Jerry Allen. New York: Harper,
          1966.

          Jimmy Rose.

1886.1   Melville, Herman. THE PIAZZA TALES. By Herman Melville.
          New York: Dix & Edwards; London: Sampson Low, Son
          and Co., 1856.

          The Lightning Rod Man.

1887   Melville, Herman. GREAT SHORT WORKS OF HERMAN MELVILLE.
          Introduction by Jerry Allen. New York: Harper,
          1966.

          The Lightning Rod Man.

1888   Melville, Herman. MARDI AND A VOYAGE THITHER. By Herman
        Melville, author of TYPEE and OMOO. London:
        Richard Bentley, 1849.

1889   Melville, Herman. MARDI: AND A VOYAGE THITHER. By
        Herman Melville. New York: Harper and Bros.,
        Publishers, 1849.

1890   Melville, Herman. MARDI, AND A VOYAGE THITHER, by
        Herman Melville. London: Constable & Co., 1922.

1891   Melville, Herman. MARDI, AND A VOYAGE THITHER. By
        Herman Melville. Boston: The St. Botolph Society,
        1923.

1891.1 Melville, Herman. MARDI, AND A VOYAGE THITHER.
        Boston: L. C. Page, 1923.

1892   Melville, Herman. MARDI, AND A VOYAGE THITHER. Raymond
        M. Weaver, ed. New York: 1925.

1892.1 Melville, Herman. ROMANCES OF HERMAN MELVILLE: TYPEE,
        OMOO, MARDI, MOBY DICK, WHITE JACKET, ISRAEL POTTER,
        REDBURN. New York: The Pickwick Publishers, Inc.,
        1928.

1893   Melville, Herman. MARDI AND A VOYAGE THITHER. Introduction
        by Bruce Franklin. New York: Capricorn Books, 1964.

1894   Melville, Herman. MARDI: AND A VOYAGE THITHER.
        Afterword by Henry Popkin. New York: The New
        American Library, 1964. Signet Classics.

1894.1 Melville, Herman. MARDI. Traduit de l'anglais par
        Rose Celli. Paris: Gallimard, 1968. Les Classiques
        Anglais.

1895   Melville, Herman. MARDI. Vol. 3. THE WRITINGS OF
        HERMAN MELVILLE. Harrison Hayford, Hershel Parker,
        and G. Thomas Tanselle, eds. Historical Note by
        Elizabeth Foster. Evanston and Chicago: Northwestern
        University Press, and The Newberry Library, 1969.

1896   Melville, Herman. THE WHALE. By Herman Melville,
        author of TYPEE, OMOO, REDBURN, MARDI, WHITE
        JACKET. London: Richard Bentley, 1851. 3 vols.

        Published October 18, 1851. 500 copies were
        printed.

        Vol. I has half-title on which the story is
        described as THE WHALE OR MOBY DICK.

1897   Melville, Herman. MOBY DICK; OR, THE WHALE. By
        Herman Melville, Author of TYPEE, OMOO, REDBURN,
        MARDI, WHITE-JACKET. New York: Harper and Bros.
        Publishers, 1851. 1 vol.

        The American text contains thirty-five passages
        not included in Bentley's edition.

1897.1 Melville, Herman. MOBY-DICK; OR, THE WHALE. By Herman
        Melville. New York: Harper and Bros., 1863.

1898   Melville, Herman. MOBY-DICK; OR THE WHITE WHALE, by
        Herman Melville. Boston: Dana Estes & Co., 1892.

1898.1 Melville, Herman. MOBY-DICK; OR, THE WHITE WHALE.
        New York, Chicago: United States Book Company,
        1892.

1899   Melville, Herman. MOBY DICK; OR, THE WHITE WHALE, by
        Herman Melville; illustrated by I. W. Taber.
        New York: C. Scribner's Sons, 1899.

1900   Melville, Herman. MOBY DICK. Introduction by George
        Louis Becke. London: Putnam, 1901.

1901   Melville, Herman. MOBY DICK; OR, THE WHITE WHALE, by
        Herman Melville. Ernest Rhys, ed. London: J. M.
        Dent & Co.; New York, E. P. Dutton & Co., 1907.
        Everyman's Library.

1902   Melville, Herman. MOBY DICK OR THE WHALE By Herman
        Melville. Introduction by Viola Meynell.
        London: Oxford University Press, 1920. World's
        Classics.

1902.1 Melville, Herman. MOBY DICK; OR, THE WHALE, by
        Herman Melville. Introduction by Viola Meynell.
        London, New York: H. Milford, 1921. World's
        Classics.

1903   Melville, Herman. MOBY DICK; OR, THE WHITE WHALE.
        By Herman Melville. Ernest Rhys, ed. London
        and Toronto: J. M. Dent & Sons, Ltd.; New York:
        E. P. Dutton & Co., 1921. Everyman's Library.

1904   Melville, Herman. MOBY DICK; OR, THE WHITE WHALE,
        by Herman Melville. Illustrated by Mead Schaeffer.
        New York: Dodd, Mead and Company, 1922.

1905   Melville, Herman. MOBY-DICK; OR, THE WHALE, by
        Herman Melville. London: Constable and Company,
        Ltd., 1922.

1906   Melville, Herman. MELVILLE'S MOBY DICK; OR, THE WHITE
        WHALE. Abridged with Biographical Introduction
        and Notes by Hattie L. Hawley. New York: The
        Macmillan Company, 1924.

1907   Melville, Herman. MOBY DICK; OR, THE WHALE, by Herman
        Melville. Introduction by Raymond M. Weaver, ed.
        New York: A. & C. Boni, 1925.

1908   Melville, Herman. MOBY DICK; OR, THE WHITE WHALE,
        by Herman Melville. Abridged by A. E. W. Blake.
        Illustrations by Rowland Hilder. New York:
        A. A. Knopf, 1926.

1909   Melville, Herman. MOBY DICK, by Herman Melville.
        Introduction by Raymond M. Weaver. New York:
        Modern Library, 1926.

1910   Melville, Herman. MOBY DICK. Abridged and with
        Introduction, Notes, and Exercises by William
        S. Ament, ed. Illustrated by Sears Gallagher.
        Boston and New York: Ginn and Company, 1928.

1911   Melville, Herman. MOBY DICK, by Herman Melville.
        Adapted with Notes and Glossary by Sylvia
        Chatfield Bates. Foreword by John H. Finley.
        Illustrated by I. W. Taber. New York, Chicago:
        C. Scribner's Sons, 1928.

1912   Melville, Herman. MOBY DICK; OR, THE WHITE WHALE.
        Earl Maltby Benson, ed. Boston, New York:
        Allyn and Bacon, 1928.

1913   Melville, Herman. MOBY DICK. Illustrated by
        John D. Whiting. New York: J. H. Sears &
        Company, 1928.

1913.1 Melville, Herman. ROMANCES OF HERMAN MELVILLE: TYPEE,
        OMOO, MARDI, MOBY DICK, WHITE JACKET, ISRAEL POTTER,
        REDBURN. New York: The Pickwick Publishers, Inc.,
        1928.

1914   Melville, Herman. MOBY DICK. Introduction by Ralph
        Dow. New York: The Macmillan Company, 1929.

1914.1 Melville, Herman. MOBY DICK. Cesare Pavese, ed.
Roma?: 193-?

First edition in Italian.

1915 Melville, Herman. MOBY DICK; OR, THE WHALE, by Herman
Melville. Illustrated by Rockwell Kent. New York:
Random House, 1930.

1915.1 Melville, Herman. MOBY DICK; OR, THE WHALE, by Herman
Melville. Illustrated by Rockwell Kent. Chicago:
The Lakeside Press, 1930.

1916 Melville, Herman. MOBY DICK; OR, THE WHITE WHALE, by
Herman Melville. Introduction by William McFee.
Notes by M. Dodge Holmes. Illustrations by
Anton Otto Fischer. Philadelphia, Chicago:
The John C. Winston Company, 1931.

1916.1 Melville, Herman. MOBY DICK. Introduction by C. H. St.
L. Russell. New York: 1931.

1917 Melville, Herman. MOBY-DICK; OR, THE WHALE by Herman
Melville. Woodcuts by Howard Simon. New York:
A. and C. Boni, 1931.

1917.1 Melville, Herman. MOBY DICK; OR, THE WHALE, by Herman
Melville. Illustrations by Alfred Staten Conyers.
Akron, Ohio, New York: The Saalfield Publishing
Company, 1931.

1918 Melville, Herman. MOBY DICK by Melville. Illustrated
by Raymond Bishop. New York: A. & C. Boni, Inc.,
1933.

1919 Melville, Herman. MOBY DICK by Herman Melville.
Ernest Rhys, ed. London: J. M. Dent & Sons,
Ltd.; New York: E. P. Dutton & Co., Inc., 1933.
Everyman's Library.

1920 Melville, Herman. MOBY DICK; OR, THE WHALE, by Herman
Melville. Illustrated by Rockwell Kent. De Luxe
ed. Garden City, New York: Garden City Publishing
Co., Inc., 1937.

1921 Melville, Herman. MOBY DICK, ROMAN. Jean Giono and
Joan Smith. Traduit de l'anglais par Lucien
Jacques. Paris: Gillimard, 1941, 1956.

1922 Melville, Herman. MOBY DICK; OR, THE WHALE. Introduction
by Clifton Fadiman. Illustrations by Boardman
Robinson. New York: Heritage Press, 1943, 1956.

1923   Melville, Herman. MOBY-DICK. Introduction by Montgomery
           Belgion. London: The Cresset Press, 1946.

1924   Melville, Herman. MOBY-DICK; OR THE WHALE. Willard
           Thorp, ed. New York: Oxford University Press,
           1947.

1925   Melville, Herman. MOBY DICK. Introduction by Newton
           Arvin. New York: Holt, Rinehart and Winston,
           1948, 1957, 1966.

1926   Melville, Herman. MOBY DICK; OR, THE WHALE. Chicago:
           Encyclopaedia Britannica, 1948, 1955. Great Books
           of the Western World.

1927   Melville, Herman. MOBY DICK; OR, THE WHITE WHALE.
           Introduction by Maxwell Geismar. New York:
           Washington Square Press, 1949, 1961.

1928   Melville, Herman. MOBY DICK. Introduction by Somerset
           Maugham, ed. Philadelphia: Winston, 1949.

1929   Melville, Herman. DE JACHT OP DE WITTE WALVIS. Vertaling:
           A. v. d. Vet. Tekeningen: Rein Snapper. Amsterdam,
           Wereld-Bibliotheek, 195-

           (Avontuur en techniekreeks, no. 25)

1930   Melville, Herman. MOBY DICK. Introduction by Clifton
           Fadiman. New York: Harper and Brothers, 1950.
           Modern Classics.

1931   Melville, Herman. MOBY DICK; OR, THE WHALE. Introduction
           by Leon Howard. New York: The Modern Library, 1950.

1932   Melville, Herman. MOBY DICK. Introduction by Alfred
           Kazin, ed. Boston: Houghton Mifflin, 1950, 1956.

1933   Melville, Herman. MOBY DICK. Introduction by Sherman
           Paul. New York: E. P. Dutton, 1950; London:
           Dent, 1954. Everyman's Library.

1934   Melville, Herman. MOBY DICK. Introduction by Raymond M.
           Weaver, ed. New York: 1950.

1935   Melville, Herman. MOBI-DIK. Translated into Hebrew by
           Elijah Bortniker. Illustrated by Rockwell Kent.
           Tel Aviv, Israel: Newman Publishing House, 1951-
           1952.

1936	Melville, Herman. MOBY-DICK; OR, THE WHALE. Introduction by James Hanley. London: Macdonald & Co., 1952; Macdonald Illustrated Classics. Series, No. 21; New York: Coward-McCann, 1953.
1937	Melville, Herman. MOBY DICK. Luther S. Mansfield and Howard P. Vincent, eds. New York: Hendricks House, 1952, 1962.
1938	Melville, Herman. MOBY-DICK. Oxford: Oxford University Press, 1952. The World's Classics.
1939	Melville, Herman. MOBY-DICK. Translated into Japanese by Nishijari Tanaka. 2 vols. Tokyo(?): Sincho Sha Publishing Co., 1952.
1940	Melville, Herman. MOBY-DICK. Simplified and adapted by Robert J. Dixson, with exercises for study and vacabulary drill. New York: Regents Publishing Co., 1953.
1941	Melville, Herman. MOBY-DICK. Adaptation d'Eliezer Fournier. Illustrations de M. F. de Christen. Tours: Mame, 1953.
1942	Melville, Herman. MOBY-DICK; OR, THE WHITE WHALE. Introduction by J. N. Sullivan. London: Collins New Classics, 1953, 1955, 1956; New York: W. W. Norton and Company, 1953. Collins Classics.
1943	Melville, Herman. MOBY-DICK. Chicago: Benjamin H. Sanborn & Co., 1953. An abridged and simplified version for sixth and seventh grades.
1944	Melville, Herman. MOBY-DICK. Oxford: Oxford University Press, 1953. First appeared in World Classics edition in 1920 and reprinted ten times through 1946. Frequency of early printings (five through 1925) dates the Melville renaissance.
1944.1	Melville, Herman. MOBY-DICK, a 16 r. p. m. record playing one hour. Los Angeles: Audio Book Co., 1953.

1945 Melville, Herman. MOBY-DICK. Translated into German
by Richard Mummendey. Berlin: Deutsche Buch-
Gemeinschaft, 1954.

1946 Melville, Herman. MOBY DICK. Texte francais de Jean
Muray. Illustrated de Paul Durand. Paris:
Hachette, 1954.

1947 Melville, Herman. MOBY-DICK. ILI BIJELI KIT. Translated
into Croatian by Zlatko Gorjan and Josip Tabak.
Zagreb: Kultura, 1954.

1947.1 Melville, Herman. MOBY DICK. Introduction by Leon
Howard. Zagreb: Kultura, 1954.

1948 Melville, Herman. MOBI-DIK. Translated into Serbian by
M. S. Nedic. Belgrade: Izdavocko Preduzece, 1954.

1949 Melville, Herman. MOBY-DICK. Vol. 48 of GREAT BOOKS OF
THE WESTERN WORLD. Robert M. Hutchins, et al, eds.
Chicago: Encyclopedia Britannica, 1955.

1950 Melville, Herman. MOBY-DICK. Translated into German by
Thesi Mutzenbecher. Hamburg: Claassen Verlag, 1955.

1951 Melville, Herman. MOBY-DICK. Translated into Japanese
by Tomoji Abe. Tokyo: Chikuma Shobo, 1955. Vol. 3.
(Vols. 1 and 2 published in 1950).

1952 Melville, Herman. MOBY-DICK; OR, THE WHITE WHALE.
New York: Grosset, 1955.

1953 Melville, Herman. MOBY-DICK; OR, THE WHALE. New York:
Signet, 1955. New American Library.

1954 Melville, Herman. MOBY-DICK; OR, THE WHITE WHALE.
Abridged with Introduction by Maxwell Geismar, ed.
New York: Pocket Books, 1956.

1955 Melville, Herman. MOBY-DICK; OR, THE WHALE. Introduction
by Alfred Kazin, ed. Boston: Houghton Mifflin Co.,
1956.

1956 Melville, Herman. MOBY DICK. Adapted for Young Readers
by Felix Sutton. Illustrated by H. B. Vestal.
New York: Grosset & Dunlap, 1956.

1957   Melville, Herman. MOBY-DICK. Translated into Japanese
by Akira Tomita. Tokyo(?): Kadokawa Shoten, 1956.

1958   Melville, Herman. MOBY-DICK; OR, THE WHALE. Boston:
Houghton Mifflin, 1956. Riverside Editions.

1959   Melville, Herman. MOBY-DICK. London(?): Singer, 1956.

1960   Melville, Herman. MOBY DICK. New York: The Dell
Publishing Company, 1956.

1961   Melville, Herman. MOBY-DICK. London: Dean, 1957.

1962   Melville, Herman. MOBY-DICK. Adapted by Felix Sutton.
London: Publicity Products, 1957.

1963   Melville, Herman. MOBY-DICK. London (?): Murray's
Sales and Service, 1957.

1964   Melville, Herman. MOBY DICK; OR, THE WHALE. G., and
M. W. Thomas, eds. London: Ginn & Co., 1957, 1962.

1965   Melville, Herman. MOBY DICK (la balena bianca)
riduzione per la gioventù a cura di A. Nutini;
illustrazioni di T. Lemmi. 5th ed. Firenze,
Casa Editrice Marzocco, 1957.

Adapted for juveniles.

1966   Melville, Herman. MOBY DICK. Tradução de Adalberto
Rochsteiner e Monteiro Lobato. 4. ed. São Paulo,
Companhia Editora Nacional, 1957.

1967   Melville, Herman. MOBY DICK; LA BALLENA BLANCA.
Juventud, 1957.

1968   Melville, Herman. MOBY DICK, DER WEISSE WAL. Illustriert
von Herbert Pridöhl. Deutsche Ubersetzung, Nachwort
und Anmerkungen von Richard Mummendey. Berlin:
Deutsche Buch-Gemeinschaft, 1957.

1969   Melville, Herman. MOBY DICK O LA BALENA BIANCA.
Introduction by Cecarina Melandri Minoli, ed.
Torino: Unione Tipografica--Editrice Torinese,
1958. 2 vols.

1970   Melville, Herman. MOBY DICK. Barcelona, Buenos Aires,
Bogotá, Editorial Bruguera, 1958.

1971	Melville, Herman. MOBY DICK. Introduction by William M. Gibson, ed. New York: Dell Publishing Co., 1959.
1972	Melville, Herman. MOBY DICK; O, LA BALLENA. Tr. de Guillermo Guerrero Estrella, Hugo E. Richart y Alejandro Rosa. México: Universidad Nacional Autónoma de México, 1960.
1973	Melville, Herman. MOBY DICK; OR, THE WHITE WHALE. Introduction by Denham Sutcliffe. New York: New American Library, 1961.
1973.1	Melville, Herman. MOBY DICK, CZYLI BIALY WIELORYB. Przelozyl Bronislaw Zielinski. Warszawa: Panstwowy Instytut, 1961.
1973.2	Melville, Herman. MOBI DIK: TLI BELYI KIT. Illius. Rokuella Kenta. Per. s angliskogo i prim. I. M. Bernshtein. Predisl. A. I. Startseva. Poslesl. B. A. Zenkovicha. 2. izd. Moskva, Geografizdat, 1961, 1962.
1974	Melville, Herman. MOBY DICK. Introduction by Sherman Paul. London: Dent; New York: E. P. Dutton, 1961.
1975	Melville, Herman. MOBY DICK. New Introduction by Quentin Anderson. New York: Collier Books, 1962.
1976	Melville, Herman. MOBY DICK. Afterword by Clifton Fadiman. Illustrated by Robert Shore. New York: Macmillan Co., 1962.
1977	Melville, Herman. MOBY DICK SAU BALENĂ ALBA IN ROMÎNESTE DE SERBAN ANDRONESCU. Bucureşti, R. P. R. Editura Tineretului, 1962.
1978	Melville, Herman. MOBY-DICK, OR, THE WHALE. Luther S. Mansfield and Howard P. Vincent, eds. New York: Hendricks House, 1962.
1979	Melville, Herman. MOBI DIK, ILI P LIIA KIT. Prevede ot angliiski Neviana Pozeva. Sofiia, Narodna Mladezh, 1962.
1980	Melville, Herman. MOBY-DICK, OR, THE WHALE. New York: Russell and Russell, 1963. 2 vols.

1981   Melville, Herman. MOBY DICK; ELLER, DEN VITA VALEN.
       Till svenska av Hugo Hultenberg. Stockholm:
       Prisma, 1963.

1982   Melville, Herman. MOBY-DICK. Introduction by Charles
       Feidelson, Jr., ed. Indianapolis: Bobbs-Merrill,
       1964. Library of Literature.

1983   Melville, Herman. MOBY DICK. Adaptacion: Ramón Conde
       Obregón. Cubierta e ilustraciones interiores:
       Vincente B. Ballestar. Barcelona: I. D. A. G.,
       1964.

1984   Melville, Herman. MOBY DICK, ROMAN. 5. ed. Hamburg:
       Claassen, 1964.

1985   Melville, Herman. MOBY DICK. Adapted and Retold by
       Frank L. Beals from Melville's Famous Story.
       San Antonio: Naylor Co., 1965.

1986   Melville, Herman. MOBY DICK; OR, THE WHALE. Afterword
       by Jerry Allen. New York: Harper & Row, 1966.

1987   Melville, Herman. MOBY DICK AND OTHER WORKS. Byrne R.
       Fone with George Marcell. New York: Barrister
       Publishing Co., 1966.

1988   Melville, Herman. MOBY-DICK, OR THE WHALE.
       An authoritative text. Reviews and letters by
       Melville. Analogues and sources. Criticism.
       Pictorial materials prepared by John B. Putnam.
       Harrison Hayford and Hershel Parker, eds.
       1st ed. New York: W. W. Norton, 1967.

1989   Melville, Herman. MOBY DICK. Bilbao, Editorial Fher,
       1967.

       NARRATIVE OF A FOUR MONTHS RESIDENCE....   See TYPEE

1990   Melville, Herman. OMOO: A NARRATIVE OF ADVENTURES IN
       THE SOUTH SEAS. By Herman Melville, author of
       TYPEE. New York: Harper and Brothers, Publishers.
       London: John Murray, 1847.

1990.1   Melville, Herman. OMOO: A NARRATIVE OF ADVENTURES IN THE SOUTH SEAS, being a sequel to the RESIDENCE IN THE MARQUESAS ISLANDS. By Herman Melville, author of TYPEE. London: John Murray, 1847.

        The Preface is dated New York, January 28, 1847. Contemporary announcements of Murray's "Colonial and Home Library" speak of an issue of this book in two parts, "sewed," and numbered respectively 43 and 44 of the series. To judge by their numbering in the Library, they postdate the edition above described.

1991   Melville, Herman. OMOO: A NARRATIVE OF ADVENTURES IN THE SOUTH SEAS. 3rd ed. New York: Harper & Brothers, 1847.

1992   Melville, Herman. OMOO: A NARRATIVE OF ADVENTURES IN THE SOUTH SEAS. By Herman Melville.... 5th ed. New York: Harper & Brothers, 1847.

1993   Melville, Herman. OMOO: A NARRATIVE OF ADVENTURES IN THE SOUTH SEAS. A sequel to TYPEE...by Herman Melville. London: J. Murray, 1849.

1994   Melville, Herman. OMOO: A NARRATIVE OF ADVENTURES IN THE SOUTH SEAS. 6th ed. New York: Harper & Brothers, 1850.

1994.1   Melville, Herman. OMOO: A NARRATIVE OF ADVENTURES IN THE SOUTH SEAS. By Herman Melville.... 6th ed. New York: Harper & Brothers, 1855. Repr. of the 1850 edition.

1995   Melville, Herman. OMOO: A NARRATIVE OF ADVENTURES IN THE SOUTH SEAS. A sequel to TYPEE; OR, THE MARQUESAS ISLANDERS. By Herman Melville. New ed. London: J. Murray, 1861.

1996   Melville, Herman. OMOO: A NARRATIVE OF ADVENTURES IN THE SOUTH SEAS. By Herman Melville.... 6th ed. New York: Harper & Brothers, 1863. Repr. of 1850 ed.

1997   Melville, Herman. OMOO; A NARRATIVE OF ADVENTURES IN THE SOUTH SEAS. A sequel to TYPEE by Herman Melville. New York: United States Book Company, 1892.

1998   Melville, Herman. OMOO. Appendix by Marie Clothilde Balfour. London: John Lane, 1904.

1999   Melville, Herman. OMOO. Introduction by W. Clark Russell,
        ed. New York: 1904.

2000   Melville, Herman. OMOO, A NARRATIVE OF ADVENTURES IN
        THE SOUTH SEAS, by Herman Melville. Ernest Rhys, ed.
        London: J. M. Dent & Co., New York: E. P. Dutton
        & Co., 1907. Everyman's Library.

2000.1 Melville, Herman. OMOO. Introduction by Ernest Rhys.
        New York: 1908.

2001   Melville, Herman. OMOO. W. Clark Russell, ed.
        New York: E. P. Dutton, 1911. New Universal Library.

2002   Melville, Herman. OMOO, A NARRATIVE OF ADVENTURES IN
        THE SOUTH SEAS, by Herman Melville. Ernest Rhys, ed.
        London & Toronto: J. M. Dent & Sons, Ltd., New York:
        E. P. Dutton & Co., 1921.

2003   Melville, Herman. OMOO; A NARRATIVE OF ADVENTURES IN
        THE SOUTH SEAS, by Herman Melville. London:
        Constable and Company, Ltd., 1922.

2004   Melville, Herman. OMOO; A NARRATIVE OF ADVENTURES IN
        THE SOUTH SEAS, by Herman Melville. London, New
        York: H. Milford, 1924.

2005   Melville, Herman. OMOO, by Herman Melville. Illustrated
        by Mead Schaeffer. New York: Dodd, Mead and Company,
        1924.

2006   Melville, Herman. OMOO, A NARRATIVE OF ADVENTURES IN
        THE SOUTH SEAS, by Herman Melville. Ernest Rhys, ed.
        London and Toronto: J. M. Dent & Sons, Ltd., New
        York: E. P. Dutton & Co., 1925.

2006.1 Melville, Herman. ROMANCES OF HERMAN MELVILLE: TYPEE,
        OMOO, MARDI, MOBY DICK, WHITE JACKET, ISRAEL POTTER,
        REDBURN. New York: The Pickwick Publishers, Inc.,
        1928.

2007   Melville, Herman. OMOO; A NARRATIVE OF ADVENTURES IN
        THE SOUTH SEAS. Garden City, New York: Doubleday,
        195-? Dolphin Books.

2008   Melville, Herman. OMOO. Boston: L. C. Page, 1951.

2009   Melville, Herman. OMOO. Harrison Hayford and Walter
       Blair, eds. New York: Hendricks House, 1957.

2010   Melville, Herman. OMOO, A NARRATIVE OF ADVENTURES IN
       THE SOUTH SEAS. New York: Grove Press, 1958.
       Evergreen Books.

2011   Melville, Herman. OMOO. Perevod s angliĭskogo T. L. i
       V. I. Rovinskikh. Moskva, Gos. izd-vo geografiche-
       skoĭ lit-ry, 1960.

2012   Melville, Herman. OMOO. New Introduction by Van Wyck
       Brooks. Wood engravings by Reynolds Stone. Oxford,
       England: Printed for members of the Limited Editions
       Club, 1961.

2013   Melville, Herman. OMOO; A NARRATIVE OF ADVENTURES IN
       THE SOUTH SEAS. New York: Russell & Russell,
       1963.

2014   Melville, Herman. OMOO. Introduction by Van Wyck Brooks.
       New York: Heritage, 1967.

2015   Melville, Herman. OMOO: A NARRATIVE OF ADVENTURES IN
       THE SOUTH SEAS. Harrison Hayford, Hershel Parker,
       and G. Thomas Tanselle, eds. Historical Note by
       Gordon Roper. Evanston and Chicago: Northwestern
       University Press and The Newberry Library, 1968.

2016   Melville, Herman. "The Paradise of Bachelors and the
       Tartarus of Maids," Harper's New Monthly Magazine,
       1855.

2017   Melville, Herman. SELECTED TALES AND POEMS by Herman
       Melville. Introduction by Richard Chase, ed.
       New York: Holt, Rinehart and Winston, 1950.

       Paradise of Bachelors and Tartarus of Maids.

2018   Melville, Herman. GREAT SHORT WORKS OF HERMAN MELVILLE.
       Introduction by Jerry Allen. New York: Harper &
       Row, Publishers, 1966. A Perennial Classic.

       Paradise of Bachelors and Tartarus of Maids.

2019   Melville, Herman. THE PIAZZA TALES. By Herman Melville.
       New York: Dix and Edwards, 1856.

       The Piazza.

2020　Melville, Herman.　GREAT SHORT WORKS OF HERMAN MELVILLE.
　　　　Introduction by Jerry Allen.　New York:　Harper &
　　　　Row, Publishers, 1966.　A Perennial Classic.

　　　　The Piazza.

2021　Melville, Herman.　THE PIAZZA TALES.　By Herman Melville,
　　　　author of TYPEE, OMOO, etc.　New York:　Dix and
　　　　Edwards.　London:　Sampson Low, Son and Co., 1856.

　　　　The Piazza
　　　　BARTLEBY
　　　　BENITO CERENO
　　　　The Lightning Rod Man
　　　　The Encantadas; or Enchanted Islands
　　　　The Bell Tower

　　　　Published in May or June, 1856.　It is doubtful
　　　　whether copies of this book were ever actually issued
　　　　in England, despite the fact that Sampson Low and
　　　　Company advertised the book at 9s. in June, 1856.

2022　Melville, Herman.　THE PIAZZA TALES, by Herman Melville.
　　　　London, Bombay:　Constable and Company, Ltd., 1923.

2023　Melville, Herman.　THE PIAZZA TALES by Herman Melville.
　　　　Drawing by Benj Greenstein.　New York:　The Elf
　　　　Publishers, 1929.

　　　　Of this edition, seven hundred and fifty copies
　　　　were printed for sale in the United States and England,
　　　　and the type destroyed.

2024　Melville, Herman.　PIAZZA TALES.　Introduction by
　　　　Egbert S. Oliver, ed.　New York:　Hendricks House,
　　　　Farrar Straus, 1948.

2025　Melville, Herman.　BILLY BUDD AND THE PIAZZA TALES.
　　　　Garden City, New York:　Dolphin Books, 1956, 1961.

2026　Melville, Herman.　THE PIAZZA TALES.　New York:　Russell
　　　　and Russell, 1963.

2027　Melville, Herman.　PIERRE: OR THE AMBIGUITIES.　By
　　　　Herman Melville.　New York:　Harper and Bros.,
　　　　Publishers, 1852.

2028   Melville, Herman. PIERRE: OR THE AMBIGUITIES. By Herman Melville. London: Sampson Low, Son and Co., 1852.

Published in November, 1852, this English edition is as scarce as, if not scarcer than, the American edition, the bulk of which was destroyed by fire.

2029   Melville, Herman. PIERRE: OR, THE AMBIGUITIES. By Herman Melville. New York: Harper and Brothers, 1855.

2030   Melville, Herman. PIERRE: OR, THE AMBIGUITIES, by Herman Melville. London, Bombay: Constable and Company, 1923.

2031   Melville, Herman. PIERRE, OR, THE AMBIGUITIES. Preface by H. M. Tomlinson and Introduction by John Brooks Moore. New York: E. P. Dutton and Co., 1929.

2032   Melville, Herman. PIERRE, OR THE AMBIGUITIES. Robert S. Forsythe, ed. New York: Alfred A. Knopf, 1930, 1941. Americana Deserta Series.

2033   Melville, Herman. PIERRE; OR, THE AMBIGUITIES. Introduction by Henry A. Murray, ed. New York: Hendricks House, Farrar, Straus & Cudahy, Inc., 1949.

2034   Melville, Herman. PIERRE, OR THE AMBIGUITIES. H. A. Murray, ed. New York: Hendricks House, 1957.

2035   Melville, Herman. PIERRE; OR, THE AMBIGUITIES. New York: Grove Press, 1957. Evergreen Books.

2035.1 Melville, Herman. PIERRE; OR, THE AMBIGUITIES. London: Nelson, Foster & Scott, 1957.

2036   Melville, Herman. PIERRE, OR THE AMBIGUITIES. New York: Russell and Russell, 1963.

2037   Melville, Herman. PIERRE; OR THE AMBIGUITIES. Foreword by Lawrance Thompson. New York: New American Library, 1964.

2037.1 Melville, Herman. PIERRE. Harrison Hayford, Hershel Parker, and G. Thomas Tanselle, eds. Evanston and Chicago: Northwestern and The Newberry Library, 1971.

2038   Melville, Herman. GREAT SHORT WORKS OF HERMAN MELVILLE.
        Introduction by Jerry Allen. New York: Harper
        and Row, 1966. A Perennial Classic.

        A Poor Man's Pudding and a Rich Man's Crumbs.

2039   Melville, Herman. REDBURN: HIS FIRST VOYAGE. BEING THE
        SAILOR BOY CONFESSIONS AND REMINISCENCES OF THE
        SON OF A GENTLEMAN IN THE MERCHANT SERVICE. By
        Herman Melville. Author of TYPEE, MARDI, etc.
        London: Richard Bentley, 1849. 2 vols.

        This book was published on September 29, 1849.
        The English edition predates the American one. 750
        copies were printed.

2040   Melville, Herman. REDBURN: HIS FIRST VOYAGE. BEING THE
        SAILOR BOY CONFESSIONS AND REMINISCENCES OF THE SON
        OF A GENTLEMAN IN THE MERCHANT SERVICE. By Herman
        Melville, Author of TYPEE, MARDI. New York:
        Harper and Bros., Publishers, 1849. 1 vol.

        A book issued, REDBURN: OR THE SCHOOLMASTER OF
        A MORNING, New York, 1845, is of doubtful authorship.

2041   Melville, Herman. REDBURN: HIS FIRST VOYAGE. New York:
        Harper and Brothers, 1850.

2042   Melville, Herman. REDBURN: HIS FIRST VOYAGE. BEING
        THE SAILOR-BOY CONFESSIONS AND REMINISCENCES OF
        THE SON-OF-A-GENTLEMAN, IN THE MERCHANT SERVICE.
        By Herman Melville.... New York: Harper &
        Brothers, 1855.

2043   Melville, Herman. REDBURN; HIS FIRST VOYAGE: BEING THE
        SAILOR-BOY CONFESSIONS AND REMINISCENCES OF THE SON
        OF A GENTLEMAN IN THE MERCHANT SERVICE, by Herman
        Melville. London: Constable and Company, Ltd.,
        1922.

2044   Melville, Herman. REDBURN; HIS FIRST VOYAGE. Boston:
        L. C. Page, 1924.

2045   Melville, Herman. REDBURN, HIS FIRST VOYAGE: BEING THE
        SAILOR BOY CONFESSIONS AND REMINISCENCES OF THE
        SON-OF-A-GENTLEMAN IN THE MERCHANT SERVICE, by
        Herman Melville.... Illustrated by Frank T.
        Merrill. Boston: The St. Botolph Society,
        1924.

2046   Melville, Herman. REDBURN, HIS FIRST VOYAGE. Introduction
        by Raymond Weaver, ed. New York: A. & C. Boni,
        1924.

2046.1 Melville, Herman. ROMANCES OF HERMAN MELVILLE: TYPEE,
OMOO, MARDI, MOBY DICK, WHITE JACKET, ISRAEL POTTER,
REDBURN. New York: The Pickwick Publishers, Inc.,
1928.

2047 Melville, Herman. REDBURN. Introduction by William
Plomer. London: Jonathan Cape, 1937.

2048 Melville, Herman. REDBURN: HIS FIRST VOYAGE: BEING THE
SAILOR BOY CONFESSIONS AND REMINISCENCES OF THE
SON-OF-A-GENTLEMAN IN THE MERCHANT SERVICE. Garden
City, New York: Doubleday & Company, Inc., 1957.
Doubleday Anchor Books.

2049 Melville, Herman. LA NAVE DI VETRO. Introduction by
Giancarlo Vigorelli, ed. Bologna: Capelli, 1957.

2050 Melville, Herman. REDBURN, HIS FIRST VOYAGE.
Harrison Hayford, Hershel Parker, and G. Thomas
Tanselle, eds. Historical Note by Hershel Parker.
Evanston and Chicago: Northwestern University
Press and The Newberry Library, 1969.

2051 Melville, Herman. GREAT SHORT WORKS OF HERMAN MELVILLE.
Introduction by Jerry Allen. New York: Harper and
Row, 1966. A Perennial Classic.

The Two Temples.

2052 Melville, Herman. TYPEE: A PEEP AT POLYNESIAN LIFE
DURING A FOUR MONTHS RESIDENCE IN A VALLEY OF THE
MARQUESAS WITH NOTICES OF THE FRENCH OCCUPATION
OF TAHITI AND THE PROVISIONAL CESSION OF THE
SANDWICH ISLANDS TO LORD PAULET. By Herman
Melville. Part One. (Part Two.) New York:
Wiley and Putnam; London: John Murray, 1846.
2 vols.

2053 Melville, Herman. NARRATIVE OF A FOUR MONTHS RESIDENCE
AMONG THE NATIVES OF A VALLEY OF THE MARQUESAS
ISLANDS: OR A PEEP AT POLYNESIAN LIFE. By Herman
Melville. London: John Murray, 1846. 1 vol.

A volume in Murray's "Colonial and Home Library"
(No. 15), subsequently named TYPEE.

"The Story of Toby," published separately the
same year, later added to the book as an appendix.

2054 Melville, Herman. TYPEE: A PEEP AT POLYNESIAN LIFE
DURING A FOUR MONTHS RESIDENCE IN A VALLEY OF THE
MARQUESAS. Revised Edition with a Sequel. By
Herman Melville. New York: Wiley and Putnam,
London: John Murray, 1847. 1 vol.

2054.1   Melville, Herman. TYPEE: OR A NARRATIVE OF A FOUR
MONTHS RESIDENCE AMONG THE NATIVES OF A VALLEY
OF THE MARQUESAS ISLANDS: OR A PEEP AT POLYNESIAN
LIFE. By Herman Melville. London: John Murray,
1847. 1 vol.

2055   Melville, Herman. TYPEE: A PEEP AT POLYNESIAN LIFE.
Revised edition with a Sequel. New York: Wiley
and Putnam, 1848.

2056   Melville, Herman. TYPEE: A PEEP AT POLYNESIAN LIFE....
Revised edition with a sequel. New York: Harper
and Brothers, 1849.

2057   Melville, Herman. TYPEE: A PEEP AT POLYNESIAN LIFE,
DURING A FOUR MONTHS RESIDENCE IN A VALLEY OF THE
MARQUESAS. Revised edition with a sequel. By
Herman Melville. New York: Harper & Brothers,
1857.

2058   Melville, Herman. TYPEE: A PEEP AT POLYNESIAN LIFE.
Revised with a sequel. New York: 1860.

2059   Melville, Herman. TYPEE; OR, A NARRATIVE OF A FOUR
MONTHS' RESIDENCE AMONG THE NATIVES OF A VALLEY
OF THE MARQUESAS ISLANDS; OR, A PEEP AT POLYNESIAN
LIFE. By Herman Melville. New edition. London:
J. Murray, 1861.

2060   Melville, Herman. TYPEE: A REAL ROMANCE OF THE SOUTH
SEAS. Biographical and Critical Introduction by
Arthur Stedman, ed. New York: United States
Book Co., 1892.

2061   Melville, Herman. TYPEE: A NARRATIVE OF A FOUR MONTHS'
RESIDENCE AMONG THE NATIVES OF A VALLEY OF THE
MARQUESAS ISLANDS; OR, A PEEP AT POLYNESIAN LIFE.
By Herman Melville. New edition, with a memoir of
the author and illustrations. London: John Murray,
1893.

2062   Melville, Herman. TYPEE. Introduction by Arthur
Stedman. Boston: 1900.

2063   Melville, Herman. TYPEE. Introduction by W. P. Trent, ed.
Boston: Heath & Co., 1902.

2064   Melville, Herman. TYPEE. Introduction by W. Clark
Russell. New York: 1904.

2065   Melville, Herman. TYPEE; A NARRATIVE OF THE MARQUESAS
ISLANDS, by Herman Melville. London: J. M. Dent
& Co.; New York: E. P. Dutton & Co., 1907.

2066   Melville, Herman. TYPEE. W. Clark Russell, ed.
New York: E. P. Dutton & Co., 1911. New
Universal Library.

2067   Melville, Herman. TYPEE, A ROMANCE OF THE SOUTH SEAS,
by Herman Melville. Introduction and glossary by
Sterling Andrus Leonard, ed. New York: Harcourt,
Brace and Howe, 1920.

        Chapter III omitted from this edition.

2068   Melville, Herman. TYPEE, A NARRATIVE OF THE MARQUESAS
ISLANDS, by Herman Melville. London & Toronto:
J. M. Dent & Sons, Ltd.; New York: E. P. Dutton
& Co., 1921.

2069   Melville, Herman. TYPEE; A PEEP AT POLYNESIAN LIFE
DURING A FOUR MONTHS' RESIDENCE IN A VALLEY OF
THE MARQUESAS, WITH NOTICES OF THE FRENCH
OCCUPATION OF TAHITI AND THE PROVISIONAL CESSION
OF THE SANDWICH ISLANDS TO LORD PAULET, AND A
SEQUEL, THE STORY OF TOBY, by Herman Melville.
London: Constable and Company, Ltd., 1922.

2070   Melville, Herman. TYPEE, by Herman Melville.
Illustrations by Mead Schaeffer. New York:
Dodd, Mead and Company, 1923.

2071   Melville, Herman. TYPEE, by Herman Melville. London,
New York: H. Milford, 1924. World's Classics.

2072   Melville, Herman. TYPEE, A NARRATIVE OF THE MARQUESAS
ISLANDS, by Herman Melville. Ernest Rhys, ed.
London and Toronto: J. M. Dent & Sons, Ltd.,
New York: E. P. Dutton & Co., 1930. Everyman's
Library.

2073   Melville, Herman. TYPEE; OR, A PEEP AT POLYNESIAN LIFE,
by Herman Melville. Philadelphia: D. McKay, 1930.

2074   Melville, Herman. TYPEE; A NARRATIVE OF THE MARQUESAS
ISLANDS, by Herman Melville. Illustrated by
Guido Boer. New York: Aventine Press, 1931.

2075   Melville, Herman. TYPEE, by Herman Melville. New York:
W. J. Black, Inc., 1932.

2076   Melville, Herman. TYPEE; A ROMANCE OF THE SOUTH SEAS,
by Herman Melville. Introduction by Raymond Weaver.
Illustrations by Miguel Covarrubias. New York:
The Limited Editions Club, 1935. Reprinted, New
York: Heritage Press, 1963.

2077   Melville, Herman. PARAÍSO DE CANIBAIS; NARRATIVA DE
UMA ESTADIA DE QUATRO MESES ENTRE OS INDIGENAS DAS
ILHAS MARQUESAS. Traduzido do inglês por F. Dos
Reis e Lima e Joao de Oliveira. Lisboa,
Portugália Editora, 194-?

2078   Melville, Herman. TYPEE; OR, A PEEP AT POLYNESIAN LIFE,
by Herman Melville. Front. by Ellis Silas.
Philadelphia: D. McKay Company., n. d. First
published in this edition, 1940.

2079   Melville, Herman. TYPEE. Traducción directa del inglés
por Abraham Schijman. Buenos Aires: Editorial
Ayacucho, 1945.

2080   Melville, Herman. TYPEE. Roman traduit de l'anglais
par Pierre Verdier. Paris: La Centaine, 1945.

2080.1 Melville, Herman. TYPEE. Biographical and Critical
Introduction by Arthur Stedman, ed. Boston:
L. C. Page, 1950.

2081   Melville, Herman. TYPEE, A PEEP AT POLYNESIAN LIFE.
New York: Avon Publications, 195-?

2081.1 Melville, Herman. TYPEE. Introduction by Robert
Gibbings. London: 1951.

2082   Melville, Herman. TYPEE. Translated into Japanese by
Fukuo Hashimoto. Tokyo (?): Hayakawa Shobo, 1953.

2083   Melville, Herman. TYPEE. New York: Avon Red and Gold
Library, 1956.

2084   Melville, Herman. TYPEE. New York: Grosset & Dunlap,
1957?

2085   Melville, Herman. TYPEE and BILLY BUDD. Introduction
by Milton R. Stern. New York: E. P. Dutton, 1958.
Dutton Everyman Paperbacks.

2086   Melville, Herman. TAIPI. Perevod s Angliiskogo i
       obrabotka L. G. Shpet. Moskva, Gos. Izd-vo
       Geograficheskoi Lit-ry, 1958.

       In Cyrillic characters.

2087   Melville, Herman. TYPEE. Prevedla Gitica Jakopin.
       Koper, Lipa, 1958.

2088   Melville, Herman. TYPEE: A REAL ROMANCE OF THE SOUTH
       SEAS. Introduction by C. Merton Babcock. New York:
       Harper and Brothers, 1959. Harper's Modern Classics.

2089   Melville, Herman. TYPEE. London: Oxford University
       Press, 1959. The World's Classics.

2090   Melville, Herman. TYPEE. Illustrated by Mead Schaeffer.
       New York: Dodd, Mead & Co., 1959.

2091   Melville, Herman. TYPEE: A PEEP AT POLYNESIAN LIFE
       DURING A FOUR MONTHS' RESIDENCE IN A VALLEY OF
       THE MARQUESAS, WITH NOTICES OF THE FRENCH
       OCCUPATION OF TAHITI AND THE PROVISIONAL CESSION
       OF THE SANDWICH ISLANDS TO LORD PAULET. Garden
       City, New York: Dolphin Books, 1961.

2092   Melville, Herman. BILLY BUDD and TYPEE. Introduction
       by Maxwell Geismar. New York: Washington Square
       Press, 1962.

2093   Melville, Herman. TYPEE, A PEEP AT POLYNESIAN LIFE
       DURING A FOUR MONTHS' RESIDENCE IN A VALLEY OF
       THE MARQUESAS. /New York?/: West Virginia Pulp
       and Paper Co., 1962.

2094   Melville, Herman. TYPEE: A PEEP AT POLYNESIAN LIFE
       DURING A FOUR MONTHS' RESIDENCE IN A VALLEY OF THE
       MARQUESAS, WITH NOTICES OF THE FRENCH OCCUPATION
       OF TAHITI AND THE PROVISIONAL CESSION OF THE
       SANDWICH ISLANDS TO LORD PAULET, AND A SEQUEL,
       THE STORY OF TOBY. New York: Russell & Russell,
       1963.

2095   Melville, Herman. TYPEE. Introduction by Clifton
       Fadiman. New York: Bantam Books, 1964.

2096   Melville, Herman. TYPEE. Afterword by Harrison Hayford.
       New York: New American Library, 1964. Signet
       Classics.

2097   Melville, Herman. MELVILLE: THE BEST OF MOBY DICK,
       TYPEE, AND BILLY BUDD. Foreword by Edward Ellsberg.
       New York: Platt & Munk, 1964.

2098   Melville, Herman. TYPEE, A PEEP AT...MARQUESAS. WITH
        NOTICES OF THE FRENCH...TO LORD PAULET. Introduction
        by Clara Thomas. New York: Airmont Publishing Co.,
        1965.

2099   Melville, Herman. TAIPI. ABENTEUER IN DER SÜDSEE.
        (Übertragung und Nachwort von Ilse Hecht.)
        Vollständige Ausg. 4. Aufl. Leipzig: Dieterich,
        1967.

2100   Melville, Herman. TYPEE: A PEEP AT POLYNESIAN LIFE.
        Harrison Hayford, Hershel Parker, and G. Thomas
        Tanselle, eds. Historical Note by Leon Howard.
        Evanston and Chicago: Northwestern University
        Press and The Newberry Library, 1968.

        THE WHALE - See MOBY DICK

2101   Melville, Herman. WHITE JACKET: OR THE WORLD IN A
        MAN OF WAR. By Herman Melville. London: Richard
        Bentley, 1850. 2 vols.

        Published January 23, 1850. The English edition
        predates the American one. 1,000 copies were printed.

        Vol. I, pp. iii and iv contain a preface dated
        October, 1849, and different in content from the note
        on p. iv of the American edition, dated March, 1850.

2102   Melville, Herman. WHITE JACKET: OR THE WORLD IN A
        MAN OF WAR. By Herman Melville. Author of
        TYPEE, OMOO, MARDI and REDBURN. New York:
        Harper and Bros., Publishers; London: Richard
        Bentley, 1850. 1 vol.

2103   Melville, Herman. WHITE-JACKET; OR, THE WORLD IN A
        MAN-OF-WAR. By Herman Melville.... New York:
        Harper & Brothers, 1855.

2104   Melville, Herman. WHITE-JACKET; OR, THE WORLD IN A
        MAN-OF-WAR, by Herman Melville.... New York;
        Chicago: United States Book Company, 1892.

2105   Melville, Herman. WHITE JACKET; OR, THE WORLD IN A MAN-OF-WAR, by Herman Melville. London: Constable and Company, Ltd., 1922.

2106   Melville, Herman. WHITE JACKET; OR, THE WORLD IN A MAN-OF-WAR, by Herman Melville. Introduction by Carl Van Doren. New York: 1924; London: Oxford University Press, 1929. World's Classics.

2106.1 Melville, Herman. ROMANCES OF HERMAN MELVILLE: TYPEE, OMOO, MARDI, MOBY DICK, WHITE JACKET, ISRAEL POTTER, REDBURN. New York: The Pickwick Publishers, Inc., 1928.

2107   Melville, Herman. WHITE-JACKET. Boston: L. C. Page, 1950.

2108   Melville, Herman. WHITE JACKET; OR, THE WORLD IN A MAN-OF-WAR. Introduction by William Plomer. London: John Lehmann, 1952; New York: Grove Press, 1956. Evergreen Books.

2109   Melville, Herman. VESTE BLANCHE. Adaptation d'Eliezer Fournier. Paris: Delagrave, 1957.

2110   Melville, Herman. WHITE JACKET, OR THE WORLD IN A MAN-OF-WAR. New York: Russell & Russell, 1963.

2111   Melville, Herman. WHITE-JACKET, OR THE WORLD IN A MAN-OF-WAR. Introduction by A. R. Humphreys, ed. London: Oxford University Press, 1966.

2112   Melville, Herman. WHITE-JACKET. Hennig Cohen, ed. New York: Holt, Rinehart & Winston, 1967.

2113   Melville, Herman. WHITE-JACKET; OR THE WORLD IN A MAN-OF-WAR. Harrison Hayford, Hershel Parker, and G. Thomas Tanselle, eds. Historical Note by Willard Thorp. Evanston and Chicago: Northwestern University Press and The Newberry Library, 1970.

2114   Melville, Herman. MELVILLE'S OATH OF ALLEGIANCE AS INSPECTOR OF CUSTOMS (1866). ESQ, 47 (2nd Qt., 1967), 129.

2115   "The Melville Room in the Berkshire Athenaeum," BSL,
        47 (Winter, 1957), 9.

2115.1 THE MELVILLE SOCIETY NEWSLETTER. A quarterly publication
        of exchange of information on life and works of
        Herman Melville. Tyrus Hillway, Secretary. Colorado
        State College, Greeley, Colorado.

2115.2 Melville, Herman. MOBY DICK. New York: The Dell
        Publishing Company, 1956.

        A comic book containing photographs of Gregory
        Peck. (No. 717 of Movie Classic Series).

2116   Menard, Wilmon. "A Forgotten South Sea Paradise,"
        Asia, 33 (September, 1933), 457-463; (October, 1933),
        510.

2117   Mencken, H. L. THE AMERICAN LANGUAGE: AN INQUIRY INTO
        THE DEVELOPMENT OF ENGLISH IN THE UNITED STATES.
        New York: Alfred A. Knopf, 1936, p. 261n.

        Mencken noted that when Melville's MOBY DICK was
        brought out in England, many changes were made in the
        text in order to get rid of "Americans" and American
        spellings. In Chapter XVI alone there were 106
        variations.

2118   Mendel'son, M. Ot "Taipi" do Bikini /From TYPEE to
        Bikini7, Literaturnaia gazeta, July 27, 1946.

2119   Mendilow, A. A. TIME AND THE NOVEL. Introduction by
        J. Isaacs. London, New York: Peter Nevil, Ltd.,
        1952, p. 213.

2120   Mengeling, Marvin E. "MOBY-DICK: The Fundamental
        Principles," ESQ, 38 (1st Qt., 1965), 74-87.

        Polarities (optimism vs. pessimism, head vs.
        heart, etc.) are keys to MOBY DICK.

2121   Merchant, Norris. "The Artist and Society in Melville,"
        Views, 4 (1957), 56-57.

2121.1 /Merchant Marine Cadet Corps Educational Unit7. AMERICANS
        WHO HAVE CONTRIBUTED TO THE HISTORY AND TRADITIONS OF
        THE UNITED STATES MERCHANT MARINE (1943).

2122   Merrifield, Richard. "White Whale," Yankee, 19
        (February, 1955), 41.

2123   Messenger, William E. "Conrad and Melville Again,"
        Conrad, 2 (Winter, 1969-70), 53-64.

        Comparison of Conrad and Melville.

2124   Metcalf, Eleanor Melville. HERMAN MELVILLE: CYCLE AND
        EPICYCLE. Cambridge, Mass.: Harvard University
        Press, 1953.

        Rev. by Charles Anderson, AL, 26 (1954), 262-264.

2125   Metcalf, Eleanor Melville, ed. HERMAN MELVILLE: JOURNAL
        OF A VISIT TO LONDON AND THE CONTINENT, 1849-1850.
        London: Cohen & West, Ltd., 1949; Cambridge: Harvard
        University Press, 1949.

        Rev. by Charles Anderson, AL, 21 (1949), 250-251.

2126   Metcalf, Eleanor Melville. "A Pilgrim by Land and Sea,"
        HB, 3 (1927), 3-11.

        Two letters to Melville's children printed in
        children's magazine by his grand-daughter, Mrs. Eleanor
        Melville Metcalf.

2127   Metzger, Charles R. "Melville's Saints: Allusions in
        BENITO CERENO," ESQ, 58 (1970), 88-90.

        Melville alludes to St. Mary, St. Nicholas,
        St. Dominic, St. Francis, and St. Bartholomew.
        Since all "suffered versions of Bartholomew's
        martyrdom," by virtue of their exposure to evils
        of slavery perhaps all bear some "kinship" to this
        saint.

2128   Meyer, Donald. "The Dissolution of Calvinism," PATHS
        OF AMERICAN THOUGHT. Arthur M. Schlesinger, Jr.,
        and Morton White, eds. London: Chatto & Windus,
        1964, passim.

        Remarks which place Melville in his theological
        milieu.

2129   Meynell, Viola. "A Great Story Teller: Herman Melville,"
        LivA, 304 (1920), 715-720.

        A justification of her forthcoming edition of
        MOBY DICK.

2130   Meynell, Viola. "Herman Melville," DubR, 166 (January-
        March, 1920), 96-105.

2131   Meynell, Viola. Introduction, MOBY DICK. London:
        Oxford University Press, 1920.

        Many credit this edition with setting the vogue
        for the Melville revival. It was first published in
        1920, reprinted in 1921, 1922 (twice), 1923, 1925,
        1929, 1930, 1935, 1938, 1945, and 1946; reset in 1952
        and reprinted in 1955, 1957, 1958, 1963 (three times),
        and 1966. The repeated publications indicate the
        book's significance.

2132   Middleton, John A. "Shark-Talk: The Uses of Dialogue
        in MOBY DICK," DAI, 30 (Ind.: 1970), 4995A.

2133   Milano, Paolo. IL LETTORE DI PROFESSIONE. Milano:
        Feltrinelli, 1960.

        Melville and others.

2134   Milford, H. S. "The Text of TYPEE," TLS, (May 27, 1936),
        355.

2134.1 Miller, Edwin H., ed. A CENTURY OF WHITMAN CRITICISM.
        London and Bloomington, Indiana: Indiana University
        Press, 1969, passim.

        Comparisons of Melville and Whitman.

2135   Miller, Edwin H. WALT WHITMAN'S POETRY: A PSYCHOLOGICAL
        JOURNEY. New York: Houghton Mifflin Co., 1968,
        passim.

2136   Miller, F. De Wolfe. "Another Chapter in the History
        of the Great White Whale," MELVILLE AND HAWTHORNE
        IN THE BERKSHIRES: A SYMPOSIUM. Howard P. Vincent,
        ed. Kent, Ohio: Kent State University Press,
        1968, pp. 109-117.

        A new analogue of MOBY DICK, a newspaper excerpt
        of 1843 from a work by William Comstock which has not
        been located.

2137   Miller, F. DeWolfe. "Melville, Whitman, and the Forty
        Immortals," ENGLISH STUDIES IN HONOR OF JAMES
        SOUTHALL WILSON. Charlottesville, Va.: 1951,
        pp. 23-24.

2138   Miller, James E., Jr. "The Achievement of Melville,"
        UKCR, 26 (Autumn, 1959), 59-67.

2139   Miller, James E., Jr. "BILLY BUDD: The Catastrophe of Innocence," MLN, 73 (March, 1958), 168-176.

2139.1 Miller, James E., Jr. "BILLY BUDD: The Catastrophe of Innocence," in READER'S GUIDE TO HERMAN MELVILLE. New York: Farrar, Straus and Cudahy, 1962, pp. 218-228.

2140   Miller, James E., Jr. "The Complex Figure in Melville's Carpet," ArQ, 15 (Autumn, 1959), 197-210.

       The major theme in the Melville canon: man must compromise with his ideals so he can come to terms with the evil in himself and in the universe.

2141   Miller, James E., Jr. THE CONFIDENCE-MAN: His Guises," PMLA, 74 (March, 1959), 102-111.

2142   Miller, James E., Jr. "Hawthorne and Melville: No! in Thunder," QUESTS SURD AND ABSURD. Chicago: Chicago University Press, 1967, pp. 186-208.

       Interpretation of Hawthorne's much-quoted notebook entry of 1856 concerning Melville.

2143   Miller, James E., Jr. "Hawthorne and Melville: The Unpardonable Sin," PMLA, 70 (March, 1955), 91-114.

       Pride of the intellect, "losing touch with humanity," becomes the unpardonable sin. A common pattern for commission of the unpardonable sin is repeated in MOBY DICK.

       Cf. Henry G. Fairbanks. "Sin, Free Will, and 'Pessimism' in Hawthorne," PMLA, 71 (1956), 975-89; Joseph T. McCullen and John C. Guilds, "The Unpardonable Sin in Hawthorne: A Re-Examination," NCF, 15 (1960), 221-237.

2143.1 Miller, James E., Jr. "Hawthorne and Melville: The Unpardonable Sin," QUESTS SURD AND ABSURD: ESSAYS IN AMERICAN LITERATURE. Chicago: Chicago University Press, 1967, pp. 209-238.

2144   Miller, James E., Jr. "The Many Masks of MARDI," JEGP, 58 (July, 1959), 400-413.

2145   Miller, James E., Jr. "Melville's Quest in Life and
        Art," SAQ, 58 (Autumn, 1959), 587-602.

2146   Miller, James E., Jr. "Melville's Search for Form,"
        BuR, 8 (December, 1959), 260-276.

        Elements which Melville synthesized in MOBY DICK.

2147   Miller, James E., Jr. "MOBY-DICK: The Grand Hooded
        Phantom," AION-SG, 2 (1959), 141-165.

2148   Miller, James E., Jr. A READER'S GUIDE TO HERMAN
        MELVILLE. New York: Farrar, Straus and Cudahy,
        1962; London: Thames and Hudson, 1962.

        Three categories of Melville's characters: those
        who wear masks (either nefariously or innocently); the
        "maskless men"; and the seekers who must "decide with
        what face to confront the world."

2149   Miller, James E., Jr. "REDBURN and WHITE-JACKET:
        Initiation and Baptism," NCF, 13 (March, 1959),
        273-293.

2150   Miller, James E., Jr. "Uncharted Interiors: The American
        Romantics Revisited," ESQ, 35 (1964), 34-39.

        The meeting ground of Emerson, Thoreau, and
        Whitman is in their transcendental mysticism--spirit;
        the meeting ground of Poe, Hawthorne, and Melville in
        their psychological drama--mind.

2151   Miller, James E., Jr., and Bernice Slote, eds.
        THE DIMENSIONS OF THE SHORT STORY. New York:
        Dodd, Mead, 1964, pp. 539-545.

2152   Miller, Paul W. "Sun and Fire in Melville's MOBY DICK,"
        NCF, 13 (September, 1958), 139-144.

2153   Miller, Perry. "An American Language," NATURE'S NATION.
        Cambridge: Harvard University Press, 1967, pp.
        208-301.

2154   Miller, Perry. "The Common Law and Codification in
        Jacksonian America," PAPS, 103 (1959), 463-468.

2155   Miller, Perry, ed. "Hawthorne and His Mosses,"
        GOLDEN AGE OF AMERICAN LITERATURE. Selected and
        edited with Introduction and Notes. New York:
        George Braziller, Inc., 1959, pp. 407-419.

2155.1 Miller, Perry. THE LIFE OF THE MIND IN AMERICA.
New York: Harcourt, Brace & World, Inc., 1965,
passim.

2156 Miller, Perry. "Melville and Transcendentalism,"
VQR, 29 (Autumn, 1953), 556-575.

The fundamental concepts in MOBY DICK and PIERRE
are man in nature, defiantly and unrepentantly
Transcendental.

2156.1 Miller, Perry. "Melville and Transcendentalism,"
NATURE'S NATION. Cambridge, Mass.: The Belknap
Press of Harvard University, 1967, pp. 184-196.

Melville and Emerson were both aware of a
"configuration of ideas" which, popularly identified
with Germany, "challenged the regnant ethic and
aesthetic of nature...Emerson...gave over reading
romances as a waste of time, but Melville had no
recourse but to write romances that would destroy
romance...."

2157 Miller, Perry. "Melville and Transcendentalism,"
MOBY DICK CENTENNIAL ESSAYS. Tyrus Hillway and
Luther S. Mansfield, eds. Dallas: Southern
Methodist University Press, 1953, pp. 123-152.

2158 Miller, Perry. THE RAVEN AND THE WHALE: THE WAR OF
WORDS AND WITS IN THE ERA OF POE AND MELVILLE.
New York: Harcourt, Brace, 1956.

Melville accepted as the "terms of his problem"
precisely the terms his contemporaries proposed. If
then he is relegated to the solitude of failure, the
tragedy is not so much his overreaching as "an
inescapable collapse of the structures his society
provided him...with no allowance for alternatives...."
Cf. John Gerlach," Messianic Nationalism in
the Early Works of Herman Melville: Against Perry
Miller," ArQ, 28 (1972), 5-26.

Rev. by Willard Thorp, AL, 29 (1957), 97-98;
Daniel Aaron, NEQ, 29 (1956), 538-541.

2159 Miller, Ruth. "But Laugh or Die: A Comparison of THE
MYSTERIOUS STRANGER and BILLY BUDD," LitHY, 11, 1
(1970), 25-29.

2160   Miller, Wayne Charles. "Herman Melville and the
         Dissection of the Military World: A Warning
         to America," AN ARMED AMERICA: ITS FACE IN
         FICTION. New York: New York University Press,
         1970, pp. 29-52.

         Melville the first to analyze the military
         structure as a microcosm of the "authoritarian state."

2161   Millgate, Michael. AMERICAN SOCIAL FICTION: JAMES TO
         COZZENS. New York: Barnes & Noble, Inc., 1965,
         passim.

         In THE CONFIDENCE MAN, as in PIERRE, Melville
         leaves no doubt of his attitude towards the increasing
         commercialization of American society.

2162   Millgate, Michael. "Melville and Marvell: A Note on
         BILLY BUDD," ES, 49 (1968), 47-50.

2163   Millhauser, M. "The Form of MOBY-DICK," JAAC, 13
         (June, 1955), 527-532.

         For better understanding, the work should be
         approached as a tragedy.

2164   Mills, Gordon H. "American First Editions at Texas
         University: Herman Melville, VII (1819-1891),"
         UTLC, 4 (1951), 89-92.

2165   Mills, Gordon H. "The Castaway in MOBY-DICK," UTSE,
         29 (1950), 231-248.

         The problem of fate in MOBY DICK. Analysis and
         summary of views.

2166   Mills, Gordon H. "Herman Melville (1819-1891),"
         UTLC, 4 (Summer, 1951), 89-92.

2167   Mills, Gordon H. "The Significance of 'Arcturus' in
         MARDI," AL, 14 (1942), 158-161.

         The recognition of Arcturus as "a representation
         of an impartial and detailed criticism of man" gives
         significance to a symbolic interpretation of MARDI.

2168   Mills, Nicolaus C. "The Discovery of Nil in PIERRE and
         JUDE THE OBSCURE," TSLL, 12 (1970), 249-262.

         Both Melville and Hardy are preoccupied with
         "nothingness." Pierre's and Jude's despair is
         not tragic but a reflection of a world in which
         sacrifice is without a metaphysical justification.

2169   Mills, Nicolaus C. "Prison and Society in 19th Century American Fiction," WHR, 24 (Autumn, 1970), 325-331.

In BARTLEBY the "restrictiveness" of the prison is symbolic of society outside prison.

2170   Milne, Gordon. THE AMERICAN POLITICAL NOVEL. Norman, Okla.: Oklahoma University Press, 1956, passim.

BILLY BUDD, the "tragedy of spirit and law in a world of necessity."

2171   Milne, Gordon. GEORGE WILLIAM CURTIS AND THE GENTEEL TRADITION. Bloomington, Indiana: Indiana University Press, 1956, pp. 57, passim.

Melville and Curtis were often linked together at this period, partly because the work of both appeared in the same magazine, partly because their writings showed resemblances.

2172   Minnigerode, Meade, ed. SOME PERSONAL LETTERS OF HERMAN MELVILLE AND A BIBLIOGRAPHY. New York: The Brick Row Book Shop, 1922; repr., Freeport, New York: Books for Libraries Press, 1969.

2173   Minoli, Cecarina Melandri, ed. Introduction, MOBY DICK O LA BALENA BIANCA. Torino: Unione Tipografico-Editrice Torinese, 1958. 2 vols.

2174   Mitchell, Charles. "Melville and the Spurious Truth of Legalism," CentR, 12 (1968), 110-126.

2175   Mitchell, Donald G. AMERICAN LANDS AND LETTERS. New York: Charles Scribner's Sons, 1899, II, 235.

2176   Mitchell, Edward. "From Action to Essence: Some Notes on the Structure of Melville's THE CONFIDENCE-MAN," AL, 40 (March, 1968), 27-37.

The structure is one of constancy of activity rather than constancy of character. The distinction resulting from such a structure implies that without confidence there would be neither confidence men nor victims, in short, no humanity.

2177   Mize, George E. "Evert Duyckinck: Critic to His Times," ESQ, 55 (2nd Qt., 1969), 89-95.

2178   Mizener, Arthur. "Herman Melville: MOBY DICK,"
        TWELVE GREAT AMERICAN NOVELS. New York: New
        American Library, 1967, pp. 19-33.

        Rev. by William Braswell, AL, 40 (1968), 423-24.

2178.1 /MOBY DICK/. Photoplay title: THE SEA BEAST (A Warner
        Brothers screen classic starring John Barrymore).
        New York: Grosset & Dunlap, 1926.

2178.2 MOBY DICK (1955). Produced and Directed: John Huston, sc.:
        Ray Bradbury and John Huston. From the novel by
        Herman Melville. ph.: Oswald Morris and John Huston).
        mus.: Philip Stainton. des.: Ralph Brinton,
        ed.: Russell Lloyd. players: Gregory Peck, Richard
        Basehart, Leo Genn, James Robertson Justice, Harry
        Andrews, Bernard Miles, Orson Welles.

2179   Mogan, Joseph J., Jr. PIERRE and MANFRED: Melville's
        Study of the Byronic Hero," PELL, 1 (Summer, 1965),
        230-240.

2180   Molinoff, Katherine. "Conrad's Debt to Melville:
        James Wait, Donkin and Belfast of the 'Narcissus,'"
        Conrad, 1, iii (Summer, 1969), 119-122.

        Apparently Conrad took three sailors from
        Melville's REDBURN, dividing Sailor Jackson into
        Wait and Donkin.

2181   Monroe, Harriet. "A Discussion with Hart Crane,"
        Poetry, 29 (1926), 34-41.

        Harriet Monroe, editor of Poetry, accepted
        Crane's poem "At Melville's Tomb" and printed her
        exchange of letters with Crane about it.

2182   Montague, Gene B. "Melville's BATTLE PIECES," UTSE,
        35 (1956), 106-115.

2183   Montale, Eugenio, ed. Introduzione, BILLY BUDD,
        GABBIERE DI PARROCCHETTO. 5th ed. Milano:
        Bompiani, 1965.

        Montale introduced BILLY BUDD to Italian
        readers.

2183.1 Montale, Eugenio. "An Introduction to BILLY BUDD (1942),"
        SR, 68 (July, 1960), 419-422.

        English translation of Montale's Introduction
        to the 1942 Italian edition of BILLY BUDD.

2184   Monteiro, George. "BARTLEBY THE SCRIVENER and Melville's
        Contemporary Reputation," SB, 24 (1971), 195-196.

        A reference to this work in the June 1880 Atlantic
        Monthly.

2185   Monteiro, George. "Elizabeth Shaw Melville as Censor,"
        ESQ, 62 (1971), 32-33.

        Elizabeth Shaw Melville's complaint about two
        Melville letters in Rose Hawthorne Lathrop's
        MEMORIES OF HAWTHORNE (1897).

2186   Monteiro, George. "Melville and Keats," ESQ, 31
        (2nd Qt., 1963), 55.

        Keats as a possible source for the term Jemmy Legs
        in BILLY BUDD.

2186.1 Monteiro, George. "Mather's Melville Book," SB, 25
        (1972), 226-227.

        On November 20, 1906, Ferris Greenslet wrote to
        Frank Jewett Mather, Jr., to report that the authorities
        at Houghton-Mifflin did not believe enough interest in
        Melville existed to warrant the publication of Mather's
        biography of him.

2187   Moore, Jack B. "Ahab and Bartleby: Energy and Indolence,"
        SSF, 1 (Summer, 1964), 291-294.

        Themes of the two works related to a two-stanza
        poem published in TIMOLEON, "Fragments of a Lost
        Gnostic Poem of the Twelfth Century."

2188   Moore, John Brooks, ed. Introduction. PIERRE, OR THE
        AMBIGUITIES. Preface by H. M. Tomlinson. New York:
        E. P. Dutton, 1929.

        Rev. by Weldan Stone, AL, 2 (1930), 462-64.

2188.1 Moore, John Brooks. "Review of Lewis Mumford's
        HERMAN MELVILLE," AL, 1 (1929), 215-217.

2189   Moorman, Charles. "Melville's PIERRE and the Fortunate
        Fall," AL, 25 (March, 1953), 13-30.

        PIERRE is Melville's reworking of the myth of the
        Fall of Man and its tradition of felix culpa.

        Cf., James Kissane. "Imagery, Myth, and Melville's
        PIERRE," AL, 26 (1955), 564-572.

2190   Moorman, Charles. "Melville's Pierre in the City,"
            AL, 27 (January, 1956), 571-577.

            Continuation of Moorman's previous article
        (AL, 25 (1953), 13-30), to defend the myth approach
        to PIERRE, and to correct the contention of James
        Kissane (AL, 26 (1955), 564-72) that this approach
        cannot explain ending of the novel.

2191   Mordell, Albert. "Frank T. Bullen and Herman Melville,"
            ToJ, 6 (1960), 77-83.

            Criticism of MOBY DICK in Bullen's novel, THE
        CRUISE OF THE CACHALOT (1898).

2192   Mordell, Albert. "Melville and 'WHITE-JACKET,'" SatRL,
            7 (1931), 946.

2193   Morehead, Barbara. MELVILLE'S USE OF THE NARRATOR IN
            MOBY-DICK. Diss. Chicago: 1951.

2194   Morison, Samuel Eliot. "How to Read MOBY-DICK," Life,
            40 (June 25, 1956), 57-58, 61-62, 67-68.

2195   Morison, Samuel Eliot, ed. "Melville's 'Agatha' Letter
            to Hawthorne," NEQ, 2 (1929), 296-307.

2196   Morpurgo, J. E. "Herman Melville and England," Month,
            n. s., 4 (1950), 18-186.

            Melville successful in England because he found
        America's frontier also England's--on the seas.

2197   Morris, Lloyd R. "The Life of Herman Melville,"
            Outlook, 130 (1922), 149-150.

2198   Morris, Lloyd R. "Melville: Promethean " Open Court,
            45 (September, 1931), 513-526; (October, 1931),
            621-635.

            Repetition of the "Ethan Brand" theory.

2199   Morris, Lloyd R. THE REBELLIOUS PURITAN: PORTRAIT OF
            MR. HAWTHORNE. New York: Harcourt, Brace & Company,
            1927, pp. 243-251, passim.

2200   Morris, Wright. "The High Seas: Herman Melville,"
            THE TERRITORY AHEAD. New York: Harcourt, Brace
            & Co., 1958; Atheneum, paperback, 1963, pp.
            67-77.

2201   Morris, Wright. "The Lunatic, the Lover, and the Poet," KR, 27 (Autumn, 1965), 727-737.

2202   Morsberger, Robert E. "'I Prefer Not To': Melville and the Theme of Withdrawal," UCQ, 10 (November, 1964), 24-29.

2203   Mosher, Bernard, and Douglass Wigmore. "The Mobled Dick: An Imperfect Summary of MOBY-DICK Maliciously Compiled from Sundry Authentic Accounts Published by the Best Contradictory Authorities," excerpt in MOBY-DICK AS DOUBLOON: ESSAYS AND EXTRACTS (1851-1970), Hershel Parker and Harrison Hayford, eds. New York: W. W. Norton & Company, Inc., 1970, pp. 363-366.

2204   Moss, Sidney P. "'Cock-A-Doodle-Doo!' and Some Legends in Melville Scholarship," AL, 40 (May, 1968), 192-210.

The story, a "companion piece" to BARTLEBY, represents the opposite position. Where Bartleby is defeated by life and withdraws into death, the narrator of "Cock-A-Doodle-Doo!" defies and denies death, "while exulting in life."

2205   Mott, Frank Luther. A HISTORY OF AMERICAN MAGAZINES, 1741-1850. New York; London: D. Appleton and Company, 1930, passim.

Melville's reviewers.

2206   Mower, George R. "The Kentucky Tragedy: A Source for PIERRE," KFR, 15 (1969), 1-2.

2207   Mugridge, Donald H., and Blanche P. McCrum. A GUIDE TO THE STUDY OF THE UNITED STATES OF AMERICA: REPRESENTATIVE BOOKS REFLECTING THE DEVELOPMENT OF AMERICAN LIFE AND THOUGHT. Washington: Library of Congress, 1960, passim.

2208   Mulqueen, James E. "Conservatism and Criticism: The Literary Standards of the American Whigs, 1845-1852," AL, 41 (1969), 355-372.

The relationship between political and literary principles of American Whigs; and the Whig reaction to Melville's PIERRE.

2209   Mumford, Lewis. AESTHETICS, A DIALOGUE. New York: Troutbeck, 1925.

2209.1   Mumford, Lewis. THE GOLDEN DAY: A STUDY OF AMERICAN
             EXPERIENCE AND CULTURE. New York: Boni and
             Liveright, 1926, pp. 142-153.

         The white whale as the external force of Nature
and Destiny.

2210   Mumford, Lewis. HERMAN MELVILLE: A STUDY OF HIS LIFE
             AND VISION. New York: Harcourt, Brace, 1929;
             New York: Literary Guild, 1929. New edition,
             slightly revised, New York: Harcourt, Brace,
             and World, 1962.

2211   Mumford, Lewis. "The Significance of Herman Melville,"
             NR, 56 (1928), 212-214.

         Melville is significant because his life and work
reflect the "tragic sense of life," which should lead
us to impose meaning on our transitory existence.

2212   Mumford, Lewis. "The Writing of MOBY-DICK," AmM, 15
             (1928), 482-490.

         The conditions under which MOBY DICK was written
and effect of the writing upon Melville.

2213   Mumford, Lewis. "The Young Olympian," SatRL, 5
             (1928), 514-515.

2214   Munson, Gorham. STYLE AND FORM IN AMERICAN PROSE.
             Garden City, New York: Doubleday, Doran, 1929,
             pp. 135-149.

         MARDI.

2215   Murray, Henry A. "Bartleby and I," MELVILLE ANNUAL,
             1965: A SYMPOSIUM: BARTLEBY THE SCRIVENER.
             Howard P. Vincent, ed. (Kent Stud. in Eng. III).
             Kent, Ohio: Kent State University Press, 1966,
             pp. 3-24.

         Meaning of the "I," and a dialogue between the
attorney, the psychologist, the author, the scrivener,
the biographer, the first critic, the second critic,
and the historian.

2216   Murray, Henry A. "In Nomine Diaboli," NEQ, 24 (December,
             1951), 435-452.

         A psychological interpretation of MOBY DICK.

2217   Murray, Henry A., ed. Introduction, PIERRE: OR, THE AMBIGUITIES. New York: Hendricks House, Farrar Straus, 1949.

2218   Murray, Henry A. "Personality and Creative Imagination," ENGLISH INSTITUTE ESSAYS, 1942. New York: Columbia University Press, 1943, pp. 139-162.

2219   Murray, Henry A. "Prelude," MELVILLE AND HAWTHORNE IN THE BERKSHIRES: A SYMPOSIUM. Howard P. Vincent, ed. Kent, Ohio: Kent State University Press, 1968, pp. 1-3.

2219.1 Murray, Henry A. "Review of HERMAN MELVILLE," NEQ, 2 (July, 1929), 523-526.

        A review of Lewis Mumford's HERMAN MELVILLE.

2220   Murry, John Middleton. "The End of Herman Melville," JOHN CLARE AND OTHER STUDIES. London: Peter Nevill, 1950, pp. 208-212.

2221   Murry, John Middleton. "Herman Melville's Silence," TLS, 1173 (1924), 433.

2222   Murry, John Middleton. THE PROBLEM OF STYLE. London: 1922.

2222.1 Murry, John Middleton. SON OF WOMAN: THE STORY OF D. H. LAWRENCE. New York: Jonathan Cape and Harrison Smith, 1931, pp. 265-272.

2223   Myers, Franklin G. HERMAN MELVILLE: MOBY DICK. New York: Barnes & Noble, 1966.

2224   Myers, Henry Alonzo. ARE MEN EQUAL? AN INQUIRY INTO THE MEANING OF AMERICAN DEMOCRACY. New York: Putnam's, 1945, pp. 46-56.

2225   Myers, Henry Alonzo. "Captain Ahab's Discovery: The Tragic Meaning of MOBY DICK," NEQ, 15 (March, 1942), 15-34.

2226   Myers, Henry Alonzo. "The Tragic Meaning of MOBY-DICK," TRAGEDY: A VIEW OF LIFE. Ithaca: Cornell University Press, 1956, pp. 57-77.

2227   Myers, Margaret. "Mark Twain and Melville," MTJ, 14 ii (1968), 5-8.

2228   Naddell, Sara Anne. MOBY DICK - With a Reader's Guide.
         AMSCO School Publications, 1970.

2229   Narita, Shigehisa. "Melville on Arnold," SELit, (1966),
         41-53.

         Survey of the marking and annotation in Melville's
         copies of five works of Matthew Arnold.

2230   Naruse, Takeshi. "Bartleby's Denial: On the Meaning
         of 'Prefer Not To,'" EiT, 1 (February, 1962),
         50-60.

2230.1   Narveson, Robert. "The Name Claggart in BILLY BUDD,"
         AS, 43 (October, 1968), 229-232.

2231   Nash, J. V. "Herman Melville, 'Ishmael' of American
         Literature," Open Court, 40 (1926), 734-742.

2231.1   Nash, Roderick. WILDERNESS AND THE AMERICAN MIND.
         New Haven and London: Yale University Press, 1967,
         p. 152.

2232   Nathanson, Leonard. "Melville's BILLY BUDD, Chapter 1,"
         Expl, 22 (May, 1964), Item 75.

         Billy's thrashing of Red Whiskers prefigures his
         killing of Claggart. Red Whiskers is in the tradition
         of the popular folk devil or the Vice.

2233   Nault, Clifford A., Jr. "Melville's Two-Stranded Novel:
         An Interpretation of MOBY-DICK as an Enactment of
         Father Mapple's Sermon and the Lesser Prophecies,
         with an Essay on Melville's Interpretation,"
         DA, 22 (Wayne State: 1961), 1979-80.

2234   Neal, Myrna. MELVILLE AND THE THEATRE. Diss. Texas
         Wesleyan College: 1955.

2234.1   Neider, Charles, ed. SHORT NOVELS OF THE MASTERS.
         New York: Rinehart, 1948, pp. 9-11.

         BENITO CERENO.

2235   Nelson, John Herbert. THE NEGRO CHARACTER IN AMERICAN
         LITERATURE. New York: Lawrence, 1926. First AMS
         Edition, 1970, p. 29.

2236   Nelson, Lowry, Jr. "Night Thoughts on the Gothic Novel,"
         YR, 52 (December, 1962), 236-257.

         Comparison of MOBY DICK with FRANKENSTEIN and
         WURTHERING HEIGHTS. Ahab as a Gothic hero.

2237   Nelson, Raymond J. "The Art of Herman Melville: The
            Author of PIERRE," YR, 59 (1970), 197-214.

            DON QUIXOTE is Melville's chief model for PIERRE,
        and the book is "about" literature, rather than "about"
        Melville.

2238   Newbery, Ilse Sofie Magdalene. "THE ENCANTADAS:
            Melville's INFERNO," AL, 38 (1966), 49-68.

            Comparison with Dante's "various circles of
        damnation." The central theme which "binds the cycle
        together and connects it with other PIAZZA TALES" is
        the effect of evil on life.

2239   Newbery, Ilse Sofie Magdalene. "The Unity of Melville's
            PIAZZA TALES," DA, 26 (Br. Columbia U.: 1966),
            4668.

            Evidence, drawn chiefly from the introductory
        sketch, "The Piazza" (written specially for the
        published volume) that Melville intended the tales,
        as collected, to show thematic unity.

2240   Newcomer, Alphonso G. AMERICAN LITERATURE. Chicago:
            Scott, Foresman and Company, 1901, p. 128.

            Influence of early tales of adventure on Melville.

2241   Newman, Robert G. "An Early Berkshire Appraisal of
            MOBY DICK," AQ, 9 (Fall, 1957), 365-366.
            In Greylock Sentinel, North Adams, Mass.,
        December 13, 1851.

2242   Nichol, John W. "Melville and the Midwest," PMLA, 66
            (September, 1951), 613-625.

2243   Nichol, John W. "Melville's '"Soiled" Fish of the Sea,'"
            AL, 21 (1949), 338-339.

            F. O. Matthiessen, in his discussion of Melville's
        artistry, has been misled by what is probably a misprint
        ("soiled" for "coiled") in the Constable edition.

            Cf., F. O. Matthiessen, AMERICAN RENAISSANCE,
        pp. 390-395; and Richard D. Altick. THE ART OF LITERARY
        RESEARCH. New York: 1963, p. 50.

2244   Nichols, Martha F. "Sun Imagery in the Novels of Herman
            Melville," DA, 29 (Tulane: 1968), 1904A.

            There are four types of sun images on which success
        or failure in achieving a quest or resolving a conflict
        depends on "an understanding of the multiplicity of
        reality."

2245   Nicol, Charles. "The Iconography of Evil and Ideal in
            BENITO CERENO," ATQ, 7 (Summer, 1970), 25-31.

            Melville, "while sympathetic to the plight of
            slaves, is generally unsympathetic toward Babo's
            revolt because it merely gives another turn to the
            circle of bloodshed."

2246   Nikoljukin, A. N. "Die amerikanische Romantik und unsere
            Epoche," ZEITSCHRIFT FUR ANGLISTIK UND AMERIKANISTIK,
            15, 4 (1967), 347-374.

            A common feature of the American romantics is their
            protest against the capitalistic way of life in the
            United States.

2247   Nilon, Charles H. BIBLIOGRAPHY OF BIBLIOGRAPHIES IN
            AMERICAN LITERATURE. New York: R. R. Bowker, 1970.

2248   Nilon, Charles H. SOME ASPECTS OF THE TREATMENT OF NEGRO
            CHARACTERS BY FIVE REPRESENTATIVE AMERICAN NOVELISTS:
            COOPER, MELVILLE, TOURGÉE, GLASGOW, FAULKNER. Diss.
            Wisconsin: 1952.

2249   Noble, David W. "The Jeremiahs: James Fenimore Cooper,
            Nathaniel Hawthorne, Herman Melville," THE ETERNAL
            ADAM AND THE NEW WORLD GARDEN: THE CENTRAL MYTH IN
            THE AMERICAN NOVEL SINCE 1830. New York: George
            Braziller, 1968, pp. 1-47.

            Comparison of THE SCARLET LETTER and MOBY DICK in
            theme and allegory of the "myth of the New World Eden."

2250   Noel, Daniel C. "The Portent Unwound: Religious and
            Psychological Development in the Imagery of Herman
            Melville, 1819-1851," DA, 28 (Drew: 1967), 1791A.

            The development of Melville's correlative religious
            and psychological orientation from his earliest years
            through completion of MOBY DICK (1851) is portended in
            the imagery of his writing, reading and marginalia.
            Emphasis is on the configurations of "circle," "line,"
            and "spiral."

2250.1 Nogueira, Rui, ed. MELVILLE ON MELVILLE. New York:
            Viking Press, 1971.

2250.2 Nogueira, Rui, ed. MELVILLE ON MELVILLE. London:
            Secker & Warburg for the British Film Institute,
            1971.

2251   Noone, John B., Jr. "BILLY BUDD: Two Concepts of Nature," AL, 29 (November, 1957), 249-262.

Ideological reading in terms of Hobbes, Locke, and Rousseau.

2251.1   Norlin, George. THE QUEST OF AMERICAN LIFE. Boulder, Col.: UCS, Series B. Studies in Humanities, 2 (March, 1945).

2252   Norman, Liane. "Bartleby and the Reader," NEQ, 44 (March, 1971), 22-39.

By manipulating the reader, the most important character, so that he must identify with the lawyer and also judge the lawyer's shortcomings, Melville forces him to discover how far he will go to assure individual freedom of a person who makes no social contribution. Melville thus presents tension between the democratic-Christian dream of the selfhood of man and the reality of the self-interest of men.

Cf., David Shusterman. "The 'Reader Fallacy' and 'Bartleby the Scrivener,'" NEQ, 45 (1972), 118-124.

2253   Northrup, C. S. "Herman Melville," A MANUAL OF AMERICAN LITERATURE. Theodore Stanton, ed. New York: G. P. Putnam's Sons, 1909, pp. 164-165.

Melville's masterpiece was MOBY DICK; in an "uneven ...strained, Carlylesque style, it nevertheless fills the reader with the fascination of the sea...."

2254   Notoya, Ginsaku. "Angry God and Silent God—On the Symbolic Meaning of MOBY-DICK," Critica, 6 (September, 1962), 2-18.

The rejection of Ahab's rebellion by Ishmael and Melville.

2255   Núñez, Estuardo. "Delano, el primer viajero norteamericano en el Perú," Ipna, 6 (1954), 35-41.

2256   Núñez, Estuardo. "Herman Melville en la américa latina," CuaAm, 68 (March-April, 1953), 209-221.

Melville's contacts with Latin America and particularly his indebtedness to Delano.

2257   Núñez, Estuardo. "Herman Melville en el Perú," MdS, 27 (May-June, 1953), 14-16; repr., in Panorama, 3 (1954), 25.

Contacts, impressions, and reminiscences of Peru in Melville's writings.

2258   Nye, Russel B. AMERICAN LITERARY HISTORY: 1607-1830.
New York: Alfred A. Knopf, Inc., 1970. A Borzoi
Book.

Melville's place in the literary history of the
nation.

2259   Oates, J. C. "Melville and the Manichean Illusion,"
TSLL, 4 (Spring, 1962), 117-129.

By the time of writing BILLY BUDD, Melville had
"drifted into a sort of 'Nihilism.'" In WHITE-JACKET
and MOBY DICK, the heroes have freedom of choice; in
PIERRE choice is a fantasy, which is carried to nihilism
and despair in THE CONFIDENCE-MAN.

2260   O'Brien, Edward J. "The Fifteen Finest Short Stories,"
Forum, 79 (1928), 908-914.

BENITO CERENO, the "noblest short story" in American
literature.

2261   O'Brien, Fitz-James. "Our Authors and Authorship:
Melville and Curtis," PutM, 9 (April, 1857), 384-393.

2262   O'Brien, Fitz-James. "Our Young Authors--Melville,"
PutM, 1 (February, 1853), 155-164.

TYPEE was "healthy," OMOO "nearly so," MARDI was
"excusable wildness," but MOBY DICK, and even more,
PIERRE, "inexcusable insanity."

2263   O'Connor, William Van. "Melville on the Nature of Hope,"
UKCR, 22 (Winter, 1955), 123-130.

Melville was "profoundly interested in the nature
of hope as a human phenomenon."

2264   O'Connor, William Van. "The Novel and the 'Truth' about
America," STUDIES IN AMERICAN CULTURE: DOMINANT
IDEAS AND IMAGES. Joseph J. Kwiat and Mary C.
Turpie, eds. Minneapolis: Minnesota University
Press, 1960, pp. 74-83.

ISRAEL POTTER is based on a "chapbook autobiography,"
but a few chapters reveal that this is a "picaresque tale."

2265   O'Connor, William Van. "Plotinus Plinlimmon and the
Principle of Name-Giving," THE GROTESQUE: AN
AMERICAN GENRE AND OTHER ESSAYS. Carbondale:
Southern Illinois University Press, 1962, pp. 92-97.

Melville's sources for names.

2266   O'Daniel, Therman B. "Herman Melville as a Writer of Journals," CLAJ, 4 (December, 1960), 94-105.

2267   O'Daniel, Therman B. "An Interpretation of the Relation of the Chapter Entitled "The Symphony' to MOBY DICK as a Whole," CLAJ, 2 (September, 1958), 55-57.

2268   O'Dea, Richard J. "THE FATHERS: A Revaluation," TCL, 12 (July, 1966), 87-95.

    Comparison of Allen Tate with Melville and others.

2269   O'Donnell, Charles R. "The Mind of the Artist: Cooper, Thoreau, Hawthorne, Melville," DA, 17 (Syracuse: 1957), 1752.

2269.1   O'Farrell, Mairin. "Patrick Kavanagh Looks at Writing and Writers," IrishD, 80 (July, 1964), 15-19.

2270   Ogata, Toshihiko. "On MOBY-DICK," JosB, 14 (March, 1962), 35-55.

    Innocence and evil.

2270.1   Oglesby, Carl. "Melville, or Water Consciousness & Its Madness: A Fragment from a Work-in-progress," TriQ, No. 23/24 (Winter/Spring, 1972), pp. 123-141.

2271   Okamoto, Katsumi. "The End of Melville--As Seen Through BILLY BUDD," Geibun, 2 (March, 1962), 1-20.

2272   Olenjeva, B. "Amerikans'ka novela epoxy romantyzmu," RLž, 11 (1967), 45-55.

    The American short story during the romantic period.

2273   Oliver, Egbert S. "'Cock-A-Doodle-Doo!' and Transcendental Hocus-Pocus," NEQ, 21 (1948), 204-216.

    This story, a companion piece to BARTLEBY, is a parody of Thoreauvian Transcendentalism, particularly of a passage, "Monday," in A WEEK ON THE CONCORD AND MERRIMAC RIVERS.

2274   Oliver, Egbert S. HERMAN MELVILLE AND THE IDEA OF PROGRESS. Diss. Washington U.: 1940.

2275   Oliver, Egbert S. "Herman Melville's Lightning-Rod Man," PhilF, 35 (June, 1956), 4-5, 17.

2276   Oliver, Egbert S. "To Light the Gay Bridals: One Aspect
         of MOBY-DICK," ESQ, 35 (1st Qt., 1964), 30-34.

         Melville's imagination in the creative process
         "embodies...the great Romantic antithesis of life in
         struggle against death."

2277   Oliver, Egbert S. "Melville's Goneril and Fanny Kemble,"
         NEQ, 18 (1945), 489-500.

         The Goneril of THE CONFIDENCE MAN grew out of
         Melville's knowledge of Fanny Kemble, a near neighbor
         in Lenox for the six years preceding the writing of
         this savage caricature, rather than out of the novelist's
         disillusionment.

2278   Oliver, Egbert S. "Melville's Picture of Emerson and
         Thoreau in THE CONFIDENCE MAN," CE, 8 (1946), 61-72.

         Melville's satirical treatment of Emerson and
         Thoreau, as Mark Winsome and his disciple, Egbert,
         reveals the warmth, humor, and practicality of his
         thinking.

2279   Oliver, Egbert S. "Melville's Tartarus," ESQ, 28,
         Melville Supplement, (1962), 23-25.

2280   Oliver, Egbert S., ed. THE PIAZZA TALES by Herman
         Melville. New York: Hendricks House, Farrar
         Straus, 1948.

         Rev. by Robert E. Spiller, AL, 21 (1950), 138.

2281   Oliver, Egbert S. "A Second Look at Bartleby," CE, 6
         (1945), 431-439.

         In his withdrawal from society, Bartleby portrays
         Thoreau, not Melville.

2282   Oliver, Egbert S. STUDIES IN AMERICAN LITERATURE.
         New Delhi: Eurasia Publishing House, 1965.

2283   Olson, Charles. CALL ME ISHMAEL. New York: Reynall &
         Hitchcock, 1947. Repr. New York: Grove, 1958.

         An interpretation of Melville's purpose, sources,
         and method of composition.

         Revs., C. R. Anderson, AL, 19 (1948), 376-77;
         Walter E. Bezanson, NEQ, 20 (1947), 410-13;
         Willard Thorp, "More About Melville," SatRL,
         30 (1947), 36.

2284   Olson, Charles. "David Young, David Old," WR, 14 (1949), 63.

2285   Olson, Charles. "Equal, That Is, to the Real Itself," ChicagoR, 12 (1958), 98-104.

Rev.-art., Milton R. Stern's THE FINE HAMMERED STEEL.

2286   Olson, Charles. "Lear and MOBY DICK," TwYr, 1 (1938), 165-189.

Melville's debt to KING LEAR, and his union of democracy and Christianity.

2287   Olson, Charles. "Materials and Weights of Herman Melville," NR, 127 (September 8, 1952), 20-21; (September, 15, 1952), 17-18, 21.

An attack on the Mansfield-Vincent edition.

2288   Olson, Charles. "Melville et Shakespeare, ou la Découverte de MOBY-DICK," TM, 7 (October, 1951), 647-676.

2288.1 ONE HUNDRED INFLUENTIAL AMERICAN BOOKS PRINTED BEFORE 1900: CATALOGUE AND ADDRESSES: Exhibition at The Grolier Club, April 18-June 16, 1946. New York: The Grolier Club, 1947. Repr., New York: Kraus Reprint Corporation, 1967, pp. 10, 16, 93-94.

2289   Onís, Jose de. "Messianic Nationalism in the Literature of the Americas: Melville and the Hispanic World," PROCEEDINGS OF THE IVth CONGRESS OF THE INTERNATIONAL COMPARATIVE LITERATURE ASSOCIATION. Francois Jost, ed. Fribourg, 1964. 2 vols. The Hague: Mouton, 1966, I, 229-236.

2290   Opitz, E. A. "Herman Melville: An American Seer," ContempR, 972 (1946), 348-353.

Notes on the British popularity of Melville, particularly the reception of TYPEE as a sociological tract.

2291   Orians, C. H. "Censure of Fiction in American Romances and Magazines," PMLA, 52 (1937), 195-214.

2292   Ortego, Philip D. "The Existential Roots of BILLY BUDD," ConnR, 4, 1 (1970), 80-87.

Melville presents no absolute truth or moral example, but simply tries to show what man is: "his own victim, not God's."

2293 Orth, Ralph H. "An Early Review of THE CONFIDENCE-MAN," ESQ, 43 (2nd Qt., 1966), 48.

An early review appeared in the Burlington Free Press, April 25, 1857.

2294 Osborne, Frances Thomas. "Herman Melville Through a Child's Eye," BNYPL, 69 (December, 1965), 655-660.

Reminiscences of Melville's granddaughter.

2295 Osbourn, R. V. "The White Whale and the Absolute," EIC, 6 (April, 1956), 160-170.

If MOBY DICK is interpreted in philosophical, instead of psychological or theological terms, it will reveal Melville's metaphysical interests at the time he wrote it.

2295.1 Osterling, A. Presentation, NOBEL LECTURES, INCLUDING PRESENTATION SPEECHES AND LAUREATES' BIOGRAPHIES - LITERATURE - 1901-1967. Horst Frenz, ed. Amsterdam, London, New York: Published for the Novel Foundation by Elsevier Publishing Company, 1969, pp. 497-500.

Comparison of Hemingway and Melville.

2296 Overton, Grant. "Hawthorne - Melville," AN HOUR OF THE AMERICAN NOVEL. Philadelphia: 1929.

2297 Owen, W. J. B. "Reply to Brewer," MLN, 68 (1953), 214-216.

2298 Owlett, F. C. "Herman Melville (1819-1891): A Centenary Tribute," London Bookman, 56 (August, 1919), 164-167.

An appreciative tribute.

2298.1 P., B. A. "Ageless and Edible," AN&Q, 7 (December, 1947), 141.

Reference to a note by James D. Hart in the Melville Society Newsletter (August 7, 1947), apropos Melville's likening himself to a seed taken out of an Egyptian pyramid: the novelist may have come on this idea through G. P. R. James, who was then living at Stockbridge.

2299   Packard, Robert Joslin. "A Study of Herman Melville's CLAREL," DA, 24 (Columbia: 1963), 2018-19.

2300   Paéz, Ramiro. "BENITO CERENO: La historia del motín del barco negrero en la bahía de Arauco," RdPac, 4, iv (1967), 106-116.

        Commentary on the action and conspectus of interpretation on three levels: metaphysical, sociological, and psychological.

2301   Paéz, Ramiro. "MOBY DICK, la historia de la persecución de la ballena blanca," Athenea, 152, No. 402 (1963), 149-155.

2302   Pafford, Ward, and Floyd C. Watkins. "BENITO CERENO: A Note in Rebuttal," NCF, 7 (June, 1952), 68-71.

        Argument that Babo's wound is self-inflicted.

        Rebuttal to Tom Burns Haber. "A Note on Melville's BENITO CERENO," NCF, 6 (1951), 146-147.

2303   Page, C. A. Introduction, ISRAEL POTTER. New York: L. C. Page & Co., 1925.

2304   Page, Frederick. "Letter to the Editor," Nation&Ath, 29 (1921), 433.

2305   Pagnini, Marcello. "Struttura ideologica e struttura stilistica in MOBY-DICK," SA, 6 (1960), 87-134.

2306   Palmer, R. R. "Herman Melville and the French Revolution," AHRF, 26 (1954), 254-256.

        Melville's unfavorable opinion of the French Revolution in BILLY BUDD the influence of an uncle, Thomas Melville, who had lived in France, 1790-c1811.

2307   Paltsits, Victor H. "A Bibliography," LitRNYEP, June 9, 1923, p. 752.

2308   Paltsits, Victor H., ed. "Family Correspondence of Herman Melville, 1830-1904. In the Gansevoort-Lansing Collection," BNYPL, 33 (July, 1929), 507-525; (August, 1929), 575-625. Repr. New York: New York Public Library, 1929.

        Copies or extracts of over one hundred letters.

        Notes by Henry Gansevoort of Melville's lecture on "Statuary in Rome," pp. 14-16.

2309   Paltsits, Victor H. "Herman Melville's Background and
          New Light on the Publication of TYPEE," BOOKMEN'S
          HOLIDAY. New York: New York Public Library, 1943,
          pp. 248-268.

2310   Pannwitt, Barbara, ed. THE ART OF SHORT FICTION.
          Boston: Ginn, 1964, pp. 244-246.

          BARTLEBY, THE SCRIVENER.

2311   Parke, John. "Seven MOBY-DICKS," NEQ, 28 (1955), 319-338.

          The seven "layers" on which MOBY DICK may be read:
       the physical adventure, the spiritual exaltation of
       hazardous voyaging, the interaction of husbandmen and
       nature, the pride and retribution, the nemesis of self-
       mutilation, the confrontation with chaos, and Ahab's
       inability "to locate and objectify evil in himself, or
       to accept it and deal with it prudently as part of the
       entire created world."

2311.1 Parke, John. "Seven MOBY-DICKS," INTERPRETATIONS OF
          AMERICAN LITERATURE. C. Feidelson and P. Brodtkorb,
          eds. New York: Oxford University Press, 1959,
          pp. 84-101.

2311.2 Parker, Hershel. "BENITO CERENO and CLOISTER-LIFE:
          A Re-Scrutiny of a 'Source,'" SSF, 9 (Summer,
          1972), 221-232.

          Argument against H. Bruce Franklin's contention
       in THE WAKE OF THE GODS that William Stirling's
       CLOISTER-LIFE OF THE EMPEROR CHARLES THE FIFTH was
       a source for BENITO CERENO.

2312   Parker, Hershel, ed. Foreword, THE CONFIDENCE-MAN: HIS
          MASQUERADE. New York: W. W. Norton & Company, 1971.

2313   Parker, Hershel, ed. "Gansevoort Melville's 1846 London
          Journal," BNYPL, 69 (December, 1965), 633-654;
          70 (January-February, 1965), 36-49, 113-131.

          Gansevoort Melville's 1846 London diary provides
       an account of Gansevoort's arrangement for publication
       of TYPEE.

2314   Parker, Hershel. "Gansevoort Melville's Role in the
          Campaign of 1844," NYHSQ, 49 (April, 1965), 143-173.

2315   Parker, Hershel. "Herman Melville and Politics:
          A Scrutiny of the Political Milieu of Herman
          Melville's Life and Works," DA, 24 (Northwestern:
          1964), 5390-91.

2316   Parker, Hershel. "Melville and the Transcendentalists:
A Chronology," THE CONFIDENCE-MAN: HIS MASQUERADE.
New York: W. W. Norton & Company, Inc., 1971,
pp. 254-263.

2317   Parker, Hershel. "Melville's Salesman Story," SSF, 1
(1964), 154-158.

    "The Lightning-Rod Man" would have been read at
the time of its publication as a story in a well-known
genre--the humorous salesman story in which the type
figure is a Yankee pedlar. Melville's salesman is not
a Satanic figure but a character out of the folklore of
the time.

2318   Parker, Hershel. "Melville's Satire of Emerson and
       Thoreau: An Evaluation of the Evidence," ATQ, 7
       (Summer, 1970), 61-67.

    Cf., Elizabeth S. Foster. Introduction, THE
CONFIDENCE MAN. New York: Hendricks House, 1954;
    Sidney P. Moss. "'Cock-A-Doodle-Doo!' and Some
Legends in Melville Scholarship," AL, 40 (1968), 192-210;
    Egbert S. Oliver. "'Cock-A-Doodle-Doo!' and
Transcendental Hocus-Pocus," NEQ, 21 (1948), 204-216;
    Egbert S. Oliver. "Melville's Picture of Emerson
and Thoreau in 'THE CONFIDENCE MAN,'" CE, 8 (1946),
61-72.

2319   Parker, Hershel. "The Metaphysics of Indian-Hating,"
       NCF, 18 (September, 1963), 165-173.

    In each of his novels from TYPEE to BILLY BUDD,
Melville satirized the "failure of Christians to be
Christian." The final irony is that modern readers
may have become insensitive to his satire.

2319.1 Parker, Hershel, ed. "The Metaphysics of Indian-hating,"
       THE CONFIDENCE MAN: HIS MASQUERADE. New York:
       W. W. Norton and Company, 1971, pp. 323-331.

2320   Parker, Hershel. "New Cross-Lights on Melville in the
       1870's," ESQ, 39 (2nd Qt., 1965), 24-25.

    An article in Harper's New Monthly Magazine,
January, 1873, "The Sailors' Snug Harbor," presents
a pen portrait of Thomas Melville, Herman Melville's
youngest brother.

2321   Parker, Hershel, ed. THE RECOGNITION OF HERMAN MELVILLE:
       SELECTED CRITICISM SINCE 1846. Ann Arbor: Michigan
       University Press, 1967. Repr., Ann Arbor Paperbacks,
       1970.

    Rev. by Howard Kerr, SSF, 9 (1972), 103-105.

2322   Parker, Hershel. "A Reexamination of MELVILLE'S REVIEWERS,"
AL, 42 (May, 1970), 226-232.

Hetherington "so gravely misrepresents the tone and
content of many important reviews as to invalidate quite
significant sections of his book."

Cf., Hugh W. Hetherington. MELVILLE'S REVIEWERS:
BRITISH AND AMERICAN, 1846-1891. Chapel Hill: 1961.

2323   Parker, Hershel. "Species of 'Soiled Fish,'" CEAAN, 1
(1968), 11-12.

2323.1 Parker, Hershel. "'The Story of China Aster": A Tentative
Explication," in THE CONFIDENCE-MAN: HIS MASQUERADE.
Hershel Parker, ed. New York: W. W. Norton & Co.,
1971, pp. 353-356.

2324   Parker, Hershel. "Three Melville Reviews in the London
Weekly Chronicle," AL, 41 (January, 1970), 584-589.

Previously uncollected English reviews of Melville's
works, MARDI, THE WHALE, and ISRAEL POTTER.

2324.1 Parker, Hershel. "Trafficking in Melville," (rev.art.)
MLQ, 33 (May, 1972), 54-66.

2325   Parker, Hershel, and Harrison Hayford, eds. MOBY-DICK
AS DOUBLOON: ESSAYS AND EXTRACTS (1851-1970).
New York: W. W. Norton & Co., 1970.

"...fullest collection of criticism ever assembled
on an American literary work," including an annotated
list of books and articles on MOBY DICK from 1921 to
1969.

2326   Parkes, Henry Bamford. THE AMERICAN EXPERIENCE: AN
INTERPRETATION OF THE HISTORY AND CIVILIZATION OF
THE AMERICAN PEOPLE. New York: Alfred A. Knopf,
1947, pp. 200-205, passim.

"MOBY DICK is not only the greatest book written
by an American; it is also the greatest American book...."

2327   Parkes, Henry Bamford. "Freedom and Order in Western
Literature," DenverQ, 4 (Summer, 1969), 1-18.

Places Melville in his historical, literary and
social milieu.

2328   Parkes, Henry Bamford. "Poe, Hawthorne, Melville: An Essay in Sociological Criticism," PR, 16 (February, 1949), 157-165.

Melville, as well as Hawthorne and Poe, commonly dealt with characters who show isolation and immaturity, two traits which seem to have marked the American of the 1840's and which anticipate twentieth-century American traits.

2329   Parks, Aileen Wells. "Leviathan: An Essay in Interpretation," SR, 47 (Winter, 1939), 130-132.

In MOBY DICK, Melville "foretold the doom of a culture and a civilization." Ahab symbolizes the rugged individualist and the whale represents industrialism.

2329.1 Parrington, Vernon Louis. AMERICAN DREAMS: A STUDY OF AMERICAN UTOPIAS. New York: Russell & Russell, Inc., 2nd edition. Englarged with Postscript, 1964, p. 137.

2329.2 Parrington, Vernon Louis. THE BEGINNINGS OF CRITICAL REALISM IN AMERICA; 1860-1920. New York: Harcourt, Brace and Company. (Completed to 1900 only). 1930, p. 14, passim.

2330   Parrington, Vernon Louis. "Herman Melville, Pessimist," MAIN CURRENTS IN AMERICAN THOUGHT: THE ROMANTIC REVOLUTION IN AMERICA, 1800-1860. New York: Harcourt, Brace & Co., 1927, II, 258-267, passim.

2330.1 Paston, George. AT JOHN MURRAY'S, RECORDS OF A LITERARY CIRCLE, 1843-1892. London: 1932.

2331   Patrick, Walton R. "Melville's BARTLEBY and the Doctrine of Necessity," AL, 41 (1969), 39-54.

Melville's allusions in the story are to Jonathan Edwards and Joseph Priestley.

2332   Pattee, Fred Lewis. THE DEVELOPMENT OF THE AMERICAN SHORT STORY: AN HISTORICAL SURVEY. New York and London: Harper and Brothers, 1923, pp. 153-154.

2333   Pattee, Fred Lewis. THE FIRST CENTURY OF AMERICAN LITERATURE. New York and London: D. Appleton-Century Company, 1935, passim.

2334   Pattee, Fred Lewis. "Herman Melville," AmM, 10 (1927), 33-43.

Melville is Taji in MARDI. He is also Jack Chase, Jackson, Paul Jones, and Ahab.

2334.1   Pattee, Fred Lewis. "Herman Melville," THE NEW
         AMERICAN LITERATURE: 1890-1930. New York:
         Century Company, 1930, pp. 359-383.

2335   Pattee, Fred Lewis. "Melville and Whitman," THE
        FEMININE FIFTIES. New York, London: D. Appleton-
        Century Company, 1940, pp. 28-49.

2336   Patterson, Frank M. "The San Dominick's Anchor,"
        AN&Q, 3 (October, 1964), 19-20.

2337   Paul, Sherman. "Hawthorne's Ahab," N&Q, 196 (June 9,
        1951), 255-257.

        Ethan Brand and Ahab.

2338   Paul, Sherman, ed. Introduction, MOBY DICK. New York,
        Dutton; London: Dent, 1950, 1961.

2338.1 Paul, Sherman. Introduction, MOBY DICK. London: Dent,
        1954. Everyman's Library.

2339   Paul, Sherman. "Melville's 'The Town-Ho's Story,'"
        AL, 21 (1949), 212-221.

        The ship-as-society, a recurrent symbol in
        Melville's work, in "The Town-Ho's Story" becomes a
        stage on which is acted one possible failure in human
        institutions.

2340   Paul, Sherman. "Morgan Neville, Melville, and the Folk
        Hero," N&Q, 194 (June 25, 1949), 278.

        Melville's use of Mike Fink.

2341   Pavese, Cesare. AMERICAN LITERATURE: ESSAYS AND OPINIONS.
        Trans. with Introduction by Edwin Fussell. Berkeley:
        California University Press, 1970.

        Contains an essay on Melville.

2342   Pavese, Cesare. "F. O. Matthiessen," LA LETTERATURA
        AMERICANA E ALTRI SAGGI. 3rd ed. Torino: Giulio
        Einandi, 1959, pp. 177-187.

2343   Pavese, Cesare. "Herman Melville," LA LETTERATURA
        AMERICANA E ALTRI SAGGI. 3rd ed. Torino:
        Giulio Einandi, 1959, pp. 77-101.

2344   Pavese, Cesare. "Herman Melville," LaCul, 11 (1932),
        83-93.

| 2345 | Pavese, Cesare. LA LETTERATURA AMERICANA E ALTRI. SAGGI. Milan: 1953, passim. |

| 2346 | Pavese, Cesare. LA LETTERATURA AMERICANA E ALTRI SAGGI. 3rd ed. Torino: Giulio Einandi, 1959, passim. |

| 2347 | Pavese, Cesare. "The Literary Whaler (1932)," SR, 68 (Summer, 1960), 407-418. |

| 2348 | Payne, John. "Herman Melville," VIGIL AND VISION, NEW SONNETS. London: The Villon Society, 1903, p. 62. |

| 2349 | Pearce, Howard D. "The Narrator of 'Norfolk Isle and the Chola Widow,'" SSF, 3 (Fall, 1965), 56-62.

THE ENCANTADAS. |

| 2350 | Pearce, Roy Harvey. THE CONTINUITY OF AMERICAN POETRY. Princeton, New Jersey: Princeton University Press, 1961, passim. |

| 2351 | Pearce, Roy Harvey. "Melville's Indian-Hater: A Note on the Meaning of THE CONFIDENCE-MAN," PMLA, 67 (December, 1952), 942-948.

There seems no way out of the darkness: only by seeing nature as entirely evil can one resist the confidence-man, but to do so makes life a continual celebration of black hatred. |

| 2352 | Pearce, Roy Harvey. "The Metaphysics of Indian-Hating: Leatherstocking Unmasked," HISTORICISM ONCE MORE: PROBLEMS AND OCCASIONS FOR THE AMERICAN SCHOLAR. Princeton: Princeton University Press, 1969, pp. 109-136, passim.

An understanding of Melville's Indian-hater is a means of understanding "not only that archetypal figure Leatherstocking but also his continuing shape-shifting progeny...." |

| 2353 | Pearson, Norman Holmes. "The American Writer and the Feeling for Community," ES, 43 (October, 1962), 403-412. |

| 2354 | Pearson, Norman Holmes. "BILLY BUDD: 'The King's Yarn,'" AQ, 3 (Summer, 1951), 99-114.

A study of sources with emphasis on Milton and the Bible.

Cf., "A Caution about Sources," MELVILLE'S BILLY BUDD AND THE CRITICS. William T. Stafford, ed. Belmont, Calif.: 1961, pp. 142-143. |

2354.1   Pearson, Norman Holmes. "Literary Forms and Types Or a Defense of Polonius," ENGLISH INSTITUTE ANNUAL: 1940. New York: AMS Press, Inc., 1965, pp. 61-72.

2355   Pease, Zephaniah W. "'Historical Address,' One Hundredth Anniversary of the New Bedford Post Society," NBMM, (May 19, 1930).

2356   Peckham, Morse. "Hawthorne and Melville as European Authors," MELVILLE AND HAWTHORNE IN THE BERKSHIRES: A SYMPOSIUM. Howard P. Vincent, ed. Kent, Ohio: Kent State University Press, 1968, pp. 42-62.

2356.1   Peckham, Morse. "Hawthorne and Melville as European Authors," THE TRIUMPH OF ROMANTICISM. Columbia, South Carolina: South Carolina University Press, 1970, pp. 153-175.

2357   Peckham, Morse. "Toward a Theory of Romanticism," PMLA, 66 (1951), 5-23.

Peckham's influential views of Romanticism have affected Melville criticism. Therefore, his further works should be consulted:

"Toward a Theory of Romanticism: II. Reconsiderations," SIR, 1, i (1961), 1-8;
THE TRIUMPH OF ROMANTICISM. Columbia, S. C.: 1970;
BEYOND THE TRAGIC VISION; THE QUEST FOR IDENTITY IN THE NINETEENTH CENTURY. New York: G. Braziller, 1962.

2358   Percival, M. O. A READING OF MOBY DICK. Chicago: Chicago University Press, 1950.

A Jungian and Kierkegaardian reading in terms of Ahab, concerned with the psychology of anxiety.

Rev. by Nathalia Wright, AL, 22 (1949), 520-21; Sherman Paul, NEQ, 23 (1950), 530-33.

2358.1   Percival, M. O. "Captain Ahab and MOBY DICK," STUDIES IN MOBY-DICK. Howard P. Vincent, comp. Columbus, Ohio: Charles E. Merrill Publishing Company, 1969, pp. 116-122.

2359   Pérez Gállego, Cándido. "MOBY DICK como alegoría política," PSA, 44 (1967), 205-16.

2360   Perkins, George. "Death by Spontaneous Combustion in Marryat, Melville, Dickens, Zola, and Others," Dickensian, 60 (Winter, 1964), 57-63.

Similar accounts of death are found in Melville and other nineteenth-century authors.

2361   Perosa, Sergio. Introduzione, L'UOMO DI FIDUCIA.
         Venezia, Neri Pozza, 1961.

         THE CONFIDENCE MAN is an "anatomia" and has much
in common with morality plays.

2362   Perrine, Laurence. "The Nature of Proof in the
         Interpretation of Poetry," EJ, 51 (September,
         1962), 393-398.

         Interpretation of Melville's "The Night-March."

2363   Perry, Robert L. "BILLY BUDD: Melville's PARADISE LOST,"
         MQ, 10 (1969), 173-185.

         Billy's resemblance to prelapsarian Adam and Eve:
Apropos Milton's phrase in Aeopagitica, "knowledge of
good and evil," Billy's "real tragic flaw" is naive
"innocence due to ignorance...that Milton condemned."

2364   Peters, Robert L. "Melville's MOBY DICK," Expl, 16
         (April, 1958), Item 44.

         Bulkington is "ballast for the good in Ahab,"
a "good," which Melville does not intend that we forget.

2365   Petrullo, Helen B. "The Neurotic Hero of TYPEE,"
         AI, 12 (Winter, 1955), 317-323.

         TYPEE, a pre-Freudian literary work, is a "neat,
but unconscious, symbolic representation of a psychological process."

2366   Petty, George R., and William M. Gibson. PROJECT OCCULT:
         THE ORDERED COMPUTER COLLATION OF UNPREPARED LITERARY
         TEXT. New York: New York University Press, 1970.

2367   Peyre, Henry. WRITERS AND THEIR CRITICS: A STUDY OF
         MISUNDERSTANDING. Ithaca, New York: Cornell
         University Press, 1944, passim.

         References which place Melville in his literary
and cultural milieu.

2368   Phelps, Leland R. "MOBY DICK in Germany," CL, XI (Fall,
         1959), 349-355.

2369   Phelps, Leland R. A PRELIMINARY CHECK-LIST OF FOREIGN
         LANGUAGE MATERIALS ON THE LIFE AND WORKS OF HERMAN
         MELVILLE. Melville Society Special Publication
         Number 2 (December, 1960).

2369.1   Phelps, Leland R. A PRELIMINARY CHECK-LIST OF WORKS OF
         HERMAN MELVILLE IN TRANSLATION. Melville Society
         Special Publication Number 2, Part 2 (April, 1961).

2369.2   Phelps, Leland R. A PRELIMINARY CHECK-LIST OF FOREIGN
         MATERIALS ON THE LIFE AND WORKS OF HERMAN MELVILLE.
         Evanston: Northwestern University, 1960.

2370   Phelps, Leland R. "The Reaction to BENITO CERENO and
         BILLY BUDD in Germany," Sym, 13 (Fall, 1959), 294-
         299.

         Thomas Mann's reaction to BILLY BUDD.

2371   Philbrick, Thomas L. "Another Source for WHITE-JACKET,"
         AL, 29 (January, 1958), 431-439.

         A further source: William McNally's EVILS AND
         ABUSES IN THE NAVAL AND MERCHANT SERVICE, EXPOSED; WITH
         PROPOSALS FOR THEIR REMEDY AND REDRESS. Boston: Cassady
         & March, 1839.

2372   Philbrick, Thomas L. JAMES FENIMORE COOPER AND THE
         DEVELOPMENT OF AMERICAN SEA FICTION. Cambridge,
         Mass.: Harvard University Press, 1961, passim.

         An excellent perspective for the study of
         Melville's works.

         Rev., Harry Hayden Clark, JEGP, 62 (1963), 236-38;
         Donald A. Ringe, NEQ, 35 (1962), 428-429.

2373   Philbrick, Thomas L. "Melville's 'Best Authorities,'"
         NCF, 15 (September, 1960), 171-179.

         Sources of WHITE-JACKET.

2374   Phillips, Barry. "'The Good Captain': A Reading of
         BENITO CERENO," TSLL, 4 (Summer, 1962), 188-197.

2375   Piamonte, Guido. "Musica al radio: il mondo di Melville
         rievocato da Britten," FLe, 48 (December 16, 1951),
         6.

2376   Pickering, James H. "Melville's 'Ducking' Duyckinck,"
         BNYPL, 70 (November, 1966), 551-552.

         Irving as the source for Melville's name for
         Evert Duyckinck.

         Cf., Heyward Ehrlich. "A Note on Melville's 'Men
         Who Dive,'" BNYPL, 69 (1965), 661-664; and Ehrlich's
         "'Diving and Ducking Moralities': A Rejoinder,"
         BNYPL, 70 (1966), 552-553.

2377   PICTURE BOOK OF AMERICAN AUTHORS. New York: Sterling
        Publishing Co., Inc., 1962. Visual History Series,
        pp. 26-27.

2378   Pierre-Quint, Léon. "Herman Melville," Preuves, 195
        (1967), 47-51.

2379   Pilkington, William T. "'BENITO CERENO' and the American
        National Character," Discourse, 8 (Winter, 1965),
        49-63.

        Delano, in the aspects of his personality and
his pattern of thought, represents Melville's view of
the American national character.

2380   Pilkington, William T. "BENITO CERENO and the 'Valor-
        Ruined Man' of MOBY-DICK," TSLL, 7 (Summer, 1965),
        201-207.

2381   Pilkington, William T. "Melville's BENITO CERENO: Source
        and Technique," SSF, 2 (Spring, 1965), 247-255.

        Melville changes the date of events described in
Delano's NARRATIVE from 1805 to 1799, a time crucial
to the conflicts between the old and new order. Don
Benito's emotional devastation is also emphasized
without suggestion of recovery.

2382   Pinkerton, Helen. "BILLY BUDD" SoR, 4 (Summer, 1968),
        717. (Poem).

2383   Piper, Henry Dan, ed. A MANY-WINDOWED HOUSE: COLLECTED
        ESSAYS ON AMERICAN WRITERS AND AMERICAN WRITING.
        Introduction by Henry Dan Piper. Carbondale and
        Edwardsville: Southern Illinois University Press,
        1970.

        Rev. by John Lydenberg, AL, 43 (1972), 673-675.

2384   Piroué, Georges. "Connaissance et méconnaissance de
        Melville," TA, 54 (June, 1952), 156-159.

2385   Pitt, A. Stuart. "Moody Ahab and His Heaven-Insulting
        Purpose," HistN, 4 (October, 1956), 23-27.

2386   Pitz, Henry C. "A Painter of Themes: Gil Wilson,"
        AmArt, 21 (April, 1957), 30-35.

        Illustrations for MOBY DICK.

2387   Pivano, Fernanda. "Alcune fonti del MOBY DICK," FLe,
        10 (March 8, 1953), 4.

2388   Pivano, Fernanda. "MOBY DICK di Herman Melville,"
        Conv, 15 (1943), 209-243.

2388.1 Pizer, Donald, ed. "The American Public and 'Popular'
        Fiction," THE LITERARY CRITICISM OF FRANK NORRIS.
        Austin: University of Texas Press, 1964, p. 125.

2389   Pizer, Donald. REALISM AND NATURALISM IN NINETEENTH-
        CENTURY AMERICAN LITERATURE. Preface by Harry T.
        Moore. Carbondale and Edwardsville: Southern
        Illinois University Press, 1966, p. 5.

        The contrast between appreciation of literature
        in the days of Melville and the late nineteenth century.

2390   Plomer, William, ed. Introduction. BILLY BUDD, FORETOPMAN.
        London: John Lehmann, Ltd., 1947, pp. 7-10.

        BILLY BUDD, a "final protest against the nature of
        things."

2391   Plomer, William, ed. Introduction, REDBURN. London:
        1937.

2392   Plomer, William, ed. SELECTED POEMS OF HERMAN MELVILLE.
        London: The Hogarth Press, 1943.

2393   Plomer, William, ed. Introduction, WHITE JACKET. London:
        John Lehmann, 1952; New York: Grove Press, 1956.

2394   Plumstead, A. W. "BARTLEBY: Melville's Venture into a
        New Genre," MELVILLE ANNUAL 1965, A SYMPOSIUM:
        BARTLEBY THE SCRIVENER. Howard P. Vincent, ed.
        (Kent Stud. in Eng., III). Kent, Ohio: Kent State
        University Press, 1966, pp. 82-93.

        BARTLEBY and BENITO CERENO are emerging as classics
        of the American short story genre.

2395   Plumstead, A. W. "Puritanism and Nineteenth Century
        American Literature," QQ, 70 (1963), 209-222.

        Puritan influence on Hawthorne and Melville.

2396   Plumstead, A. W. TIME'S ENDLESS TUNNEL: A STUDY OF
        HERMAN MELVILLE'S CONCERN WITH TIME. Diss.
        Rochester, 1960.

2397   Pochmann, Henry A. "Herman Melville," GERMAN CULTURE
        IN AMERICA: PHILOSOPHICAL AND LITERARY INFLUENCES,
        1600-1900. Madison: University of Wisconsin Press,
        1957, 436-440, passim.

2398   Poenicke, Klaus. "Der Drachentöter und das Menschenbild
        des Naturalismus," JA, 15 (1970), 88-100.

        Moby Dick as the legendary dragon and Ahab the
        dragon-slayer, but the legend is perverted by sacrifice
        of the community. The dragon fighters (the national,
        racial, and social groups) claim to be the champions
        of "healthy elementary forces," and thus the naturalist
        authors prepared the way for militant leftish and fascist
        ideologies.

2399   Poenicke, Klaus. "A View from the Piazza: Herman
        Melville and the Legacy of the European Sublime,"
        CLS, 4 (1967), 267-281.

        "The Piazza," title story of Melville's PIAZZA
        TALES, enacts "a quest into the heart of American
        experience." However, Melville reacted against
        "romantic American landscape ideology" based primarily
        on the "aesthetics of the infinite...."

2400   Poggi, Valentina. "PIERRE: Il 'Kraken' di Melville,"
        SA, 10 (1964), 71-100.

        Chapter LIX ("Squid") of MOBY DICK shows Pierre
        confronted by ambiguities as frightful as the terror
        which the apparition of the faceless squid aroused in
        the Pequod crew. Melville's remarks about "krakens" in
        a letter (1851) show he was thinking of a formless,
        chance-like apparition of life (PIERRE) which would be
        related to MOBY DICK as the kraken is to the leviathan.

2401   Poirier, Richard. "A Literature of Law and Order,"
        PR, 36 (1969), 189-204.

        MOBY DICK as one example of literature since mid-
        nineteenth century offering multiplicity of patterns,
        myths, meanings, but which does not present reality of
        life of the characters.

2402   Poirier, Richard. A WORLD ELSEWHERE: THE PLACE OF STYLE
        IN AMERICAN LITERATURE. New York: Oxford University
        Press, 1966, passim.

        Rev. by Robert E. Spiller, AL, 39 (1968), 582-584.

2402.1 Polk, James. "Melville and the Idea of the City,"
UTQ, 41 (Summer, 1972), 277-292.

"Melville's emphasis upon the fallen City is the
more sobering when we consider the larger role of the
city-image in the development of the American
imagination...."

2403 Pollock, Thomas Clark. THE NATURE OF LITERATURE: ITS
RELATION TO SCIENCE, LANGUAGE AND HUMAN EXPERIENCE.
New York: Gordian Press, Inc., 1965, pp. 136-137,
passim.

Through the symbol of the whale, as well as through
such characters as Ahab, Starbuck, and Pip, Melville
evoked in the mind of the reader the experience he was
attempting to express.

2404 Pommer, Henry F. "Herman Melville and the Wake of the
Essex," AL, 20 (1948), 290-304.

Melville's use of the Essex, which was sunk by a
whale, as a source for MOBY DICK.

2405 Pommer, Henry F. THE INFLUENCE OF MILTON ON HERMAN
MELVILLE. Diss. Yale: 1946.

2406 Pommer, Henry F. "Melville as Critic of Christianity,"
FI, 102 (February 24, 1945), 121-123.

America's most pessimistic major author reminds
us that "the great despisers" are "the great adorers."

2407 Pommer, Henry F. "Melville's 'The Gesture' and the
Schoolbook Verses," AN&Q, 6 (January, 1947), 150-151.

. Melville's verses, identified by T. O. Mabbott
in the Melville Society Newsletter, December 14, 1946,
are identified as the work of other writers, but another
manuscript poem by Melville is disclosed in a copy of
CLAREL.   •

2408- Pommer, Henry F. MILTON AND MELVILLE. Pittsburgh:
Pittsburgh University Press, 1950.

Milton's influence on language, themes, and
characters in Melville. Also, comparisons of Ahab
and Milton's Satan.

Revs. by Leon Howard, NCF, 6 (1951), 76;
Sherman Paul, NEQ, 24 (1951), 550-552; Robert C.
Ryan, Sym, 10 (1971), 230-240; Robert Spiller,
AL, 23 (1951), 384-385.

2409   Pope, Martin L. THE WANDERING QUEST: A STUDY OF HERMAN
        MELVILLE. Diss. Columbia: 1965.

2410   Popkin, Henry. Afterword, MARDI: AND A VOYAGE THITHER.
        New York: The New American Library, 1964. Signet
        Classics.

2411   Pops, Martin Leonard. THE MELVILLE ARCHETYPE. Kent,
        Ohio: Kent State University Press, 1970.

        A Jungian analysis of the development of
        Melville's imagination throughout his entire career.

2412   Pops, Martin Leonard. "The Winding Quest: A Study of
        Herman Melville," DA, 28 (Columbia: 1968), 4141A.

        Melville as "a religious artist" whose personae
        are engaged in "a quest for the Sacred" often involving
        a "sexual correlative."

2412.1 Porte, Joel. EMERSON AND THOREAU: TRANSCENDENTALISTS IN
        CONFLICT. Middletown, Conn.: Wesleyan University
        Press, 1966, p. 38.

        If Bartleby was meant to be "the type of the artist,"
        Emerson was not prepared to cry with Melville, "Ah,
        Bartleby! Ah, humanity!...."

2413   Porte, Joel. "Melville," THE ROMANCE IN AMERICA: STUDIES
        IN COOPER, POE, HAWTHORNE, MELVILLE, AND JAMES.
        Middletown, Conn.: Wesleyan University Press, 1969,
        pp. 152-192.

        Melville came to a "dead end as a romancer" in the
        mid-1850's, but BILLY BUDD reasserts the essential realism
        of romance by pointing to that "something ineluctably and
        terrifyingly mysterious at the bottom of human experience,"
        which had long fascinated Melville.

        Revs. Nina Baym, JEGP, 68 (1969), 723-27;
        Lawrence Buell, NEQ, 43 (1970), 331-33; Harry Hayden
        Clark, AL, 43 (1971), 310-11.

2414   Postman, Neil. "Teaching Novel and Film," EngRec, 14
        (October, 1963), 41-44.

        BILLY BUDD as a novel and movie.

2415   Potter, David. "The Brodhead Diaries, 1846-1849,"
        JRUL, 11 (December, 1947), 21-27.

2416   Potter, David. "Reviews of MOBY-DICK," JRUL, 3 (June,
          1940), 62-65.

2417   Potter, George W. "An Old Sailor Swears Revenge on a
          Sea Dog," PEB, 95 (November 13, 1957), 41.

          Discussion of a bitter statement about Tom Melville,
          Herman Melville's brother, pencilled on a preliminary leaf
          of a copy of the first edition of REDBURN owned by the
          Providence Athenaeum.

2418   Poulet, Georges. STUDIES IN HUMAN TIME. Trans. Elliott
          Coleman. Baltimore: Johns Hopkins University Press,
          1956, pp. 337-341.

2419   Powell, Lawrence C. "The Alchemy of Books," AmLAB, 46
          (1952), 266-272.

2420   Powell, Lawrence C. "My Melville," ISLANDS OF BOOKS.
          Los Angeles: Ward Ritchie Press, 1951, pp. 68-74.

2421   Powell, Lawrence C. "Of Whales and Grass," BOOKS IN MY
          BAGGAGE. Cleveland: World Publishing Company, 1960,
          pp. 49-55.

2422   Powers, William. "Bulkington as Henry Chatillon," WAL,
          3 (1968), 153-155.

          Bulkington as "a tribute to both the substance and
          the spirit" of Parkman's Portrayal of the guide in THE
          CALIFORNIA AND OREGON TRAIL which Melville had reviewed
          in 1849.

2423   Powys, John Cowper. "Melville and Poe," ENJOYMENT OF
          LITERATURE. New York: Simon and Schuster, 1938,
          pp. 379-390.

2424   Praz, Mario. THE HERO IN ECLIPSE IN VICTORIAN FICTION.
          Trans. by Angus Davidson. London, New York, Toronto:
          Geoffrey Cumberlege, Oxford University Press, 1956,
          pp. 455-456, passim.

          Herman Melville was "haunted" by the portrait of
          Beatrice Cenci, "as can be seen in the last two books
          of his novel PIERRE, and in certain lines of CLAREL...."

2425   Praz, Mario. THE ROMANTIC AGONY. Trans. from Italian
        by Angus Davidson. Cleveland, New York: The
        World Publishing Company. Maridian Books, 1933,
        1956, 1968, p. 449.

        The alleged portrait by Guido Reni "haunted" Melville;
        evidence given by his JOURNAL UP THE STRAITS; The Colophon,
        1935, p. 133; and PIERRE, Book XXVI; as well as CLAREL,
        Vol. 2.

2426   Price, Lawrence Marsden. THE RECEPTION OF UNITED STATES
        LITERATURE IN GERMANY. Chapel Hill: North Carolina
        University Press, 1966, pp. 127-130, passim. (North
        Carolina University Studies in Comparative Literature,
        No. 39).

        Contains bibliography of Melville items in German,
        and a survey of Melville's reception in Germany.

2427   Priestley, J. B. LITERATURE AND THE WESTERN MAN. New York:
        Harper & Brothers, 1960, pp. 237-239, passim.

        Very adverse criticism.

2428   Pritchard, John Paul. CRITICISM IN AMERICA: AN ACCOUNT
        OF THE DEVELOPMENT OF CRITICAL TECHNIQUES FROM THE
        EARLY PERIOD OF THE REPUBLIC TO THE MIDDLE YEARS OF
        THE TWENTIETH CENTURY. Norman, Oklahoma: Oklahoma
        University Press, 1956, pp. 98-99, passim.

        G. W. Peck, writing in 1847 of Melville's OMOO,
        longed for the "good old days" when Democracy, "the
        one progressive principle," had not "subverted sound
        religion and philosophy."

2429   Pritchett, V. S. "The Best Generation," American
        Literature Number. NStm, 56 (1958), 1434.

        The vagrant irresponsible young men in Kerouac's
        ON THE ROAD are in British eyes, an extension of the
        literary idea that organized society is evil as seen
        in Melville and others.

2430   Pritchett, V. S. "Without the Whale," NStm, 55 (1958),
        504-505.

        General essay on Melville's works.

2431   Procter, Page S., Jr. "A Source for the Flogging
          Incident in WHITE-JACKET," AL, 22 (May, 1950),
          176-177.

          A possible source in William Leggett's story,
"Brought to the Gangway," published in the New York
Mirror, 11 (April 19, 1834), 329-331.

          Cf., Keith Huntress, "Melville's Use of a Source
for WHITE JACKET," AL, 17 (March, 1945), 66-74.

2432   Purcell, James M. "Melville's Contribution to English,"
          PMLA, 56 (September, 1941), 797-808.

          Two lists of 180 words show Melville's contribution
to and influence upon the formation of the English
vocabulary.

2433   Putnam, George H. A MEMOIR OF GEORGE PALMER PUTNAM.
          New York: 1903.

2434   Putnam, John B. "Whaling and Whalecraft: A Pictorial
          Account," MOBY-DICK. Harrison Hayford and Hershel
          Parker, eds. New York: W. W. Norton, 1967, pp.
          509-528.

2435   Putzel, Max. "The Source and the Symbols of Melville's
          'BENITO CERENO,'" AL, 34 (May, 1962), 191-206.

          Melville's adaptation of Amasa Delano's NARRATIVE
OF VOYAGES AND TRAVELS.

2436   Quennell, Peter. "The Author of MOBY-DICK," NStm, 33
          (1929), 604.

2437   Quigly, I. "BILLY BUDD," /Motion picture version7
          Spec, 209 (September 28, 1962), 437.

2438   Quinn, Arthur Hobson. "The Creator of MOBY DICK,"
          YR, n. s., 16 (October, 1922), 205-209.

          An article-review of Raymond Weaver's biography
of Melville.

2439   Quinn, Arthur Hobson. "Herman Melville and the Exotic
          Romance," AMERICAN FICTION: AN HISTORICAL AND
          CRITICAL SURVEY. New York: Appleton-Century-Crofts,
          Inc., 1936, 1951, 1964, pp. 149-158, passim.

2439.1   Quinn, Arthur Hobson. "The Romance of the Frontier,"
          THE LITERATURE OF THE AMERICAN PEOPLE. New York:
          Appleton-Century, 1951, pp. 243-247.

2440   Quinn, Patrick. "The Ishmael Complex," Cw, 64 (August 3, 1956), 444-446.

2441   Quinn, Patrick. "Poe's 'Imaginary Voyage,'" HudR, 4 (Winter, 1952), 562-585.

        ARTHUR GORDON PYM influenced Melville in his writing of MOBY DICK, especially as to use of whiteness.

        Cf., W. H. Wells, "MOBY DICK and Rabelais," MLN, 38 (1923), 123.

2442   Quint, Leon-Pierre. "Herman Melville," *Preuves*, 17 (May, 1967), 47-51.

2443   Radiguet, Max. LES DERNIERS SAUVAGES. Paris: 1929.

2444   Rahv, Philip. "The Dark Lady of Salem," PR, 8 (1941), 362-381.

2445   Rahv, Philip, ed. DISCOVERY OF EUROPE: THE STORY OF AMERICAN EXPERIENCE IN THE OLD WORLD. Boston: Houghton Mifflin, 1947.

2446   Rahv, Philip, ed. EIGHT GREAT AMERICAN SHORT NOVELS. New York: Berkeley, 1963, pp. 10-11.

        BARTLEBY, THE SCRIVENER.

2447   Rahv, Philip, ed. "Introduction: The Native Bias," LITERATURE IN AMERICA: AN ANTHOLOGY OF LITERARY CRITICISM. Cleveland and New York: World Publishing Company, 1957, 1967, pp. 11-22.

2448   Rahv, Philip. "Melville and His Critics," PR, 17 (September-October, 1950), 732-775.

        A review-article of Newton Arvin's HERMAN MELVILLE.

2449   Rahv, Philip. "Melville and His Critics," IMAGE AND IDEA: TWENTY ESSAYS ON LITERARY THEMES. Norfolk, Conn.: New Directions, 1957, pp. 182-187.

2449.1   Raleigh, John Henry. "Eugene O'Neill," *Ramparts*, 2 (1964), 72-87.

        O'Neill in the "great dark tradition" of Melville and others.

2450   Raleigh, John Henry. MATTHEW ARNOLD AND AMERICAN CULTURE.
          Berkeley and Los Angeles: California University
          Press, 1961, passim.

          Matthew Arnold's influence on Melville.

2451   Raleigh, John Henry. "The Novel and the City: England
          and Fiction: England and America in the Nineteenth
          Century," VS, 11, iii (March, 1968), 291-328.

          The city in REDBURN, PIERRE, BARTLEBY, and
          ISRAEL POTTER.

2451.1   Raleigh, John Henry. "Revolt and Revaluation in
          Criticism, 1900-1930," THE DEVELOPMENT OF AMERICAN
          LITERARY CRITICISM. Floyd Stovall, ed. Chapel
          Hill, North Carolina: North Carolina University
          Press, 1955, pp. 159-198, passim.

          A factor operating in "the efflorescence of American
          literary studies" was the rediscovery of complex and
          hitherto obscure literary figures such as Melville.

2452   Ramakrishna, P. "Moral Ambiguity in Herman Melville's
          'BENITO CERENO,'" Crit&R, (1966), 136-145.

2453   Rampersad, Arnold. MELVILLE'S ISRAEL POTTER: A PILGRIMAGE
          AND PROGRESS. Bowling Green, Ohio: Bowling Green
          University Popular Press, 1969.

          Relation of ISRAEL POTTER to Melville's previous
          work.

          Rev. by Walter Bezanson, AL, 43 (1971), 133-135.

2454   Randall, D. A., and J. T. Winterich. "One Hundred Good
          Novels. Melville, Herman: MOBY DICK," PubW, 137
          (1940), 255-257.

          Collations and notes.

2455   Rasco, Lavon. "The Biographies of Herman Melville:
          A Study in Twentieth Century Biography," DA, 17
          (Northwestern: 1957), 357.

2456   Rathbun, John W. "BILLY BUDD and the Limits of Perception,"
          NCF, 20 (June, 1965), 19-34.

          The final chapters are an "ironic epilogue"
          showing the impact of Billy's death on the state,
          Captain Vere, and the seamen.

2457   Ray, Richard E. "'BENITO CERENO': Babo as Leader,"
           ATQ, 7 (1970), 31-37.

        The story is neither a study of pure evil nor a
condemnation of slavery. The central figure is Babo,
an unusually intelligent leader "doing his duty" when
the opportunity presents itself.

2458   Read, Herbert Edward. ENGLISH PROSE STYLE. London:
           Bell, 1942; new ed., 1952; repr., Boston: Beacon,
           1955, pp. 164-165, 198-200.

        Passages from MOBY DICK and BILLY BUDD used for
stylistic analysis.

2459   Read, Herbert Edward. THE NATURE OF LITERATURE. New York:
           Horizon Press, 1956, p. 226.

        The relationship between Melville and Hawthorne.

2460   Redman, Ben Ray. "New Editions," SatRL, 32 (1949), 28.

        The reader should not be baffled by THE CONFIDENCE
MAN, but should simply enjoy the story.

2460.1   Reed, Henry. "Books in General," NS&N (May 31, 1947),
           397.

        Melville cherished his "ambiguities" to the end.

2460.2   Reed, Henry. MOBY-DICK, A PLAY FOR RADIO. London: 1947.

2461   Reed, Walter L. "Meditations on the Hero-Narrative Form
           in Carlyle, Kierkegaard, and Melville," DAI, 31
           (Yale: 1970), 1288A.

2462   Rees, John O., Jr. "Spenserian Analogues in MOBY-DICK,"
           ESQ, 18 (3rd Qt., 1972), 174-178.

        Influence of Canto 12, Book II, of FAERIE QUEENE,
particularly upon Chapter 133, "The Chase - First Day."

2463   Rees, Robert A. "Melville's Alma and THE BOOK OF MORMON,"
           ESQ, 43 (2nd Qt., 1966), 41-46.

        The parallel between Alma of MARDI and two characters
of the same name in THE BOOK OF MORMON.

2464   Reeves, Paschal. "The 'Deaf Mute' Confidence Man:
        Melville's Imposter in Action," MLN, 75 (January,
        1960), 18-20.

        An impersonator, who posed as a deaf mute in
Fayetteville, North Carolina, April 1850, provides a
counterpart for the deaf mute in THE CONFIDENCE MAN.

2465   Regan, Charles L. "Melville's Horned Woman," ELN, 5
        (September, 1967), 34-39.

        The account of the woman with a horn growing out
of her forehead, described in Chapter 61 of WHITE JACKET,
resembles the portrait of Margaret Owyn published in
London, 1588.

        Melville may also have known of the "horned woman"
through Marston's play THE MALCONTENT.

2466   Reich, Charles A. "The Tragedy of Justice in BILLY BUDD,"
        YR, 56 (Spring, 1967), 368-389.

        In BILLY BUDD, Melville examines the theme of
justice in terms of a three-part problem in law:
first, the legal standards; second, Vere's reactions
to a conflict between natural and social law; and
third, society's standards.

2467   Reid, B. L. "Old Melville's Fable," MR, 9 (1968),
        529-546.

        BILLY BUDD in terms of scriptural analogy in
the tradition of Milton and Hawthorne, forming "a trap
of the archetype of the Fall of man," "a parable of
man in the trap which is the world."

2467.1 Reid, B. L. "Old Melville's Fable," TRAGIC OCCASIONS:
        ESSAYS ON SEVERAL FORMS. Port Washington, New York:
        Kennikat Press, 1971, pp. 137-162.

2467.2 Reid, B. L. "Leviathan Is the Text," TRAGIC OCCASIONS:
        ESSAYS ON SEVERAL FORMS. Port Washington, New York:
        Kennikat Press, 1971, pp. 95-135.

2468   Reinert, Otto. "Bartleby the Inscrutable: Notes on a
        Melville Motif," AMERICANA NORVEGICA: NORWEGIAN
        CONTRIBUTIONS TO AMERICAN STUDIES. Sigmund Skard
        and Henry H. Wasser, eds. Vol. I, Oslo: Gyldendal
        Norsk Forlag: Philadelphia: Pennsylvania University
        Press, 1966, pp. 180-205.

        BARTLEBY related to earlier as well as to later
works of Melville.

2469   Reiss, John P., Jr. "Problems of the Family Novel: Cooper, Hawthorne, and Melville," DAI, 30 (Wis.: 1969), 1178A-79A.

2470   Reist, John S., Jr. "Surd Evil and Suffering Love," Universitas, 2 (Fall, 1964), 81-90.

A theological consideration of BILLY BUDD.

2471   Renvoisé, Jean-Paul. "BILLY BUDD: Opéra de Benjamin Britten," EA, 18 (October-December, 1965), 367-382.

M. Renvoise's account of the way the librettists, Eric Crozier and E. M. Forster, solved their problems in adapting the tale.

Britten was moved to compose the opera after he read the brief account of BILLY BUDD in Forster's ASPECTS OF THE NOVEL.

2471.1   Resink, G. J. "Samburan Encantada," ES, 47 (February, 1966), 35-44.

Comparison of Conrad and Melville.

2472   Resink, G. J. "Samburan Encantada," Conrad, 1, ii (1968), 37-44.

Comparison of Conrad and Melville.

2472.1   Reynolds, Cuyler. ALBANY CHRONICLES. Albany: 1906.

2472.2   Reynolds, Cuyler, ed. HUDSON-HOHAWK GENEALOGICAL AND FAMILY MEMOIRS. New York: 1911.

2473   Reynolds, J. N. MOCHA DICK, OR THE WHITE WHALE OF THE PACIFIC. Introduction by L. L. Balcolm. New York: 1832.

A possible source for MOBY DICK.

2473.1   Reynolds, J. N. MOCHA DICK. KbM, May, 1839.

2473.2   Reynolds, J. N. VOYAGE OF THE U. S. FRIGATE POTOMAC.

2474   Reynolds, Michael S. "The Prototype for Melville's Confidence-Man," PMLA, 86 (October, 1971), 1009-1013.

Parallels between the New York Herald's story and Melville's character in THE CONFIDENCE MAN.

2475   Rhys, Ernest. Editor's Note, MOBY DICK: OR THE WHITE
        WHALE. London: J. M. Dent, 1907.

2476   Rhys, Ernest. Introduction, OMOO. New York: 1908.

2477   Ribalow, Harold U. "How Palestine Influenced Herman
        Melville's Writings," JewN (August 30, 1957), 10.
        Repr. from the Jerusalem Post.

2477.1 Rice, Howard C., Jr., et al. "MOBY DICK by Herman Melville:
        A Century of an American Classic 1851-1951: Catalogue
        of an Exhibition Princeton University Library October
        15-December 15, 1951," PULC, 13 (Winter, 1952), 63-
        118.

2478   Rice, Julian C. "MOBY DICK and Shakespearean Tragedy,"
        CentR, 14, 4 (1970), 444-468.

        The theme of mortal inter-indebtedness offsets
        the tragic pessimism, as does the ability of Ishmael
        to endure through relativism and an acceptance of human
        fraility.

2478.1 Richardson, Charles F. AMERICAN LITERATURE, 1607-1885.
        New York: G. P. Putnam's Sons, 1889, II, 403-405.

        "...Melville made some essays in the same direction
        /as W. S. Mayo in KALOOLAH/, but failed completely for
        lack of a firm thought and a steady hand...."

2478.2 Richardson, Charles F. "Herman Melville," ENCYCLOPAEDIA
        BRITANNICA. 10th ed. New York: The Encyclopaedia
        Britannica Company, 1902, VI, 631.

2479   Richie, Donald. "Herman Melville," SCE, 10 (November,
        (1955), 33-40.

        A biographic article with interpretative summaries
        of the romances before MOBY DICK.

2479.1 Ricks, Beatrice, Joseph D. Adams, and Jack O. Hazlerig,
        comps. NATHANIEL HAWTHORNE: A REFERENCE
        BIBLIOGRAPHY, 1900-1971. Boston: G. K. Hall & Co.,
        1972, passim.

2480   Rideout, Walter B. INSTRUCTOR'S MANUAL FOR "THE
        EXPERIENCE OF PROSE." New York: Crowell, 1960,
        pp. 15-16.

        BENITO CERENO.

2481   Ridge, George Ross, and Davy S. Ridge. "A Bird and a
        Motto: Source for 'BENITO CERENO,'" MissQ, 13
        (Winter, 1959-1960), 22-29.

2482   Riegel, O. W. "The Anatomy of Melville's Fame," AL, 3
        (1931), 195-203.

        The revival of interest in Melville in the "twenties"
        was not the first. At least four or five movements sought
        to reawaken interest in this American writer.

        Cf., William Braswell. "A Note on 'The Anatomy of
        Melville's Fame,'" AL, 5 (1934), 360-364.

2483   Riffaterre, Michael. "Criteria for Style Analysis,"
        Word, 15 (1959), 172.

        Analysis of Melville's verbal style in MOBY DICK.

2484   Rimonte, Nilda. "Notes on Starbuck and Stubb," DilR,
        13 (October, 1965), 420-424.

        Starbuck, Ahab, and Stubb serve as a kind of
        Greek chorus in MOBY DICK. They are complementary.

2485   Ritchie, M. C. "Herman Melville," QQ, 37 (1930), 36-61.

2486   Rizzardi, Alfredo. "Anglo-American Literature," Conv,
        31 (1963), 368-370.

        Review-article of Warner Berthoff's THE EXAMPLE
        OF MELVILLE.

2487   Rizzardi, Alfredo. LA CONDIZIONE AMERICANA: STUDI SU
        POETI NORD-AMERICANI. Bologna: Cappelli, 1959.

        On Melville and others.

2488   Rizzardi, Alfredo. "La Poesia di Herman Melville,"
        SA, 1 (1955), 159-203.

2489   Rizzardi, Alfredo. "La poesia Melvilliana," FLe, 10
        (March 8, 1953), 4-5.

2490   Robbins, J. Albert, ed. AMERICAN LITERARY SCHOLARSHIP:
        AN ANNUAL, 1968. Durham, North Carolina: Duke
        University Press, 1970.

2490.1 Robbins, J. Albert, ed. AMERICAN LITERARY SCHOLARSHIP:
        AN ANNUAL, 1969. Durham, North Carolina: Duke
        University Press, 1971.

2491   Roberts, Morley. "The Sea in Fiction," QQ, 37 (1930),
         18-35.

         Melville, the greatest novelist of the sea.

2491.1   Roberts, Morley. W. H. HUDSON: A PORTRAIT. New York:
         E. P. Dutton and Company, 1924, p. 131.

2491.2   Robertson, R. B. OF WHALES AND MEN. New York: 1954.

2492   Robillard, Douglas. "Theme and Structure in Melville's
         JOHN MARR AND OTHER SAILORS," ELN, 6 (1969), 187-
         192.

         Unity of theme is provided by the poet-sailor Marr
         who turns to the sea for understanding. Thus, the sea
         becomes the central symbol and theme of the story.

2493   Rockwell, Frederick S. "DeQuincey and the Ending of
         MOBY DICK," NCF, 9 (1954), 161-168.

2494   Rogers, Robert. "Fair Maid and Femme Fatale,"
         A PSYCHOANALYTIC STUDY OF THE DOUBLE IN LITERATURE.
         Detroit, Michigan: Wayne State University Press,
         1970, pp. 133-137.

         PIERRE.

2495   Rogers, Robert. "The 'Ineludible Gripe' of BILLY BUDD,"
         L&P, 14 (1964), 9-22.

         Repr., LITERATURE IN CRITICAL PERSPECTIVES.
         Walter K. Gordon, ed. New York: Appleton-
         Century-Crofts, 1968, pp. 732-740.

         A psychological reading of Billy as unconscious
         rebel.

2495.1   Rogers, Robert. "The Opposing Self," A PSYCHOANALYTIC
         STUDY OF THE DOUBLE IN LITERATURE. Detroit, Michigan:
         Wayne State University Press, 1970, pp. 67-70.

         BARTLEBY.

2495.2   Rogers, Robert. "Psychomachia: The Soul Battle,"
         A PSYCHOANALYTIC STUDY OF THE DOUBLE IN LITERATURE.
         Detroit, Michigan: Wayne State University Press,
         1970, pp. 146-159.

         BILLY BUDD.

2496 Rohrberger, Mary. "Point of View in 'BENITO CERENO':
   Machinations and Deceptions," CE, 27 (April, 1966),
   541-546.

   Delano's viewpoint is necessary to involve the
reader in the mystery, and then to maintain the reader's
involvement until the recognition is accomplished. When
Delano's viewpoint is no longer necessary, it is discarded.

2497 Roper, Gordon. "Before MOBY DICK," UCM, 48 (October,
   1955), 4-9.

   The "Toby correspondence" in full.

2498 Roper, Gordon. AN INDEX OF MELVILLE'S MARDI, MOBY-DICK,
   PIERRE, AND BILLY BUDD. Diss. Chicago: 1944.

2499 Roper, Gordon. "Melville's MOBY DICK, 1851-1951,"
   DR, 31 (Autumn, 1951), 167-179.

   The changing reputation of MOBY DICK.

2500 Roper, Gordon. "On Teaching MOBY DICK," ESQ, 28,
   Melville Supplement (3rd Qt., 1962), 2-4.

2501 Rose, Edward J. "Melville, Emerson, and the Sphinx,"
   NEQ, 36 (June, 1963), 249-258.

   Comparison of Chapter LXX of MOBY DICK (Ahab's
monologue on the sperm-whale's head) and Emerson's
poem "The Sphinx" illustrates the differences between
Melville's thought and Emerson's.

2502 Rose, Edward J. "'The Queenly Personality': Walpole,
   Melville, and Mother," L&P, 15 (Fall, 1966), 216-
   229.

   Parallels between Horace Walpole's play, THE
MYSTERIOUS MOTHER, and Melville's PIERRE.

2503 Rosen, Bruce John. "TYPEE and OMOO: Melville's Literary
   Apprenticeship," DA, 27 (N. Y. U.: 1966), 461A-
   462A.

2504 Rosen, Roma. "Melville's Use of Shakespeare's Plays,"
   DA, 23 (Northwestern: 1963), 3356.

2505 Rosenbach, A. S. W., ed. Introduction, MOBY DICK.
   London, New York: 1929.

2506   Rosenberry, Edward H. "Awash in Melvilliana," NEQ, 33
            (December, 1960), 525-528.

            Review of recent publications.

2507   Rosenberry, Edward H. THE COMIC SPIRIT IN THE ART OF
            HERMAN MELVILLE. Diss. Delaware: 1953.

2508   Rosenberry, Edward H. "Israel Potter, Benjamin Franklin,
            and the Doctrine of Self-Reliance," ESQ, 28,
            Melville Supplement (1962), 27-29.

2509   Rosenberry, Edward H. MELVILLE AND THE COMIC SPIRIT.
            Cambridge, Mass.: Harvard University Press, 1955,
            pp. 105-115. Repr., New York: Octagon Books,
            1969.

            The "comic threads" are as "vital as the tragic
            ones to the rich suggestiveness" of MOBY DICK.

            Revs., Henry Grattan, NEQ, 29 (1956), 559-560;
            Luther S. Mansfield, AL, 28 (1956), 239-40; Robert C.
            Ryan, Sym, 10 (1971), 230-40.

2510   Rosenberry, Edward H. "Melville and His Mosses," ATQ,
            7 (1970), 47-51.

            Elements of both "I and My Chimney" and "The
            Apple-Tree Table" derive from a recollection or re-
            reading of Mosses from an Old Manse.

2511   Rosenberry, Edward H. "Melville's Burgundy Club Sketches,"
            HLB, 12 (1958), 253-267.

2512   Rosenberry. Edward H. "Melville's Ship of Fools,"
            PMLA, 75 (December, 1960), 604-608.

            THE SHIP OF FOOLS by Sebastian Brant (1458-1521),
            the prototype of Melville's THE CONFIDENCE MAN.

2513   Rosenberry, Edward H. "The Problem of BILLY BUDD,"
            PMLA, 80 (December, 1965), 489-498.

            Repr., in LITERATURE IN CRITICAL PERSPECTIVES.
            Walter K. Gordon, ed. New York: Appleton-Century-
            Crofts, 1968, pp. 762-773; and in TWENTIETH CENTURY
            INTERPRETATIONS OF BILLY BUDD. Howard P. Vincent, ed.
            Englewood Cliffs, New Jersey: 1971, pp. 48-55.

            The irony in BILLY BUDD is not satiric, but rather
            Aristotelian—reversal of fortune, "irony of fate."

2514   Rosenberry, Edward H. "Queequeg's Coffin-Canoe: Made in TYPEE," AL, 30 (January, 1959), 529-530.

2515   Rosenfeld, William. "The Divided Burden: Common Elements in the Search for a Religious Synthesis in the Works of Theodore Parker, Horace Bushnell, Nathaniel Hawthorne, and Herman Melville," DA, 22 (Minn.: 1962, 4019.

2516   Rosenfeld, William. "Uncertain Faith: Queequeg's Coffin and Melville's Use of the Bible," TSLL, 7 (Winter, 1966), 317-327.

The images of spiritual rebirth in passages about Ishmael, Bulkington, and Queequeg relate to words of Jesus to Nicodemus in John: 3.

2517   Rosenheim, Frederick. "Flight from Home: Some Episodes in the Life of Herman Melville," AI, 1 (1940), 1-30.

2518   Rosenthal, Bernard. "Elegy for Jack Chase," SRom, 10 (Summer, 1971), 213-229.

"...The dedication of BILLY BUDD to Jack Chase,... heralds Melville's lament for a world where the symbolic presence of Jack Chase has yielded to that of John Claggart....Whatever else it may be, BILLY BUDD is a deliberate farewell to that quest for a spiritually ordered world which first received artistic form in TYPEE, where Melville's hero discovered cannibalism instead of innocence...."

2519   Rosenthal, Bernard. "Melville, Marryat, and the Evil-Eyed Villain," NCF, 25 (1970), 221-224.

2520   Rosenthal, M. L., and A. J. M. Smith. EXPLORING POETRY. New York: Macmillan, 1955, pp. 373, 667.

"Billy in the Darbies"
"The Portent"

2521   Ross, Danforth. THE AMERICAN SHORT STORY. Minneapolis: Minnesota University Press, 1961, pp. 15-16.

BARTLEBY.

2522   Ross, Morton L. "Captain Truck and Captain Boomer," AL, 37 (November, 1965), 316.

Boomer's "mania" for introduction may be drawn from a character in Cooper's HOMEWARD BOUND.

2522.1   Roth, Russell. "The Inception of a Saga: Frederick
Manfred's BUCKSKIN MAN," SDR, 7, iv (Winter,
(1969-1970), 87-99.

2523   Rothfork, John. "The Sailing of the Pequod: An
Existential Voyage," ArQ, 28 (1972), 55-60.

2524   Rothschild, Herbert, Jr. "The Language of Mesmerism in
'The Quarter-Deck' Scene in MOBY DICK," ES, 53
(June, 1972), 235-238.

2525   Roudiez, Leon A. "Camus and MOBY DICK," Sym, 15
(Spring, 1961), 30-40.

      Cf., Leon A. Roudiez, "Strangers in Melville and
Camus," FR, 31 (1958), 217-226.

2526   Roudiez, Leon A. "Strangers in Melville and Camus,"
FR, 31 (January, 1958), 217-226.

      Repr., as "Les Étrangers chez Melville et Camus,"
RLM, 8 (1961), 343-357.

      Comparison of Camus's L'ÉTRANGER with BILLY BUDD.

      Cf., Leon A. Roudiez, "Camus and MOBY DICK,"
Sym, 15 (1961), 30-40.

2527   Rourke, Constance M. AMERICAN HUMOR: A STUDY OF THE
NATIONAL CHARACTER. New York: Harcourt, Brace,
1931, pp. 191-200; repr., New York: Doubleday
Anchor, 1953, pp. 154-160, passim.

      The humor in MARDI, MOBY DICK, OMOO, and TYPEE.

2528   Rouse, H. Blair. "Democracy, American Literature, and
Mr. Fast," EJ, 36 (1947), 321-323.

2529   Rousseaux, André. "MARDI," FL, 5 (1950), 2.

      An interpretation of Melville's novel in which
the author places Melville "as high as Poe."

2530   Rousseaux, André. "A travers l'oeuvre de Melville,"
FL, 6 (August 11, 1951), 2.

2530.1   Routh, H. V. TOWARDS THE TWENTIETH CENTURY. New York:
1937.

2531   Rovit, Earl. "Fathers and Sons in American Fiction,"
        YR, 53 (Winter, 1963), 248-257.

        Melville had read Hawthorne's tale of "the
unpardonable sin" and in writing to Hawthorne, Melville
felt no need to spell out his motto. The substitution
of "devil" for "father" was a masquerade that Melville
and Hawthorne "knew well how to play," both having had
to cope with their years of adolescence without the
presence of actual fathers.

2531.1 Rovit, Earl. "HE SENT FORTH A RAVEN: The Curse and
        the Covenant," MissQ, 12 (1959), 23-45.

        Comparison of certain referents in the novel of
Elizabeth M. Roberts with MOBY DICK.

2531.2 Rovit, Earl. THE PLAYER KING. New York: Harcourt,
        Brace and World, 1965, p. 173.

        Reference to BARTLEBY.

2532   Rowland, Beryl. "Melville's Bachelors and Maids:
        Interpretation Through Symbol and Metaphor,"
        AL, 41 (1969), 389-405.

2533   Rowland, Beryl. "Melville's Waterloo in 'Rich Man's
        Crumbs,'" NCF, 25 (September, 1970), 216-221.

        Certain curious factual errors in Melville's
sketch.

2533.1 Rubenstein, Gilbert M. "The Businessman in Literature,
        Par I," AmBC, 17 (April, 1967), 24-26, 30-31.

        Satan is the first "businessman" in Western
literature, for he sold Eve "a bill of goods." He
is the serpentine prototype of literary businessman
in the New Testament, and in Melville and others.

2534   Rubin, Joseph Jay. "Melville's Reputation, 1847," N&Q,
        176 (1939), 298.

2534.1 Rubin, Louis D., Jr. THE CURIOUS DEATH OF THE NOVEL:
        ESSAYS IN AMERICAN LITERATURE. Baton Rouge:
        Louisiana State University Press, 1967, pp. 277-278,
        passim.

2535   Rubin, Louis D., Jr. THE TELLER OF THE TALE. Seattle:
        Washington University Press, 1967, p. 212.

        Ishmael is Melville, for besides being in the story
he can also stand aside and tell us "what it means." He
is both a character and the author's surrogate.

2536   Rubin, Louis D., Jr., and John Rees Moore, eds.
        "Herman Melville," THE IDEA OF AN AMERICAN NOVEL.
        New York: Thomas Y. Crowell Company, 1961, pp.
        216-229, passim.

        Letters from Melville to Hawthorne.

2537   Rukeyser, Muriel. THE LIFE OF POETRY. New York:
        A. A. Wyn, 1949, pp. 25-26, 68-73.

2537.1 Rukeyser, Muriel. WILLARD GIBBS. Garden City, New York:
        Doubleday Doran, 1942, pp. 353-357.

2538   Ruland, Richard. "Melville and the Fortunate Fall:
        Typee as Eden," NCF, 23 (1968), 312-323.

        The Edenic imagery of TYPEE is employed ironically.
    Typee is no paradise but a part of the world, its
    "insulation and Edenic innocence" making it an impossible
    place for Tommo to live and still retain his identity.

2539   Ruland, Richard. THE REDISCOVERY OF AMERICAN LITERATURE:
        PREMISES OF CRITICAL TASTE, 1900-1940. Cambridge,
        Mass.: Harvard University Press, 1967, passim.

        Critical survey of the period and analysis of
    interest in Melville.

        Rev. by Benjamin T. Spencer, AL, 40 (1968), 235-36.

2540   Runden, John P. IMAGERY IN MELVILLE'S SHORTER FICTION,
        1853-1856. Diss. Indiana: 1952.

2541   Runden, John P., ed. MELVILLE'S "BENITO CERENO": A TEXT
        FOR GUIDED RESEARCH. Boston: Heath, 1965, pp. 119-
        121.

2542   Russell, C. H. St. L. Introduction, MOBY DICK. New
        York: 1931.

2543   Russell, Frank A. AMERICAN PILGRIMAGE. New York:
        Dodd, Mead, 1942, pp. 119-133.

2543.1 Russell, Frank A. SHOULD OLD ACQUAINTANCE. New York:
        1943.

2544   Russell, Jack. "ISRAEL POTTER and 'Song of Myself,'"
        AL, 40 (1968), 72-77.

        Certain parallels suggest that Whitman may have
    been influenced by Melville's novel.

2545   Russell, Michael. POLYNESIA: OR, AN HISTORICAL ACCOUNT
       OF THE PRINCIPAL ISLANDS IN THE SOUTH SEAS.
       Edinburgh: 1845.

2546   Russell, Thomas. "Yarn for Melville's TYPEE," PQ, 15
       (1936), 16-29.

2547   Russell, W. Clark. "A Claim for American Literature,"
       NAR, 154 (February, 1892), 138-149.

       When he, Herman Melville, "died the other day,
       men who could give you the names of fifty living
       American poets and perhaps a hundred living American
       novelists owned that they had never heard of Herman
       Melville."

2548   Russell, W. Clark, ed. Introduction, OMOO. New York:
       1904.

2549   Russell, W. Clark. Introduction, TYPEE. New York: 1904.

2550   Russell, W. Clark. Letter to Herman Melville, July 21,
       1886, published in The New York World, October 11,
       1891, p. 26.

       Russell wrote: "Your reputation here /England/
       is very great."

2550.1 Russell, William Clark. AN OCEAN TRAGEDY. 1889.

       Inscribed to Herman Melville.

2551   Russell, W. Clark. "Sea Stories," ContempR, 46 (September,
       1884), 356-359.

       MOBY DICK, Melville's finest work.

2552   Rust, R. Dilworth. "Vision in MOBY DICK," ESQ, 33
       (4th Qt., 1963), 73-75.

       If Ahab's destruction can be seen in terms of his
       "increasing blindness (both physical and spiritual),
       Ishmael's salvation can be traced to his increasing
       vision."

2553   Ryan, Robert C. "'Weeds and Wildings Chiefly: With A
       Rose or Two' by Herman Melville: Reading Text and
       Genetic Text. Edited from the Manuscripts. With
       Introduction and Notes," DA, 28 (Northwestern: 1967),
       2262A.

2554   Rysten, Felix S. A. "False Prophets in Fiction: Camus,
       Dostoevsky, Melville, and Others," DA, 29 (Southern
       California: 1969), 3586A-87A.

2555   Sackman, Douglas. "The Original of Melville's Apple-Tree Table," AL, 11 (1940), 448-451.

The same occurrence described in Timothy Dwight's TRAVELS IN NEW ENGLAND AND NEW YORK (New Haven: 1821), II, 398, and in D. D. Field, ed., A HISTORY OF BERKSHIRE COUNTY, MASS. (Pittsfield: 1829).

Melville mentions in "Hawthorne and His Mosses" having read Dwight's TRAVELS. It is also likely that he read Field's HISTORY OF BERKSHIRE COUNTY because he was interested in Berkshire County affairs.

2556   Sadleir, Michael. "Bibliography of the First Editions of the Prose Works of Herman Melville," THE WORKS OF HERMAN MELVILLE. London: Constable, 1923, Vol. 12, 337-358.

2557   Sadleir, Michael. "Herman Melville: Essay and Bibliography," EXCURSIONS IN VICTORIAN BIBLIOGRAPHY. London: Chaundy & Cox, 1922, pp. 215-234.

2558   Sadleir, Michael. "Letter to the Editor," Nation&Ath, 29 (1921), 396.

2559   Saeki, Shoichi. "Shosetsuka Melville to Shin-hihyo," EigoS, 115 (1969), 472-473.

Melville the novelist.

2560   Sale, Arthur. "Captain Vere's Reasons," CamJ, 5 (October, 1951), 3-18.

Billy Budd's death as ironic.

2561   Sale, Arthur. "The Glass Ship: A Recurrent Image in Melville," MLQ, 17 (June, 1956), 118-127.

2561.1   Salt, H. S. "Herman Melville," LitGuide, n. s. 311 (1922), 70.

2562   Salt, H. S. "Herman Melville," UnR, 4 (May, 1889), 78.

2563   Salt, H. S. "Herman Melville," ScAR, 2 (June-December, 1889), 186-190.

It is hard to account for "the indifference of the present generation to Herman Melville's writings."

2564   Salt, H. S. "Marquesan Melville," GentM, 272 (March, 1892), 248-257.

"...The increasing transcendentalism of Melville's later thought was accompanied and reflected by a corresponding complexity of language, the limpid simplicity...in TYPEE and OMOO and WHITE JACKET being now succeeded by...fantastic word-painting...."

2565   Salvidge, Stanley. "Herman Melville and Liverpool,"
        <u>Spec</u>, 139 (1927), 88-89.

2565.1 San Juan, Epifanio, Jr. "Spatial Orientation in American
        Romanticism," E-WR, 2, 1 (Spring-Summer, 1965),
        33-55.

2566   Sanborn, Franklin Benjamin. MEMORABILIA OF HAWTHORNE,
        ALCOTT, AND CONCORD. Kenneth Walter Cameron, ed.
        Hartford: Transcendental Books, 1970.

2567   Sandberg, A. "Erotic Patterns in 'The Paradise of
        Bachelors and the Tartarus of Maids,'" L&P, 18,
        1 (1968), 2-8.

        The diptych conveys the narrator's "pleasure in
        the bachelors' world and his recoil from the world of
        women"; although he leaves "no doubt as to the world
        he wants," he never understands his motivation.

2567.1 Sander, Lucille A. "Melville's Symbolism of the Pipe,"
        ESQ, 59 (1970), 4-7.

        "There is no smoking near the end of MOBY DICK;
        there are no peaceful souls, no dreamy musings; only
        passion and fear."

2568   Sanders, Thomas E. THE DISCOVERY OF FICTION. Dallas,
        Texas; Palo Alto, Calif.; Oakland, New Jersey:
        Scott, Foresman and Company, 1967, pp. 237-238, 621.

        Parallel between the whale of MOBY DICK and the
        turtle in Paul Brodeur's "The Turtle."

2568.1 Santayana, George. THE LETTERS OF GEORGE SANTAYANA.
        Daniel Cory, ed. New York: Charles Scribner's
        Sons, 1955, p. 224, 229.

        "...I tried the other day to read MOBY DICK, but
        in spite of much skipping, I have got stuck in the
        middle. Is it such a masterpiece as they say?...."

2569   Satterfield, John. "Perth: An Organic Digression in
        MOBY DICK," MLN, 74 (February, 1959), 106-107.

        An epic interpretation of MOBY DICK. Perth is
        modeled on Hephaestus, the ancient Greek god of fire
        and metalworking.

2570   Scherman, David E., and Rosemarie Redlich. "Herman
        Melville," A CHRONICLE OF AMERICAN WRITERS FROM
        1607-1952 WITH 173 PHOTOGRAPHS OF THE AMERICAN
        SCENE THAT INSPIRED THEM. New York: Dodd, Mead
        & Co., 1952, pp. 71-73.

2571   Scherting, Jack. "The Bottle and the Coffin: Further
            Speculation on Poe and MOBY-DICK," PN, 1, i-ii
            (1968), 22.

        Melville probably read "MS. Found in a Bottle,"
        and "traces" of the story were incorporated into
        MOBY DICK.

2572   Schiffman, Joseph. Afterword, THREE SHORTER NOVELS.
            Quentin Anderson, ed. New York: Harper, 1962.

2573   Schiffman, Joseph. "Critical Problems in Melville's
            'BENITO CERENO,'" MLQ, 11 (September, 1950),
            317-324.

2574   Schiffman, Joseph. HERMAN MELVILLE: THE WORLD A SHIP.
            New York: McGraw-Hill Book Co., (Tape Recordings
            in English), 1969.

2575   Schiffman, Joseph. "Melville's Final Stage, Irony: A Re-
            examination of BILLY BUDD Criticism," AL, 22
            (1950), 128-136.

        A review of various interpretations of the "theme
        of acceptance."

2576   Schlesinger, Arthur M., Jr., and Morton White, eds.
            PATHS OF AMERICAN THOUGHT. London: Chatto &
            Windus, 1964, passim.

        References place Melville in the cultural milieu
        of his time.

2577   Schless, H. H. "Flaxman, Dante, and Melville's PIERRE,"
            BNYPL, 64 (February, 1960), 65-82.

        Several of the ambiguities of PIERRE may be resolved
        by application of the DIVINE COMEDY, particularly the
        Inferno.
                            o
        Also, a number of images in PIERRE are inspired by
        the illustrations from John Flaxman's OEUVRE COMPLET,
        particularly those of the lone fir tree up into which
        Pierre gazes, and the description of Isabel, as well as
        Pierre's trip to the city.

2578   Schless, H. H. "MOBY DICK and Dante: A Critique and
            Time Scheme," BNYPL, 65 (May, 1961), 289-312.

        Dante's DIVINE COMEDY one of several profound
        influences on MOBY DICK.

2579   Schneider, Herbert Wallace. "At Sea," A HISTORY OF
            AMERICAN PHILOSOPHY. New York: Columbia University
            Press, 1946; 2nd printing, 1947, pp. 293-301, passim.

2580   Schroeder, Fred E. H. "'Enter Ahab, Then All': Theatrical Elements in Melville's Fiction," DR, 46 (Summer, 1966), 223-232.

Three general theatrical techniques employed in MOBY DICK, BENITO CERENO, and BILLY BUDD: Use of the nineteenth-century "picture-frame" stage; use of semi-operatic choruses and bombastic speeches; and use of theatrical sudden disclosures which are intensified by means of carefully contrived visual focal points.

2581   Schroeter, James. "REDBURN and the Failure of Mythic Criticism," AL, 39 (November, 1967), 279-297.

"Redburn's rejection of Bolton and Jackson, and Melville's rejection of the genteel and 'Jacksonian' viewpoints seem both to stem from Melville-Redburn's striving for balance and independence...."

2582   Schroth, Evelyn. "Melville's Judgment on Captain Vere," MQ, 10 (1969), 189-200.

The man Melville "would have govern" is "the balanced man," "the whole man—with instinct and reason joined and head and heart reigning together," such as Nelson; Vere, by contrast, governs merely "by norms of social expediency," having "mechanized the finer instincts of his soul to the routinized enforcement of 'forms.'"

2583   Schultz, Donald D. "Herman Melville and the Tradition of the Anatomy: A Study in Genre," DAI, 30 (Vanderbilt: 1970), 4463A.

2583.1 Schulz, Max F., William D. Templeman, and Charles R. Metzger, eds. ESSAYS IN AMERICAN AND ENGLISH LITERATURE PRESENTED TO BRUCE ROBERT McELDERRY, JR. Athens, Ohio: Ohio University Press, 1967.

2584   Schwartz, Arthur M. "The American Romantics: An Analysis," ESQ, 35 (1964), 39-44.

Hawthorne, Poe, and Melville should be considered negative Romantics, according to the Morse Peckham definition. Hawthorne and Melville, not having fashioned cosmologies, show their paralysis.

2585   Scoresby, William, Jr. AN ACCOUNT OF THE ARCTIC REGIONS, WITH A HISTORY AND DESCRIPTION OF THE NORTHERN WHALE-FISHERY. Edinburgh and London: 1820.

2585.1   Scoresby, William, Jr.   JOURNAL OF A VOYAGE TO THE NORTHERN
         WHALE-FISHERY: INCLUDING RESEARCHES AND DISCOVERIES
         ON THE EASTERN COAST OF WEST GREENLAND, MADE IN THE
         SUMMER OF 1822, IN THE SHIP BAFFIN OF LIVERPOOL.
         Edinburgh and London: 1823.

         An influence on Melville.

2586   Scott, Nathan A., Jr.   THE BROKEN CENTER: STUDIES IN THE
         THEOLOGICAL HORIZON OF MODERN LITERATURE. New Haven
         and London: Yale University Press, 1966, passim.

         Melville's "tragic vision" and its relation to
         the twentieth century.

2586.1   Scott, Nathan A., Jr.   "Judgment Marked by a Cellar: The
         American Negro Writer and the Dialectic of Despair,"
         DenverQ, 2, ii (Summer, 1967), 5-35.

         The cultural basis of Negro literature is not found
         in the African jungle, but, as with Hawthorne, Melville,
         and others, in the mythic, secularized Calvinist pattern
         of the "wounded Adam."

2587   Scott, Nathan A., Jr., ed.   THE TRAGIC VISION AND THE
         CHRISTIAN FAITH. New York: Association Press,
         1957.

2588   Scott, Sumner W. D.   "Some Implications of the Typhoon
         Scenes in MOBY DICK,"   AL, 12 (1940), 91-98.

         Nautical matters and the drama involved in
         Chapters 118 to 125, the typhoon scenes.

         Cf., Lincoln Colcord, "Notes on MOBY DICK,"
         Freeman, 5 (August, 1922), 559-62; (August 30, 1922),
         585-587.

2589   Scott, Sumner, W. D.   THE WHALING BACKGROUND OF MOBY DICK.
         Diss. Chicago: 1950.

2590   Scott, Wilbur S.   "The Archetypal Approach: Literature
         in the Light of Myth," FIVE APPROACHES OF LITERARY
         CRITICISM: AN ARRANGEMENT OF CONTEMPORARY CRITICAL
         ESSAYS. New York: London: The Macmillan Company,
         1963.

2591   Scott, Wilbur S.   MELVILLE'S ORIGINALITY: A STUDY OF
         SOME OF THE SOURCES OF MOBY-DICK. Diss. Princeton:
         1943.

2592   Scudder, Harold H.   "Hawthorne's Use of TYPEE," N&Q,
         187 (October, 1944), 184-186.

2593   Scudder, Harold H. "Melville's BENITO CERENO and Captain
        Delano's Voyages," PMLA, 43 (1928), 502-532.

        Source of Melville's story in Chapter 18 of
        Captain Amasa Delano's narrative of voyages, 1817.

2593.1 Scully, Vincent. THE EARTH, THE TEMPLE, AND THE GODS.
        New Haven: 1962, pp. 6-7.

2593.2 THE SEA BEAST. Photoplay title for MOBY DICK. (A Warner
        Brothers Screen Classic Starring John Barrymore).
        New York: Grosset & Dunlap, 1926.

2594   Sealts, Merton M., Jr. "Approaching Melville through
        'Hawthorne and His Mosses,'" ESQ, 28, Melville
        Supplement (3rd Qt., 1962), 12-15.

        Excerpts from Melville's critical paper provide
        themes for study of MOBY DICK.

2595   Sealts, Merton M., Jr. "Did Melville Write 'October
        Mountain'?" AL, 22 (May, 1950), 178-182.

        History of the error that Melville reviewed THE
        SCARLET LETTER.

2596   Sealts, Merton M., Jr. "The Ghost of Major Melvill,"
        NEQ, 30 (September, 1957), 291-306.

        Melville's uncle may have been one of the many
        prototypes for some aspects of BILLY BUDD.

2597   Sealts, Merton M., Jr. "Herman Melville's 'I and My
        Chimney,'" AL, 13 (May, 1941), 142-154.

        The chimney is Melville's heart and soul; the
        secret closet is his feared hereditary bent toward
        insanity; the Scribe is O. W. Holmes; Dacres is his
        father. The whole sketch is an allegorical account
        of the circumstances leading to Melville's examination
        for possible insanity in 1852.

2598   Sealts, Merton M., Jr. "Herman Melville's Reading in
        Ancient Philosophy," DA, 30 (Yale: 1969), 1574A-
        1575A.

2599   Sealts, Merton M., Jr. "Melville," AMERICAN LITERARY
        SCHOLARSHIP: AN ANNUAL: 1967. James Woodress, ed.
        Durham, North Carolina: Duke University Press, 1969,
        pp. 32-54.

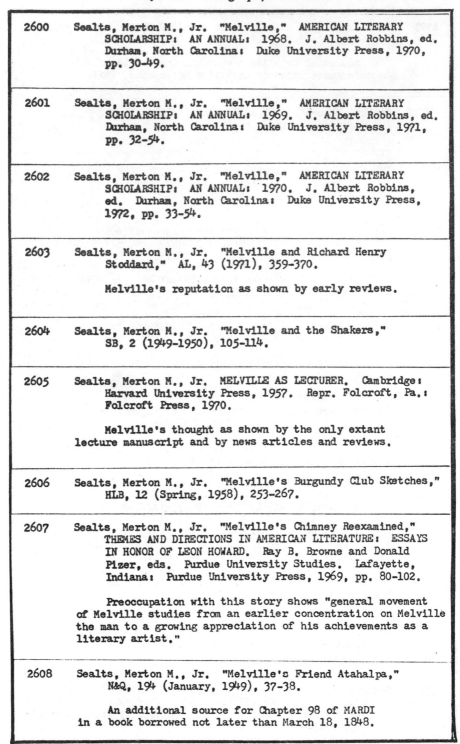

2600   Sealts, Merton M., Jr. "Melville," AMERICAN LITERARY
             SCHOLARSHIP: AN ANNUAL: 1968. J. Albert Robbins, ed.
             Durham, North Carolina: Duke University Press, 1970,
             pp. 30-49.

2601   Sealts, Merton M., Jr. "Melville," AMERICAN LITERARY
             SCHOLARSHIP: AN ANNUAL: 1969. J. Albert Robbins, ed.
             Durham, North Carolina: Duke University Press, 1971,
             pp. 32-54.

2602   Sealts, Merton M., Jr. "Melville," AMERICAN LITERARY
             SCHOLARSHIP: AN ANNUAL: 1970. J. Albert Robbins,
             ed. Durham, North Carolina: Duke University Press,
             1972, pp. 33-54.

2603   Sealts, Merton M., Jr. "Melville and Richard Henry
             Stoddard," AL, 43 (1971), 359-370.

             Melville's reputation as shown by early reviews.

2604   Sealts, Merton M., Jr. "Melville and the Shakers,"
             SB, 2 (1949-1950), 105-114.

2605   Sealts, Merton M., Jr. MELVILLE AS LECTURER. Cambridge:
             Harvard University Press, 1957. Repr. Folcroft, Pa.:
             Folcroft Press, 1970.

             Melville's thought as shown by the only extant
             lecture manuscript and by news articles and reviews.

2606   Sealts, Merton M., Jr. "Melville's Burgundy Club Sketches,"
             HLB, 12 (Spring, 1958), 253-267.

2607   Sealts, Merton M., Jr. "Melville's Chimney Reexamined,"
             THEMES AND DIRECTIONS IN AMERICAN LITERATURE: ESSAYS
             IN HONOR OF LEON HOWARD. Ray B. Browne and Donald
             Pizer, eds. Purdue University Studies. Lafayette,
             Indiana: Purdue University Press, 1969, pp. 80-102.

             Preoccupation with this story shows "general movement
             of Melville studies from an earlier concentration on Melville
             the man to a growing appreciation of his achievements as a
             literary artist."

2608   Sealts, Merton M., Jr. "Melville's Friend Atahalpa,"
             N&Q, 194 (January, 1949), 37-38.

             An additional source for Chapter 98 of MARDI
             in a book borrowed not later than March 18, 1848.

2609   Sealts, Merton M., Jr. "Melville's 'Geniality,'"
ESSAYS IN AMERICAN AND ENGLISH LITERATURE PRESENTED
TO BRUCE ROBERT McELDERRY, JR. Max F. Schulz, with
William D. Templeman and Charles R. Metzger, eds.
Athens: Ohio University Press, 1967, pp. 3-26.

      Cf., excerpt: "The Dialogue in Chapter 30" in
THE CONFIDENCE MAN HIS MASQUERADE. Hershel Parker, ed.
New York: W. W. Norton & Co., 1971, p. 331.

      Melville's repeated use of the word "genial" and
its cognates reveals "one persistent strain of sensibility
linking his years at sea, his career as an author, and
the retrospective musings of his late private writing."
MARDI "most fully expresses Melville's fondness for genial
conviviality." THE CONFIDENCE MAN "most caustically
exposes its weakness and dangers."

2610   Sealts, Merton M., Jr. "Melville's 'Neoplatonical
Originals,'" MLN, 67 (February, 1952), 80-86.

      Thomas Taylor's translation of THE SIX BOOKS OF
PROCLUS ON THE THEOLOGY OF PLATO (London, 1816),
provided Melville in MARDI and THE CONFIDENCE MAN with
material for satire of "oracular gibberish."

2611   Sealts, Merton M., Jr. "Melville's Reading: A Check List
of Books Owned and Borrowed," HLB, 2 (Spring, 1948),
141-163; (Autumn, 1948), 378-392; 3 (Winter, 1949),
119-130; (Spring, 1949), 268-277; (Autumn, 1949),
407-421; 4 (Winter, 1950), 98-109; 6 (Spring, 1952),
239-247.

2612   Sealts, Merton M., Jr. MELVILLE"S READING: A CHECK-LIST
OF BOOKS OWNED AND BORROWED. Madison: Wisconsin
University Press, 1966. Revised and enlarged pub.
of HLB, 2-4 (1948-1950); 6 (1952).

      Records of Melville's library, and lists of books
borrowed, his reading in early years and at sea.

      Rev. by Roger E. Stoddard, NEQ, 40 (1967), 612-613.

2613   Sealts, Merton M., Jr. "The Publication of Melville's
PIAZZA TALES," MLN, 59 (January, 1944), 56-59.

      From the incomplete correspondence between Melville
and his publishers, a portion of the bibliographical
history of PIAZZA TALES (1856) is reconstructed.

      Two letters are printed.

2613.1 Sears, Clara Endicott. DAYS OF DELUSION. Boston: 1924.

2614 Sedgwick, Henry Dwight. "Reminiscences of Literary
Berkshire," CentM, 50 (1895), 562.

2615 Sedgwick, William Ellery. HERMAN MELVILLE: THE TRAGEDY
OF MIND. Cambridge, Mass.: Harvard University
Press, 1944.

A study of Melville's thought as reflected in the
divergent and expanding nature of his search for truth.

Revs. Luther S. Mansfield, AL, 17 (1945), 90-93;
Willard Thorp, SatRL, 27 (1944), 11; NEQ, 18 (1945),
101-104.

2616 Seelye, John D. "The Contemporary 'Bartleby,'" ATQ, 7
(Summer, 1970), 12-18.

The story is a series of satirical thrusts at
Melville's own contemporaries: Irving and the Whigs
in the complacent attorney, the Transcendentalists, as
sketched in Emerson's essay about them, in Bartleby
himself.

2617 Seelye, John D. "The Golden Navel: The Cabalism of
Ahab's Doubloon," NCF, 14 (March, 1960), 350-355.

The golden doubloon nailed to the Pequod's mast
represents the "golden navel," the center of life, of the
ship and its crew who gather around to interpret the
significance of the coin.

2618 Seelye, John D., ed. Introduction, ARTHUR GORDON PYM,
BENITO CERENO, AND RELATED WRITINGS. Philadelphia:
J. B. Lippincott, 1967.

2619 Seelye, John D. Introduction and Bibliography,
THE CONFIDENCE-MAN: HIS MASQUERADE. Facsim. of
1st ed. San Francisco: Chandler, 1967.

Facsimile of first edition, plus contemporary
illustrations of "Yankee Peddlers, confidence-men,
and itinerant preachers."

2620 Seelye, John D. THE IRIDESCENT SCABBARD: MELVILLE'S
IRONIC MODE. Diss. Claremont Graduate School:
1961.

2621   Seelye, John. MELVILLE: THE IRONIC DIAGRAM. Evanston,
          Illinois: Northwestern University Press, 1970.

          Melville regarded his own art as "a system of
tensions produced by diagrammatic contrasts, a
paradoxical structure which would accommodate his
search for belief and express his capacity for doubt."

          Revs. Robert C. Ryan, Sym, 10 (1971), 230-240;
Willard Thorp, AL, 42 (1971), 573-574.

2622   Seelye, John D. "'Spontaneous Impress of Truth':
          Melville's Jack Chase: A Source, an Analogue,
          a Conjecture," NCF, 20 (March, 1966), 367-376.

          Jack Gunn, the captain of the starboard watch of
the main-topmen in William Leggett's tale "A Watch in
the Main-Top" of TALES AND SKETCHES OF A COUNTRY
SCHOOLMASTER, 1829, is "an analogue so close to Jack
Chase as to put the authenticity of Melville's portrait
/of Chase/ in doubt."

2623   Seelye, John D. "The Structure of Encounter: Melville's
          Review of Hawthorne's Mosses," MELVILLE AND
          HAWTHORNE IN THE BERKSHIRES: A SYMPOSIUM. Howard
          P. Vincent, ed. Kent, Ohio: Kent State University
          Press, 1968, pp. 63-69.

2624   Seelye, John D. "Timothy Flint's 'Wicked River' and
          THE CONFIDENCE-MAN," PMLA, 78 (March, 1963),
          75-79.

          Apparently Melville made use of Timothy Flint's
RECOLLECTIONS OF THE LAST TEN YEARS (1826) and his
HISTORY AND GEOGRAPHY OF THE MISSISSIPPI VALLEY (1828)
in writing the description of the river which he
evidently intended to use in the novel but discarded.

2625   Seelye, John D. "'Ungraspable Phantom': Reflections of
          Hawthorne in PIERRE and THE CONFIDENCE-MAN,"
          SNNTS, 1, iv (1969), 436-443.

          "...Although the cozening conversation on the
Mississippi riverboat is but one in a series of friend-
ships doomed from the start, it seems to bear more than
an incidental relation to Melville's estrangement from
Hawthorne."

2625.1 Seldes, Gilbert. THE STAMMERING CENTURY. New York:
          1928.

2625.2 Seldon, Annette Peters. A CRITICAL ANALYSIS OF THE
          STORIES OF HERMAN MELVILLE. Diss. Indiana: /n. d./

2626   Seltzer, Leon F. "Camus's Absurd and the World of
Melville's CONFIDENCE-MAN," PMLA, 82 (March, 1967),
14-27.

As: the story itself is "nihilistic," or even an
"anti-novel," so its "trickster-hero (or anti-hero)" is
intended "to be taken as a nihilist of tremendous
lucidity," a "natural successor" to Ahab and Pierre,
who passes "beyond absurd reasoning to absurd action."

2627   Seltzer, Leon F. "Like Repels Like: The Case of
Conrad's Antipathy for Melville," Conrad, 1
(1969), 101-105.

2628   Seltzer, Leon F. "The Vision of Melville and Conrad:
A Comparative Study," DA, 29 (S. U. N. Y., Buffalo:
1968), 613A-14A.

The two writers are linked in terms of a common
"nihilistic perspective" that affects both subject
matter and technique. Each speaks in behalf of an
ideal of human solidarity, "man's greatest resource
against an alien universe as well as his own perilous
egoism."

2629   Seltzer, Leon F. THE VISION OF MELVILLE AND CONRAD:
A COMPARATIVE STUDY. Athens: Ohio University
Press, 1970.

The "spiritual kinship" between the two authors.

Rev. by Edmund A. Bojarski, CEA (November, 1971), 31.

2630   Semmens, John Edward. "Point of View in the Early and
Later Fiction of Herman Melville," DA, 26 (Notre
Dame: 1965), 1028.

Beginning with BARTLEBY, Melville's handling of
point of view is characterized by authorial disengage-
ment. By standing apart, he was able "to give attention
to structural demands that his subjective involvement
in the early fiction had prevented."

2631   Senescu, Betty Cobey. "Melville's MOBY DICK," Expl,
25 (1967), Item 78.

Ahab's death accidental and unheroic.

2632   Sewall, Richard B. "Ahab's Quenchless Feud: The
        Tragic Vision in Shakespeare and Melville,"
        CompD, 1 (Fall, 1967), 207-218.

        "Shakespeare, for all the demands of the commercial
        theatre, was part Greek in his sense of tragedy, and had
        he lived to see Melville's work, would have sensed at
        once a kinship of vision and purpose...."

2633   Sewall, Richard B. "MOBY DICK," in THE VISION OF
        TRAGEDY. New Haven: Yale University Press, 1959,
        pp. 92-105; repr. as Yale Paperbound, 1962.

2634   Shafer, Robert E. "Teaching Sequences in Hawthorne and
        Melville," THE TEACHER AND AMERICAN LITERATURE:
        PAPERS PRESENTED AT THE 1964 CONVENTION OF THE
        NATIONAL COUNCIL OF TEACHERS OF ENGLISH. Champaign,
        Illinois: 1965, pp. 110-114.

        Survey of the available anthologies in American
        literature, and their respective merits.

2635   Shapiro, Charles, ed. TWELVE ORIGINAL ESSAYS ON GREAT
        AMERICAN NOVELS. Detroit: Wayne State University
        Press, 1958.

        MOBY DICK.

        Rev. by Alexander Cowie, AL, 30 (1958), 389-90.

2635.1 Sharrock, Roger. "Absorbing Japan," TLS, August 8,
        1958, p. 446.

        After the time of St. Francis Xavier, the image
        of Japan in European minds was that of an alien
        civilization as seen in (among other references)
        Melville's allusion in MOBY DICK to the "impenetrable
        Japans."

2636   Shattuck, Roger. "Two Inside Narratives: BILLY BUDD and
        L'ETRANGER," TSLL, 4 (Autumn, 1962), 314-320.

        BILLY BUDD is anything but "a testament of
        acceptance."

2637   Shaw, Richard O. "The Civil War Poems of Herman
        Melville," LH, 68 (Spring, 1966), 44-49.

2638   Sherbo, Arthur. "Melville's Portuguese Catholic Priest,"
       AL, 26 (January, 1955), 563-564.

       Father Jerome Lobo, author of A VOYAGE TO
       ABYSSINIA (trans. into English by Samuel Johnson),
       and Abbé Joachim Legrand, who translated and continued
       Father Lobo's history of Abyssinia.

       Cf., Millicent Bell, "Pierre Bayle and MOBY DICK,"
       PMLA, 66 (1951), 626-648.

2639   Sherman, Stuart B., John Birss, and Gordon Roper, comps.
       MELVILLE BIBLIOGRAPHY, 1952-1957. Providence,
       Rhode Island: Providence Public Library, 1959.

2640   Sherwood, John C. "Vere as Collingwood: A Key to
       BILLY BUDD," AL, 35 (January, 1964), 476-484.

       Captain Vere may be the portrait of a historical
       figure whom Melville admired: Cuthbert, Baron
       Collingwood. Collingwood, vice-admiral and second in
       command at Trafalgar, was well known in the nineteenth
       century.

2641   Shimada, Taro. "An Essay on MOBY-DICK," Pursuit, 1
       (December, 1962), 67-83.

       The problem of viewpoint.

2642   Shimada, Taro. "MOBY DICK ni tsuite," EigoS, 115
       (1969), 476-478.

       A study of MOBY DICK.

2643   Shimura, Masami. "'The Tartarus of Maids' no Sekai,"
       EigoS, 115 (1969), 487-488.

       The world of "Tartarus of Maids."

2644   Shneidman, Edwin S. "The Deaths of Herman Melville,"
       MELVILLE AND HAWTHORNE IN THE BERKSHIRES: A
       SYMPOSIUM. Howard P. Vincent, ed. Kent, Ohio:
       Kent State University Press, 1968, pp. 118-143.

       After MARDI, Melville's "most vital dialogue of
       the mind concerned itself with whether or not he could
       fully live, express himself openly, be printed publicly,
       be read widely, be adjudged fairly; or whether he would
       need to print himself privately,...."

2645   Shneidman, Edwin S. "Orientations toward Death," THE STUDY OF LIVES. Robert W. White, ed. New York: Atherton Press, 1963, pp. 221-227.

"...Captain Ahab's demise was goal-seeking behavior that made obsessed life or subintentioned death relatively unimportant to him, compared with the great press for the discharge of his monomania of hate...."

2646   Short, Raymond W. Introduction, FOUR GREAT AMERICAN NOVELS. New York: Henry Holt and Co., 1946.

Comparisons with Shakespeare.

BILLY BUDD.

2647   Short, Raymond W. "Melville as Symbolist," UKCR, 15 (Autumn, 1949), 38-49.

Melville's method "allows his symbols to accumulate meaning in the course of their use," so that "a single meaning attached to them often has at least a partial validity."

2647.1   Short, Raymond W. "Melville as Symbolist," INTERPRETATIONS OF AMERICAN LITERATURE. C. Feidelson and P. Brodtkorb, eds. New York: Oxford University Press, 1959, pp. 102-113.

2648   Short, Raymond W., and Richard B. Sewall. A MANUAL OF SUGGESTIONS FOR TEACHERS USING "SHORT STORIES FOR STUDY," 3rd ed. New York: Holt, 1956, pp. 46-49.

BARTLEBY, THE SCRIVENER.

2649   Shroeder, John W. "'Some Unfortunate Idyllic Love Affair': The Legends of Taji and Jay Gatsby," BBr, 22 (1968), 143-153.

MARDI as source.

2650   Shroeder, John W. "Sources and Symbols for Melville's CONFIDENCE-MAN," PMLA, 66 (June, 1951), 363-380.

Sources and symbols which went into THE CONFIDENCE-MAN: Parallels between Melville's story and Hawthorne's "The Celestial Railroad"; and certain allegorical characters traced to Spenser, and reptilian symbolism to Milton.

2650.1   Shroeder, John W.   "Sources and Symbols for Melville's
          CONFIDENCE-MAN," THE CONFIDENCE-MAN: HIS
          MASQUERADE. Hershel Parker, ed. New York:
          W. W. Norton & Company, Inc., 1971, pp. 298-316.

2651   Shulman, Robert. "Melville's Thomas Fuller: An Outline
          for Starbuck as an Instance of the Creator as
          Critic," MLQ, 23 (December, 1962), 337-352.

          Thomas Fuller's HOLY AND PROFANE STATE, which
          Melville read in Spril, 1849, helped in shaping MOBY
          DICK.

2652   Shulman, Robert. "Melville's 'Timoleon': From
          Plutarch to the Early Stages of BILLY BUDD," CL,
          19 (Fall, 1967), 351-361.

          Melville in BILLY BUDD employed themes from
          Plutarch's LIFE OF TIMOLEON which he did not use in
          "Timoleon." Both BILLY BUDD and "Timoleon" show "how
          pervasively during the 1880's Melville was concerned
          with the figure of the suffering martyr, typically
          under the aspect of tragedy, not redemption."

2653   Shulman, Robert. "Montaigne and the Techniques and
          Tragedy of Melville's BILLY BUDD," CL, 16
          (Fall, 1964), 322-330.

          Employment of Montaigne on Vere's side was "a
          useful strategy for winning initial approval for a
          character who will later strain that acceptance.
          Actually, Vere responded to a limited range of the
          Essays: "...Montaigne's own celebration of the values
          of compassion, freedom, personal loyalty, private
          integrity, and individual conscience serve to remind
          us of what Vere has disregarded."

2654   Shulman, Robert. "The Serious Functions of Melville's
          Phallic Jokes," AL, 33 (May, 1961), 179-194.

          The employment of sexual imagery in Melville's
          work.

2654.1   Shulman, Robert. "The Style of Bellow's Comedy,"
          PMLA, 83 (March, 1968), 109-117.

          Bellow in THE ADVENTURES OF AUGIE MARCH and
          HERZOG has consciously or unconsciously adapted many
          elements of form and style of Melville and others.

2655   Shulman, Robert. "Toward MOBY-DICK: Melville and Some Baroque Worthies," DA, 20 (Ohio State: 1960), 3731-32.

     Rabelais's bearing on the phallic puns and black rites in MOBY DICK.

2656   Shurr, William H. "The Symbolic Structure of Herman Melville's CLAREL," DAI, 30 (N. C., Chapel Hill: 1970), 3477A.

2657   Shusterman, David. "The 'Reader Fallacy' and BARTLEBY THE SCRIVENER," NEQ, 45 (1972), 118-124.

     Cf., Liane Norman, "Bartleby and the Reader," NEQ, 44 (1971), 22-39.

2658   Silberman, Donald Joseph. "Form and Point of View in Melville's Fiction," DA, 27 (SUNY Buffalo: 1966), 187A.

2659   Simboli, David. "BENITO CERENO as Pedagogy," CLAJ, 9 (December, 1965), 159-164.

2659.1   Simon, Howard. Woodcuts. MOBY DICK: OR, THE WHALE. N. Y. A., and C. Boni, 1931.

2659.2   Simon, Jean. A HERMAN MELVILLE ANTHOLOGY. Paris: 1946.

2660   Simon, Jean. HERMAN MELVILLE, MARIN, METAPHYSICIEN ET POÈTE. Diss. Paris: 1941.

2660.1   Simon, Jean. HERMAN MELVILLE: MARIN, MÉTAPHYSICIEN ET POÈTE. Paris: Boivin et Cie, 1939.

     Said to be the first to introduce Melville to the French public.

2661   Simon, Jean. LA POLYNÉSIE DANS L'ART ET LA LITTÉRATURE DE L'OCCIDENT. Paris: 1939.

2662   Simon, Jean. "Recherches Australiennes sur Herman Melville," RAA, 13 (1935), 114-129.

     Abstract of the research of J. W. Earnshaw into the background of OMOO.

2663   Simon, Jean. "Traveaux récents sur Herman Melville," EA, 6 (February, 1953), 40-49.

     A bibliography and critical survey of recent books on Melville.

2664   Simonds, William Edward. A STUDENT'S HISTORY OF AMERICAN
        LITERATURE. Boston: Houghton Mifflin Company, 1909,
        p. 304.

        "...Melville was...master of a brilliant style
which gave his writings a distinction still retained."

2665   Simonson, Harold P. INSTRUCTOR'S MANUAL TO ACCOMPANY
        "TRIO: A BOOK OF STORIES, PLAYS, AND POEMS.
        New York: Harper & Row, 1965, pp. 24-25.

        BARTLEBY THE SCRIVENER

2666   Simpson, Eleanor E. "Melville and the Negro: From
        TYPEE to BENITO CERENO," AL, 41 (1969), 19-38.

        Survey of Melville's treatment of non-whites
and of slavery in his fiction up to 1855--"increasing
originality in his portrayals" and "decreasing reliance
on literary convention and popular stereotypes."

        Cf., Sidney Kaplan, "Herman Melville and the
American National Sin," JNH, 41 (October, 1956),
311-338; JNH, 42 (January, 1957), 11-37.

2667   Singleton, Gregory H. "Ishmael and the Covenant,"
        Discourse, 12 (1969), 54-67.

        Ishmael in relation to "covenant" theology:
Like his biblical prototype, Ishmael is "in a peculiar
relationship to a covenanted people," the crew of the
Pequod, led by Ahab. The outsider, he is neither entirely
of the covenant nor completely separated from it, until
the final catastrophe, being "in community with the crew,
mankind, and nature," but excluded from "the covenant
of death aboard the Pequod." Ishmael's survival is
"Melville's final irony,...his greatest inversion of
the Christian-Calvinist cosmology--the salvation by
exclusion."

2667.1 Sisk, John P. "MAKING IT IN AMERICA," Atl, 224, vi
        (December, 1969), 63-68.

        MAKING IT by Norman Podhoretz illustrates a
"thoroughly respectable American tradition," concerning the American desire for commercial success and
its counterpart. From Franklin onward such books have
been written by such writers as Melville and others.

2668   Skard, Sigmund. AMERICAN STUDIES IN EUROPE: THEIR
        HISTORY AND PRESENT ORGANIZATION. 2 vols.
        Philadelphia: Pennsylvania University Press,
        1958, passim.

        Melville and other American writers in European
        countries.

2669   Skard, Sigmund. "The Use of Color in Literature,"
        PrAPS, 90 (1946), 163-249.

2670   Slater, Judith. "The Domestic Adventurer in Melville's
        Tales," AL, 37 (November, 1965), 267-279.

        The narrator "learns to accept the dark truth of
        the north exposure, but he is still able to enjoy the
        illusion of beauty." However, he "falls short of the
        truly comprehensive perspective which can look steadily
        on a universe in which good and evil live side by side
        day and night." He lives in "a divided realm and suffers
        from his inability to reconcile the halves."

2671   Slochower, Harry. "Freudian Motifs in MOBY DICK,"
        Complex, 3 (Fall, 1950), 16-26.

        "Sex-allusions are particularly crowded in the
        descriptions of the White Whale. They point to Moby
        Dick as a male-female, father-mother figure."

2672   Slochower, Harry. "MOBY DICK: The Myth of Democratic
        Expectancy," AQ, 2 (1950), 259-269.

        "...our American beginnings contain the elements
        of the universal myth. We began as an interracial
        commune and with the need for reconstructing old forms.
        There is danger that our unity will become petrified
        into airless conformity and that our freedom will
        disintegrate into capriciousness...."

2672.1 Slochower, Harry. "MOBY DICK: The Myth of Democratic
        Expectancy," DISCUSSIONS OF MOBY DICK. Milton R.
        Stern, ed. Boston: Heath, 1960, pp. 45-51.

2673   Slochower, Harry. "The Quest for an American Myth:
        MOBY DICK," MYTHOPOESIS: MYTHIC PATTERNS IN
        THE LIBERARY CLASSICS. Detroit: Wayne State
        University Press, 1970, pp. 223-245.

        Melville "at once continues the American Myth
        of unlimited possibilities and expresses disenchantment
        with it," and through Ahab "gives us both the threat
        and the promise of the American quest."

        Cf., Graham Burns, "The Unshored World of MOBY
        DICK," CR, 13 (1970), 68-83.

2674   Smalley, Amos. "I Killed MOBY-DICK," ReadD, 70 (June,
         1957), 172-180.

         An introduction recalling the legend of the
         white whale and Melville's classic, with an account
         of the actual capture and killing of a white whale
         about 1892.

2674.1   Smith, H. D., Lieut. "The Mutiny on the Somers," AmMag,
         8 (June, 1888), 109-114.

2675   Smith, Henry Nash. "The Image of Society in MOBY DICK,"
         MOBY DICK CENTENNIAL ESSAYS. Tyrus Hillway and
         Luther S. Mansfield, eds. Dallas: Southern
         Methodist University Press, 1953, pp. 59-75.

2676   Smith, Henry Nash. "Origins of a Native American Literary
         Tradition," THE AMERICAN WRITER AND THE EUROPEAN
         TRADITION. Margaret Denny and William H. Gilman, eds.
         Minneapolis: Minnesota University Press, 1950, pp.
         63-77.

2677   Smith, Herbert F. "Melville's Master in Chancery and
         His Recalcitrant Clerk," AQ, 17 (Winter, 1965),
         734-741.

         The narrator in BARTLEBY has enlarged his "snug
         business" in becoming Master in Chancery. The main
         concern of Chancery law is with "principles of absolute
         instead of relative justice." The new Master hired
         Bartleby because of the increased work. Now he is
         challenged in his legal thinking by Bartleby. The
         story takes on additional meaning when one recognizes
         why Melville placed the narrator in the new office.
         Even the key word, "prefer," relates to the Master's
         obligations.

2678   Smith, J. E. A. BIOGRAPHICAL SKETCH OF HERMAN MELVILLE.
         Written for the Evening Journal. Pittsfield,
         Massachusetts, 1891.

         An early biographical sketch.

2679   Smith, J. E. A. THE HISTORY OF PITTSFIELD, MASSACHUSETTS,
         FROM THE YEAR 1800 TO THE YEAR 1876. Springfield,
         Mass.: C. W. Bryan and Co., 1876, pp. 399-400.

         Contains an account of Major Thomas Melville
         written by Herman Melville but not signed.

2680   [Smith, J. E. A.] TACHCONIC, THE ROMANCE AND BEAUTY OF
        THE HILLS. Boston: 1879, p. 318.

        Contains an account of the meeting of Hawthorne
        and Melville and their seeking shelter together in a
        rainstorm.

2681   Smith, Nelson J. STUDY GUIDE TO MELVILLE'S MOBY DICK.
        Pennant Key-indexed Study Guide. Philadelphia:
        Educational Research Associates, 1967.

2682   Smith, Paul. "BENITO CERENO and the Spanish Inquisition,"
        NCF, 16 (1962), 345-349.

2683   Smith, Paul. "THE CONFIDENCE-MAN and the Literary
        World of New York," NCF, 16 (March, 1962), 329-337.

2684   Smylie, James. "BILLY BUDD: The Work of Christ in
        Melville," RinL, 33 (Spring, 1964), 286-296.

        "Dominant theological lines of the Nineteenth
        Century" present in BILLY BUDD.

2685   Smyth, Clifford. "A Letter from Herman Melville,"
        IntlBR, 3 (1924), 25, 65.

2686   Snell, George. "Herman Melville: The Seeker,"
        THE SHAPERS OF AMERICAN FICTION, 1798-1947.
        New York: E. P. Dutton, 1947, pp. 60-78.

        WHITE JACKET offers "an undeviating matter-of-fact
        report of life."

        Rev. by Kenneth B. Murdock, AL, 20 (1949), 461-65.

2687   Snyder, Oliver. "A Note on BILLY BUDD," Accent, 11
        (Winter, 1951), 58-60.

        BILLY BUDD as "a great political Mystery drama."
        Billy and Claggart represent the lower class; their
        struggle is parallel to that of the French Revolution.

2688   Solomont, Susan, and Ritchie Darling. BARTLEBY.
        Amherst, Mass.: Green Knight Press, 1969.

2689   "Some Melville Letters," N&A, 29 (1921), 712-713.

        Eight letters by Melville to James Billson
        between October, 1884, and December, 1888.

2690   Sowder, William J. "Melville's 'I and My Chimney':
A Southern Exposure," MissQ, 16 (1963), 128-145.

Allegorically the story presents the history of slavery in the South from late 18th century to mid-19th century. The chimney represents slavery.

2691   Spangler, Eugene R. "Harvest in a Barren Field:
A Counterpoint," WR, 14 (Summer, 1950), 305-307.

"There is hardly a greater need in American letters today than for...a carefully analytical body of criticism on Melville," and the greatest tragedy is "the calibre of criticism being published."

Cf., James B. Hall, "MOBY DICK: Parable of a Dying System," WR, 14 (Summer, 1950), 223-226.

2691.1   Spears, Monroe K. DIONYSUS AND THE CITY: MODERNISM IN TWENTIETH-CENTURY POETRY. New York: Oxford University Press, 1970, passim.

2692   Spector, Robert D. "Melville's BARTLEBY and the Absurd,"
NCF, 16 (September, 1961), 175-177.

2693   Spectorsky, Auguste C., ed. "His First Voyage: REDBURN,"
BOOK OF THE SEA. New York: Appleton-Century-Crofts, 1954, pp. 452-455.

2693.1   Spencer, Benjamin T. "'Beautiful Blood and Beautiful Brain': Whitman and Poe," ESQ, 35 (1964), 45-49.

2694   Spencer, Benjamin T. THE QUEST FOR NATIONALITY: AN AMERICAN LITERARY CAMPAIGN. Syracuse University Press, 1957, passim.

2694.1   Spencer, Benjamin T. "The Smiling Aspects of Life and a National American Literature," ENGLISH INSTITUTE ESSAYS - 1949. Alan S. Downer, ed. New York: AMS Press, Inc., 1965, 117-146.

2695   Sperling, Hellmuth. HERMAN MELVILLE ALS KRITIKER SEINER ZEIT. Diss. Humboldt-Universitat Berlin: 1953.

2696   Spilka, Mary, Kingsley Widmer, and Arthur Efron. "Controversy on Lawrence and the Academy," Paunch, 27 (October, 1966), 83-96.

Public letters on institutionalism vs. individualism with long digression about BILLY BUDD.

2697   Spiller, Robert E. "Melville: Our First Tragic Poet,"
        SatRL, 33 (November, 1950), 24-25.

2698   Spiller, Robert E. THE OBLIQUE LIGHT: STUDIES IN
        LITERARY HISTORY AND BIOGRAPHY. London: Collier-
        Macmillan, Ltd., New York: Macmillan Company, 1968,
        passim.

        Melville and others "had each discovered...that
        American literature must be a reinterpretation of the
        eternal issues in human experience in terms of life in
        contemporary America...."

2699   Spiller, Robert E. "Romantic Crisis: Herman Melville,"
        THE CYCLE OF AMERICAN LITERATURE. New York:
        Macmillan, 1955, pp. 89-99; repr., New York:
        Mentor Books, 1957, pp. 76-91.

        Rev. by Norman Holmes Pearson, AL, 28 (1957),
        545-546.

2699.1 Spiller, Robert E. THE THIRD DIMENSION: STUDIES IN
        LITERARY HISTORY. London: Collier-Macmillan, Ltd.,
        New York: Macmillan Company, 1965, passim.

2700   Spiller, Robert E., and Willard Thorp, Thomas H. Johnson,
        and Henry Seidel Canby, eds. "Herman Melville,"
        LITERARY HISTORY OF THE UNITED STATES. New York:
        The Macmillan Company, (Revised Edition in one
        volume), 1960, pp. 441-471, passim.

2700.1 Spiller, Robert, Willard Thorp, Thomas H. Johnson,
        Henry Seidel Canby, Richard M. Ludwig, eds.
        LITERARY HISTORY OF THE UNITED STATES: BIBLIOGRAPHY.
        London and New York: Macmillan, 1946, 1963.

2701   Spininger, Dennis J. "Paradise and the Fall as Theme
        and Structure in Four Romantic Novels: Tieck's
        WILLIAM LOVELL, Chateaubriand's ATALA and RENÉ,
        Melville's TYPEE," DA, 29 (Wis.: 1969), 4469A-
        70A.

2702   Spofford, William K. "Melville's Ambiguities: A Re-
        evaluation of 'The Town-Ho's Story,'" AL, 41
        (1969), 264-270.

        The Story is "a microcosmic presentation" of
        issues that both chapter and book leave indeterminate:
        Is God just or unjust? Is the whale agent or principal?

2703   Springer, Haskell S., comp. HERMAN MELVILLE: BILLY BUDD.
         Columbus, Ohio: Charles E. Merrill Studies. Charles
         E. Merrill Co., 1970.

2704   Springer, Norman. "Bartleby and the Terror of
         Limitation," PMLA, 80 (September, 1965), 410–
         418.

         "It is one of Melville's successes that he forces
         us to see and feel this yawning incomprehensibility the
         narrator faces, an incomprehensibility great in its
         effect because it is so carefully surrounded by all the
         concrete paraphernalia of the comprehensible...."

2705   Stafford, John. "Henry Norman Hudson and the Whig Use
         of Shakespeare," PMLA, 66 (1951), 649–661.

         Background for Melville's use of Shakespeare in
         his essay on Hawthorne and in MOBY DICK.

2706   Stafford, John. THE LITERARY CRITICISM OF "YOUNG
         AMERICA": A STUDY IN THE RELATIONSHIP OF POLITICS
         AND LITERATURE 1837-1850. Berkeley and Los
         Angeles: California University Press, English
         Studies, No. 3, 1952; New York: Russell & Russell,
         1952; reissued, 1967, passim.

2707   Stafford, William T. "An Annotated Checklist of Studies
         of BILLY BUDD," MELVILLE'S BILLY BUDD AND THE
         CRITICS. William T. Stafford, ed. 2nd ed. Belmont,
         Calif.: Wadsworth, 1968, pp. 263–272.

2707.1   Stafford, William T., ed. MELVILLE'S BILLY BUDD AND THE
         CRITICS. San Francisco: Wadsworth Publishing Co.,
         1961; 2nd ed. Belmont, Calif.: Wadsworth, 1968.

2708   Stafford, William T. "The New BILLY BUDD and the
         Novelistic Fallacy: An Essay-Review," Herman
         Melville Special Number, MFS, 8 (1962), 306–311.

2709   Stallman, Robert W., and Arthur Waldhorn, eds. AMERICAN
         LITERATURE: READINGS AND CRITIQUES. New York:
         Putnam, 1961.

2710   Stallman, Robert W., and R. E. Watters. THE CREATIVE
         READER. New York: The Ronald Press, 1954, pp.
         334–338.

         Notes and questions for discussion of BILLY BUDD.

2711   Stanford, Raney. "The Romantic Hero and That Fatal
        Selfhood," CentR, 12 (1968), 430-454.

        The romantic hero places Ahab in the line of
        descent from the traditional hero to the romantic
        rebel-hero to the modern anti-hero.

2712   Stanonik, Janez. "Did Melville Ever See an Albino?"
        AL, 43 (1972), 637-638.

2713   Stanonik, Janez. MOBY DICK: THE MYTH AND THE SYMBOL,
        A STUDY IN FOLKLORE AND LITERATURE. Ljubljana,
        Yugoslavia: Ljubljana University Press, 1962.

        Possibility of an "UR-MOBY-DICK" in the form of
        a folk-tale known to Melville, now lost. As evidence:
        certain details in a French account, "Le Cachalot blanc,"
        by Jules Lecomte (1837), and three novels about whale-
        hunts by Charles M. Newell.

            Revs., by Merton M. Sealts, AL, 35 (1963), 376-77;
        Owen Thomas, NEQ, 37 (1964), 117-118.

2714   Stanton, Robert. "TYPEE and Milton: Paradise Well
        Lost," MLN, 74 (May, 1959), 407-411.

2715   Stanzel, Franz. "Der Ich-Roman: MOBY-DICK," Chapter
        III of DIE TYPISCHEN ERZÄHLSITUATIONEN IM ROMAN:
        DARGESTALLT AN TOM JONES, MOBY-DICK, THE
        AMBASSADORS, ULYSSES. u. a. (Wiener Beiträge
        zur enge. Phil., Bd. 63. Wien: W. Braumüller,
        1956.

            Rev. by Joseph Warren Beach, AL, 28 (1956), 250-
        252.

2716   Stanzel, Franz. DIE TYPISCHEN ERZAHLSITUATIONEN IN
        ROMAN: DARGESTELLT AN TOM JONES, MOBY DICK, THE
        AMBASSADORS, ULYSSES. Diss. Wien: 1956.

2716.1 Stanzel, Franz. NARRATIVE SITUATIONS IN THE NOVEL:
        TOM JONES, MOBY DICK, THE AMBASSADORS, ULYSSES.
        Trans. by J. P. Pusack. Indiana: 1971.

2717   Star, Morris. "A Checklist of Portraits of Herman
        Melville," BNYPL, 71 (September, 1967), 468-473.

            Contemporary descriptions of Melville's personal
        appearance and chronological survey of the known
        paintings, photographs, and prints, brief characteriza-
        tion and location of each.

2717.1   Star, Morris. "Melvillo's Markings in Walpole's
                 ANECDOTES OF PAINTING IN ENGLAND," PBSA, 66
                 (July-September, 1972), 321-327.

2718   Star, Morris. "Melville's Use of the Visual Arts,"
                 DA, 25 (Northwestern: 1964), 2988.

                 Influence on Melville of the visual arts,
         particularly painting.

2719   Starke, A. H. "A Note on Lewis Mumford's Life of
                 Herman Melville," AL, 1 (1929), 304-305.

                 Mumford's misconception of the meeting between
         Melville and Hawthorne in London in 1856.

2720   Starr, Nathan Comfort. THE SEA IN THE ENGLISH NOVEL
                 FROM DEFOE TO MELVILLE. Diss. Harvard: 1928.

2721   Startsev, A. German Melvili i ego "MOBI DIK,"
                 MELVILLE, H. MOBI DIK ILI BELYI KIT. Moscow:
                 1961, pp. 9-20. 2nd ed. Moscow: 1962.

2722   Stavig, Richard Thorson. "Melville's BILLY BUDD: A
                 New Approach to the Problem of Interpretation,"
                 DA, 14 (Princeton: 1954), 822-823.

2723   Stavrou, C. N. "Ahab and Dick Again," TSLL, 3 (Autumn,
                 1961), 309-320.

                 For Ahab, Moby Dick was the embodiment of evil;
         and in his relentless pursuit of "the all-destroying
         but unconquering whale," Ahab represents the indomitable
         spirit of man.

2724   Stawell, F. M. "Time, Imagination, and the Modern
                 Novelist," NC&A, 107 (1930), 274-284.

2725   Stedman, Arthur. "Herman Melville's Funeral," NYDT
                 (October 1, 1891).

2726   Stedman, Arthur, ed. Introduction, TYPEE: A REAL
                 ROMANCE OF THE SOUTH SEA. Boston: 1892; New York:
                 American Publishers Corporation, 1892; repr.,
                 Boston: L. C. Page, 1950.

2727   Stedman, Arthur. "Marquesan Melville," NYW, 32
                 (October 11, 1891), 26.

2727.1 Stedman, Arthur. "Melville of Marquesas," RevR, 4 (1891), 428-430.

2728 Stedman, Arthur. "Poems by Herman Melville," CentM, 22 (1892), 104-105.

2729 Stedman, Edmund Clarence. POETS OF AMERICA. Boston and New York: Houghton Mifflin Company. The Riverside Press, Cambridge: 1885, p. 49.

"There is native fire in the lyrics of Melville...."

2729.1 Stedman, Edmund Clarence, and Ellen Mackay Hutchinson, eds. A LIBRARY OF AMERICAN LITERATURE FROM THE EARLIEST SETTLEMENT TO THE PRESENT TIME. 11 Vols. New York: 1889, VII, 464-478.

2729.2 Stegner, Wallace, ed. THE AMERICAN NOVEL FROM JAMES FENIMORE COOPER TO WILLIAM FAULKNER. New York: Basic Books, Inc., 1965, passim.

2730 Stein, William Bysshe. "Bartleby: The Christian Conscience," MELVILLE ANNUAL 1965, A SYMPOSIUM: BARTLEBY THE SCRIVENER. Howard P. Vincent, ed. Kent Studies in English, III. Kent, Ohio: Kent State University Press, 1966, pp. 104-112.

Melville's development of BARTLEBY is rigidly controlled by the subject of the story--"the moral relativism (or pragmatic Christianity) of nineteenth-century America."

2731 Stein, William Bysshe. "'BILLY BUDD': The Nightmare of History," Criticism, 3 (Summer, 1961), 237-250.

The "tone" of the narrator and the conflict between fact (history) and fable (myth) in the tale.

2732 Stein, William Bysshe. "Melville and the Creative Eros," LHB, 1, No. 2 (1960), 13-26.

On "After the Pleasure Party."

2733 Stein, William Bysshe. "Melville Roasts Thoreau's Cock," MLN, 74 (March, 1959), 218-219.

2734 Stein, William Bysshe. "Melville's Chimney Chivy," ESQ, 35 (2nd Qt., 1964), 63-65.

The religious imagery in the tale suggests a debate on religious faith.

2735   Stein, William Bysshe. "Melville's Cock and the Bell
        of Saint Paul," ESQ, 27 (2nd Qt., 1962), 5-10.

        On "Cock-a-doodle-doo!"

2736   Stein, William Bysshe. "Melville's Comedy of Faith,"
        ELH, 27 (December, 1960), 315-333.

        In "The Piazza" the narrator can and should offer
        Marianna the human contact she need, and the confrontation
        with her is the real opportunity to test the narrator's
        faith.

2737   Stein, William Bysshe. "Melville's Eros," TSLL, 3
        (Autumn, 1961), 297-308.

        "The Paradise of Bachelors" and "The Tartarus
        of Maids" ironically explore the narcissism and
        emotional self-destruction of the male who has turned
        from eros and its implications of normal affection and
        spiritual love.

2738   Stein, William Bysshe. MELVILLE'S POETRY AND ITS
        IMAGERY. Bollingen Fellowship: 1954.

2739   Stein, William Bysshe. "Melville's Poetry: Its Symbols
        of Individuation," L&P, 7 (May, 1957), 21-26.

2740   Stein, William Bysshe. "Melville's Poetry: Two Rising
        Notes," ESQ, 27 (1962), 10-13.

2741   Stein, William Bysshe. "The Moral Axis of BENITO
        CERENO," Accent, 15 (Summer, 1955), 221-233.

        An analysis of the tale's religious, ritualistic
        overtones and its mood of bleak despair.

2742   Stein, William Bysshe. "The Motif of the Wise Old
        Man in BILLY BUDD," WHR, 14 (Winter, 1960), 99-
        101.

2743   Stein, William Bysshe. "The Old Man and the Triple
        Goddess: Melville's 'The Haglets,'" ELH, 25
        (March, 1958), 43-59.

        A close analysis of the poem.

2744   Stein, William Bysshe. THE POETRY OF MELVILLE'S LATE
         YEARS: TIME, HISTORY, MYTH, AND RELIGION. Albany:
         New York State University Press, 1970.

         An intensive examination of JOHN MARR AND OTHER
SAILORS; TIMOLEON; "Weeds and Wildings, with a Rose or
Two," and "Marquis de Grandvin."

         Revs. by Lawrence Buell, NEQ, 44 (1971), 517-519;
Robert C. Ryan, Sym, 10 (1971), 230-240; Howard P.
Vincent, AL, 44 (1972), 325-327.

2745   Stein, William Bysshe. "Time, History, and Religion:
         A Glimpse of Melville's Late Poetry," ArQ, 22
         (Summer, 1966), 136-145.

2746   Stencel, Michelle M. "Knowledge in the Novels of
         Herman Melville," DAI, 30 (S. C.: 1970), 4956A-
         57A.

2747   Stern, Madeline B. "The House of Expanding Doors: Ann
         Lynch's Soirees, 1846," NYH, 23 (1942), 42-51.

2748   Stern, Milton R. THE FINE HAMMERED STEEL OF HERMAN
         MELVILLE. Urbana, Illinois: Illinois University
         Press, 1957.

         Revs., Charles Olson, ChiR, 12 (1958), 98-104;
Howard P. Vincent, AL, 31 (1959), 84-86.

2749   Stern, Milton R., ed. Introduction, DISCUSSIONS OF
         MOBY DICK. Boston: D. C. Heath & Co., 1960.

2750   Stern, Milton R., ed. Introduction, TYPEE and BILLY
         BUDD. New York: E. P. Dutton, 1958.

2751   Stern, Milton R. "Melville's Tragic Imagination: The
         Hero without a Home," PATTERNS OF COMMITMENT IN
         AMERICAN LITERATURE. Marston LaFrance, ed.
         Published in association with Carleton University
         by Toronto University Press, 1967, pp. 39-52.

         "...Melville's vision tends toward the naturalistic
and the existential in its sense of death, or the consciousness thereof, as a basis of value...."

2752   Stern, Milton R. "MOBY DICK, Millennial Attitudes, and
         Politics," ESQ, 54 (1st Qt., 1969), 51-60.

         MOBY DICK, a "deeply political novel," as well as
a metaphysical one—a study of man and democracy, of
power and command, of humanity and despotism.

2753   Stern, Milton R. "A New Harpoon for the Great White
        Whale," ClearH, 30 (1956), 564-565.

2754   Stern, Milton R. "Some Techniques of Melville's Perception,"
        PMLA, 73 (June, 1958), 251-259.

2755   Stern, Milton R. "The Theme and Craft of Herman Melville,"
        DA, 15 (Michigan State: 1955), 1859-60.

2756   Stern, Milton R. "The Whale and the Minnow: MOBY DICK
        and the Movies," CE, 17 (May, 1956), 470-473.

        The usefulness of comparison for teaching
        MOBY DICK.

2757   Sternlicht, Sanford. "Sermons in MOBY DICK," BSUF, 10,
        1 (1969), 51-52.

        Not Father Mapple addressing his congregation, but
        Fleece preaching to the sharks delivers "the true sermon
        of life as Melville saw it" in his "darkly pessimistic
        view of man's role and fate."

2758   Stevens, Aretta J. "The Edition of Montaigne Read by
        Melville," PBSA, 62 (1st Qt., 1968), 130-134.

2759   Stevens, Harry R. "Melville's Music," Musicology, 2
        (July, 1949), 405-421.

        Melville's writing reveals sensitive appreciation
        of music and a complex use of musical materials.

2760   Stevens, Virginia. "Thomas Wolfe's America," Mainstream,
        11 (1958), 1-24.

        Wolfe felt, as did Melville, that America needed
        "a radical affirmation of the heart."

2761   Stevenson, Robert Louis. THE LETTERS OF ROBERT LOUIS
        STEVENSON. Sidney Colvin, ed. New York: 1911;
        London: William Heinemann, Ltd., 1924, III, 203,
        254, passim.

2761.1 Stevenson, Robert Louis. THE WORKS OF ROBERT LOUIS
        STEVENSON. New York: 1912, IX, 25-26

2762   Stevick, Philip. THE THEORY OF THE NOVEL. New York:
        The Free Press; London: Collier-Macmillan, Ltd.,
        1967, passim.

2763   Stewart, George R. "The Two MOBY-DICKS," AL, 25
         (January, 1954), 417-448.

         A study of the shift from what internal evidence
         indicates was Melville's original plan "to something
         less simple which afterwards became--doubtless after
         several more shifts--our present complex and ever-
         challenging MOBY-DICK."

         Cf., Edward Stone, "MOBY-DICK and Shakespeare:
         A Remonstrance," SQ, 7 (1956), 445-448.

2764   Stewart, Randall. AMERICAN LITERATURE AND CHRISTIAN
         DOCTRINE. Baton Rouge: Louisiana State University
         Press, 1958, pp. 98-102, passim.

         Cf., THE TRAGIC VISION AND THE CHRISTIAN FAITH.
         Nathan A. Scott, Jr., ed. New York: Association Press,
         1957, pp. 257-262.

2765   Stewart, Randall, ed. THE AMERICAN NOTEBOOKS BY
         NATHANIEL HAWTHORNE. New Haven: 1932, passim.

2766   Stewart, Randall. "A Doctrine of Man," MissQ, 12
         (1959), 4-9.

         Melville and Hawthorne insisted on "man's
         imperfection, his non-perfectibility, his fallibility";
         their tragic heroes were men torn by internal conflict.

2767   Stewart, Randall, ed. THE ENGLISH NOTEBOOKS BY
         NATHANIEL HAWTHORNE: BASED UPON THE ORIGINAL
         MANUSCRIPTS IN THE PIERPONT MORGAN LIBRARY.
         New York: Russell & Russell, Inc., 1962, pp.
         432, 433, 435, passim.

2768   Stewart, Randall. "Ethan Brand," SatRL, 5 (1929), 967.

         Correction of Lewis Mumford's statement that
         Hawthorne had Melville in mind when he wrote "Ethan
         Brand" by showing that the story was published several
         months before Hawthorne and Melville became acquainted.

2768.1 Stewart, Randall. "Hawthorne's Contributions to THE
         SALEM ADVERTISER," AL, 5 (1934), 327-341.

         Hawthorne's reviews of books, including a review
         in THE SALEM ADVERTISER, March 25, 1846, of Melville's
         TYPEE.

2769   Stewart, Randall. "Herman Melville, 1819-1891: Loyalty
        to the Heart," AMERICAN CLASSICS RECONSIDERED:
        A CHRISTIAN APPRAISAL. Harold C. Gardiner, ed.
        New York: Scribners, 1958, pp. 210-228.

2770   Stewart, Randall. "Melville and Hawthorne," SAQ, 51
        (July, 1952), 436-446.

2771   Stewart, Randall. "Melville and Hawthorne," MOBY DICK
        CENTENNIAL ESSAYS. Tyrus Hillway and Luther S.
        Mansfield, eds. Dallas: Southern Methodist
        University Press, 1953, pp. 153-164.

2772   Stewart, Randall. "Melville and Hawthorne,"
        REGIONALISM AND BEYOND. ESSAYS OF RANDALL STEWART.
        George Core, ed. Foreword by Norman Holmes Pearson.
        Nashville: Vanderbilt University Press, 1968,
        pp. 113-125, passim.

2773   Stewart, Randall. NATHANIEL HAWTHORNE: A BIOGRAPHY.
        New Haven: Yale University Press, 1948, pp. 107-112,
        passim.

2774   Stewart, Randall. "A Populous World," YR, 37 (Spring,
        1948), 542-544.

        An article-review of THE TIMES OF MELVILLE AND
        WHITMAN by Van Wyck Brooks.

2775   Stewart, Randall. "Two Approaches to Melville," VQR,
        28 (Autumn, 1952), 606-609.

        The "two approaches" are Lawrance Thompson's
        MELVILLE'S QUARREL WITH GOD and Merrell Davis's
        MELVILLE'S MARDI: A CHARTLESS VOYAGE.

2776   Stewart, Randall. "The Vision of Evil in Hawthorne and
        Melville," THE TRAGIC VISION AND THE CHRISTIAN
        FAITH. Nathan A. Scott, Jr., ed. New York:
        Association Press, 1957, pp. 238-263.

        Repr., substantially in AMERICAN LITERATURE AND
        CHRISTIAN DOCTRINE. Baton Rouge: Louisiana State
        University Press, 1958, pp. 73-102.

2776.1 Stewart, Randall, and Dorothy Bethrum, eds. CLASSIC
        AMERICAN FICTION. Chicago: Scott, Foresman & Co.,
        1954, pp. 180-183.

2777   Stitt, Peter A. "Herman Melville's BILLY BUDD: Sympathy
        and Rebellion," ArQ, 28 (1972), 39-54.

2778 Stockton, Eric W. "A Commentary on Melville's 'The Lightning-Rod Man,'" PMASAL, 40 (1955), 321-328.

2779 Stoddard, Richard Henry. "Herman Melville," NYM&E (October 8, 1891), 5.

2780 Stoddard, Richard Henry. "My Life in the Custom-House," RECOLLECTIONS PERSONAL AND LITERARY. Ripley Hitchcock, ed. New York: 1903, pp. 142-144.

  Melville as an Inspector of Customs.

2781 Stoddard, Richard Henry. Obituary of Melville, New York Critic, 16, n. s. (November 4, 1891), 272.

2782 Stokes, Gary. "The Dansker, Melville's Manifesto on Survival," EJ, 57 (October, 1968), 980-981.

  The Dansker is a mouthpiece for Melville's own "detached view of his conception of the story" and to "give some insight into what is required for survival in a world inhospitable to innocence."

2783 Stoll, Elmer E. "Symbolism in MOBY-DICK," JHI, 12 (June, 1951), 440-465.

  "...It /MOBY DICK/ is not by any means to be accounted an immortal masterpiece; nor does it much remind me...of Aeschylus, Dante, Shakespeare, or even the two Russians of our latter day...."

2784 Stoller, L. "American Radicals and Literary Works of the Mid-Nineteenth Century: An Analogy," NEW VOICES IN AMERICAN STUDIES. Ray B. Browne, Donald M. Winkleman, and Allen Hayman, eds. Lafayette, Indiana: Purdue University Studies, 1966, pp. 13-20.

2785 Stone, Edward. "Bartleby and Miss Norman," SSF, 9 (Summer, 1972), 271.

  Thomas Hood's "Miss Norman" (1852) a possible source for Melville's story.

2786 Stone, Edwatd. A CERTAIN MORBIDNESS: A VIEW OF AMERICAN LITERATURE. Carbondale and Edwardsville: Southern Illinois University Press, 1969.

  Rev. by Glenn O. Carey, SSF, 7 (1970), 672-674; Russel B. Nye, AL, 43 (1971), 499-500.

2787　　Stone, Edward. "The Devil is White," ESSAYS ON
DETERMINISM IN AMERICAN LITERATURE. Sydney J.
Krause, ed. (Kent Studies in English, No. 1)
Kent, Ohio: Kent State University Press, 1964,
pp. 55-66.

Rabelais noted in the sixteenth century that the
color white possessed an "enigmatic ability" to evoke
two opposing feelings.

2788　　Stone, Edward, ed. "Herman Melville--MOBY DICK,"
WHAT WAS NATURALISM? MATERIALS FOR AN ANSWER.
New York: Appleton-Century-Crofts, Inc., 1959,
pp. 63-69, passim.

Chapter 42, "The Whiteness of the Whale," given
as one of the illustrations of the use of "naturalism."

2789　　Stone, Edward. "Melville's Pip and Coleridge's Servant
Girl," AL, 25 (November, 1953), 358-360.

BIOGRAPHIA LITERARIA (1847), I, Part II, a probable
source for anecdote in MOBY DICK.

2790　　Stone, Edward. "MOBY-DICK and Shakespeare: A Remonstrance,"
SQ, 7 (Autumn, 1956), 445-448.

Answer to George R. Stewart, "The Two MOBY-DICKS,"
AL, 25 (1954), 417-448.

2791　　Stone, Geoffrey. "Claggart--II," MELVILLE'S BILLY
BUDD AND THE CRITICS. William T. Stafford, ed.
Belmont, California: Wadsworth Publishing Co.,
1961, pp. 159-160; rev. 2nd ed., 1969, pp. 218-
219.

2792　　Stone, Geoffrey. "Herman Melville: 1819-1891: Loyalty
to the Heart," AMERICAN CLASSICS RECONSIDERED: A
CHRISTIAN APPRAISAL. Harold C. Gardiner, ed. New
York: Scribners, 1958, pp. 210-228.

2793　　Stone, Geoffrey. MELVILLE. New York: Sheed & Ward,
1949.

Revs., R. W. B. Lewis, HudR, 2 (1949), 612;
Sherman Paul, NEQ, 23 (1950), 405-407; Willard
Thorp, AL, 22 (1949), 356-357.

2794　　Stone, Harry. "Dickens and Melville Go to Chapel,"
Dickensian, 54 (Winter, 1958), 50-52.

Comparison of Edward Thompson Taylor and his
chapel, the Seaman's Bethel, in Dickens' AMERICAN
NOTES (1842) and Melville's MOBY DICK (1851).

2795   Stone, Herbert Stuart, comp. FIRST EDITION OF AMERICAN
        AUTHORS: A MANUAL FOR BOOK LOVERS. Introduction
        by Eugene Field. Kennebunkport, Maine: Milford
        House, Inc., 1970, pp. 137-138.

2796   Stonier, G. W. "Enigma of a Very Good, Very Bad Writer,"
        NS&N, 27 (February 5, 1944), 95.

2797   Stout, Janis. "Melville's Use of the Book of Job,"
        NCF, 25 (June, 1970), 69-83.

        The Job motif in Melville's work indicates
        questioning and defiance but finally humility and
        acceptance. This is the pattern of MOBY DICK, where
        Ishmael, who survives, more nearly resembles Job than
        does Ahab. Although Joban defiance takes precedence
        over resignation in PIERRE and THE CONFIDENCE-MAN,
        BILLY BUDD shows the acceptance prefigured in Ishmael.

2798   Stovall, Floyd. "Contemporaries of Emerson," AMERICAN
        IDEALISM. Norman, Oklahoma: Oklahoma University
        Press, 1943, pp. 55-78, passim.

2798.1 Stovall, Floyd, ed. Introduction. THE DEVELOPMENT OF
        AMERICAN LITERARY CRITICISM. Chapel Hill: North
        Carolina University Press, 1955, pp. 3-13, passim.

2799   Stovall, Floyd, ed. "Melville," EIGHT AMERICAN AUTHORS:
        A REVIEW OF RESEARCH AND CRITICISM. New York:
        Modern Language Association of America, 1956, 1963,
        pp. 207-270.

        Rev. by Randall Stewart, AL, 30 (1958), 119-121.

2800   Strachey, J. St. Loe. "Herman Melville," London
        Spectator, 70 (June 24, 1893), 858-859.

        "...Though Mr. Melville wrote at a time when
        English insolence and pig-headedness, and Yankee
        bumptiousness, made a good deal of ill-blood between
        the two peoples, he at heart feels that, on the sea
        at least, it is the English kin against the world...."

2801   Strachey, J. St. Loe. "Herman Melville: Mariner and
        Mystic," Spectator, 127 (May 6, 1922), 559-560.

        "...I well remember some thirty years ago writing
        a review in the Spectator on a new edition of Melville's
        works....A reference thereto shows that a Melville boom
        was then proceeding....There was quite a furor over
        Melville in those days. All the young people worshipped
        him...."

2802   Strandberg, Victor H. "God and the Critics of Melville,"
        TSLL, 6 (Autumn, 1964), 322-333.

        Attack on Lawrance Thompson's MELVILLE'S QUARREL
        WITH GOD as it relates to MOBY DICK and BILLY BUDD.

2803   Stratman, Carl J. "Unpublished Dissertations in the
        History and Theory of Tragedy, 1889-1957," BB, 22
        (1958), 161-164.

2804   Strauch, Carl F., ed. "Critical Symposium on American
        Romanticism," ESQ, 35 (2nd Qt., 1964), 2-60.

2805   Strauch, Carl F. "Ishmael: Time and Personality in
        MOBY-DICK," SNNTS, 1, iv (Winter, 1969), 468-483.

        In pairing Ishmael and Queequeg, Melville "is
        suggesting that for survival modern man should ally
        himself with the primitive."

2806   Strauch, Carl F. "The Problem of Time and the Romantic
        Mode in Hawthorne, Melville, and Emerson," ESQ,
        35 (2nd Qt., 1964), 50-60.

        "...Ishmael does hover over Descartesian vortices,
        but the plain narrative fact is that the vortex shoots
        him up, with Queequeg's coffin, for survival. Life
        refuses to die, and belief is woven into the very fabric
        of life...."

2807   Strout, Cushing, ed. INTELLECTUAL HISTORY IN AMERICA:
        CONTEMPORARY ESSAYS ON PURITANISM, THE ENLIGHTENMENT
        AND ROMANTICISM. New York, Evanston and London:
        Harper & Row, 1968, I, passim.

2808   Stuart, Charles. "BILLY BUDD. The Novel by Melville.
        The Score by Benjamin Britten," WorldR, (January,
        1952), 9-14.

2809   Sühnel, Rudolf. "Melvilles BILLY BUDD: Eine Interpreta-
        tion," SuL, 3 (1959), 125-144.

2810   Sühnel, Rudolf. "Melvilles MOBY-DICK: Versuch einer
        Deutung," NS, 5 (December, 1956), 553-561.

2811   Suits, Bernard. "BILLY BUDD and Historical Evidence:
        A Rejoinder," NCF, 18 (December, 1963), 288-291.

        Rejoinder to Ray B. Browne, "BILLY BUDD: Gospel
        of Democracy," NCF, 17 (1963), 321-337.

2812   Sullivan, J. N. Introduction, MOBY-DICK, OR THE WHALE. New York: E. P. Dutton and Company, 1950.

2813   Sullivan, J. N. Introduction, MOBY-DICK. London: Collins New Classics, 1953.

2814   Sullivan, J. W. N. "Herman Melville," TLS, 1123 (July 26, 1923), 493-495.

"...It is possible that MOBY DICK is a great work of art....And possibly there are some to whom Ahab, Starbuck and the rest...are credible and satisfying sea heroes. But as the great whale grows more imminent even the most resolutely realistic reader must have strange qualms. Is this a ship, are these men, and is the great whale really a whale...."

2815   Sullivan, J. W. N. "Herman Melville," ASPECTS OF SCIENCE, SECOND SERIES. New York: Knopf, 1926, pp. 190-205.

2816   Sullivan, Sister Mary Petrus. "MOBY DICK: Chapter 129, 'The Cabin,'" NCF, 20 (September, 1965), 188-190.

If Ahab had responded to Pip's need for love, he might have been able to save his soul by re-establishing a connection with humanity and sharing in the faith that sustained the boy.

2816.1   Summerhayes, Donald C. THE RELATION OF ILLUSION AND REALITY TO FORMAL STRUCTURE IN SELECTED WORKS OF FICTION BY NATHANIEL HAWTHORNE, MELVILLE, AND JAMES. Diss. Yale: n. d.

2817   Sumner, D. Nathan. "The American West in Melville's MARDI and THE CONFIDENCE-MAN," RS, 36 (1968), 37-49.

The two works show evidence that by 1857 Melville had moved from "at least a qualified optimism" regarding the future of the United States, to "almost complete pessimism," one contributing factor being failure of the American West to meet its share of responsibilities for solving national problems.

2818   Sundermann, Karl H. HERMAN MELVILLES GEDANKENGUT: EINE KRITISCHE UNTERSUCHUNG SEINER WELTANSCHAULICHEN GRUNDLAGEN. Diss. Berlin, 1937.

2819   Sundermann, Karl K. HERMAN MELVILLES GEDANKENGUT: EINE
KRITISCHE UNTERSUCHUNG SEINER WELTANSCHAULICHEN
GRUNDIDEEN. Berlin: Verlag Arthur Collignon, 1937.

> Almost a concordance of Melville's ideas. The
> book is divided into three major parts: the religious
> element, the philosophical, and the historical elements
> in Melville's works.

> Revs. by William Braswell, AL, 10 (1938), 104-107;
> Charles J. Olson, Jr., NEQ, 12 (1939), 154-156.

2820   Sutcliffe, Denham. Afterword, MOBY DICK: OR, THE
WHITE WHALE. New York: New American Library,
1961.

2821   Sutcliffe, Denham. "Christian Themes in American Fiction,"
ChS, 44 (1961), 304-305.

> BILLY BUDD.

2822   Sutton, Felix. MOBY DICK. Adapted for young readers.
Illustrated by H. B. Vestal. New York: Grosset
& Dunlap, 1956.

2823   Sutton, Walter. "Melville and the Great God Budd,"
PrS, 34 (Summer, 1960), 128-133.

> Buddhism in BILLY BUDD. The story read also in
> terms of Schopenhauer.

2824   Sutton, Walter. "Melville's 'Pleasure Party' and the
Art of Concealment," PQ, 30 (July, 1951), 316-327.

2825   Sutton, Walter. MODERN AMERICAN CRITICISM. Englewood
Cliffs, New Jersey: Prentice-Hall, Inc., 1963,
passim.

2826   Swanson, Donald R. "The Exercise of Irony in BENITO
CERENO," ATQ, 7 (Summer, 1970), 23-25.

2827   Swanson, Donald R. "The Structure of THE CONFIDENCE-MAN,"
CEA, 30, viii (1968), 6-7.

> The story's "intricate design," narrative chapters,
> digressions, and interpolated tales, intentionally
> reflect inconsistencies of the real world.

2828   Sweetser, Margaret S. HERMAN MELVILLE'S CONCEPTION OF
THE GREAT WRITER AND HIS EXPERIMENTS IN LITERARY
MANNERS. Diss. Minnesota: 1952.

2829   Swingle, L. J. "Answers to Blake's TYGER: A Matter of
        Reason or of Choice?" CP, 2 (1969), 61-71.

        The Tyger's world is existential like Melville's
        in THE CONFIDENCE MAN.

2830   Swinnerton, Frank. "The Londoner," New York <u>Bookman</u>,
        53 (May, 1921), 239.

        "...only lately have the quidnuncs discovered the
        latter book /MOBY DICK/, of which a new edition has just
        appeared in "The World Classics" with an introduction by
        Viola Meynell....'MOBY DICK' has been formally 'found'
        and placed as one of the masterpieces of all time...."

2831   Taglioni, Eleonora. "Ulisse Abbandonato: Herman
        Melville," NA, 493 (1965), 382-393.

2832   Takamura, Katsuji. "Melville no Shosetsu-gun," EigoS,
        115 (1969), 474-475.

        The novels of Herman Melville.

2833   Tanimoto, Taizo. "Ahab, a Tragic Hero, and the Leading
        Characters in MOBY-DICK: Melville and Ahab,"
        E&AL, 7 (October, 1962), 48-67.

2834   Tanimoto, Taizo. "Melville ni okeru Sukui," EigoS,
        115 (1969), 489-490.

        Salvation in Melville.

2835   Tanimoto, Taizo. "Pierre, The Shepherd: The Meaning
        of Saddle Meadows in Melville's PIERRE," DosL, 24
        (March, 1966), 23-40.

        Melville deliberately balanced the "artificiality,
        the stylized conventionality of pastoral" in the early
        chapters dealing with the Glendinning estate against
        the urban "world of actual life" where Pierre, "the
        helpless shepherd of the pastoral world," is subsequently
        defeated.

2836   Tanner, Tony. THE REIGN OF WONDER: NAIVETY AND REALITY
        IN AMERICAN LITERATURE. London; New York: Cambridge
        University Press, 1965, passim.

2837   Tanselle, G. Thomas. "The First Review of TYPEE,"
        AL, 34 (January, 1963), 567-571.

        The "first review" in the short-lived New York
        <u>Weekly News</u>, March 21, 1846, praised the book on
        grounds of its dramatic story and style.

2838   Tanselle, G. Thomas. "A Further Note on 'Whiteness' in
         Melville and Others," PMLA, 81 (1966), 604.

         The whitness in MOBY DICK is associated with
         "the emptiness and neutrality of external nature,"
         not with "annihilation."

              Cf. Harry Tucker, Jr. "A Glance at 'Whiteness'
         in Melville and Camus," PMLA, 80 (1965), 605; and
         William M. Manly. "Journey to Consciousness: The
         Symbolic Pattern of Camus's L'ETRANGER," PMLA, 79
         1964), 321-328.

2839   Tanselle, G. Thomas. "Herman Melville's Visit to
         Galena in 1840," JISHS, 53 (Winter, 1960), 376-388.

2840   Tanselle, G. Thomas. "Melville Writes to the New
         Bedford Lyceum," AL, 39 (November, 1967), 391-392.

              A previously unpublished Melville letter, October 3,
         1857, to William P. S. Cadwell involves arrangement for
         Melville's lecture at the New Bedford (Massachusetts)
         Lyceum, February 23, 1858.

2841   Tanselle, G. Thomas. "The Sales of Melville's Books,"
         HLB, 17 (April, 1969), 195-215.

              Records of Melville's publishers are important in
         tracing his popularity during his lifetime. Papers at
         Harvard provide complete accounts for Wiley and Putnam,
         as well as for Harpers. Records are available also for
         Putnam, Dix and Edwards, John Murray, Richard Bentley
         and Longman, Brown, Green, and others.

2842   Tanselle, G. Thomas. "Textual Study and Literary
         Judgment," PBSA, 65 (2nd Qt., 1971), 109-122.

              Examples taken from the editing of Melville's
         works indicate some of the ways in which literary
         judgment necessarily plays a major role in decisions
         both about substantives and about accidentals.

2843   Tanselle, G. Thomas. "TYPEE and DeVoto Once More,"
         PBSA, 62 (4th Qt., 1968), 601-604.

              Cf., Bernard DeVoto. "Editions of TYPEE," SatRL,
         5 (1928), 406; and G. Thomas Tanselle, "TYPEE and DeVoto:
         A Footnote," PBSA, 64 (1970), 207-209.

2844   Tanselle, G. Thomas. "TYPEE and DeVoto: A Footnote,"
         PBSA, 64 (2nd Qt., 1970), 207-209.

              Cf., Bernard DeVoto. "Editions of TYPEE," SatRL,
         5 (1928), 406; and G. Thomas Tanselle, "TYPEE and
         DeVoto Once More," PBSA, 62 (1968), 601-604.

2845   Targ, William. "MOBY-DICK: The Great American Novel,"
         BOUILLABAISSE FOR BIBLIOPHILES. Cleveland: World
         Publishing Co., 1955, pp. 299-307.

2846	Taylor, Walter Fuller. "Herman Melville," A HISTORY OF AMERICAN LTTERS. New York: American Book Co., 1936, pp. 131-140. Revised as THE STORY OF AMERICAN LETTERS. Chicago: Regnery, 1956, pp. 119-128.
2847	TeSelle, Sallie McFague. LITERATURE AND THE CHRISTIAN LIFE. London and New Haven: Yale University Press, 1966, pp. 170, 178-181.
2848	Thakur, D. "The Tales of Melville," LCrit, 8, iv (1969), 39-53.
2849	"Thersites." "Talk on Parnassus," NYTBR, 54 (May 24, 1949), 7, 27. Henry James, Herman Melville, and Franz Kafka in an imaginary conversation.
2850	Thody, Philip, ed. With Notes. Trans. by Ellen Conroy Kennedy. LYRICAL AND CRITICAL ESSAYS. New York: Knopf, 1968, p. 355. Camus refers to MOBY DICK.
2851	Thomas, Clara. Introduction, TYPEE. New York: Airmont Publishing Co., 1965.
2852	Thomas, G., and M. W., eds. MOBY DICK: OR, THE WHALE. Illus. by Exell. London: Ginn & Co., 1957, 1962.
2853	Thomas, Henri. "Herman Melville d'après son Journal de Bord," Critique, 8 (October, 1952), 833-846.
2854	Thomas, Russell. "Melville's Use of Some Sources in THE ENCANTADAS," AL, 3 (1932), 432-456. A study of Melville "in his workshop, searching through his Spenser, his Collins, or his Chatterton, selecting poetical gems" and altering or polishing them for his purpose.
2855	Thomas, Russell. "Yarn for Melville's TYPEE," PQ, 15 (January, 1936), 16-29. Parallel passages from TYPEE and Charles S. Stewart's A VISIT TO THE SOUTH SEAS.... (1831).
2856	Thompson, Lawrance. Foreword, PIERRE: OR THE AMBIGUITIES. New York: New American Library, 1964.
2857	Thompson, Lawrance. MELVILLE'S QUARREL WITH GOD. Princeton: Princeton University Press, 1952. Cf., Victor H. Strandberg, "God and the Critics of Melville," TSLL, 6 (1964), 322-333. Revs., by William H. Gilman, AL, 24 (1953), 558-61; Leo Marx, NCF, 7 (1952), 138-140.

2857.1　Thompson, Lawrance. "MOBY DICK: One Way to Cut In," <u>Carrell</u>, 3 (December, 1962), 1-12.

　　　　　Two interwoven plots, one concerning Ahab and Moby Dick, the other concerning Ishmael.

2857.2　Thompson, W. R. "Melville's 'The Fiddler': A Study in Dissolution," TSLL, 2 (Winter, 1961), 492-500.

　　　　　Hautboy, like Bartleby, is the artist in conflict with society. It is questionable whether the fall here is fortunate, for Hautboy, in his descent and in his return to "the world of men," has sacrificed his artistic integrity. His capitulation leaves him only "a husk of a man...who has lost his way by trading the inward reality for the outward illusion."

2857.3　Thompson, W. R. "'The Paradise of Bachelors and the Tartarus of Maids': A Reinterpretation," AQ, 9 (Spring, 1957), 34-45.

2858　　Thorp, Willard. Afterword, BILLY BUDD AND OTHER TALES. New York: New American Library. Signet Classics. 1961.

2859　　Thorp, Willard. "American Writers as Critics of Nineteenth-Century Society," THE AMERICAN WRITER AND THE EUROPEAN TRADITION. Margaret Denny and William H. Gilman, eds. Minneapolis: Minnesota University Press, 1950, pp. 90-105.

　　　　　"...Every one of his important works, from TYPEE to BILLY BUDD, contains...a social theme. Except for Whitman, he was the most ardent democrat of the writers of the mid-century...."

2860　　Thorp, Willard. "Did Melville Review THE SCARLET LETTER?" AL, 14 (November, 1942), 302-305.

　　　　　The review in the <u>Literary World</u>, March 30, 1850, often attributed to Melville, was probably written by Evert A. Duyckinck.

　　　　　Cf., David V. Erdman and Ephim G. Fogel, eds. EVIDENCE FOR AUTHORSHIP. Ithaca, New York: Cornell University Press, 1966, p. 516; and R. E. Watters, "Melville's 'Isolatoes,'" PMLA, 60 (1945), 1138n.

2861　　Thorp, Willard. "'Grace Greenwood' Parodies TYPEE," AL, 9 (1938), 455-457.

　　　　　Evidence of Melville's contemporary vogue is that "Grace Greenwood" (Sara Jane Lippincott, journalist) contributed a group of parodies of thirteen well-known authors of the day, the eighth of which is Melville.

2862   Thorp, Willard. HERMAN MELVILLE. New York: American
       Writers Series, 1938.

       Rev. by F. Barron Freeman, NEQ, 12 (1939), 609-610.

2863   Thorp, Willard. "Herman Melville," LITERARY HISTORY
       OF THE UNITED STATES. Robert E. Spiller, et al,
       eds. New York: Macmillan, 1948, I, 441-471.
       Revised edition, New York: Macmillan, 1955.

2864   Thorp, Willard. "Herman Melville's Silent Years,"
       UR, 3 (1937), 254-262.

2865   Thorp, Willard, ed. Introduction, HERMAN MELVILLE:
       REPRESENTATIVE SELECTIONS. American Writer Series.
       New York: American Book Company, 1938.

       Rev. by Robert S. Forsythe, AL, 11 (1939), 92-95.

2866   Thorp, Willard, ed. Introduction, MOBY-DICK, OR THE
       WHALE. New York: Oxford University Press, 1947.

2867   Thorp, Willard. "The Literary Scholar as Chameleon,"
       LITERARY VIEWS: CRITICAL AND HISTORICAL ESSAYS.
       Carroll Camden, ed. Chicago: University of
       Chicago Press. Published for William Marsh Rice
       University, 1964, pp. 159-173.

       "...many nineteenth-century writers who may never
have heard of les symbolistes were practicing symbolism and
had some notion of what they were doing....MOBY DICK is a
plum-pudding of symbols, from the sea and bipolarities,
the doubloon, and the try-works down to Ahab's pipe and
Queequeg's idol Yojo."

2868   Thorp, Willard. "Melville," AMERICAN LITERARY
       SCHOLARSHIP: AN ANNUAL: 1963. James Woodress, ed.
       Durham, North Carolina: Duke University Press, 1965,
       pp. 29-40.

2869   Thorp, Willard. "Melville," AMERICAN LITERARY
       SCHOLARSHIP: AN ANNUAL: 1964. James Woodress, ed.
       Durham, North Carolina: Duke University Press, 1966,
       pp. 32-42.

2870   Thorp, Willard. "Melville," AMERICAN LITERARY
       SCHOLARSHIP: AN ANNUAL: 1965. James Woodress, ed.
       Durham, North Carolina: Duke University Press, 1967,
       pp. 28-44.

2871   Thorp, Willard. "Melville," AMERICAN LITERARY
       SCHOLARSHIP: AN ANNUAL: 1966. James Woodress, ed.
       Durham, North Carolina: Duke University Press, 1968,
       pp. 25-39.

2872   Thorp, Willard. "More About Melville," SatRL, 30
        (May 24, 1947), 36.

        An essay-review of Charles Olson's CALL ME
        ISHMAEL. New York: 1958.

2873   Thorp, Willard. "Redburn's Prosy Old Guide Book,"
        PMLA, 53 (1938), 1146-1156.

        In writing the eleven Liverpool chapters in
        REDBURN, Melville borrowed from THE PICTURE OF LIVERPOOL:
        OR STRANGER'S GUIDE. Also, Identification of seven of
        the nine guidebooks listed in REDBURN.

2874   Thorp, Willard. Review-article of Charles Olson's
        CALL ME ISHMAEL, MLN, 63 (February, 1948), 141-142.

        The question of whether there were "two MOBY DICK'S"
        is merely hypothesis.

2875   Thorp, Willard. "The Teacher and New Approaches to
        American Literature," THE TEACHER AND AMERICAN
        LITERATURE: PAPERS PRESENTED AT THE 1964 CONVENTION
        OF THE NATIONAL COUNCIL OF TEACHERS OF ENGLISH.
        Lewis Leary, ed. Champaign, Ill.: 1965, pp. 3-10.

        "...We found we could penetrate Melville's re-
        discovered MOBY DICK as his contemporaries could not,
        because we recognized that the story moves on several
        levels which are intricately related: the narrative, the
        technological,...the psychological, the symbolic, the
        mythic, and the metaphysical....The only danger...is that
        we may overdo the matter and lead our students to believe
        that a poet or dramatist never makes a simple, direct
        statement,...and that all is ambiguity, ambivalence,
        paradox, wit and irony...."

2876   Thorp, Willard, Merle Curti, Carlos Baker, eds.
        "Herman Melville," AMERICAN ISSUES. Chicago;
        Philadelphia; New York: J. B. Lippincott Co.,
        1941, I, 426, 584; II, 431, 446.

2877   Thurman, Howard K. HERMAN MELVILLE: HUMANITARIAN AND
        CRITIC OF POLITICS. Diss. Iowa: 1950.

2878   Thurston, Jarvis, O. B. Emerson, Carl Hartman, and
        Elizabeth V. Wright. SHORT FICTION CRITICISM:
        A CHECKLIST OF INTERPRETATIONS SINCE 1925 OF
        STORIES AND NOVELETTES (AMERICAN, BRITISH,
        CONTINENTAL, 1800-1958). Denver: Alan Swallow,
        1960, pp. 154-162, 253-255.

2879   Tick, Stanley. "Forms of the Novel in the Nineteenth
        Century: Studies in Dickens, Melville, and George
        Eliot," DA, 27 (San Diego, Calif.: 1966), 1349A-
        50A.

2880   Tillyard, E. M. W. "Melville: 'MOBY DICK,'" THE EPIC
        STRAIN IN THE ENGLISH NOVEL. Fair Lawn, New Jersey:
        Essential Books, Inc., 1958, pp. 119-120.

            "...MOBY DICK, though a great book, remains something
        of an oddity. It is individual, not choric. It reflects
        the spirit of a great and strange man, but it does not
        interpret the 'accepted unconscious metaphysic' of a
        group."

2881   Tilton, Eleanor M. "Melville's 'Rammon': A Text and
        Commentary," HLB, 13 (Winter, 1959), 50-91.

2882   Tindall, William York. "The Ceremony of Innocence,"
        GREAT MORAL DILEMMAS IN LITERATURE, PAST AND
        PRESENT. R. M. MacIver, ed. New York: Harper
        & Row, Publishers, 1956, pp. 73-81.

            "We may say that BILLY BUDD is a vision of man in
        society, a vision of man's moral quandary,...a vision
        of confronting what confronts us, of man thinking things
        out with all the attendant confusions and uncertainties
        ...."

2883   Tindall, William York. THE LITERARY SYMBOL. New York:
        Columbia University Press, 1955; New York: Mentor
        Books, 1957; Bloomington: Indiana University Press,
        1960, passim.

            Critical approaches to symbolism of the white whale.

2884   Tomita, Akira. "How to Read MOBY-DICK," RikR, 16
        (1955), 1-16, 53-55.

2885   Tomlinson, H. M. "A Clue to 'MOBY DICK,'" LitRNYEP, 2
        (November 5, 1921), 141-142.

            The "clue" is recognition that the novel is a work
        of "pure genius and therefore sui generis."

2886   Tomlinson, H. M. THE FACE OF THE EARTH. Indianapolis:
        Bobbs-Merrill, 1950.

            Personal appreciation of Herman Melville.

2887　Tomlinson, H. M. GIFTS OF FORTUNE. London: William
　　　　Heinemann, Ltd., 1926, pp. 108-109.

　　　　Comparison of MOBY DICK and MACBETH.

2888　Tomlinson, H. M. Preface, PIERRE. New York:
　　　　E. P. Dutton, 1929.

2889　Tomlinson, H. M. "Two Americans and a Whale," HarpMM,
　　　　152 (April, 1926), 618-621.

2890　Tomlinson, H. M. "The World of Books," N&A, 29
　　　　(June 4, 1921), 363.

2891　Tomlinson, H. M. "The World of Books," London Athenaeum,
　　　　33 (April 7, 1923), 17.

2892　Tomlinson, T. B. "Faulkner and American Sophistication,"
　　　　MelbCR, 7 (1964), 92-103.

　　　　Comparison of Faulkner's style with Melville's
　　　　BILLY BUDD.

2893　Tompkins, Jane P. "Studies in Melville's Prose Style,"
　　　　DA, 28 (Yale: 1967), 246A.

　　　　A study of selected works and parts of works from
　　　　1838 to 1852, relating "facts of style" to Melville's
　　　　"habits of thought, thematic concerns, and larger
　　　　structural patterns."

2893.1　Townsend, Harvey Gates. PHILOSOPHICAL IDEAS IN THE
　　　　UNITED STATES. New York: American Book Co., 1934;
　　　　Octagon Books, Inc., 1968, p. 133.

2893.2　Trask, Georgianne Sampson, and Charles Burkhart, eds.
　　　　STORYTELLERS AND THEIR ART. New York: Doubleday
　　　　& Company, 1963, pp. 259-278.

2894　Travis, Mildred K. "The Idea of Poe in PIERRE," ESQ,
　　　　50 (1st Qt., 1968), 59-62.

2895　Travis, Mildred K. "MARDI: Melville's Allegory of
　　　　Love," ESQ, 43 (2nd Qt., 1966), 88-94.

　　　　Leaving the factual approach to love and marriage
　　　　in TYPEE, Melville treated these themes allegorically
　　　　in MARDI, with allusions to Spenser and the Greek
　　　　myths.

2896 Travis, Mildred K. "Melville's Furies: Technique in
MARDI and MOBY DICK," ESQ, 47 (2nd Qt., 1967),
71-73.

The ships which the Pequod meets are the Greek
Furies, warning against the chase.

2897 Travis, Mildred K. "Melville's 'Furies' Continued in
PIERRE," ESQ, 62 (Winter, 1971), 33-35.

2898 Travis, Mildred K. "Spenserian Analogues in MARDI and
THE CONFIDENCE MAN," ESQ, 50 (1st Qt., 1968),
55-58.

Three scenes in MARDI seem to have had their origin
in Spenser's Bower of Bliss, Garden of Adonis, and
Temple of Venus. THE CONFIDENCE MAN seems to have come
from PROSOPOPOEIA: OR MOTHER HUBBERD'S TALE.

2899 Treeman, Elizabeth. CORRIGENDA TO BILLY BUDD.
Cambridge, Mass.: Harvard University Press, 1953.

2900 Trent, W. P. A HISTORY OF AMERICAN LITERATURE. New York:
Appleton, 1929, passim.

2901 Trent, W. P., ed. Introduction, TYPEE. Boston:
D. C. Heath, 1902.

2902 Trent, W. P., and John Erskine. "Melville," GREAT
AMERICAN WRITERS. New York: Henry Holt and
Company, 1912, pp. 56-57.

2903 Trent, William P., John Erskine, Stuart P. Sherman, and
Carl Van Doren, eds. "Melville," A SHORT HISTORY
OF AMERICAN LITERATURE: BASED UPON THE CAMBRIDGE
HISTORY OF AMERICAN LITERATURE. New York: G. P.
Putnam's Sons (The Knickerbocker Press), 1922,
pp. 198-201.

2904 Trent, William P., John Erskine, Stuart P. Sherman, and
Carl Van Doren, eds. "Melville's Autobiographical
Romances," and "Melville's Later Work," THE CAMBRIDGE
HISTORY OF AMERICAN LITERATURE. New York: The
Macmillan Company; Cambridge, England: at the
University Press, 1917; repr., 1965.

2904.1 TRES ESCRITORES NORTEAMERICANOS: HERMAN MELVILLE,
EDITH WHARTON, GERTRUDE STEIN. Traducción Angela
Figuera. Madrid: Gredos, 1962 (UMPAW HO, 12, 13).

2904.2　Trilling, Lionel. "Contemporary American Literature in
Its Relation to Ideas," THE AMERICAN WRITERS AND
THE EUROPEAN TRADITION. Margaret Denny and
William H. Gilman, eds. Minneapolis: Minnesota
University Press, 1950, pp. 132-153.

2905　Trilling, Lionel. THE MIDDLE OF THE JOURNEY. New York:
The Viking Press, 1947.

Gifford Maxim, a character in the novel, argues
that not only are Captain Vere and Billy symbolically
"pure Spirit and Law in the world of Necessity,
respectively, but also God the Father and both Christ
and Christ in Adam."

2906　Trimpi, Helen P. "Conventions of Narrative Romance in
MOBY DICK," SoR, 7 (January, 1971), 115-129.

2907　Trimpi, Helen P. "Demonology and Witchcraft in MOBY DICK,"
JHI, 30 (October-December, 1969), 543-562.

2908　Trimpi, Helen P. ROMANCE STRUCTURE AND HERMAN MELVILLE'S
USE OF DEMONOLOTY AND WITCHCRAFT IN MOBY-DICK.
Diss. Harvard: 1966.

2909　Tsuru, Shigeto. "Japanese Images of America," PATHS OF
AMERICAN THOUGHT. Arthur M. Schlesinger, Jr., and
Morton White, eds. London: Chatto & Windus, 1964,
p. 515.

Melville and Japan.

2910　Tucker, Harry, Jr. "A Glance at 'Whiteness' in Melville
and Camus," PMLA, 80 (December, 1965), 605.

Camus's symbolic use of "whiteness" in L'ETRANGER
similar to Melville's use in MOBY DICK.

Cf., William M. Manly, "Journey to Consciousness:
The Symbolic Pattern of Camus's L'ETRANGER," PMLA, 79
(1964), 321-328; and G. Thomas Tanselle, "A Further
Note on 'Whiteness' in Melville and Others," PMLA, 81
(1966), 604.

2910.1　Tuckerman, Henry T. "Authors in Berkshire," Philadelphia
American Literary Gazette and Publishers' Circular,
2 (November 16, 1863), 38-40.

2911　Tudor, Stephen. "Four for Melville," ESQ, 59 (Spring,
1970), 3.

Four "poems" entitled TYPEE, MOBY DICK, BARTLEBY
THE SCRIVENER, and BILLY BUDD, respectively.

2912   Tuerk, Richard. "Melville's 'BARTLEBY' and Isaac
D'Israeli's CURIOSITIES OF LITERATURE, Second
Series," SSF, 7 (Fall, 1970), 647-649.

D'Israeli's book is not the primary source for
BARTLEBY, but it does make clearer some parts of the
story and illustrates Melville's skill in appropriating
material from literary sources.

2913   Turlish, Lewis A. "A Study of Teleological Concepts in
the Novels of Herman Melville," DAI, 30 (Michigan:
1970), 3922A.

2914   Turnage, Maxine. "Melville's Concern with the Arts in
BILLY BUDD," ArQ, 28 (1972), 74-82.

2915   Turner, Arlin. "Recent Scholarship on Hawthorne and
Melville," THE TEACHER AND AMERICAN LITERATURE:
PAPERS PRESENTED AT THE 1964 CONVENTION OF NATIONAL
COUNCIL OF TEACHERS OF ENGLISH. Lewis Leary, ed.
Champaign, Ill.: 1965, pp. 95-109.

Outline of the landmark biographies and critical
works which began to appear in the late twenties and
continues.

2916   Turner, Darwin T. "Smoke from Melville's Chimney,"
CLAJ, 7 (December, 1963), 107-113.

Melville, angered by the charges of immorality
against his earlier work, playfully "executed an
enjoyable literary hoax" in his short story.

2917   Turner, Darwin T. "A View of Melville's 'Piazza,'"
CLAJ, 7 (September, 1963), 61-62.

The story develops two themes: "an individual
must embrace the good and the evil of life without
seeking escape" and "isolation from humanity is
dangerous and debilitating."

2918   Turner, David Reuben. HERMAN MELVILLE'S MOBY DICK.
New York: Arco, 1969.

2919   Turner, Frederick W., III. "Melville and Thomas Berger:
The Novelist as Cultural Anthropologist," CentR,
13 (Winter, 1969), 101-121.

2920   Turner, Frederick W., III. "Melville's Post-Meridian
          Fiction," MASJ, 10 (Fall, 1969), 60-67.

          Treatment of BARTLEBY, THE ENCANTADAS, BENITO
          CERENO, ISRAEL POTTER, and THE CONFIDENCE-MAN as
          exploratory studies of the American scene in which
          Melville, seeking an explanation for the poor reception
          of MOBY DICK and PIERRE, found the source of failure in
          his country's culture and national character.

2920.1   Turner, Lorenzo Dow. ANTI-SLAVERY SENTIMENT IN AMERICAN
          LITERATURE PRIOR TO 1865. Port Washington, New
          York: 1929; Kennikat Press, Inc., 1966, pp. 50-51.

2921   Tutt, Ralph M. "'Jimmy Rose'--Melville's Displaced
          Noble," ESQ, 33 (4th Qt., 1963), 28-32.

          "The story is no pathetic portrait of a fallen
          aristocrat; it is a statement of tragic flaw in the
          American character."

2922   Tuveson, Ernest Lee. "The Creed of the Confidence-Man,"
          ELH, 33 (1966), 247-270.

          A "new religion," like the eighteenth-century
          philosophy of "Tout est bien," is the optimistic creed
          which the confidence-man promulgates. The faith of
          confidence appears to be in essence "a confidence-game
          played on the human race and especially on the American
          segment of it...by mankind itself." However, there still
          remains "a psychic need for confidence"; stripped of it,
          man "confronts the blank, terrible universe with no
          spiritual shield."

2922.1   Tuveson, Ernest Lee. REDEEMER NATION. Chicago:
          Chicago University Press, 1968.

2923   Tyler, Parker. "Milly and Billy as Proto-Finnegans,"
          EVERY ARTIST HIS OWN SCANDAL: A STUDY OF REAL
          AND FICTIVE HEROES. New York: Horizon Press,
          1964, pp. 239-255.

          On James's Milly Theale and Billy Budd.

2924   Tynan, Kenneth. "Moby Dick, adapted by Orson Welles
          from Herman Melville's Novel at the Duke of York's
          London," CURTAINS: SELECTIONS FROM THE DRAMA
          CRITICISM AND RELATED WRITINGS. Atheneum, 1961,
          pp. 255-256.

2925   Underwood, Francis H. "Melville," A HANDBOOK OF ENGLISH
          LITERATURE: AMERICAN AUTHORS. Boston: Lee and
          Shepard, 1872, p. 458.

2926   "An Unpublished Letter from Herman Melville to Mrs. Hawthorne in Explanation of MOBY-DICK," AMERICAN ART ASSOCIATION - ANDERSON GALLERIES CATALOGUE OF SALE, No. 3911. New York: 1931, p. 9.

        Portion of a four-page letter dated January 8, 1852.

2927   Untermeyer, Louis. "Herman Melville," AMERICAN POETRY FROM THE BEGINNING TO WHITMAN. New York: Harcourt, Brace & Co., 1931, pp. 547-562.

2928   Untermeyer, Louis. "Herman Melville," MAKERS OF THE WESTERN WORLD. New York: Simon and Schuster, 1955, pp. 47-59.

2929   Ustinov, Peter. BILLY BUDD (Screen Play from novel by Herman Melville, and play by Louis O. Coxe and Rovert Chapman, 1962.

        Cf., Review-article by Pauline Kael, "BILLY BUDD," FilmQ, 16 (Spring, 1963), 53-56.

2930   Van Cromphout, Gustaaf. "Herman Melville's REDBURN Considered in the Light of the Elder Henry James's THE NATURE OF EVIL," RLV, 29 (1963), 117-126.

2931   Vancura, Zdenek. "The Negro in the White Man's Ship: A Critical Triptych," PragSE, 8 (1959), 73-97.

2932   Vanderhaar, Margaret M. "A Re-Examination of 'BENITO CERENO,'" AL, 40 (May, 1968), 179-191.

        The "public" or social meaning of the story in Melville's day and now has particular reference to slavery and its "brutalizing, dehumanizing effects" on both master and slave.

2933   VanDerhoff, Jack. A BIBLIOGRAPHY OF NOVELS RELATED TO AMERICAN FRONTIER AND COLONIAL HISTORY. Troy, New York: The Whitston Publishing Company, 1971, pp. 315-316.

        MOBY DICK and ISRAEL POTTER.

2934   Van Der Krolf, J. M. "Zen and the American Experience," VBQ, 25 (Autumn, 1959), 122-132.

2935   Vande Kieft, Ruth M. "'When Big Hearts Strike Together': The Concussion of Melville and Sir Thomas Browne," PLL, 5 (1969), 39-50.

2936   Van Doren, Carl. THE AMERICAN NOVEL: 1789-1939.
New York: 1921. Rev. and Enlarged, New York:
Macmillan, 1940, passim.

2937   Van Doren, Carl. "Contemporaries of Cooper," CAMBRIDGE
HISTORY OF AMERICAN LITERATURE. New York: 1917,
I, 320-323.

2938   Van Doren, Carl, ed. Foreword, BILLY BUDD, BENITO
CERENO AND THE ENCHANTED ISLES. New York:
The Readers Club, Inc., 1942.

2939   Van Doren, Carl, ed. Introduction, WHITE JACKET.
New York: 1924, 1929.

2940   Van Doren, Carl. "Lucifer from Nantucket. An Introduction
to MOBY DICK," Century, 110 (August, 1925), 494-501.

Transcendentalism in Melville.

2941   Van Doren, Carl. "Melville before the Mast," CentM,
108 (1924), 272-277.

WHITE-JACKET

2942   Van Doren, Carl. "Mocha Dick," ROVING CRITIC. New York:
Knopf, 1923, pp. 97-99.

2943   Van Doren, Carl. "Mr. Melville's MOBY DICK," New York
Bookman, 59 (April, 1924), 154-157.

2944   Van Doren, Carl. "A Note of Confession," Nation, 127
(1928), 622.

An apology for having omitted Melville's shorter
novels in earlier articles.

2945   Vann, J. Don. "A Checklist of Melville Criticism,
1958-1968," SNNTS, 1, iv (1969), 507-530.

2946   Van Nostrand, Albert D. "The Linked Allegories of
MOBY DICK," EVERYMAN HIS OWN POET: ROMANTIC
GOSPELS IN AMERICAN LITERATURE. New York:
McGraw, 1968, pp. 113-140, passim.

2947   Van Patten, Nathan. "Herman Melville," AN INDEX TO
BIBLIOGRAPHIES AND BIBLIOGRAPHICAL CONTRIBUTORS
RELATING TO THE WORK OF AMERICAN AND BRITISH
AUTHORS, 1923-1932. London: Oxford University
Press, Humphrey Milford; Stanford, Calif.:
Stanford University Press, 1934, pp. 172-174.

2948   Van Vechten, Carl. "A Belated Biography," LitRNYEP, 3 (1921), 316.

2949   Van Vechten, Carl. "The Later Work of Herman Melville," DD, 3 (1922), 9-20.

2949.1 Van Vechten, Carl. "The Later Work of Herman Melville," EXCAVATIONS: A BOOK OF ADVOCACIES. New York: Alfred Knopf, 1926. Repr., Freeport, New York: Books for Libraries Press, 1971, pp. 65-88.

2950   Vargish, Thomas. "Gnostic Mythos in MOBY DICK," PMLA, 81 (June, 1966), 272-277.

       Melville probably obtained his knowledge of the mythos from Andrew Norton's THE EVIDENCES OF THE GENUINENESS OF THE GOSPELS (1844).

2951   Vernon, John. "Melville's 'The Bell-Tower,'" SSF, 7 (Spring, 1970), 264-276.

       Bannadonna is a scientist displeased with the imperfection of mankind. In seeking to correct these imperfections through technology, scientists seal themselves off from humanity and offend nature by transgressing the bounds she has set upon mankind. Then the bell falls, the tower is toppled, and nature reclaims the scene.

2952   Verucci, Valeria. "'The Bell Tower' di Herman Melville," SA, 9 (1964), 89-120.

2953   Victor, Alexander O. "Five Inches of Books," YULG, 22 (1948), 127-128.

2954   Vigorelli, Giancarlo, ed. Introduction, LA NAVE DI VETRO. Bologna: Capelli, 1957.

2955   Vincent, Howard P. "And Still They Fall from the Masthead," MELVILLE AND HAWTHORNE IN THE BERKSHIRES: A SYMPOSIUM. Howard P. Vincent, ed. Kent, Ohio: Kent State University Press, 1968, pp. 144-155.

       In WHITE-JACKET, the "man-of-war world" is very present, but the story is about "how White-Jacket sees his world and what he does with it, what it does with him."

2956   Vincent, Howard P., comp. CHARLES E. MERRILL STUDIES IN MOBY-DICK. Columbus, Ohio: Charles E. Merrill, 1969.

2957   Vincent, Howard P., comp. CHECKLIST OF HERMAN MELVILLE. Columbus, Ohio: Charles E. Merrill, 1969.

2958   Vincent, Howard P., ed. COLLECTED POEMS OF HERMAN MELVILLE. Chicago: Packard and Company, Hendricks House, 1947.

     Rev., by William Braswell, AL, 19 (1948), 366-368.

2959   Vincent, Howard P., gen. ed. COMPLETE WORKS OF HERMAN MELVILLE. Chicago and New York: Hendricks House, 1947.

2960   Vincent, Howard P. GUIDE TO HERMAN MELVILLE. Columbus, Ohio: Charles E. Merrill, 1969.

2961   Vincent, Howard P., comp. HERMAN MELVILLE: MOBY DICK. Charles E. Merrill Studies. Columbus, Ohio: Charles E. Merrill, 1969.

2961.1   Vincent, Howard P., ed. Introduction, TWENTIETH CENTURY INTERPRETATIONS OF BILLY BUDD: A COLLECTION OF CRITICAL ESSAYS. Englewood Cliffs, New Jersey: Prentice-Hall, Inc., 1971.

2962   Vincent, Howard P. "Ishmael, Writer and Art Critic," THEMES AND DIRECTIONS IN AMERICAN LITERATURE. Ray B. Browne and Donald Pizer, eds. Purdue University Studies. Lafayette, Indiana: Purdue University Press, 1969, pp. 69-79.

2963   Vincent, Howard P., ed. MELVILLE AND HAWTHORNE IN THE BERKSHIRES. Kent, Ohio: Kent State University Press, 1968.

     A printing of most of the talks delivered at the 1966 Melville-Hawthorne conference, and two papers written subsequently.

     Rev., by Harry Hayden Clark, AL, 41 (1969), 284-285.

2964   Vincent, Howard P., ed. MELVILLE ANNUAL 1965, A SYMPOSIUM: BARTLEBY THE SCRIVENER. Kent Studies in English III. Kent, Ohio: Kent State University Press, 1966.

     Revs., Richard H. Fogle, AL, 39 (1967), 114-115; Walton R. Patrick, SSF, 5 (1967), 299-301.

2965   Vincent, Howard P. THE TAILORING OF MELVILLE'S WHITE-
        JACKET. Evanston, Illinois: Northwestern University
        Press, 1970.

              Revs., by William Braswell, AL, 43 (1971), 451-452;
        Robert C. Ryan, Sym, 10 (1971), 230-240.

2966   Vincent, Howard P. THE TRYING-OUT OF MOBY-DICK. Boston:
        Houghton Mifflin, 1949; repr., Carbondale: Southern
        Illinois University Press, 1965.

              Revs., Henry A. Murray, NEQ, 23 (1950), 527-530;
        Sherman Paul, NEQ, 25 (1952), 423-24; Willard Thorp,
        AL, 22 (1949), 355-56.

2967   Vincent, Howard P. "WHITE-JACKET: An Essay in
        Interpretation," NEQ, 22 (September, 1949), 304-
        315.

              WHITE-JACKET represents Melville's experiment in
        symbolism. The jacket, itself symbolic, becomes the
        object of scorn, and the shipmates' final rejection of
        the jacket at the auction represents the rejection of
        the owner as well. White Jacket's fall from the yardarm
        is caused by his garment, symbolizing the Fall of Man
        and a Christian rebirth.

2968   Violette, W. L. "MOBY DICK: A Study in Symphonic Prose,"
        LC, (Mysore, India), 4 (Summer, 1960), 19-23.

2968.1 Virtanen, Reino. "Emile Montegut as a Critic of
        American Literature," PMLA, 63 (1948), 1265-1275.

              "Of Melville, he [Montegut] noted only ISRAEL
        POTTER, and allowed himself to be superseded by
        E. D. Forgues, whose article on MOBY DICK is perhaps
        more sensitive and penetrating than that of any non-
        American of the time."

              Cf., E. D. Forgues, "MOBY DICK, La Chasse à la
        Baleine," RDM, 1 (February 1, 1853), 491-514.

2969   Vittorini, Elio. "'Herman Melville,' An Outline of
        American Literature," SR, 68 (Summer, 1960),
        433-434.

2970   Vogel, Dan. "The Dramatic Chapters in MOBY DICK,"
        NCF, 13 (December, 1958), 239-247.

              A Study of the dramatic structure of MOBY DICK,
        showing inter-relationships between stage directions,
        expositions, characters, soliloquies, and action.

2971   Vogel, Dan. "Melville's Shorter Published Poetry:
        A Critical Study of the Lyrics in MARDI, of
        BATTLE PIECES, JOHN MARR and TIMOLEON," DA, 17
        (New York University: 1957), 367-368.

2972   Vogelback, Arthur L. "Shakespeare and Melville's
            BENITO CERENO," MLN, 67 (February, 1952), 113-116.

        Babo in Melville's story seems modeled on Iago
        as an incarnation of evil. Both characters illustrate
        the mystery of evil.

2972.1 Vogler, Thomas A. "INVISIBLE MAN: Somebody's Protest
            Novel," IowaR, 1, ii (Spring, 1970), 64-82.

        Comparison of Ellison's novel with the work of
        Melville and others.

2973   Von Abele, Rudolph. "Melville and the Problem of Evil,"
            AmM, 65 (November, 1947), 592-598.

        Melville's morality was based upon the need of
        choosing actions which result in the least evil. "'As
        well hate a seraph as a shark. Both were made by the
        same hand.' This...is the answer to the problem; it is
        Melville's final reconciliation to the world."

2973.1 Von Hagen, Victor Wolfgang, ed. THE ENCANTADAS, OR THE
            ENCHANTED ISLES. With Introduction, Critical
            Epilogue, and Bibliographical Notes. Burlingame,
            Calif.: Wm. P. Wreden, 1940.

2973.2 Von Hagen, Victor. EQUADOR AND THE GALAPAGOS ISLANDS.
            Norman, Oklahoma: 1949.

2973.3 Von Hagen, Victor Wolfgang, ed. "Herman Melville,"
            GREEN WORLD OF THE NATURALISTS: A TREASURY OF
            FIVE CENTURIES OF NATURAL HISTORY IN SOUTH
            AMERICA. Selected and Annotated with Biographical
            Sketches and Introduction. New York: Greenberg,
            1948, pp. 201-202.

2974   Wadlington, Warwick. "Ishmael's Godly Gamesomeness:
            Selftaste and Rhetoric in MOBY-DICK," ELH, 39
            (June, 1972), 309-331.

        "The audience awareness that Ishmael evinces is
        a reflection of /Melville's/ increasing ambivalence
        toward his reading public and his growing sense of
        the effect his readers had on his role as a serious
        writer."

2975	Wadlington, Warwick. "The Theme of the Confidence Game in Certain Major American Writers," DA, 28 (Tulane: 1968), 3691A.

In BENITO CERENO, MOBY DICK, and THE CONFIDENCE MAN, there is an interrelation of the problem of belief, the limitations and uncertainty of human knowledge, and the theme of leadership, brought together in terms of a "grimly comic" confidence game.

2976	Wagenknecht, Edward. "The Ambiguities of Herman Melville," CAVALCADE OF THE AMERICAN NOVEL FROM THE BIRTH OF THE NATION TO THE MIDDLE OF THE TWENTIETH CENTURY. New York: Henry Holt, 1952, pp. 58–81.

2977	Wagenknecht, Edward. "Our Contemporary, Herman Melville," CE, 11 (1950), 301-308.

2977.1	Wagenknecht, Edward. "Our Contemporary, Herman Melville," EJ, 39 (1950), 121-128.

2978	Wagenknecht, Edward. NATHANIEL HAWTHORNE: MAN AND WRITER. New York: Oxford University Press, 1961, pp. 107-108, passim.

2978.1	Wagenknecht, Edward. WILLIAM DEAN HOWELLS: THE FRIENDLY EYE. New York: Oxford University Press, 1969, pp. 26, 28.

Melville's BATTLE-PIECES (1867) drew a severe review from Howells on the ground that "not having felt what he described, Melville could not hope to move others."

2979	Wager, Willis. AMERICAN LITERATURE: A WORLD VIEW. New York: New York University Press; London: London University Press, Ltd., 1968, pp. 110-115, passim.

2980	Waggoner, Hyatt H. "Hawthorne and Melville Acquaint the Reader with Their Abodes," SNNTS, 2, iv (Winter, 1970), 420-424.

Similar treatment of subject by Melville and Hawthorne.

2981	Waggoner, Hyatt H. "Herman Melville," AMERICAN POETS: FROM THE PURITANS TO THE PRESENT. Boston: Houghton Mifflin Company, 1968, pp. 227-235.

2982   Waggoner, Wyatt Howe. "A Possible Verse Parody of
         MOBY-DICK in 1865," AN&Q, 2 (April, 1942), 3-6.

2983   Wagner, Vern. "Billy Budd as Moby Dick: An Alternate
         Reading," STUDIES IN HONOR OF JOHN WILCOX.
         A. Doyle Wallace and Woodburn O. Ross, eds.
         Detroit: Wayne State University Press, 1958,
         pp. 157-174.

2984   Wainger, B. M. "Herman Melville: A Study in Disillusion,"
         UCB, 25 (January, 1932), 35-62.

         Herman Melville's story is one of "disillusionment
         and defeat in man's struggle with society and in his
         struggle with nature."

2985   Wais, Kurt. "Die Errettung aus dem Schiffbruch: Melville,
         Mallarmé und einige deutsche Voraussetzungen,"
         DVLG, 34 (1960), 21-45.

2985.1 Wais, Kurt. "Die Errettung aus dem Schiffbruch: Melville:
         Mallarmé und einige deutsche Voraussetzungen,"
         COMPARATIVE LITERATURE: PROCEEDINGS OF THE SECOND
         CONGRESS OF THE INTERNATIONAL COMPARATIVE LITERATURE
         ASSOCIATION. Warner P. Friederich, ed. (UNCSCL,
         Nos. 23, 24), 2 Vols. Chapel Hill: North Carolina
         University Press, 1959, I, 294-309.

2985.2 Walcutt, Charles C. AMERICAN NATURALISM: A DIVIDED
         STREAM. Minneapolis: 1956, p. 290.

         Melville's relationship to the Naturalists.

2986   Walcutt, Charles C. "The Fire Symbolism in MOBY DICK,"
         MLN, 59 (1944), 304-310.

         Ahab's cry, "Oh! thou clear spirit of clear
         fire..." (Chapter CXIX) is more than melodrama. It
         is "the key which explains many paradoxical and
         confusing references to fire and enables us to
         relate the fire symbolism to the central meaning of
         the story."

2987   Walcutt, Charles C. MAN'S CHANGING MASK: MODES AND
         METHODS OF CHARACTERIZATION IN FICTION. Minneapolis:
         Minnesota University Press, 1966, pp. 102-123,
         passim.

         An analysis of MOBY DICK.

2988   Walcutt, Charles C. "The Soundings of MOBY-DICK,"
         ArQ, 24 (Summer, 1968), 101-116.

2989   Walker, Warren S. "A Note on Nathaniel Ames," AL, 26 (1954), 239-241.

2990   Walker, Warren S. TWENTIETH-CENTURY SHORT STORY EXPLICATION: INTERPRETATIONS, 1900-1960, INCLUSIVE OF SHORT FICTION SINCE 1800. Hamden, Conn.: Shoe String Press, 1951, Supplement I, 1961-1963, Pub., 1963; Supplement II, 1963-1964, pub., 1965. Rev. ed., 1967.

2991   Walker, William E., and Robert L. Welker, eds. REALITY AND MYTH: ESSAYS IN AMERICAN LITERATURE IN MEMORY OF RICHARD CROOM BEATTY. Nashville: Vanderbilt University Press, 1964, passim.

2992   Walser, Richard. "Another Early Review of TYPEE," AL, 36 (January, 1965), 515-516.

On March 21, 1846, the Spirit of the Times, a New York sporting weekly, reviewed Melville's TYPEE favorably.

2993   Walter, Josef. HERMANN MELVILLE'S INFLUENCE UPON GERSTÄCKER'S SOUTH SEA NOVELS. Diss. Freiburg (Schweiz), 1952.

2994   Ward, A. C. AMERICAN LITERATURE, 1880-1930. New York: The Dial Press, 1932, pp. 20ff.

An analysis of Melville laudatory, yet critical.

2995   Ward, Joseph A. "The Function of the Cetological Chapters in MOBY-DICK," AL, 28 (May, 1956), 164-183.

The primary purpose of the cetological chapters is knowledge, with relatedness the key to knowledge, and symbolism the approach. To know one thing fully is to know the universe, and the whale links all worlds.

2996   Ward, Joseph A. "Melville and Failure," ESQ, 33 (4th Qt., 1963), 43-48.

Failure is an important motif in Melville's fiction. "The fall from security is a descent from illusion to reality."

2997   Ward, Joseph Thomas. "Herman Melville: The Forms and Forces of Evil," DA, 20 (Notre Dame: 1960), 2786-2787.

2998   Ward, Robert S. "Longfellow and Melville: The Ship and the Whale," ESQ, 22 (1st Qt., 1961), 57-63.

2999   Warner, Rex. Introduction, BILLY BUDD AND OTHER STORIES.
         London: John Lehmann, Ltd., 1951.

2999.1   Warren, Austin. THE NEW ENGLAND CONSCIENCE. Ann Arbor:
         Michigan University Press, 1966, passim.

3000   Warren, Robert Penn, ed. Introduction, SELECTED POEMS
         OF HERMAN MELVILLE: A READER'S EDITION. New York:
         Random House, 1970.

3000.1   Warren, Robert Penn. "Melville the Poet," SELECTED
         ESSAYS OF ROBERT PENN WARREN. New York: Random
         House, Inc., 1958, pp. 184-198.

3001   Warren, Robert Penn. "Melville the Poet," KR, 8
         (1946), 208-223.

         Melville did not learn his craft, but if his
         poetry is, on the whole, a poetry of shreds and patches,
         many of the patches are of a "massy and kingly fabric."

3002   Warren, Robert P. "Melville's Poems," SoR, 3 (Autumn,
         1967), 799-855.

3003   Warren, Robert Penn. "Some Recent Novels," SoR, 1
         (Winter, 1936), 624.

         "...MOBY DICK is, with very slight and mechanical
         qualification, quite as 'regional' as THE SCARLET LETTER
         ...."

3004   Watkins, Floyd C. "Melville's Plotinus Plinlimmon and
         Pierre," REALITY AND MYTH: ESSAYS IN AMERICAN
         LITERATURE IN MEMORY OF RICHARD CROOM BEATTY.
         William E. Walker, and Robert L. Welker, eds.
         Nathville, Tenn.: Vanderbilt University Press,
         1964, pp. 39-51.

3005   Watkins, Floyd C. "Note on Melville's Three Twin Sons,"
         AS, 30 (1955), 152.

         Melville's dialectal usage of _twin_ for _triplet_
         in Chapter 53 of REDBURN.

3006   Watson, Charles N., Jr. "Characters and Characterizations
         in the Works of Herman Melville," DAI, 31 (Duke:
         1970), 372A.

3007   Watson, Charles N., Jr. "Melville's Agatha and Hunilla:
A Literary Reincarnation," ELN, 6 (1968), 114-118.

       Parallels suggest that Melville transformed parts
of the Agatha Robertson story into the character of
Hunilla in the eighth sketch of THE ENCANTADAS.

3008   Watson, Charles N., Jr. "Melville's Jackson: Redburn's
Heroic 'Double,'" ESQ, 62 (1971), 8-10.

       "...it is no more true of Jackson than of Ahab
that he is a card-board villain, a manifestation of
pure evil....each of them embodies the complex mixture
of resignation and rebellion, compassion and misanthropy,
that is characteristic of Melville's own searching
intelligence."

3009   Watson, E. L. Grant. "Melville's PIERRE," NEQ, 3
(1930), 195-234.

       If one would understand Melville, one must
understand this book before all the others. PIERRE
was "the center of Melville's being, and the height
of his achievement...."

3010   Watson, E. L. Grant. "Melville's Testament of
Acceptance," NEQ, 6 (1933), 319-327.

       Cf., Roger Shattuck, "Two Inside Narratives:
BILLY BUDD and L'ETRANGER," TSLL, 4 (1962), 314-320.

3011   Watson, E. L. Grant. "MOBY DICK," LonMer, 3 (December,
1920), 180-186.

       Comparison with Ibsen's WHEN WE DEAD AWAKEN.

3012   Watters, Reginald E. "Boston's Salt-Water Preacher,"
SAQ, 45 (1946), 350-361.

       An account of Father Edward Taylor with whom
Father Mapple is sometimes identified.

3013   Watters, Reginald E. "The Meanings of the White Whale,"
UTQ, 20 (1951), 155-168.

3014   Watters, Reginald E. "Melville's Isolatoes," PMLA, 60
(December, 1945), 1138-1148.

       Throughout his work, Melville indicates that
happiness is not obtainable in isolation, but in shared
experiences. In his criticism of the voluntary
Isolato, Melville may have had in mind Donne's metaphor:
"No Man is an Island...."

3015   Watters, Reginald E. "Melville's Metaphysics of Evil,"
         UTQ, 9 (January, 1940), 170-182.

         In early novels, Melville sees implacable evil in
         external nature, but in later work, especially BILLY BUDD,
         he sees man is free "to imprint his pattern upon the
         blackness of the cosmos" and that love alone gives value
         to that pattern.

3016   Watters, Reginald E. "Melville's Sociality," AL, 17
         (March, 1945), 33-49.

         Acceptance of an "embracing sociality."

3017   Watts, Robert Alan. "The 'Seaward Peep': Ahab's
         Transgression," UR, 31 (December, 1964), 133-138.

         The ocean in MOBY DICK represents a concept known
         by many names: the Platonic Absolute, or ultimate
         reality, or the Oversoul. The concept of Oversoul was
         contemporary to Melville and important in the American
         Romantic tradition.

3018   A Wayfarer. "A Testimonial for MOBY-DICK," London
         Nation, 28 (January 22, 1921), 572.

         "...there never was such a book,...I put its
         author with Rabelais, Swift, Shakespeare...."

3019   Weaks, Mabel. "Long Ago and 'Faraway': Traces of
         Melville in the Marquesas in the Journals of
         A. G. Jones, 1854-1855," BNYPL, 52 (July, 1948),
         362-369.

3020   Weaks, Mabel. "Some Ancestral Lines of Herman Melville
         as Traced in Funeral and Memorial Spoons,"
         NYG&BR, 80 (October, 1949), 194-197.

3021   Weathers, Willie T. "MOBY DICK and the Nineteenth-Century
         Scene," TSLL, 1 (Winter, 1960), 477-501.

         Parallels between MOBY DICK and the political
         scene and other events of the time.

3022   Weathers, Winston. "Melville and the Comedy of
         Communications," Etc, 20 (1963), 411-420.

         Melville's TYPEE is a quest for a paradise of
         perfect communication in primitive simplicity. The
         quest is unsuccessful, but Melville continues it in
         OMOO, MOBY DICK, BARTLEBY, and BILLY BUDD, ending
         in tragic despair.

3023   Weaver, Raymond M., ed. BILLY BUDD AND OTHER PROSE
        PIECES. London: Constable and Company, 1924;
        New York: Russell & Russell, 1963.

3024   Weaver, Raymond M. "The Centennial of Herman Melville,"
        New York *Nation*, 109 (August 2, 1919), 145-146.

        "Born in hell-fire, and baptized in an unspeakable
        name, MOBY DICK...reads like a great opium dream. The
        organizing theme of the book is the hunting of Moby-Dick
        ...by the monomaniac Captain Ahab...."

3024.1 Weaver, Raymond M. "The Centennial of Herman Melville,"
        ONE HUNDRED YEARS OF THE NATION: A CENTENNIAL
        ANTHOLOGY. Henry M. Christman and Abraham Feldman,
        eds. New York: Macmillan, 1965, pp. 113-118.

3025   Weaver, Raymond M. "Herman Melville," *Bookman*, 54
        (1921), 318-326.

        Nearly the whole of the first chapter of Weaver's
        HERMAN MELVILLE, MARINER AND MYSTIC. New York: 1921.

3026   Weaver, Raymond M. "Herman Melville," AMERICAN WRITERS
        ON AMERICAN LITERATURE. John Macy, ed. New York:
        1931, pp. 190-206.

3027   Weaver, Raymond M. HERMAN MELVILLE: MARINER AND MYSTIC.
        Introduction by Mark Van Doren. New York: George
        H. Doran Company, 1921; repr., New York: Pageant
        Books, 1961.

        An important work in the Melville Revival of the
        1920's.

3028   Weaver, Raymond M. Introduction, ISRAEL POTTER. New
        York: Boni, 1924.

3029   Weaver, Raymond M., ed. Introduction, MARDI AND A
        VOYAGE THITHER. New York: A. & C. Boni, 1925.

3030   Weaver, Raymond M., ed. Introduction, MOBY DICK.
        New York: A. & C. Boni, 1924, 1925, 1926, 1950.

3031   Weaver, Raymond M., ed. Introduction, REDBURN, HIS
        FIRST VOYAGE. New York: A. & C. Boni, 1924.

3032   Weaver, Raymond M., ed. Introduction, SHORTER NOVELS OF
        HERMAN MELVILLE. New York: Liveright Pub. Corp.,
        1928, 1956; New York: Grosset and Dunlap, 1957;
        Greenwich, Conn.: Fawcett Publication, 1960.

3033   Weaver, Raymond M., ed. Introduction, TYPEE. Illustrated
       by Miguel Covarrabias. New York: The Limited
       Editions Club, 1935; repr., New York: Heritage
       Press, 1963.

3034   Weaver, Raymond M., ed. JOURNAL UP THE STRAITS,
       OCTOBER 11, 1856-MAY 5, 1857. New York: The
       Colophon, 1935.

3035   Weaver, Raymond M. "Journal of Melville's Voyage in
       the Clipper Ship Meteor," NEQ, 2 (1929), 120-139.

3035.1 Webb, Walter Prescott. HISTORY AS HIGH ADVENTURE.
       Edited with Introduction by E. C. Barksdale.
       Austin: Publication of the Jenkins Garrett
       Foundation by The Pemberton Press, 1969, pp.
       187-188.

       Melville's description in MARDI quoted at length
       wherein Melville speaks of the fact that "the old powers
       had filled up with population and had overflowed their
       borders...."

3035.2 Weber, Alfred. Introduction, BILLY BUDD, FORETOPMAN
       by Herman Melville. Karlsruhe: G. Braun, 1961.

3036   Weber, L. Sherwood, et al. FROM HOMER TO JOYCE: A
       STUDY GUIDE TO THIRTY-SIX GREAT NOVELS. New York:
       Holt, 1959, pp. 210-217.

       MOBY DICK.

3037   Weber, Walter. HERMAN MELVILLE: EINE STILISTISCHE
       UNTERSUCHUNG. Basel: Philographischer Verlag,
       1937.

3038   Weber, Walter. "Some Characteristic Symbols in Herman
       Melville's Works," RES, 1 (1949), 217-224.

3039   Weeks, Donald. "Two Uses of MOBY DICK," AQ, 2 (Summer,
       1950), 165-176.

3040   Wegelin, Oscar. "Herman Melville As I Recall Him,"
       Colophon, n. s., 1 (Summer, 1935), 21-24.

       Account of the sale of Melville's library.

3041   Weidman, Jerome. "MOBY-DICK: An Appreciation,"
       Holiday, 19 (February, 1956), 50-51, 80, 82, 84,
       87-89.

3042   Weir, Charles, Jr. "Malice Reconciled: A Note on
        Herman Melville's BILLY BUDD," UTQ, 13 (April,
        1944), 276-285.

        In BILLY BUDD, Melville's "symbolic art reaches
        its highest peak," for here he reconciles evil with
        universal justice.

3043   Weisert, John J. "Thomas Edgerton Browne and John Ross
        Browne in Kentucky," FCHQ, 36 (1962), 329-339.

        John Ross Browne (c.1821-1875), whose Etchings
        of a Whaling Cruise in 1846 anticipated Melville's work.

3044   Weisinger, Herbert, and Adrian J. Jaffe, eds. THE
        LAUREATE FRATERNITY: AN INTRODUCTION TO LITERATURE.
        Evanston: Row, Peterson, 1960, pp. 142-143.

        BILLY BUDD.

3045   Weissbuch, Ted N. "A Note on the Confidence-Man's
        Counterfeit Detector," ESQ, 19 (2nd Qt., 1960),
        16-18.

3046   Weissbuch, Ted N., and Bruce Stillians. "Ishmael the
        Ironist: The Anti-Salvation Theme in MOBY DICK,"
        ESQ, 31 (2nd Qt., 1963), 71-75.

3047   Wellek, Rene, and Austin Warren. THEORY OF LITERATURE.
        New York: Harcourt, Brace & World, Inc., 1942,
        1947, 1949, 1956, passim.

3047.1 Welles, Orson. MOBY DICK, Adapted by Orson Welles.
        London: 1956.

3048   Wells, Henry W. "A Religious Quest," THE AMERICAN WAY
        OF POETRY. New York: Columbia University Press,
        1943, pp. 78-88.

        CLAREL expresses American transcendental idealism
        under which Melville "chafed severely but from which he
        never escaped, so firmly had the harpoon of mysticism
        pierced his breast...."

3049   Wells, Henry W. "Herman Melville's CLAREL," CE, 4
        (1943), 478-483.

3050   Wells, Henry W. "An Unobtrusive Democrat, Herman
            Melville," SAQ, 43 (January, 1944), 46-51.

           The "social-mindedness" in his novels reveals that
in Melville the common man found a humanitarian spokes-
man.

3051   Wells, W. H. "MOBY DICK and Rabelais," MLN, 38 (1923),
            123.

           Rabelais's parallels for "whiteness" of the whale.

           Cf., Patrick H. Quinn, "Poe's 'Imaginary Voyage,'"
HudR, 4 (1952), 562-585.

3052   Welsh, Alexander. "A Melville Debt to Carlyle," MLN,
            73 (November, 1958), 489-491.

           The "silly sheep" passage in Chapter 69 of
MOBY DICK.

3052.1   Wendell, Barrett. A LITERARY HISTORY OF AMERICA.
            New York: Charles Scribner's Sons, 3rd ed., 1901,
            p. 229.

3053   Werge, Thomas. "MOBY-DICK and the Calvinist Tradition,"
            SNNTS, 1 (Winter, 1969), 484-506.

           In MOBY DICK, the epistemological emphasis and
even the book's total coherence "are inseparable from
the preoccupations, language and dialectic of the
Calvinist tradition" to which it "consistently refers
and on which it consciously depends."

3054   Werge, Thomas. "MOBY-DICK: Scriptural Source of
            'Blackness and Darkness,'" AN&Q, 9 (1970), 6.

3055   Werge, Thomas. "The Persistence of Adam: Puritan
            Concerns and Conflicts in Melville and Mark Twain,"
            DA, 28 (Cornell: 1968), 3653A-54A.

           MOBY DICK is central in location of the influence
in Melville of the Augustinian or Puritan conception of
original sin as a corruption of nature.

3055.1   West, Ray B., Jr. "The American Short Story at Mid-Century,"
            THE SHORT STORY IN AMERICA. Los Angeles, Chicago,
            New York: Gateway Editions, Inc., 1952, pp. 1-25.

3056   West, Ray B., Jr. "Primitivism in Melville," PrS, 30
            (Winter, 1956), 369-385.

3057   West, Ray B., Jr. "The Unity of BILLY BUDD," HudR,
         5 (Spring, 1952), 120-127.

         "...BILLY BUDD as a unified work not only is not
         marred by digressions and irrelevancies, it is a
         triumph of architectonic structure...."

3057.1   West, Ray B., Jr. THE WRITER IN THE ROOM: SELECTED
         ESSAYS. Michigan State University Press, 1969.

3057.2   Westbrook, Max. "Stephen Crane and the Personal
         Universal," MFS, 8 (1963), 351-360.

         The heroes in Crane, Melville and others are
         "united by the common theme of the personal universal,
         a theme which suggests that the worlds they inhabit
         are not strictly naturalistic."

3058   Wheeler, Otis. "Humor in MOBY DICK: Two Problems,"
         AL, 29 (May, 1957), 203-206.

         The comic role passes from Ishmael and Queequeg as
         their humor gives way to more sublime themes. Though
         this splits MOBY DICK structurally, it enhances its
         tragic grandeur.

3059   Whipple, A. B. C. "The Whaleman Novelist," YANKEE
         WHALERS IN THE SOUTH SEAS. Garden City, New York:
         Doubleday & Co., 1954, pp. 40-54.

         Two chapters deal with Melville.

3060   White, Edgar Walter. "BILLY BUDD," Adelphi, 28
         (1st Qt., 1952), 492-498.

         A favorable comparison of Benjamin Britten's
         opera with Melville's novel.

3061   White, Morton Gabriel, and Lucia White. "Bad Dreams
         of the City: Melville, Hawthorne, and Poe,"
         THE INTELLECTUAL VERSUS THE CITY: FROM THOMAS
         JEFFERSON TO FRANK L. WRIGHT. Cambridge:
         Harvard University Press, 1962, pp. 36-53.

3061.1   White, Morton Gabriel, and Lucia White. "The Intellectual
         versus the City," PATHS OF AMERICAN THOUGHT. Arthur
         M. Schlesinger, Jr., and Morton White, eds. London:
         Chatto & Windus, 1964, p. 257.

3062   White, Viola C. SYMBOLISM IN THE WRITINGS OF HERMAN
         MELVILLE. Diss. North Carolina: 1934.

3063   WHITE WHALE AND WOEFUL SEA. *Life*, 40 (June 25, 1956),
       50-53.

       Photos and brief text about the John Huston film.

3064   White, William. "Herman Melville: A New Source?"
       N&Q, 180 (June 7, 1941), 403.

       Melville may have used Dr. Louis A. Baker's
       HARRY MARTINGALE: OR, ADVENTURES OF A WHALEMAN IN
       THE PACIFIC. (Boston, 1848).

3065   White, William. "One Man's Meat: Societies and
       Journals Devoted to a Single Author," AmBC, 8
       (1957), 22-24.

       Pertinent bibliography as to journals and news-
       letters devoted to Melville and others.

3066   Widmer, Kingsley. "BARTLEBY," THE LITERARY REBEL.
       Preface by Harry T. Moore. Carbondale and
       Edwardsville: Southern Illinois University Press,
       1965, pp. 48-59.

3067   Widmer, Kingsley. "Melville's Radical Resistance: The
       Method and Meaning of BARTLEBY," SNNTS, 1 (Winter,
       1969), 444-458.

3068   Widmer, Kingsley. "The Negative Affirmation: Melville's
       'Bartleby,'" MFS, 8 (1962), 276-286.

       The attorney stands for a "superficial, benevolent
       nationalism" on which the life of mid-nineteenth century
       American society was based.

3069   Widmer, Kingsley. "The Perplexed Myths of Melville:
       BILLY BUDD," *Novel*, 2 (Fall, 1968), 25-35.

       Vere is "the second-rate made Captain"; Billy and
       Claggart are "stupid goodness versus depraved rationality,
       a cut-down Christ against a hopped-up Satan."

3070   Widmer, Kingsley. "The Perplexity of Melville: BENITO
       CERENO," SSF, 5 (1968), 225-238.

       An "ambivalent view of the good but terribly
       limited representative American."

3071   Widmer, Kingsley. THE WAYS OF NIHILISM: A STUDY OF
        HERMAN MELVILLE'S SHORT NOVELS. A Publication of
        the California State Colleges. Los Angeles:
        Anderson, Ritchie & Simon, 1970.

        "...The nihilistic implications of Melville's
        fables,...deny ameliorist possibilities...."

3071.1 Wigod, Jacob. "The Quest for Eden in American
        Literature," Orient/West, 7 (1962), 71-79.

        Ahab typical of those who leave society to
        confront present reality.

3071.2 Wild, Bernadette. "Malcolm Lowry: A Study of the
        Sea Metaphor in UNDER THE VOLCANO," UWR, 4
        (Fall, 1968), 46-60.

        Lowry's work suggests Melville's MOBY DICK,
        as well as Conrad's LORD JIM and Goethe's FAUST.

3072   Wiley, Elizabeth. "Four Strange Cases," Dickensian,
        58 (May, 1962), 120-125.

        WIELAND and REDBURN as sources of the spontaneous
        combustion in BLEAK HOUSE.

3072.1 Wiley, Lulu R. THE SOURCES AND INFLUENCES OF THE NOVELS
        OF CHARLES BROCKDEN BROWN. New York: Vantage Press,
        1950, pp. 239-243.

3073   Willett, Maurita. "The Letter A, Gules, and the Black
        Bubble," MELVILLE AND HAWTHORNE IN THE BERKSHIRES:
        A SYMPOSIUM. Howard P. Vincent, ed. Kent, Ohio:
        Kent State University Press, 1968, pp. 70-78.

        Comparison of THE SCARLET LETTER and MOBY DICK.

3074   Willett, Maurita. "The Silences of Herman Melville,"
        ATQ, 7 (1970), 85-92.

        The use of Silence in authors Melville is known
        to have read, notably Shakespeare and Carlyle, indicates
        the remarkable range and variety of the idea in Melville's
        own writing.

3075   Willett, Ralph W. "Nelson and Vere: Hero and Victim in
        BILLY BUDD, SAILOR," PMLA, 82 (October, 1967), 370-
        376.

        Melville deliberately contrasted Vere as an
        upholder of existing laws, and Nelson, an heroic maker
        of a new Order for society.

3076   Williams, David Park. "Hook and Ahab: Barrie's
               Strange Satire on Melville," PMLA, 80 (December,
               1965), 484-488.

         Barrie made extensive use of passages from
         Melville in writing PETER AND WENDY and PETER PAN.

3076.1   Williams, Harold, ed. ONE WHALING FAMILY. Boston:
               Houghton Mifflin Co., 1964.

         Journals and papers of members of the Williams
         family. The son's account of his experiences in the
         Pacific and Arctic in the whaleship <u>Florence</u> (1873-1874)
         question the picturesque whaleboat race in Melville's
         MOBY DICK.

3077   Williams, John Brindley. "The Impact of Transcendentalism
               on the Novels of Herman Melville," DA, 26 (So. Calif.:
               1965), 1052-1053.

         Although Melville criticized the Transcendental
         religious faith in a benevolent nature, his writings
         show an interest in Emersonian self-reliance and in
         the "portrayal of symbolic correspondences between
         nature and the mind." In many respects, Melville was
         in agreement with Transcendental ethics.

3078   Williams, Mentor L. "Horace Greeley Reviews OMOO,"
               PQ, 27 (January, 1948), 94-96.

         Greeley's review in the New York <u>Tribune</u>,
         June 8, 1847.

3079   Williams, Mentor L. "Park Benjamin on Melville's
               MARDI," AN&Q, 8 (December, 1949), 132-134.

3080   Williams, Mentor L. "Some Notices and Reviews of
               Melville's Novels in American Religious
               Periodicals, 1846-1847," AL, 22 (May, 1950),
               119-127.

         Reaction to Melville in several popular religious
         journals.

3081   Williams, Mentor L. "Two Hawaiian Americans Visit
               Herman Melville," NEQ, 23 (1950), 97-99.

         "Pilgrimage" students of Titus Munson Coan and
         John Thomas Gulick to Herman Melville at Arrowhead in
         spring of 1859, when he had visibly entered his "long
         quietus."

3081.1   Williams, Stanley T. THE AMERICAN SPIRIT IN LETTERS.
               Vol. XI OF THE PAGEANT OF AMERICA: A PICTORIAL
               HISTORY OF THE UNITED STATES. Ralph Henry
               Gabriel, ed. New Haven: Yale University Press,
               1926.

3081.2 Williams, Stanley T. "Cosmopolitanism in American
Literature before 1880," THE AMERICAN WRITER
AND THE EUROPEAN TRADITION. Margaret Denny and
William H. Gilman, eds. Minneapolis: Minnesota
University Press, 1950, pp. 45-62.

3082 Williams, Stanley T. "'Follow Your Leader': Melville's
BENITO CERENO," VQR, 23 (Winter, 1947), 61-76.

Leading characters follow "inner impulses" of
their natures: Delano, complacent towards the presence
of good or evil; Don Benito, overcome by the presence
of evil, and Babo, the symbol of evil itself. The plan
shows that Melville was not a "formless, prolix writer
incapable of patterns."

3083 Williams, Stanley T. "Melville," EIGHT AMERICAN
AUTHORS: A REVIEW OF RESEARCH AND CRITICISM.
Floyd Stovall, ed. New York: Modern Language
Association of America, 1956, Norton, 1963,
pp. 207-270.

3084 Williams, Stanley T. THE SPANISH BACKGROUND OF AMERICAN
LITERATURE. 2 Vols. New Haven: Yale University
Press, 1955, I, 224-227, 394-396, passim.

3085 Williams, Stanley T. "Spanish Influence on American
Fiction: Melville and Others," NMQ, 22 (Spring,
1952), 5-14.

3086 Williams, Stanley T. "Who Reads an American Book?"
VQR, 28 (1952), 518-531.

3087 Willibald, Jutta. DER EINFLUSZ UND DIE AUFNAHME HERMAN
MELVILLES IN DER DEUTSCHEN UND FRANZÖSISCHEN
LITERATUR. Diss. Freie Universitat, Berlin:
1956.

3088 Willis, Samuel. "Private Allegory and Public Allegory
in Melville," THE CONFIDENCE-MAN: HIS MASQUERADE.
Hershel Parker, ed. New York: W. W. Norton &
Company, 1971, pp. 285-286.

3089 Willson, Lawrence. "Yet Another Note on MOBY DICK,"
DR, 35 (Spring, 1955), 5-15.

MOBY DICK is "in a very real sense" Melville's
PARADISE LOST, his attempt to "justify God's ways to
man."

3090   Wilmer, Herbert. "Aspects of American Fiction: A Whale,
            A Bear, and A Marlin," AMERICANA-AUSTRIACA:
            FESTSCHRIFT DES AMERIKA-INSTITUTS DER UNIVERSITÄT
            INNSBRUCK ANLÄSSLICH SEINES ZEHNJÄHRIGEN BESTEHENS.
            Klaus Lanzinger, ed. (Beiträge zur Amerikakunde,
            Band 1.) Wien, Stuttgart: W. Braumuller Univ.-Verl,
            1966, pp. 229-246.

            The works discussed are MOBY DICK, "The Bear,"
            and THE OLD MAN AND THE SEA.

3090.1   Wilson, Carroll Atwood. THIRTEEN AUTHOR COLLECTIONS OF
            THE NINETEENTH CENTURY AND FIVE CENTURIES OF
            FAMILIAR QUOTATIONS. Jean C. S. Wilson and
            David A. Randall, eds. New York: Scribner's,
            1950, I, 305-316.

3091   Wilson, Edmund. "John Singleton Mosby, 'The Grey Ghost,'"
            NY, 34 (February 14, 1959), 117-136.

            Works by and about Mosby, including Melville's
            poem, "The Scout toward Aldie."

3092   Wilson, Edmund. PATRIOTIC GORE: STUDIES IN THE
            LITERATURE OF THE AMERICAN CIVIL WAR. New York:
            Oxford University Press, 1962, pp. 323-327,
            635-637, passim.

3093   Wilson, Edmund, ed. THE SHOCK OF RECOGNITION. Garden
            City, New York: Doubleday & Company, 1943; Farrar,
            Straus, 1955, passim.

3093.1   Wilson, Edmund. "A Treatise on Tales of Horror,"
            NY, 20 (1944), 67-70, 73-74.

3093.2   Wilson, Edmund. "A Treatise on Tales of Horror,"
            CLASSICS AND COMMERCIALS: A LITERARY CHRONICLE
            OF THE FORTIES. New York: Farrar, Straus, 1950,
            pp. 172-181.

3094   Wilson, G. R., Jr. "BILLY BUDD and Melville's Use of
            Dramatic Technique," SSF, 4 (1967), 105-111.

            The "multiple meaning" of the story would not have
            been possible had Melville "further dramatized any
            important action."

3095   Wilson, Gilbert. "MOBY-DICK and the Atom," BAS, 8
            (August, 1952), 195-197.

3096   Wilson, Harry B. "The Double View: Melville's 'The
        Lightning-Rod Man,'" APPROACHES TO THE SHORT STORY.
        Neil D. Isaacs and Louis H. Leiter, eds.
        San Francisco: Chandler, 1963, pp. 16-23.

3097   Wilson, J. S. "Henry James and Herman Melville,"
        VQR, 21 (1945), 281-286.

3098   Wimsatt, William K., Jr., and Cleanth Brooks. LITERARY
        CRITICISM: A SHORT HISTORY. New York: Alfred A.
        Knopf, 1957, pp. 587-588, 679-680, passim.

3099   Winans, Edward R., and James Paris. HERMAN MELVILLE'S
        BILLY BUDD. New York: Monarch Press, Inc., 1965.
        Thor Publications.

        An excellent aid for teaching or research:
        summary of story, character analyses, critical commen-
        taries, essay questions, glossary of nautical terms,
        notes on the style of BILLY BUDD, and bibliography and
        guide to research.

3100   Winterich, John T. "Mystic Adventurer: Herman Melville,"
        WRITERS IN AMERICA: 1842-1967. With Illustrations
        by Fritz Kredel. An Informal Glance at Some of
        the Authors Who Have Flourished Since the Establish-
        ment of the Davey Company One Hundred and Twenty-five
        Years Ago. Jersey City, New Jersey: The Davey
        Company, 1968, pp. 47-50.

3101   Winterich, John T. "Romantic Stories of Books, Second
        Series, IV: MOBY-DICK," PubW, 116 (1929), 2391-
        2394.

3102   Winters, Yvor. "Herman Melville and the Problems of
        Moral Navigation," IN DEFENSE OF REASON. Denver:
        Alan Swallow, 1947, pp. 200-233.

3102.1 Winters, Yvor. "Herman Melville and the Problems of
        Moral Navigation," MAULE'S CURSE: SEVEN STUDIES
        IN THE HISTORY OF AMERICAN OBSCURANTISM. Norfolk:
        New Directions, 1938, pp. 53-89.

        The works of Melville support the thesis that
        refined alienation from reality is an important step
        in the direction of obscurantism.

3102.2 Wish, Harvey. SOCIETY AND THOUGHT IN EARLY AMERICA:
        A SOCIAL AND INTELLECTUAL HISTORY OF THE AMERICAN
        PEOPLE THROUGH 1865. New York, London, Toronto:
        Longmans, Green & Co., 1950, pp. 451, 464.

        Melville had to await the twentieth century for
        a "full sympathic hearing." His novels seemed "too
        pessimistic for the optimistic 1850's...."

3103   Witherington, Paul. "The Art of Melville's TYPEE,"
        ArQ, 26 (1970), 136-150.

        TYPEE, though experimental, is an artistic novel,
        revealing the origin of some of Melville's artistic
        dilemmas of idea and form. In TYPEE Melville tried out
        narrative rhythm, symbolism, narrative focus, and setting;
        and the careful balance of ambiguity, begun in TYPEE,
        became his trademark.

3104   Withim, Phil. "BILLY BUDD: Testament of Resistance,"
        MLQ, 20 (June, 1959), 115-127.

        Melville dedicated BILLY BUDD to Jack Chase who
        fought for human rights. If revolution succeeds, man
        can be free from hereditary tyranny, but if it fails,
        man becomes a Billy Budd suffering tyranny's abuses
        because, innocent and trusting, he has failed to resist.
        Cf., E. L. Grant Watson, "Melville's Testament of
        Acceptance," NEQ, 6 (1933), 319-327.

3104.1 "Without the Whale," NStm, 55 (April 19, 1958), 504-505.

3105   Witte, W. "The Sociological Approach to Literature,"
        MLR, 36 (1941), 86-94.

3106   Wolfe, Don M. THE IMAGE OF MAN IN AMERICA. New York:
        Thomas Y. Crowell Company, 2nd edition, 1970,
        pp. 357, passim.

        Comparison of Hemingway and Melville.

3106.1 Wolfe, Thomas. THE LETTERS OF THOMAS WOLFE. Elizabeth
        Nowell, ed. New York: Charles Scribner's Sons,
        1956, p. 254.

        "As to MOBY DICK, I read that magnificent work for
        the first time about six months ago in America in order
        to understand something about this man Melville that I
        had been imitating...."

3107   Wolfrum, Max D. "Responsible Failure in Melville,"
        DAI, 31 (Wash U.: 1970), 1821A.

3108   Wolpert, Bernard M. "The Melville Revival: A Study of
        Twentieth Century Criticism through Its Treatment
        of Herman Melville," DA, 18 (Ohio State: 1958),
        1800-1802.

3109   Woodberry, George E. NATHANIEL HAWTHORNE. Boston and
        New York: Houghton Mifflin Company. The Riverside
        Press, 1902, pp. 207, 221, 256.

        Julian Hawthorne's description of Melville's visits.

3110   Woodress, James. DISSERTATIONS IN AMERICAN LITERATURE,
       1891-1955. With Supplement 1956-1961. Durham,
       North Carolina: Duke University Press, 1962,
       pp. 31-33.

3111   Woodress, James. DISSERTATIONS IN AMERICAN LITERATURE,
       1891-1966. Newly revised and enlarged with the
       assistance of Marian Koritz. Durham, North
       Carolina: Duke University Press, 1968.

3112   Woodruff, Stuart C. "Melville and His Chimney,"
       PMLA, 75 (June, 1960), 283-292.

3113   Woodruff, Stuart C. "Stubb's Supper," ESQ, 43
       (2nd Qt., 1966), 46-48.

       Melville's "horrible vultureism of earth" is
       illustrated in the activity of the sharks around Stubb's
       captured whale and in the behavior of mankind, but "moral
       cannibalism," hinted at in Fleece's sermon to the sharks,
       is particularly evident in Stubb's mistreatment of Fleece.

3114   Woodson, Thomas. "Ahab's Greatness: Prometheus as
       Narcissus," ELH, 33 (September, 1966), 351-369.

       Ahab is a Prometheus whose fire consumes him.
       He is also a Narcissus, who, "because he could not
       grasp the tormenting, mild image he saw in the
       fountain, plunged into it, and was drowned."

3115   Woodson, Thomas. "Thoreau on Poverty and Magnanimity,"
       PMLA, 85 (January, 1970), 21-34.

       Comparison of Billy with Thoreau's John Brown.

3116   Woodward, C. Vann. "A Southern Critique for the Gilded
       Age," THE BURDEN OF SOUTHERN HISTORY. Baton Rouge:
       Louisiana State University Press, 1960, pp. 109-140.

3117   Woolf, Leonard. "Herman Melville," N&A, 33 (1923), 688.

       Symbolism in MARDI and MOBY DICK.

3118   Wright, Lyle H. "Herman Melville," AMERICAN FICTION:
       1774-1850: A CONTRIBUTION TOWARD A BIBLIOGRAPHY.
       Rev. ed. San Marino, Calif.: Huntington Library,
       1948, pp. 197-198.

3119   Wright, Lyle H. "Herman Melville," AMERICAN FICTION:
       1851-1875: A CONTRIBUTION TOWARD A BIBLIOGRAPHY.
       San Marino, Calif.: Huntington Library, 1957,
       pp. 228-229.

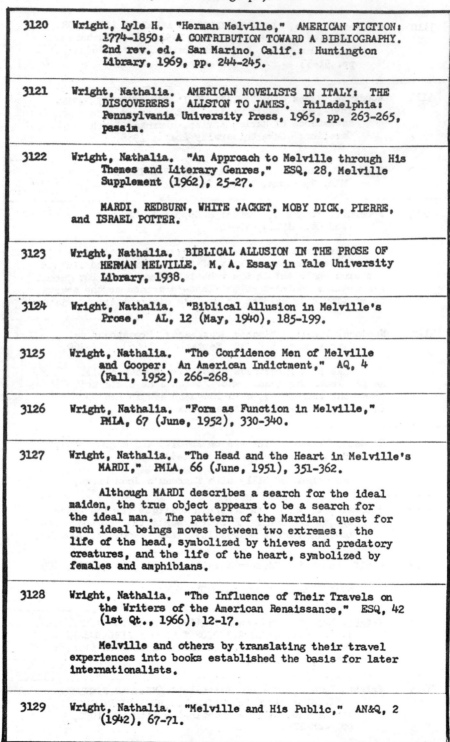

3120   Wright, Lyle H. "Herman Melville," AMERICAN FICTION:
        1774-1850: A CONTRIBUTION TOWARD A BIBLIOGRAPHY.
        2nd rev. ed. San Marino, Calif.: Huntington
        Library, 1969, pp. 244-245.

3121   Wright, Nathalia. AMERICAN NOVELISTS IN ITALY: THE
        DISCOVERERS: ALLSTON TO JAMES. Philadelphia:
        Pennsylvania University Press, 1965, pp. 263-265,
        passim.

3122   Wright, Nathalia. "An Approach to Melville through His
        Themes and Literary Genres," ESQ, 28, Melville
        Supplement (1962), 25-27.

        MARDI, REDBURN, WHITE JACKET, MOBY DICK, PIERRE,
        and ISRAEL POTTER.

3123   Wright, Nathalia. BIBLICAL ALLUSION IN THE PROSE OF
        HERMAN MELVILLE. M. A. Essay in Yale University
        Library, 1938.

3124   Wright, Nathalia. "Biblical Allusion in Melville's
        Prose," AL, 12 (May, 1940), 185-199.

3125   Wright, Nathalia. "The Confidence Men of Melville
        and Cooper: An American Indictment," AQ, 4
        (Fall, 1952), 266-268.

3126   Wright, Nathalia. "Form as Function in Melville,"
        PMLA, 67 (June, 1952), 330-340.

3127   Wright, Nathalia. "The Head and the Heart in Melville's
        MARDI," PMLA, 66 (June, 1951), 351-362.

        Although MARDI describes a search for the ideal
        maiden, the true object appears to be a search for
        the ideal man. The pattern of the Mardian quest for
        such ideal beings moves between two extremes: the
        life of the head, symbolized by thieves and predatory
        creatures, and the life of the heart, symbolized by
        females and amphibians.

3128   Wright, Nathalia. "The Influence of Their Travels on
        the Writers of the American Renaissance," ESQ, 42
        (1st Qt., 1966), 12-17.

        Melville and others by translating their travel
        experiences into books established the basis for later
        internationalists.

3129   Wright, Nathalia. "Melville and His Public," AN&Q, 2
        (1942), 67-71.

3130   Wright, Nathalia. "Melville and 'Old Burton,' with
         BARTLEBY as an Anatomy of Melancholy," TSL, 15
         (1970), 1-13.

         Robert Burton's THE ANATOMY OF MELANCHOLY exerted
a stylistic and thematic influence on Melville. In
BARTLEBY, Melville depicted three main types, many of
the symptoms, and most of the major causes of melancholy
according to Burton.

3131   Wright, Nathalia. MELVILLE'S USE OF THE BIBLE. Diss.
         Yale, 1949.

3132   Wright, Nathalia. MELVILLE'S USE OF THE BIBLE. Durham,
         North Carolina: Duke University Press, 1949; New
         York: New edition, incl., "Appendix: MOBY DICK:
         Jonah's or Job's Whale," Octagon Books, 1969,
         pp. 189-194.

         The Bible and Apocrypha as Melville's sources for
symbols, language, and ideas.

3133   Wright, Nathalia. "MOBY DICK: Jonah's or Job's Whale?"
         AL, 37 (May, 1965), 190-195.

3134   Wright, Nathalia. "MOSSES FROM AN OLD MANSE and MOBY
         DICK: The Shock of Discovery," MLN, 67 (June, 1952),
         387-392.

         Hawthorne as an influence on Melville's use of
fire imagery in MOBY DICK.

3135   Wright, Nathalia. "A Note on Melville's Use of Spenser:
         Hautia and the Bower of Bliss," AL, 24 (March,
         1952), 83-85.

         Parallels between the last episode of MARDI and
THE FAERIE QUEENE, Book II, Canto xii.

3136   Wright, Nathalia. "PIERRE: Herman Melville's INFERNO,"
         AL, 32 (May, 1960), 167-181.

3137   Wright, Nathalia. "A Source for Melville's CLAREL:
         Dean Stanley's SINAI AND PALESTINE," MLN, 62
         (February, 1947), 110-116.

         Melville found in SINAI AND PALESTINE "confirmation
of his own observations of the scene and support for his
own spiritual longings," and also "a rationalization of
the discrepancy between reality and the ideal which he,
too, tried to make."

3137.1 Wyllie, J. C. "Harper Records," UVBSSN, 37 (September, 1957).

      Publisher's records of books by Melville and others.

3137.2 Wyrick, Green D., ed. THE AMERICAN NOVEL: TWO STUDIES. Emporia: Graduate Division of the Kansas State Teachers College, 1965.

      See Saada Ishag, "Herman Melville as an Existentialist: An Analysis of TYPEE, MARDI, MOBY DICK, and THE CONFIDENCE MAN," ESRS, 14, ii (December, 1965), 5-41, 60-62.

3138 Yaggy, Elinor. PIERRE: KEY TO THE MELVILLE ENIGMA. Diss. Washington U.: 1946.

3139 Yaggy, Elinor. "Shakespeare and Melville's PIERRE," BPLQ, 6 (January, 1954), 43-51.

      For PIERRE Melville borrowed more from Romeo and Juliet than from Hamlet.

3140 Yamaya, Saburo. "The Inner Struggle in Melville's PIERRE," JH, 3 (1958), 101-120.

3141 Yamaya, Saburo. "Melville's 'Inland Voyage to Fairyland,'" ESSAYS IN ENGLISH AND AMERICAN LITERATURE: IN COMMEMORATION OF PROFESSOR TAKEJIRO NAKAYAMA'S SIXTY-FIRST BIRTHDAY. Tokyo: Shohakusha, 1961, XIV, 185-285.

3142 Yamaya, Saburo. "A New Interpretation of Melville's MOBY-DICK," SEL, (1961), 59-81.

3143 Yamaya, Saburo. "Poe, Hawthorne, and Melville's BENITO CERENO," SELit, 4 (March, 1961), 21-32.

3144 Yamaya, Saburo. "The Stone Image of Melville's PIERRE," SELit, 34 (Spring, 1957), 31-57.

3145 Yankowitz, Susan. "Lowell's BENITO CERENO: An Investigation of American Innocence," YT, 2 (1968), 81-90.

      A contrast of the psychological and philosophical elements of Melville's narration with the overt sociological and political content of Lowell's dramatization.

3146 Yates, Norris. "An Instance of Parallel Imagery in Hawthorne, Melville, and Frost," PQ, 36 (April, 1957), 276-280.

Image of the woodpile in all three authors.

ISRAEL POTTER.

3147 Yates, Norris. "A Traveller's Comments on Melville's TYPEE," MLN, 69 (December, 1954), 581-583.

An account by E. K. Drayton, doctor of the U. S. S. St. Mary's, published in the New York Spirit of the Times (May 24, 1856), of a visit to Nukuhiva in 1855, with remarks on the "romance" of TYPEE versus the reality of Polynesian life.

3148 Yeager, Henry J. "Melville's Literary Debut in France," MQ, 11 (Summer, 1970), 413-425.

In the first years of the decade 1846 to 1856, France welcomed the new and the foreign. French dissatisfaction with its own government aroused interest in America, its people and its political system. For such reasons, Melville was reviewed by eminent critics such as Philarète Chasles. In the closing years of the decade, Melville's popularity declined.

3149 Yellin, Jean Fagan. "Black Masks: Melville's BENITO CERENO," AQ, 22 (Fall, 1970), 678-689.

The moral theme of the story emerges from Melville's use of three Negro stereotypes: the stock plantation view of the black as inferior; the standard abolitionist view of him as victim; and the commonplace view of him as an exotic primitive. After lifting the black masks, Melville suggests that the true Negro has no voice in America, just as he has no recognized face.

3150 Yoder, B. A. "Poetry and Science: 'Two Distinct Branches of Knowledge' in BILLY BUDD," SoRA, 3 (1969), 223-239.

Older criticism of the story shows it either as a final acceptance of the Christian way of life or as an ironic indictment of that way. Newer interpretation is that Melville is treating an unsolvable moral dilemma. This interpretation goes back to the Christian interpretation with modifications.

3151   Young, James Dean. "The Nine Gams of the Pequod,"
        AL, 25 (January, 1954), 449-463.

            Used as a frame of reference, these nine
    meetings at sea enable the reader to gain new
    insights into the structure and significance of
    the narration.

3152   Young, Philip. THREE BAGS FULL: ESSAYS IN AMERICAN
        FICTION. New York: Harcourt Brace, 1972.

            Discussion of various characters of American
    fiction, including Melville's Tommo.

3153   Yu, Beongcheon. "Ishmael's Equal Eye: The Source of
        Balance in MOBY DICK," ELH, 32 (March, 1965),
        110-125.

            The anguished Melville of 1856, incapable of
    either belief or disbelief, is no longer the Melville
    who created Ishmael, but the Melville who has somehow
    lost Ishmael's "equal eye."

3153.1 Zabel, Morton D., ed. LITERARY OPINION IN AMERICA:
        ESSAYS ILLUSTRATING THE STATUS, METHODS, AND
        PROBLEMS OF CRITICISM IN THE UNITED STATES IN
        THE TWENTIETH CENTURY. 3rd ed. rev. New York:
        Harper, 1962. Torchbooks.

3154   Zanetti, Emilia. "Berg, il Mahogonny, e il Billy Budd
        tratto da Melville," FLe, 30 (September 18, 1949,
        4.

3155   Zelocchi, Rosanna. "Herman Melville, Poeta della guerra
        e della Natura," FLe, 16 (May 21, 1961), 5.

3156   Zenkevich, B. A. Posleslovie /Afterword7, Melville,
        Mobi Dik ili Belyi Kit /MOBY-DICK, or The White
        Whale7. Moscow: 1961; 2nd ed., Moscow: 1962,
        pp. 834-839.

3157   Ziegler, Arthur. "MOBY DICK," in FROM HOMER TO JOYCE:
        A STUDY GUIDE TO THIRTY-SIX GREAT BOOKS.
        J. Sherwood Weber, ed. New York: Holt, 1959,
        pp. 210-217.

            Bibliography and list of editions.

3158 Zimmerman, Michael. "Herman Melville in the 1920's:
       An Annotated Bibliography," BB, 24 (1964-65),
       Part I, 117-120; Part II, 139-144.

       Melville criticism in periodicals in the 1920's,
       with a section on book references, chapters, anthologies,
       and histories of American literature in the 1920's, as
       well as a section on various reprints of Melville's
       work in the 1920's.

3159 Zimmerman, Michael. "Herman Melville in the 1920's:
       A Study in the Origins of the Melville Revival,
       with an Annotated Bibliography," DA, 25 (Columbia:
       1964), 1224.

       Description of and reasons for the revival of
       interest in Melville in the 1920's. It was the
       Melville rebel, the philosopher, and the psychologist
       who particularly attracted readers at that time.

3160 Zink, David D. "Bartleby and the Contemporary Search
       for Meaning," ForumH, 8 (Summer, 1970), 46-50.

       Bartleby's failure to find in his work a meaningful
       reason for existence connects Melville's story with
       modern existential philosophy. If Bartleby's case
       seemed singular in Melville's time, but would today
       be recognized as a problem in American culture, that
       fact serves to illustrate Melville's modernity.

3161 Zink, Karl E. "Herman Melville and the Forms—Irony
       and Social Criticisms in BILLY BUDD," Accent, 12
       (Summer, 1952), 131-139.

3162 Zirker, Priscilla Allen. "Evidence of the Slavery
       Dilemma in WHITE-JACKET," AQ, 18 (Fall, 1966),
       477-492.

       "Though the spirit of egalitarianism infuses
       Melville's WHITE JACKET, even this social document
       of the year 1849 was affected by an ideology which
       implicitly and in practice denied egalitarianism—
       specifically as applied to the Negro."

3163 Zirker, Priscilla Allen. "The Major and Minor Themes
       of Melville's WHITE-JACKET," DA, 27 (Cornell:
       1966), 1799A-1800A.

       The major theme is egalitarianism; the minor
       theme is hatred of war, seen against the slavery
       question in 1849. "The minor theme, disassociated
       from assumptions of man's perfectibility, partially
       undercuts the ebullient major theme and captures the
       conclusion of the narrative."

3164   Zolla, Elémire. "Il linguaggio di PIERRE," SA, 3
         (1957), 63-97.

3165   Zolla, Elémire. "Melville dinanzi al Risorgimento ed
         alla Guerra di Secessione," ITALIA E STATI
         UNITI NELL'ETA' DEL RISORGIMENTO E DELLA GUERRA
         CIVILE: ATTI DEL II SYMPOSIUM DI STUDI AMERICANI.
         Firenze, 27-29 Maggio 1966. Firenze: "La Nuova
         Italia," 1969, pp. 7-18.

3166   Zolla, Elémire. "Melville e l'Abbandono dello Zodiaco,"
         Par, 11 (August, 1960), 3-41.

         MOBY DICK.

3166.1   Zolla, Elémire. "Melville y el abandono del zodíaco,"
         PSA, 26 (1962), 13-45, 121-153.

3167   Zolla, Elémire. "La struttura e le fonti di CLAREL,"
         SA, 10 (1964), 101-134.

Subject Index

Subject Index

Absolute and Absolutism: 675, 838, 2748, 2991

Absurd and Absurdity: 1031, 1114, 1168, 1313, 2626, 2692, 3071

The "Acceptance" Thesis   See BILLY BUDD

Achilles, Shield of: 942

Acushnet (ship) (See Dolly): 50, 113, 566, 649, 900, 972, 1136,
     1185, 2124, 2210, 2403, 2700, 2793, 2966, 3027

Adam: 131, 212, 512, 1004, 1279, 1534, 1660, 2249, 2363, 2408,
       2586.1, 2615, 2748, 2857, 3055, 3132

Adam, the American Adam: 399, 475, 1534, 1534.1

Adams, Henry: 159, 1257, 1545, 2615, 2764, 2793, 2966

Adams, William Henry Davenport, BURIED CITIES OF CAMPANIA: OR,
           POMPEII AND HERCULANEUM (1868): 1257, 1545

Addison, Joseph: 1257, 1545, 1688, 2764

Adler, George J.: 1257, 1545, 2397, 2793

Aeschylus: 2615, 2966

Affirmation - See Faith

Afghanistan, Battle in: 1311

Agassiz, Louis: 211, 2793

Agatha Letter: 113, 217, 777, 925, 1134, 1174, 1185, 1257, 1461,
       1527, 2195, 2621, 2772, 3007, 3132

Ahab: 50, 113, 122, 126, 127, 129, 134, 159, 168, 178, 217, 228,
233, 279, 279.1, 291, 303, 310, 313, 334, 352, 359, 410, 430,
458, 507, 512, 525, 534, 537, 540, 558, 575, 578, 586, 607,
624, 629, 630, 637, 649, 689, 693, 701, 746, 764, 768, 793,
810, 829, 864, 885, 887, 909, 910, 911, 935, 958, 970, 985,
1027, 1031, 1036, 1058, 1070, 1089, 1112, 1158, 1160, 1170,
1174, 1182, 1185, 1215, 1218, 1230, 1235, 1258, 1278, 1289,
1308, 1324, 1327, 1347, 1360, 1379, 1383, 1383.1, 1383.2,
1388, 1395, 1431, 1457, 1476, 1481, 1500, 1501, 1525, 1550,
1631, 1640, 1645, 1657, 1658, 1660, 1683, 1683.1, 1694, 2140,
2178, 2187, 2202, 2203, 2210, 2216, 2225, 2236, 2249, 2254,

2270.1, 2283, 2326, 2329, 2334, 2334.1, 2337, 2350, 2358,
2358.1, 2364, 2380, 2385, 2398, 2403, 2408, 2427, 2439, 2478,
2484, 2501, 2552, 2568, 2578, 2609, 2617, 2629, 2631, 2632,
2645, 2673, 2700, 2711, 2723, 2748, 2751, 2752, 2786, 2793,
2816, 2833, 2857.1, 2872, 2946, 2962, 2966, 2970, 2985.2,
2986, 3011, 3016, 3017, 3021, 3027, 3039, 3076, 3102, 3102.1,
3114, 3124, 3132, 3133, 3153

Ahab, King, Biblical Character: 3124, 3132

Aiken, Conrad: 24, 25, 2350

Ainsworth, William Harrison: 1174, 1545

Akenside, Mark. PLEASURES OF THE IMAGINATION (1744): 2857

Albany, New York: 1185, 1474, 2472.1, 2793

Albany Academy: 1185, 2793, 3027

Albino (See Whale): 2712

Alcott, Bronson: 26, 1545, 2210, 3027

Aleema (MARDI): 113, 649, 2748, 3132

Alienation in American Literature: 568, 811, 909, 910

Allegory: 134, 150, 212, 216, 278, 286, 322, 359, 449, 477, 507, 573, 575, 666, 829, 864, 945, 988, 989, 1039, 1235, 1236, 1348, 1518, 2427, 2615, 2772, 2857, 2895, 2946, 2987, 3071, 3088

Allen, Ethan (ISRAEL POTTER): 512, 1185, 1257, 1501, 1601, 2411, 2793, 2857

Allston, Washington: 415

Allusion(s): 1555, 1577

Alma (MARDI): 649, 887, 2210, 2463, 2615, 2793, 3132

Ambergris: 50, 649, 932

Ambiguity: 163, 199, 418, 471, 484, 517, 633, 638, 698, 1390, 1502, 1575, 1622, 1671, 2120, 2210, 2400, 2452, 2460.1, 2502, 2629, 2702, 2976, 2995, 3149

Ambition, Melville's Secret Ambition: 2210

American Adam (See Adam, American)

American Books Published in Great Britain before 1848: 41, 684

American Character: 2326, 2379, 2921

American Civilization: 621, 1406, 2326, 2353

American Culture (Also see Culture): 50, 292, 293, 294, 323, 418, 519, 546, 865, 2209, 2209.1, 2381, 2534.1, 2798.1, 2920

American Democracy (See also Democracy): 927, 1477, 2224, 2339, 2672, 2672.1

The American Dream: 33, 478, 818, 972, 1406, 1618, 1630, 2329.1, 2672, 2672.1

American Epic (See also Epic, Democratic; and Epic Tradition): 1596

The American Experience: 2445, 2934

American First Editions (See Richard Curle)

American Humor (See Humor): 2527

American Idealism (See Idealism): 2798

American Imagination (See Imagination): 2402.1

American Innocence (See also Innocence): 600, 789, 794, 3145

American Life (See Culture): 323, 2398, 2399, 2401, 2403, 2698

American Literary Tradition: 2676, 2694, 2694.1, 2698, 2699, 2699.1

American Myth (See also Myth): 2673

American National Sin: 1362.1, 1363, 1364, 1365, 2666

American Novel: 590, 1298, 2729.2, 2936, 3137.2

American Public and Popular Fiction: 2388.1

American Radicals of the Nineteenth Century: 2784

American Renaissance: 7, 15, 18, 542, 1046, 2539, 2699.1, 3128

American - The Representative American: 3070

American Romanticism (See also Romanticism): 17, 320, 419, 1027, 1036, 1549.1, 1634, 2246, 2565.1, 3017

American Short Story: 931, 2394, 3055.1

American Society in Nineteenth Century: 2210, 2350, 2352, 2353

American Studies (See also Literary History): 1655.2

American Tradition: 326, 1211, 1262, 1649, 2667.1

American Utopia (See American Dream)

The American Writer: 2353, 2377, 2383, 2668

American Writer and the European Tradition: 1001, 1247, 2668, 3081.2

Americanisms: 39, 148, 2615

Ames, Nathaniel, A MARINER'S SKETCHES (Providence, 1831): 43, 50, 972, 1257, 2408, 2793, 2965, 2966, 2989

Anarchy: 1268

Anatomy, a form of prose fiction: 914, 2583

Anglicanism: 298

Animal Imagery: 573, 1422

Animism: 159

Ann Alexander (a whaleship sunk by a whale): 1545, 2966

Anthropomorphism: 159

Anti-Hero (See Hero): 2626

"Anti-novel": 2626

Anti-Salvation Theme: 3046

Anti-Transcendentalism (See Transcendentalism): 1221

"Apathy and Enthusiasm": 113

Apocalypse, Melville's interest in: 3132

Apocalyptic Temper: 35

Appearance: 697 (See Reality and Illusion)

"The Apple-Tree Table": 113, 217, 493, 644, 713.1, 800.1, 817,
841, 1185, 1215, 1257, 1370, 1501, 1520, 1545, 1620, 2210,
2411, 2510, 2555, 2793

"The Apple-Tree Table," Editions: 493, 1814

The Apollo Myth: 701, 887

April Fools' Day: 701, 887

Aranda, Don Alexandro (BENITO CERENO): 1185

Aranson, Jack (Play: MOBY DICK): 1358.1

Archeology: 159

Archetype(s) and Archetypal Patterns: 159, 2411, 2590

Archipelago, Mardian: 649

Architecture, Melville's symbolic use of: 1554 (See also
Cottage and Temple)

Arcturion (ship - MARDI): 113, 649, 701, 1185, 1545, 2748, 2793,
3132

Aristotle and Aristotelian: 217, 632, 1149, 1257, 2413, 2793, 2966, 3132

Arnold, Matthew: 35.1, 217, 243, 512, 810, 887, 1257, 2229, 2408, 2411, 2450, 2615, 2764, 2793, 2857, 2965, 2966, 3027, 3132, 3150

Arrowhead, Pittsfield: 1174, 1185, 2124, 2172, 2408, 2793, 3027

Art (See also "Craft"): 159, 244, 276, 359, 558, 588, 938, 972, 1072, 1091, 1185, 1193, 1444, 2145, 2210, 2413, 2914, 2962

Art, Melville's: 2237, 2413

Art of Fiction: (See also Craft of Fiction): 700, 2893.2

Art of the Novel: 723

Artist: 588, 677, 1630, 1728, 2269, 2412, 2413

Artist, Melville's Theories of: 159, 172, 185, 415, 430, 499, 512, 516, 641, 662, 677, 808, 972, 1352, 1630, 1730, 2121, 2412, 2413, 2952

The Artist as Devil: 2413

Articles of War: 1315, 2210, 2748

Aster, China: 2323.1, 3132

Astor, John Jacob: 641, 1257

Astronomy: 649, 887

Atavism, Melville's interest in: 159

Atheism: 134, 2748

Atufal: 1185

Aunt Charity (MOBY DICK): 217

Aurelius, Marcus: 27

Australia - and Melville: 1273

Authority: 215, 457, 458, 460, 461, 478, 1051, 1052, 1235, 1268,
    1467, 2160, 3071

Autobiography and Autobiographical: 50, 199, 701, 899, 972,
    1233, 1561

Avatar: 329, 887

Avengers, Three (MARDI): 1501

Avery, Latham B., the original of Mad Jack: 50

Azzageddi, demon of Babbalanja (MARDI): 1501, 2793

Babbalanja (MARDI): 113, 217, 649, 701, 887, 1174, 1185, 1501,
    1700, 2210, 2615, 2748, 2793, 3132

Babo (BENITO CERENO): 217, 701, 887, 1185, 1257, 2245, 2302,
    2435, 2457, 2793, 2972, 3071

Bachelor's Delight (ship): 1185

Bachofen, Johann Jakob: 132

Bacon, Francis: 154.1, 649, 1257, 2615, 3132

Baker, Dr. Louis A. HARRY MARTINGALE: OR, ADVENTURES OF A
        WHALEMAN IN THE PACIFIC (Boston: 1848): 161.1, 3064

Balance (Also see Structure): 1655

Ballads and Songs of the Sea: 468

Balzac, Honoré de: 113, 1257, 1545, 3132

Bannadonna ("The Bell Tower"): 781, 1630, 2951, 2952

Baptism: 2149

Bardianna (MARDI): 113, 1501

Bardianna, authority of Babbalanja: 649

Barrie, Sir James Matthew: 3076

Barrymore, John: 525

Barth, John. THE SOT-WEED FACTOR: 1535

BARTLEBY THE SCRIVENER: 5, 11, 113, 123, 217, 232, 234, 248,
250, 289.1, 389, 412, 512, 565, 567, 640, 641, 643, 651, 658,
671, 698, 713, 735, 748, 779, 803, 804, 810, 813, 815, 838,
841, 887, 908, 909, 930, 965, 965.1, 1052, 1060, 1076, 1077,
1078, 1160, 1174, 1185, 1215, 1227, 1235, 1246, 1255, 1257,
1304, 1317, 1323.1, 1379, 1425, 1434, 1451, 1501, 1514, 1520,
1527, 1535, 1545, 1591.1, 1644, 1658, 1677, 1725, 1726, 2169,
2174, 2184, 2187, 2201, 2202, 2204, 2210, 2215, 2230, 2252,
2273, 2280, 2281, 2310, 2331, 2366, 2394, 2402, 2411, 2413,
2446, 2451, 2468, 2495.1, 2521, 2531.2, 2572, 2607, 2615, 2616,
2621, 2629, 2630, 2648, 2657, 2665, 2677, 2688, 2692, 2704,

2730, 2785, 2793, 2825, 2911, 2912, 2920, 2944, 2964, 3014,
3022, 3066, 3067, 3068, 3070, 3071, 3130, 3160

BARTLEBY THE SCRIVENER, Editions: 515, 1815, 1815.1, 1815.2,
1816, 1816.1, 2572, 3032

Bartleby, the Attorney: 5, 135, 217, 372, 640, 670, 803, 887,
  894, 938, 1185, 1527, 1644, 2140, 2202, 2615, 2677, 2704,
  2786, 3067, 3068, 3132

BARTLEBY THE SCRIVENER - Film: 289, 289.1, 1073

BARTLEBY THE SCRIVENER - Opera: 1541

Bartlett, W. H. FORTY DAYS IN THE DESERT, ON THE TRACK OF THE
  ISRAELITES: OR, A JOURNEY FROM CAIRO...TO MOUNT SINAI AND
  PETRA: 1257

BATTLE-PIECES AND ASPECTS OF THE WAR: 113, 159, 217, 400, 512,
  547, 620, 651, 685, 900, 925, 1049, 1052, 1093, 1174, 1179,
  1185, 1255, 1257, 1365, 1412, 1501, 1520, 1528, 1535, 1539,
  1545, 1551, 1552, 1650, 1677, 1679, 1727, 2124, 2172, 2182,
  2210, 2408, 2411, 2603, 2621, 2615, 2700, 2793, 2971, 2978.1,
  2981, 3000, 3000.1, 3027, 3132

BATTLE-PIECES..., Editions: 547, 1104, 1361, 1788.1

Baudelaire, Charles: 113, 2793

Bayle, Pierre. DICTIONNAIRE HISTORIQUE ET CRITIQUE (1734-1738):
  192, 193, 701, 810, 887, 892, 893, 1072, 1257, 1545, 2124,
  2748, 2793, 2857, 2952, 2966, 3132

Beale, Thomas. THE NATURAL HISTORY OF THE SPERM WHALE (1839):
  50, 113, 181.1, 1185, 1257, 1545, 2793, 2966

Beaumont and Fletcher. WIT WITHOUT MONEY: 720

Beckford, William. VATHEK: 306, 1312, 1545, 2793

BEHEMOTH - See Cornelius Mathews

Belief (See Faith)

The Bell of Saint Paul (and "Cock-a-Doodle-Doo"): 2735

"The Bell Tower": 113, 117, 159, 217, 512, 651, 781, 815, 821, 841, 880, 1049, 1061, 1174, 1185, 1257, 1365, 1454, 1501, 1520, 1535, 1545, 1618, 1626, 1630, 2210, 2280, 2411, 2413, 2248, 2951, 2952

"The Bell Tower" - Editions: 515, 1816.1, 1817, 1818

Bello, King (MARDI): 1501

Bellow, Saul: 2654.1

Bembo (OMOO): 113, 1501

Bennet, George, and Daniel Tyerman. JOURNAL OF VOYAGES AND TRAVELS (1832): 1326

Bennett, Frank DeBell. NARRATIVE OF A WHALING VOYAGE ROUND THE GLOBE (1840): 1326

BENITO CERENO: 9, 113, 159, 213, 217, 301, 305, 372, 378, 387, 412, 416, 460, 470, 472, 509, 512, 645, 651, 667, 700, 701, 731, 747, 771, 780, 789, 810, 816, 821, 834, 841, 843, 850, 879, 887, 929, 936, 965, 965.1, 972, 1026, 1047, 1048, 1049, 1050, 1052, 1055, 1075, 1078, 1081, 1112, 1149, 1174, 1185, 1215, 1227, 1255, 1257, 1304, 1306, 1320, 1362.1, 1363, 1365, 1379, 1435.1, 1446, 1469, 1488, 1501, 1511, 1520, 1535, 1545, 1581, 1583, 1618, 1623, 1674, 1677, 1725.1, 1726, 2127, 2174, 2210, 2234.1, 2245, 2260, 2280, 2300, 2302, 2311.2, 2332, 2336, 2343, 2356, 2356.1, 2370, 2374, 2379, 2380, 2381, 2394, 2411, 2435, 2439, 2452, 2457, 2480, 2481, 2496, 2541, 2572,

2573, 2580, 2593, 2621, 2629, 2659, 2666, 2682, 2741, 2776.1, 2793, 2826, 2847, 2920, 2932, 2944, 2965, 2972, 2975, 3070, 3071, 3082, 3102, 3102.1, 3132, 3143, 3145, 3149

BENITO CERENO - Editions: 515, 661.1, 950, 1047, 1375, 1652,
    1818.1, 1819, 1820, 1821, 1822, 1822.1, 1823, 1824, 1825,
    1826, 1827, 1828, 1829, 1830, 2572, 2618, 2938, 3032

Benito Cereno (Character):   113, 570, 657, 701, 887, 894, 2140,
    2381, 3132

Benito Cereno - Play: 556, 1306, 1583, 3145

Benjamin, Park: 3079

Berger, Thomas.   LITTLE BIG MAN (1964):   2919

Berkshire and Berkshire County: 254, 255, 303, 371, 372, 800.1,
    1174, 1539, 1545, 1638, 1673, 2124, 2158, 2210, 2219, 2241,
    2555, 2614, 2793, 2910.1, 2966, 3027

THE BIBLE, Melville's Use of (See also Christianity):   188, 398,
    455, 466, 512, 683, 701, 810, 887, 1257, 1332, 1641, 1694,
    2124, 2287, 2347, 2354, 2397, 2408, 2516, 2772, 2793, 2797,
    2857, 3054, 3123, 3124, 3131, 3132

Bibliography: 37, 40, 50, 186, 280, 281, 310, 314, 328, 338,
    359, 412, 421, 497, 514, 528, 540, 549, 576, 577, 615, 654.1,
    745, 746, 751, 754, 785, 786, 787, 804, 810, 815, 816, 818,
    847, 849, 900, 923.1, 959, 994, 995, 1003, 1006.1, 1053, 1087,
    1106, 1117, 1174, 1184.1, 1185, 1190, 1192.1, 1200, 1205.1,
    1250, 1291, 1328, 1329.1, 1337, 1428, 1490, 1491, 1492, 1545,
    1548, 1667, 2172, 2247, 2250.1, 2287, 2307, 2312, 2366, 2369,
    2369.1, 2369.2, 2426, 2428, 2479.1, 2506, 2536, 2541, 2556,
    2557, 2572, 2575, 2599, 2600, 2601, 2602, 2604, 2605, 2611,
    2612, 2613, 2619, 2621, 2639, 2660.1, 2662, 2663, 2700.1, 2703,
    2707, 2717, 2744, 2748, 2793, 2795, 2799, 2803, 2804, 2846,

Bibliography, cont.

2862, 2863, 2865, 2868, 2869, 2870, 2871, 2878, 2904, 2904.1,

2933, 2937, 2945, 2947, 2957, 2961.2, 2973.1, 2990, 3065, 3071,

3080, 3083, 3090.1, 3099, 3110, 3111, 3118, 3119, 3120, 3137.1,

3157, 3158, 3159

Bildad, Captain (MOBY DICK): 178, 217, 1058, 1185, 2966, 3027, 3132

Biography and Biographical: 9, 30, 34, 50, 63, 104, 113, 177, 217,

238, 275, 303, 315, 317, 321, 336, 338, 351, 367, 371, 372,

512, 531, 615, 651, 713, 744, 801, 802, 896, 900, 954, 958,

971, 972, 975, 1014, 1021, 1122, 1125, 1128, 1138, 1152, 1174,

1176, 1185, 1206.1, 1214, 1232, 1248, 1250, 1251, 1252, 1253,

1254, 1254.1, 1255, 1256, 1257, 1271, 1291, 1292.1, 1327, 1369,

1405, 1442, 1473, 1474, 1479, 1480, 1545, 1612, 1635, 1506, 1587,

1599, 1601, 1611, 1662.1, 1681, 1717, 1717.1, 2124, 2175, 2186.1,

2197, 2199, 2207, 2210, 2211, 2212, 2213, 2294, 2320, 2354.1,

2369, 2369.1, 2369.2, 2397, 2436, 2438, 2439, 2448, 2455, 2472.1,

2472.2, 2479, 2517, 2566, 2570, 2603, 2607, 2609, 2678, 2744,

2747, 2748, 2765, 2767, 2773, 2779, 2780, 2857, 2862, 2864,

2872, 2927, 2948, 2984, 3020, 3027, 3040, 3081, 3100, 3153

BILLY BUDD: 9, 47, 59, 59.1, 60, 93, 107, 113, 117, 121, 126.1,

129, 131, 159, 168, 203, 214, 215, 216, 217, 218, 221, 234,

251, 278, 287, 302, 307, 309, 315, 336, 338, 357, 360, 389,

390, 397, 399, 412, 420, 436, 455, 458, 478, 483, 491, 492,

510, 512, 516, 535, 536, 555, 593, 594.1, 601, 645, 666, 673,

681, 692, 700, 703, 704, 715, 719, 742, 748, 749, 766, 782,

810, 826, 827, 835, 836, 841, 846, 851, 877, 887, 891, 899,

900, 902, 904, 905, 909, 910, 918, 921, 924, 925, 944, 954,

958, 962, 972, 981, 990, 1003, 1007, 1049, 1052, 1078, 1079,

1080, 1083, 1135, 1146, 1162, 1168, 1171.2, 1174, 1184, 1185,

BILLY BUDD, cont.

1194, 1212, 1227, 1255, 1257, 1262, 1279, 1290, 1291, 1304,
1314, 1315, 1321, 1357.1, 1379, 1390, 1402, 1411, 1418, 1433,
1434, 1466, 1468, 1501, 1502, 1509, 1511, 1512, 1520, 1531.1,
1534, 1534.1, 1545, 1576, 1618, 1625, 1655, 1660, 1661, 1675,
1677, 1685, 1699, 1700, 1716, 1724, 1726, 1729, 2124, 2125,
2135, 2139, 2139.1, 2140, 2159, 2160, 2170, 2172, 2174, 2202,
2207, 2210, 2220, 2221, 2230.1, 2232, 2251, 2259, 2271, 2292,
2306, 2326, 2350, 2354, 2356, 2356.1, 2363, 2370, 2382, 2408,
2411, 2413, 2414, 2427, 2437, 2439, 2456, 2458, 2466, 2467,
2467.1, 2470, 2471, 2471.1, 2472, 2495, 2495.2, 2498, 2513,
2518, 2526, 2539, 2560, 2575, 2580, 2596, 2615, 2621, 2615,

2629, 2633, 2636, 2640, 2646, 2652, 2653, 2684, 2687, 2696,
2700, 2702, 2703, 2707.1, 2708, 2710, 2718, 2722, 2731, 2742,
2748, 2764, 2772, 2777, 2782, 2793, 2802, 2809, 2811, 2819,
2821, 2823, 2825, 2836, 2857, 2859, 2882, 2892, 2899, 2905,
2911, 2914, 2923, 2929, 2944, 2961.1, 2961.2, 2966, 2969, 2977,
2977.1, 2983, 3010, 3014, 3015, 3016, 3022, 3027, 3042, 3044,
3056, 3057, 3060, 3070, 3071, 3075, 3092, 3094, 3099, 3102,
3102.1, 3104, 3107, 3115, 3124, 3132, 3150, 3154, 3161

BILLY BUDD, Editions: 126.1, 515, 594.1, 599.1, 782, 897, 897.1,
898, 950, 1146, 1384, 1499, 1652, 1831, 1832, 1832.1, 1832.2,
1833, 1834, 1835, 1836, 1837, 1838, 1839, 1840, 1841, 1842,
1843, 1844, 1845, 1846, 1847, 1848, 1848.1, 1849, 1850, 1851,
1852, 2183, 2183.1, 2390, 2646, 2750, 2858, 2938, 2999, 3023,
3032, 3035.2

BILLY BUDD, "Acceptance" Thesis: 777, 835, 921, 1078, 1675, 2210,
2575, 2615, 2636, 2797, 2857, 2865, 3010, 3042; Resistance,
3104

Billy Budd (character): 426, 510, 887, 894, 972, 1194, 1418, 1509, 1640, 1699, 2140, 2408, 2466, 2467, 2467.1, 2470, 2495, 2560, 2687, 2700, 2905, 2923, 2983, 3010, 3069, 3102, 3102.1, 3104, 3115

Billy Budd as Adam: 1279, 1534, 1534.1, 2363, 2456, 2748, 2905, 3132

Billy Budd and Apollo: 887

Billy Budd and "The Birthmark," (Hawthorne): 2764

Billy Budd and John Brown: 3115

BILLY BUDD, Buddhism in: 2823

Billy Budd as Christ: 492, 1279, 2456, 2684, 2748, 2764, 2905

Billy Budd as Isaac: 2456

Billy Budd as Moby Dick: 2983

Billy Budd and Oedipus: 3044

Billy Budd and Othello: 3044

Billy Budd as Peacemaker: 2748

Billy Budd, Execution of (See also Hanging Scene, and "Billy Budd Theme"): 169, 436, 452, 601, 681, 1315, 1520, 1545, 1715, 2139, 2139.1, 2456, 2560, 2776

BILLY BUDD, Father Figure in: 2495.1

BILLY BUDD, Film and Play: 385, 495, 496, 595, 596, 597, 598, 599, 599.1, 601, 663, 1357, 1376, 2414, 2437, 2929

BILLY BUDD, Freudian Reading of: 2495

BILLY BUDD, The Hanging Scene (See also Execution of Billy Budd, and the "Billy Budd Theme"): 169, 436, 451, 452, 512, 681, 981, 1675, 2575

Billy Budd, Irony in His Death: 2560

BILLY BUDD, Miltonic strains and parallels: 970, 2354, 2363, 2408, 2467

BILLY BUDD, Opera: 93, 355, 852, 853, 945, 1006, 1321, 1357, 2471, 2808, 3060

BILLY BUDD, Political Mystery Drama: 2687

BILLY BUDD, "Resistance Thesis" (See also "Acceptance Thesis"): 3104

BILLY BUDD, Sources (See also Bible, Melville's Reading, and Names): 47, 49, 50, 1411, 1646.1, 2674.1

BILLY BUDD, Son Figure in: 2495.1

BILLY BUDD and THE TEMPEST: 1661

"Billy Budd Theme": 47, 436, 897, 1007, 1545, 1715, 2611, 2612

BILLY BUDD, Christian Themes in: 2821

BILLY BUDD, Theological Concepts in (See also Bible and Christianity): 59, 59.1

Billy Budd as Unconscious Rebel: 2495

BILLY BUDD, The Wise Old Man, Motif of: 2742

Bird Imagery (See also Imagery and Symbols): 701, 1404, 1600

Bird, Robert Montgomery. NICK OF THE WOODS (Character parallels with Confidence-man): 1085

Black Guinea (CONFIDENCE-MAN): 887

Blackness (See Power of)

Blackness, Melville's (See also Melancholy, Pessimism, and
Nihilism): 965, 965.1, 2210, 3015, 3054

Blake, William: 217, 260, 359, 900, 1545, 2124, 2210, 2358,
2408, 2819, 2829, 2857, 2966, 3027

Bland (WHITE JACKET): 113, 217, 701, 1185, 2408, 3132

Bligh, Captain: 113, 3027

Blindness: 701, 2552

Blondes (See also Whiteness): 479

"Body and Soul" Metaphor (See also Allegory, Imagery, Symbols):
1550

Bolton, Harry (REDBURN): 113, 217, 456, 701, 972, 1185, 1501,
1553, 2615

Bon Homme (ship): 1185

Book Promotion: 498

Books Belonging to Melville (See also Melville's Reading):
442, 701, 1170, 1203, 1257, 1666, 2397, 2417, 2611, 2612,
3040

Books - Guide Books: 701

Books, Rare (See Exhibitions and Editions, First and Textual)

Booksellers and Melville: 1496

Booktrade in the Nineteenth Century: 994

Boomer, Captain (MOBY DICK): 2522

Browning, Robert: 113, 1545, 2356, 2356.1, 2615, 2793, 3027

Brownson, Orestes. THE SPIRIT-RAPPER (1854): 1370

Bryant, William Cullen: 113, 1257, 1545, 2124, 2793, 3027

Buccaneers, Melville's: 1340

Buchanan, Robert: 1174, 1185, 1257, 1545, 2124, 2793, 3027

Buddhism: 159, 887, 2823

Bulkington (MOBY DICK): 217, 359, 507, 510, 512, 586, 701, 1501, 2364, 2422, 2516, 2615, 2748, 2857, 3021

Bullen, Frank T. THE CRUISE OF THE CACHALOT ROUND THE WORLD AFTER SPERM WHALES: 70, 2191

Bulwer-Lytton, Edward. THE LAST DAYS OF POMPEII and PELHAM: 1174, 1257, 1545

Bunger, Dr. (MOBY DICK): 113

Bunyan, John: 217, 322, 2453, 2793, 2857, 3027, 3057

Burial Customs, Naval: 325

Burke, Edmund: 390, 1545, 3027

Burton, Robert. THE ANATOMY OF MELANCHOLY: 113, 649, 701, 1072, 1174, 1185, 1257, 1545, 2124, 2512, 2793, 2857, 2966, 3027, 3062, 3130

The Businessman in Western Literature: 2533.1

Butler, Fanny Kemble: 512, 972, 1185, 1257, 1545, 2124, 2793, 3027

Butler, Samuel. HUDIBRAS: 364, 1545, 2124, 2793, 3027

Cave (See Symbols): 512, 1036

Cenci, Beatrice: 474, 1257, 2424, 2425

Cenci Portrait: 1521, 2424, 2425

Centenary, Melville's: 68, 1666, 2298, 3024, 3024.1

Cervantes Saavedra, Miguel de: 701, 1215, 1257, 1516, 1517, 2237, 2408, 2615, 2793

Cetology: 1058, 1185, 2946, 2995

Chamois, whalingboat (MARDI): 649

Chance (See also Freedom of Will): 359, 2966

Channing, William Ellery: 1174, 1545, 2408

Chapman, John Jay: 1245

Characters (Categories of Melville's Characters): 2148

Characters, Light and Dark: 284

Characterization (See also Style): 3006, 3124, 3132

Charles V: 887

Chase, Jack (WHITE JACKET): 113, 217, 507, 508, 512, 900, 1174, 1185, 1257, 1501, 1683, 2210, 2334, 2334.1, 2411, 2518, 2615, 2622, 2793, 2965, 3027, 3104, 3132

Chase, Owen. NARRATIVE OF THE MOST EXTRAORDINARY AND DISTRESSING SHIPWRECK OF THE WHALE-SHIP ESSEX, OF NANTUCKET: WHICH WAS ATTACKED AND FINALLY DESTROYED BY A LARGE SPERMACETI-WHALE, IN THE PACIFIC OCEAN:

113, 717, 1257, 1297, 1545, 1713, 2124, 2966

Chase, Owen, of the Essex (Character): 113, 512, 1185, 1257, 2793

Chasles, Victor Euphémion Philarète: 386, 1174, 1257, 1545,
2793, 3027, 3148

Cheever, Henry T. THE WHALE AND HIS CAPTORS: 113, 1295, 2408,
2966

Chesterfield, Lord: 649, 972, 1545

The Chola Woman: 248, 1257

Christ: 131, 251, 309, 397, 468, 492, 512, 649, 666, 701, 803,
810, 887, 1279, 1532.1, 2408, 2463, 2516, 2578, 2684, 2748,
2793

Christ Figures in BARTLEBY, BENITO CERENO, BILLY BUDD, CONFIDENCE-
MAN, PIERRE: 887

Christian Analyses (See Christianity): 2769, 2792

The Christian Conscience: 2730

Christian Doctrine (See Christianity): 59, 59.1, 2764, 2776

Christian Faith (See Christianity)

Christianity: 50, 134, 159, 329, 332, 333, 415, 477, 512, 534,
810, 822, 887, 1171.2, 1183, 1651, 1729, 2156, 2156.1, 2157,
2210, 2286, 2319, 2397, 2406, 2463, 2587, 2615, 2667, 2694,
2730, 2776, 2793, 2821, 2847, 3071, 3132, 3150

The City, Melville's Treatment of: 159, 1697, 2190, 2249,
2402.1, 2451, 2691.1, 3061, 3061.1

The Civil War: 7, 113, 837, 1179, 1209, 1551, 1552, 1655.2,
2210, 2615, 2793

Civil War Poems, Melville's (See Poetry): 2637

"Cock-a-Doodle-Doo!" - Editions: 1547, 1852.1, 1852.2, 1853

Coffin (See also Symbolism): 1508, 1695, 1708, 2514, 2516, 2571

Colbrook (Character, WHITE JACKET): 113, 1501

Coleridge, Samuel Taylor: 106, 113, 217, 322, 359, 649, 810, 1174, 1257, 1545, 1688, 2356, 2356.1, 2408, 2411, 2789, 2793, 2857, 2965, 2966, 3024, 3027, 3132

Colloquial Style (See Language): 352

Colnet, James. A VOYAGE TO THE SOUTH ATLANTIC AND ROUND CAPE HORN INTO THE PACIFIC: 731, 1257, 1340, 2966

Color, Use of (See also Blackness, Whiteness, and Symbolism): 28, 70, 605, 606, 943, 2669, 2787, 3132

The Comic Spirit: 2507, 2509

Comic Tradition in American Literature (See also Literary History, and Literary Tradition): 1600

COMMERCIAL REGULATIONS MADE BY THE PRINCIPLE /sic/ CHIEFS OF THE SAMOAN GROUP OF ISLANDS (1839): 445

Commercialization of American Society (See also Civilization, Industrialization, and Society): 2161

Commitment in American Literature: 1462

Common Law (See also Authority, Law, and Society): 2154

The Common Man (See also Democracy, Hero, Humanitarianism): 2178, 2453, 2581, 2859, 3050

Communication: 813, 1435, 2748, 3022

The Community (See also Democracy): 1042, 1043, 1046, 2353, 2398

Communities, Ideal - Rejected: 182

Compassion (See also Civilization, Humanitarianism, Society):
107

The Complex Passion: 242

Comstock, William: 2136

Concordance to Biblical Allusions in MOBY DICK (See Bible):
1332

Confession, as Form of Prose Fiction: 919

"Confidence" Creed: 2922

Confidence, Melville's Lack of: 230, 2210

THE CONFIDENCE-MAN: 9, 32, 50, 65, 113, 150, 157, 159, 205, 206,
214, 215, 217, 222, 230, 234, 235, 291, 308, 318, 328, 329, 391,
405, 454, 469, 484, 507, 510, 512, 518, 530, 546, 548, 569, 580,
610, 615, 651, 697, 698, 700, 701, 702, 713, 721, 732, 795, 810,
841, 868, 869, 870, 872, 885, 887, 891, 900, 903, 909, 910, 925,
958, 972, 1021, 1044, 1049, 1052, 1058, 1085, 1110, 1132, 1132.1,
1148, 1174, 1183, 1185, 1212, 1215, 1217, 1235, 1255, 1257,
1269, 1291, 1313, 1319, 1331, 1365, 1371, 1379, 1385.1, 1464,
1501, 1511, 1520, 1531, 1532.1, 1535, 1539, 1545, 1584, 1621,
1650, 1655, 1677, 1685, 1698, 1703, 2124, 2135, 2141, 2156,
2156.1, 2157, 2161, 2172, 2176, 2204, 2210, 2259, 2273, 2277,

THE CONFIDENCE-MAN, cont.

2278, 2293, 2312, 2316, 2318, 2319, 2319.1, 2351, 2352, 2356, 2356.1, 2361, 2408, 2411, 2413, 2427, 2439, 2460, 2464, 2474, 2507, 2509, 2525, 2526, 2539, 2609, 2610, 2615, 2621, 2624, 2625, 2626, 2629, 2650, 2650.1, 2683, 2700. 2748, 2793, 2817, 2825, 2827, 2829, 2857, 2859, 2898, 2920, 2922, 2936, 2965, 2975, 2977, 2977.1, 3014, 3016, 3027, 3045, 3088, 3102, 3102.1, 3107, 3124, 3125, 3132

THE CONFIDENCE-MAN, Editions: 548, 870, 881, 923, 1054, 1854, 1855, 1856, 1857, 1858, 1859, 1860, 1861, 1862, 1863, 1864, 1865, 2312, 2361, 2619, 2960

The Confidence-Man in American Literature: 1210, 2975

THE CONFIDENCE-MAN and Hawthorne's "The Celestial Railroad": 512, 868, 869, 870, 2650, 2862

THE CONFIDENCE-MAN and the Story of Charlemont: 701, 1371, 1501

The Confidence-Man, Anti-hero or Hero: 356, 2626

The Confidence-Man (Various Identities): 150, 157, 205, 219, 329, 512, 870, 2140, 2141, 2204, 2273, 2278, 2413, 2650

The Confidence Man, the Cosmopolitan as: 701, 887

The Confidence-Man, the Devil as: 219, 870, 2650

The Confidence-Man, Emerson as: 702, 870, 1183, 2204, 2273, 2278, 2318, 2949, 2949.1

THE CONFIDENCE-MAN, Emerson as Mark Winsome: 868, 2318

THE CONFIDENCE-MAN, The Mute as Avatar or Christ-Figure: 329, 484, 512, 697, 868, 869, 870, 1044, 1291, 1621, 2141, 2259, 2413, 2509, 2857

Cooper, James Fenimore: 47, 113, 159, 217, 247, 263, 661, 812, 925, 972, 1174, 1257, 1545, 1655.1, 2156, 2156.1, 2157, 2253, 2372, 2408, 2522, 2551, 2615, 2793, 2857, 2966, 3027

Copyright (See also International Copyright): 41, 262, 440, 994, 1174

Corporal Punishment, Articles of War: 50

Corposants (See MOBY DICK)

Cosmology: 2667

Cosmopolitanism (See also City, Community, Society): 701, 1331, 3081.2

The Cottage and the Temple (See also Imagery and Symbolism): 1554

Cowley, William Ambrosia. VOYAGE AROUND THE GLOBE: 701, 731

Counterfeiting (WHITE JACKET): 701

Covenant and Covenant Theology: 2667

The Craft of Fiction (See also the Art of Fiction): 276, 277, 690, 700

The Craft of Melville: 2755

Crane, Hart: 181, 204, 217, 471, 602, 603, 766, 924, 1532, 2181, 2411

Crébillon, Claude Prosper Jolyot de: 1340

Criticism, General: 24, 25, 35, 61, 77, 84, 87, 94, 110, 166, 167, 183, 211, 218, 236, 252, 312, 314, 362, 394, 395, 417, 427, 432, 433, 434, 448, 465, 511, 513, 514, 523, 527, 528, 529, 539, 541, 559, 562, 582, 589, 609, 612, 626, 627, 659, 696, 736, 738, 744, 757, 784, 788, 795, 831.1, 833, 842, 863, 873, 895, 897, 906, 920, 933, 967, 997, 1010, 1013, 1022, 1032, 1120, 1128, 1165.1, 1177, 1181, 1205, 1222, 1229, 1240, 1285, 1303, 1305, 1344, 1347, 1419, 1450, 1451.1, 1462, 1494, 1515, 1526, 1537, 1548, 1560, 1586, 1593, 1600, 1601, 1618, 1626, 1636, 1637, 1643, 1658, 1662.1, 1665, 1671.1, 1672, 1678, 1680, 1684, 2137, 2138, 2155.1, 2166, 2209, 2219, 2242, 2285, 2291, 2296, 2321, 2324.1, 2325,

2329.2, 2333, 2334, 2334.1, 2341, 2344, 2345, 2346, 2347, 2383, 2395, 2419, 2428, 2429, 2429.1, 2436, 2448, 2449, 2451.1, 2454, 2455, 2460.1, 2486, 2491, 2506, 2528, 2530.1, 2539, 2559, 2574, 2575, 2581, 2583.1, 2599, 2600, 2601, 2602, 2635, 2668, 2691, 2709, 2774, 2783, 2796, 2798.1, 2799, 2825, 2842, 2848, 2862, 2863, 2868, 2869, 2870, 2871, 2900, 2903, 2904, 2904.1, 2927, 2928, 2949, 2949.1, 2960, 2973, 2976, 2979, 2994, 3003, 3025, 3026, 3027, 3036, 3038, 3047, 3057.1, 3083, 3084, 3086, 3093 3098, 3108, 3116, 3141, 3153.1

Criticism, Early Twentieth-Century: 1617, 2186.1, 2367, 2478.2, 2530.1, 2977.1, 2994

Criticism, European - General: 23, 44, 62, 73, 110, 132, 162, 202, 224, 225, 227, 251, 279.1, 282, 308, 345, 386, 399, 405, 414, 417, 425, 428, 429, 431, 432, 433, 434, 447, 448, 454, 484.1, 484.2, 484.3, 484.4, 485, 485.1, 485.2, 488, 489, 519, 520, 521, 531, 539, 562, 582, 600, 630, 660, 664, 748, 749, 825, 831, 849, 876, 877, 878, 896, 906, 937, 976, 977, 978, 979, 980, 1011, 1033, 1059, 1060, 1061, 1062, 1064, 1078, 1099, 1100, 1113, 1160, 1164, 1165, 1249, 1251, 1252, 1253, 1254, 1256, 1265, 1288, 1317, 1322, 1355, 1372, 1393, 1417, 1420, 1439, 1454, 1455, 1456, 1460, 1464, 1465, 1466, 1467, 1470, 1471, 1472, 1473, 1478, 1517, 1530,

1547, 1548, 1563, 1564, 1565, 1566, 1567, 1591, 1643, 1671, 1678, 1689, 1690, 1691, 1692, 1693, 1832, 1857.1, 2118, 2133, 2173, 2246, 2255, 2256, 2257, 2272, 2288, 2289, 2300, 2301, 2305, 2341, 2342, 2343, 2344, 2345, 2346, 2347, 2359, 2361, 2369, 2369.1, 2369.2, 2375, 2378, 2384, 2387, 2388, 2397, 2398, 2400, 2424, 2425, 2442, 2443, 2479, 2487, 2488, 2489, 2530, 2559, 2642, 2643, 2660, 2660.1, 2661, 2662, 2663, 2695, 2715, 2716, 2721, 2809, 2810, 2818, 2819, 2831, 2832, 2834, 2853, 2952, 2985, 2985.1, 3037, 3087, 3090, 3154, 3155, 3156, 3164, 3165, 3166.1, 3167

Criticism, French: 386, 519, 520, 521, 849, 895, 1322, 1521, 1522, 1643, 1689, 1690, 1691, 1692, 1693, 2384, 2443, 2526, 2530, 2660, 2660.1, 2661, 2662, 2663, 2968.1, 3148

Criticism, German and Austrian: 1177, 1186, 1249, 1355, 1456, 1464, 1465, 1633, 2156.1, 2368, 2370, 2397, 2426, 2695, 3087, 3090

Criticism, Italian (See also Dante): 484.1, 484.3, 484.4, 485.2, 1565, 1566, 1567, 1666.1, 1668, 1669, 1671, 1769.1, 2133, 2173, 2342, 2343, 2344, 2345, 2346, 3165

Criticism - Literary Criticism of "Young America": 2706

Criticism - "New Criticism": 916, 2559

Criticism, Nineteenth-Century Views: 362, 1013, 1568, 2253, 2261, 2262, 2367, 2478.1, 2486, 2729.1, 2861, 2910.1, 2925, 2992, 3078, 3080, 3086

Criticism, Past and Present Comparison: 55, 74, 95, 97, 176, 340, 499, 527, 1120, 1126, 1229, 1303, 1345, 1346, 1387, 1589, 1610, 1655.2, 2258, 2326, 2328, 2329.2, 2367, 2389, 2428, 3098, 3102.2

Criticism, Russian: 3156

The Cross (See Symbolism): 159, 902

Crucifixion (See Christianity, Cross, and Symbolism): 902, 1532.1, 3124, 3132

Culture (See American Culture): 512

Curtis, George William: 113, 217, 1257, 1545, 2171

Customs Office (See Melville as Inspector of Customs): 1174, 1185, 2210, 2780

Cuthbert, Baron Collingwood, British Admiral: 2640

Cuticle, Dr. Cadwallader (WHITE JACKET): 113, 1185, 2210, 2465, 2615, 2793, 2965, 2966, 3132

Daggoo (MOBY DICK): 113, 217, 1185, 1369, 1501, 2210, 2358, 2615, 2966, 3132

Dahlberg, Edward. AIMS FOR OBLIVION: 239, 262, 625, 626

Dana, Richard Henry, Jr. TWO YEARS BEFORE THE MAST: 113, 217, 300, 636, 900, 972, 1107, 1108, 1136, 1174, 1185, 1257, 1545, 1590, 2124, 2210, 2240, 2551, 2793, 2966, 3027

Dana, Richard Henry, Sr.: 50, 217, 1174, 1257, 1545, 2124, 2210, 2551, 2965

Daniel, Book of: 810, 3132

Dansker (CONFIDENCE-MAN): 159, 704, 1314, 2748, 2782, 3132

Dante, Alighieri: 113, 159, 217, 233, 242, 428.1, 512, 982, 984, 1008, 1185, 1257, 1518, 1523, 1668, 1669, 2200, 2217, 2238, 2408, 2453, 2577, 2578, 2615, 2748, 2793, 2819, 2857, 2966, 3027, 3132, 3136

The Dark Tradition (See also Power of Blackness): 1597.1, 2449.1

Darkness (See Blackness, Dark Tradition, and Power of Blackness): 701

Darwin, Charles: 50, 883, 900, 1174, 1185, 1257, 1498, 1545, 2793, 3027

The Dead Letter Office (See BARTLEBY): 1174

The Deaf Mute (See Mute, THE CONFIDENCE-MAN): 2464

Death: 50, 359, 701, 791, 1058, 1511, 1431, 2210, 2360, 2644, 2645, 2857

Death, Spiritual, and Rebirth (See also Death): 320

Defoe, Daniel: 649, 900, 1174, 1257, 1545, 3027

Deism: 1410

Delano, Captain Amasa (Character, BENITO CERENO): 113, 217, 472, 570, 657, 701, 789, 1071, 1185, 1215, 1257, 1501, 1306, 1391, 1469, 1623, 2374, 2379, 2496, 2793, 3027, 3071, 3149

Delano, Captain Amasa. NARRATIVE OF VOYAGES AND TRAVELS (Boston: 1817): 113, 556, 879, 887, 936, 1257, 2256, 2435, 2593

Democracy and the Democratic Experience: 14, 113, 145, 231, 232, 233, 390, 477, 492, 512, 864, 927, 986, 1026, 1477, 1559, 1626, 1675, 1677, 1729, 2286, 2326, 2330, 2428, 2528, 2581, 2615, 2672, 2672.1, 2748, 2793, 2798, 2811, 2859, 3050

Democratic Expectancy: 2672, 2672.1

Democratic Faith (See also Democracy and the Democratic Experience): 927, 2252, 2353, 2672, 2672.1

The Democratic Imagination: 175, 516, 695

The Democratic Protest: 864

The Democratic Tradition and American Literature (See also Literary History and Literary Tradition): 772, 2528

Demonism and Demonic (See Devil, Satan): 168, 946, 947, 1031, 1302, 2629, 2907

Depravity, Innate: 680, 1520, 2764, 2857

DeQuincey, Thomas: 1257, 1545, 2210, 2493, 2793

Despair: 359, 2168

Despotic Command: 458, 879

Destiny: 2209.1

Determinism (See also Naturalism): 927, 1446.1, 1640

Development of Melville's Work: 50, 62, 113, 588, 701, 1220, 1223, 1247, 1265, 1414, 1428, 1658, 2250, 2475, 2492, 2503, 2534.1, 2974, 3103, 3107

Development of Melville through MOBY DICK: 44, 2974

Devil (See also Demon, Diabolism, Satan): 131, 887, 1021, 2232,
2531, 2787, 2793, 2857

Diabolism (See Devil, Satan): 1026

Dialect, Negro (See Language, Vocabulary): 352

Dialogue: 352, 392, 556, 2132

Dichotomies, Good and Evil: 460

Dickens, Charles: 50, 113, 217, 649, 900, 1174, 1257, 1545,
2360, 2650, 2793, 2794, 3071, 3072

Dickinson, Emily: 113, 217, 2350, 2411, 2615, 2748

Diction (See Dialect, Language, Vocabulary): 972, 2182, 2243

Digressions (See Structure, Style): 701, 846

Disguise (See Masks, Symbolism): 701

Disillusionment (See Blackness, Despair, Pessimism): 2857, 2984

Disraeli, Benjamin: 113, 1545, 2793, 3132

Disraeli, Isaac. THE CURIOSITIES OF LITERATURE: 1257, 1545,
2408, 2793, 2912

Dissertations, Dissertation Abstracts, and Dissertation Abstracts
International: 49, 153, 156, 172, 173, 179, 187, 197, 206,
207, 214, 240, 246, 255, 285, 297, 309, 317, 332, 344, 345,
346, 347, 358, 403, 407, 449, 450, 457, 467, 473, 533, 542,
543, 545, 579, 605, 609, 614, 631, 646, 648, 655, 667, 672,
674, 700, 719, 721, 725, 732, 733, 737, 749, 755, 764, 770,
775, 805, 808, 809, 827, 842, 866, 869, 884, 888, 898, 926,
971, 992, 993, 1022, 1033.1, 1035, 1037, 1038, 1039, 1042,
1057, 1065, 1074, 1086, 1088, 1128, 1147, 1152, 1157, 1162, 1164,
1166, 1171, 1175, 1188, 1206, 1210, 1212, 1220, 1222, 1239, 1274,
1275, 1288, 1298, 1302, 1329, 1334, 1350, 1362.1, 1398, 1404,

Dissertations, Abstracts, International. cont.

1414, 1422, 1429, 1439, 1447, 1500, 1555, 1577, 1588, 1624,

1632, 1633, 1636, 1655, 1662.2, 1705, 1717, 1726, 1730, 2132,

2193, 2233, 2234, 2239, 2244, 2248, 2250, 2269, 2274, 2299,

2315, 2396, 2405, 2409, 2412, 2455, 2461, 2469, 2498, 2503,

2504, 2507, 2515, 2540, 2554, 2583, 2589, 2591, 2598, 2620,

2625.2, 2628, 2630, 2655, 2656, 2658, 2660, 2695, 2701, 2716,

2718, 2720, 2722, 2746, 2755, 2803, 2816.1, 2818, 2828, 2877,

2879, 2893, 2908, 2913, 2971, 2975, 2993, 2997, 3006, 3025,

3055, 3062, 3077, 3107, 3108, 3110, 3111, 3131, 3138, 3159,

3163

Dissolution (See also Determinism, Despair): 2857.2

Dolly, whalingship (See Acushnet): 1185, 2793

Dominora (MARDI): 1185

Don Quixote (See Miguel Cervantes)

Dostoievsky, Feodor Mikhailovich: 113, 536, 909, 910, 911,

1043, 2411, 3071

Doubloon (See also MOBY DICK): 359, 517, 701, 942, 1005, 2325,

2423, 2617, 2748, 2867, 3021

Doubt (See Despair, Disillusionment): 839

Doughty, Charles Montagu: 583

Downing, Andrew Jackson: 1554

Dread (See Disillusionment, Despair): 359

Dream (See Illusion, Imagination, Vision): 701

Druidic Rites and Priests: 887

Dualism: 453, 912, 1031, 1553, 1622, 2625

Ducasse, Isidore, Comte de Lautréamont. LES CHANTS DE MALADOROR:
159

Dramatic Form and Technique (See Art, Structure, Style):
276, 277

Dreiser, Theodore: 812, 2615

Duyckinck, Evert: 50, 113, 335, 635, 649, 701, 810, 900, 972,
1127, 1174, 1185, 1257, 1545, 1635, 2124, 2177, 2210, 2408,
2411, 2615, 2706, 2748, 2793, 2857, 2860, 2966, 3027, 3071,
3088, 3132

Duyckinck, Evert, "Diving and Ducking": 726, 728, 2376

Duyckinck, George: 649, 1174, 1185, 1257, 2124, 2210, 1545,
2408, 2793, 2966

Dwight, Timothy. TRAVELS IN NEW ENGLAND AND NEW YORK (New Haven:
1821): 713.1, 2555

Early Work of Melville (See Biography and also Development of
Melville): 677

Earnshaw, J. W.: 2662

Earth: 359

East, and Near East (See Oriental): 809, 810

East Indian Religions and Mythologies (See Hindu and Oriental
Religions and Mythologies): 439

Economics, Literary Treatment of (See also Literary History and
Literary Tradition): 499, 502, 503

Eden: 512, 876, 1072, 2408, 2538, 3071.1, 3132

Edmund (<u>King</u> <u>Lear</u>) (See also Shakespeare): 1645

Edwards, Jonathan: 2331, 2408, 2793

Egalitarianism: 3162, 3163

Egbert (THE CONFIDENCE-MAN): 2278, 2316

Egypt and Egyptian Mythology: 701, 810, 3132

Elijah (MOBY DICK): 1185, 1694, 3132

Eliot, George (Pseud., Marian Evans): 701, 1174, 1545

Eliot, T. S.: 113, 359, 2615

Elizabethan - Jacobean Perspective: 721

Ellis, William. POLYNESIAN RESEARCHES. 2 Vols., 1829; 4 Vols.,
    1853: 1185, 1326

Ellison, Ralph. THE INVISIBLE MAN: 32, 301, 1535, 2972.1

Emerson, Ralph Waldo: 113, 217, 285, 335, 359, 512, 586, 589,
    649, 854, 868, 870, 887, 900, 1036.1, 1174, 1185, 1215, 1257,
    1372, 1391, 1545, 1634, 1653, 1677, 2124, 2156, 2156.1, 2157,
    2172, 2202, 2204, 2210, 2273, 2278, 2316, 2318, 2408, 2411,
    2501, 2508, 2615, 2748, 2764, 2793, 2819, 2857, 2965, 2966,
    3016, 3027, 3071, 3077, 3132

Emerson Idiom: 1634

Empiricism: 296

THE ENCANTADAS: 50, 113, 117, 159, 217, 248, 324, 372, 512, 651,
    720, 731, 810, 815, 841, 883, 925, 1040, 1049, 1052, 1061, 1127,
    1174, 1185, 1223, 1257, 1263, 1272, 1340, 1341, 1365, 1379,
    1520, 1527, 1535, 1545, 1582, 1677, 2124, 2210, 2238, 2280,
    2356, 2356.1, 2408, 2411, 2439, 2472, 2572, 2621, 2629, 2793,
    2854, 2920, 2944, 2973.1, 3007, 3102, 3102.1, 3132

THE ENCANTADAS, Editions: 515, 1865.1, 1866, 1867, 1868, 1868.1, 1869, 1870, 2572, 2938, 2973.1, 3032

THE ENCANTADAS, Sources: 1263, 2854, 3007

Enceladus (PIERRE): 217, 512, 1069, 1185, 2615, 2793

The Enlightenment: 2356, 2356.1

Enoch Mudge: 750

Environment, Man's (See also Civilization, Society): 380

Epic, Democratic (See also Democracy): 516

Epic, Spiritual (See also Christianity, Literary History, and Literary Tradition): 526

Epic and Epic Romance (See also Romance): 516, 517, 563, 593, 1027, 1207, 1308, 1470

Epic Tradition: 1308, 1596

Epicureanism: 988

Epistemology and Epistemological Effort: 15

Essex, whaleship: 113, 506, 1185, 1257, 1297, 2124, 2404, 2793, 2966

Ethan Brand, Melville as: 35.1, 111, 383, 408, 2198, 2210, 2212, 2260, 2768, 2772

"Ethan Brand," Melville on: 175, 1027, 1656, 1657, 2337, 2615

Ethics and Ethical: 536

Etymology (See also Language and Vocabulary): 143, 438

The Eucharist (See Christianity, Sacrament, and Sacramentalism): 159

Europe, Influence on Melville: 662

European Response to American Books in the Nineteenth-Century:

   994, 996, 1001, 1002, 1522, 2445, 2668, 2676, 2979, 3081.2

Eve: 2363, 2408, 3132

Evil: 33, 107, 342, 516, 608, 645, 682, 740, 931, 935, 1070,

   1278, 1302, 1344, 1446, 1582, 2140, 2210, 2245, 2270, 2429,

   2470, 2478, 2578, 2581, 2615, 2772, 2776, 2973, 2997, 3015,

   3082, 3098, 3133

Evolution, Theory of, and Melville: 579

Exhibitions (See also Books and Manuscripts): 281, 421, 695,

   1009, 2288.1, 2417, 2428, 2477.1, 2926

Existentialism: 296, 359, 361, 490, 589, 670, 672, 811, 909,

   1313, 1481, 1572.1, 2292, 2523, 2629, 2751, 2829, 3071

"Expanding" Symbol: 384

Expediency vs. Morality: 990

Experience, Aspects of: 15, 244, 317, 453, 1045, 2403, 2413,

   2698

Experience, Role of in Melville's Writing: 315, 317, 478, 653,

   2403, 2698

Experiment(s): 435

Expressions (See Dialect, Language, Vocabulary): 147

Fable: 2731

Fact as Spiritual Symbol (See Symbolism): 616, 912

The Faerie Queene (See also Edmund Spenser): 2462, 2857, 3135

Failure, Theme of (See also Themes): 453, 1434

Fairyland: 348

Faith (See also Christ and Christianity): 318, 557, 680, 839,
888, 893, 1237, 1343, 2210, 2397, 2615

Fall of Innocence (See also Fall of Man, Felix Culpa, and
Innocence): 790, 836, 886, 910, 2621, 2701, 2748

Fall of Man (See Fall of Innocence, Felix Culpa or "Fortunate
Fall, and Innocence): 512, 701, 518, 1424, 2189, 2363, 2413,
2467, 2701, 2857

Fallacy, Novelistic: 1106, 2708

Falsgrave, Rev. (PIERRE): 217

Fascism and Fascistic Ideologies: 2398

"Fast-Fish and Loose-Fish" (MOBY DICK): 1185, 1594, 2946

Fatalism: 127, 359, 1015, 1505

Fate (See also Free Will): 989, 1228, 2165, 2966

The Fates: 1724

Father, Search for: 473, 909

The Father Figure (Also see Paternity): 512, 2531

Father Mapple (See Mapple, Father)

Fathers and Sons in American Fiction: 512, 2531

Faulkner, William: 16, 174, 217, 362, 406, 773, 774, 812, 1058,
1535, 2352, 2748, 2772, 2892, 2966

Faust and Faustian: 228, 1072, 1525, 1630, 1631, 2270.1, 2836,
2857, 3132

Fire, Symbol of (See Fire Imagery and Fire Worship): 359, 512, 701, 1656, 2152, 2569, 2986, 3134

Fire Worship: 190, 810, 1312, 1457, 2986

The Fisher King: 693

FitzGerald, Edward. OMAR KHAYYÁM: 810

Flask (MOBY DICK): 129, 988, 989, 1185, 2210, 2615, 2966

Flaubert, Gustave: 113, 359

Flaxman, John (1755-1826). Illustrator of OEUVRE COMPLET.
   (See Dante also): 2577, 2578

Fleece (MOBY DICK): 217, 1185, 1501, 2757, 2946, 2966, 3113

Flint, Timothy. RECOLLECTIONS OF THE LAST TEN YEARS (1826) and
   HISTORY AND GEOGRAPHY OF THE MISSISSIPPI VALLEY (1828): 2624

Flogging: 2, 50, 113, 566, 900, 1174, 1185, 2431, 2965, 3071

Flower Symbol (See Persian Poetic Imagery, Imagery, and Symbolism):
   353, 647, 648, 649, 667, 733, 775, 810, 829, 988, 989, 1024

Folk Hero (See Hero): 2340

Folklore: 137, 142, 145, 389, 512, 518, 544, 592, 594, 2317, 2340,
   2713

The Fool: 472, 518

Forest Symbol: 159

Forgues, E. D.: 1521, 2968.1

Form (See also Structure and Style): 409, 701, 844, 1065, 2146,
   2214, 3126

Fortunate Fall (See also Fall of Innocence, Fall of Man, and Felix Culpa): 1424, 2189, 2538

Fouqué, Friedrich Heinrich Karl (See Yillah, MARDI): 2397

The Four Elements and Melville: 455

The Four Squires (MOBY DICK): 129

Franklin, Benjamin: 512, 2544, 2615, 2793, 3027, 3132

Franklin, Benjamin (ISRAEL POTTER): 701, 1185, 1215, 1501, 1257, 2411, 2508, 2793, 3027

Fraser, James B. MESOPOTAMIA AND ASSYRIA: 113, 810

Free Press (the Press in MOBY DICK as symbol for Free Press): 469

Freedom of Will: 561, 589, 838, 983, 1228, 1640, 2143, 2143.1, 2331, 2408, 2829, 2966

French Influence on Melville: 728

French Reputation, Melville's (See Criticism, French): 63, 386, 849, 1257, 1545, 2968.1, 3148

French Revolution, Melville's Opinion of: 2306, 3071

Freud, Sigmund: 156, 359, 471, 512, 2216, 2411, 2495, 2671, 2793, 2857, 2966, 3132

Fright: 5

The Frontier, America's and England's: 2196

Frost, Robert, 217, 918, 2411, 2966

The Fugitive Slave Act (1850) in Connection with the Sims Case: 864

Fuller, Margaret: 217, 649, 922, 972, 1174, 1236.1, 1257, 2793, 2966, 3027

Fuller, Thomas. HOLY AND PROFANE STATES: 2651

The Furies (See Greek Furies)

Gabriel (MOBY DICK): 113, 1185, 2408, 3132

Galapagos Islands (THE ENCANTADAS): 50, 1185, 2973.2

Galena, Illinois, Melville's Visit to: 1185, 2839

Gall, Franz Joseph: 126

The Gams (Pequod): 1020, 3151

The Gansevoorts of Albany: 113, 649, 1257, 1396, 2124, 2210, 2793

Gansevoort, Catherine (Grandmother): 972, 1257, 1545, 2124

Gansevoort, Catherine (Cousin): 1257, 1545, 2124

Gansevoort, Guert, Lieutenant (Melville's cousin): 47, 50, 113, 972, 1153, 1185, 1257, 2124, 2793

Gansevoort, Henry (or "Hunn"): 972, 1185, 1257, 1545, 2124

Gansevoort, Herman (Uncle after whom Melville was named): 113, 217, 649, 810, 972, 1257, 1545, 2124

Gansevoort, Herman (Infant cousin): 1257

Gansevoort, Leonard (Great-uncle): 113, 972, 1257, 1545, 2793

Gansevoort, Leonard (Cousin): 50, 113, 972, 1257, 1545, 2124

Gansevoort, Mary A.: 113, 972, 1257, 1545, 2124

Gospels (See Bible and Christianity): 3132

Gothic, The American Gothic: 1632

Gothicism: 113, 116, 117, 159, 201, 309, 310, 512, 525, 727, 789,
791, 1215, 1289, 1356, 1439, 1440, 1632, 1695, 2216, 2236, 2593.1,
3093.1, 3093.2

Grape Imagery (See Persian Poetry Imagery)

Gray, Thomas: 1340, 1545, 2124, 2265

Greece: 810

The Greek Chorus: 2484

The Greek Furies: 2896, 2897

Greek Mythology and Myths (See also Mythology, Western): 2895,
2896, 2897, 3132

Greeks: 3132

Greeley, Horace: 1174, 1257, 1545

Green Imagery (See also Color, Use of, and Imagery): 2748

Greenbush, New York (where Melville taught school): 1185

Greene, Richard Tobias: 50, 113, 159, 442, 649, 999, 1028, 1174,
1185, 1257, 1545, 2124, 2210, 2213, 2793, 2966, 3027, 3132

Greenwood, Grace, pseud. (See Sara Jane Lippincott)

Griggs, George (Melville's brother-in-law): 1545, 2124

Griggs, Helen Maria Melville (Mrs. George Griggs, Melville's sister):
1545, 2124

The Grotesque: 1088, 2201

Guide Books: 701, 2873

Guilt, Theme of (See also Themes): 649, 670, 1685, 2764

Guilt and Innocence (See also Good and Evil, and Innocence):
2764

Guinea (WHITE JACKET): 1294

Guy, Captain (OMOO): 1501

Hakluyt, Richard: 649, 2966, 3027

Hall, Judge James: 65, 3088

An Hamitic Dream: 628, 629

Hamlet and "Hamletism" (See also Shakespeare): 512, 701, 810,
2615, 2748, 2857, 2966, 3132

Handbooks, Manuals, and Reader's Guides (See also Teaching Aids):
671, 933, 962, 1014, 1047, 1056, 1109, 1110, 1129, 1323.1,
1549, 1591.1, 2148, 2228, 2253, 2480, 2648, 2665, 2681, 2710,
2795, 2925

Hanging (See Hanging Scene, BILLY BUDD)

"The Happy Failure": 113, 217, 324, 810, 841, 1049, 1185, 1223,
1257, 1365, 1501, 1520, 1545, 1598, 2411, 3132

"The Happy Failure," Editions: 1873

Hardy, Lem (OMOO): 1501

Hardy, Thomas: 113, 900, 1185, 2168, 3027

Hart, Joseph C. MIRIAM COFFIN: OR, THE WHALE FISHERMAN (1834):
1109.1, 1266, 2966

Hawthorne's Works, Characters, or Phrases (Influence or Parallels)
in Relation to Melville:

"The Artist of the Beautiful" and "The Bell Tower": 1630
THE BLITHEDALE ROMANCE: 113, 182, 1257, 1592
"The Celestial Railroad": 2650
"Chiefly about War Matters": 1528
"Ethan Brand": 1656, 1657, 2764, 2966
"The Gentle Boy": 913, 914
THE HOUSE OF THE SEVEN GABLES: 2124
"My Kinsman, Major Molineux," 1413
"No! in Thunder": 178, 2142
"The Old Apple Dealer": 1527
Roger Chillingworth: 637
THE SCARLET LETTER: 2124, 2249, 3073
SEPTIMIUS FELTON: 545, 1257
"The Seven Vagabonds": 1464
TWICE-TOLD TALES: 2124
"The Unpardonable Sin": 1650, 2124, 2531, 2966
"Young Goodman Brown": 235, 1258, 1764, 2772

Hawthorne, Sophia (Mrs. Nathaniel Hawthorne): 113, 217, 900,

1174, 1185, 1257, 2124, 2210, 2411, 2615, 2762, 2772, 2793,

2926, 2966, 3027

Hawthorne, Una: 2124, 3027

Hazlitt, William: 2793

Head and Heart (See also Heart): 187, 338, 2120, 3127

Heans, Sir Williams: 1172

Heart: 85, 338, 2748, 2792

Hebrew(s): 810, 3132

Hegel, Georg Wilhelm Friedrich: 2397

Heine, Heinrich: 810, 1257

Hell: 2408, 3132

Hemingway, Ernest: 251, 812, 1165.1, 2295.1, 3106

Hephaestus, Greek God of Fire and Metalcraft (Perth, MOBY DICK):

2569

Heritage of Europe and America, Influence on Melville: 662, 1247

Herodotus: 810

Hero: 127, 128, 159, 165, 185, 356, 396, 399, 404, 507, 677, 701, 729, 970, 1221, 1360, 1500, 1501, 2120, 2178, 2478, 2626, 2859, 2923, 3075, 3132

Hero as Artist: 1730

Hero - Byronic Hero: 2179, 2857

Hero - in Eclipse in Victorian Fiction: 2424

Hero - The Fairy Hero of Spenser: 1623

Hero - Folk Hero: 2340

Hero - Greek Tragic Hero: 127, 128

Hero - Neurotic Hero (TYPEE): 2365

Hero - Romantic Rebel Hero: 2711

Hero-Savior: 389

Hero - Self-reliant Hero: 586

Hero - Tragic Hero: 159, 2615, 2766, 2833

Hero - Trickster: 2626

Hero-Narrative Form: 2461

Heroic Ideal: 399, 955, 956, 1052

Heroic Tragedy (See also Tragedy): 1184

Heroines: 479

Hesiod. WORKS AND DAYS: 113, 649, 1545

Heterodoxy: 188

Higginson, Thomas Wentworth: 722

The Highlander, ship: 1185, 1257, 3027, 3132

Hindu Mythology: 159, 3132

Hindu Poetry: 552

Hine, Ephraim Curtis. THE HAUNTED BARQUE (1848). (See as to
    Lemsford, WHITE JACKET): 1133

Hinduism (See also Religion): 810

The Hispanic World and Melville: 665

History: 832, 1344, 2615, 2731, 2744, 2745, 2752, 2807, 3000.1,
    3035.1

Hoadley, Catherine Gansevoort (Melville's sister): 1185, 1545,
    2124

Hobbes, Thomas. LEVIATHAN: OR, THE MATTER, FORME, AND POWER OF A
    COMMONWEALTH ECCLESIASTICALL AND CIVILL. London: 1651:
    .379, 1210.1, 2251, 2793, 2857, 3027

Hodgskin, Thomas. "Abolition of Impressment": 1211.1, 2373

Holmes, Jane. MEADOW BROOK: 292

Holmes, Oliver Wendell, Jr., Chief Justice: 113, 927, 1174,

The Holy Land: 810, 1185, 2615

Homer, 96, 512, 649, 1257, 1534, 1534.1, 1536, 2124, 2408, 2615,
    3132

Homosexuality: 62, 239, 512, 625, 790, 791, 794

Honolulu: 50, 113, 159, 855, 975

Hood, Thomas: 2785

Hope (See also Christ, Christianity, and Faith): 2263

Hope, Thomas. ANASTASIUS; OR MEMOIRS OF A GREEK: 1312

Hopkins, Gerard Manley: 2411

The Horned Woman (WHITE JACKET): 2465

Horror, Tales of (See Gothic)

Howells, William Dean: 480, 482, 1174, 1545, 2615

Hudson, William Henry. IDLE DAYS IN PATAGONIA (1917): 422,
    1282, 1282.1

The Human Condition: 5, 66

Humanism: 197, 391.1, 2615

Humanitarianism: 972, 2609, 2877, 3050

Hume, David: 217

Humor: 108, 221, 248, 359, 392, 517, 639, 758, 814, 830, 866,
    871, 972, 1114, 1183, 1185, 1339, 1348, 1349, 1455, 1639, 2159,
    2317, 2423, 2527, 2694, 2987, 3058

Hunilla: 217, 389, 895, 1185, 1527, 2349, 2615, 3007, 3132

Hymn(s): 180

Hypocrisy: 50, 972

Ideals and Idealism: 2140, 2615, 2748, 2798

Idealism, American: 475, 477, 478, 904, 905, 1700, 2798, 2991,
    3004, 3048

Ideea (OMOO): 1501

Ignorance: 988, 989, 1582, 2363

"Il Penserosa" (See Milton)

Illusions: 1581, 2816.1, 2996

Illustrators: 1399

Imagination: 29, 73, 106, 116, 159, 286, 348, 517, 625, 695, 972, 1057, 1577, 2210, 2218, 2402.1, 2615, 2724

Imagination, Democratic (See also American Imagination): 695, 2402.1

Immaturity: 2328

Immortality (See also Christ, Christianity, Faith, and Religion): 972, 2615

Imperfectibility of Man: 2991, 3004

Imperialism: 1446

Impotence (See also Ahab): 113

Impressment: 1211.1, 2373

Impressionism: 972

Incest, Theme of (See also Themes): 474, 1102

Income, Melville's from Literary Efforts: 502, 503

Indian-Hating (See also CONFIDENCE-MAN): 701, 870, 2319, 2319.1, 2351, 2352, 2353, 2615, 2650, 3132

Indian Imagery (See also Imagery): 2650

Indirection, Tactics of: 318

Individualism: 134, 478, 533, 927, 1460, 2329, 2748

The Indomitable, ship (BILLY BUDD): 1185, 2748, 2793, 3132

Industrialism (See also Society and Technology): 819, 820, 821, 823, 1082, 1447, 2161, 2210, 2329, 2857.3

Infamy: 513

Infidel (See also Atheism): 680

Influences on Melville (See also Criticism: European, French, German; and Literary Tradition): 33, 243, 246, 2156.1

Initiation: 797, 886, 1443, 2149, 2581

Innocence (See also Fall of Innocence; Fall of Man; *Felix Culpa*): 131, 426, 513, 653, 771, 789, 790, 794, 797, 886, 1045, 1071, 1534, 1581, 1661, 1662, 1724, 2139, 2139.1, 2159, 2270, 2581, 2764, 2882, 3071, 3090

Innocence, American (See American Innocence): 600, 789, 794, 3145

Insanity, Melville's Fear of: 359, 870, 972, 1542, 2210, 2597, 2615, 2650, 3088

Inscrutability, Melville on: 2397

International Copyright: 41, 262, 440, 994, 1174

Internationalism in Literature: 3128

Interpolations: 1084

Interpretations (See Particular Works): 236, 672

Intuition, Melville's: 85

Irony: 150, 359, 701, 768, 835, 1058, 1183, 2178, 2351, 2352, 2513, 2575, 2620, 2826, 2857, 3071, 3075, 3161

Israel (See Holy Land)

ISRAEL POTTER: 50, 113, 151, 159, 217, 248, 391, 399, 484.4,
485.2, 512, 540, 651, 691, 701, 728, 769, 810, 894, 900, 925,
958, 1052, 1166, 1174, 1185, 1212, 1215, 1255, 1257, 1284,
1379, 1406, 1501, 1507, 1520, 1545, 1601, 1677, 1696, 1711,
2124, 2125, 2156.1, 2172, 2210, 2264, 2324, 2356, 2356.1, 2408,
2411, 2439, 2451, 2453, 2508, 2544, 2615, 2621, 2629, 2700,
2793, 2919, 2920, 2933, 2968.1, 3014, 3027, 3102, 3102.1, 3122,
3132, 3146

ISRAEL POTTER, Editions: 1448, 1493, 1876, 1876.1, 1876.2, 1877,
1878, 1878.1, 1878.2, 1879, 1880, 1881, 1882, 1883, 1884,
1884.1, 2303, 3028

Israel Potter. THE LIFE AND REMARKABLE ADVENTURES OF ISRAEL
POTTER (Providence: 1824): 1711, 2453, 2793

Italian Publications (See Criticism: Italian): 163

Italy: 484.2, 485.2, 810, 2408, 2424, 2793

Jack Chase (See Chase, Jack)

Jacket Motif: 57, 117, 701, 2967

Jackson, Andrew: 113, 957, 1257, 1545, 2793, 3027, 3132

Jackson (REDBURN): 113, 217, 1185, 1501, 2334, 2334.1, 2615,
2629, 2793, 3008, 3027

Jacksonian American, or Jacksonian Politics: 1185, 2154, 2249,
2251.1, 2706, 2966

James, G. P. R.: 1185, 2298.1, 2793

James, Henry: 113, 217, 512, 608, 701, 812, 1079, 1174, 1185,
1335, 2793, 2857, 2923, 2930, 2965, 3097

JOURNAL OF MELVILLE'S VOYAGE IN A CLIPPER SHIP, THE METEOR,
Editions: 1765

JOURNAL OF A VISIT TO EUROPE AND THE LEVANT: 810, 925, 973,
1240, 1241, 1501, 1768

JOURNAL OF A VISIT TO EUROPE AND THE LEVANT, Editions: 1240, 1768

JOURNAL OF A VISIT TO LONDON AND THE CONTINENT, 1849-1850: 925,
1501, 2124, 2125, 2408

JOURNAL OF A VISIT TO LONDON AND THE CONTINENT, 1849-1850, Editions:
1766, 1769

JOURNAL UP THE STRAITS, OCTOBER 11, 1865, TO MAY 5, 1857:
484.1, 484.2, 485.2, 512, 1765, 2124, 2408, 2425, 2579, 2793,
3034, 3132

JOURNAL UP THE STRAITS, OCTOBER 11, 1865, TO MAY 5, 1857, Editions:
1767

Journey, Melville's (See Quest): 85

Judaism (See CLAREL, Jews): 810

Jude of JUDE THE OBSCURE (See Thomas Hardy): 2168

Judges, Book of: 159, 3132

Julia, ship (fictional name for Lucy Ann, whaler, in OMOO):
50, 113, 857, 1185, 2793, 2966, 3027, 3132

Jung, Carl Gustav: 159, 740, 887, 1026, 1089, 2210, 2358,
2358.1, 2411

Jungfrau, vessel: 1185

Jupiter (See also Zeus): 887, 3132

Justice: 1007, 2466, 3042

Lamb, Charles: 113, 567, 887, 1257, 1545, 2124, 2793, 3027

Landscape: 2399

Language (See also Vocabulary): 39, 96, 113, 138, 141, 145, 147, 148, 222, 223, 241, 277, 352, 363, 414, 555, 556, 830, 872, 874, 887, 972, 1027, 1036.1, 1058, 1159, 1246, 1302, 1420, 1532.1, 1560, 1675.1, 1677, 1690, 1708, 2117, 2153, 2156.1, 2243, 2403, 2432, 2483, 2524, 2564, 2610, 2761

Lansing, Catherine Gansevoort (Cousin): 1545, 2124

Lathrop, Rose Hawthorne. MEMORIES OF HAWTHORNE (1897): 2185

Latin America and Melville: 2256, 2257

Lavater, Johann Kaspar: 126

Law, Melville's Influence on: 1224, 2222.1, 2466

Law and Order: 685, 687, 1594, 2154, 2159, 2401

Lawrence, D. H.: 113, 1185, 1482, 1483, 1484, 1485, 1486, 1487, 2411, 3027, 3071

Laws, Samoan for Ships: 445

The Leatherstocking, Archetypal Figure: 2352

Lecomte, Jules. LE CACHALOT BLANC (1837): 2713

Leconte de Lisle, Charles Marie: 159

Lectures by Melville: 1, 20, 83, 100, 261, 272, 273, 437, 650, 708, 1197, 1458, 1556, 1557, 2124, 2172, 2308, 2408, 2605, 2700, 2840

Ledyard (BENITO CERENO): 113, 810, 1050

Leg, Symbol (See Symbolism): 701, 1504, 1558

Life in a <u>Man-of-War</u>: 1049, 1296

Light and Rock, Symbols (See Symbolism): 309

Light as Symbol (See Symbolism): 359, 701

"The Lightning-Rod Man": 113, 217, 324, 412, 512, 651, 815, 820,
841, 1061, 1174, 1185, 1215, 1223, 1257, 1415, 1416, 1501,
1520, 1523, 1545, 2210, 2275, 2280, 2317, 2332, 2411, 2413,
2748, 2778, 3096

"The Lightning-Rod Man," Editions: 1886.1, 1887

Linguistic Theory (See also Language): 874

Lippincott, Sara Jane (See Pseud., "Grace Greenwood"): 1174,
1545, 2861

Literal Interpretations: 1518, 1523

Literary History: 6, 32, 33, 35, 35.1, 58, 61, 74, 75, 76, 79,
499, 500, 504, 511, 513, 526, 527, 529, 530, 535, 536, 544,
546, 568, 593, 609, 615, 620, 684, 722, 746, 772, 831.1, 832,
865, 902, 920, 927, 1639, 1646, 1655.2, 1671.1, 1675, 1677,
1680, 1857.1, 2249, 2251.1, 2253, 2258, 2394, 2395, 2396, 2397,
2399, 2401, 2402, 2403, 2428, 2439.1, 2447, 2448, 2449, 2451.1,
2486, 2530.1, 2534.1, 2539, 2570, 2673, 2676, 2683, 2694, 2694.1,
2698, 2699, 2699.1, 2729.2, 2798.1, 2828, 2867, 2976, 2979,
2980, 2981, 2994, 3052.1, 3081.1, 3102.2, 3116, 3148, 3153.1

Literary Tradition (See also Literary History): 159, 1356, 2667,
2676, 2683, 2694, 2694.1

Liverpool, and Melville: 113, 1174, 1185, 2565, 2793, 3027,
3132

Liverpool - THE PICTURE OF LIVERPOOL: OR A STRANGER'S GUIDE.
(Liverpool: Jones & Wright, 1808): 2873

Lobo, Father Jerome. A VOYAGE TO ABYSSINIA. Trans. and continued
by Abbé Joachim Legrand. (Trans. into English by Samuel
Johnson): 2638

Locke, John: 296, 649, 1545, 2251, 2411, 2793, 2966, 3132

Lombardo (MARDI): 1501, 2210

London, Jack: 1433, 1545, 2793

Loneliness: 131, 1385.1

Long Ghost (OMOO): 50, 649, 678, 1174, 1185, 1257, 1501, 2793,
3027

Longfellow, Henry Wadsworth: 109, 1174, 1257, 1545, 2124, 2793,
2998, 3027

Loomings: 701

Love: 5, 794, 2463, 2470, 2615, 2649, 2734, 2895

Love Imagery (See Persian Poetic Imagery): 810

Love, Romantic (Lack of as Theme): 594, 744, 791

Love Scenes, Early (PIERRE): 331

Lowell, James Russell: 211, 1174, 1257, 1545, 2793, 3027

Lowell, Robert (Play: BENITO CERENO): 556

Lowry, Malcolm: 684.1, 1584, 3071.2

Loyalty to the Heart: 2792

Lucett, Edward. ROVINGS IN THE PACIFIC FROM 1837 TO 1849 WITH
A GLANCE AT CALIFORNIA. (London: 1851): 2, 862, 1174,
1545, 1589.1

Lucian. TRUE HISTORY: 113, 119, 1416, 2857

Lucy (PIERRE): 887, 1185, 2189, 2210, 2615

Lucy Ann, ship: 50, 113, 1185, 1503, 1545, 2793

Luke (Marked in Melville's Bible): 3132

Luther, Martin: 2397, 2615

"Lycidas": (See Milton)

Lyricism, Melville's: 455

The Machine as Symbol (See Symbolism also): 864, 889, 947, 1626,
     1656, 1657, 2952

Mackintosh, Maria Hoadley (Mrs. William H. Mackintosh - niece):
     1545, 2124

MacMechan, Archibald: 524, 1174, 1185, 1257, 1545, 2210, 2411,
     2966, 3027

Macpherson, James. OSSIAN and FINGAL: 649, 1257, 1545

Macrocosm and Microcosm: 841

Mad Jack (WHITE JACKET): 50, 113, 2615

Madness: 701, 2270.1, 2857

Magazinist, Melville as: 1275

Magic: 578, 1219

Mallarmé, Stéphane: 2985, 2985.1

Man, Modern, 33, 909

Man and His Environment (See also Civilization and Society): 380

Manfred, Frederick. BUCKSKIN MAN: 2522.1

Manfred and Pierre (Byronic Heroes): 2179

Manicheanism: 113, 2793, 3071

Manichean Illusion (See Manicheanism): 2259, 3171

Mann, Thomas: 2370, 3132

Manners, American: 519

Manners, Melville as Novelist of Manners: 516, 519

Manuals (See Handbooks; also Teaching Aids)

The Mansion as Symbol (See Symbolism): 2353

Manuscripts - Collections: 82, 1009, 1092, 2115

Mapple, Father (MOBY DICK): 50, 113, 129, 217, 244, 359, 811, 864, 1115, 1159, 1185, 1244, 1501, 1559, 1608, 1664, 2210, 2233, 2757, 2793, 2857, 2966, 3012, 3027, 3102, 3102.1, 3132, 3133

MARDI: 50, 113, 115, 119, 149, 159, 168, 175, 185, 212, 217, 229, 268, 284, 285, 309, 310, 315, 321, 338, 339, 346, 372, 454, 455, 458, 471, 478, 479, 500, 507, 509, 512, 560, 641, 647, 648, 649, 651, 652, 654, 660, 677, 711, 713, 727, 739, 777, 805, 810, 830, 864, 871, 885, 887, 900, 957, 958, 972, 1014, 1019, 1036, 1039, 1049, 1063, 1072, 1148, 1162, 1174, 1185, 1191, 1201, 1202, 1215, 1233, 1255, 1257, 1276, 1291, 1313, 1364, 1365, 1379, 1404, 1446, 1471, 1475, 1501, 1520, 1523, 1524, 1545, 1640, 1664, 1675.1, 1677, 1700, 1716, 1728, 1730, 2124, 2125, 2144, 2156.1, 2167, 2172, 2177, 2205, 2210, 2214, 2324, 2330, 2334, 2334.1, 2397, 2404, 2408, 2410, 2411, 2413, 2427, 2439, 2463, 2498, 2507, 2509, 2527, 2529, 2563, 2564, 2608, 2609, 2610, 2615, 2621, 2629, 2649, 2698, 2700, 2748, 2754, 2793, 2817, 2857, 2859, 2862, 2895, 2896, 2898, 2920.1, 2965, 2966, 2971, 2977, 2977.1, 3014, 3015, 3016, 3027, 3029, 3035.1, 3079, 3102, 3102.1, 3117, 3122, 3124, 3127, 3130, 3132, 3135

MARDI, Editions: 162, 882, 1139, 1888, 1889, 1890, 1891, 1891.1, 1892, 1892.1, 1893, 1894, 1894.1, 1895, 2410, 2865, 3029

Mardi, Land and People: 649, 1501

MARDI, Sources (See also Sources, General): 268, 1039, 1326, 2463

MARDI, Symbolism (See Symbolism): 3117

Marginalia, Melville's: 587, 588

Margoth (CLAREL): 1185

Marheyo (Melville's Host in Taipi-Vai): 113, 1501

Marine Imagery (See also Imagery): 159

Mariners and Mariners' Life Sketches: 43, 101

Marjora (MARDI): 113

Marlowe, Christopher: 1545, 3132

Marnoo (TYPEE): 113

Marquesas: 50, 113, 202, 265, 414, 649, 856, 900, 976, 1094, 1096, 1185, 2727, 2727.1, 2748, 2793, 3019, 3027

Marquesan Language, Melville's Use of: 414, 830

Marryat, Frederick: 50, 113, 155, 649, 692, 900, 972, 1174, 1185, 1257, 1523, 1545, 1612, 1613, 1715, 2360, 2373, 2519, 2966, 3027

Marston, John. The Malcontent: 2465

Marvell, Andrew: 47, 113, 1644.1, 2162, 2857

Marx, Leo. THE MACHINE IN THE GARDEN (1964) and PARABLE OF THE WALLS: 1174, 3071

Masefield, John: 584, 972, 1660.1, 2210, 2290, 2298, 2793, 3027

Media, King (MARDI): 113, 649, 887, 1185, 1501, 2210, 2615, 2748

Medusa: 512

Mehevi (TYPEE): 1501

Melancholy: 667, 972, 2450, 3130

Melanchton, Philipp: 2397

Melodrama in Melville's Work: 972

Melville, Herman (See Biography): 113, 1185, 1257, 1545, 2124, 2210, 3027

Melville in Baltimore: 968, 969

Melville in England: 714

Melville, Inspector in Custom House: 1174, 1185, 2210, 2780

Melville, the "Ishmael" of American Literature: 2231, 2535

Melville as Lecturer (See also Lectures): 1185

Melville - "Two Melvilles": 543

Melville Scholarship and Research (See also Dissertations and Dissertation Abstracts): 217, 788, 1667, 2204, 2490, 2491.1, 2541, 2599, 2600, 2601, 2602, 2662, 2868, 2869, 2870, 2871, 2915, 3083, 3099

Melville's Contribution to Magazines: 1185, 2172

Melville's Family Tree: 2124

Melville, Allan (Melville's great grandfather): 3027
Melville, Allan (Melville's father): 113, 649, 972, 1185,
     1257, 1545, 2124, 2210, 2408, 2411, 2793, 3027
Melville, Allan (Melville's brother): 113, 649, 810, 972, 1185,
     1257, 1545, 2124, 2210, 2793, 3027
Melville, Anna Marie Priscilla (cousin): 1185, 1545, 2124, 3027
Melville, Augusta (Melville's sister): 113, 649, 972, 1185,
     1257, 1545, 2124, 2793, 3027
Melville, Catherine Bogart (sister-in-law): 1257, 1545, 2124
Melville, Catherine Gansevoort Melville (sister): 113, 649,
     972, 1185, 1257, 1545, 2124, 2793
Melville, Elizabeth (Bessie) (Melville's daughter): 1185, 1257,
     1545, 2124, 2793
Melville, Elizabeth Shaw (Melville's wife): 113, 810, 972, 1174,
     1185, 1215, 1257, 2124, 2185, 2210, 2408, 2411, 2793, 3027
Melville, Frances (Melville's daughter): 113, 972, 1185, 1257,
     1545, 2124, 2793

Melville, Frances Priscilla (Melville's sister): 649, 972,
     1185, 1257, 1545, 2124, 3027
Melville, Francoise Fleury (aunt): 2124
Melville, Gansevoort (Melville's brother): 113, 649, 810, 972,
     1185, 1257, 1538, 1545, 2124, 2210, 2313, 2314, 2411, 2793,
     3027
Melville, Helen Marie (See Griggs, Helen Maria Melville (Melvill's
     sister): 113, 649, 810, 972, 1185, 1257, 1545, 2124, 3027
Melville, Henry (cousin): 1257, 1545
Melville, Jane Dempsey (sister-in-law): 1257, 2124
Melville, Lucy (niece): 1545, 2124
Melvill, Lucy (aunt): 972, 1545
Melvill, Malcolm (Melville's son): 113, 512, 649, 972, 1185,
     1257, 1545, 2124, 2210, 2793, 3027
Melville, Marie Gansevoort (niece): 1257, 2124, 2793
Melville, Mrs. Allan (nee Maria Gansevoort, Melville's mother):
     113, 649, 1185, 1257, 1545, 1677, 2124, 2210, 2411, 3027
Melville, Mary (Mrs. John DeWolf) (Aunt): 1257, 2124
Melville, Nancy (aunt): 113, 2411, 2793
Melvill, Priscilla (aunt): 649, 972, 1257, 1545, 2124
Melville, Priscilla, II (cousin): 1257

Melvill, Robert (cousin): 1185, 1257, 1545, 2124
Melville, Sophia Thurston (sister-in-law): 1257, 1545, 2124
Melville, Stanwix (Melville's son): 113, 1130, 1185, 1257,
     1545, 2124, 2210, 2793
Melville, Thomas (Melville's great-great-grandfather): 972,
     1545
Melville, Major Thomas (Melville's grandfather): 113, 532, 972,
     1185, 1257, 1545, 2124, 2679, 2793, 3027
Melville, Thomas (Melville's uncle): 113, 649, 972, 1185, 1257,
     1545, 2124, 2306, 2596, 2793, 3027
Melville, Thomas (Melville's brother): 113, 649, 972, 1185,
     1545, 1677, 2124, 2320, 2411, 2417, 2793, 3027
Melville, Thomas Wilson (cousin): 113, 649, 925, 972, 1257, 1544,
     1545, 2793
Melvill, Mrs. Thomas (Mrs. A. A. Hobart): 1545
Melville, Thomas, Jr.: 972, 1545

(See also Gansevoort, Griggs, Hoadley, Shaw)

Melville's Funeral: 2725

Melville's Nineteenth-Century Reputation: 10, 13, 26, 27, 46, 50,
   51, 101, 176, 200, 372, 401, 402, 468.1, 500, 501, 524, 589,
   684, 709, 713, 724, 744, 1174, 1175, 1176, 1185, 1333, 1539,
   1568, 1569, 1570, 1571, 1572, 1579, 2184, 2196, 2321, 2534,
   2547, 2548, 2549, 2550, 2551, 2563, 2564, 2603, 2679, 2729.1,
   2761, 2761.1, 2841, 2861, 3080, 3129, 3148

Melville's Obituary: 2781

Melville's Reading: 50, 243, 442, 552, 649, 703, 807, 892, 1203,
   1257, 1312, 1407, 1536, 1669, 2124, 2397, 2598, 2608, 2611,
   2612, 2717.1, 3074, 3132

Melville-Hawthorne Conference in 1966: 2963

Melville Society Newsletter: 2115.1

Memnon": 154.1, 2615

The Memnon Stone, or The Terror Stone (PIERRE): 810, 887, 1069,
   2615, 2748, 3132

Mephistopheles (See Devil, Satan): 228

Mercier, James. LIFE IN A MAN-OF-WAR: 1185

Merchant Marine, Americans Who Contributed to: 2121.1

Meredith, George: 113, 217, 1174, 3024

Mervyn, Arthur: 1355.1

Mesmerism, Language of: 2524

Metamorphosis: 701

Metaphors (See also Imagery and Symbolism): 113, 813, 1058, 1219,
   1550, 2532

Metaphysical and Metaphysics: 329, 415, 603, 690, 2319, 2660, 2660.1

Metcalf, Frances Melville Thomas (Herman Melville's Daughter): 113

Meteor, ship: 81, 1185, 2793, 3035

Meter: 2182

Microcosm (See also Macrocosm): 1704

Miguel (REDBURN): 2360

Milieu, Melville's: 113, 231, 232, 238, 249, 294, 327, 365, 370, 372, 375, 407, 419, 465, 482, 535, 620, 621, 622, 669, 889, 916, 1432, 1444, 1453, 1459, 1477, 1477.1, 1511, 1536.1, 1639, 2128, 2158, 2169, 2175, 2207, 2208, 2209, 2224, 2231.1, 2251.1, 2313, 2314, 2315, 2326, 2327, 2333, 2367, 2575, 2576, 2694, 2893.1, 2904.2, 3021, 3061, 3061.1, 3160

A Military World and Military Necessity (See Authority): 1577, 2160

Miller, Joaquin: 917

Millthorpe (PIERRE): 1501

Milton, John - Allusions, Influence, Parallels: 113, 512, 637, 701, 810, 887, 900, 970, 1072, 1185, 1230, 1545, 1677, 1686, 2216, 2354, 2363, 2405, 2408, 2467, 2615, 2650, 2714, 2857, 3027, 3089

Mirror Symbolism (See Symbolism): 701

Miscellaneous Recognition: 4, 130, 132, 147, 160, 166, 167, 194, 225, 231, 236, 252, 282, 293, 295, 323, 325, 326, 327, 345, 354, 362, 373, 401, 448, 541, 609, 612, 669, 736, 738, 743, 778, 798, 863, 896, 1013, 1030, 1216, 1270, 1280, 1281, 1292.1, 1298, 1300, 1307, 1318, 1414, 1463, 1479, 2266, 2269.1, 2284, 2285, 2291, 2296, 2297, 2298.1, 2304, 2341, 2355, 2377, 2378, 2419, 2420, 2442, 2444, 2485,2511, 2537.1, 2543, 2543.1, 2561.1, 2562, 2613.1, 2625.1, 2659.2, 2729.1, 2774, 2779, 2796, 2849, 2886, 2893.2, 2922.1, 2953, 2973.3, 2977, 2977.1, 3059, 3081, 3081.1, 3141

Misogynist, Melville as: 625

Missions and Missionaries: 3, 4, 50, 69, 103, 159, 311, 649, 668, 890, 1174, 1185, 2210, 2748, 2793, 3080, 3132

Moa Artua, Typee God: 887

MOBY DICK: 9, 12, 13, 14, 19, 22, 24, 27, 29, 33, 37, 39, 44, 49, 50, 58, 64, 71, 74, 91, 92, 99, 104, 108, 109, 113, 114, 117, 122, 124, 219, 134, 136, 146, 148, 149, 159, 161, 168, 173, 175, 179, 180, 181, 185, 188, 191, 192, 193, 198, 209, 214, 215, 217, 221, 228, 229, 232, 233, 234, 238, 244, 245, 248, 267, 276, 277, 279.1, 286, 287, 291, 295, 299, 301, 303, 304, 306, 307, 310, 312, 320, 321, 322, 330, 334, 338, 342, 343, 344, 349, 352, 353, 366, 372, 374, 377, 380, 392, 396, 399, 404, 406, 409, 411, 413, 420, 422, 423, 425, 428, 430, 431, 443, 444, 454, 455, 458, 462, 464, 466, 469, 477, 478, 479, 484.3, 484.4, 485, 485.1, 486, 499, 500, 512, 516, 517, 524, 526, 530, 531, 533, 534, 538, 540,

MOBY DICK, cont.

544, 545, 553, 558, 559, 561, 563, 571, 572, 574, 578, 581, 584, 586, 591, 592, 593, 594, 603, 611, 615, 621, 624, 625, 628, 629, 632, 639, 645, 649, 651, 662, 664, 676, 679, 683, 693, 696, 699, 700, 701, 706, 707, 712, 713, 715, 717, 719, 721, 723, 740, 741, 742, 752, 753, 756, 759, 762, 763, 764, 773, 774, 776, 777, 793, 794, 795, 799, 805, 806, 810, 811, 828, 829, 831, 848, 849, 851, 854, 859, 864, 865, 871, 874, 885, 887, 889, 896, 900, 907, 909, 910, 911, 913, 914, 920, 925, 927, 928, 932, 935, 940, 943, 946, 947, 956, 957, 958, 970, 983, 985, 986, 988, 989, 996, 1003, 1005, 1020, 1023, 1025, 1027, 1031, 1034, 1036, 1049, 1052, 1057, 1058,

1072, 1082, 1084, 1089, 1099, 1105, 1111, 1112, 1127, 1151, 1157, 1159, 1162, 1163, 1164, 1165, 1169, 1171, 1173, 1174, 1178, 1182, 1185, 1199, 1207, 1215, 1218, 1219, 1221, 1227, 1228, 1230, 1233, 1235, 1237, 1247, 1249, 1257, 1258, 1259, 1266, 1278, 1282, 1282.1, 1286, 1287, 1289, 1290, 1291, 1295, 1304, 1308, 1311, 1312, 1313, 1323, 1325, 1332, 1343.1, 1347, 1348, 1351, 1354, 1358.1, 1365, 1366, 1367, 1373, 1374, 1379, 1380, 1381, 1382, 1383, 1385.1, 1386, 1388, 1389, 1390, 1396, 1399, 1401.1, 1420, 1421, 1423, 1431, 1436, 1437, 1438, 1441, 1449, 1450, 1452, 1455, 1457, 1465, 1470, 1471, 1475.1, 1470, 1481, 1482, 1483, 1486, 1487, 1489, 1495, 1505, 1506, 1513, 1515, 1516,

MOBY DICK, cont.

1518, 1520, 1523, 1525, 1529, 1530, 1534, 1534.1, 1539, 1545,
1550, 1584, 1585, 1591, 1594, 1604, 1607, 1609, 1612, 1613,
1631, 1640, 1641, 1642, 1645, 1646, 1648, 1650, 1654, 1657,
1658, 1660, 1660.1, 1663, 1664, 1670, 1675.1, 1677, 1681, 1683,
1685, 1688, 1694, 1695, 1700, 1702, 1704, 1707, 1708, 1709,
1712, 1713, 1716, 1722, 1728, 1730, 1944.1, 2115.2, 2117, 2119,
2120, 2124, 2125, 2129, 2130, 2131, 2132, 2135, 2136, 2146,
2147, 2152, 2156, 2156.1, 2163, 2165, 2172, 2178, 2189, 2191,
2193, 2194, 2199, 2203, 2207, 2209.1, 2210, 2212, 2216, 2220,
2223, 2225, 2226, 2228, 2233, 2236, 2240, 2241, 2253, 2254,
2259, 2267, 2269.1, 2270, 2270.1, 2276, 2283, 2286, 2288, 2295,

2295.1, 2298, 2301, 2305, 2311, 2324, 2325, 2326, 2329, 2330,
2338, 2338.1, 2343, 2347, 2350, 2354.1, 2356, 2356.1, 2358,
2358.1, 2359, 2364, 2380, 2386, 2387, 2388, 2397, 2398, 2400,
2401, 2302, 2403, 2404, 2408, 2411, 2413, 2416, 2423, 2427,
2428, 2430, 2434, 2436, 2438, 2439, 2441, 2454, 2458, 2462,
2467, 2467.2, 2473, 2473.1, 2475, 2477.1, 2478, 2483, 2484,
2491.1, 2493, 2495.1, 2497, 2498, 2499, 2500, 2501, 2507, 2509,
2514, 2516, 2522, 2524, 2525, 2527, 2531.1, 2539, 2551, 2552,
2563, 2564, 2567.1, 2568, 2568.1, 2569, 2570, 2571, 2579, 2580,
2586, 2588, 2589, 2591, 2593.2, 2594, 2609, 2615, 2621, 2629,

MOBY DICK, cont.

2631, 2633, 2635, 2638, 2641, 2642, 2647, 2651, 2655, 2659.1,
2664, 2671, 2672, 2673, 2674, 2675, 2681, 2694.1, 2698, 2700,
2705, 2712, 2713, 2715, 2716, 2716.1, 2718, 2721, 2723, 2748,
2749, 2751, 2752, 2754, 2756, 2757, 2762, 2763, 2764, 2772,
2783, 2787, 2788, 2789, 2793, 2794, 2797, 2800, 2802, 2805,
2806, 2810, 2814, 2816, 2819, 2822, 2825, 2830, 2833, 2836,
2845, 2847, 2850, 2857, 2857.1, 2859, 2872, 2875, 2876, 2880,
2884, 2885, 2887, 2889, 2896, 2902, 2906, 2907, 2908, 2910,
2911, 2918, 2924, 2926, 2927, 2933, 2936.1, 2940, 2943, 2946,
2950, 2955, 2956, 2961, 2962, 2965, 2966, 2968, 2969, 2970,
2974, 2975, 2977, 2977.1, 2981, 2982, 2983, 2986, 2987, 2988,

2991, 2994, 2995, 3003, 3004, 3011, 3013, 3014, 3015, 3016,
3017, 3018, 3021, 3022, 3024, 3030, 3039, 3041, 3046, 3047,
3051, 3052, 3053, 3054, 3055, 3056, 3027, 3036, 3058, 3073,
3076, 3076.1, 3089, 3090, 3092, 3095, 3100, 3101, 3102, 3102.1,
3102.2, 3106, 3106.1, 3113, 3117, 3122, 3124, 3130, 3132, 3133,
3134, 3142, 3151, 3153, 3157, 3166

MOBY DICK, Editions: 37, 38, 42, 58, 96, 114, 184, 189, 281, 694,
759, 760, 761, 776, 951, 952, 953, 966, 979, 1097, 1098, 1118,
1140, 1260, 1261, 1301, 1381, 1399, 1682, 1719, 1896, 1897,
1897.1, 1898, 1898.1, 1899, 1900, 1901, 1902, 1902.1, 1903,
1904, 1905, 1906, 1907, 1908, 1909, 1910, 1911, 1912, 1913, 1913.1,
1914, 1914.1, 1915, 1915.1, 1916, 1916.1, 1917, 1917.1, 1918,
1919, 1920, 1921, 1922, 1923, 1924, 1925, 1926, 1927, 1928, 1929,
1930, 1931, 1932, 1933, 1934, 1935, 1936, 1937, 1938, 1939, 1940,
1941, 1942, 1943, 1944, 1944.1, 1945, 1946, 1947, 1947.1, 1948,
1949, 1950, 1951, 1952, 1953, 1954, 1955, 1956, 1957, 1958,
1959, 1960, 1961, 1962, 1963, 1964, 1965, 1966, 1967, 1968, 1969,

MOBY DICK, Editions, cont.

1970, 1971, 1972, 1973, 1973.1, 1973.2, 1974, 1975, 1976, 1977, 1978, 1979, 1980, 1981, 1982, 1983, 1984, 1985, 1986, 1987, 1988, 1989, 2173, 2338, 2338.1, 2505, 2812, 2813, 2820, 2822, 2842, 2850, 2960, 3030, 3047.1

MOBY DICK, Baptism of Fire and Sperm: 794

MOBY DICK, Centenary of: 447, 2477.1

MOBY DICK, Changing Reputation of: 2499

MOBY DICK: Chapel of Edward Thompson Taylor in Dickens' AMERICAN NOTES, and MOBY DICK: 1794, 2966

MOBY DICK, Conclusion of: 707, 1608

MOBY DICK, Corposants in: 444

MOBY DICK, Dante's Influence: 2578

MOBY DICK, Demonology and Witchcraft in: 2907, 2908

MOBY DICK, Ending of and Thomas DeQuincey: 2493

MOBY DICK, Epic Interpretation: 2569

MOBY DICK, Fate and Fatalism in: 127, 983, 1505, 1677, 2165, 2283, 2966

MOBY DICK, Film: 525, 960, 1017, 1187; theatre, 1358.1; 1609, 2178.1, 2178.2; photoplay, 2593.2; 2756, 2924, 3063

MOBY DICK, Fire Symbolism: 2986, 3134

MOBY DICK, The Free Press in America, Chapter 53 as Symbol of: 469

MOBY DICK, Freudian Motifs: 2671

MOBY DICK, Humor in: 3058

MOBY DICK, Iron Crown of Lombardy: 1421

MOBY DICK, Language of: 39, 1027, 1036.1, 1058, 1420, 2524

MOBY DICK and Lear: 63, 765, 1476, 1497, 1525, 1645, 2220, 2286, 2478

MOBY DICK, Linguistic Devices in (Also see Language): 1058, 1420, 2483

MOBY DICK as Love Story: 794

MOBY DICK and Macbeth: 2887

MOBY DICK, "Mast-head" Chapter: 12, 2748

MOBY DICK as Narrative Romance: 2906

MOBY DICK and the ODYSSEY: 1534, 1534.1

MOBY DICK, and Paradise Lost: 3089

MOBY DICK, Play for Radio: 2460.2

MOBY DICK and Poe: 2571

MOBY DICK, Polarities in: 2120

MOBY DICK as Political Fable: 1159, 1584

MOBY DICK and Political Views of Melville: 1159

MOBY DICK and THE SCARLET LETTER: 3037

MOBY DICK - Seven MOBY DICKS (See also Two MOBY DICKS): 2311, 2311.1

MOBY DICK, The Shadow in: 943, 1089

MOBY DICK and Edmund Spenser: 2462

MOBY DICK and Swedenborg: 2358

MOBY DICK and The Tempest: 2220

MOBY DICK - Three MOBY DICKS: 864

MOBY DICK, Twentieth-Century Relevance: 1475.1

MOBY DICK - Two MOBY DICKS (See also Seven MOBY DICKS): 864,
988, 989, 1128, 1257, 1264, 1937, 2283, 2321, 2325, 2763,
2790, 2833, 2857.1, 2874, 2966, 3058

MOBY DICK and an Ur-MOBY DICK: 2713

MOBY DICK and "Young Goodman Brown" (Hawthorne's Story): 2764

MOBY DICK, Sources: 506, 707, 943, 1109.1, 1157, 1266, 1295,
1324, 1325, 1607, 1608, 2136, 2404, 2473, 2473.1, 2522, 2571,
2591, 2713, 2966, 3054

MOBY DICK, Structure: 113, 244. 359, 425, 734, 2163, 2305, 2970

MOBY DICK, Symbolism: 9, 194, 244, 1169, 1185, 1550, 1659, 1681,
2210, 2401, 2567.1, 2783, 2789, 2987, 3117

MOBY DICK, Teaching Aids (See also Handbooks and Manuals, and
General Teaching Aids): 9, 146, 2500, 2681, 2875

MOBY DICK, Themes (See Themes, General): 334, 947, 2401, 3046,
3122

MOCHA DICK: 34, 50, 113, 716, 854, 940, 941, 2473.1, 2793, 2942,
2966

Modern Man (See Man, Modern)

The Modern Novelist: 2724

Modernity of Melville: 777

Mohammed: 810, 3132

Mohi, the Historian (MARDI): 113, 1185, 1501, 2615, 2793, 3132

Monism: 841, 844, 1031

The Monitor, warship: 1257, 1528

"The Monkey-Rope": 312

Monologue: 763

Monomania: 645

Montaigne, Michel Eyquem Seigneur de: 1257, 1409, 1545, 2615,
    2653, 2758, 2857, 2966, 3027

Montégut, Emile: 386, 2968.1, 3027

Moore, Thomas: 1257, 1312, 1545, 2793

Morality and Moral Interpretations (See also Christianity,
    Criticism, and Themes): 113, 642, 741, 990, 1518, 2292, 2973

More, Thomas: 364, 1545

Moredock, Colonel John (CONFIDENCE-MAN): 701, 1501, 2351, 2352,
    3132

Morewood, John and Sarah (Melville's neighbors): 65, 1185, 1257,
    1545

Mormon, Book of: 2463, 2793

Morris, William: 2124, 2356, 2356.1

Mortmain (CLAREL): 1185

Mosby, John Singleton: 3091, 3092

Moses: 701, 2615, 3132

Navel - Golden Navel (See also Doubloon): 2617

Necessity, Doctrine of: 2331

Negative Capability: 359

The Negro (Also see Slavery): 301, 387, 392, 512, 789, 850, 864,
　　887, 932, 991, 1026, 1049, 1362.1, 1363, 1364, 1365, 1582,
　　2235, 2435, 2586.1, 2666, 2932, 3070, 3149, 3162

The Negro in American Fiction: 301, 387, 789, 2235, 2248, 2586.1,
　　2931

Nehemiah (CLAREL): 1185, 3132

Nelson, Viscount Horatio, British Admiral: 990, 1083, 3075

Neoclassicism in America, Decline of: 1161

Neoplatonic and Neoplatonists, Melville's Use of: 2347, 2610,
　　3132

The Neversink, ship (See United States frigate): 48, 50, 113,
　　1029, 1185, 1704, 2793, 3132

Neville, Morgan: 2340

The New Criticism: 512, 1449

New England and Melville: 1177

New Testament (See Bible): 2124, 3132

New York and Melville: 113, 1636, 1637, 2210, 2240

Newell, A. M. PÉHE NÚ-E - THE TIGER WHALE OF THE PACIFIC: 267

Newell, Charles M. THE VOYAGE OF THE FLEETWING: 71, 2713

Nichols, Thomas L. FORTY YEARS OF AMERICAN LIFE (London: 1864):
　　21

Obscenity (See also Humor): 359

Obscurantism: 3102, 3102.1

Occult: 2366

Ocean, as Metaphor and Symbol: 2748

ODYSSEY (See also Homer, and MOBY DICK): 1534

Oedipus (See also Greek Tragic Hero): 512, 2615

Office-Seeker, Melville as (See Biography): 1138

Oh-Oh (MARDI): 1501, 3132

Old Combustibles (WHITE JACKET): 1501

The Old and the New Order: 2381

Old Testament (See Bible): 3132

OMOO: 10, 36, 41, 46, 50, 51, 105, 113, 117, 159, 162, 164, 168, 175, 217, 226, 321, 372, 458, 461, 512, 521, 527, 649, 651, 660, 677, 678, 701, 713, 730, 805, 810, 830, 857, 858, 862, 887, 890, 900, 925, 927, 958, 972, 994, 996, 1003, 1014, 1049, 1052, 1084, 1116, 1122, 1174, 1185, 1215, 1227, 1235, 1247, 1255, 1257, 1291, 1365, 1368, 1379, 1484, 1485, 1501, 1503, 1506, 1520, 1545, 2124, 2156.1, 2172, 2177, 2199, 2207, 2208, 2210, 2240, 2335, 2408, 2411, 2413, 2427, 2428, 2439, 2503, 2527, 2548, 2564, 2615, 2621, 2629, 2662, 2664, 2700, 2748, 2793, 2857, 2902, 2927, 2965, 2966, 3014, 3022, 3027, 3078, 3102, 3102.1, 3102.2, 3132

OMOO, Editions: 368, 369, 1137, 1141, 1990, 1990.1, 1991, 1992, 1993, 1994, 1995, 1996, 1997, 1998, 1999, 2000, 2000.1, 2001, 2002, 2003, 2004, 2005, 2006, 2006.1, 2007, 2008, 2009, 2010, 2011, 2012, 2013, 2014, 2015, 2476, 2548, 2865

"On the Morning of Christ's Nativity" (See Milton)

O'Neill, Eugene: 2449.1

Onomatopoetic words (Also see Language and Music): 148

Opposition (See Balance and Structure): 1655

Optimism: 738, 1059, 1114, 1391, 1572.1, 2120, 2615

Oratory: 1677

Ordeal, Religious Ordeal of the Nineteenth-Century: 893

Order, Christian and Metaphysical: 415

Organic Form: 844, 2146

Organic Principle (See also Structure): 1677

Orient, Orientalism, and Oriental Religion: 159, 810, 1312

Original Sin (See also Fall of Man, and "Fortunate Fall"):
    1170, 1520, 2615, 2748, 2764, 2772, 2857, 3055

Orme, Daniel (See under "Daniel Orme" in Poems and Short Works)

Orpheus: 512

Osgood, Frances S. POETRY OF FLOWERS: 113, 648, 649

Osiris: 887, 1072, 3132

Othello (See Shakespeare): 1158

Outsider(s): 279

Oversoul (Also see Emerson): 3017

Pacificism: 214, 215

Paine, Thomas: 390, 2857

Painters and Painting: 366, 1116, 1701, 2717.1, 2718, 2962

Palace, Tragedy in: 491

Palm as Symbol (See also Symbolism): 159

Palestine: 113, 2477

Parable(s) (See also Bible): 989, 1082, 1584

"The Paradise of Bachelors": 113, 327, 512, 900, 1519, 1677, 2210, 2408, 2411, 2609

"The Paradise of Bachelors," Editions: 515

"The Paradise of Bachelors and The Tartarus of Maids": 113, 217, 324, 393, 512, 651, 658, 841, 1185, 1257, 1379, 1520, 1545, 2532, 2567, 2621, 2737, 2793, 2857.3

"The Paradise of Bachelors and The Tartarus of Maids," Editions: 2016, 2017, 2018

Paradise, Loss of: 212, 1519, 2363, 2701

Paradise (to be) Regained: 475

PARADISE LOST and PARADISE REGAINED (See Milton): 2408

Paradox: 1058, 1504, 2210

The Parcae: 378, 2203, 2358

Parallels (See Sources): 1715

Park, Mungo (BENITO CERENO): 113, 810, 1050

Parki, brigantine (MARDI): 649

Parkman, Francis. THE CALIFORNIA AND OREGON TRAIL (Reviewed by Melville in 1849): 2422, 3016

Parricide: 512

Parsee (MOBY DICK): 159, 228, 1312, 1457

The Past, Melville's Interest in: 3132

The Pastoral and Pastoralism: 516, 2835

Pater, Walter: 2356, 2356.1

Paternity: 63

Patriotism: 2615

Patronage, Government: 441

Paul, the Apostle (See Bible): 2857, 3132

Pearson, Tobias: 638

Pease, Captain Valentine (of the Acushnet): 113, 1185

Peleg, Captain (MOBY DICK): 217, 359, 1058, 1185, 1501, 2615, 2966, 3027, 3132

Pequod, Meaning of the Name: 343, 438, 989, 1163, 3132

Pequod, whaler (MOBY DICK): 50, 113, 129, 217, 244, 310, 343, 438, 701, 887, 935, 972, 989, 1036, 1157, 1159, 1185, 1348, 1720, 2124, 2178, 2210, 2358, 2400, 2523, 2667, 2793, 2866, 2896, 2966, 2970, 3027, 3092, 3151

Pequot Names in American Literature: 438, 1163

Periodicals and Publishers:

General References: 113, 421, 1174, 1257, 2158, 2205, 2841
Academy (London): 1174, 1545
Advertiser (Boston): 1174
Advertiser (Newark): 1174
Albany Journal: 1174
Albion (English Magazine founded in U. S.): 1174, 1545
American (Baltimore): 1174, 1545
American Courier (Philadelphia): 1174
American Literary Gazette: 1174
American Magazine: 1257, 2793
American Review: 50, 1174, 2793
American Whit Review: 113, 1174
Anglo-American (New York): 1174, 1545
Anglo-American (Toronto): 1174
Argus (Albany): 1174, 1257
Athenaeum: 649, 1174, 2793, 2965
Atlantic Monthly: 113, 259, 1174, 1185, 1257, 1595, 2793
Atlas (London): 1174, 1545
Atlas (New York): 1174

Periodicals and Publishers, cont.

Bee (Boston): 1174
Bell's Weekly Messenger: 1174
Bentley, Richard, Publisher: 217, 649, 961, 972, 1063, 1174,
    1257, 1333, 2966
Bentley's Miscellany: 200, 217, 649, 1063, 1174, 1185, 1257,
    1545, 2124, 2210, 2793, 2841, 2965, 2966, 3027
Berkshire County Eagle: 1174, 1185, 1257
Berkshire Evening Journal: 1185
Blackwood's Edinburgh Magazine: 649, 1174, 1545, 2793
Britannia: 1174
Chamber's Edinburgh Journal: 1174
Christian Examiner (Boston): 1174
Christian Observatory (Boston): 1174
Christian Parlor Magazine: 1174
Christian Union and Religious Memorial: 1174
Citizen (New York): 1174
Commercial Advertiser (New York): 1174, 1257, 2124
Constable and Company: 1185
Cosmopolitan Magazine: 1257, 2793
Courant (Hartford): 1174
Courier (Buffalo): 1174

Critic (London): 1174, 2793
Culturist and Gazette: 1257
Curtis, George William: 1174, 1185, 3027
Daily Tribune: 1174, 1257
Democratic Press and Lansingburgh Advertiser: 1174, 1185,
    1257, 2124
Democratic Review: 50, 810, 1174, 1257, 2706
Dix and Edwards, Publishers: 1174, 1185, 1257, 2793, 2841
Eclectic Review: 50, 1174
Edinburgh Journal (See Chambers): 50
Examiner, The (London): 1174, 2793
Frank Leslie's Illustrated Weekly: 2124
Friend (Journal of Honolulu): 3
Gazette (Salem; Lansingburgh): 1174, 1257
Gentleman's Magazine: 1174
Godey's Lady's Book: 113, 1174
Graham's Magazine: 113, 217, 649, 1174
Greeley, Horace: 1174, 1257, 1545, 2793, 3078
Harper and Brothers, Publishers: 1174, 1185, 1257, 2124,
    2841, 2966
Harper's Family Library: 50, 649

Periodicals and Publishers, cont.

Harper's Magazine: 113, 649, 1174, 1185, 1257, 2124, 2210
Harper's New Monthly Magazine: 217, 2793, 2966
Herald (New York): 1174, 1257
Holden's Dollar Magazine: 1174, 1257, 2124, 2966
John O'London's Weekly: 2124
Knickerbocker Magazine: 50, 113, 649, 810, 1174, 1257, 1545
    2966
Library of American Books (Wiley & Putnam): 1174
Literary World (Boston and New York): 50, 113, 649, 1174,
    1185, 1257, 1545, 2124, 2210, 2408, 2793, 2965, 2966
Littell's Living Age: 113, 1174, 1545
London Examiner and Literary Gazette: 1174, 1545, 2124
London Weekly Chronicle: 2324
Mercury (New Bedford): 1174
Microscope: 1257
Morning Courier and New York Enquirer: 1174, 1257
Mudie's Select Library: 996
Murray, Henry A.: 1545, 2408, 2793
Murray, John: 684, 1174, 1185, 1545, 2793, 2841
Murray - House of Murray, Publishers: 810, 994, 1257, 1545,
    2124, 2210, 2330.1, 3027

New York Evening Post: 1174, 2124
New York Times: 1174, 1545, 2124
North American Review: 1545
North British Review: 1545
North Western Gazette and Galena Advertiser: 1257, 1545
New York Review: 2706
Osgood's Literary World (See Literary World): 2124
Penny Magazine, The: 1545, 2793
Pittsfield Sun, The: 1545
Post (Boston): 1174, 2124
Putnam, George Palmer, Publisher: 1174, 1257, 1545, 2433, 2841
Putnam's Magazine: 1174, 1257
Putnam's Monthly Magazine: 113, 217, 810, 887, 1174, 1185,
    1257, 1545, 2793
Quarterly Review: 1174
Review des Deux Mondes: 1545, 2793
Ripley, George: 1174, 1257
Salem Advertiser: 2793
Scottish Art Review: 1174, 2124
Scribner, Charles: 1257, 2124

Southern Literary Messenger: 113, 1174
Southern Quarterly Review: 113, 1174
Spectator, The: 1174, 2793
Springfield Republican: 1539
Sun (New York): 1174, 1257
Times (London; New York): 1174, 1257
United States Democratic Review (See Democratic Review)
United States Magazine and Democratic Review: 1545, 2793
Whig Review: 2706
Wiley and Putnam, Publishers (See George Palmer Putnam): 50,
    1174, 1257, 1545, 2124, 2793, 2841
Yankee Doodle: 1174, 1257, 1545

"The Piazza": 159, 324, 412, 453, 651, 686, 841, 887, 900, 925, 1185, 1257, 2399, 2408, 2413, 2471.1, 2472, 2621, 2736, 2980

"The Piazza," Editions: 1815.1, 2019, 2020

PIERRE: 46, 50, 51, 66, 78, 113, 117, 137, 153, 154, 159, 168, 177, 179, 185, 196, 199, 203, 214, 215, 217, 232, 233, 248, 276, 277, 284, 285, 291, 310, 315, 331, 337, 338, 341, 344, 415, 418, 455, 459, 471, 474, 478, 479, 500, 504, 512, 557, 593, 633, 638, 645, 649, 653, 675, 698, 700, 701, 713, 721, 727, 777, 795, 805, 810, 824, 828, 841, 860, 861, 885, 887, 891, 900, 907, 925, 927, 956, 958, 972, 984, 1008, 1015, 1035, 1036, 1036.1, 1040, 1049, 1052, 1058, 1065, 1067, 1068, 1069, 1074, 1102, 1134, 1148, 1171.1, 1171.2, 1174, 1183, 1185, 1198, 1212, 1215, 1226, 1233, 1247, 1257, 1291, 1365, 1379, 1396, 1401, 1413, 1417, 1424,

1431, 1449, 1465, 1501, 1511, 1520, 1539, 1545, 1561, 1592, 1631, 1635, 1648, 1650, 1675, 1675.1, 1677, 1685, 1686, 1693, 1700, 1701, 1710, 1716, 1728, 1730, 2124, 2135, 2156, 2156.1, 2161, 2168, 2172, 2179, 2189, 2190, 2199, 2206, 2208, 2210, 2216, 2220, 2237, 2259, 2262, 2326, 2330, 2356, 2356.1, 2397, 2400, 2402, 2408, 2411, 2413, 2424, 2425, 2427, 2439, 2451, 2495.2, 2498, 2501, 2502, 2507, 2509, 2539, 2564, 2577, 2579, 2615, 2621, 2625, 2629, 2700, 2744, 2748, 2754, 2777, 2793, 2819, 2825, 2835, 2836, 2857, 2879, 2894, 2897, 2917, 2927, 2946, 2965, 2966, 2977, 2977.1, 2991, 3004, 3009, 3014, 3015, 3016, 3027, 3071, 3081.2, 3102, 3102.1, 3122, 3124, 3130, 3132,

3136, 3138, 3139, 3140, 3144, 3164

PIERRE, Editions: 860, 1142, 2027, 2028, 2029, 2030, 2031, 2032, 2033, 2034, 2035, 2036, 2037, 2188, 2217, 2856, 2888

PIERRE, Sources: 1413

PIERRE, Style and Structure: 154, 1065, 1226, 2237

Pierre (Glendinning): 887, 1501, 1185, 2140, 2168, 2400, 2615, 2793, 3004, 3124

Pip (MOBY DICK): 113, 129, 217, 359, 701, 756, 797, 864, 887, 932, 1089, 1127, 1185, 1369, 1457, 1501, 2210, 2403, 2615, 2748, 2789, 2793, 2816, 2946, 2966, 2970, 3132

Pipe Symbolism: 553, 2567.1, 2609, 2867

Pitch: 318, 887, 1698, 3124, 3132

Pittsfield, Massachusetts: 113, 1174, 1185, 1257, 1271, 1539, 1635, 2124, 2210, 2793, 3027, 3132

Plath, Sylvia: 1234

Plato and Platonism: 581, 649, 808, 887, 988, 1545, 2347, 2411, 2610, 2615, 2819, 2857, 2966, 3027, 3132

PLINLIMMON: 113, 217, 459, 701, 887, 1040, 1066, 1174, 1183, 1185, 2210, 2265, 2748, 2793, 2857, 3004, 3132

Pliny, NATURAL HISTORY: 2966

Plotinus: 2857

Plots and Characters, Study of: 933, 3124

Plutarch: 887, 1257, 2652, 2857

Podhoretz, Norman. MAKING IT IN AMERICA: 2667.1

Poe, Edgar Allan: 34, 113, 224, 565, 649, 900, 972, 1116, 1174, 1185, 1257, 1545, 1695, 2411, 2423, 2441, 2529, 2571, 2615, 2693.1, 2793, 2894, 2965, 3071, 3143

Poetry, Melville's (Analyses): 106, 120, 171, 195, 210, 227, 363, 435, 449, 450, 467, 512, 551, 593, 655, 656, 680, 685, 687, 688, 705, 837, 840, 845, 896, 900, 925, 933, 980, 993, 1011, 1093, 1113, 1178, 1185, 1209, 1257, 1274, 1329, 1329.1, 1330, 1445, 1447.1, 1501, 1532, 1540, 1551, 1552, 1605, 1606, 1662.2, 1676, 1677, 1679, 2210, 2362, 2407, 2408, 2487, 2488, 2489, 2520, 2537, 2615, 2637, 2660, 2660.1, 2697, 2728, 2729, 2738, 2739, 2740, 2744, 2745, 2793, 2824, 2881, 2927, 2971, 2981, 3000, 3000.1, 3001, 3002, 3048, 3132

Poetry, Melville's, Editions: 227, 241, 515, 550, 1533, 1676, 1777.1, 1778, 1779, 1780, 1781, 1782, 1783, 1784, 1785, 1786, 1787, 1788, 1789, 1789.1, 1790, 1791, 1792, 1793, 1794, 1795, 1796, 1797, 1798, 2392, 2865, 2958

Poetry about Melville: 193.1, 602, 2348

POEMS, LECTURES, SHORT WORKS BY HERMAN MELVILLE:

"The Admiral of the White": 1257, 2744
"The AEolian Harp": 113, 1257, 2744, 2966
"After the Pleasure Party": 113, 512, 925, 1185, 1257, 2210, 2732, 2744, 2824
"An Afternoon in Naples in the Time of Bomba: with an Introduction Merging into a Symposium of Old Masters at Delmonica's": 1257
"The Age of Antonines": 1257, 2408
"Always with Us!": 1257, 2744
"The Ambuscade": 2744
"America": 2411
"The American Aloe on Exhibition": 2411, 2744
"Amorosa" (to "Rosamond"): 810, 1257, 2744
"Apathy and Enthusiasm": 2408
"The Apparition": 1257, 2744
"The Archipelago": 649, 1545, 2744
"Armies of the Wilderness" (BATTLEPIECES): 2408
"Art": 1257, 2358, 2413, 2966, 3132

POEMS, LECTURES, SHORT WORKS BY HERMAN MELVILLE, cont.

POEMS, LECTURES, SHORT WORKS BY HERMAN MELVILLE, cont.

"A Ground Vine": 2744
"The Haglets" (from JOHN MARR): 113, 159, 1257, 1545, 1651,
    2210, 2411, 2743, 2744
"Hearth-Roses": 2744
"Hearts-of-Gold": 2744
"Herba Santa" (from TIMOLEON): 1651, 2744
"The House-Top": 1257
"Immolated": 1257, 1545, 2793
"In a Bye-Canal": 113, 2744
"In a Church in Padua": 1545, 2744
"In a Garret": 1257, 2411, 2744
"In the Desert" (TIMOLEON): 810, 2408, 2744
"In the Hall of Marbles": 1257, 2744
"In the Old Farm-House": 1257
"In the Pauper's Turnip-Field": 1257
"In the Prison Pen": 2411
"Inscription for Rip Van Winkle": 1257, 2744
"Inscription for the Slain at Fredericksburg": 1257
"Iris": 1257, 2744
"The Isles at Large": 2411

"Jack Roy": 1257, 2744
"The Lake": 113, 2615
"Lamia's Song": 2411, 2744
"Lee in the Capitol": 113, 400, 1257, 2793
"L'Envoi" ("The Return of Sire de Nesle"): 113, 2744, 2793
"L'Envoi" (The "Rose Farmer"): 2744
"The Little Good-Fellows": 1257, 2744
"The Loiterer": 2744
"Lone Founts": 1257, 2744
"Lonie": 1257
"Look-out Mountain": 1257
"The Lover and the Syringa-Bush": 2744
"Lyon": 2793
"Madam Mirror": 1677, 2744
"Madcaps": 1257, 2744
"Madonna of the Trefoil": 2411
"Magian Wine": 2744
"The Maid's Tragedie": 2411
"The Maldive Shark" (JOHN MARR): 1185, 1257, 1651, 2411, 2744,
    2981

POEMS, LECTURES, SHORT WORKS BY HERMAN MELVILLE, cont.

POEMS, LECTURES, SHORT WORKS BY HERMAN MELVILLE, cont.

"Travel Pieces": 1257
"Travelling: Its Pleasures, Pains, and Profits" (Lecture):
    1185, 1257
"Trophies of Peace": 113, 925, 1257, 1545, 2744
"The Tropical Summer: A Sonnet": 2411
"The Tuft of Kelp": 2411, 2744
"The Two Temples": 113, 159, 217, 324, 818, 841, 887, 1185,
    1257, 1545, 1618, 1677, 2408, 2411, 2793
"The Two Temples," Editions: 2051
"Under the Ground": 2744
"Under the Rose": 810, 1257, 2411
"The Vial of the Attar": 2744
"The Victor of Antietam": 1257
"A Way-Side Weed": 2744
"The Weaver": 2411, 2744
"When Forth the Shepherd Leads the Flock": 2744
"Wild Strawberry Hunters" (See "Madcaps"): 1257
"The Wise Virgins to Madam Mirror": 2744

Point of View: 153, 173, 700, 770, 909, 910, 1036, 1309, 2496,

    2630, 2641, 2658

Polarity: 1022

Political Mystery Drama (BILLY BUDD): 2687

Political Novel: 2170

Political Symbolism: Fable or Fact: 287, 390, 620, 1159, 1418,

    1552, 1584, 1677, 2208, 2210, 2251, 2314, 2315, 2359, 2687,

Pollard, Captain George, of the _Essex_: 113

Polynesia and Polynesian Life: 50, 102, 311, 372, 649, 810, 887,

    1095, 1096, 1174, 2545, 2661, 3027, 3132, 3147

Pomaree (OMOO): 1501

"Poor Man's Pudding and Rich Man's Crumbs": 113, 217, 324, 810,

    841, 1185, 1223, 1257, 1545, 1677, 2411, 2793

"Poor Man's Pudding and Rich Man's Crumbs," Editions: 2038

Pope, Alexander: 1687, 2408, 2411

The Reader (as a character in the story): 2252, 2657

Reading, Melville's (See Melville's Reading)

The Reading Public: 501, 502, 503, 2388.1, 2389

Realism: 399, 419, 480, 482, 701, 812, 876, 947, 972, 1148, 1185, 1221, 1438, 1718, 2210, 2329.2, 2335, 2389, 2615, 2814, 2827, 2978.1

Reality: 812, 1148, 2244, 2252, 2401, 2686, 2816.1, 2836, 2996, 3004

Reason: 839, 2397, 2615, 2829

Rebellion: 56, 214, 215, 275, 655, 691, 814, 909, 1525, 2495, 2777, 3071

Rebirth, Spiritual: 2516

Reconstruction - after the Civil War: 1552

REDBURN: 50, 57, 113, 115, 117, 203, 217, 234, 257, 316, 372, 399, 456, 481, 509, 512, 608, 649, 651, 653, 677, 701, 717, 727, 806, 810, 841, 878, 886, 900, 925, 927, 934, 957, 958, 971, 972, 974, 1018, 1045, 1048, 1049, 1052, 1072, 1084, 1127, 1143, 1174, 1185, 1244, 1255, 1257, 1291, 1297, 1365, 1379, 1437, 1442, 1443, 1467, 1477.1, 1501, 1520, 1534, 1534.1, 1545, 1553, 1613.1, 1650, 1662, 1677, 1685, 1687, 1696, 1697, 2124, 2125, 2135, 2149, 2156.1, 2172, 2180, 2210, 2360, 2397, 2408, 2411, 2413, 2417, 2439, 2451, 2495.1, 2509, 2581, 2615, 2621, 2629, 2693, 2698, 2700, 2744, 2748, 2793, 2857, 2873, 2927, 2930, 2965, 2966, 3008, 3016, 3027, 3031, 3072, 3122, 3124, 3132

REDBURN, Editions: 2039, 2040, 2041, 2042, 2043, 2044, 2045, 2046, 2046.1, 2047, 2048, 2049, 2050, 2391, 2954, 3031

Redburn (character): 113, 1501, 1553, 2629, 2873, 3008

REDBURN, Sources (See General Sources): 1467

Redemption (Also see Christianity and Faith): 797

Red Whiskers (BILLY BUDD): 2232

Reformation: 149

Reformed Protestant Dutch Church: 180

THE REFUGEE (ISRAEL POTTER published under such title): 1185

Regionalism: 3003

Rejection Thesis: 820

Relativism and Relativity: 1622, 2748, 2991, 3004

Religion (Also see Buddhism, Christianity, Egyptian belief,
  Fire Worship, Hinduism, Islamism, Judaism, Belief of the
  Shakers, Transcendentalism, Yezidis)

Religion, Melville's Treatment of: 175, 338, 339, 398, 512, 644,
  701, 744, 887, 892, 972, 988, 989, 1046, 1185, 2250, 2615,
  2744, 2745, 2748, 2904.2, 2995, 2991

Religious Imagery (Also see Imagery): 2734, 3070

Religious Interpretations (See Morality and Moral Interpretations):
  o50, 113, 872, 981, 1228, 2701, 2730, 2734, 2741, 2744

Religion, Oriental: 159

Religious Synthesis: 2515

Rembrandt, Harmenszoon van Ryn: 1257, 2411

Reni, Guido (Also see his alleged portrait of Beatrice Cenci):
  2424, 2425

Reptilian Symbolism (Also see Symbolism): 2650

Reputation, Melville's Nineteenth-century (See under Melville)

"Resistance" Thesis (See "Acceptance" and Rejection: BILLY BUDD):
3104

Responsibility, Moral (See Morality and Moral): 2292

Resurrection, Recurrent Theme in Melville: 2966

Revelation: 701, 3132

The Revelation of St. John the Divine: 829

Revenge Motif: 645, 1058

Reviews by Melville and Miscellaneous Writing (See also Poems,
Sketches, and Short Works): 257.1, 258, 751, 1799, 1800, 1801,
1802, 1803, 1804, 1805, 1806, 1807, 1808, 1809, 1810, 1811,
1812, 1813, 2408, 2422, 2511, 2623, 2862

Reviews of Melville's Works – Too numerous to list, but see:
1173, 1174, 1175

Revival of Melville Interest in 1920's: 68, 74.1, 75, 76, 77, 79,
81, 86, 90, 91, 92, 97, 104, 196, 199, 252, 256, 321, 322, 351,
364, 374, 463, 464, 493, 494, 526, 558, 563, 583, 612, 633, 668,
752, 753, 851, 861, 900, 935, 940, 989, 1013, 1119, 1206.1, 1280,
1335, 1352, 1353, 1453, 1484, 1586, 1611, 1616, 1648, 1664, 1665,
1672, 1674, 1711, 1718, 1737, 1773, 1774, 1821, 1892, 1909, 2031,
2046, 2067, 2106, 2129, 2130, 2131, 2172, 2188.1, 2197, 2209.1,
2210, 2211, 2212, 2213, 2214, 2219.1, 2260, 2298, 2304, 2307,
2308, 2330, 2436, 2438, 2482, 2505, 2557, 2558, 2561.1, 2719,
2768, 2801, 2885, 2890, 2891, 2936, 2941, 2943, 2944, 2948,

Revival of Melville Interest in 1920's, cont.

2949, 2949.1, 3011, 3024, 3025, 3027, 3051, 3081.1, 3101, 3117, 3158, 3159

Revival of Melville Interest - "Four or Five Revivals": 340, 2482

Revival of Melville Interest - "Fourth" Revival: 1613.2, 2482

Revival of Melville Interest - "Two Revivals": 1185

Reynolds, J. N. MOCHA DICK, OR THE WHITE WHALE OF THE PACIFIC. (New York: 1832) (Also see MOCHA DICK): 34, 50, 113, 649, 854, 941, 1127, 2473, 2473.1, 2966

Reynolds, J. N. VOYAGE OF THE U. S. FRIGATE POTOMAC: 1257, 1545, 2473.2

Rhetoric (See also Diction, Language, Vocabulary): 9, 808, 1726

Rhythm (Also see Prose Style and Language): 1677

"Rich Man's Crumbs" (See "Poor Man's Pudding and Rich Man's Crumbs"): 2533

Riga, Captain (REDBURN): 113, 217, 1501

Rights of Man, ship (BILLY BUDD): 492, 887, 2700, 2748, 3132

Rimbaud, Arthur: 113, 159, 583

Ringbolt, Captain (John Codman). SAILOR'S LIFE AND SAILOR'S YARNS. (Reviewed by Melville): 1257, 1467

Ritual: 159

Roberts, Elizabeth Madox. HE SENT FORTH A RAVEN: 2531.1

Robin (See Hawthorne, Melville's Debt to): 653

Rockwell, Julius, Melville's Letter to: 554

Rolfe (CLAREL): 1185

Romance, Elegiac: 396

Romance - Narrative Romance: 2906

Romance, Oriental: 810

Romance, South Seas: 50, 52, 449, 919, 2291, 2698, 2699

Romantic Mode: 2806

Romantic Sensibility: 1036.1

Romantic Tradition: 3132

Romanticism: 249, 290, 294, 308, 320, 382, 642, 685, 701, 887, 810, 972, 1171.3, 1289, 1377, 1378, 1629, 2150, 2225, 2272, 2330, 2356, 2356.1, 2357, 2399, 2584, 2699, 2699.1, 2793, 2804, 2807, 2893.1

Romanticism, Negative: 18, 2584, 2764

Rome: 484.2, 485.2, 2793

Rosa, Salvator: 2718

The Rose Bud or Bouton de Rose, French whaling ship: 1185

Roses and Rose Imagery: 353, 810

Rose-Window Symbol: 309

Rousseau, Jean-Jacques: 50, 159, 1174, 1257, 1545, 2251, 2330, 2411, 2857, 3027

Royce, Josiah: 927

Russell, G. W. (A. E.): 2358

Russell, Michael. POLYNESIA: OR, AN HISTORICAL ACCOUNT OF THE PRINCIPAL ISLANDS OF THE SOUTH SEAS. (1845): 2545

Russell, W. Clark. AN OCEAN TRAGEDY (1889): 1185

Russian Publication of Melville: 64, 162, 969, 1002, 1323, 1548

Ruth (CLAREL): 113, 1185

Sacrament (See also Eucharist): 159, 512

Sacrifice: 50, 1457

Saddle Meadows: 2748, 2793, 2835, 3132

Sailor Savage, Theme of: 159

Sailor, Symbol of: 1704

Saints, Melville's Allusion to: 2127

Salinger, Jerome David. CATCHER IN THE RYE: 217, 934

Salon, First American Salon: 1562

Salt, Henry S.: 1167, 1185, 1257, 2124

Salvation (See also Christianity, Redemption, and Resurrection):
    2834

Samoa (MARDI): 113, 887, 2748

Samoa, King of Media (MARDI): 1501, 2615

Samoan Laws (1839) - for Naval Vessels: 445

Samuel Enderby, vessel (MOBY DICK): 113, 1185

San Dominick, ship (BENITO CERENO): 657, 701, 887, 1185, 1365,
    2336, 2793

Sandwich Islands (See Hawaiian Islands): 50

Santayana, George: 2568.1

THE SEA BEAST (See MOBY DICK Film): 2178.1, 2593.2

Sea (Ballads, Imagery, Symbolism): 86, 101, 133, 144, 145, 159, 288, 359, 455, 468, 526, 806, 845, 904, 905, 989, 2200, 2372, 2491, 2492, 2551, 2720, 2969, 3071, 3071.2

Search for Father-Figure (See Father-Figure): 473, 909

The Self in Melville: 2402

The "Self" and "Not-Self": 315, 317

Self-Parody: 2413

Self-Reliance: 1052, 2508

Selfridge, Thomas O., Rear-Admiral: 53

Seneca: 339, 1257, 1545

Sensibility (See Romantic Sensibility)

Sentimental Years: 327

Serapis, ship: 1185, 1257

Serenia (MARDI): 1185, 1640, 3132

Sermon, Use of: 811, 864, 1559, 1664, 2757, 2946, 3092

Sermon on the Mount: 887, 2748, 2793, 3132

Serpent Image: 487, 2189

Sex, Allusions and Motifs (See also Freudian Motifs): 880, 2412, 2502, 2532, 2567, 2654, 2671, 2857.3

Sexual Immaturity: 2328, 2567

Shadrach, Account Marked in Melville's Bible: 3132

Shaftesbury, Third Earl of: 2857

Shorty (OMOO): 113, 1257, 1501

Silence, Use of: 701

Silence, Melville's: 79, 3074

Similitude, Dark: 721

Simms, William Gilmore: 487, 649, 1174, 1276, 1545, 2966

Sims Case: 864

Sin (See also Evil, and Original Sin): 988, 989, 1008, 2143,
    2143.1, 2408, 2772

Sin - American National Sin: 1362.1, 1363, 1364, 1365

Sin - Unpardonable Sin (Also see Hawthorne): 1650, 2124, 2531,
    2966

Siva: 534, 885, 887

Skelton, John. PHILIP SPARROW: 652

Skepticism: 892, 893, 2615, 2798

Slavery: 7, 472, 657, 686, 771, 804, 821, 864, 1149, 1159, 1320,
    1362.1, 1363, 1364, 1365, 1446, 1149, 1582, 1623, 2127, 2210,
    2245, 2457, 2615, 2666, 2690, 2920.1, 2932, 3070, 3162, 3163

Smith, H. D., Lieut. "The Mutiny on the Somers" (1888): 2674.1

Smith, Joseph Edwards Adams. HISTORY OF PITTSFIELD, MASSACHUSETTS.
    (1876): 1174, 1185, 1556, 2124, 2966, 3027

Smollett, Tobias: 50, 113, 512, 678, 1185, 1257, 1430, 1545,
    1612, 1613, 2793, 3024, 3027

Social Convention: 459, 701

Social Commitment: 938

Social Criticism: 151, 244, 499, 533, 600, 620, 645, 658, 662, 701, 972, 992, 1038, 1185, 1217, 1314, 1319, 1352, 1353, 1536.1, 2161, 2210, 2281, 2328, 2397, 2398, 2429, 2466, 2752, 2932, 2973, 3016, 3042, 3050, 3105, 3125, 3161

Society: 236, 251, 294, 370, 426, 499, 533, 542, 600, 658, 741, 1379, 1418, 1509, 1601, 1677, 2121, 2169, 2210, 2329.1, 2339, 2350, 2353, 2397, 2398, 2466, 2675, 2752, 2857.2, 2859, 2984, 3075, 3102.2

"Soiled Fish" (WHITE JACKET): 35.1, 1677, 2243, 2323

Soliloquies: 359

Solitude: 235, 537, 540, 3016

Solomon: 2615, 2748, 3132

Somers, ship: 47, 113, 1135, 1257, 1411, 1545, 2674.1, 2793

Somers Mutiny (See Lieut. H. D. Smith): 121, 1135, 1675

Sophocles: 1545, 2586, 2615, 2966

Sources: 32, 47, 50, 54, 65, 154.1, 159, 161.1, 181.1, 190, 192, 268, 339, 512, 671, 713.1, 780, 800.1, 887, 942, 1109.1, 1150, 1157, 1185, 1211.1, 1295, 1296, 1326, 1448, 1467, 1542, 1607, 1644.1, 1696, 1723, 2354, 2371, 2381, 2464, 2465, 2473, 2481, 2519, 2555, 2571, 2585, 2585.1, 2591, 2593, 2597, 2625, 2650, 2713, 2785, 2789, 2966, 3054, 3064

South Seas (See also Polynesia): 2, 3, 49, 50, 52, 54, 372, 654.1, 810, 998, 1185, 2116, 2966, 3027

Southey, Robert: 649, 1545, 1607

Soviet Criticism of Melville: 825

Space, Influence on Imagination: 29

Spain and Spanish Influence on Melville: 664, 665, 3084, 3085

Spanish Inquisition: 213, 2682

Space as Symbol: 244, 435, 512, 2565.1

Specksnyder: 170, 676

Speech (See Dialect and Language): 222

Speech, Marquesan: 159

Spenser, Edmund: 649, 810, 1185, 1255, 1257, 1263, 1341, 1623, 2408, 2462, 2650, 2772, 2793, 2857, 2895, 2898, 2966, 3027, 3135

Sperm, Baptism of: 794

Spiritualism: 1401

Sprague, Dr. William: 1602

Squires, Three (MOBY DICK): 1501

Stage and Screen, Melville on: 755

Stanley, Dean. SINAI AND PALESTINE: 3137

St. John: 192, 1620

St. John, Grave of: 192

St. Lawrence, vessel: 1185

Stanley, Glendinning (PIERRE): 1185, 1501

Structure (See also Style): 376, 702, 1086, 1655, 1699, 1705, 2701, 3167

Structure, Picaresque: 701

Stubb (MOBY DICK): 113, 129, 217, 988, 1185, 1348, 1501, 2484, 2615, 2793, 2966, 2970, 3113, 3132

Style (See also Structure): 119, 148, 376, 411, 500, 512, 874, 887, 972, 1065, 1185, 1220, 1226, 1597, 1670, 1690, 2156.1, 2214, 2222, 2356, 2356.1, 2402, 2458, 2483, 3124, 3132

Style - "Plain Style": 2156.1

"Submission" Theme (See also Themes): 1527

Suffering: 2470

Sufism (The Persian Poets and the Sufi Mystics): 810

Sumner, Charles: 1185, 1257, 1411, 1545

The Sun: 359, 2152, 2244

Sun-gods - Alma, Apollo, Cosmopolitan, Osiris, Taji, Yillah: 887

Superman: 392

Supernaturalism: 145, 3132

Survival: 2782

Swedenborg, Emanuel: 988, 989, 1257, 1545, 2748

Swift, Jonathan: 113, 119, 649, 830, 1174, 1215, 1257, 1545, 2615, 2793, 2857, 2966, 3027

Swinburne, Algernon Charles: 2356, 2356.1

Thoreau, Henry David: 113, 159, 217, 348, 644, 701, 870, 887, 900, 1174, 1185, 1372, 1545, 2202, 2204, 2210, 2273, 2278, 2281, 2316, 2318, 2411, 2615, 2733, 2748, 2793, 2965, 2966, 3027, 3115

Time: 1504, 2396, 2418, 2578, 2724, 2744, 2745, 2805, 2806, 2857, 3004

TIMOLEON: 8, 113, 651, 887, 900, 1174, 1185, 1255, 1257, 1535, 1545, 1651, 1677, 1679, 2124, 2172, 2187, 2210, 2408, 2411, 2615, 2621, 2652, 2744, 2793, 2857, 2971, 3000, 3027

TIMOLEON, Editions: 1798.1

Timonism: 2210

Timrod, Henry: 159

Titan(s): 887, 1397

Toby, Story of (TYPEE) (See also Richard Tobias Greene): 50, 271, 900, 999, 1174, 1185, 1501, 2210, 2497, 2615, 2748, 2793, 3027 3132

Tocqueville, Alexis de. DEMOCRACY IN AMERICA: 217, 530, 701, 1041, 1161, 1545, 2124

Tolstoy, Leo Nikolaevich: 113, 303, 3071

Tom Brown (WHITE JACKET): 1706

Tomahawk Pipe (See also Pipe): 553

Tome, Dr. Robert: 42

Tommo (OMOO and TYPEE): 701, 1185, 1501, 2538, 2748, 2793, 3152

Tone: 1226

Tortoise - Gallapagos Tortoise, Symbol of: 159

Tortoise Hunting: 50, 2124

Totalitarian State (See Authority and Social Criticism): 2160

Tower, Symbol of: 159, 512

"The Town Ho's Story": 50, 113, 217, 218, 315, 359, 701, 815, 859, 864, 925, 948, 1185, 1441, 1642, 2339, 2702, 2763, 2793, 2857, 3151

Tower, Archetype of: 159

Tradition, Nineteenth-Century (See also Literary Tradition): 1534

Tradition, Literary (See Literary History and Literary Tradition): 746, 2429, 2439, 2447, 2448, 2449

Traditionalist, Aesthetic: 2448

Tragedy: 413, 632, 674, 1184, 1374, 1534, 1730, 2163, 2286, 2615, 2633, 2748

Tragedy, Classic: 1308

Tragic Flaw: 1724, 2363, 2921

Tragic Hero (See also Hero): 2615

Tragic Phase of Melville: 1685

Tragic Poet - Melville America's First: 2697

Tragic Sense of Life: 2210, 2211

Tragic Vision: 737, 955, 956, 1162, 1449, 2226, 2586, 2587, 2632, 2633, 2776, 2966

The Trail, Legend of: 693

Tyerman, Daniel, and George Bennet. JOURNAL OF VOYAGES AND

  TRAVELS. (1832): 1326

TYPEE: 10, 21, 26, 41, 46, 50, 51, 102, 103, 105, 113, 140, 149,

  168, 217, 234, 271, 292, 321, 338, 372, 402, 424, 458, 461, 500,

  507, 512, 520, 521, 527, 572, 649, 651, 660, 677, 701, 713, 717,

  727, 742, 777, 805, 810, 814, 830, 841, 862, 876, 887, 900, 917,

  922, 925, 972, 976, 994, 996, 1003, 1014, 1028, 1035, 1049, 1052,

  1064, 1084, 1090, 1103, 1126.1, 1174, 1185, 1215, 1227, 1235,

  1243, 1247, 1255, 1257, 1291, 1295, 1313, 1316, 1318, 1339, 1379,

  1484, 1485, 1501, 1506, 1520, 1534, 1534.1, 1539, 1545, 1573,

  1574, 1575, 1640, 1650, 1677, 1685, 2118, 2124, 2125, 2134,

  2135, 2156.1, 2172, 2177, 2199, 2210, 2213, 2240, 2290, 2309,

  2313, 2329.1, 2335, 2348, 2356, 2356.1, 2365, 2397, 2403, 2408,

  2411, 2413, 2427, 2439, 2503, 2514, 2518, 2527, 2538, 2546,

  2549, 2563, 2564, 2592, 2615, 2621, 2629, 2664, 2666, 2700,

  2701, 2714, 2718, 2744, 2748, 2754, 2793, 2800, 2837, 2843,

  2844, 2768.1, 2855, 2857, 2859, 2861, 2895, 2911, 2927, 2965,

  2966, 2981, 2992, 2995, 3014, 3022, 3027, 3102, 3102.1, 3102.2,

  3103, 3107, 3132, 3147, 3162

TYPEE, Editions: 140, 668, 949, 953, 963, 1126.1, 1144, 1510,

  2052, 2053, 2054, 2054.1, 2055, 2056, 2057, 2058, 2059, 2060,

  2061, 2062, 2063, 2064, 2065, 2066, 2067, 2068, 2069, 2070,

  2071, 2072, 2073, 2074, 2075, 2076, 2077, 2078, 2079, 2080,

  2080.1, 2081, 2081.1, 2082, 2083, 2084, 2085, 2086, 2087, 2088,

  2089, 2090, 2091, 2092, 2093, 2094, 2095, 2096, 2097, 2098,

  2099, 2100, 2549, 2726, 2750, 2851, 2865, 2901, 3033

TYPEE, A One-Act Radio Play: 424

Vangs, Captain (TYPEE): 113

Variety, Non-narrative Chapters: 113

Vavona (MARDI): 1501

Veils (See also Illusions): 1581

Venton, Captain Henry, of the Lucy Ann: 113

Vere (BILLY BUDD): 113, 217, 483, 491, 492, 673, 701, 704, 836, 852, 887, 1079, 1083, 1162, 1185, 1194, 1314, 1315, 1409, 1640, 1644.1, 1660, 1699, 1716, 2174, 2202, 2210, 2292, 2456, 2466, 2467, 2467.1, 2470, 2513, 2560, 2582, 2615, 2640, 2653, 2700, 2748, 2793, 2857, 2905, 3069, 3071, 3075, 3132

Verhaeren, Émile: 159

Versification, Melville's: 2210

Vigny, Alfred de, SERVITUDE ET GRANDEUR MILITAIRES (1835): 217, 1576, 2640

The Villain (in Marryat and Melville): 2519

Vindictiveness, Pathological: 637

Vine (CLAREL): 113, 1185, 2210, 2615, 3132

Violence, the Novel of: 915

Virgil: 113, 1185, 1545, 2408, 2966

Vishnu, Hindu Mythology of: 159, 534, 701, 810, 885, 887, 2966

Vision: 316, 347, 356, 671, 806, 1058, 2210, 2552, 2628, 2629

Vision - Tragic Vision: 2633

Visual Arts - Influence on Melville: 2718

Vivenza (MARDI): 113, 2210

The White Whale: 37, 50, 80, 122, 159, 204, 233, 256, 279, 299, 306, 322, 372, 377, 381, 384, 402, 404, 422, 479, 507, 517, 534, 540, 573, 603, 645, 699, 701, 796, 810, 829, 864, 887, 941, 964, 1031, 1058, 1070, 1162, 1170, 1187, 1190, 1218, 1224, 1234, 1394, 1431, 1436, 1546, 1568, 1621, 1631, 2122, 2136, 2209.1, 2210, 2295, 2301, 2324, 2329, 2348, 2403, 2408, 2423, 2427, 2430, 2439, 2568, 2654, 2671, 2674, 2700, 2712, 2753, 2756, 2787, 2788, 2793, 2883, 2889, 3013, 3104.1

Whiteness (Also see Color): 159, 279, 306, 307, 322, 359, 422, 479, 512, 606, 701, 864, 909, 910, 1024, 1031, 1070, 1258, 1282, 1282.1, 1394, 1631, 1633.1, 2178, 2210, 2441, 2615, 2787, 2788, 2793, 2838, 2910, 3051

White – Non-White: 1033.1

Whitman, Walt: 113, 217, 274, 359, 512, 844, 1058, 1174, 1179, 1185, 1257, 1545, 1677, 2135, 2124, 2134.1, 2210, 2330, 2408, 2411, 2544, 2615, 2693.1, 2748, 2793, 3024, 3132

Wilkes, Captain Charles. NARRATIVE OF THE UNITED STATES EXPLORING EXPEDITION (Philadelphia: 1845): 50, 1257, 1324, 1325, 1326, 2966

Wilson, Charles B., English Consul (OMOO): 50, 1501

Wilson, Gil (Painter): 2386

Winsome, Mark (CONFIDENCE MAN): 868, 2278, 2316, 3132

Wisdom of Solomon: 3132

Wise, Lt. Henry: 50, 159, 998

Witchcraft: 2907, 2908